Writing in Context

PARAGRAPHS AND ESSAYS

WITH READINGS

Writing in Context

PARAGRAPHS AND ESSAYS

WITH READINGS

Laurie G. Kirszner

University of the Sciences in Philadelphia

Stephen R. Mandell

Drexel University

Bedford / St. Martin's

Boston ■ New York

For Bedford/St. Martin's

Developmental Editor: Mikola De Roo
Senior Production Editor: Harold Chester
Senior Production Supervisor: Joe Ford
Marketing Manager: Brian Wheel
Art Direction and Cover Design: Lucy Krikorian
Text Design: Wanda Kossak and Wanda Lubelska
Copy Editor: Alice Vigliani
Photo Research: Alice Lundoff
Cover Photos: (left to right) David Young-Wolff/PhotoEdit; David Frazier/Photo
    Researchers; Esbin-Anderson/The Image Works; Paul Barton/CORBIS Stock Market
Composition: Monotype Composition Company, Inc.
Printing and Binding: R.R. Donnelly & Sons Co.

President: Joan E. Feinberg
Editorial Director: Denise B. Wydra
Editor in Chief: Nancy Perry
Director of Marketing: Karen R. Melton
Director of Editing, Design, and Production: Marcia Cohen
Managing Editor: Erica T. Appel

Library of Congress Control Number: 2002112829

8 7 6 5 4 3
f e d c b a

For information, write: Bedford/St. Martin's, 75 Arlington Street, Boston,
MA 02116   (617-399-4000)

ISBN: 0-312-40630-4 (Instructor's Annotated Edition)
      0-312-40467-0 (Student Edition with Readings)

Acknowledgments
Acknowledgments and copyrights appear at the back of the book on pages 688–89,
which constitute an extension of the copyright page.

Preface for Instructors

When we wrote our paragraph-to-essay developmental workbook, *Writing First: Practice in Context*, we wanted it to reflect our priorities as teachers as well as the importance of writing in college and in the wider world. In and out of the classroom, writing comes first, and we believe that students master writing skills best by learning and practicing them in the context of their own writing. The first developmental workbook to teach grammar in context, *Writing First* quickly became a best-seller quite simply because its approach to writing works. *Writing in Context: Paragraphs and Essays* makes this same innovative approach to the process of writing paragraphs and essays available in a smaller, convenient worktext format.

In *Writing in Context*, writing gets constant emphasis: the book begins with thorough coverage of the writing process, and most chapters begin with writing prompts. Extensive writing practice is central not only to the writing process chapters but to the grammar chapters as well. In addition to an abundance of traditional practice exercises, each grammar chapter includes a unique three-step sequence of writing and editing prompts (Seeing and Writing/Flashback/Revising and Editing) that guides students in applying the chapter's concepts to a piece of their own writing. One thing our years in the classroom have taught us is that students learn writing skills best in the context of their own written work. Here, by moving from their own writing to mastery exercises and back to their own work, students learn more effectively and more purposefully.

Our goals in *Writing in Context* are the same as they have been in our other textbooks: to motivate students to improve their writing for college and for everyday life and to give them the tools they need to do so. It is our hope that by practicing skills in the context of their own writing, students will come to see writing as something at which they can succeed. To achieve our goals, we worked hard to keep the text flexible enough to support a variety of teaching styles and to meet the needs of individual students. We wrote this book for adults—our own interested, concerned, hardworking students—and we tailored the book's approach and content to them. Consequently, we avoid exercises that present writing as a seemingly dull, pointless, and artificial activity, and we do our best to offer fresh, contemporary examples, writing assignments, and student passages. In the book's style and tone, we try to show respect for our audience—to treat college students as adults who can take responsibility for their own learning and for their development as writers.

Organization

Writing in Context: Paragraphs and Essays has a flexible organization that permits instructors to teach topics in the order that works best for them and their students. The book is divided into an introduction and four sections: "Writing Paragraphs and Essays," "Revising and Editing Your Writing," "Becoming a Critical Reader," and "Learning Research Skills." The introduction explains and illustrates active reading strategies that students can use to get the most out of their college reading and to write effective responses. The first section provides a comprehensive discussion of the process of writing paragraphs and essays. The second section presents a thorough review of sentence skills, grammar, punctuation, mechanics, and spelling. The third section reinforces critical reading skills and includes nineteen professional essays, each illustrating a particular pattern of development. The fourth section prepares students to do research. It gives a brief overview of the research process (including information on both print and Internet sources); illustrates and explains MLA documentation style; and includes an annotated, fully documented student research paper. The appendix, "Strategies for College Success," provides help with skills that students will need in other courses, such as developing effective study strategies, taking notes, completing homework, taking exams, giving oral presentations, managing their time well, and applying for jobs.

Features

Supporting the emphasis on writing in *Writing in Context* are innovative features designed to make students' writing practice meaningful, productive, and enjoyable.

The text's process approach guides students step by step through the writing process, providing comprehensive coverage in a flexible format. Eleven chapters on paragraph development (Units One and Two) feature many examples of student and professional writing, with separate chapters on each method of paragraph development. Unit One, "Focus on Paragraphs," also contains explanatory material and exercises that help students understand the role of the topic sentence in structuring a paragraph. A comprehensive treatment of essay writing (Unit Three, "Focus on Essays") starts with Chapter 12, "Writing an Essay," in which the thesis statement is a major focal point along with material that explains and illustrates the process of preparing a formal outline. Chapter 13, "Introductions and Conclusions," offers guidance rarely found in developmental writing texts. In Chapter 14, "Patterns of Essay Development," each pattern is illustrated by a student essay.

Unique "writing in context" activities let students apply each new concept to their own writing.   Most chapters begin with a *Seeing and Writing* activity, a writing prompt accompanied by a photo or other visual images. Then, a series of *Flashback* exercises encourages students to practice skills introduced in the chapter in the context of their first *Seeing and Writing* response. At the end of the chapter, a *Revising and Editing* activity guides students through a final look at their *Seeing and Writing* responses.

Both native and nonnative writers get the grammar help they need.   Thorough, accessible grammar explanations are complemented by clear, helpful examples. The book also offers stronger ESL coverage than any competing text: Chapter 30, "Grammar and Usage Issues for ESL Writers," discusses concerns of special interest to nonnative writers and includes over a dozen exercises.

Each chapter offers numerous opportunities for practice and review.   Easy-to-grade *Practices* following each section of every chapter form a strand of mastery exercises that let students hone specific skills. *Visual writing prompts* in Chapter 14's essay assignments serve as additional sources of inspiration for writing. *Self-Assessment Checklists* and *Chapter Review* activities enable students to think critically about their writing as they revise and edit it. *Collaborative Activities* offer creative options for student-centered classroom learning. Finally, *Answers to Odd-Numbered Exercise Items* at the end of the book let students check their own work as they practice and review.

Writing in Context **helps students make the connection between reading and writing.**   The book's introduction, "Reading for College," guides students step by step through the reading process, includes a sample annotated reading from a college textbook, and contains exercises that allow students to practice previewing, highlighting, annotating, outlining, and summarizing on college textbook readings. Chapter 35, "Readings for Writers," contains nineteen professional readings that illustrate the patterns of development covered in the paragraph and essay chapters of the book. Selections focus on timely topics likely to be of interest to students—for example, the relationship between "wife-beater" T-shirts and domestic violence, and the debate over requiring Americans to carry national ID cards.

A vocabulary enhancement strand begins most chapters.   Word Power boxes accompanying each *Seeing and Writing* prompt introduce two or three words (along with their definitions) that students might use in their responses. This feature enables students to expand their vocabularies in a nonthreatening way—in the context of their own writing.

Writing in Context **respects students as serious writers.**   The text has more student writing than any other developmental textbook: numerous paragraph-length examples as well as thirty-three complete essays provide realistic models. The tone and level of explanatory material, as well as the subject matter of examples and exercises, acknowledge the diverse interests, ages, and experiences of developmental writers.

Writing in Context **helps students learn the research skills they need to find and incorporate outside sources into their writing.** Unit Nine, "Writing with Sources," introduces students to the process of doing research for their college writing assignments. This two-chapter unit begins with an overview of the research process (including information on both print and Internet sources); illustrates and explains MLA documentation style; and includes an annotated, fully documented student research paper.

An appendix on developing effective academic study strategies covers skills that students can use in other courses. Appendix A, "Strategies for College Success" (unique in books of this type), gives students practical strategies for approaching note-taking, exams, oral presentations, time management, and job applications, as well as tips for adjusting to college life.

Writing in Context **makes information easy to find and use.** The engaging full-color design supports the text's pedagogy and helps students find information quickly. *Focus boxes* highlight key concepts and important information, *quick reference tabs* make the book easy to navigate, *marginal cross-references* to other parts of the book help students find and review key information, and *Computer Tips* highlight helpful advice for students writing with computers. For students who need additional practice with specific skills, *marginal cross-references to the Exercise Central online exercise collection* direct them to a unique database of exercise items.

Ancillaries

Writing in Context is accompanied by a comprehensive teaching support package that includes the following items:

- The *Instructor's Annotated Edition* provides answers to the Practice exercises.
- *Classroom Resources for Instructors Using WRITING IN CONTEXT* offers advice for teaching developmental writing as well as chapter-by-chapter pointers for using *Writing in Context* in the classroom and sample answers to essay questions.
- *Teaching Developmental Writing: Background Readings* offers more than two dozen professional articles on topics of interest to developmental writing instructors, accompanied by suggestions for practical applications to the classroom.
- Exercise Central, the largest collection of grammar exercises available with any writing text, includes multiple-exercise sets on every grammar

topic to give students all the practice they need. Exercise Central can be accessed via the World Wide Web at <www.bedfordstmartins.com/exercisecentral>.

- *Diagnostic and Mastery Tests to Accompany* WRITING IN CONTEXT offers diagnostic and mastery tests complementing the topic coverage in *Writing in Context*. This volume's perforated pages enable instructors to copy the material and distribute it to students.

- *Supplemental Exercises to Accompany* WRITING IN CONTEXT offers additional grammar exercises (including material from the Exercise Central online exercise collection). Like *Diagnostic and Mastery Tests,* this book has perforated pages to make it easier for instructors to copy and distribute the exercises to students.

- *Transparency Masters to Accompany* WRITING IN CONTEXT, including student writing samples from the text, are available as a printed package and as files downloadable from the Web site.

- The *Writing in Context* Web site <www.bedfordstmartins.com/writingin context> features downloadable versions of two print ancillaries, *Classroom Resources for Instructors Using* WRITING IN CONTEXT and *Diagnostic and Mastery Tests to Accompany* WRITING IN CONTEXT, downloadable forms (including the transparency masters, with customizable versions of the Peer Assessment Checklists), links to helpful writing sites, and access to the Exercise Central grammar exercise collection.

Acknowledgments

In our work on *Writing in Context,* we have benefited from the help of a great many people.

Franklin E. Horowitz of Teachers College, Columbia University, drafted an early version of Chapter 30, "Grammar and Usage Issues for ESL Writers," and his linguist's insight continues to inform that chapter. Linda Stine and Linda Stengle of Lincoln University devoted energy and vision to the preparation of *Classroom Resources for Instructors.* Susan Bernstein's work on the compilation and annotation of *Teaching Developmental Writing* reflects her deep commitment to scholarship and teaching. We are very grateful for their contributions.

We are grateful to Fran Weinberg for her meticulous work as she helped us adapt and prepare the book's final manuscript as well as for her contributions to the chapter on research and to the appendix. We thank Judith Lechner for her thorough work on Exercise Central and the accompanying exercise book. Carol Sullivan and Mark Gallaher, longtime friends and colleagues, made valuable contributions to the book's exercises, and we thank them as well.

Writing in Context could not exist without our students, whose words appear on almost every page of the book in sample sentences, paragraphs, and essays. Our thanks go to Lis Bare, Kevin Bey, Dan Brody, Susan Burkhart, Michelle Cooper, Daniel Corey, Shannon Cornell, Mark Cotharn, Sutapa Das, Megan Davia, Demetrius Davis, Andrea DeMarco, Kim DiPialo, Jerry Doyle, Ann Duong, Thaddeus Eddy, Mohamad Faisal, John Fleeger, Richard Greene, Linda Grossman, Monica Han, Catherine Hartman, Beth Haurin, Russ Hightower, Keith Jackson, Nisha Jani, Panhej Jolanpretra, Willa Kincaid, Nicholas Kinlaw, Serge Komanawski, Meredith Krall, Peter Likus, George Lin, Jennifer Loucks, Dan Lynn, Krishna Mahajan, Toni-Ann Marro, Felicia May, Jeremy McDonald, Matt McDonald, Michael McManus, Timothy E. Miles, Kelly Miller, Kristin Miller, Hiro Nakamura, Miniinah Neal, Samantha Nguyen, Rob O'Neal, Karoline Ozols, Nirav Patel, Doreen Queenan, James Ramos, Linda Richards, Cheri Rodriguez, Allison Rogers, Christina Rose, Terry Simons, Todd Slunt, Rizwana Syed, Deborah Ulrich, Lisa Van Hoboken, Jason Varghese, Jason Walsh, Jen Weber, Scott Weckerly, Kristin Whitehead, Janice Williams, Teren Williams, Tom Woller, Alisha Woolery, Mai Yoshikawa, and Jessica Zimmerman.

Instructors throughout the country have contributed suggestions and encouragement at various stages of the book's development. For their collegial support, we thank Linda Austin, McLennan Community College; Carol Talbot Baron, Northern Essex Community College; Susan Brant, College of the Canyons; Vilma Chemers, Roosevelt University; Helen Chester, Milwaukee Area Technical College; Eileen Eliot, Broward Community College; Jacqueline Gray, St. Charles Community College; Johanna Grimes, Tennessee State University; Deanne Gute, University of Northern Iowa; Adam Heidenreich, Roosevelt University; Carra Leah Hood, Southern Connecticut State University; Robin Ikegami, Sacramento City College; Enid Leonard, Lane Community College; Janene Lewis, Huston-Tillotson College; Jane Long, Southwestern Oklahoma State University; Donna Maurer, North Shore Community College; Samuel McLeary, Southeastern Community College; David Merves, Miami-Dade Community College; Ronald Miazga, Kalamazoo Valley Community College; Katherine Ellen Perrault, University College of the Fraser Valley; Michael Ritterbrown, Glendale College; Meredith Anne Serling, Southeastern Community College; Joyce Stoffers, Southwestern Oklahoma State University; Rebecca Suarez, University of Texas–El Paso; Janet Turk, Lamar University; Lucilia Valerio, University of Massachusetts–Lowell; Linda Varvel, Anoka-Ramsey Community College; Ted Walkup, Clayton College and State University; Margaret Whalen, Mt. San Antonio College; and Jayne Williams, Texarkana College.

At Bedford/St. Martin's, we thank president Joan Feinberg, who believed in this project and gave us support and encouragement from the outset. We thank Nancy Perry, editor in chief and our longtime friend, who continues to earn our respect as well as our affection. We also thank Greg Johnson, associate editor, for his diligent work on the book's ancillaries; Joanna Imm, associate editor, for helping with numerous tasks, big and small; Erica Appel, managing editor, and Harold Chester, senior project editor, for guiding the book ably through production; Lucy Krikorian, art director, for overseeing the beautiful and innovative design; and New Media editors Harriet Wald and Coleen O'Hanley for their work on the *Writing in Context* Web site. Thanks also go to Joe Ford, senior production supervisor; Karen Melton, director of marketing; and Brian Wheel, marketing manager. Our biggest thanks go to our editor, Mika De Roo. Her insights, energy, and thoroughness have gone a long way toward making this book as good as it could possibly be.

We are grateful, too, for the continued support of our families—Mark, Adam, and Rebecca Kirszner and Demi, David, and Sarah Mandell. Finally, we are grateful for the survival and growth of the writing partnership we entered into in 1975, when we were graduate students. We had no idea then of the wonderful places our collaborative efforts would take us. Now, we know.

Laurie G. Kirszner
Stephen R. Mandell

Contents

REVISING AND EDITING YOUR WRITING   227

UNIT FOUR   Writing Effective Sentences   227

UNIT FIVE   Solving Common Sentence Problems   319

BECOMING A CRITICAL READER   545

UNIT EIGHT   *Reading Essays*   *545*

LEARNING RESEARCH SKILLS   611

UNIT NINE   Writing with Sources   611

CHAPTER 36 Writing a Research Paper   613

A Student's Guide to Using
Writing in Context

What *Writing in Context* Can Do for You

It is no secret that writing will be very important in most of the courses you take in college. Whether you write lab reports or English papers, midterms or final exams, your ability to organize your thoughts and express them in writing will help to determine how well you do. In other words, succeeding at writing is the first step toward succeeding in college. Perhaps even more important, writing is a key to success outside the classroom. On the job and in everyday life, if you can express yourself clearly and effectively, you will stand a better chance of achieving your goals and making a difference in the world around you.

Whether you write as a student, as an employee, as a parent, or as a concerned citizen, your writing almost always has a specific purpose. For example, when you write an essay, a memo, a letter, or a research paper, you are writing not just to complete an exercise but to give other people information or to tell them your ideas or opinions. That is why, in this book, we do not ask you simply to do grammar exercises and fill in blanks; in each chapter, we also ask you to apply the skills you are learning to a piece of your own writing.

As teachers—and former students—we know how demanding college can be and how hard it is to juggle assignments with work and family responsibilities. We also know that you do not want to waste your time or money. That is why in *Writing in Context* we make information easy to find and use and provide many different features to help you become a better writer.

The following sections describe the key features of *Writing in Context*. If you take the time now to familiarize yourself with these features, you will be able to use the book more effectively later on.

How *Writing in Context* Makes Information Easy to Find and Use

Brief table of contents   Inside the front cover is a brief table of contents that summarizes the topics covered in this book. This feature can help you find a particular chapter quickly.

Detailed table of contents   The table of contents that starts on page xiii provides a detailed breakdown of the book's topics. Use this table of contents to find a specific part of a particular chapter.

Index   The index, which appears at the back of the book starting on page 690, enables you to locate all the available information about a particular topic. The topics appear in alphabetical order; so, for example, if you wanted to find out how to use commas, you would find the *C* section and look up the word *comma*. (If the page number following a word is **boldfaced**, that tells you that on that page you can find a definition of the word.)

List of Self-Assessment Checklists   On page xxx is a list of checklists designed to help you write, revise, and fine-tune the paragraphs and essays you compose. Use this list to help you find the checklist that is most useful for the particular writing assignment you are working on.

A handy cross-referencing system   Often, an *italicized marginal cross-reference* will point you to another section of the book (for example, "*See 28A and 28B*"). At the tops of most pages of *Writing in Context*, you will find *quick-reference tabs* consisting of green-and-blue boxes, each containing a number and a letter. This information tells you which chapter you have turned to and which section of that chapter you are looking at. Together, the cross-references and the tabs help you find information quickly. For example, if a cross-reference in the text suggests, "*See 9A for more on classification*," you can use the tabs to help you locate section 9A.

---

10 A
Definition   **113**

wearing shorts, low-cut shirts, tank or halter tops, sandals, flip-flops, jeans, or T-shirts.

Melissa Morris (student)

The topic sentence introduces the term the paragraph will define. The paragraph goes on to define the term, using several short examples to illustrate the definition. The paragraph ends with negation—telling what the term *business casual* does not mean.

The following paragraph defines a piece of gymnastics equipment—the pommel horse.

For information on how to write a definition essay, as well as a list of transitions suitable for definition paragraphs and essays, see 14H.

How *Writing in Context* Can Help You Become a Better Writer

Preview boxes   Each chapter starts with a list of key concepts that will be discussed in the chapter. Looking at these boxes before you skim the chapter will help you get an overview of the chapter.

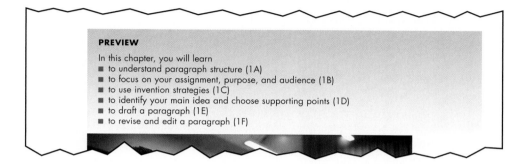

> **PREVIEW**
>
> In this chapter, you will learn
> - to understand paragraph structure (1A)
> - to focus on your assignment, purpose, and audience (1B)
> - to use invention strategies (1C)
> - to identify your main idea and choose supporting points (1D)
> - to draft a paragraph (1E)
> - to revise and edit a paragraph (1F)

Seeing and Writing activities   Most chapters include a three-part writing activity that helps you apply specific skills to your own writing. Those chapters start with a *Seeing and Writing* assignment that asks you to write about a particular topic. (An accompanying photograph or other visual is included to stimulate your writing.) Beside each assignment, a Word Power box lists two or three vocabulary words (and their definitions) that you might find useful as you write your response. Throughout the chapter, *Flashback* exercises help you analyze your *Seeing and Writing* response so you can identify and correct specific writing problems. Finally, a *Revising and Editing* exercise asks you to fine-tune your writing. (See, for example, pages 229, 232, and 239 in Chapter 15.)

Focus boxes   Throughout the book, boxes with the word *Focus* in a red banner highlight useful information, identify key points, and explain difficult concepts.

FOCUS   **Placing Topic Sentences**

A topic sentence can appear anywhere in a paragraph—at the beginning, in the middle, or at the end. For the time being, however, you should place your topic sentences at the beginning of your paragraphs. This strategy will keep you on track as you write. In addition, by telling readers what your paragraph will be about, your topic sentence will help readers follow your ideas.

xxviii

A STUDENT'S
GUIDE TO USING
*WRITING IN
CONTEXT*

Self-Assessment Checklists Chapters 1, 3–12, and 14 include Self-Assessment Checklists that give you a handy way to check your work and measure your progress. Use these checklists to help you revise your writing before you hand it in.

 SELF-ASSESSMENT CHECKLIST:

Writing a Narrative Paragraph

Unity

- Does your topic sentence tell readers what the main idea of the paragraph is?
- Is your topic sentence specific enough?
- Do all details and events support your topic sentence?

Development

- Should you add more events or details to make your narrative clearer or livelier?

Computer Tips and marginal notes *Computer Tips* in the running text help you make effective use of your computer as you write. *Word Power* boxes define words you might choose to include in your Seeing and Writing response. Finally, if you need additional practice with specific skills, *marginal cross-references to the Exercise Central online exercise collection* have been added to the text.

Computer Tip

Try hitting the Enter or Return key after each sentence of your paragraph. Isolating each detail and example in this way can help you evaluate the amount and kind of support you have used in your paragraph.

▶ **Word Power**

curriculum
all the courses offered by a school

elective
a course that is not required

ON THE WEB
For more practice, visit Exercise Central: www.bedford stmartins.com/ writingincontext

Answers to Odd-Numbered Exercise Items   Starting on page 675, you will find answers for some of the Practice items in the book. When you need to study a topic independently or when your instructor has you complete a Practice but not hand it in, you can consult these answers to see if you are on the right track.

How *Writing in Context* Can Help You Succeed in Other Courses

In a sense, this whole book is all about succeeding in other courses. After all, as we said earlier, writing is the key to success in college. But *Writing in Context* also includes specific sections at the end of the book that you may find especially useful in courses you take later on in college. We have designed these sections so you can use them on your own as well as with your instructor's help.

Appendix A, "Strategies for College Success"   This practical guide offers specific, useful information on a wide variety of important topics, such as note-taking, study skills, oral presentations, time management, and job applications.

List of correction symbols   The chart on the last page of the book lists marks that many instructors use when evaluating and marking student papers. Becoming familiar with these symbols will help you get the most out of your instructor's comments on your work.

Self-Assessment Checklists for Writing Paragraphs and Essays

Units 1–3 of *Writing in Context* include a number of Self-Assessment Checklists designed to help you write, revise, and fine-tune your paragraphs and essays. You can use these checklists both in your writing course and in other courses that include written assignments. The following list shows the page number for each checklist.

Writing in Context

PARAGRAPHS AND ESSAYS

WITH READINGS

Introduction: Reading for College

PREVIEW

In this chapter, you will learn
- how to preview a passage (IA)
- how to highlight a passage (IB)
- how to annotate a passage (IC)
- how to outline a passage (ID)
- how to summarize a passage (IE)

Reading is essential to all your college courses. In addition to your textbooks, you will be reading other books (both fiction and nonfiction); newspapers, magazines, and journals (in print and online); essays, short stories, lab notes, class handouts, and many other pieces of writing. To get the most out of your college reading, you should approach it in a practical way by asking yourself what your reading can offer you. You should also approach your reading critically, commenting on, questioning, evaluating, and even challenging what you read. In other words, you must be an active reader.

Being an **active reader** means participating in the reading process: approaching a reading assignment with a clear understanding of your purpose, previewing a passage, highlighting and annotating it, and perhaps outlining and summarizing it to help you understand what you are reading.

In order to understand your purpose for reading, start by answering some questions.

Questions about Purpose

- Why are you reading?
- Will you be expected to discuss the assigned reading in class or in a conference with your instructor?
- Will you have to write about what you are reading? If so, will you be expected to respond informally (for example, in a journal entry) or more formally (for example, in an essay)?
- Will you be tested on the material?

Once you understand your purpose, you are ready to begin reading.

A Previewing a Passage

When you **preview,** you skim a passage in order to get a sense of the writer's main idea and key supporting points and, if possible, the emphasis of the passage. As you preview, it is helpful to keep in mind the Questions about Purpose that are listed above.

In an essay, article, or chapter that is complete in itself, the title, the first paragraph (which often contains a purpose statement or overview), and the last paragraph (which often contains a restatement) are usually the best places to look for the author's main ideas, key supporting points, and emphasis. In a textbook passage, however, you need to look for clues to the writer's message in both the passage's **visual signals** (the way the passage looks on the page) and its **verbal signals** (the words and phrases the writer uses to convey order and emphasis).

Using Visual Signals

- Look at the first sentence of each paragraph.
- Look at section headings.
- Look at *italicized* and **boldfaced** words.
- Look at numbered lists.
- Look at bulleted lists (like this one).
- Look at illustrations (graphs, charts, tables, photographs, and so on).
- Look at boxed information.
- Look at information in color.

Using Verbal Signals

- Look for phrases that signal emphasis ("The *primary* reason"; "The *most important* idea").
- Look for repeated words and phrases.
- Look for words that signal addition (*also, in addition, furthermore*).
- Look for words that signal time sequence (*first, after, then, next, finally*).
- Look for words that identify causes and effects (*because, as a result, for this reason*).
- Look for words that introduce examples (*for example, for instance*).
- Look for words that signal comparison (*likewise, similarly*).
- Look for words that signal contrast (*unlike, although, in contrast*).
- Look for words that signal contradiction (*however, on the contrary*).
- Look for words that signal a narrowing of the writer's focus (*in fact, specifically, in other words*).
- Look for words that signal summaries or conclusions (*to sum up, in conclusion*).

◆ PRACTICE I-1

The following passage from an introductory psychology textbook defines and illustrates the term *attribution*. In preparation for class discussion and for other activities later in this chapter, preview the passage. Use visual and verbal signals to help you identify the passage's main idea and key supporting points.

ATTRIBUTION
Explaining Behavior

Attribution refers to the process of explaining people's behavior. What are the fundamental attribution error, the actor-observer discrepancy, and the self-serving bias? How do these biases shape the attributions we make?

As you're studying in the college library, the activities of two workers catch your attention. The two men are trying to lift and move a large file cabinet. "Okay, let's lift it and tip it this way," one guy says with considerable authority. In unison, they heave and tip the file cabinet. When they do, all four file drawers come flying out, bonking the first guy on the head. As the file cabinet goes crashing to the floor, you bite your lip to keep from laughing and think to yourself, "Yeah, they're obviously a pair of 40-watt bulbs."

Why did you arrive at that conclusion? After all, it's completely possible that the workers were not dimwits. Maybe the lock on the file drawers broke. Or maybe there was some other explanation for their mishap.

Attribution is the process of inferring the cause of someone's behavior, including your own. Psychologists also use the word *attribution* to refer to the explanation you make for a particular behavior. The attributions you make have a strong influence on your thoughts and feelings about other people.

If your attribution for the file cabinet incident was that the workers were not very bright, you demonstrated a pattern that occurs consistently in explaining the behavior of other people. *We tend to spontaneously attribute the behavior of others to internal, personal characteristics, while downplaying or underestimating the effects of external, situational factors.* This bias is so common in individualistic cultures that it's called the **fundamental attribution error** (Ross, 1977). Even though it's entirely possible that situational forces are behind another person's behavior, we tend to automatically assume that the cause is an internal, personal characteristic.

The fundamental attribution error plays a role in a common explanatory pattern called **blaming the victim**. The innocent victim of a crime, disaster, or serious illness is blamed for having somehow caused the misfortune or for not having taken steps to prevent it. For example, many people blame the poor for their dire straits, the sick for bringing on their illness, and battered women and rape survivors for somehow "provoking" their attackers. Hindsight makes it seem as if the victim should have been able to predict and prevent what was going to happen (Carli & Leonard, 1989).

Along with the fundamental attribution error, a second bias contributes to unfairly blaming the victim of misfortune. People have a strong need to believe that the world is fair—that "we get what we deserve and deserve what we get." Social psychologist Melvin Lerner (1980) calls this the **just-world hypothesis**. Blaming the victim reflects the belief that, because the world is just, the victim must have done *something* to deserve his or her fate.

Why do we have a psychological need to believe in a just world? Well, if you believe the world is unfair, then no one—including you—is safe from tragic twists of fate and chance, no matter how virtuous, careful, or conscientious you may be (Thornton, 1992). Hence, blaming the victim and believing the just-world hypothesis provide a way to psychologically defend yourself against the threatening thought, "It could just as easily have been me."

—Don H. Hockenbury and Sandra K. Hockenbury, *Psychology*, Second Edition

B   Highlighting a Passage

After you have previewed an assigned reading, read through it carefully, highlighting as you read. When you **highlight**, you use a combination of underlining and symbols to identify important material. This active-reading strategy will help you to identify the writer's main ideas so you can make connections among these ideas when you reread.

Your highlighting should be selective. Remember, you will eventually be rereading every highlighted word, phrase, and sentence, so highlight only the most important information—for instance, definitions, examples, and reviews.

Your highlighting will be most effective if you use a variety of symbols. When you reread—for example, when you are preparing to take an exam or write a paper—each symbol will convey different information to you. The number and kinds of highlighting symbols you use are up to you. All that matters is that your symbols are clear and easy to remember.

Here is how a student highlighted a passage from an introductory American history textbook. The passage focuses on the position of African Americans in society in the years immediately following World War II. Because the passage includes no visual signals apart from the section heading, the student looked carefully for verbal signals.

BLACK PROTEST AND THE POLITICS OF CIVIL RIGHTS

"I spent four years in the army to free a bunch of Frenchmen and Dutchmen," an African American corporal declared, "and I'm hanged if I'm going to let the Alabama version of the Germans kick me around when I get home." Black men and women constituted 16 percent of military personnel in World War II, well above their 10 percent presence in the general population. African American soldiers and civilians alike resolved that the return to peace would not be a return to the racial injustices of prewar America. Their political clout had grown with the migration of 2 million African Americans to northern and western cities, where they could vote and make a difference. Even in the South, the proportion of blacks who cast ballots in local and national elections inched up from 2 percent to 12 percent in the 1940s. Pursuing civil rights through the courts and Congress, the National Association for the Advancement of Colored People (NAACP) counted half a million members.

In the postwar years, individuals broke through the color barrier, achieving several "firsts" for African Americans. Jackie Robinson integrated major league baseball when he took over second base for the Brooklyn Dodgers in 1947, braving abuse from fans and players to win the Rookie of the Year Award. In 1950, Ralph J. Bunche won the Nobel Peace

Prize for his contributions to the United Nations, and Gwendolyn Brooks earned the Pulitzer Prize for poetry. A vibrant black culture, including top musicians such as Louis Armstrong, Ella Fitzgerald, and Mahalia Jackson appealed to audiences black and white.

**   Still, in most respects African Americans found that little had changed. Although a number of states and cities outside the South enacted laws regarding fair employment practices in the 1940s—even as the federal government ended its wartime antidiscrimination program— African Americans struggled to hold on to the gains they had made dur-

① ing the war. Federal housing programs for the poor and non-poor alike encouraged discrimination against blacks, and violence sometimes

② greeted those who tried to move into white areas. Postwar Detroit saw 120 incidents of arson, cross burnings, and physical attacks in neighborhoods undergoing racial transition. As African Americans migrated to northern

③ and western cities, they found themselves crowded into what were rapidly becoming ghettos.

✓✓   Things were worse in the South, where violence greeted blacks'

④ attempts to assert their rights. White men with guns turned back Medgar Evers (who would become a key civil rights leader in the 1960s) and four other veterans who were trying to vote in Mississippi. A mob lynched

⑤ Isaac Nixon for voting in Georgia, and an all-white jury acquitted the men accused of his murder. Governors, U.S. senators, and other southern politicians routinely intimidated potential voters with threats of economic retaliation and violence.

                    —James L. Roark et al., *The American Promise,* Second Edition

The student who highlighted this passage was preparing for a meeting of her study group. Because the class would be taking a midterm the following week, each member of the study group needed to understand the material very well. The student began her highlighting by placing check marks beside two important advances for African Americans cited in paragraph 1 and by drawing arrows to specific examples of blacks' political influence. (Although she thought she knew the meaning of the word *clout,* she circled it anyway to remind herself to check its meaning in a dictionary.)

In paragraph 2, she boxed the names of prominent postwar African Americans and underlined their contributions, also underlining (and starring) the key phrase "'firsts' for African Americans." She then underlined and double-starred the passage's main idea—the first sentence of paragraph 3—numbering the examples in paragraphs 3 and 4 that supported this idea, and drawing an arrow pointing from the main idea to the list of examples. She also underlined "Things were worse in the South" in paragraph 4 and placed a double check beside it to make it stand out.

◆ PRACTICE 1-2

Reread the passage from the psychology textbook (pages 3–4). As you read, highlight the article by underlining and starring its most important ideas and, if you like, drawing lines and arrows to connect related ideas. Be sure to circle any unfamiliar words and put question marks in the margin beside them.

C Annotating a Passage

As you highlight, you should also **annotate** what you are reading. Annotating a passage involves making notes—questions, reactions, reminders, ideas for writing or discussion—in the margins or between the lines. Keeping this kind of informal record of ideas as they occur to you can help to prepare you for class discussion and exams.

As you read a passage, answering the following questions will help you to make useful annotations.

Questions for Annotating
- What is the passage's main idea?
- What other ideas are important? Why?
- What relationships do you see between ideas?
- Do you understand the passage's vocabulary?
- Do you understand the passage's ideas?

The following passage reproduces the student's highlighting of the American history textbook from pages 5–6 and illustrates her annotations.

I C

BLACK PROTEST AND THE POLITICS OF CIVIL RIGHTS

Achievements of African Americans:

"I spent four years in the army to free a bunch of Frenchmen and Dutchmen," an African American corporal declared, "and I'm hanged if I'm going to let the Alabama version of the Germans kick me around when I get home." Black men and women constituted 16 percent of military per-

Military

✓ sonnel in World War II, well above their 10 percent presence in the general population. African American soldiers and civilians alike resolved that the return to peace would not be a return to the racial injustices of prewar

Politics

✓ America. Their political clout had grown with the migration of 2 million African Americans to northern and western cities, where they could vote and make a difference. Even in the South, the proportion of blacks who cast ballots in local and national elections inched up from 2 percent to 12 percent in the 1940s. Pursuing civil rights through the courts and Congress, the National Association for the Advancement of Colored People (NAACP) counted half a million members.

Sports; world politics, literature, music

* In the postwar years, individuals broke through the color barrier, achieving several "firsts" for African Americans. Jackie Robinson integrated major league baseball when he took over second base for the Brooklyn Dodgers in 1947, braving abuse from fans and players to win the Rookie of the Year Award. In 1950, Ralph J. Bunche won the Nobel Peace Prize for his contributions to the United Nations, and Gwendolyn Brooks earned the Pulitzer Prize for poetry. A vibrant black culture, including top musicians such as Louis Armstrong, Ella Fitzgerald, and Mahalia Jackson appealed to audiences black and white.

Why?? (prejudice?)

** Still, in most respects African Americans found that little had changed. Although a number of states and cities outside the South enacted laws regarding fair employment practices in the 1940s—even as the federal government ended its wartime antidiscrimination program—African Americans struggled to hold on to the gains they had made dur-

① ing the war. Federal housing programs for the poor and non-poor alike encouraged discrimination against blacks, and violence sometimes   *Discrimination*

② greeted those who tried to move into white areas. Postwar Detroit saw 120 incidents of arson, cross burnings, and physical attacks in neighborhoods   *Violence* undergoing racial transition. As African Americans migrated to northern

③ and western cities, they found themselves crowded into what were rapidly becoming ghettos.

✓✓   Things were worse in the South, where violence greeted blacks'   *South = worse*

④ attempts to assert their rights. White men with guns turned back Medgar Evers (who would become a key civil rights leader in the 1960s) and four other veterans who were trying to vote in Mississippi. A mob lynched

⑤ Isaac Nixon for voting in Georgia, and an all-white jury acquitted the men accused of his murder. Governors, U.S. senators, and other southern politicians routinely intimidated potential voters with threats of economic retaliation and violence.

> —James L. Roark et al., *The American Promise,* Second Edition

In her annotations, this student put some of the writer's key ideas into her own words and recorded questions she hoped to discuss in her study group.

◆ PRACTICE I-3

Reread the passage from the psychology textbook (pages 3–4). As you reread, refer to the Questions for Annotating (page 7). Use them to guide you as you write down your own thoughts and questions in the margins. Be sure to take time to look up any unfamiliar words you have circled and to write down brief definitions or synonyms. Think of these annotations as your preparation for discussing the passage in class.

◆ PRACTICE I-4

Exchange books with another student, and read his or her highlighting of the psychology passage. How are your written responses similar to the other student's? How are they different? Do your classmate's responses help you see anything new about the passage?

D   Outlining a Passage

Outlining is another technique you can use to better understand a passage you are reading. Unlike a **formal outline**, which follows strict conventions, an **informal outline** enables you to list and arrange a passage's ideas quickly and easily. After you have finished an informal outline of a passage, you should be able to see at a glance which ideas are more important than others and how ideas are related.

FOCUS   Making an Informal Outline

1. Write or type the passage's main idea across the top of a sheet of paper. (This will remind you of the passage's focus and help to keep your outline on track.)
2. At the left margin, write down the most important idea of the first paragraph or first section of the passage.
3. Indent the next line a few spaces, and list the examples or details that support this idea.
4. As ideas become more specific, indent further. (Ideas that have the same degree of importance are indented the same distance from the left margin.)
5. Repeat the process with each paragraph or section of the passage.

   ▢ You can use the Tab key to help you set up your outline.

The student who highlighted and annotated the passage on pages 8–9 made the following informal outline to help her understand its content.

Main idea: Although African Americans had achieved
a lot by the end of World War II, they still
faced prejudice and violence.

African Americans as a group had made significant
advances.
　　Many had served in military.
　　Political influence was growing.
　　　　More African Americans voted.
　　　　NAACP membership increased.
Individual African Americans had made significant
advances.
　　Sports: Jackie Robinson
　　World politics: Ralph Bunche
　　Literature: Gwendolyn Brooks
　　Music: Louis Armstrong, Ella Fitzgerald,
　　　　Mahalia Jackson
Despite these advances, much remained the same for
African Americans.
　　They faced discrimination in public
　　　　housing.
　　Racial integration led to violence.
　　They were pushed into ghettos.
　　Southern blacks faced violence and even
　　　　lynching if they tried to vote.

◆ PRACTICE I-5

Working on your own or in a small group, make an informal outline of the
passage from the psychology textbook. Refer to your highlighting and annotations as you construct your outline. When you have finished, check to make
certain that your outline clearly indicates the emphasis of the passage and the
relationships among its ideas.

E Summarizing a Passage

Once you have highlighted and annotated a passage, you may want to try
summarizing it. A **summary** retells, *in your own words*, what a passage
is about. A summary condenses a passage, so it generally leaves out all but
the main idea, key supporting points, and examples. A summary omits minor
details and stylistic devices, and it does *not* include your own ideas or opinions.

FOCUS   **Writing a Summary**

1. Review your outline.
2. Consulting your outline, restate the passage's main idea *in your own words*.
3. Consulting your outline, restate the passage's supporting points. Add connecting words and phrases between sentences where necessary.
4. Reread the original passage to make sure you haven't left out anything significant.

NOTE: To avoid accidentally using the exact language of the original, do not look at the passage while you write your summary.

The student who highlighted, annotated, and outlined the passage from the history textbook wrote the following summary.

> Although African Americans had achieved a lot by the end of World War II, they still faced prejudice and even violence. As a group, they had made significant advances, which included military service and increased participation in politics, as indicated by voting and NAACP membership. Individual African Americans also made significant advances. For example, Jackie Robinson integrated baseball, Ralph Bunche won the Nobel Peace Prize, Gwendolyn Brooks won the Pulitzer Prize for poetry, and artists like Louis Armstrong, Ella Fitzgerald, and Mahalia Jackson were very popular with white as well as black audiences. Despite these advances, however, much remained the same for African Americans after World War II. They faced discrimination even in public housing, and attempts at racial integration often led to violence. As a result, many African Americans found themselves pushed into ghettos. Conditions in the South were even worse: here, African Americans still faced the threat of violence and even lynching if they tried to vote.

◆ **PRACTICE I-6**

On a separate sheet of paper, write a brief summary of the passage from the psychology textbook. Use your outline to guide you—and remember to keep your summary short and to the point. Note: Your summary will probably be about one quarter to one third the length of the original passage.

◆ PRACTICE I-7

Choose one of the following passages from textbooks in various academic fields. Assuming that you are preparing for a test, go through the process of previewing, highlighting, annotating, outlining, and summarizing presented in this chapter.

GLOBAL WARMING MAY CAUSE SPECIES EXTINCTIONS

Atmospheric scientists predict that, as a result of increasing concentra-   1
tions of CO_2 and other greenhouse gases in the atmosphere (see Chapter 56), average temperatures in North America will increase 2°–5°C by the end of the twenty-first century. If the climate warms by only 1°C, the average temperature currently found at a certain location will shift 150 km to the north. To remain in the temperature regime to which they are accustomed, species will have to shift their ranges 150 km to the north. Species will need to shift their ranges as much as 500–800 km in a single century if the climate warms 2°–5°C. Some habitats, such as alpine tundra, could be eliminated from many areas as forests expand up the mountain slopes.

Conservation biologists are attempting to predict the effects of global   2
warming on North American species. Trees might be especially vulnerable to climate change because they grow for long periods before they begin to reproduce, and their seeds typically move only very short distances (Figure 58.15).

If Earth warms as predicted, climatic zones will not simply shift north-   3
ward. New climates will develop, and some existing climates will disappear. New climates are certain to develop at low elevations in the tropics because a warming of even 2°C would result in climates near sea level that are hotter than those found anywhere in the humid tropics today. Adaptation to those climates may prove difficult for many tropical organisms.

— William K. Purves et al., *Life: The Science of Biology,* Sixth Edition

---

Publicity refers to one type of PR communication: messages that   1
spread information about a person, corporation, issue, or policy in various media. Public relations today, however, involves many communication strategies besides publicity. In fact, much of what PR specialists do involves dealing with negative or unplanned publicity. For example, when documents and audiotapes surfaced in the fall of 1996 revealing that certain top executives at Texaco had made racist remarks, an intense PR campaign began. It employed a range of tactics, including paid TV advertising, major news conferences, and meetings with regional Texaco distributors. The Denny's chain of restaurants encountered similar negative publicity

throughout the 1990s, particularly after six African American Secret Service agents were refused service in one of the restaurants in 1993. However, by 2000 the chain had improved its image so much that *Fortune* magazine listed it as one of the country's fifty best companies for minorities.

Because it involves multiple forms of communication, **public relations** is difficult to define precisely. It covers a wide array of actions, such as shaping the image of a politician or celebrity, repairing the image of a major corporation, establishing two-way communication between consumers and companies, and molding wartime propaganda. Broadly defined, *public relations* refers to the entire range of efforts by an individual, an agency, or any organization attempting to reach or persuade audiences.   2

The social and cultural impact of public relations, like that of advertising, has been immense. In its infancy, PR helped convince many American businesses of the value of nurturing the public, who had been redefined as purchasers rather than as producers of their own goods. PR also set the tone for the corporate image-building that characterized the economic environment of the twentieth century and transformed the profession of journalism by complicating the way "facts" could be interpreted. Perhaps PR's most significant effect, however, has been on the political process in which individuals and organizations—on both the Right and the Left—hire *spin doctors* to shape their media image.   3

—Richard Campbell, *Media and Culture*, Third Edition

Plot

Since the short story is defined as a prose narrative usually involving one unified episode or a sequence of related events, plot is basic to this literary form. **Plot** is the sequence of events in a story and their relation to one another. Writers usually present the events of the plot in a coherent time frame that the reader can follow easily. As we read, we sense that the events are related by causation, and their meaning lies in this relation. To the casual reader, causation (or why something in the plot happened next) seems to result only from the writer's organization of the events into a chronological sequence. A more thoughtful reader understands that causation in the plot of a memorable short story reveals a good deal about the author's use of the other elements of fiction as well, especially characterization. . . .   1

A short story can dramatize the events of a brief episode or compress a longer period of time. Analyzing why a short story is short, the critic Norman Friedman suggests that it "may be short not because its action is inherently small, but rather because the author has chosen—in working with an episode or plot—to omit certain of its parts. In other words, an action may be large in size and still be short in the telling because not all of it is there." A short story can describe something that happens in a few minutes or encompass action that takes years to conclude. The narrative possibilities are endless, as the writer may omit or condense complex episodes to intensify their dramatic effect or expand a single incident to make a relatively long story.   2

Regardless of length, the plot of a short story usually has what critics   3
term an **end orientation**—the outcome of the action or the conclusion of
the plot—inherent in its opening paragraphs. As Mark Twain humorously
observed, "Fiction is obliged to stick to possibilities. Truth isn't." The novelist may conclude a single episode long before the end of a novel and then
pick up the thread of another narrative, or interpret an event from another
angle in a different character's point of view, linking episode to episode
and character to character so that each illuminates the others. But a story
stops earlier. As Poe recognized in 1842, its narrative dramatizes a single
effect complete unto itself.

The events in the plot of a short story usually involve a conflict or   4
struggle between opposing forces. When you analyze a plot, you can often
(but not always) see it develop in a pattern during the course of the narration. Typically you find that the first paragraphs of the story or **exposi-
tion** give the background or setting of the conflict. The **rising action**
dramatizes the specific events that set the conflict in motion. Often there
is a **turning point** in the story midway before further **complications** pro-
long the suspense of the conflict's resolution. The **climax** is the emotional
high point of the narration. In the **falling action**, the events begin to wind
down and point the reader toward the **conclusion** or **dénouement** at the
end of the story, which resolves the conflict to a greater or lesser degree.
Sometimes the conclusion introduces an unexpected turn of events or a
surprise ending. In successful stories the writer shapes these stages into a
complex structure that may impress you with its balance and proportion.

—Ann Charters and Samuel Charters, *Literature and Its Writers,* Second Edition

UNIT ONE

Focus on Paragraphs

Writing a Paragraph

PREVIEW

In this chapter, you will learn
- to understand paragraph structure (1A)
- to focus on your assignment, purpose, and audience (1B)
- to use invention strategies (1C)
- to identify your main idea and choose supporting points (1D)
- to draft a paragraph (1E)
- to revise and edit a paragraph (1F)

■ SEEING AND WRITING

What do you think is the primary purpose of college—to give students a general education or to prepare them for careers? Look at the picture above, and think about this question carefully as you read the pages that follow. This is the topic you will be writing about as you move through this chapter.

▶ **Word Power**
primary
most important

aspiration
a strong desire for high achievement; an ambitious goal

19

Writing is not just something you do to get a grade in school; writing is a life skill. If you can write clearly, you can express your ideas convincingly to others—in school, on the job, and in the community. Writing tasks take many different forms. In college, you might write a single paragraph, an essay exam, a short paper, or a long research paper. At work, you might write a memo, a proposal, or a report. In your daily life as a citizen of your community, you might write a letter asking for information, explaining a problem, or complaining about a service. Writing is important. If you can write, you can communicate; if you can communicate effectively, your writing is likely to get a response.

A   Understanding Paragraph Structure

This chapter takes you through the process of writing a **paragraph**. A paragraph can be part of a longer piece of writing, as it is in an essay, or it can stand alone, as it does in a one-paragraph classroom exercise or an exam answer. Because paragraphs play a part in almost every writing task, learning to write a paragraph is an important step in becoming a competent writer.

A paragraph is unified by a single main idea. The **topic sentence** states the main idea, and the rest of the sentences in the paragraph **support** the main idea. Often a final concluding statement gives readers a summary of the paragraph's main idea.

Paragraph

TOPIC SENTENCE   A paragraph consists of a **topic sentence** and **support**. The topic sentence states the main idea of the paragraph. This idea unifies the paragraph. The other sentences in the paragraph provide support. These sentences present details, facts, and examples. At the end of the paragraph is a final **concluding statement**, a sentence that sums up the paragraph's main idea. Many paragraphs follow this general structure.

SUPPORT

CONCLUDING
STATEMENT

Note that the first sentence of a paragraph is **indented**, starting about one-half inch (five spaces) from the left-hand margin. Every sentence begins with a capital letter and, in most cases, ends with a period. Sometimes a sentence ends with a question mark or an exclamation point.

◆ PRACTICE 1-1

Bring two paragraphs to class: one from a newspaper or magazine and one from a textbook. Compare your paragraphs with those brought in by other students. What features do all your paragraphs share? How do the paragraphs differ from one another?

B   Focusing on Your Assignment, Purpose, and Audience

In college, a writing task usually begins with an assignment that gives you a topic to write about. Instead of plunging in headfirst and starting to write, take time to consider some questions about your **assignment** (*what* you are expected to write), your **purpose** (*why* you are writing), and your **audience** (*for whom* you are writing). Finding out the answers to these questions at this point will save you time in the long run.

Questions about Assignment, Purpose, and Audience

Assignment

■   What is your assignment?
■   Does your instructor require a maximum (or minimum) number of words or pages?
■   When is your assignment due?
■   Will you be expected to complete your assignment at home or in class?
■   Will you be expected to work on your own or with others?
■   Will you be allowed to revise after you hand in your assignment?

Purpose

■   Are you expected to express your personal reactions—for example, to tell how you feel about a piece of music or a news event?
■   Are you expected to present information—for example, to answer an exam question, describe a process in a lab report, or summarize a story or essay you have read?
■   Are you expected to argue for or against a position on a controversial issue?

Audience

■   Who will read your paper—just your instructor, or other students, too?
■   Do you have an audience beyond the classroom—for example, your supervisor at work or your landlord?
■   How much will your readers know about your topic?
■   Will your readers expect you to use formal or informal language?

◆ PRACTICE 1-2

Each of the following writing tasks has a different audience and purpose. Think about how you would approach each task. (Use the Questions about Assignment, Purpose, and Audience, listed above, to help you decide on the best strategy.) Discuss your responses with your class or in a small group.

1. For the other students in your writing class, describe your best or worst educational experience.

2. For the instructor of an introductory psychology course, discuss the effects that early educational experiences have on a student's performance throughout his or her schooling.

3. Write a short letter to your community's school board in which you try to convince members to make two or three specific changes that you believe would improve the schools you attended or those your children might attend.

4. Write a letter to a work supervisor—either past or current—telling what you appreciate about his or her supervision and how it has helped you develop and grow as an employee.

C   Using Invention Strategies

Once you know what, why, and for whom you are writing, you can begin to experiment with different invention strategies. **Invention**—sometimes called *prewriting* or *discovery*—is the process of finding material to write about. This process is different for every writer.

Stella Drew, a student in an introductory writing course, was given this assignment.

> Write a paragraph that answers the following questions: Should community service—unpaid work in the community—be a required part of the college curriculum? Why or why not? Try to write at least five or six sentences.

Before she drafted her paragraph, Stella used a variety of invention strategies to help her come up with ideas. The pages that follow illustrate the four strategies she used: *freewriting, brainstorming, clustering,* and *journal writing.* If at any stage of your writing process you run out of ideas, return to the invention strategies you found most helpful, and use them to help you find more material.

▶ **Word Power**
curriculum
all the courses offered by a school

elective
a course that is not required

Freewriting

When you **freewrite**, you write for a set period of time—perhaps five minutes—without stopping, even if what you are writing doesn't seem to have a point or a direction. Your goal is to relax and let ideas flow without worrying about whether or not they are logical. In fact, you might try not looking at what you write while you write. Try "invisible freewriting" by turning off your monitor or tilting your laptop screen so that you cannot read it. Then, when you have finished, you can look at the monitor to see what you have written. You can freewrite without a topic in mind, but sometimes you will focus your attention on a topic. This strategy is called **focused freewriting**.

Once your freewriting is completed, underline any ideas you think you might be able to use. If you find an idea you want to explore further, freewrite again, using that idea as a starting point.

Here is Stella's focused freewriting on the topic of whether or not community service should be a required part of the college curriculum.

> *Community service. Community service. Sounds like what you do instead of going to jail. Service to the community — service in the community. Community center. College community — community college. Community service — I guess it's a good idea to do it — but when? In my spare time — spare time — that's pretty funny. So after school and work and all the reading and studying I also have to do <u>service</u>? Right. And what could I do anyway? Work with kids. Or <u>homeless</u> people. Old people? Sick people? Or not people — maybe animals. Or work for a political candidate. Does that count? But when would I do it? Maybe other people have time, but I don't. OK idea, could work — but not for me.*

Freewriting

◆ PRACTICE 1-3

Reread Stella's freewriting on the topic of community service for college students. If you were advising her, what ideas would you suggest she explore further? Underline these ideas in her freewriting.

◆ PRACTICE 1-4

Now it is time for you to begin the work that will result in a finished paragraph. (You already have your assignment from the Seeing and Writing box on page 19: to write about whether the primary purpose of college is to educate students or to prepare them for careers.) Your first step is to freewrite about your topic. Use a blank sheet of lined paper, and write for at least five minutes without stopping. If you have trouble thinking of something to write, keep recopying the last word you have written until something else comes to mind.

◆ PRACTICE 1-5

Reread the freewriting you did for Practice 1-4. Underline any ideas you think you might use in your paragraph. Then, choose one of these ideas and use it as a starting point for another focused freewriting exercise.

Brainstorming

When you **brainstorm**, you record all the ideas about your topic that you can think of. Unlike freewriting, brainstorming is often scattered all over the page. You don't have to use complete sentences; single words or phrases are fine. You can underline, star, or box important points. You can also ask questions, list points, and draw arrows to connect ideas.

Stella's brainstorming on the topic of community service appears on the next page.

> **FOCUS** **Collaborative Brainstorming**
>
> You often brainstorm on your own, but at times you may find it helpful to do **collaborative brainstorming**, working with other students to find ideas. Sometimes your instructor may ask you and another student to brainstorm together. At other times, the class might brainstorm as a group while your instructor writes ideas on the board that the class can later evaluate. However you brainstorm, your goal is the same: to come up with as much material about your topic as you can.

◆ PRACTICE 1-6

Reread Stella's brainstorming on community service (page 25). How is it similar to her freewriting on the same subject (page 23)? How is it different? If you were advising Stella, which ideas would you suggest that she cross out as she continues to explore her subject?

◆ PRACTICE 1-7

On a piece of *unlined* paper, brainstorm about your assignment: What do you think is the primary purpose of college—to give students a general education or to prepare them for careers? (Begin by writing your topic, "The purpose of college," at the top of the page.) Write quickly, without worrying about using complete sentences. Try writing on different parts of the page, making lists, and drawing arrows to connect related ideas. When you have finished, look over what you have written. Which ideas are the most interesting? As you brainstormed, did you come up with any new ideas that you did not discover while freewriting?

◆ PRACTICE 1-8

Working as a class or in a group of three or four students, practice collaborative brainstorming. First, decide as a group on a topic for brainstorming. (Your in-

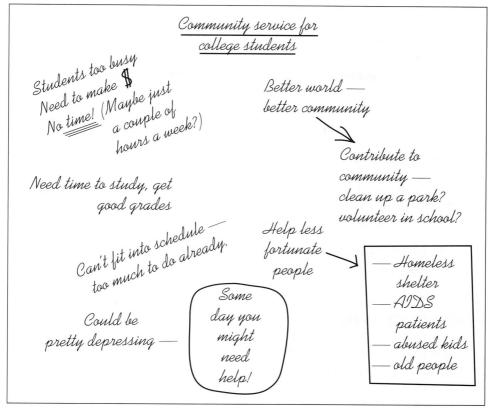

Brainstorming

structor may choose a topic for you.) Next, choose one person to write down ideas on a blank sheet of paper or on the board. (If your group is large enough, you might choose two people to write down ideas and have them compare notes at the end of the brainstorming session.) Then, discuss the topic informally, with each member contributing at least one idea. After fifteen minutes or so, review the ideas that have been written down. As a group, try to identify interesting connections among ideas and suggest ideas that might be explored further.

Clustering

Clustering, sometimes called *mapping*, is another useful invention strategy. When you cluster, you begin by writing your topic in the center of a sheet of paper. Then, you branch out, writing related ideas on the page in groups, or clusters, around the topic. As you add new ideas, you circle them and draw lines to connect the ideas to one another and to the topic at the center. (These lines will look like spokes of a wheel or branches of a tree.) As you move from the center to the corners of the page, your ideas will get more and more specific.

▶ **Word Power**

cluster

a group of items that occur close together; a bunch

Sometimes, one branch of your cluster will give you all the material you need; at other times, you may decide to write about the ideas from several branches—or to choose one or two from each branch. If you find you need additional material after you finish your first cluster, you can cluster again on a new sheet of paper, this time beginning with a topic from one of the branches.

Stella's clustering on the topic of community service for college students appears on the next page.

◆ PRACTICE 1-9

Reread Stella's clustering on community service (next page). How is it similar to her brainstorming on the same subject (page 25)? How is it different? If you were advising Stella, which branches of the cluster diagram would you say seem most promising? Why? Can you add any branches? Can you extend any of her branches further? Write your additions on Stella's cluster diagram. Then, discuss them with your class or in a small group.

◆ PRACTICE 1-10

Try clustering on the Seeing and Writing assignment: What do you think is the primary purpose of college—to give students a general education or to prepare them for careers? Begin by writing the topic in the center of a blank sheet of unlined paper. Circle the topic, and then branch out with specific ideas and examples, continuing to the edge of the page if you can. When you have finished, look over what you have written. What are the most interesting ideas in your cluster diagram? Which branches seem most promising as the basis for further writing? What new ideas have you come up with that your freewriting and brainstorming did not suggest?

Journal Writing

A **journal** is a notebook in which you keep an informal record of your thoughts and ideas. In a journal, you can reflect, question, summarize, or even complain. When you are involved in a writing project, your journal is a place where you jot down ideas to write about and where you think on paper about your assignment. Here you can try to resolve a problem, restart a stalled project, argue with yourself about your topic, or critique a draft. You can also try out different versions of sentences, keep track of details or examples, or keep a record of potentially useful things you read, see, or hear.

Once you have started making regular entries in your journal, take the time every week or so to go back and reread what you have written. You may

Clustering

find material you want to explore in further journal entries—or even an idea
for a paper.

Computer Tip

You can try keeping a journal on your computer by making entries at the same time every
day—when you check your e-mail, for example.

FOCUS **Journals**

Here are some subjects you can write about in your journal.

■ *Your school work*

You can use your journal to explore ideas for writing assignments. When you get a specific assignment, you can write a journal entry in which you record your thoughts about it and try to decide what you might write about. Your journal can also be a place where you think about what you have learned, ask questions about concepts you're having trouble understanding, and examine new ideas and new ways of seeing the world. Writing regularly in a journal about what you're studying in school can even help you become a better student.

■ *Your job*

In your journal, you can record job-related successes and frustrations, examine conflicts with coworkers, or note how you handled problems on the job. Reading over these entries can help you to understand your strengths and weaknesses and to become a more effective employee. As an added bonus, you may discover work-related topics to write about in school.

■ *Your ideas about current events*

Expressing your opinions in your journal can be a good way to explore complex ideas or just to let off steam. Your entries may spur you to write letters to your local or school newspaper or to public officials—and even to become involved in community projects or political activities.

■ *Your impressions of what you see around you*

Many professional and amateur writers carry their journals with them everywhere so that they can record any interesting or unusual things they observe in the course of their daily lives. Rather than relying on memory, they jot down images of memorable people, places, or events as soon as possible after they observe them. If you get into the habit of recording such impressions, you can later incorporate them into stories or other pieces of writing.

■ *Aspects of your personal life*

Although you may not want to record the intimate details of your life if your instructor plans to collect your journal, such entries are the most common of all in a private journal. Writing about relationships with family and friends, personal problems, hopes and dreams—all the details of your life—can help you to reach a better understanding of yourself and others.

Here is Stella's journal entry on the topic of community service for college students.

> *I'm not really sure what I think about community service. I guess I think it sounds like a good idea, but I still don't see why we should have to do it. I can't fit anything else into my life. I guess it would be possible if it was just an hour or two a week. And maybe we could get credit and a grade for it, like a course. Or maybe it should just be for people who have the time and want to do it. But if it's not required, will anyone do it?*

Journal Entry

◆ PRACTICE 1-11

Buy a notebook to use as a journal. (Your instructor may require a specific size and format, particularly if he or she is going to collect journals at some point.) Set a time to write for fifteen minutes or so in your journal—during your lunch break, for example, or before you go to bed. Make entries daily or several times a week, depending on your schedule and your instructor's suggestions. For your first journal entry, write down your thoughts about the topic you have been working on in this chapter: the primary purpose of college.

D Identifying Your Main Idea and Choosing Supporting Points

When you think you have enough material to write about, you can move on to the next stage of the writing process: finding a main idea to develop into a paragraph and selecting and organizing the points that will support that idea most effectively.

Identifying Your Main Idea

Begin by looking over what you have already written. As you read through your freewriting, brainstorming, clustering, and journal entries, look for your **main idea**—the central point that your material seems to support. The sentence that states this main idea and gives your paragraph its focus will be the paragraph's **topic sentence**.

Stella Drew thought her notes supported the idea that community service requires time and commitment but is basically worthwhile. She stated this idea in a sentence.

For more on topic sentences, see 2A.

Community service takes time, but it is so important that college students should be required to do it.

Choosing Supporting Points

After you identify your main idea, review your notes again. This time, look for the specific points (facts, reasons, and examples) that provide **support** for your main idea. Write or type the topic sentence that states this main idea at the top of a blank page. As you review your notes, list all the supporting points you think you might be able to use.

Stella chose the following points from her notes to support her paragraph's main idea.

```
Main idea: Community service takes time, but it is so
important that college students should be required to
do it.
```

- Community service helps people.
- Community service can help the world.
- Community service helps the community.
- College students are busy, and community service takes a lot of time.
- Community service can teach students about careers and about life.
- Community service can be upsetting or depressing.

Ordering Supporting Points

Once you have made a list of points you can use, arrange them in the order in which you plan to present them, as Stella did in the following list.

```
Main idea: Community service takes time, but it is so
important that college students should be required to
do it.
```

- Community service takes a lot of time.
- Students need time for family and friends, for studying, and for working.
- Community service can be depressing and upsetting.
- Community service helps the community.
- Community service can be part of a student's education.
- Community service can make the world a better place.

◆ PRACTICE 1-12

In Practices 1-4, 1-7, and 1-10, you practiced freewriting, brainstorming, and clustering. Now, you are ready to write a paragraph about your topic. Look over the invention exercises you have done, and try to find one main idea that your material can support. Write a sentence that expresses this idea on the following lines.

_____

_____

_____

Now, reread your invention exercises, and list the points you believe will support your main idea most effectively. Also list any new points you think of.

_____

_____

_____

_____

_____

_____

Look over the material you listed above, making sure each point supports your main idea. Arrange your points below in the order in which you plan to write about them.

1. _____

2. _____

3. _____

4. _____

5. _____

6. _____

7. _____

1 E

E   Drafting Your Paragraph

Once you have found a main idea for your paragraph, selected the points you will discuss, and arranged them in the order in which you plan to write about them, you are ready to write a first draft.

In a first draft, your goal is to get your ideas down on paper. Begin with a topic sentence stating your paragraph's main idea. Then, keeping an eye on the list of points you plan to discuss, write or type without worrying about correct wording, spelling, or punctuation. If a new idea—one that is not on your list—occurs to you, write it down. Don't worry about where it goes or whether it fits with the other ideas. Your goal is not to produce a perfect piece of writing but simply to create a working draft. When you revise, you will have a chance to rethink ideas and rework sentences.

Because you will revise this first draft—adding or crossing out words and phrases, reordering ideas and details, clarifying connections between ideas, and rephrasing—you should leave plenty of room for revision. Leave wide margins, triple-space, and leave extra space in places where you might need to add material. Feel free to be messy and to cross out; remember, the only person who will see this draft is you.

When you have finished your first draft, don't start revising right away. Take a break, and think about something—anything—else. Then, return to your draft, and read it with a fresh eye.

Here is the first draft of Stella's paragraph on the topic of community service for college students.

Why Community Service Should Be Required

Community service takes time, but it is so important that college students should be required to do it. When college students do community service, they volunteer their time to do good for someone or for the community. Working in a soup kitchen, raking leaves for senior citizens, and reading to children are all examples of community service. Community service can require long hours and take time away from studying and jobs. It can also force students to deal with unpleasant situations, but overall it is rewarding and helpful to others. Community service is good for the community and can be more fulfilling than playing sports or participating in clubs. Community service can also be an important part of a college education. Students can even discover what

they want to do with their lives. Community service
can also make the world a better place.

First Draft

◆ PRACTICE 1-13

Reread Stella's draft paragraph. If you were advising her, what would you suggest that she change in the draft? What might she add? What might she cross out? Be prepared to discuss your ideas with your class or in a small group.

◆ PRACTICE 1-14

Using the material you came up with for Practice 1-12, draft a paragraph that states your main idea and supports it with specific points. Be sure to leave wide margins and skip lines. (If you type your draft, you can triple-space.) When you are finished, give your paragraph a title.

| F | **Revising and Editing Your Paragraph** |

Revision is the process of reseeing, rethinking, reevaluating, and rewriting your work. Revision involves much more than substituting one word for another or correcting a comma here and there. Often, it means moving sentences, adding words and phrases, and even changing the direction or emphasis of your ideas. To get the most out of the revision process, begin by carefully rereading your draft with a critical eye, using the checklist below to guide your revision.

✔️ SELF-ASSESSMENT CHECKLIST: Revising Your Paragraph

- Have you stated your main idea clearly in your topic sentence?
- Do you have enough points to support your paragraph's main idea, or do you need to look back at your notes or try another invention strategy to find additional supporting material?
- Do you need to explain anything more fully or more clearly?
- Do you need to add more examples or details?

(continued on the following page)

(continued from previous page)

- Should you cross out any examples or details?
- Does every sentence say what you mean?
- Can you combine any sentences to make your writing smoother?
- Should you move any sentences?
- Are all your words necessary, or can you cut some?
- Should you change any words?
- Does your paragraph end with a sentence that sums up its main idea?

FOCUS   Editing

Don't confuse revision with editing. Revision often involves extensive rewriting and rearranging, and it can be hard work. Editing comes after revision.

When you **edit**, you should concentrate on the surface features of your writing, checking for clarity and for correct grammar, punctuation, mechanics, and spelling. For example, be sure you have indented the first sentence, and check to make sure every sentence begins with a capital letter and ends with a period. You should also proofread carefully for typographical errors that a computer spell checker may not identify.

Although editing is a lot less comprehensive than revision, it is a vital last step in the writing process. Many readers will not take your work seriously if it contains grammatical or mechanical errors. Correctness goes a long way toward establishing your competence and authority with your audience.

Guided by the Self-Assessment Checklist on page 33, Stella revised her paragraph, writing her changes in by hand on her typewritten draft.

```
        Why Community Service Should Be Required
     Community service takes time, but it is so impor-
tant that college students should be required to do
it. When college students do community service, they
```

~~volunteer their time to~~ do good for someone or for the
community. ~~Working~~ *For example, they work* in a soup kitchen, ~~raking~~ *rake* leaves
for senior citizens, ~~and reading~~ *or read* to children ~~are all~~
~~examples of community service.~~ *These activities* Community service can
require long hours and take time away ^*important things like* from studying
and jobs. ~~It can also force students to deal with un-~~ *However, community service is worth the time it takes.*
~~pleasant situations, but overall it is rewarding and~~
~~helpful to others.~~ Community service is ~~good for the~~
~~community and~~ *for students* can be more fulfilling ^than ^playing *other college*
activities, such as
sports or participating in clubs. Community service
can also be an important part of a college education.
learn about themselves, about their communities, and about their world,
Students can even discover what they want to do with *and*
they
their lives. ^*Finally,* Community service can ~~also~~ make the *can*
world a better place. *For all these reasons, community service*
should be a required part of the ^college curriculum.

Revised Draft

When she revised, Stella didn't worry about being neat. She crossed
out, added material, and made major changes in her words, sentences, and
ideas. Then, she edited her paragraph, checking punctuation, mechanics
and spelling, and looking for typos. The final typed version of Stella's paragraph appears below.

```
        Why Community Service Should Be Required

        Community service takes time, but it is so impor-        Topic sentence
tant that college students should be required to do
it. When college students do community service, they do
good for someone or for the community. For example, they
work in a soup kitchen, rake leaves for senior citizens,
or read to children. These activities can require long
```

Support

hours and take time away from important things, like studying and jobs. However, community service is worth the time it takes. Community service can be more fulfilling for students than other college activities, such as playing sports or participating in clubs. Community service can also be an important part of a college education. Students can learn about themselves, about their communities, and about their world, and they can even discover what they want to do with their lives. Finally, community service can make the world a better place.

Concluding statement

For all these reasons, community service should be a required part of the college curriculum.

◆ PRACTICE 1-15

Reread the final draft of Stella's paragraph about community service for college students (see previous page), and compare it with her first draft (page 32). What changes did she make? Which do you think are her most effective changes? Why? Note your thoughts on the lines below. Then, with your class or in a small group, discuss your reaction to the final typed paragraph.

_____

_____

_____

_____

_____

◆ PRACTICE 1-16

Use the Self-Assessment Checklist on page 33 to evaluate the paragraph you drafted for Practice 1-14. What additions can you make to support your main idea more fully? Should you cross out anything because it doesn't support your main idea? Can you state anything more clearly? On the following lines, list some of the changes you might make in your draft.

_____

_____

_____

_____

_____

_____

_____

_____

Now, revise your draft. Cross out unnecessary material and material you want to rewrite, and add new and rewritten material between the lines and in the margins. After you finish your revision, edit your paragraph, checking grammar, punctuation, mechanics, and spelling—and look carefully for typos. When you are satisfied with your paragraph, print out a clean copy, and hold onto it for the Seeing and Writing exercise that opens Chapter 2.

2 *Fine-Tuning Your Paragraph*

PREVIEW

In this chapter, you will learn
- to write effective topic sentences (2A)
- to write unified paragraphs (2B)
- to write well-developed paragraphs (2C)
- to write coherent paragraphs (2D)

▶ **Word Power**

pragmatic
practical;
active rather
than passive

■ SEEING AND WRITING

Make a copy of the final draft of the paragraph that you wrote and revised in Chapter 1. You will continue to work on your paragraph as you go through this chapter.

A   Writing Effective Topic Sentences

As you learned in Chapter 1, a paragraph is a group of related sentences that develops one central idea. Every paragraph includes a topic sentence that states the paragraph's main idea. This topic sentence helps guide readers, and it also helps keep writers on track as they write.

The Topic Sentence in the Paragraph

The topic sentence is the most general sentence of your paragraph. The rest of the sentences in your paragraph support the topic sentence with details, facts, and examples. Many paragraphs also include a concluding statement that sums up the paragraph's main idea.

> <u>Although most people do not know it, the modern roller coaster got its start in Coney Island in Brooklyn, New York.</u> The first economically successful roller coaster, the first high drop, and the first circuit coaster were all pioneered in Coney Island. In 1888, the Flip Flap Railway, which featured a circular loop, was built. This coaster was the first to go upside down, but it had a habit of injuring people's necks. In 1901, the Loop-the-Loop, which provided a safer ride than the Flip Flap Railway, was built. From 1884 through the 1930s, over thirty roller coasters were constructed in Coney Island. The most famous coaster in history, the Cyclone, was built at a cost of $100,000 in 1926. Although it opened in 1927, it is still the standard by which all other roller coasters are measured. It has steep drops, lots of angular momentum, and only a lap belt to hold riders in their seats. Still in operation, the Cyclone is the most successful ride in Coney Island history. It is also the last survivor of the classic wooden roller coasters that once drew crowds to Coney Island. Because of the innovations that took place there, Coney Island made possible the many high-tech roller coasters in amusement parks today.

Topic sentence

Support (details, facts, examples)

Concluding statement

Revising Topic Sentences

The first step toward writing a good paragraph is learning to write an effective topic sentence. When you revise, keep in mind the following three characteristics of effective topic sentences.

1. ***A topic sentence should be a complete sentence.*** Like any sentence, it must contain a subject and a verb and state a complete thought. Remember that there is a difference between a **topic** and a **topic**

sentence. The *topic* is what the paragraph is about; the *topic sentence* is the sentence that presents the paragraph's **main idea**—the idea the paragraph will develop.

Topic	Topic Sentence
Television violence	Violent television shows have a negative effect on my younger brother.
Animal testing	One reason not to buy products tested on animals is that most animal testing is not necessary.
Heroes	My heroes are people who take action instead of waiting for others to act.

2. *A topic sentence should be more than just an announcement of what you plan to write about*. It should make a point about the topic the paragraph discusses.

Announcement	Topic Sentence
In this paragraph I will write about the problems my first credit card caused.	When I got my first credit card, I had no idea of the problems it would cause.

3. *A topic sentence should present an idea that you can discuss in a single paragraph*. If your topic sentence is too broad, you will not be able to discuss it in just one paragraph. If your topic sentence is too narrow (for example, if it is a statement of fact), you will not be able to say much about it.

TOPIC SENTENCE TOO BROAD   Students with jobs have special needs.

TOPIC SENTENCE TOO NARROW   The tutoring center closes at 5 p.m.

EFFECTIVE TOPIC SENTENCE   Because many students have jobs, the tutoring center should remain open until 9 p.m.

FOCUS　**Placing Topic Sentences**

A topic sentence can appear anywhere in a paragraph—at the beginning, in the middle, or at the end. For the time being, however, you should place your topic sentences at the beginning of your paragraphs. This strategy will keep you on track as you write. In addition, by telling readers what your paragraph will be about, your topic sentence will help readers follow your ideas.

◆ **PRACTICE 2-1**

Underline the topic sentence in each of the following paragraphs.

1. Genetically modified crops, created by adding a desired trait from one plant to another, can be very beneficial. "Golden rice," for example, was created when scientists took genes from daffodils and other small plants and put them into a strain of rice. These genes gave the rice a golden color. More important, the new genes enabled the rice to produce beta-carotene, which produces vitamin A. The Swiss scientist who created golden rice wanted to produce a product containing this vitamin because he knew that about three hundred million people in China suffer from vitamin A deficiencies. The lack of vitamin A can cause a person to become sick easily or even to go blind, but in China vitamins are not easily available, and they are expensive. So, if the rice the Chinese people depend on already contains a vitamin that they need, eating the rice might solve a number of medical problems.

2. In the mid-nineteenth century, steamboats were an important means of transportation in America. Initially, these boats carried cargo and passengers between river towns. In some towns, passengers were met at the wharf by stagecoaches that carried them to their final destinations. In other towns, a railroad line came within walking distance of the wharf. Americans were pleased with this new type of transportation. Trips that had taken weeks by horse and carriage could now be completed in days.

3. During the American Civil War, a notorious camp was built at Andersonville, Georgia, to house prisoners of war. The Confederates selected the site because it was far from Richmond, Virginia, their capital, and near fresh water and a railroad. Although the prison was built to house 10,000 prisoners, the number of inmates grew to over 32,000. There was no shelter from the weather, no source of fresh water (except for a small stream that ran through the camp and was also used as a sewer), no clothing other than what the prisoners arrived in, and no fruit or vegetables. Many simply dug holes in the ground to live in. Because of these conditions, nearly a third of the prisoners died of disease. Today, the Andersonville National Historic Site, built on the land occupied by the old prison, is a monument to all Americans who have been prisoners of war.

◆ **PRACTICE 2-2**

Rearrange the following sentences into a logical paragraph by placing a *1* in front of the topic sentence, a *2* in front of the next sentence, and so on.

_____ By the end of the war, the game had spread throughout the country, and standard rules had been established.

_____ The first official baseball game was played in New York City in 1846.

_____ In that game, the Knickerbocker Baseball Club played a team made up of its own members.

_____ Although baseball is now seen as "America's pastime," it did not catch on right away.

_____ Soldiers even played baseball behind their own lines and in prisoner-of-war camps.

_____ Between 1846 and the start of the Civil War, interest in the game grew slowly.

_____ Several years after the war, in 1871, the first professional baseball league was formed.

_____ During the war, however, the popularity of the game increased enormously.

◆ PRACTICE 2-3

Read the following items. Put a check mark next to each one that has all three characteristics of an effective topic sentence.

Examples:

The common cold. _____

Many people are convinced that large doses of vitamin C will prevent the common cold. _✔_

1. Global warming, a crisis for our cities. _____

2. If something is not done soon, the city of New Orleans may be under water by the year 2010. _____

3. In this paragraph, I will discuss global warming. _____

4. Computers and college students. _____

5. Colleges should make sure that every student has access to a computer.

_____

◆ PRACTICE 2-4

Decide whether each of the following statements could be an effective topic sentence for a paragraph. If a sentence is too broad, write "too broad" in the blank following the sentence. If the sentence is too narrow, write "too narrow" in the blank. If the sentence is an effective topic sentence, write "OK" in the blank.

Example: Thanksgiving always falls on the fourth Thursday in November. ___*too narrow*___

1. Computers are changing the world. _____

2. There are five computer terminals in the campus library. _____

3. The computer I use at work makes my job easier. _____

4. Soccer is not as popular in the United States as it is in Europe.

   _____

5. Americans enjoy watching many types of sporting events on television.

   _____

6. There is one quality that distinguishes a good coach from a mediocre

   one. _____

7. Vegetarianism is a healthy way of life. _____

8. Uncooked spinach has fourteen times as much iron as steak does.

   _____

9. Fast-food restaurants are finally beginning to respond to the growing

   number of customers who are vegetarians. _____

10. There are many different kinds of cars to choose from. _____

◆ PRACTICE 2-5

The following paragraphs do not have topic sentences. Think of a topic sentence that expresses each paragraph's main idea, and write it on the lines above the paragraphs.

Example: *Possible answer: Early rock and roll was a creation of both*

black and white performers.

Early 1950s African-American musicians included performers such as Johnny Ace, Big Joe Turner, and Ruth Brown. Groups like the Drifters and the Clovers were also popular. By the mid-1950s, white performers such as Bill Haley and the Comets, Jerry Lee Lewis, and Elvis Presley imitated African-American music. Although their songs did not have the heavy backbeat and explicit lyrics that most black music had, their music appealed to a white audience. Eventually, this combination of black and white musical styles became known as rock and roll.

1. _____

_____

Most Americans own televisions. In fact, more people watch television than read magazines and newspapers. Television has even replaced going to the movies as the most popular form of entertainment. Not surprisingly, recent surveys have shown that most Americans get their news from television. Moreover, as anyone in the book industry knows, the best way for a book to become a best-seller is for it to be promoted on a popular television show. For example, a book that was endorsed by Oprah Winfrey was almost sure to become an instant best-seller. Finally, Americans spend many hours a day staring at their televisions, just trying to unwind.

2. _____

_____

First, you have to find a suitable job to appy for. Once you decide to apply, you have to type your résumé and send it to your prospective employer. Then, when you are invited in for an interview, you need to decide what you are going to wear. At the interview, you need to speak slowly and clearly and answer all questions directly and honestly. After the interview, you need to send a note to the person who interviewed you, thanking him or her. Finally, if everything goes well, you will get a letter or a telephone call offering you the job.

3. _____

_____

There are no written records left by the Native Americans themselves. Most of the early settlers were more interested in surviving than in writing about the Native Americans. In addition, as the westward expansion took place, the Europeans encountered the Native Americans in stages, not all at once. Also, the Native Americans spoke at least fifty-eight different languages, which made it difficult for the Europeans to communicate with them. Most important, by the time scholars decided to study Native American culture, many of the tribes no longer existed. Disease and war had wiped them out.

■ SEEING AND WRITING: Flashback

Look back at the paragraph you wrote for the Seeing and Writing exercise on page 38. Does your paragraph have an effective topic sentence? If necessary, revise the topic sentence so that it states the main idea of your paragraph more clearly. (If your paragraph does not have a topic sentence, add one now.)

B   Writing Unified Paragraphs

An effective paragraph focuses on a single main idea. A paragraph is **unified** when all its sentences support the main idea stated in the topic sentence.

Understanding Unity

To write a unified paragraph, state your main idea clearly in the topic sentence. Then, make sure the rest of the sentences in your paragraph relate directly to this idea.

> The population problem is one of the biggest causes for concern for scientists. In 1900, there were 1.6 billion people on earth, a quarter of today's population. In 1900, the average life expectancy was also much shorter than it is now. In some places, it was only twenty-three years. By the year 2000, the world's population had grown to over 6 billion. Today, average life expectancy worldwide is almost sixty-five years. This means that billions of people are living longer and using more of the earth's resources. The low death rate, combined with a high birth rate, is adding the equivalent of one new Germany to the world's population each year. According to a United Nations study, if present trends continue, by 2050 the world's population will be so large (between 7.3 and 10.5 billion) that most people in the world will be malnourished or starving.

Topic sentence

The paragraph above is unified. The topic sentence states the paragraph's main idea, and the rest of the sentences present specific details to support the main idea.

Revising Paragraphs for Unity

A paragraph lacks unity when its sentences wander from the main idea. When you revise, you can make sure your paragraphs are unified by rewriting or deleting sentences that do not support the main idea that your topic sentence states.

 Computer Tip

Try boldfacing or underlining the topic sentence of a paragraph before you start to revise.

Paragraph Not Unified

> The changing economic picture has led many people to move away from the rural Pennsylvania community where I was raised. Over the years, farmland has become more and more expensive. Years ago, a family could buy each of its children twenty-five acres on which they could start farming. Today, the price of land is so high that the average farmer cannot afford to buy this amount of land. I am tired of seeing my friends move away. After I graduate, I intend to return to my town and get a job

Topic sentence

there. Even though many factories have moved out of the area, I think I can get a job. My uncle owns a hardware store, and he told me that after I graduate, he will teach me the business. I think I can contribute something to the business and to the town.

This paragraph is not unified. After presenting one reason why people are moving away, the writer wanders from his paragraph's main idea, instead complaining about his friends and discussing his own future plans. These digressions do not support the topic sentence.

The following revised paragraph is unified. It discusses only what the topic sentence promises: the reasons why people have moved away from the writer's hometown.

Paragraph Unified

Topic sentence   <u>The changing economic picture has led many people to move away from the rural Pennsylvania community where I was raised.</u> Over the years, farmland has become more and more expensive. Years ago, a family could buy each of its children twenty-five acres on which they could start farming. Today, the price of land is so high that the average farmer cannot afford to buy this amount of land, and those who choose not to farm have few alternatives. They just cannot get good jobs anymore. Factories have moved out of the area and have taken with them the jobs that many young people used to get after high school. As a result, many eighteen-year-olds have no choice but to move to Pittsburgh to find employment.

◆ PRACTICE 2-6

The following paragraphs are not unified because some sentences do not support the topic sentence. Cross out any sentences in each paragraph that do not belong.

1. The one possession I could not live without is my car. In addition to attending school full time, I hold down two part-time jobs that are many miles from each other, from where I live, and from school. Even though my car is almost twelve years old and has close to 120,000 miles on it, I couldn't manage without it. I'm thinking about buying a new car, and I always check the classified ads, but I haven't found anything I want that I can afford. If my old car breaks down, I guess I'll have to, though. I couldn't live without my portable tape recorder because I use it to record all the class lectures I attend. Then I can play them back while I'm driving or during my breaks at work. Three nights a week and on weekends, I work as a counselor at a home for teenagers with problems, and my other job is in the tire department at Sam's. Without my car, I'd be lost.

2. Studies conducted by Dr. Leonard Eron over the last thirty years suggest that the more television violence children are exposed to, the more

aggressive they are as teenagers and adults. In 1960, Eron questioned parents about how they treated their children at home, including how much television their children watched. There is more violence on television today than there was then. Ten years later, he interviewed these families again and discovered that whether teenage sons were aggressive depended less on how they had been treated by their parents than on how much violent television programming they had watched as children. Returning in 1990, he found that these same young men, now in their thirties, were still more likely to be aggressive and to commit crimes. Researchers estimate that a child today is likely to watch 100,000 violent acts on television before finishing elementary school.

3. Libraries today hold a lot more than just books. Of course, books still outnumber anything else on the shelves, but more and more libraries are expanding to include other specialized services. For example, many libraries now offer extensive collections of tapes and compact discs, ranging from classical music to jazz to country to rock. Many have also increased their holdings of videotapes, both instructional programs and popular recent and vintage movies. Some libraries also stock DVDs. However, most people probably still get more movies from video stores than from libraries. In addition, the children's section often has games and toys young patrons can play with in the library or even check out. Most important, libraries are offering more and more computerized data services, which can provide much more detailed and up-to-date information than printed sources. These expanding nonprint sources are the wave of the future for even the smallest libraries and will allow patrons access to much more information than books or magazines ever could. People who don't know how to use a computer are going to be out of luck.

■ SEEING AND WRITING: Flashback

Look back at the paragraph that you wrote for the Seeing and Writing exercise on page 38. Review your paragraph for unity. Cross out any sentences that do not support the topic sentence. If necessary, rewrite sentences so that they support your main point.

C   Writing Well-Developed Paragraphs

A paragraph is **well developed** when it contains enough details, facts, and examples to support the topic sentence. A paragraph is not well developed when it lacks the support readers need to understand or accept its main idea.

Supporting the Topic Sentence

To determine the amount and kind of support you need, ask yourself two questions:

1. *How complicated is your main idea?* A complicated main idea will need more support than a relatively simple one. A relatively straightforward topic sentence—for example, "During the first week of school, registration is a nightmare"—would require only two or three well-chosen examples. A more far-reaching topic sentence—"Our community has to do much more to accommodate the physically challenged," for example— would call for a lot more support.
2. *How much do your readers know about your main idea?* If you know that your readers have regularly eaten food served in your school's cafeteria, you do not need to give them many examples to convince them that the food leaves much to be desired. If you think that your readers are not familiar with the food at your school, however, you have to supply more examples and possibly definitions (explaining what you mean by "mystery meat," for example) to support your point.

Revising Paragraphs for Development

A well-developed paragraph provides the support readers need to understand its points and to accept the statement the topic sentence makes. If your paragraph contains only general statements, it is not well developed. When you revise, be sure to support your general statements with details, facts, and examples.

Undeveloped Paragraph

Although pit bulls were originally bred to fight, they can actually make good pets. Today, many people are afraid of pit bulls. These dogs are sometimes mistreated. As a result, they become more aggressive. For this reason, they are misunderstood and persecuted. In fact, some cities have taken action against them. But pit bulls do not deserve their bad reputation. Contrary to popular opinion, they can make good pets.

The preceding paragraph is not well developed. It consists of general statements that leave the writer's points unclear and therefore do not provide adequate support for the main idea.

Well-Developed Paragraph

Although pit bulls were originally bred to fight, they can actually make good pets. It is true that their powerful jaws, short muscular legs, and large teeth are ideally suited to fighting, and they were used extensively for this purpose in the rural South and Southwest. It is also true that some pit bulls—especially males—can be aggressive toward other dogs. However, most pit bulls like human beings and are quite friendly.

Owners report that pit bulls are affectionate, loyal, and good with children. When pit bulls behave viciously, it is usually because they have been mistreated. As a recent newspaper article pointed out, the number of reported bites by pit bulls is no greater than the number of bites by other breeds. In fact, some dogs, such as cocker spaniels, bite much more frequently. The problem is that whenever a pit bull attacks a person, the incident is reported in the paper. But pit bulls do not deserve their reputation. Contrary to popular opinion, they can make good pets.

The paragraph is now well developed. Because general statements are clarified by examples or details, readers are more likely to accept the idea that pit bulls can make good pets.

A well-developed paragraph provides the support readers need to understand its points and to accept the statement the topic sentence makes. If your paragraph contains only general statements, it is not well developed. When you revise, be sure you support your general statements with details, facts, and examples.

Computer Tip

Try hitting the Enter or Return key after each sentence of your paragraph. Isolating each detail and example in this way can help you evaluate the amount and kind of support you have used in your paragraph.

◆ PRACTICE 2-7

Read the following paragraphs, and then write an appropriate topic sentence for each.

1. _____ The first—and simplest way—is to move out of the way of the enraged driver. If the good driver does not do this, the angry driver will probably honk the horn, flash the lights, or tailgate the slower driver. Next, when the angry driver tries to get the good driver's attention, the defensive driver should avoid making eye contact. This lessens the chance that the furious driver will try to insult the good driver and make things worse. Finally, once the angry driver has passed, the good driver must consider whether or not to call the police.

2. _____

   For example, Jim Morrison, lead singer of the Doors, has been the subject of a big-budget movie and several books since his death in July 1971. His grave in France is visited around the clock by fans, including many who were not even born when he was alive. Kurt Cobain, who committed suicide in 1994, is now the subject of several books, and his group, Nirvana, has an album that continues to sell well even though it is more than ten years old. Another example is Tupac Shakur. He was killed in 1996, but his albums still sell well, and his poetry has been collected and published. Probably the biggest sign that all three singers are still remembered fondly is the number of Web sites that try to prove they are still alive.

3. _____
_____ Some people who once turned to allergy shots now prefer to try vitamins and supplements. Others, who suffer with back problems, are trying to give up their pain relievers by visiting acupuncturists and chiropractors. Still other patients prefer to see if physical therapy can help them deal with a health problem instead of scheduling surgery. Some people also attend yoga classes to relieve stress instead of taking a prescription medication. Obviously, many patients are willing to try nontraditional methods to help them deal with their ailments.

◆ PRACTICE 2-8

Underline the supporting details, facts, and examples in each of the following paragraphs.

1. Hearing people have some misconceptions about the deaf community. First, some hearing adults might assume that everyone who is deaf considers himself to be a disabled individual who would trade anything not to be "handicapped." These people do not realize that many deaf people do not consider themselves handicapped and are very proud to be part of the deaf community. They have their own language, customs, and culture. Second, many hearing people assume that all deaf people read lips, so there is no need to learn sign language to communicate with the deaf. Lip reading—or speech reading, as many deaf people call the practice—is difficult. Not all hearing people say the same words in the same way, and facial expressions can also change the meaning of the words. If hearing people make more of an attempt to understand the deaf culture, communication between them will improve.

2. In 1996, the National Basketball Association (NBA) decided to approve a women's professional basketball league. Within fifteen months, eight teams had been formed, four in the Eastern Conference and four in the Western Conference. Next, the teams began to draft players for these teams and to select a logo and uniforms. The final logo selected, a red, white, and blue shield, showed the silhouette of a woman player dribbling the ball, with the letters "WNBA" above her. The uniforms consisted of

shorts and jerseys in the colors of the different teams. That first season, games were played in the summer, when the television sports schedule was lighter so that they could be televised during prime time. At the end of that season, the Houston Comets became the first WNBA champions. Today, the WNBA consists of sixteen teams that play 256 regular season games televised to audiences worldwide.

3. One of the largest celebrations of the passage of young girls into woman-hood occurs in Hispanic cultures. This event is called La Quinceañera, or the fifteenth year. It acknowledges that a young woman is now of mar-riageable age. The day usually begins with a Mass of Thanksgiving. The young woman wears a full-length white or pastel-colored dress and is attended by fourteen friends and relatives who serve as maids of honor and male escorts. Her parents and godparents surround her at the foot of the altar. When the Mass ends, other young relatives give small gifts to those who attended, while the Quinceañera places a bouquet of flowers on the altar of the Virgin. Following the Mass is an elaborate party, with dancing, cake, and toasts. Finally, to end the evening, the young woman dances a waltz with her favorite escort.

◆ PRACTICE 2-9

Provide two or three supporting details for each of the following topic sentences.

1. A sport utility vehicle (SUV) has advantages over a minivan.

2. Candles can help make an occasion special.

3. Home security systems protect families in several ways.

4. Conducting a successful garage sale requires organization.

5. Shopping online can save time.

◆ PRACTICE 2-10

The following two paragraphs are not well developed. On the lines that follow each paragraph, write three questions or suggestions that might help the writer develop his or her ideas more fully.

1. Other than my parents, the biggest influence on my life was probably my Aunt Sylva. When I was little, she used to baby-sit for me every day, and she always found interesting and educational things for us to do, either at home or on trips downtown. She had lived in Mexico City for

many years, and I always admired her exotic looks. As a teenager, I tried to copy the way she walked, talked, and even dressed. Even today, I often think of her when I catch myself putting on the sort of outfit she might have worn. Tragically, she died just before my eighteenth birthday.

_____

_____

_____

2. Computerized special effects have made a big difference in movies over the last ten years. Science fiction films are more spectacular than ever, and filmmakers are able to take moviegoers to places they've never been before. New special-effects techniques can also create fierce monsters, more terrifying than anything seen on the screen before. Other effects have been used in comedies to create hilarious visual jokes. It is likely that the future will bring even more impressive effects for the enjoyment of movie audiences.

_____

_____

_____

■ SEEING AND WRITING: Flashback

Look back at the paragraph you wrote for the Seeing and Writing exercise on page 38. Is your paragraph well developed? Evaluate the number and kind of details, facts, and examples you use to support your topic sentence. Then, jot down some suggestions for revision, noting the kind of material you might add to your paragraph.

D   Writing Coherent Paragraphs

A paragraph is **coherent** if all its sentences are arranged in a clear, sensible order. You can make a paragraph coherent by arranging details carefully and by supplying transitional words and phrases that show the connections between sentences.

Arranging Details

In general, you can arrange the details in a paragraph according to *time order, spatial order,* or *logical order.*

Paragraphs that are arranged in **time order** present events in the order in which they occurred. Stories, historical accounts, and instructions are generally arranged in time order.

The following paragraph presents events in time order. Specific dates as well as the words *before, once, then, finally, later,* and *after* indicate the sequence of events in the paragraph.

> In 1856, my great-great-great-grandparents, Anne and Charles McGinley, came to the United States to start a new life. Before they left Ireland, their English landlords had raised the taxes on their land so high that my ancestors could not afford to pay them. It took them three years to save the money for passage. Once they had saved the money, they had to look for a ship that was willing to take them. Then my great-great-great-grandparents were on their way. They and their ten children spent four long months on a small ship. Storms, strong tides, and damaged sails made the trip longer than it should have been. Finally, in November of 1856, they saw land, and two days later they sailed into New York Harbor. After they were admitted to the United States, they took a train to Baltimore, Maryland, where some cousins lived.

See p. 55 for a list of transitions that signal time order.

Paragraphs that are arranged in **spatial order** present details in the order in which they are seen—from top to bottom, from near to far, from right to left, and so on. Spatial order is central to paragraphs that describe something—for example, what an object, place, or person looks like.

The following paragraph presents events in spatial order. Notice how the phrases *directly in front of, next to, behind, in between, on top of, inside,* and *in the center of* help establish the order—from far to near—in which readers will view the details of the scene.

> The day I arrived at the Amish school I knew it was unlike any other school I had seen before. A long, tree-lined dirt road led to the small wooden schoolhouse. Directly in front of the school was a line of bicycles and metal scooters. A small baseball diamond had been carved into the dirt in the yard next to the schoolhouse. Behind the school, two little outhouses stood next to each other with a green water pump in between. The schoolhouse itself was a small one-story structure. White paint curled off its clapboard siding, and a short steeple, holding a brass bell, sat firmly on top of the roof. Inside the open door, a long line of black hats hung on pegs. In the center of the small schoolhouse was an iron potbellied stove surrounded by the children's desks.

See p. 55 for a list of transitions that signal spatial order.

Paragraphs that are arranged in **logical order** present ideas in a sequence that indicates why one idea logically follows another. For example, a paragraph may move from least important to most important, from general to specific, or from most familiar to least familiar.

The following paragraph presents ideas in logical order. Here, the phrases *the first rule, an even sillier rule,* and *the most ridiculous rule* establish the order in which the rules are presented—from least to most silly—and thus help readers move from one point to another.

See p. 56 for a list of transitions that signal logical order.

My high school had three rules that were silly at best and ridiculous at worst. The first rule was that only seniors could go outside the school building for lunch. In spite of this rule, many students went outside to eat because the cafeteria was not big enough to accommodate all the school's students at the same time. Understanding the problem, the teachers and the principal looked the other way as long as we returned to school before the lunch period was over. An even sillier rule was that we had to attend 95 percent of the classes for every course. This rule meant that a person could miss only about six days of class every semester. Naturally, this rule was never enforced because if it had been, half the students would have failed. The most ridiculous rule, however, was that students could not throw their hats into the air during graduation. At one point in the past—no one seems to know when— a parent had complained that a falling hat could poke someone in the eye. As a result, graduating classes were told that under no circumstance could they throw their hats. Naturally, on graduation day we did what every previous graduating class had done—ignored the rule and threw our hats into the air.

◆ PRACTICE 2-11

Read each of the following topic sentences carefully. If you were writing a paragraph introduced by the sentence, how would you arrange the supporting details—in time order, spatial order, or logical order? Write your answer in the blank following the topic sentence.

Example: It is important to keep several things in mind when shopping for a new stereo. ___*logical order*___

1. My first week at my new job began badly but ended better than I ever could have expected. _____

2. People would get along better if everyone practiced a few important rules of common courtesy. _____

3. My son's bedroom reflects his many different interests and hobbies.

   _____

4. The Mustangs are a stronger team than the Bobcats for three reasons.

   _____

5. Babies develop in amazing ways during the first three months of life.
   _____

6. When you interview for a job, keep in mind that most employers look for the same qualities in a prospective employee. _____

7. Dressing for success means looking your best from the hair on your head to the shoes on your feet. _____

8. I had always felt safe in my neighborhood until last year, when something happened that changed my attitude completely. _____

9. To protect yourself on campus after dark, you should always take the following precautions. _____

10. The new Southern Trust Bank in Gaston is one of the ugliest buildings in town. _____

Using Transitional Words and Phrases

Within a paragraph, **transitional words and phrases** often indicate the relationships among sentences. By establishing the time order, spatial order, and logical order of the ideas in a paragraph, these words and phrases enable readers to see the connections among ideas.

Transitional Words and Phrases

Some Words and Phrases That Signal Time Order

after	finally	dates (for example, "In June")
afterward	later	
at first	next	
before	now	
during	soon	
earlier	then	
eventually	today	

Some Words and Phrases That Signal Spatial Order

above	in front	on the left
behind	in the center	on the right
below	inside	on top
beside	near	over
in back	next to	under
in between	on the bottom	

Some Words and Phrases That Signal Logical Order

also	last
although	moreover
as a result	next
consequently	not only . . . but also
first . . . second . . . third	one . . . another
for example	similarly
for instance	the least important
furthermore	the most important
in addition	therefore
in fact	

Revising Paragraphs for Coherence

Because transitional words and phrases establish **coherence**, a paragraph without them is difficult to understand. You can correct this problem when you revise by including all the words and phrases that are needed to link the ideas in your paragraph.

 Computer Tip

Keep a list of transitional words and phrases in a separate file. When you revise, check this file to see if you have used the most appropriate transitions.

Paragraph without Transitional Words and Phrases

During his lifetime, Jim Thorpe faced many obstacles. Thorpe was born in 1888, the son of an Irish father and a Native American mother. He was sent to the Carlisle Indian School in Pennsylvania. "Pop" Warner, the legendary coach at Carlisle, discovered Thorpe when he saw him jump more than six feet while he was wearing street clothes. Thorpe left Carlisle to play baseball for two seasons in the newly formed East Carolina minor league. Thorpe returned to Carlisle, played football, and was named to the All-American team. Thorpe went to the Olympic games in Stockholm, where he won two gold medals. Thorpe's career took a dramatic turn for the worse when a sportswriter who had seen him play baseball in North Carolina exposed him as a professional. The Amateur Athletic Union stripped him of his records and medals. The International Olympic Committee returned Thorpe's Olympic medals to his family.

The above paragraph is not coherent because it does not include the transitional words and phrases needed to establish how the events in Jim Thorpe's life relate to one another.

Paragraph with Transitional Words and Phrases

During his lifetime, Jim Thorpe faced many obstacles. Thorpe was born in 1888, the son of an Irish father and a Native American mother. <u>In 1904</u>, he was sent to the Carlisle Indian School in Pennsylvania. <u>The next</u>

year, "Pop" Warner, the legendary coach at Carlisle, discovered Thorpe when he saw him jump more than six feet while he was wearing street clothes. Thorpe left Carlisle in 1909 to play baseball for two seasons in the newly formed East Carolina minor league. In 1911, Thorpe returned to Carlisle, played football, and was named to the All-American team. In 1912, Thorpe went to the Olympic games in Stockholm, where he won two gold medals. The next year, however, Thorpe's career took a dramatic turn for the worse when a sportswriter who had seen him play baseball in North Carolina exposed him as a professional. As a result, the Amateur Athletic Union stripped him of his records and medals. After years of appeals, the International Olympic Committee returned Thorpe's Olympic medals to his family in 1982.

The paragraph is now coherent. It contains transitional words and phrases—*in 1912, the next year,* and *after years of appeals,* for example—that establish the time order of the events in Thorpe's life.

◆ PRACTICE 2-12

Underline the transitional words and phrases in each of the following paragraphs. Then, decide what order—time order, spatial order, or logical order—the writer has chosen for arranging details in each paragraph. Write your answers in the blanks provided.

1. Alarmed that teenage girls today get only half as much exercise as boys, researchers are trying to find out why. One reason, they say, is the amount of television girls watch. But this is not an adequate explanation because boys generally watch as much television as girls do. A more important reason is that many girls do not have available to them the sorts of organized athletic programs that are available to boys. Furthermore, because both parents often work now, girls are more likely than boys to have responsibilities at home that leave them less free time to pursue physical activity. Most important, though, may be the lingering attitude that boys aren't attracted to girls who are athletic. Being "feminine," for many girls, means avoiding anything that might mess up their hair or make them sweat. Unless these habits and attitudes change, the current generation of teenage girls may grow into a generation of women plagued by serious health problems.

Order: _____

2. The high school I attended is unusual because, instead of being a single building, it is actually a campus consisting of six separate buildings located on a small hill. The building in front, which faces the street, houses administrative offices, the library, and the cafeteria. Beside the administration building is a large structure that contains the gym, a

swimming pool, and rehearsal rooms for band and chorus. In back of the administration building is a parallel building where English and foreign language classes are held. Behind this is a large grassy space flanked by two buildings that run at right angles to the English building. The building on the right is for political science and history courses, and the building on the left is for math and the sciences. At the far end of the grassy space is a small A-frame building containing the art studio and the shop. Between the buildings are covered cement walkways. Changing classes requires going from building to building, and this is usually a nice break—except in the dead of winter, when people freeze as they pass from class to class.

Order: _____

3. The Caribbean island of Puerto Rico has a complex history. Before the 1400s, the island's inhabitants for centuries were the native Arawak Indians. In 1493, Christopher Columbus and his crew were the earliest Europeans to reach the island. Fifteen years later, Ponce de Leon conquered the island for Spain, and the Spanish subjected the Arawaks to virtual slavery to develop a sugar industry. Finally, these native people were annihilated completely, slaughtered by the sword and by European diseases to which they had no immunity. The Arawaks were soon replaced by African slaves as a European plantation culture flourished. In 1898, after the Spanish-American War, the island was ceded to the United States. The next year, the United States designated Puerto Rico a colony under an American governor. Later, in 1917, Puerto Ricans were granted U.S. citizenship, and the country became a U.S. commonwealth in 1952. Since then, Puerto Ricans have debated this status, with some arguing for statehood and others for independence. For now, the island remains a commonwealth, and its citizens share most of the rights and obligations of U.S. citizenship.

Order: _____

■ SEEING AND WRITING: Flashback

Look back at the paragraph you wrote for the Seeing and Writing exercise on page 38. Are all its sentences arranged in a clear, sensible order? Is this order time, spatial, or logical? Circle the transitional words and phrases that signal this order to readers. When you have finished, add any necessary transitions to your paragraph, and rearrange sentences as needed.

■ SEEING AND WRITING: Revising and Editing

Incorporating changes and corrections from all of this chapter's flashback exercises, revise your Seeing and Writing paragraph. Then, check your work one more time to make sure your paragraph is unified, well developed, and coherent.

CHAPTER REVIEW

◆ EDITING PRACTICE

Read the following paragraphs, and evaluate each in terms of its unity, development, and coherence. First, underline each topic sentence. Then, cross out any sentences that do not support the topic sentence. Add transitional words and phrases where needed. Finally, discuss in class whether additional details and examples could be added to each paragraph.

1.   In 1979, a series of mechanical and human errors in Unit 2 of the nuclear generating plant at Three Mile Island, near Harrisburg, Pennsylvania, caused an accident that profoundly affected the nuclear power industry. A combination of stuck valves, human error, and poor decisions caused a partial meltdown of the reactor core. Large amounts of radioactive gases were released into the atmosphere. The governor of Pennsylvania immediately evacuated pregnant women from the area. People panicked and left their homes. The nuclear regulatory agency claimed that the situation was not really dangerous and that the released gases were not a health threat, but activists and local residents disputed this. The reactor itself remained unusable for more than ten

years. Massive demonstrations followed the accident, including a rally of more than 200,000 people in New York City. Some people came because the day was nice. By the mid-1980s, new construction of nuclear power plants in the United States had stopped.

2.   Cities created police forces for a number of reasons. The first reason was status: after the Civil War, it became a status symbol for cities to have a uniformed police force. A police force provided a large number of political jobs. This meant that politicians were able to promise jobs to people who would work to support them. Police forces made people feel safe. Police officers helped visitors find their way. They took in lost children and sometimes fed the homeless. They directed traffic, enforced health ordinances, and provided other services. Police officers kept order. Without a visible, uniformed police force, criminals would have made life in nineteenth-century cities unbearable.

◆ COLLABORATIVE ACTIVITIES

1. Working in a group, list the reasons that you think students decide to attend your school. After working together to arrange these reasons from least to most important, write a topic sentence that states the main idea suggested by these reasons. Finally, on your own, draft a paragraph in which you discuss the factors that lead students to attend your school.
2. In a newspaper or magazine, find an illustration or photograph that includes a lot of details. Then, write a paragraph describing what you see in the photograph. (Include enough support—details, facts, and examples—so that readers will be able to "see" it almost as clearly as you can.) Decide on a specific spatial order—from top to bottom, from left to right, or another arrangement that makes sense to you. Use that spatial order to organize the details in your draft paragraph. Finally, trade paragraphs

with another student, and offer suggestions that could improve his or her paragraph.

3. Bring to class a paragraph from a newspaper or a magazine. Working in a group, decide whether each of your paragraphs is unified, well developed, and coherent. If any paragraph does not conform to the guidelines outlined in this chapter, try as a group to rewrite it to make it more effective.

UNIT TWO

Patterns of Paragraph Development

Exemplification

PREVIEW

In this chapter, you will learn to write an exemplification paragraph.

▶ **Word Power**

adapt
to adjust to
new
surroundings

mentor
an experienced
and trusted
adviser

facilitate
to make easy

■ SEEING AND WRITING

What could your school do to make it easier for new students to adjust to college life? Look at the picture above, and then write a paragraph in which you answer this question. Make sure you review the strategies discussed in Chapter 1 before you begin.

In Chapters 1 and 2, you learned how to write paragraphs. In Chapters 3 through 11, you will become acquainted with the options you have for organizing ideas within paragraphs. As you write, you will see that your ideas tend to develop in ways that reflect how your mind works to make sense of information and communicate it to others: you give examples, tell what happened, describe physical characteristics, explain how something operates, identify causes or predict effects, identify similarities and differences, classify information into categories, define, or persuade. These methods of arranging ideas correspond to specific patterns of paragraph (and essay) development: *exemplification, narration, description, process, cause and effect, comparison and contrast, classification, definition,* and *argument.* Recognizing these patterns and understanding how they help you organize your ideas will enable you to become a more confident writer.

A Understanding Exemplification

An example is a specific illustration of a general idea. **Exemplification** is writing that explains a general statement by offering one or more specific examples. In an **exemplification paragraph**, you state a general idea in the topic sentence and then use examples to illustrate and explain it. Thus, an example is always more specific than the topic sentence of the paragraph. To be effective, examples must be *appropriate* (that is, they must support or explain your main idea), and they must be *specific* (that is, they must be precise).

You can use a number of short examples to support your topic sentence, or (if one example is particularly vivid or compelling) you can use a single extended example. In either case, you can let readers know that you are going to give an example by using *for instance* or *for example.* The following paragraph about the 1969 Woodstock festival uses a series of short examples.

Topic sentence

Series of short examples

In most respects, after all, Woodstock was a disaster. To begin with, it rained and rained for weeks before the festival, and then, of course, it rained during the festival. The promoters lost weeks of preparation time when the site had to be switched twice. They rented Yasgur's field less than a month before the concert. The stage wasn't finished, and the sound system was stitched together perilously close to the start of the show. As soon as the festival opened, the water- and food-delivery arrangements broke down, the gates and fences disintegrated, and tens of thousands of new bodies kept pouring in. (One powerful lure was the rumor that the revered Bob Dylan was going to perform; he wasn't.) In response to an emergency appeal for volunteers, fifty doctors were flown in. The Air Force brought in food on Huey helicopters, and the Women's Community Center in Monticello sent thirty thousand sandwiches. One kid was killed as he was run over by a tractor, one died of appendicitis, and another died of a drug overdose.

Hal Espen, "The Woodstock Wars"

The writer of this paragraph piles on a series of examples, one after the other, to support his paragraph's main idea. Each example gives a specific illustration of how Woodstock was a disaster: it rained, the promoters had to switch sites, water and food were not delivered as planned, and so on.

The next paragraph uses a single extended example to support its main idea—that fear can move people to take action.

Sometimes, fear can be a great motivator. Once, when I was in high school, I tried out for a part in the school play. I was surprised and thrilled when I was given one of the leads. Never for a moment, however, did I consider how long my part was or how hard I would have to work to memorize it. All I could think of was how much attention I was getting from my friends. I even ignored the warnings of the play's director, who told me I would be in trouble if I did not begin to memorize my lines. The reality of my situation finally sank in during our first dress rehearsal when I stumbled all over my lines and the rest of the cast laughed at me. That night, and for the two weeks leading up to the play, I spent hours going over my lines. Miraculously, I got through the first night of the play without missing (at least obviously missing) many of my lines. As a result of that experience, I learned two things: first, that I could do almost anything if I was frightened enough, and second, that I would never try out for another play.

Jerry Doyle (student)

Topic sentence

Single extended example

Here, a single extended example supports the topic sentence.

For information on how to write an exemplification essay, as well as a list of transitions suitable for exemplification paragraphs and essays, see 14A.

FOCUS **Exemplification**

How many examples you need in a paragraph depends on your topic sentence. A complicated, far-reaching statement might require many supporting examples to convince readers that it is reasonable. A simple, more straightforward statement would require fewer examples.

B   Writing an Exemplification Paragraph

◆ PRACTICE 3-1

Read this exemplification paragraph; then, follow the instructions on page 68.

Youthful Style?

As a teenager in the late 1960s and early 1970s, I was always pretty tolerant of radical clothing styles,

but more and more today I find myself asking, "Why do
these kids want to look so weird?" For example, I do not
understand why a boy would wear a baseball cap backwards
on his head. To me, this just looks weird, like something
a person would do and then talk in a really stupid voice
to make his friends laugh. Under the backwards cap, the boy
probably has his hair in a buzz cut, except for one long
strand of hair reaching halfway down his back. I can't
imagine who thought up this hairstyle, unless it was an ex-
monk. Furthermore, every boy I see today seems to be wearing a T-shirt that looks ten sizes too big for him and
comes down below his knees, or, if not that, he's got all
his clothes on inside out or backwards or both! Then there
are the girls. Who decided that it was attractive to combine a white T-shirt and a long, sheer, flowing skirt with
a pair of huge black jackboots? I'm so confused. It all
just makes me nostalgic for the days of frayed bell-
bottoms, tie-dyed tank tops, strands of hippie beads,
and headbands circling heads of long, stringy hair.

                                    Willa Kincaid (student)

1. Underline the topic sentence of the paragraph.

2. List the specific examples the writer uses to support her topic sentence.
   The first example has been listed for you.

   boys wearing baseball caps backwards _____

   _____

   _____

   _____

   _____

3. Circle the transitions that the writer uses to connect ideas in the
   paragraph.

◆ PRACTICE 3-2

Following are four possible topic sentences for exemplification paragraphs.
Think of three examples you could use to support each topic sentence, and be

prepared to discuss these examples with the class. For example, if you were writing a paragraph about how difficult the first week of your new job was, you could mention waking up early, getting to know your coworkers, and learning new routines.

1. I have a number of reasons for liking my neighborhood.
2. Summer jobs provide valuable opportunities for young people by allowing them to develop their interests and test their abilities.
3. Some rules and regulations are unfair.
4. Many television programs insult the intelligence of their audiences.

◆ PRACTICE 3-3

Choose one of the topics below (or one of your own choice) as the subject of an exemplification paragraph. Then, on a separate sheet of paper, use one or more of the invention strategies described in 1C to help you think of as many examples as you can for the topic you have chosen.

Effective (or ineffective) teaching	Weight training
Qualities that make a song popular	Terrible dates
Successful movies	The importance of recycling
Challenges that older students face	Role models
Why people watch reality shows	Rude behavior
Unattractive clothing styles	Politicians
Peer pressure	Acts of bravery
The benefits of e-mail	Lying

◆ PRACTICE 3-4

Review your notes from Practice 3-3, and list the examples that can help you develop a paragraph on the topic you have chosen.

_____

_____

_____

_____

◆ PRACTICE 3-5

Reread your list of examples from Practice 3-4. Now, draft a topic sentence that introduces your topic and communicates the main idea your paragraph will discuss.

_____

_____

◆ PRACTICE 3-6

Arrange the examples you listed in Practice 3-4 in a logical order — for example, from least important to most important.

1. _____

2. _____

3. _____

4. _____

◆ PRACTICE 3-7

On a separate sheet of paper, draft your exemplification paragraph. Then, using the Self-Assessment Checklist on the next page, revise your paragraph for unity, development, and coherence.

◆ PRACTICE 3-8

On a separate sheet of paper, type a final, edited draft of your exemplification paragraph.

■ SEEING AND WRITING: Revising and Editing

Look back at your response to the Seeing and Writing exercise on page 65, and evaluate it for unity, development, and coherence. Then, prepare a final, edited draft of your paragraph.

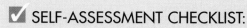

SELF-ASSESSMENT CHECKLIST:

Writing an Exemplification Paragraph

Unity

- Does your topic sentence state a general idea that can be supported with examples?

- Is your topic sentence specifically worded?

- Do all your examples support your topic sentence?

Development

- Do you need to find additional examples that more clearly support your topic sentence?

- Should you use one of the invention strategies discussed in 1C to help you come up with more ideas?

Coherence

- Are your examples arranged in an order that makes sense?

- Do you need to add transitional words or phrases?

4 *Narration*

In this chapter, you will learn to write a narrative paragraph.

Word Power

memorable
worth
remembering

moral
a lesson of a
fable or story

■ SEEING AND WRITING

Look at the picture above, which illustrates a scene from *The Three Little Pigs*. Then write a paragraph in which you retell a fairy tale or child's story that you know well. Make sure that your topic sentence states the point of the story.

A Understanding Narration

Narration is writing that tells a story. In a **narrative paragraph**, you relate a sequence of events. A narrative paragraph usually has a topic sentence that tells readers what the main idea of the paragraph is—that is, why you are telling this particular story. The rest of the paragraph develops this idea, with points arranged in time order.

In the following paragraph, writer Ron Kovic tells how he celebrated his birthday when he was a child.

> When the Fourth of July came, there were fireworks going off all over the neighborhood. It was the most exciting time of year for me next to Christmas. <u>Being born on the exact same day as my country I thought was</u> <u>really great.</u> I was so proud. And every Fourth of July, I had a birthday party and all my friends would come over with birthday presents and we'd put on silly hats and blow these horns my dad brought home from the A&P. We'd eat lots of ice cream and watermelon and I'd open up all the presents and blow out the candles on the big red, white, and blue birthday cake and then we'd all sing "Happy Birthday" and "I'm a Yankee Doodle Dandy." At night everyone would pile into Bobby's mother's old car and we'd go down to the drive-in, where we'd watch the fireworks display. Before the movie started, we'd all get out and sit up on the roof of the car with our blankets wrapped around us watching the rockets and Roman candles going up and exploding into fountains of rainbow colors, and later after Mrs. Zimmer dropped me off, I'd lie on my bed feeling a little sad that it all had to end so soon. As I closed my eyes I could still hear strings of firecrackers and cherry bombs going off all over the neighborhood.
>
> Ron Kovic, *Born on the Fourth of July*

Topic sentence

Events presented in time order

In this paragraph, all events and activities are related to the topic sentence, and transitional words and phrases—*at night, later,* and *as I closed my eyes*—clearly identify the order in which the events occurred. (Note that because narrative paragraphs tell what happened, they often rely on transitional words and phrases that indicate time, such as *after, before, now,* and *then.*)

For information on how to write a narrative essay, as well as a list of transitions suitable for narrative paragraphs and essays, see 14B.

B   Writing a Narrative Paragraph

◆ PRACTICE 4-1

Read this narrative paragraph; then, follow the instructions on page 74.

> The Trip to a Brand-New Life
>
> When I was seven, my family took a trip that changed our entire lives--the trip to America. Leaving our native Vietnam illegally, we first traveled three days in a small boat with about fifty other people. We soon ran out of

food and supplies, and I thought we would never make it, but at last we reached Malaysia. The people who met us on shore led us to a campsite where there were hundreds of other Vietnamese refugees. For nine months, my family stayed there, living in a shelter consisting of logs covered with thick plastic. During this time, we were called in to present our situation to representatives from a variety of countries so they could process our documents and decide whether to accept us as immigrants. We were among the fortunate ones accepted by the United States. Next, we were transferred to a camp in the Philippines, where the houses were more stable and the floors were cement instead of dirt. For three months, we continued to study English; then, the happy moment came when we learned that we would be leaving for America. A few days later, we were headed for New York, changing planes in several countries before reaching our destination. As the last plane landed, I was overwhelmed by the realization that my family and I had finally reached the land of our dreams. I knew that my first step on the ground would lead me to a new future and a completely new life. I was scared, but I did not hesitate.

Ann Duong (student)

1. Underline the topic sentence of the paragraph.

2. List below the major events of the narrative. The first event has been listed for you.

   The family left Vietnam and spent three days on the water.

   _____

   _____

   _____

   _____

   _____

   _____

3. Reread the narrative, circling the transitional words and phrases the writer uses to link events in time.

◆ PRACTICE 4-2

Below are four possible topic sentences for narrative paragraphs. Think of four events that could support each topic sentence, and be prepared to discuss these events with the class. For example, if you were recalling a barbecue that turned into a disaster, you could tell about burning the hamburgers, spilling the soda, and forgetting to buy paper plates.

1. One experience made me realize that I was no longer as young as I thought.

2. The first time I _____, I got more than I bargained for.

3. Even though the accident lasted only a few seconds, it seemed to last much longer.

4. I remember my reaction to one particular news event very clearly.

◆ PRACTICE 4-3

Choose one of the topics below (or one of your own choice) as the subject of a narrative paragraph. On a separate sheet of paper, use one or more of the invention strategies described in 1C to help you recall events and details about the topic you have chosen.

A difficult choice	An embarrassing situation
A frightening situation	A surprise
A time of self-doubt	A sudden understanding
A success	Something funny a friend did
An act of violence	Unexpected good luck
A lesson learned	A conflict with authority
Your happiest moment	An event that changed your life
An instance of injustice	An important decision

◆ PRACTICE 4-4

List the events you recalled in Practice 4-3 that can help you develop a narrative paragraph on the topic you have chosen.

_____

_____

_____

_____

_____

_____

◆ PRACTICE 4-5

Reread your list of events from Practice 4-4. Then, draft a topic sentence that introduces your topic and communicates the main idea your paragraph will discuss.

_____

_____

_____

◆ PRACTICE 4-6

Write down the events you listed in Practice 4-4 in the order in which they occurred.

1. _____

2. _____

3. _____

4. _____

5. _____

◆ PRACTICE 4-7

On a separate sheet of paper, draft your narrative paragraph. Then, consulting the Self-Assessment Checklist on the next page, revise your paragraph for unity, development, and coherence.

◆ PRACTICE 4-8

On a separate sheet of paper, write a final, edited draft of your narrative paragraph.

■ SEEING AND WRITING: Revising and Editing

Look back at your response to the Seeing and Writing exercise on page 72, and evaluate your paragraph for unity, development, and coherence. Then, prepare a final, edited draft of your paragraph.

☑ SELF-ASSESSMENT CHECKLIST:

Writing a Narrative Paragraph

Unity

- Does your topic sentence tell readers what the main idea of the paragraph is?

- Is your topic sentence specific enough?

- Do all details and events support your topic sentence?

Development

- Should you add more events or details to make your narrative clearer or livelier?

Coherence

- Does your narrative proceed clearly from an earlier time to a later time?

- Do you need to add transitional words or phrases?

5 *Description*

▶ **Word Power**

disregard
to ignore; to
neglect

distinctive
distinguishing;
typical of its
kind

■ SEEING AND WRITING

Look at the picture above. Then, write a paragraph in which you describe a person you encounter every day—for example, a street vendor, a bus driver, or a worker in your school cafeteria. Before you begin writing, decide what general impression you want to convey about the person you are describing.

A Understanding Description

Description is writing that paints a word picture of a person, place, or thing. In a **descriptive paragraph,** you enable readers to see what you see, hear what you hear, smell what you smell, taste what you taste, and feel what you feel. Details in a descriptive paragraph are usually arranged in *spatial order*— that is, from top to bottom, near to far, front to back, and so on.

When you write a descriptive paragraph, you try to create a single **dominant impression**—a mood or feeling that you want to communicate to readers. For example, if you were describing an old house in your neighborhood and wanted to leave readers with the impression that it was mysterious, your topic sentence would convey this idea: *The old house stands dark and alone, with just one window lit.* The rest of the sentences in the paragraph would reinforce this dominant impression.

In general, there are two kinds of descriptive paragraphs: *objective* and *subjective.* Writers use **objective description** to describe something without conveying their own emotions or opinions. This kind of description is used in technical or scientific writing but can also be used in other kinds of writing. In the following paragraph, the writer uses precise language and specific details to describe a scene to readers, but her writing does not indicate any special meaning the scene may have for her.

> Just south of Delaware Bay, where the land juts out and curves down the east coast, is a small town called Bethany Beach, Delaware. <u>One look at the beach at Bethany shows the effect of construction on the shoreline.</u> On the Atlantic side of Bethany, the white beach slopes gradually up from the ocean. In back of the beach are low rippling dunes that gradually blend into higher mounds of sand that have been planted with several types of beach grass and stubby green shrubs. The town council hoped that these plants would stabilize the dune structure and stop the erosion that threatens the beach every time there is a storm. Arching over the dunes are narrow gray boardwalks that protect the fragile dunes from the human traffic that eventually would destroy them. Behind the dunes, however, nature seems to stop. Along the Atlantic coast, as far south as Virginia Beach, the land has been divided into sandy plots, each with its own beach house or apartment. The natural flow of the beach has been interrupted by geometrical structures of shining glass and weathered gray wood.
>
> Kim DiPialo (student)

Topic sentence

Because the writer's purpose is to help readers picture the scene she describes, her description is primarily objective. The topic sentence presents the main idea of the paragraph. Then, the writer describes the beach, the dunes, and finally the area behind the dunes. Transitional words and phrases—*in back of the beach, arching over the dunes,* and *behind the dunes*—emphasize the spatial arrangement of details and connect various parts of the description. (Note that descriptive paragraphs often use transitional words and phrases that signal spatial order, such as *in front of, in back of, near,* and *next to.*) Specific visual details such as *stubby green shrubs, narrow gray boardwalks,* and *weathered gray wood* give readers a clear picture of the scene.

Writers use **subjective description** primarily to convey their feelings and opinions about a person, place, or thing, but subjective descriptions also contain specific details, just as objective descriptions do. In the following paragraph, the writer describes her impression of a building that has strong emotional associations for her.

Topic sentence

The school building was not a welcoming sight for someone used to the bright colors and airiness of tropical architecture. The building looked functional. It could have been a prison, an asylum, or just what it was: an urban school for the children of immigrants, built to withstand waves of change, generation by generation. Its red brick sides rose to four solid stories.

Specific details

The black steel fire escapes snaked up its back like exposed vertebrae. A chain link fence surrounded its concrete playground. Members of the elite safety patrol, older kids, sixth graders mainly, stood at each of its entrances, wearing their fluorescent white belts that criss-crossed their chests and their metal badges. No one was allowed in the building until the bell rang, not even on rainy or bitter-cold days. Only the safety patrol stayed warm.

Judith Ortiz Cofer, *Silent Dancing: A Partial Remembrance of a Puerto Rican Childhood*

For information on how to write a descriptive essay, as well as a list of transitions suitable for descriptive paragraphs and essays, see 14C.

In this paragraph, the topic sentence conveys the paragraph's dominant impression. The details of the paragraph are arranged in spatial order, starting with the school itself, moving to the chain link fence that surrounded the school, and ending with the children standing outside. The paragraph includes enough specific details to give readers a clear picture of the school; at the same time, it also communicates the writer's strong negative response to the building she is describing.

B   Writing a Descriptive Paragraph

◆ PRACTICE 5-1

Read this descriptive paragraph; then, follow the instructions on the next page.

                              Camaro Joe

    When I was growing up, my older sister Roxanne invari-
ably managed to come up with the greasiest lowlifes for
boyfriends, generally characterized by their lip-snarling,

cigarette-smoke-trailing, "I-just-might-die-tomorrow-and-I-might-as-well-take-someone-with-me" attitude. Usually named Mitch or Jake, these guys would hoist my delicate sister onto the backs of their black, chrome-laden motorcycles and tear off in a cloud of dirt and exhaust fumes. I particularly remember the one we called Camaro Joe, the greasy, unattractive lowlife who was Roxanne's boyfriend the summer I was twelve. When he first squealed into our driveway in a sputtering dirty-gold Camaro with a thumping stereo that shook the trees, we knew my sister had picked another winner. Joe's cowboy boots swung from his car onto the gravel of our driveway, and we watched as he launched his massive beer belly from the low seat. His waddle up to the house reminded me of a penguin. Joe was short and stocky with beady, black eyes and a thin, fuzzy mustache. He wore his black hair slicked back with grease, and a Camel cigarette hung from his lower lip as if it had been glued there. Like any good Neanderthal, he communicated mostly in grunts. My father eventually laid down the law and insisted that Roxanne stop seeing Joe, and, much to Dad's satisfaction, she did. Of course, it wasn't long before Joe was replaced by another Mitch--or was it Jake?

Susan Burkhart (student)

1. Underline the topic sentence of the paragraph.

2. In a few words, summarize the dominant impression the writer wants to give of her subject, Camaro Joe.

_____

_____

3. What are some of the details the writer uses to create this dominant impression? The first detail has been listed for you.

drives a dirty Camaro _____

_____

_____

_____

_____

_____

◆ **PRACTICE 5-2**

Each of the four topic sentences below conveys a possible dominant impression for a paragraph. Think of three details that could help support the dominant impression suggested by each topic sentence, and be prepared to discuss these details with the class. For example, to support the idea that sitting in front of a fireplace is relaxing, you could describe the crackling of the fire, the pine scent of the smoke, and the changing colors of the flames.

1. After the rainstorm, everything in the city seemed clean and new.

2. The bus was at least twenty years old and looked shabby.

3. I could see the toll that living on the streets had taken on him.

4. One of the most interesting stores I've seen sells used (or, as they say, "recycled") clothing.

◆ **PRACTICE 5-3**

Choose one of the topics below (or one of your own choice) as the subject of a descriptive paragraph. On a separate sheet of paper, use one or more of the invention strategies described in 1C to help you come up with specific details about the topic you have chosen. If you can, observe your subject directly, and write down your observations.

A favorite place from childhood	A favorite article of clothing
A place you felt trapped in	An interesting object
A quiet spot on campus	A pet
An unusual person	A building you find interesting
A place you find comforting	Your car or truck
A family member or friend	A scenic spot
A work of art	A statue or monument
A valued possession	Someone you admire
Your workplace	

◆ **PRACTICE 5-4**

List the details you came up with in Practice 5-3 that can best help you develop a descriptive paragraph on the topic you have chosen.

_____

_____

_____

_____

_____

_____

_____

◆ PRACTICE 5-5

Reread your list of details from Practice 5-4. Then, draft a topic sentence that summarizes the dominant impression you want to convey in your paragraph.

_____

_____

◆ PRACTICE 5-6

Arrange the details you listed in Practice 5-4 in spatial order. You might arrange them in the order in which you are looking at them—for example, from left to right, near to far, or top to bottom.

1. _____
2. _____
3. _____
4. _____
5. _____
6. _____
7. _____

◆ PRACTICE 5-7

On a separate sheet of paper, draft your descriptive paragraph. Then, consulting the Self-Assessment Checklist on page 84, revise your paragraph for unity, development, and coherence.

◆ PRACTICE 5-8

On a separate sheet of paper, write a final, edited draft of your descriptive paragraph.

■ SEEING AND WRITING: Revising and Editing

Look back at your response to the Seeing and Writing exercise on page 78, and evaluate your paragraph for unity, development, and coherence. Then, prepare a final, edited draft of your paragraph.

☑ SELF-ASSESSMENT CHECKLIST:

Writing a Descriptive Paragraph

Unity

- Does your topic sentence express the dominant impression you want to communicate?

- Do all the details in your paragraph support your topic sentence?

- Do all the details help to convey the dominant impression stated in your topic sentence?

Development

- Do you need to include more objective description to help readers see your subject?

- Do you need to add more subjective description to help readers understand your feelings and opinions about your subject?

Coherence

- Are your details arranged in a spatial order that makes sense?

- Do you need to add transitional words or phrases?

Process

PREVIEW

In this chapter, you will learn how to write a process paragraph.

▶ **Word Power**

compete
to work against another in pursuit of a goal

objective
a purpose or goal

penalty
a punishment or loss of advantage

■ SEEING AND WRITING

Look at the picture above, and then write a paragraph in which you explain how to play your favorite board (or other indoor) game. Assume that your readers know nothing about the game.

A   Understanding Process

A **process** is a series of steps, presented in chronological order, leading to a particular result. In a **process paragraph**, you explain how something works or tell how to do something. The topic sentence of your paragraph should identify the process (for example, "Frying chicken is easy" or "The typical job interview has three stages") and communicate the point you want to make about it. The rest of the paragraph should discuss the steps in the process, one at a time, in the order in which they occur.

In general, there are two kinds of process paragraphs: *process explanations* and *instructions*. In a **process explanation**, the writer's purpose is simply to help readers understand a process, not perform it. The following paragraph is a process explanation.

Topic sentence
Stage 1

Stage 2

Stages 3 and 4

> Once asleep, we go through four distinct stages. The first stage of sleep is marked by an easing of muscle tension and a change in brain-wave activity. This transitional stage is especially light and typically lasts about twenty minutes, during which time you may be easily awakened. In stage two, brain waves slow and slumber grows deeper. Even with the eyes taped open, we are quite literally blind during this phase and would be incapable of seeing anything—even a hand passing over the face—since the eye-brain connection has been shut off. More than half of the time devoted solely to sleep is spent in stage two, and no dreaming occurs. Stages three and four are marked by even slower brain waves, but the deepest sleep occurs in stage four. Mysteriously, the highest levels of the body's growth hormone are released during this sleep stage. After cycling back for a few minutes of stage-two sleep, dreaming begins. The first dream phase, lasting only a few minutes, is the shortest of the night. When dreaming is over, the sleeper retraces all the stages back to lighter sleep and then repeats the deep-sleep stages back to dreaming.

Mark McCuchen, *The Compass in Your Nose and Other Astonishing Facts about Humans*

The topic sentence identifies the process, and the rest of the paragraph presents the steps in strict chronological order. Throughout the paragraph, transitional words and phrases—*the first stage, in stage two,* and *stages three and four*—clearly identify individual steps in the process.

Other process paragraphs present **instructions**. Here, the writer's purpose is to give readers the information they need to actually perform a task or activity. The following paragraph gives instructions for checking a pair of in-line skates before beginning to skate.

Topic sentence

Step 1

> Now that you are the proud owner of in-lines, you must be sure your skates are fine-tuned and road-worthy, so before you roll, be sure to do the following. First, sit down and place your blades between your legs, wheels facing up. Make certain they are clean so you won't get dirty. Next, wiggle

each wheel, making certain there is no lateral play (side-to-side). If bolts are
loose, tighten them with the Allen, socket, or crescent wrench supplied by
the manufacturer. Then, spin each wheel so they all spin smoothly and
evenly. Feel and listen for any grinding. If this occurs, the bearings may
need to be cleaned or replaced. After checking the wheels, look at your
brake. Some stoppers screw on, while others have bolts on the side or
through the center. Jiggle the stopper, and if it's loose, tighten it. If it is worn,
replace it. It is best to replace your brake before you start to wear it down
to the metal, or you might strip the threads of the bolt and have to saw off
the brake, a time-consuming and difficult process. Finally, check your laces
or buckles for any wear and tear. Properly serviced, a pair of skates will have
a long life span and allow you to roll more easily and smoothly.

Step 2

Step 3

Step 4

Step 5

Joel Rappelfeld, *The Complete Blader*

Because the writer of this process paragraph expects readers to follow his instructions, he addresses them directly, using commands to tell them what to
do (for instance, "Sit down and place your blades between your legs"). He uses
clear transitional words and expressions—*next, then, after checking the
wheels*—to help readers see the exact sequence in which the steps are to be
performed. He even includes cautions and reminders ("Make certain they are
clean so you won't get dirty") and explains the purpose for some steps, such as
replacing a worn brake.

*For informa-
tion on how to
write a process
essay, as well as
a list of transi-
tions suitable
for process
essays and
paragraphs,
see 14D.*

FOCUS **Process**

Like narrative paragraphs, process paragraphs present a sequence of
events. Unlike narrative paragraphs, however, process paragraphs always describe a sequence that occurs—or should occur—in exactly the
same way every time.

B   **Writing a Process Paragraph**

◆ PRACTICE 6-1

Read this process paragraph; then, follow the instructions on page 88.

                    An Order of Fries

    I had always enjoyed the french fries at McDonald's
and other fast-food restaurants, but I never realized just

how much work goes into making them until I worked at a potato processing plant in Hermiston, Oregon. The process begins with freshly dug potatoes being shoveled from trucks onto conveyor belts leading into the plant. During this stage, workers must sort out any rocks that may have been dug up with the potatoes because these could damage the automated peelers. After the potatoes have gone through the peelers, they travel on a conveyor belt through the "trim line." Here, workers cut out any bad spots, being careful not to waste potatoes by trimming too much. Next, the potatoes are sliced in automated cutters and then fried for about a minute. After this, they continue along a conveyor belt to the "wet line." Here, workers again look for bad spots, discarding any rotten pieces. At this point, the potatoes go to a second set of fryers for three minutes before being moved to subzero freezers for ten minutes. Then, it's on to the "frozen line" for a final inspection. The inspected fries are weighed by machines and then sealed into five-pound plastic packages, which are weighed again by workers who also check that the packages are properly sealed. The bags are then packed into boxes and made ready for shipment to various McDonald's and other restaurants across the western United States. This process goes on twenty-four hours a day, to bring us consumers the tasty french fries we all enjoy so much.

Cheri Rodriguez (student)

1. Underline the topic sentence of the paragraph.

2. Is this a process explanation or instructions? How do you know?

3. List the steps in the process. The first step has been listed for you.

The potatoes are unloaded, and the rocks are sorted out.

_____

_____

_____

_____

◆ PRACTICE 6-2

Following are four possible topic sentences for process paragraphs. Think of three or four steps that explain the process each topic sentence identifies, and be prepared to discuss these steps with the class. For example, if you were explaining the process of getting a job, you could list preparing a résumé, identifying companies that are hiring, writing a job application letter, and going on an interview. Make sure each step follows logically from the one that precedes it.

1. There are four major steps in the process of making the perfect sandwich.
2. Before you begin the semester, you should set up a study routine.
3. Before you start any fitness program, set up a workout routine.
4. Discouraging unwanted attention from a coworker is a delicate process.

◆ PRACTICE 6-3

Choose one of the topics below (or one of your own choice) as the subject of a process paragraph. Use one or more of the invention strategies described in 1C to help you come up with as many steps as you can for the topic you have chosen, and list these steps on a separate sheet of paper.

Making a major purchase
Strategies for winning an
  argument
How to be popular
Buying a book or CD online
Your typical work or school day
How to discourage telemarketers
How to drop a class
Your morning routine
How to break up with someone

How to program a VCR
How to perform a particular
  household repair
Installing a computer program
How to apply for financial aid
A process involved in a hobby of
  yours
Painting a room
How to scramble eggs

◆ PRACTICE 6-4

Review your notes on the topic you chose in Practice 6-3, and decide whether to write a process explanation or a set of instructions. Then, on the lines below, choose the steps from the list you wrote in Practice 6-3 that can best help you develop a process paragraph on your topic.

_____   _____

_____   _____

_____   _____

_____   _____

◆ PRACTICE 6-5

Reread your list of steps from Practice 6-4. Then, draft a topic sentence that identifies the process you will discuss and communicates the point you will make about it.

_____

_____

_____

◆ PRACTICE 6-6

Review the steps you listed in Practice 6-4. Then, write them down in chronological order, moving from the first step to the last.

1. _____   4. _____

2. _____   5. _____

3. _____   6. _____

◆ PRACTICE 6-7

On a separate sheet of paper, draft your process paragraph. Then, consulting the Self-Assessment Checklist on page 91, revise your paragraph for unity, development, and coherence.

◆ PRACTICE 6-8

On a separate sheet of paper, write a final, edited draft of your process paragraph.

■ SEEING AND WRITING: Revising and Editing

Look back at your response to the Seeing and Writing exercise on page 85, and evaluate your paragraph for unity, development, and coherence. Then, prepare a final, edited draft of your paragraph.

✔ SELF-ASSESSMENT CHECKLIST:

Writing a Process Paragraph

Unity

- Does your topic sentence identify the process you will discuss? Does it state your main idea—the point you will make about the process?

- Is your topic sentence specifically worded?

- Have you eliminated information that does not relate directly to the process?

Development

- Have you included all the steps that readers need to know in order to understand the process?

- Do you need to explain any steps in greater detail?

- If your paragraph is a set of instructions, do you need to include any cautions or reminders?

Coherence

- Is your process explained in chronological order, or do you need to rearrange the steps?

- Do you need to add transitional words or phrases?

7 *Cause and Effect*

In this chapter, you will learn to write a cause-and-effect paragraph.

Word Power

gadget
a small, specialized mechanical or electronic device

impact
the effect of one thing on another

simplify
to make easier

■ SEEING AND WRITING

Look at the picture above. Then, write a paragraph in which you describe the impact of a particular electronic appliance or gadget on your life or the life of your family—for example, an ATM machine, a cell phone, or a television remote control. Be sure that your topic sentence identifies the item and that the rest of the paragraph discusses how it affects you or your family.

A   Understanding Cause and Effect

A **cause** is what makes a particular effect happen. An **effect** is the situation, activity, or behavior that results from a particular cause. You write **cause-and-effect paragraphs** when your purpose is to help readers understand why something happened or is happening, or when you want to show readers how one thing affects something else. You can also use cause-and-effect writing to speculate about future events.

The main difficulty you may have when planning a cause-and-effect paragraph is making sure that a **causal relationship** exists—that one event actually *caused* another event and did not just come before it in time. Another problem is considering all possible causes and effects, not just the most obvious ones. As you write, consider the importance of the causes or effects you discuss; don't make a particular cause or effect seem more significant than it actually is, just to strengthen your case.

A cause-and-effect paragraph can focus on causes or on effects. The following paragraph examines causes.

> Newspapers are folding. Paper costs are high, but loss of literate readers is much higher. Forty-five percent of adult citizens do not read newspapers. Only 10 percent abstain by choice. The rest have been excluded by their inability to read. Even the most distinguished daily papers are now written at an estimated tenth-grade level. Magazines such as the *Nation, New Republic, Time, Newsweek,* and the *National Review* are written at a minimum of twelfth-grade level. Circulation battles represent a competition for the largest piece of a diminished pie. Enlargement of that pie does not yet seem to have occurred to those who enter these increasingly unhappy competitions. The only successful major paper to be launched in the last decade, *USA Today*, relies on a simplistic lexicon, large headlines, color photographs, and fanciful weather maps that seek to duplicate the instant entertainment on TV.

Topic sentence: effect
First (minor) cause: paper costs
Second (major) cause: illiteracy

Jonathan Kozol, *Illiterate America*

The topic sentence identifies the problem the paragraph will discuss. After mentioning one relatively minor cause of the problem (the cost of paper), the paragraph goes on to analyze the primary cause of the problem—illiteracy.

The paragraph below discusses effects.

> Professional athletes are sometimes severely disadvantaged by trainers whose job it is to keep them in action. The more famous the athlete, the greater the risk that he or she may be subjected to extreme medical measures when injury strikes. The star baseball player whose arm is sore because of a torn muscle or tissue damage may need sustained rest more than anything else. But his team is battling for a place in the World Series; so the trainer or team doctor, called upon to work his magic,

Topic sentence: cause

First effect: pain
disappears

reaches for a strong dose of butazolidine or other powerful pain suppres-
sants. Presto, the pain disappears! The pitcher takes his place on the
mound and does superbly. That could be the last game, however, in which
he is able to throw a ball with full strength. The drugs didn't repair torn
muscle or cause the damaged tissue to heal. What they did was to mask
the pain, enabling the pitcher to throw hard, further damaging the torn
muscle. Little wonder that so many star athletes are cut down in their
prime, more the victims of overzealous treatment of their injuries than of
the injuries themselves.

Second effect:
muscle damaged
further

Norman Cousins,
"Pain Is Not the Ultimate Enemy"

*For information
on how to write
a cause-and-
effect essay, as
well as a list of
transitions suit-
able for cause-
and-effect
paragraphs and
essays, see 14E.*

The topic sentence identifies the cause of the problem the paragraph will consider. The paragraph then goes on to discuss two effects—the second more
important than the first—of the trainer's actions.

FOCUS   **Cause and Effect**

Be careful not to confuse the words *affect* and *effect. Affect* is a verb
meaning "to influence." *Effect* can be a verb meaning "to bring about,"
"to accomplish," or "to carry out." Usually, though, *effect* is a noun
meaning "result."

*For more on
commonly
confused words,
see 34E.*

B   **Writing a Cause-and-Effect Paragraph**

◆ **PRACTICE 7-1**

Read this cause-and-effect paragraph; then, follow the instructions on the next
page.

```
               The Ultimate High

     Some people associate running only with panting,
sweating, and plain and simple torture, but for me and other
experienced runners the effect of running is pure pleasure.
When I run, it may look as though I'm in agony, with my gap-
ing mouth, soaked brow, and constantly contracting leg mus-
cles. In fact, my daily half-hour run represents a time of
complete physical and mental relaxation. As I begin my run,
my lungs are immediately refreshed by the clean, open air.
```

The daily tensions built up in my body ease as my muscles stretch and pump, releasing all feelings of anger or frustration. I mentally dive into my run and feel as though I am lifting my feet from the pavement and ascending into the air. My mind wanders and I seem to float, daydreaming about wherever my thoughts take me. I take pride in my effort, signified by the perspiration that trickles down my face and body. After I complete my run and cool down with long, deep breaths, my body tingles and feels energized, as if I had just come off a roller coaster. I am more alert, my concentration is sharper, and my state of mind is relaxed and peaceful. I feel alive. Beginning runners initially experience soreness and fatigue rather than this kind of "high." They should be patient, however. As their bodies build up strength and tolerance, they will no longer equate running with pain but rather with relief from tension and with greater emotional well-being.

Scott Weckerly (student)

1. Underline the topic sentence of the paragraph.

2. Does this paragraph deal mainly with the causes or the effects of running? How do you know?

3. List some of the effects the writer describes. The first effect has been listed for you.

   His lungs are refreshed with clean air.

   _____

   _____

   _____

   _____

   _____

   _____

◆ PRACTICE 7-2

Following are four possible topic sentences for cause-and-effect paragraphs. Think of as many effects as you can that could result from the cause identified in each topic sentence, and be prepared to discuss these effects with the class.

For example, if you were writing a paragraph about the effects of excessive drinking on campus, you could list low grades, health problems, and vandalism.

1. Studying at the last minute can cause a number of problems.

2. Learning a second language has many advantages.

3. Walking can have some important benefits.

4. Impulse buying can have negative effects on a person's finances.

◆ PRACTICE 7-3

Think of three causes that could support each of the following topic sentences.

1. The causes of teenage pregnancy are easy to identify.

2. Chronic unemployment can have many causes.

3. Why is college tuition so expensive?

4. Athletes' high salaries can be explained by the principle of supply and demand.

5. People own pets for a variety of reasons.

◆ PRACTICE 7-4

Choose one of the following topics (or one of your own choice) as the subject of a paragraph that examines causes or effects. Then, on a separate sheet of paper, use one or more of the invention strategies described in 1C to help you think of as many causes or effects as you can for the topic you have chosen.

Why a current television show or movie is popular
Some causes (or effects) of stress
Why so many young Americans do not vote
The negative effects of credit cards
Why teenagers (or adults) drink
The reasons you decided to attend college
The effects of a particular government policy
How becoming a vegetarian might change (or has changed) your life
The benefits of home cooking
Why a particular sport is so popular
How an important person in your life influenced you
The effects of violent song lyrics on teenagers
The benefits of e-mail
Why some people find writing so difficult
The effects of a new baby on a household

The major reasons that high school or college students drop out of school
How managers can get the best (or the worst) from their employees

◆ PRACTICE 7-5

Review your notes on the topic you chose in Practice 7-4, and create a cluster
diagram. Write the topic you have chosen in the center of the page, and draw
arrows branching out to specific causes or effects.

*For more on
creating a
cluster diagram,
see 1C.*

◆ PRACTICE 7-6

Choose a few of the most important causes or effects from the cluster diagram
you made in Practice 7-5, and list them here.

_____

_____

_____

_____

_____

◆ PRACTICE 7-7

Reread your list of causes or effects from Practice 7-6. Then, draft a topic sentence that introduces your topic and communicates the point you will make
about it.

_____

_____

_____

◆ PRACTICE 7-8

List the causes or effects you will discuss in your paragraph, arranging them
in an effective order—for example, from least to most important.

1. _____

2. _____

3. _____

4. _____

◆ **PRACTICE 7-9**

On a separate sheet of paper, draft your cause-and-effect paragraph. Then, consulting the Self-Assessment Checklist below, revise your paragraph for unity, development, and coherence.

◆ **PRACTICE 7-10**

On a separate sheet of paper, write a final, edited draft of your cause-and-effect paragraph.

■ **SEEING AND WRITING:** Revising and Editing

Look back at your response to the Seeing and Writing exercise on page 92, and evaluate your paragraph for unity, development, and coherence. Then, prepare a final, edited draft of your paragraph.

☑ SELF-ASSESSMENT CHECKLIST:

Writing a Cause-and-Effect Paragraph

Unity

- Does your topic sentence clearly identify the cause or effect on which your paragraph will focus? Does it state your paragraph's main idea?

- Does all your information relate directly to the causes or effects you are discussing?

Development

- Do you need to add other important causes or effects?

- Does your audience need more information about any causes or effects you have included?

Coherence

- Are your causes and effects arranged in a logical order — for example, from least to most important?

- Do you need to add transitional words or phrases?

Comparison and Contrast

PREVIEW

In this chapter, you will learn to write a comparison-and-contrast paragraph.

▶ **Word Power**

diverge
to go in different directions; to differ

generation
a group of individuals born and living about the same time

tradition
a practice passed down from one generation to another

■ SEEING AND WRITING

Look at the picture above, which depicts a scene from the 1950s television family sitcom classic *Father Knows Best*. Then, write a comparison-and-contrast paragraph in which you explain how you think your life is different from (or the same as) the lives of the children in the picture.

A   Understanding Comparison and Contrast

A **comparison** tells how two things are similar. A **contrast** tells how they are different. A **comparison-and-contrast paragraph** can either examine just similarities or differences, or examine both similarities and differences. Sometimes, your purpose in a comparison-and-contrast paragraph is to analyze two subjects in order to clarify what makes each unique. At other times, your purpose may be to evaluate two subjects in order to determine which has greater merit or worth.

Before two things can be compared and contrasted, they need to have a **basis of comparison**—that is, they have to have enough in common so the comparison makes sense. Without at least one significant element in common, there can be no basis of comparison. For example, you would have a difficult time comparing people and bananas. (They do not share any significant characteristics.) You could, however, compare people and chimpanzees: both are mammals, both live in complex social groups, and both are capable of communication.

In general, there are two kinds of comparison-and-contrast paragraphs: *subject-by-subject* and *point-by-point comparisons*. In a **subject-by-subject comparison**, you first discuss all your points about one subject and then all your points about the other subject. When your points about the subjects correspond closely—and they often will—they should be presented in the same order. A subject-by-subject comparison has the following structure.

Subject-by-subject comparison

Subject A ——————————

    Point 1 ——————————

    Point 2 ——————————

    Point 3 ——————————

    Point 4 ——————————

Subject B ——————————

    Point 1 ——————————

    Point 2 ——————————

    Point 3 ——————————

    Point 4 ——————————

The following paragraph is an example of a subject-by-subject comparison.

Topic sentence
Subject 1 (women's
conversations)

First, it is important to note that men and women regard conversation quite differently. For women it is a passion, a sport, an activity even more important to life than eating because it doesn't involve weight gain. The first sign of closeness among women is when they find themselves engaging in endless, secretless rounds of conversation with one another. And as soon as a woman begins to relax and feel comfortable in a relationship with a man, she tries to have that type of conversation with him as well. However, the first sign that a man is feeling close to a woman is when he admits that he'd rather she please quiet down so he can hear the TV. A man who feels truly intimate with a woman often reserves for her and her alone the precious gift of one-word answers. Everyone knows that the surest way to spot a successful long-term relationship is to look around a restaurant for the table where no one is talking. Ah . . . now *that's* real love.

Subject 2 (men's conversations)

Merrill Markoe, *Men, Women, and Conversation*

This paragraph begins with a topic sentence that states the main idea of the paragraph and indicates that the paragraph will focus on differences between men and women. The writer then separately discusses women's ideas about conversation and men's ideas about conversation. The transition *however* signals the writer's shift from one subject to the other.

In a **point-by-point comparison**, you discuss each point for *both* subjects before going on to the next point. A point-by-point comparison has the following structure.

Point-by-point comparison

Point 1 _____

    Subject A _____

    Subject B _____

Point 2 _____

    Subject A _____

    Subject B _____

Point 3 _____

    Subject A _____

    Subject B _____

Point 4 _____

    Subject A _____

    Subject B _____

The following paragraph is an example of a point-by-point comparison.

After being a fan of both football and baseball for years, I have begun to understand how different these games really are. Football is much

Topic sentence

Point 1 (level of violence is different)

more violent than baseball. In football, the object is to tackle the opponent. The harder the hit, the better the tackle. As a result, many football players are injured each year. In baseball, however, violence is not the object of the game. If a player gets hurt, it is usually because of an accident, such as two players running into each other or a batter being hit by a pitch. The language used to describe each game is also different. The language of football is like the language of war: linemen "blitz," quarterbacks "throw bombs," tacklers "crush" receivers, and games end in "sudden-death" overtime. The language of baseball, however, is peaceful: hitters "bunt" or "pop up," runners "slide," and pitchers throw curves or sliders. Finally, the pace of each game is different. Football is played against the clock. When the clock runs down, the game ends, and the side with the most points wins. In baseball, however, the game does not end until nine innings have been completed or a tie has been broken. Theoretically, a game could go on for days—or even forever. Even though football and baseball are so different, I like them both. When I want to let off steam, I prefer football, and when I want to relax and sit in the sun, I like baseball.

Point 2 (language is different)

Point 3 (pace is different)

Concluding statement

Trent Patterson (student)

For information on how to write a comparison-and-contrast essay, as well as a list of transitions suitable for comparison-and-contrast paragraphs and essays, see 14F.

Like a subject-by-subject comparison, this point-by-point comparison begins with a topic sentence that states the main idea of the paragraph and indicates whether the paragraph will focus on similarities or on differences. The rest of the paragraph discusses three points of contrast, with each point made about both subjects—first for football and then for baseball—before the writer moves on to the next point. Shifts from one subject to another are signaled by the transition *however* and the words *football* and *baseball*.

> **FOCUS**   **Comparison**
>
> A subject-by-subject comparison works well if you are discussing relatively few points for each subject and if you can be sure that readers can keep these points in mind as they read. A point-by-point comparison is best for a paragraph in which you discuss many points because it enables readers to identify the individual points of the comparison as they proceed.

B   **Writing a Comparison-and-Contrast Paragraph**

◆ PRACTICE 8-1

Read this comparison-and-contrast paragraph; then, follow the instructions.

Comparing the British and
American Education Systems

The British system of education is very different from the American system. First, most American children have only one year of kindergarten, beginning at age five. Under the British system, children begin kindergarten at age four and then go on to another year of more advanced kindergarten called "preparatory" or "prep," which is comparable to American first grade. Starting in seventh grade, most American students study basic subjects separately, devoting a semester to algebra, for example, and another semester to geometry. However, under the British system, algebra, geometry, and trigonometry are taught together in a single course that is then repeated at a higher level in each grade. Also, in American high schools some classes, particularly electives, may include sophomores, juniors, and seniors. In schools run according to the British system, students at different levels, or "forms," are not mixed in classes; each form attends all its classes together. Finally, American students generally graduate after their twelfth year of school, and senior year is just another year of course work. British students, on the other hand, finish everything they need to learn in secondary school during the first term of their eleventh year of school. During the second term, they study for comprehensive final exams that cover everything they have learned for the last three and a half years. These exams, which include three separate tests for every subject, are taken during the final term.

Lisa Van Hoboken (student)

1. Underline the topic sentence of the paragraph.
2. Does this paragraph deal mainly with similarities or differences? How do you know?
3. Is this paragraph a subject-by-subject or point-by-point comparison? How do you know?
4. List some of the contrasts the writer describes. The first contrast has been listed for you.

American students start kindergarten at age five, while students in

British schools start kindergarten at age four.

_____

_____

_____

_____

_____

_____

◆ **PRACTICE 8-2**

Following are four possible topic sentences. Think of three similarities or differences for the two subjects being considered in the topic sentence, and be prepared to discuss these similarities and differences with the class. For example, if you were writing a paragraph comparing health care provided by a local clinic with health care provided by a private physician, you could discuss cost, the length of waiting time, the quality of care, and the frequency of follow-up visits.

1. My mother (or father) and I are very much alike (or different).

2. My friends and I have similar views on _____.

3. Democrats and Republicans have two very different ways of trying to solve the country's problems.

4. Two of my college instructors have very different teaching styles.

◆ **PRACTICE 8-3**

Choose one of the topics below (or one of your own choice) as the subject of a paragraph exploring similarities or differences. On a separate sheet of paper, use one or more of the invention strategies described in 1C to help you think of as many similarities and differences as you can for the topic you have chosen. (If you use clustering, create a separate cluster diagram for each of the two subjects you are comparing.)

Two popular television or radio talk-show hosts
Dog owners versus cat owners
A common perception of something versus its reality
How you act in two different situations (home and work, for example) or with two different sets of people (such as your family and your friends)
Two ads for similar products directed at different audiences
Two different bosses
Men's and women's attitudes toward dating, shopping, or conversation

Your goals when you were a child versus your goals today

Public school education versus home schooling

Two competing consumer items, such as two car models, two computer
systems, or two types of cell phones

Two relatives who have very different personalities

Two different kinds of vacations

Two generations' attitudes toward a particular issue or subject (for
example, how people in their forties and people in their teens view
religion or politics)

◆ PRACTICE 8-4

Review your notes on the topic you chose in Practice 8-3, and decide whether
to focus on similarities or differences. On the following lines, list the similarities or differences that can help you develop a comparison-and-contrast
paragraph on the topic you have selected.

_____

_____

_____

_____

_____

◆ PRACTICE 8-5

Reread your list of similarities or differences from Practice 8-4. Then, draft a
topic sentence that introduces your two subjects and suggests your purpose
for comparing or contrasting them.

_____

_____

◆ PRACTICE 8-6

Use the outlines on pages 100 and 101 to make a plan for your paragraph. If
you plan to use a subject-by-subject comparison, decide which subject you
will discuss first. If you plan to use a point-by-point comparison, decide on the
order in which you will present your points—for example, from least important to most important.

◆ **PRACTICE 8-7**

On a separate sheet of paper, draft your comparison-and-contrast paragraph. Then, consulting the Self-Assessment Checklist below, revise your paragraph for unity, development, and coherence.

◆ **PRACTICE 8-8**

On a separate sheet of paper, write a final, edited draft of your comparison-and-contrast paragraph.

■ SEEING AND WRITING: Revising and Editing

Look back at your response to the Seeing and Writing exercise on page 99, and evaluate your paragraph for unity, development, and coherence. Then, prepare a final, edited draft of your paragraph.

☑ SELF-ASSESSMENT CHECKLIST:

Writing a Comparison-and-Contrast Paragraph

Unity

  ☐ Does your topic sentence indicate whether you are stressing similarities or differences? Does it state your paragraph's main idea?

  ☐ Does all your information relate directly to the similarities or differences between your two subjects?

Development

  ☐ Is there a basis of comparison between your two subjects?

  ☐ Do you need to include more similarities? More differences?

Coherence

  ☐ Have you used a subject-by-subject or a point-by-point comparison? Is this type of comparison appropriate for your subject?

  ☐ Would arranging points in a different order be more effective?

  ☐ If your paragraph is a subject-by-subject comparison, have you treated the points for the second subject in the same order as the points for the first subject?

  ☐ Do you need to add any transitional words or phrases?

Classification

■ SEEING AND WRITING

Look at the picture above, and then write a paragraph in which you discuss the various types of fans of a particular sport.

▶ **Word Power**
enthusiastic
having or showing great excitement or interest; eager

fanatic
someone who has extreme enthusiasm for a cause

A	Understanding Classification

Classification is the activity of sorting items (people, things, ideas) into categories. In a **classification paragraph**, you tell readers how a collection of items can be sorted into categories. Each of the categories into which you classify items must be *distinct:* none of your items should fit into more than one category. For example, you would not classify novels into mysteries, romance novels, and paperbacks because a mystery or romance novel could also be a paperback.

The topic sentence of a classification paragraph identifies the subject (the group of items being discussed) and the categories into which items will be sorted. The rest of the paragraph considers the categories in the order in which they are mentioned in the topic sentence. The following is an example of a classification paragraph.

Topic sentence

Category 1

Category 2

Category 3

> I can classify my friends into three categories: those who know what they want out of life, those who don't have a clue, and those who are searching for goals. In the first category are those who know what they want; they are the most mature. They know exactly what they want to do for the rest of their lives. Although these friends will most likely be successful, they are the most predictable and therefore the most boring. In the second category are those who don't have a clue; they are the most immature. They seem to live for the minute and do not think much about the future. If there is a party the night before a big test, they will go to the party and then try to study when they get back. Although these friends can be a bad influence, they are the most fun. In the third category are those who are searching for goals; they are somewhere between the other two types when it comes to maturity. They do not know exactly what they want to do with their lives, but they realize that they should be trying to find a goal. Although these friends can sometimes be unpredictable, their willingness to try new things makes them by far the most interesting.
>
> Daniel Corey (student)

For information on how to write a classification essay, as well as a list of transitions suitable for classification paragraphs and essays, see 14G.

The topic sentence clearly identifies the paragraph's subject—friends—and the three categories into which individual friends will be sorted. The rest of the paragraph discusses these three categories, one at a time. The shift from one category to another is signaled by the transitional phrases *In the first category, In the second category,* and *In the third category.*

FOCUS Classification

Before you can classify information, you must decide what your focus will be when you choose your categories. For example, instructors can be classified according to their knowledge or their teaching ability, and computers can be classified according to their speed at processing information or their ease of use.

B Writing a Classification Paragraph

◆ PRACTICE 9-1

Read this classification paragraph; then, follow the instructions below it.

Three Kinds of Shoppers

Shoppers can be broken into three categories. The first category is made up of pragmatic shoppers; they shop because they need something. Pragmatic shoppers are purposeful. You can recognize them because they go right to the item they are looking for in the store and then leave. They do not waste time browsing or walking aimlessly from store to store. For them, shopping is definitely a means to an end. The next category is made up of recreational shoppers; they shop for entertainment. Recreational shoppers usually have too much time on their hands. For them, shopping is like going to the movies or out to dinner. They do it because it is fun. They will spend hours walking through stores looking at merchandise. More often than not, they will not buy anything. For recreational shoppers, it is the activity of shopping that counts, not the purchase itself. The third category is made up of professional shoppers; they shop because they have to. Professional shoppers are on a mission. For them, shopping is a serious business. You can see them in any mall, carrying four, five, or even six shopping bags. Frequently, an exhausted spouse who carries even more merchandise follows them. For merchants and for credit card companies, professional shoppers are a dream come true.

Kimberly Toomer (student)

1. Underline the topic sentence of the paragraph.

2. What is the subject of the paragraph? What three categories of the subject does the writer describe?

3. Circle the phrases the writer uses to introduce the three categories.

◆ PRACTICE 9-2

Classify the following groups of items into categories.

1. All the items on your desk

2. Buildings on your college campus

3. Magazines or newspapers you read

4. The various parts of a piece of equipment you use for a course or on the job

◆ PRACTICE 9-3

Choose one of the topics below (or one of your own choice) as the subject of a classification paragraph. On a separate sheet of paper, use one or more of the invention strategies described in 1C to help you classify the members of the group you have chosen into as many categories as necessary.

Drivers	Popular music
Commuters on public transportation	Fitness routines
Television shows	Popular Web sites
Employees or bosses	Part-time jobs
Parents or children	Teachers
Types of success	Popular movies
Radio stations	T-shirt slogans

◆ PRACTICE 9-4

Review the information you came up with for the topic you chose in Practice 9-3. On the following lines, list three or four categories you can develop in your paragraph.

Category 1: _____

Category 2: _____

Category 3: _____

Category 4: _____

◆ PRACTICE 9-5

Reread the list you made in Practice 9-4. Then, draft a topic sentence that introduces your subject and the categories you will discuss.

_____

_____

_____

◆ PRACTICE 9-6

List below the categories you will discuss in your classification paragraph in the order in which you will discuss them.

1. _____

2. _____

3. _____

4. _____

◆ PRACTICE 9-7

On a separate sheet of paper, write your classification paragraph. Then, consulting the Self-Assessment Checklist on the next page, revise your paragraph for unity, development, and coherence.

◆ PRACTICE 9-8

On a separate sheet of paper, write a final, edited draft of your classification paragraph.

■ SEEING AND WRITING: Revising and Editing

Look back at your response to the Seeing and Writing exercise on page 107, and evaluate your paragraph for unity, development, and coherence. Then, prepare a final, edited draft of your paragraph.

☑ SELF-ASSESSMENT CHECKLIST:

Writing a Classification Paragraph

Unity

☐ Does your topic sentence identify the categories you will discuss? Does it state your paragraph's main idea—the point your classification paragraph makes?

☐ Does all your information support your topic sentence or relate to your subject and its categories?

Development

☐ Do you need to include additional categories?

☐ Do you need to include more examples or more specific information for any category?

Coherence

☐ Do you need to rearrange categories (or details within categories)?

☐ Do you need to add transitional words or phrases?

Definition

PREVIEW

In this chapter, you will learn to write a definition paragraph.

■ SEEING AND WRITING

Look at the picture above. Then, write a one-paragraph definition of a word you learned in one of your college courses. Assume that your readers are not familiar with the term you are defining.

▶ **Word Power**
denote
to indicate; to refer to specifically

signify
to have meaning or importance

A   Understanding Definition

A **definition** explains what a term means. When you want your readers to know exactly how you are using a certain term or an unfamiliar concept, you use definition.

When most people think of definitions, they think of the one- or two-sentence **formal definitions** based on dictionary entries. These definitions have a three-part structure that includes the term to be defined, the general class to which the term belongs, and the characteristics that make the term different from all other terms in that class.

Term	Class	Differentiation
A pineapple	is a tropical plant	that has large swordlike leaves and yellow edible fruit.
Basketball	is a game	played between two teams in which the object is to put a ball through an elevated basket on the opponent's side of a rectangular court.

A single-sentence formal definition may not be enough to define an abstract concept (*envy* or *democracy*, for example), a technical term, or a complex subject. In such cases, you may need to expand this definition by writing a **definition paragraph**. A definition paragraph usually includes the three components of a formal definition, but it does not follow a particular pattern of development. It may define a term or concept by using examples, by outlining a process, or by using any of the other patterns discussed in this text. A definition paragraph may even define a term by using **negation**, telling what the term is not—for example, that a bicycle is *not* a motorized vehicle.

In a definition paragraph, the topic sentence identifies the term to be defined (and may briefly define it as well). The rest of the paragraph develops the definition by means of one or more of the patterns of development discussed in Chapters 3–9. The following paragraph defines the term *business casual*.

Many businesses allow business casual dress on Fridays; others permit it all the time. As a result, more and more people are finding themselves asking, "What is business casual?" Broadly speaking, business casual means dressing professionally but also looking relaxed. For women, this usually means wearing a skirt or slacks with a blouse or sweater. For men, it means no tie—and certainly no suit. Khakis and a short-sleeved knit shirt are popular in the summer; in other seasons, men wear a jacket over a shirt left open at the collar. Business casual, however, is not a license for being sloppy or dressing inappropriately. In other words, it does not mean

Topic sentence

Series of examples

Negation

wearing shorts, low-cut shirts, tank or halter tops, sandals, flip-flops, jeans, or T-shirts.

Melissa Morris (student)

The topic sentence introduces the term the paragraph will define. The paragraph goes on to define the term, using several short examples to illustrate the definition. The paragraph ends with negation—telling what the term *business casual* does not mean.

The following paragraph defines a piece of gymnastics equipment—the pommel horse.

For information on how to write a definition essay, as well as a list of transitions suitable for definition paragraphs and essays, see 14H.

> <u>The pommel horse is of ancient origin.</u> The Romans used it for the very practical purpose of training soldiers to mount horses. Some suggest it was used even earlier, by the bull dancers of Minoan Crete. Jumping over the bulls by doing springs off the animals' horns, these dancers surely must have practiced on something a little tamer than a live bull. Today, the pommel horse events are less exciting. The gymnast performs intricate leg-swinging movements while supporting his weight on his hands, which are either grasping the pommels or lying flat on the leather of the horse. As he swings his legs so that one follows, or "shadows," the other, the gymnast demonstrates strength, balance, and timing. Exercises such as single or double leg circles and scissors must be done continuously and in both directions. The pommel horse is difficult to master and not a favorite among gymnasts; they call it "the beast."

Topic sentence

History and background: comparison and contrast

Explanation of current function: process

Ford Hovis, *The Sports Encyclopedia*

Here, the writer defines an object in terms of its history and its current function, using comparison and contrast and process to develop his definition.

FOCUS   **Definition**

In general, avoid including a dictionary definition in your definition paragraph. After all, readers can look up a term themselves. Your definition paragraph should show how *you* define a term—not how a dictionary does.

B   **Writing a Definition Paragraph**

◆ PRACTICE 10-1

Read this definition paragraph; then, follow the instructions on the next page.

Writer's Block

Have you ever sat staring at a blank notebook page or computer screen, searching your brain for words and ideas, fidgeting with frustration, and longing to be anywhere else? If so, you probably want to know more about writer's block, a condition that afflicts ten out of ten writers at some point during their lives. Simply stated, writer's block is the inability to start a piece of writing. For nonprofessionals, writer's block almost always involves assigned writing, such as a paper for school or a report for work. (People rarely feel blocked when they are writing simply for pleasure.) Sometimes writer's block is caused by poor preparation: the writer has not allowed enough time to think and make notes that will pave the way for the actual writing of a draft. However, even prepared writers with many ideas already on paper can experience writer's block. It is comparable to being tongue-tied, only this kind of writer's block is more like being brain-tied. All the ideas keep bouncing around but will not settle into any order, and the writer cannot decide what to say first. When the agony of writer's block strikes, often the only cure is to give up and find another time to start.

Thaddeus Eddy (student)

1. Underline the topic sentence of the paragraph.

2. What is the subject of this definition?

3. In your own words, paraphrase the writer's one-sentence definition of his subject.

4. List some of the specific information the writer uses to define his subject. The first piece of information has been listed for you.

   It causes fidgeting and a desire to escape.

   _____

   _____

   _____

5. What patterns of development does the writer use in his definition?

◆ PRACTICE 10-2

Following are four possible topic sentences for definition paragraphs. Each topic sentence includes an underlined word. Decide on two possible patterns of development that you could use to expand a definition of each underlined word, and be prepared to discuss your choices with the class. For example, you could define the word *feminist* by giving examples and by telling a story.

1. During the interview, the job candidate made a <u>sexist</u> comment.

2. <u>Loyalty</u> is one of the chief characteristics of golden retrievers.

3. More than forty years after President Johnson's Great Society initiative, we have yet to eliminate <u>poverty</u> in the United States.

4. The problem with movies today is that they are just too <u>violent</u>.

◆ PRACTICE 10-3

Choose one of the topics below (or one of your own choice) as the subject of a definition paragraph. On a separate sheet of paper, use one or more of the invention strategies described in 1C to help you define the term you have chosen to discuss. Name the term, and then describe it, give examples of it, tell how it works, explain its purpose, consider its history or future, compare it to other similar things; in short, do whatever works best for defining your specific subject.

A negative quality, such as envy or dishonesty
An ideal, such as the ideal friend or ideal neighborhood
A type of person, such as a worrier or a show-off
A social concept, such as equality, opportunity, or discrimination
An important play in a particular sport or game
A hobby you pursue or an activity associated with that hobby
A technical term or specific piece of equipment that you use in your job
An object (such as an article of clothing) that is important to your
    culture or religion
A basic concept in a course you are taking
A particular style of music or dancing
A controversial subject whose definition not all people agree on, such
    as affirmative action or date rape
A goal in life, such as success or happiness

◆ PRACTICE 10-4

Review your notes for the topic you chose in Practice 10-3. On the following lines, list the details that you think you can use to develop a definition paragraph.

_____

_____

_____

_____

_____

_____

_____

◆ **PRACTICE 10-5**

Reread your notes from Practice 10-4. Then, draft a topic sentence that summarizes your main idea—the point you want to make about the term you are going to define.

_____

_____

_____

_____

◆ **PRACTICE 10-6**

List the points you will discuss in your paragraph, arranging them in an effective order.

1. _____

2. _____

3. _____

4. _____

5. _____

◆ **PRACTICE 10-7**

On a separate sheet of paper, write your definition paragraph. Then, using the Self-Assessment Checklist on the next page, revise your paragraph for unity, development, and coherence.

◆ PRACTICE 10-8

On a separate sheet of paper, write a final, edited draft of your definition paragraph.

■ SEEING AND WRITING: Revising and Editing

Look back at your response to the Seeing and Writing exercise on page 113, and evaluate your paragraph for unity, development, and coherence. Then, prepare a final, edited draft of your paragraph.

☑ SELF-ASSESSMENT CHECKLIST:

Writing a Definition Paragraph

Unity

- ☐ Do you define your term clearly in your topic sentence?
- ☐ Does your topic sentence state your paragraph's main idea—the point you want to make about the term you are defining?
- ☐ Does all your information support your topic sentence?

Development

- ☐ Do you use an appropriate pattern (or patterns) of development in your paragraph?
- ☐ Would a different pattern of development be more effective?
- ☐ Should you use negation to help you define your term?
- ☐ Do you need to include more information about your term?

Coherence

- ☐ Would arranging the information in a different order make it clearer or more interesting to readers?
- ☐ Do you need to add transitional words or phrases?

11 *Argument*

PREVIEW

In this chapter, you will learn to write an argument paragraph.

Word Power

controversy
a dispute be-
tween two
parties hold-
ing opposing
views

debate
to discuss or
argue about

refute
to prove false

■ SEEING AND WRITING

Write a paragraph in which you argue for or against one of the following
policies:

■ Censoring the Internet
■ Putting drunk drivers in jail for their first offense
■ Requiring a license for all handguns
■ Reinstituting the military draft in the United States
■ Enabling people to vote in federal elections on their home computers

Include examples from your experience or from your reading to support
your position.

A   Understanding Argument

An **argument** takes a position on a debatable subject. When you write an **argument paragraph**, your purpose is to persuade readers that your particular position has merit. The topic sentence states your position. In the rest of the paragraph, you support your position with **evidence**—*facts, examples,* and *expert opinions.* The paragraph ends with a conclusion that sums up your position.

A **fact** is information that can be verified. For example, it is a fact that A comes before G in the alphabet and that the Canadian ice hockey team won a gold medal in the 2002 Olympics. If you make the point that students are less prepared for college today than they were twenty years ago, you should support it with facts—for example, by citing SAT scores and college dropout rates. Avoid sweeping statements that are not supported by facts from encyclopedias, newspapers, or other reliable sources.

An **example** is a specific illustration of a general statement. To be convincing, an example should relate clearly to the argument you are making. For example, to support the argument that the quality of life in your neighborhood has improved recently, you could discuss a number of new businesses that have opened and several neighbors who have spent time and money improving their properties. Make sure, however, that your examples are typical, not exceptional. For instance, the fact that one new business has opened is not enough to establish that your neighborhood is improving.

An **expert** is someone who is generally recognized as knowledgeable about a particular subject. The opinion of an expert who supports your view on a subject can be very persuasive. For example, if you wanted to argue that censoring the Internet would undercut people's freedom of speech, you could quote an expert on constitutional law such as Ruth Bader Ginsburg, a justice of the United States Supreme Court. Because Ginsburg is a recognized authority on constitutional issues, her opinion carries a great deal of weight. Remember, though, that an expert in one field is not necessarily an expert in another field. For instance, Ginsburg's personal opinion about stem-cell research would have less value than the opinion of someone who has spent most of his or her life studying this subject.

The following paragraph argues against the use of Astroturf surfaces in sports stadiums.

Sports stadiums built during the 1960s and 1970s use Astroturf because it requires little maintenance and creates a uniform playing surface. But recently it has become clear that Astroturf has caused so many injuries that it should be eliminated from all pro sports stadiums. Anyone who follows baseball or football knows that Astroturf causes many knee and ankle injuries. The main reason for this situation is that it does not absorb impact the way a natural grass surface does. Astroturf consists of a layer of rough artificial grass on top of a layer of padding. Beneath these layers is a cement pad. Players who fall on Astroturf or, in the case of football, are thrown down

Topic sentence

Facts and
examples

Authority

Conclusion

onto it, risk serious injury. The New York Giants, for example, lost tight end Mark Bavaro to knee injuries caused by his falling on the artificial surface of the Meadowlands Stadium. And the Astroturf surface in Philadelphia's Veterans Stadium, long known by players to be the worst in the country, has caused the Eagles to lose a number of key players. As sports columnist Bill Lyon points out, when you sit in the stands of Veterans Stadium, you can see the gaps where sections of the Astroturf do not meet properly. When a player catches a foot in these gaps, the result can be a painful sprain or worse. The situations in Philadelphia and New Jersey are not unique. You can see the same problems in every stadium that has an Astroturf playing surface. For this reason, players, owners, and fans should insist that stadiums remove Astroturf and restore natural grass surfaces.

Toni-Ann Marro (student)

For information on how to write an argument essay, as well as a list of transitions suitable for argument paragraphs and essays, see 14I.

The paragraph begins with a sentence that gives some background. The topic sentence then states the writer's position. After stating that Astroturf causes injuries, the paragraph presents facts, examples, and comments by an expert that support the writer's position. The paragraph ends with a conclusion based on the evidence presented. Throughout the paragraph, transitional words and phrases—*the main reason, for example,* and *for this reason*—lead readers through the argument.

FOCUS   **Audience**

In addition to presenting evidence to support your argument, you need to consider the effect of your argument on your audience. Before you write, try to determine whether your readers are likely to be hostile, friendly, or neutral to your position. Let your analysis of your audience determine the approach you use.

For example, if you suspect your audience may not be receptive to your position, you might mention their possible objections in your topic sentence before stating your position. In your paragraph, you can **refute** (argue against) those objections.

> Although some people may argue that students will be shortchanged [possible objection], a core curriculum will actually benefit most students at Baker County Community College [position].

You can also address possible audience objections in the paragraph itself, stating the major argument against your position and then refuting it by showing that it is incorrect, shortsighted, or illogical. For example, for the argument outlined above, you could say that people who object to a core curriculum fail to understand that students should receive a well-rounded education, not just training for a particular job.

B   Writing an Argument Paragraph

◆ PRACTICE 11-1

Read this argument paragraph; then, follow the instructions below.

```
            Big Brother in the Workplace
     Employers should not routinely monitor the computer
use of their employees. First of all, monitoring computer
use violates an employee's privacy. Every day, employees
use their computers for work-related tasks, and every
keystroke they make is recorded. In addition, companies
routinely read employees' private e-mail files as well
as monitor the sites they visit on the Internet. This
monitoring creates an unpleasant work environment because
employees feel that someone is always watching them. At
some companies, employees have even been fired for sending
personal e-mails or for sending humorous pictures to one
another. Of course, companies that believe computers should
be used only for work-related tasks have a point. After
all, the company pays for both the computers and the
employees' time. The problem with this line of thinking,
however, is that it ignores the fact that workers need to
feel secure in order to work effectively. It therefore
makes sense that a limited use of computers for personal
reasons (to send e-mails to friends, for example) should be
allowed--just as coffee breaks are. Unless the company has
reason to suspect misuse of company computers, it should
not routinely monitor all employees' computers. Putting an
end to this type of surveillance would not only create a
more relaxed workplace, but it would also make it possible
for employees to work more efficiently.

                          Scott Rathmill (student)
```

1. Underline the topic sentence of the paragraph.

2. What controversial subject is the writer dealing with? What is the writer's position?

3. What points does the writer use to support his topic sentence?

4. List some of the evidence that the writer uses to support his points. The first piece of evidence has been listed for you.

Every keystroke an employee makes is recorded.

_____

_____

_____

5. What evidence (facts, examples, expert opinion) does the writer use to support his points?

6. What other evidence could the writer have used?

7. What opposing argument does the writer address?

8. How does the writer refute this argument?

◆ PRACTICE 11-2

Following are four topic sentences for argument paragraphs. Think of two or three points that could support each topic sentence, and be prepared to discuss them with the class. For example, if you were arguing in support of laws requiring motorcycle riders to wear safety helmets, you could say they cut down on medical costs and save lives.

1. Marijuana use for certain medical conditions should be legalized.

2. All student athletes should be paid a salary by their college or university.

3. College students caught cheating should be expelled.

4. The government should provide free health care for all senior citizens.

◆ PRACTICE 11-3

Choose one of the topic sentences from Practice 11-2. Then, list two pieces of evidence that could support each point you listed. For example, if you said that wearing safety helmets saves lives, you could list accident statistics and statements by emergency room physicians.

_____

_____

_____

◆ PRACTICE 11-4

Choose one of the topics below (or one of your own choice) as the subject of an argument paragraph. Then, on a separate sheet of paper, use one or more of the invention strategies described in 1C to help you focus on a specific issue to discuss in an argument paragraph.

An issue related to your school

Grading policies	Financial aid
Required courses	Student activity fees
Entrance requirements	Childcare facilities
Attendance policies	Sexual harassment policies
Course offerings	The physical condition of classrooms

A community issue

The need for a traffic signal, a youth center, or something else you
   think would benefit your community
An action you think local officials should take, such as changing school
   hours, cleaning up a public eyesore, or improving a specific service
A new law you would like to see enacted
A current law you would like to see repealed
A controversy you have been following in the news

◆ PRACTICE 11-5

Once you have chosen an issue in Practice 11-4, write a journal entry about your position on the issue. Consider the following questions: Why do you feel the way you do? Do you think many people share your views, or do you think you are in the minority? What specific actions do you think should be taken? What objections are likely to be raised against your position? How might you respond to these objections?

◆ PRACTICE 11-6

Review all the notes you have made for the topic you chose in Practice 11-4, and select the points that best support your position. List these points below. (You may also want to list the strongest objections to your position.)

Supporting points: _____

_____

Objections: _____

_____

◆ PRACTICE 11-7

Draft a topic sentence that clearly expresses the position you will take in your paragraph.

_____

_____

◆ PRACTICE 11-8

In the space provided, arrange the points that support your position in an order that you think will be convincing to your audience.

1. _____

2. _____

3. _____

4. _____

5. _____

◆ PRACTICE 11-9

In the space provided, list the evidence (facts, examples) that you could use to support each of your points.

Evidence for point 1: _____

_____

Evidence for point 2: _____

_____

Evidence for point 3: _____

_____

◆ PRACTICE 11-10

On a separate sheet of paper, draft your argument paragraph. Then, consulting the Self-Assessment Checklist on page 127, revise your paragraph for unity, development, and coherence.

◆ PRACTICE 11-11

On a separate sheet of paper, write a final, edited draft of your argument paragraph.

■ SEEING AND WRITING: Revising and Editing

Look back at your response to the Seeing and Writing exercise on page 120, and evaluate your paragraph for unity, development, and coherence. Then, prepare a final, edited draft of your paragraph.

☑ SELF-ASSESSMENT CHECKLIST:

Writing an Argument Paragraph

Unity

- Does your topic sentence clearly state your position?

- Is all your information directly related to your topic sentence?

- Do you need to revise your topic sentence to accommodate new ideas?

Development

- Have you made enough points to support your topic sentence?

- Do you need more facts or other evidence to convince your audience to accept any of your points?

- Have you mentioned the major arguments against your position?

- Have you refuted these arguments?

- Do you need to use one or more of the invention strategies discussed in 1C to help you come up with more ideas?

Coherence

- Would arranging ideas in a different order make your argument more convincing to readers?

- Do you need to add transitional words or phrases?

UNIT THREE

Focus on Essays

Writing an Essay

PREVIEW

In this chapter, you will learn:
- to understand essay structure (12A)
- to decide on a topic (12B)
- to use invention strategies (12C)
- to state a thesis (12D)
- to arrange ideas (12E)
- to draft an essay (12F)
- to revise and edit your essay (12G)

■ SEEING AND WRITING

What was the worst job you ever had? Look at the picture above, a famous scene from an episode of *I Love Lucy* in which Lucy and Ethel go to work at a candy factory, and think about this question carefully as you read the pages that follow. This is the topic you will be writing about as you move through this chapter. (If you have never had a job, you may write about a specific task that you disliked or a bad job that a friend or a relative has had.)

▶ **Word Power**

dehumanize
to deprive of human qualities

exploit
to make use of selfishly

*For a discus-
sion of writing
paragraphs, see
Chapter 1.*

Most of the writing you do in school will be longer than a single paragraph. Often, you will be asked to write an **essay**—a group of paragraphs on a single subject. When you write an essay, you follow the same process you do when you write a paragraph: you move from invention to selecting and arranging ideas and then to drafting, revising, and editing. Chapters 12 through 14 will show you how to apply the paragraph skills you learned in Chapters 1 through 11 to writing essays.

A   Understanding Essay Structure

Many essays have a **thesis-and-support** structure. The first paragraph of the essay—the introduction—begins with opening remarks and ends with a **thesis statement**, which presents the essay's main idea. The **body** of the essay is made up of several paragraphs that support the thesis. Each of these body paragraphs begins with a topic sentence that states the paragraph's main idea and goes on to develop it with details, facts, and examples. The last paragraph—the **conclusion**—restates the thesis in different words and offers the writer's concluding thoughts on the subject.

Essay

Opening remarks introduce the subject to be discussed.

The **thesis statement** presents the main idea of the essay, usually in the last sentence of the first paragraph.

Introduction

Topic sentence (first point)

Support (details, facts, examples)

Body paragraphs

Topic sentence (second point)

Support (details, facts, examples)

*(continued on
the following page)*

(continued from the previous page)

Topic sentence (third point)

Support (details, facts, examples)

⎤ Body paragraph
⎦

The **restatement of the thesis** summarizes the essay's main idea.

Conclusion

Closing remarks present the writer's last
thoughts on the subject.

◆ PRACTICE 12-1

Following is an essay based on the diagram above. Read the essay, and then
answer the questions that follow it.

   More and more smokers today are aware of the serious risks smoking
poses both for themselves and for the nonsmokers around them. Many of
them would like to quit but just do not think they can. However, several
strategies can help smokers achieve this goal.

   The first and easiest strategy is substituting something for the cigarette that they have gotten used to holding. Some people use a pencil, a
straw, or a coin. I have a friend who started using a Japanese fan. There
are even special products available to keep people's hands busy, such as
worry beads and small rubber balls. Almost any small object can work.

   Next, people who quit smoking need to substitute something for the
stimulation they get from cigarettes. They might chew a strongly flavored
sugarless gum, for example, or take fast, short breaths. Other people
splash their faces with ice cold water or do some light exercise. Some even
claim that standing on their heads has helped. The point is to find something that gives a physical jolt to the system.

   A third strategy is to change habits associated with smoking. For
example, people who associate cigarettes with drinking coffee might temporarily switch to tea or another beverage with caffeine, while people who
generally smoke while on the telephone might try using e-mail instead
of making long-distance calls. Unfortunately, some smoking-associated
activities are difficult to eliminate. People who associate smoking with
being in their cars obviously cannot give up driving. The point, though,
is to alter as many habits as possible to eliminate times when one would
normally reach for a cigarette.

Introduction

Thesis statement

Body paragraphs

Body paragraphs
Conclusion

Finally, most people who successfully quit smoking prepare themselves to resist temptation in moments of stress or discomfort. Rather than reaching for a cigarette, they have another sort of treat ready for themselves. Some people, understandably, choose candy or sweets of some kind, but these are not the best alternatives, for obvious reasons. A better idea is to use the money saved by not buying cigarettes to purchase something to pamper oneself with, such as expensive cologne or a personal CD player.

No one would say that it is easy to quit smoking, but this fact should not keep people from recognizing that they can kick the habit. These four antismoking strategies have worked for many ex-smokers, who recommend them highly.

1. What is the essay's thesis? Try to express it in your own words.

2. What point does the first body paragraph make? What examples support this point?

3. What point does the second body paragraph make? What examples support this point?

4. What point does the third body paragraph make? What examples support this point?

5. What point does the fourth body paragraph make? What examples support this point?

6. At what point in the conclusion does the writer restate the essay's thesis?

B   Deciding on a Topic

Most of the essays you will write in college begin as an **assignment** given to you by your instructor. The following assignments are typical of those you might be given in your composition class.

A. Discuss some things you would like to change about your school.
B. What can college students do to improve the environment?
C. Describe something you do outside of school that contributes to your education.

Because these assignments are so general, it would be difficult—if not impossible—to write about them. What specific things would you change? Exactly what could you do to improve the environment? Which activity outside of school should you write about? Answering these questions will help you narrow these assignments into **topics** that you can write about.

Assignment	Topic
Discuss some things you would change about your school.	Three things I would change to improve the quality of life at Jackson County Community College
What can college students do to improve the environment?	The campus recycling project
Describe something you do outside of school that contributes to your education.	The advantages of having a part-time job in college

For each assignment you are given, try to list several possible topics so that you have choices. For example, if you were assigned to write a four-hundred-word essay about an activity you do outside of school that contributes to your education, you could make the following list of topics.

A. The advantages of having a part-time job in college
B. Volunteering at the neighborhood community center
C. Building houses for the homeless during spring break
D. My week helping at Meals on Wheels
E. My summer job at Disney World

After you make your list, review each topic, and choose the one that you can write the best essay about. (The more you know about a topic, the more you will have to write about.) If you have difficulty coming up with a list of topics, try freewriting or brainstorming for a short period of time. If you still have difficulty, brainstorm with some of your classmates, or make an appointment with your instructor.

For more on freewriting and brainstorming, see 1C and 12C.

◆ PRACTICE 12-2

Decide whether the following topics are suitable for an essay of four or five paragraphs. If a topic is suitable, write *OK* in the blank. If it is not, write in the blank a revised version of the same topic that is narrow enough for a brief essay.

Examples: Successful strategies for quitting smoking _____*OK*_____

Horror movies _____*1950s Japanese monster movies*_____

1. Violence in American public schools _____

_____

2. Ways to improve your study skills _____

_____

12 C

3. Using pets as therapy for nursing-home patients _____

_____

4. Teachers _____

_____

5. Clothing styles _____

_____

■ **SEEING AND WRITING:** Flashback

Look back at the Seeing and Writing assignment on page 131. To narrow the topic to one you can write about, you need to decide which job to focus on. On a separate piece of paper, list all the possible jobs you could discuss.

C   Using Invention Strategies

For a full discussion of invention strategies, see 1C.

Before you start writing about a topic, you have to discover what you have to say about it. Once you have done this, you will be ready to decide on a thesis for your essay. Sometimes, ideas may come to you easily. More often, you will have to use one or more **invention strategies**, such as *freewriting* or *brainstorming*, to help you come up with ideas about your topic.

Freewriting

When you **freewrite**, you write (or type) for a fixed period of time without stopping. When you engage in **focused freewriting**, you write with a specific topic in mind. Then, you read what you have written and choose the ideas you think you can use. Following is an example of focused freewriting by a student, Kevin Coleman, on the topic "the advantages of having a part-time job in college."

```
    Working in college. I never really wanted to work,
but my parents told me that I'd have to pick up some of
my expenses. I got a student loan, but it didn't cover
everything--movies, food, etc. I began working during
my second semester. I had a bunch of part-time jobs.
Waiter. Library. Pizza truck. Some were fun--others were
pretty bad. I hated driving that pizza truck. But there
```

were some advantages. One was that I didn't have to ask
my parents for money all the time. That made them happy.
Paid half of my tuition. Working also made me happy. I
began to feel independent. Yeah--my Declaration of Independence. I saw that if things got tough, I could make
it. (Not a bad thing to know about yourself.) I wonder
if my parents knew this all along. Or is this something
that just happened? Maybe working taught me some lessons
that I didn't learn in school. I guess I'll never know.
It's not like I can really ask them. I'm running out of
things to say. The end.

◆ PRACTICE 12-3

Reread Kevin Coleman's freewriting. If you were advising Kevin, which ideas
would you suggest that he explore further? Why?

■ SEEING AND WRITING: Flashback

Choose two of the jobs you listed for the Flashback exercise on page 136.
Freewrite about each of them on separate sheets of paper. Which job
inspired the most interesting ideas? Circle the ideas that you would like
to develop further.

Brainstorming

When you **brainstorm** (either individually or in collaboration with others),
you write down (or type) all you can think of about a particular topic. You can
write in a list or in notes scattered all over a sheet of paper. After you have
recorded as much material as you can, you look over your notes to figure out
which ideas are useful and which ones are not. Here is Kevin Coleman's brainstorming on the advantages of part-time jobs for college students.

                    Advantages of a Part-Time Job
Working ever since my second year of college
Bad jobs
     Waiter--library--pizza truck driver (good tips)
Gained confidence
Helped pay tuition
Got independence

```
Bought lots of clothes
Bought photography supplies
Got a lot of satisfaction
Felt like an adult--had my own money
Brother going to college next year
Sometimes not enough time
Final exams--papers
Not enough free time
Did grades suffer? Did social life?
Always found time
Things you learn
      Responsibility
      Business
      About independence, survival skills
```

◆ PRACTICE 12-4

Reread Kevin Coleman's brainstorming. Which ideas would you advise him to explore further? Why?

■ SEEING AND WRITING: Flashback

Review the freewriting you did in the Flashback exercise on page 137. Now, on a separate piece of paper, brainstorm about the job that inspired the most interesting ideas. What ideas about the job did you get from brainstorming that you did not get from freewriting?

D   Stating Your Thesis

After you have used invention strategies to gather information about your topic, you have to decide exactly what you want to say about it. By choosing and rejecting ideas and by identifying connections among the ideas you keep, you can decide on the point you want your essay to make. You can then express this point in a **thesis statement**: a single sentence that clearly expresses the main idea that you will discuss in the rest of your essay.

Topic	Thesis Statement
Three things I would change about Jackson County Community College	If I could change three things to improve Jackson County Community College, I would

Topic	Thesis Statement
	expand the food choices, decrease class size in first-year courses, and ship some of my classmates to the North Pole.
The campus recycling project	The recycling project recently begun on our campus should be promoted more actively.
The advantages of having a part-time job	A part-time job is a valuable part of any college student's education.

Like a topic sentence, a thesis statement tells readers what to expect. An effective thesis statement has two important characteristics.

For more on topic sentences, see 2A.

1. *An effective thesis statement makes a point about a topic or takes a stand on an issue; for this reason, it must do more than state a fact or announce what you plan to write about.*

   STATEMENT OF FACT Many college students work.

   ANNOUNCEMENT In this essay, I would like to present my opinion about whether college students should work.

   EFFECTIVE THESIS STATEMENT A part-time job is a valuable part of any college student's education.

A statement of fact is not an effective thesis statement because it takes no position and gives you nothing to develop in your essay. After all, how much can you say about the *fact* that many college students work? Likewise, an announcement of what you plan to discuss gives readers no indication of the position you will take on your topic. An effective thesis statement takes a stand. It could say, for example, that a part-time job is a valuable part of a college education.

2. *An effective thesis statement is clearly worded and specific.*

   VAGUE THESIS STATEMENT Television commercials are not like real life.

   EFFECTIVE THESIS STATEMENT Television commercials do not accurately portray women or minorities.

The vague thesis statement above says little about the ideas that the essay will discuss or how it will present those ideas. It does not say, for example, *why* television commercials are not realistic. The effective thesis statement is more focused. It signals that the essay will give examples of television commercials that present unrealistic portrayals of women and minorities.

Keep in mind that at this stage of the writing process your thesis statement is *tentative.* You will almost certainly change it as you write and revise your essay.

> **FOCUS** **Stating Your Thesis**
>
> You can sometimes revise a vague thesis statement by including in it a list of the specific points that it will discuss. Revised in this way, the thesis acts as a road map, telling readers what to expect as they read.
>
> VAGUE THESIS STATEMENT   Raising tropical fish is a good hobby.
>
> EFFECTIVE THESIS STATEMENT   Raising tropical fish is a good hobby because it is inexpensive, interesting, and educational.
>
> The vague thesis statement above gives readers little information about the essay to follow. The effective thesis statement, however, lays out the plan of the essay and gives readers a clear idea of what the rest of the essay will discuss.

◆ PRACTICE 12-5

In the space provided, indicate whether each of the following items is a statement of fact (*F*), an announcement (*A*), a vague statement (*VS*), or an effective thesis (*ET*).

Examples:

My commute between home and school takes an hour each way. _F_

I hate my commute between home and school. _VS_

1. Students who must commute a long distance to school are at a disadvantage compared to students who live close by. _____

2. In this paper, I will discuss why students shouldn't cheat. _____

3. Schools should establish specific policies that will discourage students from cheating. _____

4. Cheating is a problem for both students and teachers. _____

5. Television commercials are designed to sell products. _____

6. I would like to explain why some TV commercials are funny. _____

7. Single parents have a rough time. _____

8. An article in the newspaper says that young people are starting to abuse alcohol and drugs at earlier ages than in the past. _____

9. Alcohol and drug abuse are major problems in our society. _____

10. Families can use several strategies to help children avoid drugs. _____

◆ PRACTICE 12-6

A list of broad topics for essays follows. Select five of these topics, narrow them, and generate a thesis statement for each.

1. Vacations
2. Reality television
3. Tattoos
4. Music
5. Chocolate
6. Required courses
7. Computer games
8. Disciplining children
9. X games
10. Footwear

◆ PRACTICE 12-7

Label each of the following thesis statements *VS* if it is too vague, *F* if it is factual, *A* if it is an announcement, or *ET* if it is an effective thesis. On a separate sheet of paper, rewrite those that are not effective thesis statements.

1. Different types of amusement parks appeal to different types of people. _____

2. To encourage more people to vote, Election Day should be a national holiday. _ET_

3. Every fourth year, on the first Tuesday in November, the United States elects a new president. _A_

4. My paper will prove that DVDs are better than videotapes. _A_

5. The largest fish in the sea is the whale shark. _F_

6. Forty years ago, scientists believed that the dinosaurs were killed off by the arrival of a new Ice Age. _A_

7. NASCAR drivers should be forced to drive at safer speeds. _ET_

8. This paper will discuss the increase in the number of women in the military since the 1970s. _A_

9. Movies provide great entertainment. _VS_

10. Computers have made it easier for teachers and their students to communicate. _ET_

◆ PRACTICE 12-8

Rewrite the following vague thesis statements.

> **Example:** My relatives are funny.
>
>   Rewrite: _My relatives think they are funny, but sometimes their humor can be offensive._

1. Camping can be dangerous.
2. Photography is an interesting hobby.
3. Athletes are paid too much.
4. Many people get their identities from their cars.
5. A community college education has many advantages.

■ SEEING AND WRITING: Flashback

Review your freewriting and brainstorming notes from the Flashback exercises on page 137 and page 138, and draft a thesis statement for your essay.

E   Arranging Ideas

Once you have decided on a thesis statement, look over your freewriting and brainstorming again, this time to find the points that best support your thesis. Then, make a list of these points. Here is Kevin Coleman's list of supporting points about the advantages of part-time jobs for college students.

```
Job makes parents happy
Job gives satisfaction
Job provides an income
Able to buy photography supplies
Don't have to ask parents for money
Paid half of my tuition
```

Feel like an adult
Buy clothing
Brother going to college next year
Gained confidence

After you have selected the points you think will best support your thesis, arrange them in the order in which you will discuss them—for example, from general to specific, or from least important to most important. (You can first type your list of points and then keep rearranging them until the order makes sense, indenting items with the Tab key to show how they are related.) This orderly list of points can serve as a rough outline to guide you as you write. Kevin listed his points in the following order.

Job provides steady income
    Buy clothing
    Able to buy photography supplies
Job helps pay tuition
    Makes parents happy
    Brother going to college next year
    Paid half of my tuition
Job gives satisfaction
    Feel like an adult
    Gained confidence

◆ PRACTICE 12-9

Look over Kevin's list of points above. Do you think his arrangement is effective? Can you suggest any other ways he might have arranged his points?

FOCUS   **Preparing a Formal Outline**

The rough outline discussed above is all you need to plan most of your essays. However, some writers—especially when they are planning longer, more detailed essays—like to use a more formal outline. **Formal outlines** contain a combination of numbered and lettered headings. They use roman numerals, capital letters, and arabic numerals (and sometimes lower-case letters) to show the relationships among ideas. For example, the most important (and most general) ideas are assigned a roman numeral; the next most important ideas are assigned

(continued on the following page)

(continued from the previous page)
capital letters. Each level develops the idea before it, and each new level is indented. Here is a formal outline of the points that Kevin planned to discuss in his essay.

> *Thesis statement:* A part-time job is a valuable part of any student's college education.
> I. Job gives me steady income
>   A. Can buy clothing
>   B. Can buy photography supplies
> II. Job helps pay tuition
>   A. Makes parents happy
>   1. Sets example for brother
>   2. Helps parents pay for brother's tuition
>   B. Helps me pay expenses
>   1. Provides half of college tuition
>   2. Provides money for living expenses
> III. Job gives me satisfaction
>   A. Feel like an adult
>   1. Earn respect
>   2. Invest in my future
>   B. Have more confidence

■ SEEING AND WRITING: Flashback

On a separate sheet of paper, write the thesis statement you drafted in the Flashback exercise on page 142. Then, review your freewriting and brainstorming again, and list the points you plan to use to support your thesis statement. Finally, arrange these points in an order in which you can write about them. Cross out any points that do not support your thesis statement.

F   Drafting Your Essay

For a discussion of introductions and conclusions, see Chapter 13.

After you have decided on a thesis for your essay and have arranged your points in the order in which you will discuss them, you are ready to draft your essay. At this stage of the writing process, you should not worry about spelling or grammar or about composing a perfect introduction or conclusion. Your main goal is to get your ideas down so you can react to them. Remember that the draft you are writing will be revised, so leave room for your changes: write on every other line, and triple-space if you are typing. Follow your rough out-line, but don't hesitate to depart from it if you think of new points or if your ideas take an interesting or unexpected turn as you write.

As you draft your essay, remember that it should have a **thesis-and-support** structure—that is, it should state a thesis and support it with details, facts, and examples. (Because this structure enables you to present your ideas clearly and persuasively, it will be central to much of the writing you do in col-lege.) Regardless of the specific **pattern of development** you use to shape a particular essay, each of your essays should follow this basic structure.

Notice how Kevin Coleman uses a thesis-and-support structure in the first draft of his essay.

For a discussion of thesis and support, see 12A.

For a discussion of patterns of essay development, see Chapter 14.

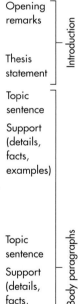

Working

Ever since I began college, I have been working. While some of my friends sat around wasting time, I have managed to hold down several part-time jobs. I have gained a lot by working. A part-time job is a valuable part of any college student's education.

Opening remarks

Thesis statement

The first reason to work is that a job provides income. I've had a number of part-time jobs, and I didn't like them all, but they did have their uses. When I want to buy books or clothes, I usually can. If an unexpected expense comes up, I can usually increase my hours so I can earn more. Last year, for example, I unexpectedly had to buy supplies for a photography course I was taking.

Topic sentence

Support (details, facts, examples)

Another reason for working is that a job helps pay tuition. Both my parents work, and they are able to make ends meet. My mother is a teacher, and my father works for an insurance company. Their jobs are demanding, and they are usually tired at the end of the day. Even so, they don't have the money to pay all my tuition. My brother will be going to college next year, and they have to save for him. Every summer, I try to earn enough money to pay part of my tuition. The jobs I hold during the year pay for most of my weekly expenses. This past year, I was able to pay almost half my tuition and almost all of my living expenses.

Topic sentence

Support (details, facts, examples)

The third reason for working is that a job gives me satisfaction. By working, I feel that I am earning the

Topic sentence

Support
(details,
facts,
examples)

respect of my parents. I am not a drain on the family, and I set a good example for my brother. I would feel horrible if I had to run to my parents every time I needed money. I would also feel like a kid, not an adult. By working, I am developing the confidence I will need when I graduate and enter the work force. Because I have been able to earn my own way, I know I can support myself no matter what happens.

Conclusion

Restatement
of thesis
Closing
remarks

I would advise any student to consider getting a part-time job. Working supplements income and helps pay tuition, and it also provides a great deal of satisfaction.

◆ PRACTICE 12-10

Reread Kevin Coleman's first draft. What changes would you suggest he make? What might he add? What might he delete?

■ SEEING AND WRITING: Flashback

On a separate sheet of paper, write a draft of an essay about the job you chose in the Flashback exercise on page 137. Be sure to include the thesis statement you developed in the Flashback exercise on page 142 as well as the points you listed in the Flashback exercise on page 144.

G   Revising and Editing Your Essay

When you **revise** your essay, you resee, rethink, reevaluate, and rewrite your work. Some of the changes you make—such as adding, deleting, or rearranging several sentences or even whole paragraphs—will be major. Others will be small—for example, adding or deleting words or phrases.

Before you begin revising, put your paper aside for a time. This "cooling-off" period allows you to put some distance between yourself and what you have written so that you can view your draft more objectively. (Keep in mind that revision is usually not a neat process. When you revise, feel free to write directly on your draft: draw arrows, underline, cross out, and write above lines and in the margins.)

When you **edit** your essay, you check grammar and sentence structure. Then, you look at punctuation, mechanics, and spelling.

Computer Tip

Revise and edit by hand on a hard copy of your essay before you type in your changes. When you take material out of your draft, move it to the end of the paper or to a separate file. Do not delete it until you are sure you do not need it.

As you revise and edit, think carefully about the questions in the two Self-Assessment Checklists that follow.

☑ SELF-ASSESSMENT CHECKLIST:
Revising Your Essay

- ☐ Does your essay have an introduction, a body, and a conclusion?
- ☐ Does your essay have a clearly worded thesis statement?
- ☐ Does your thesis statement make a point about your topic?
- ☐ Does each body paragraph have a topic sentence?
- ☐ Does each topic sentence reinforce the thesis?
- ☐ Does each body paragraph contain enough details, facts, or examples to support the topic sentence?
- ☐ Are the body paragraphs unified, well developed, and coherent?
- ☐ Do you restate your thesis or review your main points in your conclusion?
- ☐ Have you varied sentence type, structure, and length? (See Chapter 18.)
- ☐ Have you used effective parallel structure in your sentences? (See Chapter 19.)

For a discussion of how to write paragraphs that are unified, well developed, and coherent, see Chapter 2.

☑ SELF-ASSESSMENT CHECKLIST:
Editing Your Essay

Editing for Common Sentence Problems

- ☐ Have you avoided run-ons and comma splices? (See Chapter 21.)
- ☐ Have you avoided sentence fragments? (See Chapter 22.)

(continued on the following page)

(continued from the previous page)

- Do your subjects and verbs agree? (See Chapter 23.) Have you avoided illogical shifts? (See Chapter 24.)
- Have you avoided dangling and misplaced modifiers? (See Chapter 25.)

Editing for Grammar

- Are your verb forms and verb tenses correct? (See Chapters 26 and 27.)
- Have you used nouns and pronouns correctly? (See Chapter 28.)
- Have you used adjectives and adverbs correctly? (See Chapter 29.)

Editing for Punctuation, Mechanics, and Spelling

- Have you used commas correctly? (See Chapter 31.)
- Have you used apostrophes correctly? (See Chapter 32.)
- Have you used capital letters where they are required? (See Chapter 33.)
- Have you used quotation marks correctly where they are needed? (See Chapter 33.)
- Have you spelled every word correctly? (See Chapter 34.)

When he typed the first draft of his essay about the advantages of having a part-time job in college, Kevin triple-spaced so that he could write more easily in the space between the lines. Here is his draft, with his handwritten revision and editing changes.

Working

Ever since I began college, I have been working.

While some of my friends sat around wasting time, I have
Even though there have been times when I wished I didn't have to work,
managed to hold down several part-time jobs. ∧I have

                                                    can be
gained a lot by working. A part-time job ~~is~~ a valuable
                                              ; I know it has been
part of any college student's education.
                                              for me.

   The first reason to work is that a job provides
a steady source of money for day-to-day expenses.
~~income.~~ I've had a number of part-time jobs, and I
         ∧
                              Because I have a steady salary, when
didn't like them all, but they did have their uses. ~~When~~
                                                       ∧

I want to buy books or clothes, I usually can. If an

unexpected expense comes ~~up,~~ *along,* I can usually increase my

hours so I can earn more. Last year, for example, I

unexpectedly had to buy supplies for a photography

At first I thought I would have to drop the course because I couldn't afford the
course I was taking.
supplies. After talking to my boss, however, I was able to arrange to work a few
Another reason for working is that a job helps pay
extra hours and earn enough to buy the supplies I needed.
tuition. Both my parents work, and they are able to make

ends meet. ~~My mother is a teacher, and my father works~~

~~for an insurance company. Their jobs are demanding, and~~

~~they are usually tired at the end of the day. Even so,~~
But even with loans, we   *In addition, my*
~~they~~ don't have the money to pay all my tuition. ~~My~~

brother will be going to college next year, and they

have to save for him. Every summer, I try to earn

enough money to pay part of my tuition. ~~The jobs I hold~~

~~during the year pay for most of my weekly expenses.~~ This

past year, I was able to pay almost half my tuition. ~~and~~

~~almost all of my living expenses.~~
                    most important
The ~~third~~ reason for working is that a job gives me

satisfaction. By working, I feel that I am earning the

respect of my parents. I am not a drain on the family,

and I set a good example for my brother. I would feel

horrible if I had to run to my parents every time I

needed money. I would also feel like a kid, not an
                                also
adult. By working, I am developing the confidence I will

need when I graduate and enter the work force. Because I

Even though my parents have never said anything to me, I know that paying my tuition is a hardship for them.

have been able to pay my own way, *so far* I know I can support

myself no matter what happens.

I would advise any student to consider getting a
part-time job. Working ~~supplements~~ *not only provides needed* income and helps pay
tuition, *but* ~~and it~~ also ~~provides a great deal of~~ *offers* satisfac-
tion. *In my case, a job has given me the insight and the confidence I will need to succeed after I graduate.*

◆ PRACTICE 12-11

What material did Kevin Coleman add to his draft? What did he delete? Why did he make these changes? Be prepared to discuss Kevin's revisions with the class.

When his revisions and edits were complete, Kevin proofread his essay to be sure he had not missed any errors. The final revised and edited version of his essay appears below.

Working

Ever since I began college, I have been working. While some of my friends sat around wasting time, I have managed to hold down several part-time jobs. Even though there have been times when I wished I did not have to work, I have gained a lot by working. A part-time job can be a valuable part of any college student's education; I know it has been for me.

The first reason to work is that a job provides a steady source of money for day-to-day expenses. I have had a number of part-time jobs, and even though I did not like them all, they did have their uses. Because I have a steady salary, when I want to buy books or an item of clothing, I usually can. If an unexpected expense comes along, I can usually increase my hours so I can earn more. Last year, for example, I unexpectedly had to buy supplies for a photography course I was taking. At first, I thought I would have to drop the course because I could not afford the supplies. After talking to my boss, however, I was able to arrange to work a few extra hours and earn enough to buy the supplies I needed.

Another reason for working is that a job helps pay tuition. Even though my parents have never said anything to me, I know that paying my tuition is a hardship for them. Both my parents work, and they are able to make ends meet. But even with loans, they do not have the money to pay all my tuition. In addition, my brother will be going to college next year, and they have to save for him. Every summer I try to earn enough money to pay part of my tuition. This past year, I was able to pay almost half my tuition.

The most important reason for working is that a job gives me satisfaction. By working, I feel that I am earning the respect of my parents. I am not a drain on the family, and I set a good example for my brother. I would feel horrible if I had to run to my parents every time I needed money. I would also feel like a kid, not an adult. Furthermore, by working, I am developing the confidence I will need when I graduate and enter the work force. Because I have been able to pay my own way so far, I know I can support myself no matter what happens.

I would advise any student to consider getting a part-time job. Working not only provides needed income and helps pay tuition but also offers satisfaction. In my case, a job has given me the insight and the confidence I will need to succeed after I graduate.

◆ PRACTICE 12-12

Reread the final draft of Kevin Coleman's essay. Do you think this draft is an improvement over his first draft? What other changes could Kevin have made? Be prepared to discuss your evaluation of Kevin's final draft with the class.

■ SEEING AND WRITING: Flashback

Using the Self-Assessment Checklist for revising your essay on page 147 as a guide, evaluate the essay you wrote for the Flashback exercise on page 146. What points can you add to support your thesis more fully? What points can you delete? Can any ideas be stated more clearly? (You may want to get feedback by exchanging essays with another student.)

> ■ SEEING AND WRITING: Revising and Editing
>
> Now, revise the draft of your essay, writing in new material between the lines or in the margins. Then, edit this revised draft, using the Self-Assessment Checklist for editing your essay on pages 147–48 to help you find errors in grammar, sentence structure, punctuation, mechanics, and spelling. When you have finished, prepare a final draft of your essay.

CHAPTER REVIEW

◆ EDITING PRACTICE

After reading the following student essay, write an appropriate thesis statement on the lines provided. (Make sure your thesis statement clearly communicates the essay's main idea.) Then, fill in the topic sentences for the second, third, and fourth paragraphs. Finally, restate the thesis in different words in the conclusion.

Preparing for a Job Interview

I have consulted a lot of books and many Web sites that give advice on how to do well on a job interview. Some recommend practicing your handshake, and others suggest rehearsing answers to typical questions. This advice is useful, but not many books tell how to get mentally prepared for an interview. [Thesis statement:] _____

_____

_____

[Topic sentence for the second paragraph:] _____

_____

_____

Feeling good about how I look is important, so I usually wear a jacket and tie to an interview. Even if you will not be dressing this formally on the job, try to make a good first impression. For this reason, you should never come to an interview dressed in jeans or shorts. Still, you should be careful not to overdress. For example, wearing a suit or a dressy dress to an interview at a fast-food restaurant might make you feel good, but it could also make you look as if you do not really want to work there.

[Topic sentence for the third paragraph:] _____

_____

_____

Going on an interview is a little like getting ready to participate in an important sporting event. You have to go in with the right attitude. If you think you are not going to be successful, chances are that you will not be. So before I go on any interview, I spend some time building my confidence. I tell myself that I can do the job and that I will do well in the interview. By the time I get to the interview, I am convinced that I am the right person for the job.

[Topic sentence for the fourth paragraph:] _____

_____

_____

Most people go to an interview knowing little or nothing about the job. They expect the interviewer to tell them what they will have to do. Once, an interviewer told me that he likes a person who has taken the time to do his or her home-work. Since that time, I have always done some research before I go on an interview--even for a part-time job. (Most of the time, my research is nothing more than a quick look at the company Web site or a call to a person who has a job where I want to work.) This kind of research really pays off. At my last interview, for example, I was able to talk in specific terms about the job's duties and indicate which shift I would prefer. The interviewer must have been impressed because she offered me the job on the spot.

    [Restatement of thesis:] _____

_____

_____

_____

Of course, following my suggestions will not guarantee that you get a job. You still have to do well at the interview itself. Even so, getting mentally prepared for the interview will give you an advantage over people who do almost nothing before they walk in the door.

◆ COLLABORATIVE ACTIVITIES

1. On your own, find a paragraph in a magazine or a newspaper about a controversial issue that interests you. Working in a group, select one of the best paragraphs. Choose three points about the issue discussed that you could develop in a short essay, and then brainstorm about these points. Finally, write a sentence that could serve as the thesis statement for an essay.

2. Working in a group, come up with thesis statements suitable for essays on three of the following topics.

Professional sports	Gun safety
The Internet	Dressing well on a budget
Safe driving	College entrance exams
Parenthood	Bad habits
Honesty	How to prepare for a test

For information on stating a thesis, see 12D.

3. Exchange your group's three thesis statements with those of another group. Choose the best one of the other group's thesis statements. A member of each group can then read the thesis statement to the class and explain why the group chose the thesis statement it did.

Introductions and Conclusions **13**

PREVIEW

In this chapter, you will learn:
- to write an introduction (13A)
- to choose a title (13A)
- to write a conclusion (13B)

Word Power

monotonous
repetitious;
lacking in
variety

robotic
mechanical

routine
a standard
procedure to
be followed
regularly

■ SEEING AND WRITING

Look at the picture above, in which Charlie Chaplin, in the film *Modern Times* (1936), is sucked into a factory machine. Then, make a copy of the essay you wrote for Chapter 12. As you go through this chapter, you will continue to work on the introduction and conclusion of this essay.

155

When you draft an essay, you usually concentrate on the **body** because it is the largest single section and because it is the section in which you develop your ideas. A well-constructed essay, however, is more than a series of body paragraphs. It also includes an **introduction** and a **conclusion,** both of which contribute to the overall effectiveness of your writing.

A   Introductions

An introduction is the first thing people see when they read your essay. If your introduction is interesting and effective, it is likely to draw readers into your essay and make them want to read further. If it is not, readers may get bored and stop reading.

Your introduction should prepare readers for your essay by giving them the information they need to follow your discussion. For this reason, the introduction should be a full paragraph and include a **thesis statement** that presents the main idea of your essay. This statement usually appears at the end of the introductory paragraph. (In each of the examples on pages 157–60, the thesis statement is underlined.)

Here are some options you can experiment with when you write your introductions.

FOCUS   What to Avoid in Introductions

■   Do not begin your essay by announcing what you plan to write about.

Phrases to avoid

This essay is about . . .

Today I will talk about . . .

In my essay I will discuss . . .

■   Do not apologize for your ideas.

Phrases to avoid

Although I don't know much about this subject . . .

I might not be an expert but . . .

Beginning with a Direct Approach

The simplest way to start an essay is to present a few opening remarks and then list the points you will discuss. A straightforward approach, such as the one that follows, moves readers directly to the central concerns of your essay. (Once you feel comfortable with this strategy, you can experiment with other approaches.)

> Television sitcoms are a part of most people's lives. Almost everyone watches these shows at one time or another. In addition to providing entertainment, sitcoms often show characters struggling with real-life situations. By doing so, these characters convey ideas about what is right and wrong and what is acceptable and not acceptable. Unfortunately, some viewers, especially young ones, are overly influenced by what they see. That is why it is disturbing to see how many sitcoms convey unrealistic images of men and women. <u>These stereotypes not only misrepresent reality, but they also teach distorted values that make it almost impossible for real men and women to relate to one another.</u>

Thesis statement

> Amy Donohue (student)

Beginning with a Narrative

You can begin an essay with a narrative drawn from your own experience or from a current news event. If your story is interesting, it will involve readers almost immediately. Notice how the narrative in the following introduction sets the stage for an essay in which the writer discusses his experiences as a volunteer firefighter.

> On September 11, 2001, the unthinkable happened: terrorists crashed two commercial airplanes into the twin towers at the World Trade Center. Ignoring the possibility that the two one-hundred-and-ten-story towers were in danger of falling, hundreds of firefighters rushed inside the buildings to try to save as many lives as possible. Their selfless actions enabled thousands of people to get out, but half the firefighters—over three hundred—died when the twin towers collapsed. <u>Although I have never faced a catastrophe like the one in New York, as a volunteer firefighter I am ready—day or night whenever an alarm sounds—to deal with a dangerous situation.</u>

Thesis statement

> Richard Pogue (student)

Beginning with a Question (or a Series of Questions)

Using one or more questions at the beginning of your essay is an effective introductory strategy. Because readers expect you to answer the questions in your essay, they will want to read further. Notice how two questions in the following introduction catch the reader's eye.

Imagine this scene: A child is sitting under a Christmas tree opening her presents. She laughs and claps her hands as she gets a doll, a pair of shoes, and a sweater. What could spoil this picture? What information could cause the child's parents to feel guilt? The answer is this: that children from developing countries probably worked long hours in substandard conditions so this American child could receive her gifts.

Thesis statement

Megan Davia (student)

Beginning with a Definition

A definition at the beginning of your essay can give valuable information to readers. Such information can explain a confusing concept or clarify a complicated idea, as the following paragraph demonstrates.

The term *good parent* is not easy to define. Some things about being a good parent are obvious—keeping your children safe, taking them to the dentist for regular checkups, helping them with their homework, being there for them when they want to talk, and staying up at night with them when they are sick, for example. Other things are not so obvious, however. I found this out last year when I became a volunteer at my daughter's middle school. Up until that time, I never would have dreamed that one morning a week could do so much to improve my daughter's attitude toward school.

Thesis statement

Russ Hightower (student)

FOCUS **Beginning with a Definition**

Do not introduce a definition with a tired opening phrase such as "*According to Webster's . . .*" or "*The American Heritage Dictionary defines . . .*"

Beginning with a Background Statement

A background statement can provide an overview of a subject and lay the groundwork for the discussion to follow. As the following introduction illustrates, a background statement can also help prepare readers for a surprising or controversial thesis statement.

English is the most widely spoken language in the history of our planet, used in some way by at least one out of every seven human beings around the globe. Half of the world's books are written in English, and the majority of international telephone calls are made in English. English is the language of over sixty percent of the world's radio programs, many of them beamed, ironically, by the Russians, who know that to win friends and influence nations, they're best off using English. More than seventy percent of international mail is written and addressed in English, and eighty percent of all computer text is stored in English. English has acquired the largest vocabulary of all the world's languages, perhaps as many as two million words, and has generated one of the noblest bodies of literature in the annals of the human race. <u>Nonetheless, it is now time to face the fact that English is a crazy language.</u>

> Thesis statement

Richard Lederer, "English Is a Crazy Language"

Beginning with a Quotation

An appropriate saying or an interesting piece of dialogue can immediately draw readers into your essay. Notice how the quotation below creates interest and leads smoothly and logically into the thesis statement at the end of the introduction.

According to the comedian Jerry Seinfeld, "When you're single, you are the dictator of your own life. . . . When you're married, you are part of a vast decision-making body." In other words, before you can do anything, you have to discuss it with someone else. These words kept going through my mind as I thought about asking my girlfriend to marry me. The more I thought about Seinfeld's words, the more I hesitated. <u>I never suspected that I would pay a price for my indecision.</u>

> Thesis statement

Dan Brody (student)

Beginning with a Surprising Statement

You can begin your essay with a surprising or unexpected statement. Because your statement takes readers by surprise, it catches their attention. Notice in the following paragraph how a rather startling opening statement leads readers to the essay's thesis.

Some of the smartest people I know never went to college. In fact, some of them never finished high school. Even so, they know how to save twenty percent on the price of a dinner, fix their own faucets when they leak, get discounted prescriptions, get free rides on a bus to Atlantic City, use public transportation to get anywhere in the city, and live on about twenty-two dollars a day. These are my grandparents' friends. Some people would call them old and poor. <u>I would call them survivors who have learned to make it through life on nothing but a Social Security check.</u>

> Thesis statement

Sean Ragas (student)

Beginning with a Contradiction

You can begin your introduction with an idea that many people believe to be true. Then, as the following paragraph does, you can capture readers' attention by demonstrating why this idea is untrue or questionable.

Drugs and crime are so thoroughly intertwined in the public mind that to most people a large crime problem seems an inevitable consequence of drug use. But the historical link between the two is more a product of drug laws than of drugs. There are four clear connections between drugs and crime, and three of them would be much diminished if drugs were legalized. This fact doesn't by itself make the case for legalization persuasive, of course, but it deserves careful attention in the emerging debate of whether prohibition of drugs is worth the trouble.

Ethan A. Nadelmann, "Legalize Drugs"

Thesis statement (margin note)

FOCUS **Titles**

Every essay should have a **title** that suggests the subject of the essay and makes people want to read it.

Before you choose a title, reread your essay (especially your thesis statement) carefully. Then, jot down several possible titles and select the one you like the best. When you write your title, be sure to follow these guidelines.

- Capitalize all words except for articles (*a, an, the*), prepositions (*at, to, of, around,* and so on), and coordinating conjunctions (*and, but,* and so on) unless they are the first or last word of the title.
- Do not underline your title or enclose it within quotation marks.
- Center the title at the top of the first page. Double-space between the title and the first line of your essay.

As you consider a title for your paper, think about the following options.

- A title can highlight a key word or term.

Guavas
Dyslexia
Liars

(continued on the following page)

(continued from the previous page)

■ A title can be a straightforward statement.

Thirty-Eight Who Saw Murder Didn't Call the Police
The "Black Table" Is Still There

■ A title can be a question.

Who Killed the Bog Men of Denmark? And Why?
Why Fear National ID Cards?

■ A title can set a scene.

Summer Picnic Fish Fry

■ A title can establish a personal connection with readers.

The Men We Carry in Our Minds
I Have a Dream

■ A title can offer an unusual perspective.

The New Prohibitionism

■ A title can be a familiar saying or a quotation from your essay itself.

Men Are from Mars, Women Are from Venus
Slice of Life

■ A title can relate to the pattern of development used in the essay.

Three Ways to Make Your Neighborhood Better (exemplification)
The Rise and Fall of Doo-Wop (narrative)
My Grandfather (description)
How to Write an Effective Résumé (process)
Why the *Titanic* Sank (cause and effect)
Four-Year vs. Two-Year Colleges (comparison and contrast)
Types of Sports Fans (classification)
What It Means to Be Happy (definition)
Let's Stop Persecuting Smokers (argument)

For more information on patterns of essay development, see Chapter 14.

◆ **PRACTICE 13-1**

Look at the student essays in Chapter 14, locating one introduction you think is particularly effective. Be prepared to explain the strengths of the introduction you chose.

◆ **PRACTICE 13-2**

Using the different options for creating titles discussed on pages 160–61, write two titles for each of the essays described below. List your titles on a separate piece of paper.

1. A student writes an essay about three people who disappeared mysteriously: Amelia Earhart, aviator; Ambrose Bierce, writer; and Jimmy Hoffa, union leader. In the body paragraphs, the student describes the circumstances surrounding their disappearances.

2. A student writes an essay arguing against doctors' letting people select the sex of their babies. In the body paragraphs, she presents reasons that she thinks it is unethical.

3. A student writes an essay to explain why America is ready to elect a woman president. In the body paragraphs, the writer gives reasons for his beliefs.

4. A student writes an essay describing the harmful effects of steroids on student athletes. In the body paragraphs, he shows the effects on the heart, brain, and other organs.

5. A student writes an essay explaining why she joined the Navy. In the body paragraphs, she discusses her need to earn money for college tuition, her wish to learn a trade, and her desire to see the world.

■ SEEING AND WRITING: Flashback

Look back at the essay you reprinted for the Seeing and Writing exercise on page 155. Evaluate your introduction. Does it prepare readers for the essay to follow? Does it include a thesis statement? Is it likely to interest readers? On a separate sheet of paper, draft a different opening paragraph using one of the options presented in 13A. Be sure to include a clear thesis statement.

After you have finished drafting a new introduction, think of a new title that will attract your readers' attention. (Use one of the options listed in the Focus box on pages 160–61.)

B   Conclusions

Because your **conclusion** is the last thing readers see, they often judge your entire essay by its effectiveness. For this reason, conclusions should be planned, drafted, and revised with care. (Like an introduction, a conclusion is usually a full paragraph.)

Your conclusion should give readers a sense of completion. One way you can accomplish this is by restating the essay's thesis. Keep in mind, however, that a conclusion is more than a word-for-word restatement of the thesis. If you return to your thesis here, you should summarize it, expand on it, or make some general concluding remarks; then, try to end with a sentence that readers will remember.

FOCUS   **Essay Exams**

■   In essay exams, when time is limited, a one-sentence restatement of your thesis is often enough for a conclusion. Likewise, an in-class essay exam may require just a one- or two-sentence introduction.

FOCUS   **What to Avoid in Conclusions**

■   Do not introduce any new ideas. Your conclusion should summarize the ideas you discuss in your essay, not open up new lines of thought.

■   Do not apologize for your opinions, ideas, or conclusions. Apologies will undercut your reader's confidence in you.

Phrases to avoid

I may not be an expert . . .

At least that's my opinion . . .

I could be wrong, but . . .

■   Do not use overused phrases to announce your essay is coming to a close.

Phrases to avoid

In summary . . .

In conclusion . . .

Here are some options you can experiment with when you write your conclusions.

Concluding with a Restatement of Your Thesis

This no-nonsense conclusion reinforces the essay's most important ideas by restating the thesis in different words and reviewing the main points of the discussion.

> It is unfortunate that television sitcoms do not show men and women relating to each other in a meaningful way. The simplistic plots, the reliance on humor—especially sexual humor—to resolve complicated problems, and the use of male and female stereotypes do little to educate viewers. At best, television sitcoms teach viewers that sex can make any problem disappear. At worst, they reinforce behavior patterns that make it almost impossible for men and women to relate to each other. A more realistic response from characters would show viewers that honest communication could do more to resolve conflicts between men and women than stereotypical behavior can.
>
> Amy Donohue (student)

Concluding with a Narrative

A narrative conclusion can bring an event discussed in the essay to a logical, satisfying close. The following conclusion uses a narrative to tie up the essay's loose ends.

> After twenty years, the tree began to bear. Although Grandfather complained about how much he lost because pollen never reached the poor part of town, because at the market he had to haggle over the price of avocados, he loved that tree. It grew, as did his family, and when he died, all his sons standing on each other's shoulders, oldest to youngest, could not reach the highest branches. The wind could move the branches, but the trunk, thicker than any waist, hugged the ground.
>
> Gary Soto, "The Grandfather"

Concluding with a Question (or a Series of Questions)

By ending with a question, you leave readers with something to think about. However, the question should build on the thesis statement and not introduce any new issues. Notice how the conclusion below asks a series of questions before restating the essay's thesis.

> Why is it that when the sun or the moon or the stars are out, they are visible, but when the lights are out, they are invisible, and that when I

wind up my watch, I start it, but when I wind up this essay, I shall end it? English is a crazy language.

Richard Lederer, "English Is a Crazy Language"

Concluding with a Prediction

This type of conclusion not only sums up the thesis but also looks to the future. The following conclusion uses this technique to paint a troubling picture of the future of American cities.

> On that little street were the ghosts of the people who brought me into being and the flesh-and-blood kids who will be my children's companions in the twenty-first century. You could tell by their eyes that they couldn't figure out why I was there. They were accustomed to being ignored, even by the people who had once populated their rooms. And as long as that continues, our cities will burst and burn, burst and burn, over and over again.

Anna Quindlen, "The Old Block"

Concluding with a Recommendation

Once you think you have convinced readers that a problem exists, you can make recommendations in your conclusion about how the problem should be solved. Notice how the following paragraph makes a series of recommendations about a cancer drug made from the Pacific yew tree.

> Every effort should be made to ensure that the yew tree is made available for the continued research and development of taxol. Environmental groups, the timber industry, and the Forest Service must recognize that the most important value of the Pacific yew is as a treatment for cancer. At the same time, its harvest can be managed in a way that allows for the production of taxol without endangering the continual survival of the yew tree.

Sally Thane Christensen, "Is a Tree Worth a Life?"

Concluding with a Quotation

Frequently, a well-chosen quotation—even a brief one—can add a lot to your essay. In some cases, quoted speech or writing can add authority to your ideas. In others, as in the following paragraph, it can reinforce the main point of the essay.

> It was 4:25 a.m. when the ambulance arrived to take the body of Miss Genovese. It drove off. "Then," a solemn police detective said, "the people came out."

Martin Gansberg, "Thirty-Eight Who Saw Murder Didn't Call the Police"

◆ PRACTICE 13-3

Look at the student essays in Chapter 14, locating one conclusion you think is particularly effective. Be prepared to explain the strengths of the conclusion you chose.

■ SEEING AND WRITING: Flashback

Look back at your response to the Seeing and Writing exercise on page 155. Evaluate your conclusion. Is it suitable for your topic and thesis? Does it bring your essay to a clear and satisfying close that will leave a strong impression on readers? On a separate sheet of paper, try drafting a different concluding paragraph using one of the options presented in 13B.

■ SEEING AND WRITING: Revising and Editing

Reread your responses to the Flashback exercise above and the one on page 162. Are the new paragraphs you wrote more effective than the introduction and conclusion of the essay you wrote in Chapter 12? If so, substitute them for the opening and closing paragraphs of that essay.

CHAPTER REVIEW

◆ EDITING PRACTICE

The following student essay has an undeveloped introduction and conclusion. Decide what introductory and concluding strategies would be most appropriate for the essay. Then, on a separate sheet of paper, rewrite both the introduction and the conclusion to make them more effective. Finally, add an interesting title for the essay.

Although women got the right to vote in 1919, no woman had ever served on the U.S. Supreme Court until the 1980s.

However, President Reagan was determined to fulfill his campaign promise of appointing women to positions of power in his administration. So, in 1981, he nominated Sandra Day O'Connor, a relatively unknown judge from Arizona, to fill the vacancy left by retiring Associate Justice Potter Stewart. O'Connor, who had graduated with honors from Stanford law school in 1952, was unable to find a position as a lawyer because she was a woman. So she married and raised three sons. Later on, she found a position in the Arizona Attorney General's office. From that point on, she moved into increasingly responsible political and legal positions, including first an appointment and later election to the Arizona senate. After she was nominated to the Supreme Court, O'Connor was confirmed by the U.S. Senate by a vote of 99-0, quite a vote of confidence for someone who had been unable, at first, to practice her profession.

In 1993, President Clinton nominated a second woman to the Supreme Court. This woman was Ruth Bader Ginsburg, whose path to the Court was similar to O'Connor's. She, too, graduated from law school with honors yet was unable to find employment as a lawyer. She did, however, find work as a law professor and eventually became the first tenured woman law professor at Columbia. Throughout her career, Ginsburg worked hard to end discrimination against women.

In fact, she argued six cases before the Supreme Court on women's rights before her own appointment.

Although O'Connor is seen as conservative and Ginsburg as moderate, both women fight hard for the rights of women and children.

◆ COLLABORATIVE ACTIVITIES

1. Bring to class several copies of an essay you wrote for another class. Have each person in your group comment on your essay's introduction and conclusion. Revise the introduction and conclusion in response to your classmates' suggestions.

2. Find a magazine or newspaper article that interests you. Cut off the introduction and conclusion and bring the body of the article to class. Ask your group to decide on the best strategy for introducing and concluding the article. Then, collaborate on writing new opening and closing paragraphs and an interesting title.

3. Working in a group, think of interesting and appropriate titles for essays on each of the following topics. Try to use as many of the different options outlined in the Focus box on pages 160–61 as you can.

The difficulty of living with a roommate
The evils of gambling
The need for regular exercise
The joys of living in the city (or in the country)
The responsibility of having a pet
Things that make life easier
Job interviews
The obligation to vote
Celebrating the holidays
Parents (or being a parent)
Public transportation

Patterns of Essay Development **14**

As you learned in Chapters 3 through 11, writers have a variety of options for developing ideas within a paragraph. These options include *exemplification, narration, description, process, cause and effect, comparison and contrast, classification, definition,* and *argument.* When you write an essay, you can use these same strategies to help you organize your material.

In your college courses, different assignments and writing situations call for different patterns of essay development. For instance, if an exam question asked you to compare two systems of government, you would use *comparison and contrast* to structure your essay. If your lab manual asked you to explain the stages of a particular chemical reaction, you would use *process*. If an English composition assignment asked you to tell about a childhood experience, you would use *narration*. If a section of a research paper on environmental pollution called for examples of dangerous waste disposal practices, you would use *exemplification*.

Each section in this chapter defines and explains one pattern of essay development, gives examples of how it is used in typical college writing assignments, provides several options for organizing an essay, and includes a list of useful transitions. A student essay illustrates each pattern, and a list of writing topics and a Self-Assessment Checklist give you opportunities for practice and review.

A   Exemplification

For information on writing an exemplification paragraph, see Chapter 3.

Exemplification illustrates a general statement with specific examples that support it. An **exemplification essay** uses specific examples to support a thesis.

FOCUS   Topics for Exemplification

The wording of your assignment may suggest exemplification. For example, you may be asked to *illustrate* or to *give examples*.

Assignment	Thesis Statement
Education Should children be taught in only their native languages or in English as well? Support your answer with examples of specific students' experiences.	The success of students in a bilingual third-grade class suggests the value of teaching elementary-school students in English as well as in their native languages.
Literature Does William Shakespeare's *Othello* have to end tragically? Illustrate your position with references to specific characters.	Each of the three major characters in *Othello* contributes to the play's tragic ending.

For examples of exemplification essays by professional writers, see 35A.

(continued on the following page)

(continued from the previous page)

Assignment	Thesis Statement
Composition Discuss the worst job you ever had. Include plenty of specific examples to support your thesis.	My summer job at a fast-food restaurant was my all-time worst job because of the endless stream of rude customers, the many boring and repetitive tasks I had to perform, and my manager's insensitive treatment of employees.

In an exemplification essay, each body paragraph can develop a single example or discuss several related examples.

Options for Organizing Exemplification Essays

One Example per Paragraph	Several Related Examples per Paragraph
¶1 Introduction	¶1 Introduction
¶2 First example	¶2 First group of examples
¶3 Second example	¶3 Second group of examples
¶4 Third example	¶4 Third group of examples
¶5 Conclusion	¶5 Conclusion

Regardless of how many examples you select, each one should relate to your thesis, and your essay's topic sentences should make clear just how each example supports the thesis statement. In addition, transitional words and phrases should introduce each example and indicate the relationship between one example and another.

FOCUS Transitions for Exemplification

Also	Furthermore	The most important example
Besides	In addition	
Finally	Moreover	The next example
First	One example . . .	
For example	Another example	
For instance	Specifically	

The following student essay, "Fighting Fire with Fire Safety Education" by Timothy E. Miles, uses a series of examples to illustrate the need to educate children about fire safety. Some paragraphs group several brief examples together; others develop a single example. Notice how Timothy uses clear topic sentences and helpful transitions to introduce his examples and link them to one another.

Fighting Fire with Fire Safety Education

Since young children suffer more fire-related injuries and fatalities than most others do, fire safety education must be introduced at an early age. This can be done both by parents and by local fire departments. Fire safety for young children is an ongoing concern, and adults must take the responsibility for educating and protecting them.

What should small children be taught? First, they should understand what matches are and what the consequences of playing with them can be. In addition, they should be taught that matches are not toys and that they can cause great damage. Children should also be taught how to avoid contact burns from stove burners, hot liquids, and electrical appliances.

Another essential part of fire safety education for children is learning how to extinguish fires when their own clothing ignites. Many children are burned by their own clothing. The chance of injury can be prevented if they are taught how to "Stop, Drop, and Roll." One way of teaching this is for the adult to cut out a "flame" from paper and tape it lightly to the child. When the child actually stops, drops, and rolls on the ground, the "flame" will fall off, thereby "extinguishing" the "fire."

Exit drills in the home can also save lives. These drills need to include information such as how to crawl low to escape smoke, how to feel for hot doors, and how to place towels or clothing under doors to stop smoke from coming into a room. (Children should also understand that smoke and fumes, not the fire itself, cause most deaths.) Deciding on a meeting place where all family members can be accounted for is perhaps the most important.

Making sure children know the fire department phone number is another way to reduce fire-related injuries and deaths. It is very important that children know the correct number because not all areas have a 911 system. The numbers of all emergency services should be prominently posted near each phone. Children should know how to dial these numbers and should know the address from which they are calling. To practice reporting a fire, a child can use a toy phone, with an adult assuming the role of the operator.

Finally, children should be aware of what firefighters look like in their equipment. Some children, particularly very young ones, are afraid of firefighters because of their unfamiliar appearance. During a visit to any local firehouse, children can meet firefighters who can answer questions and demonstrate and explain their equipment and gear. If children are familiar with firefighters and their equipment, they will not run away from them or hide.

Of course, educating children is not enough in itself to ensure fire safety; parents and other adults must also educate themselves about what to do (and what not to do) if a fire actually occurs. For example, do not go back into a fire for any reason. Have a meeting place where family members can be accounted for. Do not try to put out a fire; instead, have someone notify the fire department immediately. In addition, adults should take the responsibility for getting children involved in fire prevention. Many children learn best by example. Handouts, displays, and videotapes are especially helpful. Demonstration and practice of exit drills in the home and of "Stop, Drop, and Roll" are also useful, particularly during special fire hazard periods such as Halloween and Christmas. Participating in drawing escape plans and making inspections of the home for potential problems also make children feel they are helping. In fact, children can sometimes see things that adults overlook.

By keeping these points in mind, children and their parents can join together to avoid potential disaster.

```
If family members learn about fire safety and if they
practice and review what they have learned on a regular
basis, lives will be saved.
```

◆ PRACTICE 14-1

1. Underline the thesis statement of "Fighting Fire with Fire Safety Education." Then, try to restate it in your own words.

2. On a separate sheet of paper, list the examples Tim uses to support his thesis. Which examples does he group together? Why? Which examples does he develop in paragraphs of their own? Why?

3. How does Tim link his examples to one another? Underline some of the transitional words that serve this purpose.

4. Is the straightforward introduction effective? How else might Tim have opened his essay?

5. Is the conclusion effective? How else could Tim have ended his essay?

6. What is this essay's greatest strength? What is its greatest weakness?

◆ PRACTICE 14-2

Following the writing process outlined in Chapter 12, write an exemplification essay on one of the following topics.

Advantages (or disadvantages) of starting college right after high school
The three best things ever invented
Who (or what) should appear on U.S. postage stamps? Why?
Advantages (or disadvantages) of being a young parent
Athletes who really are role models
Four items students need to survive in college
Messages various hip-hop artists send to listeners
Study strategies that work
Traits of a good employee
News events that concerned, troubled, or shocked you

▶ **Word Power**

manipulate
to use dishonest or devious behavior in order to exert influence

entice
to attract by appealing to hope or desire; to lure

◆ PRACTICE 14-3

On a separate sheet of paper, write an exemplification essay explaining how the advertisement on the next page appeals to its target audience. Is it effective? Why or why not? Begin by identifying the ad, the product it promotes, and the audience you think it hopes to reach. Then, state your thesis. After briefly describing the ad, give examples to support your thesis.

✅ SELF-ASSESSMENT CHECKLIST:

Writing an Exemplification Essay

- Does your introduction give readers a clear idea of what to expect? If not, revise your introduction to clarify your essay's goals.

- Does your essay include a clearly stated thesis? If not, revise your thesis statement to clarify your essay's main idea.

- Do all your examples support your thesis? Eliminate any irrelevant examples.

- Do you have enough examples to support your thesis? Add examples where necessary.

- Is each example clearly related to the essay's thesis? If not, reword your topic sentences to clarify the connection.

- Do transitional words and phrases clearly link your examples to one another? Add transitions where necessary.

- Does your conclusion sum up the main idea of your essay? If not, revise the conclusion to make this idea clear to readers.

- What problems did you experience in writing your essay? What would you do differently next time?

B   Narration

*For information
on writing
a narrative
paragraph, see
Chapter 4.*

Narration tells a story, usually presenting a series of events in chronological (time) order, moving from beginning to end. A **narrative essay** can tell a personal story, or it can recount a recent or historical event or a fictional story.

*For examples of
narrative essays
by professional
writers, see 35B.*

FOCUS   Topics for Narration

The wording of your assignment may suggest narration. For example, you may be asked to *tell, trace, summarize,* or *recount.*

Assignment	Thesis Statement
Composition Tell about a time when you had to show courage even though you were afraid.	Sometimes a person can exhibit great courage despite being afraid.
American history Summarize the events that occurred during President Franklin Delano Roosevelt's first one hundred days in office.	Although many thought they were extreme, the measures enacted by Roosevelt during his first one hundred days in office were necessary to fight the effects of the economic depression.
Political science Trace the development of the Mississippi Freedom Democratic Party.	As the Mississippi Freedom Democratic Party developed, it found a voice that spoke for equality and justice.

When you write a narrative essay, you can discuss one event or several in each paragraph of your essay.

Options for Organizing Narrative Essays

One Event per Paragraph	**Several Events per Paragraph**
¶1 Introduction	¶1 Introduction
¶2 First event	¶2 First group of events
¶3 Second event	¶3 Second group of events
¶4 Third event	¶4 Third group of events
¶5 Conclusion	¶5 Conclusion

Sometimes, to add interest to your narrative, you may decide not to use exact chronological order. For example, you might begin with the end of your story and then move back to the beginning to trace the events that led to this outcome. However you arrange the events, carefully worded topic sentences and clear transitional words and phrases will help readers follow your narrative.

FOCUS **Transitions for Narration**

After	First . . . Second . . .	Soon
As soon as	Third	Then
At the same time	Immediately	Two hours (days,
Before	Later	months, years)
Earlier	Meanwhile	later
Eventually	Next	
Finally	Now	

The following student essay, "Swing Shift" by Mark Cotharn, is a narrative that relates the events of a day in the life of a police officer. Notice that Mark uses present tense to make his dramatic, emotional story more immediate. (Paragraph 3, which moves back in time to summarize events that occurred earlier in the week, uses past tense.) Transitional words and phrases help link events in chronological order, and the mention of specific days and times also helps keep readers on track.

                    Swing Shift[1]

     I'm home now, safe within familiar walls. Sur-   1
rounded by my wife and children, I sit at my kitchen
table drinking a cold beer, trying to wake up. After the
week I've had, I wonder why I keep this job.
     Today is Thursday, and I've got to pull myself   2
together long enough for one more shift. It's eleven
o'clock in the morning, and I've got one hour to prepare
mentally for work. This was such a crazy week, I'm not
sure if I can.
     Monday it was the guy on Weeping Willow who was   3
cut up like a side of beef by two parolees. Later that

---

[1]swing **shift**   a work shift between the day and night shifts (for example, noon to 8 p.m.)

evening, there was that seventeen-year-old boy who was stabbed to death by his friend. Tuesday brought a father angry at me for giving his kid a citation. The kid didn't tell his old man I threw a bag of dope away, to give him a second chance. Wednesday was the triple gang-land execution on Holley. I will never forget the way Teto Gomez looked with most of his head gone or the way his brains decorated the yellow rose bush. But the worst part of that case was doing CPR on Robert Berassa, who had been shot fourteen times. He was wearing a white T-shirt that was turning crimson. Every time I com-pressed on his chest, my shirt turned crimson, too. It was too late; Robert was dead.

Soon I finish my beer and make my way to the   4
station. Only God can know what the day's events will bring, but I really hope it won't be much.

After a short briefing, I begin my shift on patrol.   5
Almost immediately, I find myself in pursuit of an armed robbery suspect carrying several handguns and some dyna-mite. I chase him through the city for almost twelve minutes, at speeds exceeding a hundred miles per hour, before his van quits running and comes to a stop.

I stop my unit behind his van. Then, with shotgun   6
in hand, I make my way to within twenty feet of his door. I repeat commands for him to put his hands up, but he won't listen to me. Instead, he opens his door and charges at me. I see that he has something in his hand, but I can't tell what it is. Before I know it, I hear two loud booms. The suspect falls to the ground in a pool of blood. Confused, I feel the rotorwash of a helicopter twenty feet over my head and hear the wail of approaching police cars. Still, I don't understand why the suspect dropped so suddenly until I see smoke rising from the barrel of my shotgun. The suspect is dead, clutching a stick of dynamite.

Unable to let go of my professionalism in public, I   7
immediately detach myself from all emotions or feelings. Many fellow officers come to me and call me Stud, Killer, Ice Man, Exterminator; others come to me and congratulate me on a job well done.

Later, heading back to the station, I turn off the   8
radio and listen to the silence of my thoughts. I know
when I get there I will be read my rights and interviewed like a common crook. What did I do wrong?

As I expected, I'm met at the door by a shooting   9
team from Internal Affairs. These guys are serious about
their job. If the team can find a reason to convict me,
they will. The interrogation is lengthy; I'm exhausted.
Eventually, I realize that twelve hours or so have gone
by and the questions are still coming. I recognize the
interrogation technique because it's the same one I use.

It's three o'clock in the morning. The shooting team   10
is done with me, and I'm headed out the door for home when
my chief tells me to go upstairs and talk to the department shrink. Why? I don't need a shrink; I need sleep.

The shrink is asking me stupid questions like "How   11
do you feel?" and "Are you going to be OK?" What am I
supposed to say? No? I tell her I'm just fine and that
I'll be back to work in two days.

Finally, on my way home, alone in my car, I come   12
to. My palms sweat; my chest constricts; my pulse ham-
mers. My mind races back to the intersection of Citrus
and Arrow. I can see his face; he's laughing at me. I
hear two crisp booms and see him fall.

◆ PRACTICE 14-4

1. Underline the thesis statement of "Swing Shift." Then, try to restate it in your own words.

2. Underline the specific transitional words and phrases and the references to days and times that Mark uses to link events in chronological order.

3. Where does Mark mention specific days and times?

4. What specific events and situations support Mark's thesis? On a separate sheet of paper, list as many as you can.

5. Do you think Mark's essay should have a longer, more fully developed opening paragraph, or do you like the introduction he has? Why?

6. Do you think Mark's conclusion should summarize the events his essay discusses, or is his conclusion effective? Why?

7. What is this essay's greatest strength? What is its greatest weakness?

`14 B`

◆ PRACTICE 14-5

Following the writing process outlined in Chapter 12, write a narrative essay on one of the following topics.

> The story of your education
> An ideal day
> The plot summary of a terrible book or movie
> A time when you had to make a split-second decision
> Your first confrontation with authority
> An important historical event
> A day everything went wrong
> A story from your family's history
> Your employment history, from first to most recent job
> A biography of your pet

◆ PRACTICE 14-6

▶ **Word Power**
peril
imminent
danger; risk of
harm

menacing
threatening

On a separate sheet of paper, write a narrative essay that tells the story behind the picture below.

Scene from a movie from the early 1900s in which the heroine narrowly escapes from a variety of perilous situations.

☑ SELF-ASSESSMENT CHECKLIST:
Writing a Narrative Essay

- Does your introduction make the purpose of your narrative clear to readers? Does it set the scene and introduce important characters? Develop your opening paragraph further if you need to.

- What is your essay's thesis? If necessary, revise your thesis statement to make your main idea clear.

- Have you included all the specific events you need? Tell about additional incidents, if necessary.

- Are all the events you discuss clearly related to your thesis statement? If necessary, revise your essay to clarify the relationship of each event to your essay's main idea; delete any irrelevant events.

- Are the events you discuss arranged in clear chronological order? Rearrange events if necessary to reflect the order in which they occurred.

- Do topic sentences and transitional words and phrases make the sequence of events clear? Revise if necessary to clarify this sequence.

- Does your conclusion remind readers why you have told them your story? If necessary, revise your conclusion to make your purpose clear.

- What problems did you experience in writing your essay? What would you do differently next time?

C   Description

Description tells what something looks, sounds, smells, tastes, or feels like. A **descriptive essay** uses details to give readers a clear, vivid picture of a person, place, or object.

For information on writing a descriptive paragraph, see Chapter 5.

FOCUS   Topics for Description

The wording of your assignment may suggest description. For example, it may ask you to *describe* or to *tell what an object looks like*.

(continued on the following page)

For examples of descriptive essays by professional writers, see 35C.

(continued from the previous page)

Assignment	Thesis Statement
Composition Describe a room that was important to you when you were a child.	Pink-and-white striped wallpaper, tall shelves of cuddly stuffed animals, and the smell of Oreos dominated the bedroom I shared with my sister.
Scientific writing Describe a piece of scientific equipment.	The mass spectrometer is a complex instrument, but every part is ideally suited to its function.
Art history Choose one modern painting and describe its visual elements.	The disturbing images crowded together in Picasso's *Guernica* suggest the senselessness of war.

When you plan a descriptive essay, you focus on selecting details that help your readers see what you see, feel what you feel, and experience what you experience. Your goal is to create a single **dominant impression**, a central theme or idea to which all the details relate. This dominant impression unifies the description and gives readers an overall sense of what the person, object, or scene looks like (and perhaps what it sounds, smells, tastes, or feels like). Sometimes—but not always—your details will support a thesis, making a point about the subject you are describing.

You can arrange details in a descriptive essay in many different ways. For example, you can move from least to most important details (or vice versa), from top to bottom (or from bottom to top or side to side), or from far to near (or near to far). Each of your essay's body paragraphs may focus on one key characteristic of the subject you are describing or on several related descriptive details.

Options for Organizing Descriptive Essays

Least to Most Important	Top to Bottom	Far to Near
¶1 Introduction	¶1 Introduction	¶1 Introduction
¶2 Least important details	¶2 Details at top	¶2 Distant details
¶3 More important details	¶3 Details in middle	¶3 Closer details
¶4 Most important details	¶4 Details on bottom	¶4 Closest details
¶5 Conclusion	¶5 Conclusion	¶5 Conclusion

When you describe a person, object, or scene, you can use **objective description**, reporting only what your senses of sight, sound, smell, taste, and touch tell you ("The columns were two feet tall and made of white marble"). You can also use **subjective description**, conveying your attitude or your feelings about what you observe ("The columns were tall and powerful looking, and their marble surface seemed as smooth as ice.") Many essays combine these two kinds of description.

FOCUS **Figures of Speech**

Descriptive writing, particularly subjective description, is frequently enriched by *figures of speech*—language that creates special or unusual effects.

■ A **simile** uses *like* or *as* to compare two unlike things.

Her smile was like sunshine.

■ A **metaphor** compares two unlike things without using *like* or *as*.

Her smile was a light that lit up the room.

■ **Personification** suggests a comparison between a nonliving thing and a person by giving the nonliving thing human traits.

The sun smiled down on the crowd.

As you write, use transitional words and expressions to guide readers through your description. (Many of these transitions are prepositions or other words and phrases that indicate location or distance.)

FOCUS **Transitions for Description**

Above	In front of	Outside
Behind	Inside	Over
Below	Nearby	The least
Between	Next to	important
Beyond	On	The most
In	On one side . . . On	important
In back of	the other side	Under

The following student essay, "African Violet" by Alisha Woolery, uses description to create a portrait of a family member. By combining subjective and objective description and using specific visual details, Alisha conveys a vivid impression of her great-grandmother as physically frail yet emotionally spirited.

African Violet

The black-and-white picture of my great-grand-   1
parents is a picture I often bring into my mind when
I have decided to look at the "big picture" of life and
think all the "deep thoughts." I see their faces, etched
into the contrasting grays, so young, so hopeful for
their new lives together. My mind then shifts to a more
recent picture of my great-grandma with her small, frail
body, which in the end gave her more pain than she
could handle. At this point, I realize how much she
taught me about life and death--and about everything in
between.

My great-grandfather died when I was quite young,   2
and I have only a faint memory of riding his foot like
a horse while he recited "Banbury Cross." I have to create an image of him from my relatives' fond memories.
Fortunately, however, I knew my great-grandma well, and
the conversations we had are among my favorite memories
of her. Often, I picture her sitting with me in her
parlor, telling me one of the numerous stories of her
youth.

"One time I was getting to be about sixteen years   3
old, and there was this boy who asked me on a picnic."
Her eyes brightened as she told her story. "He was older
than me, and he had a horse and buggy! And whoowee!
That was really something."

The look of astonishment on my face must have   4
been apparent because we laughed until I thought we
would keel over. There she was, ninety years old, with
absolutely no teeth, telling me how hot this boy who had
asked her out was. It was then I realized that the eyes
looking out from her aging face were the same brown eyes
that had flirted with boys, had fallen in love, and had

seen her children and her children's children's children. She had years of experience, and I had very little, but on that warm summer evening, as we sat in her living room, her story bridged the gap between generations.

When I don't picture my great-grandma telling stories, I see her on her sunporch, engaged in her one true passion: caring for her plants. She loved them all, but her favorites were small plants with dark green leaves and purple blossoms, African violets. I didn't inherit her green thumb, so the miracles she worked with plants were a constant wonder to me. Stems and leaves seemed to thrive under her gentle touch. Plants were her pride and joy, and until she was in her mid-eighties I often saw her, on hands and knees, digging around in the dirt in her front yard.

No, Grandma didn't resign herself to age and let life pass her by; she rode it for all it was worth. In fact, when I picture her, I often see her outside, behind the wheel of her car. The woman was a traffic hazard, not because she poked along as so many older folks do but because she was a speed demon! Poised for action, Grandma strapped herself into her brown 1972 Nova and sped out toward destinations unknown, with one foot on the gas and the other on the brake. I suppose, by all laws of nature, her driving escapades should have done her in, but Grandma died a peaceful death with quiet resolution and acceptance. In fact, she probably had a better outlook on the whole thing than anyone else in the family. I was only fifteen, and she was the closest person to me to die, so it was especially difficult for me to accept that our talks were simply over.

It wasn't until recently that I realized that even by her dying, Grandma was continuing to teach me about life. Now, when I picture her, I see not just her lively stories, caring hands, and daredevil spirit, but also her courage: I see how bravely she dealt with the increasing pain in her legs as her body deteriorated.

The memories of my great-grandma are very important to me, and sometimes it scares me when a detail escapes

my mind because remembering our time together and what
I've learned from her is all I have left of her. It is
virtually impossible to communicate the impact she has
had on me. The only way I feel I can repay her is by
telling her stories to my own grandchildren and great-
grandchildren someday, keeping her memory alive.

◆ PRACTICE 14-7

1. What dominant impression of her great-grandmother does Alisha convey to readers?

2. On a separate sheet of paper, list the specific visual details Alisha uses to convey her essay's dominant impression. What other details could she have included?

3. What determines the order in which details are presented in this essay? How else might Alisha have arranged details?

4. Is this essay primarily a subjective or an objective description?

5. What is this essay's greatest strength? What is its greatest weakness?

◆ PRACTICE 14-8

Following the writing process outlined in Chapter 12, write a descriptive essay on one of the following topics.

An abandoned building   A street, road, or highway
Your supervisor   A painting or photograph
A person or character who   A historical site or monument
   makes you laugh (or   An advertisement
   frightens you)   An object you cherish
Your room (or your closet   Someone whom everyone notices
   or desk)

◆ PRACTICE 14-9

On a separate sheet of paper, write a real-estate brochure for the house pictured on the next page, using your imagination to describe its setting, exterior, and interior in detail. Your goal in this descriptive essay is to provide enough positive details to interest a prospective buyer.

▶ **Word Power**

mansion
a large, stately
house

lush
characterized
by luxuriant
growth

☑ SELF-ASSESSMENT CHECKLIST:

Writing a Descriptive Essay

Does your introduction identify the subject of your description and convey your essay's dominant impression? Revise your introduction if necessary to clarify your essay's focus.

Do you describe every significant aspect of your subject in detail? If necessary, add specific details to create a more complete, more vivid picture.

Do all the details in your essay support your dominant impression? Eliminate any irrelevant details.

Are your details arranged in a definite order within your essay and within paragraphs? Would another order be more effective? Rearrange the details if necessary.

Do topic sentences and transitional words and phrases move readers smoothly from one part of your subject to another? Reword topic sentences and add transitions where necessary.

Does your conclusion leave readers with a clear sense of your essay's purpose? Revise if necessary to reinforce the dominant impression you want your description to convey.

What problems did you experience in writing your essay? What would you do differently next time?

D   Process

For information on writing a process paragraph, see Chapter 6.

A **process** is a series of chronological steps that produces a particular result. **Process essays** explain the steps in a procedure, telling how something is (or was) done. A process essay can be organized as either a *process explanation* or a set of *instructions*.

For examples of process essays by professional writers, see 35D.

> ### FOCUS   Topics for Process
>
> The wording of your assignment may suggest process. For example, you may be asked to *explain a process, give instructions, give directions,* or *give a step-by-step account.*
>
> | Assignment | Thesis Statement |
> |---|---|
> | *American government*   Explain the process by which a bill becomes a law. | The process by which a bill becomes a law is long and complex, involving numerous revisions and a great deal of compromise. |
> | *Pharmacy practice*   Summarize the procedure for conducting a clinical trial of a new drug. | To ensure that drugs are safe and effective, scientists follow strict procedural guidelines for testing and evaluating them. |
> | *Technical writing*   Write a set of instructions for applying for a student internship in a state agency. | When applying for a government internship, students must follow several important steps. |

If your purpose is simply to help readers understand a process, not actually perform it, you will write a process explanation. **Process explanations**, like the first two examples in the Focus box above, often use present tense verbs ("Once a bill *is* introduced in Congress" or "A scientist first *submits* a funding application") to explain how a procedure is generally carried out. However, when a process explanation describes a specific procedure that was completed in the past, it uses past tense verbs ("The next thing I *did*").

If your purpose is to enable readers to actually perform the steps in a process, you will write instructions. **Instructions**, like the last example in the Focus box above, always use present tense verbs in the form of commands to tell readers what to do ("First, *meet* with your adviser").

Whichever kind of process essay you write, you can either devote a full paragraph to each step of the process or group a series of minor steps together in a single paragraph.

Options for Organizing Process Essays

One Step per Paragraph	**Several Steps per Paragraph**
¶1 Introduction	¶1 Introduction
¶2 First step in process	¶2 First group of steps
¶3 Second step in process	¶3 Second group of steps
¶4 Third step in process	¶4 Third group of steps
¶5 Conclusion	¶5 Conclusion

As you write your process essay, discuss each step in the order in which it is performed, making sure your topic sentences clearly identify the function of each step or group of steps. If you are writing instructions, be sure to include any warnings or reminders you think are necessary, as well as a list of necessary equipment or materials.

Transitions are extremely important in process essays because they enable readers to follow the sequence of steps in the process and, in the case of instructions, to perform the process themselves.

FOCUS **Transitions for Process**

After that	Later	The first (second, third) step
As	Meanwhile	
As soon as	Next	The last step
At the same time	Now	Then
Finally	Once	The next step
First	Soon	When
Immediately	Subsequently	While

The following student essay, Mai Yoshikawa's "Under Water," explains the process of scuba diving. Because Mai did not think her readers would be likely to have the opportunity to try scuba diving, she did not write her essay in the form of instructions. Instead, she wrote a process explanation, using present tense verbs. Notice how clear transitions move readers smoothly through the steps of the process.

Under Water

For most people, their first scuba-diving experience in the ocean does not turn out to be a very good one, and so it was with me. Because I rushed to see the beauty of the seascape, I wasted oxygen and didn't pay much attention to the instructor. Unexpected dangers lie under water, and most first-time divers, like me, are unaware of the risk they are taking when they enter this other world. Now, as a more experienced diver, I have learned that I need to protect myself from trouble by having the right equipment and knowing how to use it correctly.

To ensure a safe dive, the first thing everyone needs to do is to assemble some basic equipment: an air tank, fins, snorkel, mask, life vest, nylon socks, weight belt, gloves, regulator, pressure and depth gauges, and, occasionally, a wetsuit. The weight belt maintains the diver's natural buoyancy; therefore, the number of weights a person carries will vary. (The lighter the diver, the more weights he or she needs.) While I am floating under water, the weight belt and the air pressure work together to enable me to stay at a certain depth without moving up and down. The nylon socks keep my fins from slipping and help me avoid foot injuries. The pressure and depth gauges are connected to the tank where I can easily reach them and check to make sure the numbers on the two instruments correspond. The gauges are set to notify me how deep I can swim with the amount of oxygen left in my tank. Once I get all this equipment and check it, I plan the day's activities and routes with the instructor. The instructor, at that point, becomes my "buddy."

The next step--a thorough, careful equipment check--is extremely important. If there are more than two divers, each person pairs up with another person. Usually someone who has had a lot of experience and knows the importance of the inspection, such as an assistant instructor or the owner of the dive shop, is available to help the amateur divers get set up. Using the buddy system, I check my partner's equipment and

make sure every part is in gear, and she checks mine
as well. First, I make sure that the mask fits my
buddy's face and that no hair is caught in the rubber
lining because any space will allow water to enter.
Next, I pull the string on her life vest, examine the
jacket as the air inflates, and listen to make sure it
holds the air with no leak. Then, I place the regulator in my mouth, and I try breathing for a while as
the oxygen from the tank flows into me each time I
inhale. Finally, I open the valve of the tank to its
fullest so that my partner will get enough oxygen as
she dives.

   As I check to make sure my equipment is working, I   4
get tense and nervous, thinking about possible accidents
that, in the worst situation, could kill me. Once this
serious phase is finished, however, I am ready for
the main event of the day: the dive itself. Usually,
the group dive lasts for two or three separate periods,
each consisting of approximately twenty to forty minutes. Changing diving spots after every swim gives me
the opportunity to enjoy different scenery. On lucky
days, I can see rare, enormous fish that I never dreamt
of viewing except on the television screen. In most
cases, the instructors give us permission to feed these
fish.

   Scuba diving is an exciting, breathtaking sport,   5
but I have learned that no matter how many times I
experience it, I have to be very careful and responsible
about the actions I take both before and after I enter
the water. But once I start swimming deep into the
ocean, I feel so small, yet so free. The fear and panic
disappear from my mind with the bubbles of oxygen that
flow out from my regulator, and my own rhythmic breathing echoes in my ears.

◆ PRACTICE 14-10

1. On a separate sheet of paper, list the major steps in the process of scuba
diving. Does the writer present them in strict chronological order?

2. What identifies Mai's essay as a process explanation rather than a set of instructions?

3. Underline some of the transitional words and phrases that link the steps in the process. Are any other transitions needed?

4. Underline Mai's thesis statement. Then, try to restate it in your own words.

5. Why does Mai open her essay with a negative experience? Is this an effective opening strategy?

6. What is the essay's greatest strength? What is its greatest weakness?

◆ **PRACTICE 14-11**

Following the writing process outlined in Chapter 12, write a process essay on one of the following topics. (Note: Before you begin, decide whether a process explanation or a set of instructions will be more appropriate for your purpose.)

> An unusual recipe
> College registration
> Finding an apartment
> Applying for a job
> Getting dressed for a typical Saturday night
> A religious ritual or cultural ceremony
> A task you often do at work
> A do-it-yourself project that didn't get done
> Your own writing process
> A self-improvement program (past, present, or future)
> How to find something on the Internet

▶ **Word Power**
priorities
most important tasks

optimum
the most favorable condition for a particular situation

◆ **PRACTICE 14-12**

List the steps involved in planning the perfect party. Then, use this list to help you write a process essay that gives step-by-step instructions in the order in which they need to be done. (Hint: You can devote separate paragraphs to tasks to be done the week before, the day before, the morning of the party, and so on.) Be sure to include cautions and warnings to help your readers avoid problems.

John Belushi, as John "Bluto" Blutarsky, in the infamous toga party scene from Animal House (1978).

✔️ SELF-ASSESSMENT CHECKLIST:

Writing a Process Essay

Does your introduction identify the process you will discuss and indicate its purpose? Revise your introduction if necessary to clarify your purpose.

Is your essay a process explanation or a set of instructions? If your strategy is not appropriate for your essay's purpose, rewrite the essay using a different strategy.

Does your thesis statement present an overview of the process? If not, revise the statement to make it as clear and specific as you can.

Do you include every important step in the process? If not, add steps that will help readers understand (or perform) the process.

Are all the steps you present necessary? Delete any irrelevant or unimportant ones.

(continued on the following page)

(continued from the previous page)

- Are the steps in the process presented in strict chronological order? Rearrange any that are out of order.

- Are related steps grouped in individual paragraphs? If not, revise to make each paragraph unified.

- Do topic sentences clearly identify major stages in the process? Do they clarify the function of each step or group of steps? Revise topic sentences as necessary.

- Do transitional words and phrases clarify the relationship between steps? If necessary, add transitions to make connections clear.

- Have you included all necessary warnings or reminders? Add cautions or clarifications as needed.

- Does your conclusion effectively sum up your process? Revise as necessary to clarify your purpose.

- What problems did you experience in writing your essay? What would you do differently next time?

E   Cause and Effect

For information on writing a cause-and-effect paragraph, see Chapter 7.

A **cause** makes something happen; an **effect** is a result of a particular cause or event. **Cause-and-effect essays** identify causes or predict effects; sometimes they do both.

FOCUS   Topics for Cause and Effect

For examples of cause-and-effect essays by professional writers, see 35E.

The wording of your assignment may suggest cause and effect. For example, the assignment may ask you to *explain why, predict the outcome, list contributing factors, discuss the consequences,* or tell what *caused* something else or how something is *affected* by something else.

Assignment	Thesis Statement
Women's studies What factors contributed to the rise of the women's movement in the 1970s?	The women's movement of the 1970s had its origins in the peace and civil rights movements of the 1960s.

(continued on the following page)

(continued from the previous page)

Assignment	Thesis Statement
Public health Discuss the possible long-term effects of smoking.	In addition to its physical effects, smoking may also have long-term social and emotional consequences.
Media and society How did television affect the lives of the first generation of viewers who grew up with it?	In its early years, television created a generation of people who learned differently from those in previous generations.

A cause-and-effect essay can focus on causes or on effects. When you write about causes, be sure to examine *all* pertinent causes. You should emphasize the cause you consider the most important, but do not forget to consider other causes that may be relevant to your topic. Similarly, when you write about effects, consider *all* significant effects of a particular cause, not just the first few that you think of.

If your focus is on finding causes, as it is in the first assignment in the Focus box on page 194, your introductory paragraph should identify the effect (the women's movement). If your focus is on predicting effects, as it is in the second and third assignments listed there, you should begin by identifying the cause (smoking, television). In the body of your essay, you can devote a full paragraph to each cause (or effect), or you can group several related causes (or effects) together in each paragraph. Be careful not to confuse *affect* (usually a verb) and *effect* (usually a noun) in your cause-and-effect essays. (See 34E.)

Options for Organizing Cause-and-Effect Essays

Identifying Causes	Predicting Effects
¶1 Introduction (identifies effect)	¶1 Introduction (identifies cause)
¶2 First cause	¶2 First effect
¶3 Second cause	¶3 Second effect
¶4 Third (and most important) cause	¶4 Third (and most important) effect
¶5 Conclusion	¶5 Conclusion

Transitions are important in cause-and-effect essays because they establish causal connections, telling readers that A caused B and not the other

way around. They also make it clear that events have a causal relationship
(A *caused* B) and not just a *sequential* one (A *preceded* B). Remember, when
one event follows another, the second is not necessarily the result of the
first.

FOCUS   **Transitions for Cause and Effect**

Accordingly	For this reason	The most impor-
Another cause	Since	tant cause
Another effect	So	The most impor-
As a result	The first (second,	tant effect
Because	third) cause	Therefore
Consequently	The first (second,	
For	third) effect	

The following student essay, "How My Parents' Separation Changed My Life"
by Andrea DeMarco, examines the effects of a significant event on the writer and
her family. Andrea begins by identifying the cause—the separation—and then
goes on to explain its specific effects on her family and on herself. Notice how
transitional words and phrases make Andrea's causal connections clear to her
readers.

How My Parents' Separation Changed My Life

Until I was ten, I lived the perfect all-American   1
life with my perfect all-American family. I lived in a
suburb of Albany, New York, with my parents, my sister
and brother, and our dog, Daisy. We had a ping-pong
table in the basement, a barbecue in the backyard, and
two cars in the garage. My dad and mom were high school
teachers, and every summer we took a family vacation.
Then, it all changed. My parents' separation made everything different.

One day, just before Halloween, when my sister was   2
twelve and my brother was fourteen (Daisy was seven),
our parents called us into the kitchen for a family conference. We didn't think anything was wrong at first;
they were always calling these annoying meetings. We
figured it was time for us to plan a vacation, talk
about household chores, or be nagged to clean our rooms.

As soon as we sat down, though, we knew this was different. We could tell Mom had been crying, and Dad's voice cracked when he told us the news. They were separating--they called it a "trial separation"--and Dad was moving out of our house.

I hardly remember what else we talked about that 3
day. But I do remember how things changed right after that. Every Halloween we always had a big jack-o'-lantern on our front porch. Dad used to spend hours at the kitchen table cutting out the eyes, nose, and mouth and hollowing out the insides. That Halloween, because he didn't live with us, things were different. Mom bought a pumpkin, and I guess she was planning to carve it up. But she never did, and we never mentioned it. It sat on the kitchen counter for a couple of weeks, getting soft and wrinkled, and then it just disappeared. I suppose Mom threw it out.

Other holidays were also different because Mom and 4
Dad were not living together. Our first Thanksgiving without Dad was pathetic. I don't even want to talk about it. Christmas was different, too. We spent Christmas Eve with Dad and our relatives on his side, and Christmas Day with Mom and her family. Of course, we got twice as many presents as usual. I realize now that both our parents were trying to make up for the pain of the separation. The worst part came when I opened my big present from Mom: Barbie's Dream House. This was something I had always wanted. Even at ten, I knew how hard it must have been for Mom to afford it. The trouble was, I had gotten the same thing from Dad the night before.

The worst effect of my parents' separation on all 5
three of us was not the big events but the disruption in our everyday lives. Dinner used to be a family time, a chance to talk about our day and make plans. But after Dad left, Mom seemed to stop eating. Sometimes she would just have coffee while we ate, and sometimes she would not eat at all. She would microwave some frozen thing for us or heat up soup or cook some hot dogs. We didn't care--after all, now she let us watch TV while we ate--but we did notice.

Other parts of our routine changed, too. Because Dad   6
didn't live with us anymore, we had to spend every Saturday and every Wednesday night at his apartment, no matter
what else we had planned. Usually he would take us to dinner at McDonald's on Wednesdays, and then we would go back
to his place and do our homework or watch TV. That wasn't
too bad. Saturdays were a lot worse. We really wanted to
be home, hanging out with our friends in our own rooms in
our own house. Instead, we had to do some planned activity
with Dad, like go to a movie or a hockey game.

My parents were separated for only eight months,   7
but it seemed like forever. By the end of the school
year, they had somehow worked things out, and Dad was
back home again. That June, at a family conference
around the kitchen table, we made our summer vacation
plans. We decided on Williamsburg, Virginia, the all-
American vacation destination. So things were back to
normal, but I wasn't, and I'm still not. Now, eight
years later, my mother and father are all right, but I
still worry they'll split up again. And I worry about
my own future husband and how I will ever be sure he's
the one I'll stay married to. As a result of what happened in my own family, it is hard for me to believe
any relationship is forever.

◆ PRACTICE 14-13

1. Underline Andrea's thesis statement. Then, try to restate it in your own words.

2. What specific effects of her parents' separation does Andrea identify? List these effects on a separate sheet of paper.

3. Underline the transitional words and phrases that make the causal connections in Andrea's essay clear to her readers.

4. Is Andrea's relatively long concluding paragraph effective? Why or why not? Do you think it should be shortened or divided into two paragraphs?

5. Is Andrea's straightforward title effective, or should she have used a more creative or eye-catching title? Can you suggest an alternative?

6. What is this essay's greatest strength? What is its greatest weakness?

◆ PRACTICE 14-14

Following the writing process outlined in Chapter 12, write a cause-and-effect essay on one of the following topics.

A teacher's positive (or negative) effect on you

Why you voted a certain way in a recent election (or why you chose not to vote)

Why the popularity of soap operas has been steadily declining

How your life would be different if you dropped out of school (or quit your job)

How a particular invention (for example, the cell phone) has changed your life

Why e-mail is so popular

A movie or book that changed the way you look at life

How a particular season (or day of the week) affects your mood

How having a child would change (or has changed) your life

How a particular event made you grow up

◆ PRACTICE 14-15

Imagine you have won a multi-million-dollar lottery. How would your life change? Write a cause-and-effect essay that discusses specific ways in which your life would be different.

▶ **Word Power**

annuity
annual payment of an allowance or income

windfall
a sudden, unexpected bit of good luck

☑ SELF-ASSESSMENT CHECKLIST:
Writing a Cause-and-Effect Essay

- ☐ Does your introduction identify the particular cause or effect on which your essay will focus? Revise your introduction if necessary to zero in on your topic.

- ☐ Does your essay focus on causes or effects? Does your thesis statement accurately convey this emphasis to readers? If not, revise your thesis statement to identify the key causes or effects that you will emphasize.

- ☐ Do you identify all causes or effects relevant to your topic? If not, revise to include all significant causes or effects.

- ☐ Do you discuss any irrelevant causes or effects? If necessary, revise to eliminate them.

- ☐ Which cause or effect is most important? Arrange causes or effects to indicate their relative importance.

- ☐ Does each body paragraph identify and explain one particular cause or effect (or several closely related causes or effects)? Revise where necessary to unify each body paragraph.

- ☐ Do your transitional words and phrases make causal connections clear? If not, revise to clarify the relationships between causes and effects.

- ☐ Does your conclusion reinforce the causal relationships you discuss? Revise to make your emphasis clearer.

- ☐ What problems did you experience in writing your essay? What would you do differently next time?

F   Comparison and Contrast

For information on writing a comparison-and-contrast paragraph, see Chapter 8.

Comparison identifies similarities; **contrast** identifies differences. **Comparison-and-contrast essays** explain how two things are alike or how they are different; sometimes, they discuss both similarities and differences.

When you organize a comparison-and-contrast essay, you can choose either a *point-by-point* or a *subject-by-subject* arrangement. A **point-by-point** compari-

FOCUS Topics for Comparison and Contrast

The wording of your assignment may suggest comparison and contrast—for example, by asking you to *compare, contrast, discuss similarities,* or *identify differences.*

For examples of comparison-and-contrast essays by professional writers, see 35F.

Assignment	Thesis Statement
Philosophy What basic similarities do you find in the beliefs of Henry David Thoreau and Martin Luther King Jr.?	Although King was more politically active, both he and Thoreau strongly supported the idea of civil disobedience.
Nutrition How do the diets of native Japanese and Japanese Americans differ?	As they become more and more assimilated, Japanese Americans consume more fats than their native Japanese counterparts do.
Literature Contrast the two sisters in Alice Walker's short story "Everyday Use."	Unlike Maggie, Dee—her more successful, better-educated sister—has rejected her family's heritage.

son alternates between the two subjects you are comparing or contrasting, moving back and forth from one subject to the other. A **subject-by-subject** comparison treats its two subjects separately, first fully discussing one subject and then moving on to consider the other subject. In both kinds of comparison-and-contrast essays, the same points are discussed in the same order for both subjects.

Options for Organizing Comparison-and-Contrast Essays

Point-by-Point Comparison	**Subject-by-Subject Comparison**
¶1 Introduction (identifies subjects to be compared or contrasted)	¶1 Introduction (identifies subjects to be compared or contrasted)
¶2 First point discussed for both subjects	¶¶2–3 First subject discussed
¶3 Second point discussed for both subjects	¶¶4–5 Second subject discussed
¶4 Third point discussed for both subjects	¶6 Conclusion
¶5 Conclusion	

The transitional words and phrases you use in a comparison-and-contrast essay tell readers whether you are focusing on similarities or differences. Transitions also help move readers through your essay from one subject to the other and from one point of similarity or difference to the next.

FOCUS   **Transitions for Comparison and Contrast**

Although	Likewise
But	Nevertheless
Even though	On the contrary
However	On the one hand . . . On the other hand
In comparison	Similarly
In contrast	Unlike
Like	Whereas

The following student essay, "Another Ordinary Day" by Nisha Jani, contrasts teenage boys and girls by going through a typical day in the lives of "Johnny" and "Jane." A point-by-point comparison, Nisha's essay alternates between her two subjects, treating the same points in the same order for each. Notice that topic sentences identify the part of the day under discussion in each paragraph and clearly signal shifts from one subject to the next.

Another Ordinary Day

"Boys are from Jupiter and get stupider/Girls are   1
from Mars and become movie stars/Boys take a bath and
smell like trash/Girls take a shower and smell like a
flower." As simple playground songs like this one suggest, the two sexes see themselves very differently.
Even though adult men and women have similar goals, values, and occupations, as children and teenagers, boys
and girls often seem to belong to two different species,
In fact, from the first moment of the day to the last,
the typical boy and girl live very different lives.

    The sun rises, and the alarm clock signals the   2
beginning of another day for Johnny and Jane, two
seventh-grade classmates. Johnny, an average thirteen-
year-old boy, wakes up late and has to hurry. He throws
on his favorite jeans, a baggy T-shirt, and a baseball
cap. Then, he goes into the kitchen, has a hearty high-
cholesterol breakfast, and runs out of the house to

school, usually forgetting some vital book or homework assignment. Jane, unlike Johnny, wakes up early. She takes a shower, blow-dries her hair, and puts on her make-up. Then, there is the moment of truth: What should she wear today? Getting dressed can be a very difficult process, one that often includes taking everything out of her closet and calling friends for advice. After she makes her decision, she helps herself to some food (probably low- or no-fat) and goes off to school.

School is a totally different experience for Johnny and Jane. Johnny will probably sit in the back of the classroom with a couple of guys, throwing paper airplanes and spitballs. These will be directed at the males they do not like and the females they think are kind of cute. (However, if their male friends ever ask the boys about these girls, they will say girls are just losers and deny that they like any of them.) On the opposite side of the classroom, however, is Jane, focused on a very different kind of activity. At first it looks as if she is vigorously copying the algebra notes that the teacher is putting on the board, but these notes have absolutely nothing to do with algebra. In actuality, she is writing about boys, clothes, and other topics that are much more important to her than the square root of one hundred twenty-one. Then, she proceeds to fold the note into a box or other creative form, which can often put origami to shame. As soon as the teacher turns around, the note is passed and the process begins all over again.

Lunch, a vital part of the school day, is also very different for Johnny and Jane. On the one hand, for Johnny and his friends, it is a time to compare baseball cards, exchange sports facts, and of course tell jokes about every bodily function imaginable. In front of them on the table, their trays are filled with pizza, soda, fries, and chips, and this food is their main focus. For Jane, on the other hand, lunch is not about eating; it is a chance to exchange the latest gossip about who is going out with whom. The girls look around to see what people are wearing, what they should do with their hair, and so on. Jane's meal is quite a bit smaller than

3

4

Johnny's: it consists of a small low-fat yogurt and half a bagel (if she feels like splurging, she will spread some cream cheese on the bagel).

After school, Johnny and Jane head in different   5
directions. Johnny rushes home to get his bike and meets up with his friends to run around and play typical "guy games," like pick-up basketball or touch football. Johnny and his friends play with every boy who shows up, whether they know them or not. They may get into physical fights and arguments; however, in the end it is all a game, and they plan to meet up again the next day. In contrast to the boys, Jane and her friends are very selective. Their circle is a small one, and they do every-thing together. Some days, they go to the mall (they will not necessarily buy anything there, but they will consider the outing productive anyway because they have spent time together). Most days, though, they just talk, with the discussion ranging from school to guys to lipstick colors. When Jane gets home, she will most likely run to the phone and talk for hours to the same three or four girls.

At the age of thirteen or fourteen, boys and girls   6
do not seem to have very much in common. Given this situation, it is amazing that boys and girls grow up to become men and women who coexist and interact as neighbors, friends, and coworkers. What is even more amaz-ing is that so many grow up to share lives and raise fam-ilies together, treating each other with love and respect.

◆ PRACTICE 14-16

1. Underline Nisha's thesis statement. Then, try to restate it in your own words.

2. Does Nisha's opening paragraph identify the subjects she will discuss? Will she focus on similarities or on differences?

3. Nisha's essay is a point-by-point comparison. What four points does she discuss for each of her two subjects?

4. Underline some transitional words and phrases Nisha uses to move read-ers from one subject (Johnny) to the other (Jane).

5. Reread Nisha's topic sentences. What do they contribute to the essay?

6. What is this essay's greatest strength? What is its greatest weakness?

◆ PRACTICE 14-17

Following the writing process outlined in Chapter 12, write a comparison-and-contrast essay on one of the following topics.

Two coworkers
Two movie heroes
How you expect your life to be different from the lives of your parents
Men's and women's ideas about their body images
Two ways of studying for an exam
Risk-takers and people who play it safe
Library research and Internet research
Country and city living (or you can compare suburban living with either)
Two popular magazines (features, ads, target audiences, pictures)
Two professional athletes

◆ PRACTICE 14-18

On a separate sheet of paper, write an essay in which you compare the following two photographs, considering both what the monuments look like and their emotional impact on you.

▶ **Word Power**
symbol
something that represents something else

Iwo Jima memorial statue at Arlington National Cemetery.

Vietnam Veterans Memorial in Washington, D.C.

☑ SELF-ASSESSMENT CHECKLIST:

Writing a Comparison-and-Contrast Essay

- Does your introduction identify the two subjects you will compare and contrast? If not, revise to make the focus of your essay clear.

- Does your essay examine similarities or differences? If necessary, revise your thesis statement to make your emphasis clear.

- Have you discussed all significant points of comparison or contrast that apply to your two subjects? Develop your discussion further if necessary.

- Are any points insignificant or irrelevant? If necessary, revise to eliminate any similarities or differences that do not support your thesis.

- Have you treated the same points for both your subjects? Revise if necessary to make your discussion balanced.

- Is your essay a point-by-point comparison or a subject-by-subject comparison? If necessary, revise to make your organization consistent with one of these two ways of organizing material.

(continued on the following page)

(continued from the previous page)

- Does each topic sentence clearly identify the subject and the point of comparison or contrast being discussed? If necessary, revise topic sentences to clarify each paragraph's focus.

- Do transitional words and phrases move readers from one subject or point to another? Add transitions where necessary.

- Does your conclusion remind readers what your two subjects are and whether you have focused on similarities or differences? If not, revise to reinforce your essay's focus.

- What problems did you experience during the process of writing your essay? What would you do differently next time?

G   Classification

Classification is the act of sorting items into appropriate categories. **Classification essays** divide a whole (your subject) into parts and sort various items into categories.

For information on writing a classification paragraph, see Chapter 9.

FOCUS   Topics for Classification

The wording of your assignment may suggest classification. For example, you may be asked to consider *kinds, types, categories, components, segments,* or *parts of a whole.*

Assignment	Thesis Statement
Business What kinds of courses are most useful for students planning to run their own businesses?	Courses dealing with accounting, management, interpersonal communication, and computer science offer the most useful skills for future business owners.
Biology List the components of the blood, and explain the function of each.	Red blood cells, white blood cells, platelets, and plasma have very distinct functions.

For examples of classification essays by professional writers, see 35G.

(continued on the following page)

(continued from the previous page)

Assignment	Thesis Statement
Education Classify elementary school children according to their academic needs.	The elementary school population includes special-needs students, students with reading and math skills at or near grade level, and academically gifted students.

As a rule, each paragraph of a classification essay examines a separate category—a different part of the whole. For example, a paragraph could focus on one kind of course in the college curriculum, one component of the blood, or one type of child. Within each paragraph, you discuss the individual items that you have assigned to a particular category—for example, accounting courses, red blood cells, or gifted students. If you consider some categories less important than others, you may decide to discuss those minor categories together in a single paragraph, devoting full paragraphs only to the most significant categories.

Options for Organizing Classification Essays

One Category in Each Paragraph	Major Categories in Separate Paragraphs; Minor Categories Grouped Together
¶1 Introduction (identifies whole and its major categories)	¶1 Introduction (identifies whole and its major categories)
¶2 First category	¶2 Minor categories
¶3 Second category	¶3 First major category
¶4 Third category	¶4 Second (and more important) major category
¶5 Conclusion	¶5 Conclusion

In a classification essay, topic sentences identify the category or categories discussed in each paragraph. Transitional words and phrases signal movement from one category to the next and may also tell readers which categories you consider most and least important.

FOCUS   **Transitions for Classification**

One kind . . .	The first (second,	The most impor-
Another kind	third) category	tant component
The final type	The last group	The next part

The following student essay, "Selling a Deam" by Rob O'Neal, classifies American car names into categories on the basis of the kind of message they communicate to consumers. Notice that Rob discusses one category in each of his body paragraphs, using clear topic sentences to identify and define each kind of car name and relate each category to the group as a whole.

Selling a Dream

The earliest automobiles were often named after the men who manufactured them--Ford, Studebaker, Nash, Olds, Chrysler, Dodge, Chevrolet, and so on. More recently, however, American car makers have been competing to see what kinds of names will sell the most cars. Many car names seem to be chosen simply for how they sound: Alero, Corvette, Neon, Probe, Caprice. Many others, however, are designed to sell specific dreams to consumers. Americans always seem to want to be, do, and become something different. They want to be tough and brave, to explore new places, to take risks. With the names that auto manufacturers choose for their cars, they appeal to Americans' deepest desires.

Some American cars are named for places people dream of traveling to. Park Avenue, Malibu, Riviera, Seville, Tahoe, Yukon, Aspen, and Durango are some model names that suggest escape--to New York City, California, Europe, the West. Other place names--Sebring, Daytona, and Bonneville, for example--are associated with the danger and excitement of car racing. And then there is the El Dorado, a car named for a fictional paradise: a city of gold.

Other car names convey rough and tough, even dangerous, images. Animal names fall into this category, with models like Ram, Bronco, and Mustang suggesting powerful, untamed beasts. (Cars named after animals, such as Mercury's Cougar, Lynx, and Bobcat and Pontiac's Impala, convey speed as well as power.) Other cars in the "rough and tough" category include those that suggest the wildness of the Old West: Wrangler and Rodeo, for example. Because the American auto industry is centered near Detroit, Michigan, where many cities have Indian names, cars named for the cities where they are manufactured have inherited these names. Thus, cars called Cadillac, Pontiac, and Cherokee recall the proud history of Indian nations, and these too might suggest the excitement of the untamed West.

The most interesting car names in terms of the   4
dream they sell, however, are those that suggest exploration and discovery. Years ago, some car names honored real explorers, like DeSoto and LaSalle. Now, model names only sell an abstract idea. Still, American car names like Blazer, Explorer, Navigator, Mountaineer, Expedition, Caravan, and Voyager (as well as the names of foreign cars driven by many Americans, such as Nissan's Pathfinder and Quest and Honda's Passport and Odyssey) have the power to make drivers feel they are blazing new trails and discovering new worlds--when in fact they may simply be carpooling their children to a soccer game or commuting to work.

Today, the car is an ordinary piece of machinery,   5
a necessity for many people. Clearly, the car is no longer seen as the amazing invention it once was. Despite the fact that most people take the existence of cars for granted, however, manufacturers still try to make consumers believe they are buying more than just transportation. But whether we drive a Malibu, Mustang, Cherokee, or Expedition--or even a "royal" LeBaron or Marquis--we eventually realize that we are driving cars, not magic carpets.

◆ PRACTICE 14-19

1. What three categories of car names does Rob discuss in his essay?

2. Is Rob's treatment of the three categories similar? Does he give the same kind of information for each kind of car name? Explain.

3. How do Rob's topic sentences move readers from one category to the next? How do they link the three categories?

4. Underline Rob's thesis statement. Then, try to restate it in your own words.

5. Should Rob have included additional examples in each category? Should he have included any additional categories? Why or why not?

6. What is this essay's greatest strength? What is its greatest weakness?

◆ PRACTICE 14-20

Following the writing process outlined in Chapter 12, write a classification essay on one of the following topics.

Types of teachers (or bosses)
Ways to lose (or gain) weight
Things that you hang on your walls
Kinds of stress
How students dress
Kinds of stores in your community shopping district or mall

Traits of oldest children, middle children, and youngest children
Kinds of desserts
Workers you encounter in a typical day
Popular music

◆ PRACTICE 14-21

Look at the picture below. Then, on a separate sheet of paper, write an essay in which you classify the food you eat. The categories you create can classify

▶ **Word Power**

gourmet
involving high-quality ingredients and skilled preparation

nutritious
healthy, nourishing

the food according to convenience, ease of preparation, healthfulness, where it is consumed, and so on.

☑ SELF-ASSESSMENT CHECKLIST:

Writing a Classification Essay

- Does your introduction give readers an overview of the subject whose categories you will discuss? If necessary, revise to clarify the subject of your classification.
- Does your thesis statement identify the categories you will discuss? If not, revise your thesis statement to clarify your essay's focus.
- Does each body paragraph discuss a single major category or a related group of minor categories? If not, revise to create unified paragraphs.
- Are any categories insignificant or irrelevant? Revise to eliminate any categories that are not central to your essay's purpose.
- Does each topic sentence identify and define the category or categories the paragraph discusses? If necessary, revise your topic sentences to clarify the focus of each paragraph.
- Have you treated each major category similarly and with equal thoroughness? If not, revise to make your discussion balanced.
- Do transitional words and phrases clearly lead readers from one category to the next? If not, revise to make your essay flow more smoothly.
- Does your conclusion review the major categories your essay discusses? If necessary, revise to sum up the categories and their relationships to your subject.
- What problems did you experience in writing your essay? What would you do differently next time?

H   Definition

For information on writing a definition paragraph, see Chapter 10.

Definition explains the meaning of a term or concept. A **definition essay** presents an *extended definition*, using other patterns of development to move beyond a simple dictionary definition.

*For examples
of definition
essays by pro-
fessional writ-
ers, see 35H.*

FOCUS   **Topics for Definition**

The wording of your assignment may suggest definition. For example,
you may be asked to *define* or *explain* or to answer the question *What is
x?* or *What does x mean?*

Assignment	Thesis Statement
Art Explain the meaning of the term *performance art*.	Unlike more conventional forms of art, *performance art* extends beyond the canvas.
Biology What did Darwin mean by the term *natural selection*?	*Natural selection,* popularly known as "survival of the fittest," is a good deal more complicated than most people think.
Psychology What is *attention deficit disorder*?	*Attention deficit disorder* (ADD), once narrowly defined as a childhood problem, is now known to affect adults as well as children.

As the thesis statements above suggest, definition essays can be developed
in various ways. For example, you can define something by telling how it
occurred (narration), by describing its appearance (description), by giving a
series of examples (exemplification), by telling how it operates (process), by
telling how it is similar to or different from something else (comparison and
contrast), or by discussing its parts (classification). Some definition essays use
a single pattern of development; others combine several patterns of development, perhaps using a different one in each paragraph.

Options for Organizing Definition Essays

**Single Pattern of
Development**

¶1 Introduction (identifies
   term to be defined)
¶2 Definition by example
¶3 Additional examples
¶4 Additional examples
¶5 Conclusion

**Combination of Several
Different Patterns of
Development**

¶1 Introduction (identifies term
   to be defined)
¶2 Definition by description
¶3 Definition by example
¶4 Definition by comparison and
   contrast
¶5 Conclusion

The kinds of transitions used in a definition essay depend on the specific pattern or patterns of development in the essay. (In addition to the transitional words and expressions listed in the following Focus box, you may also use those appropriate for the particular patterns you use to develop your definition essay. These transitions are listed in Focus boxes throughout this chapter.)

FOCUS **Transitions for Definition**

Also	One characteristic . . . Another
For example	characteristic
In addition	One way . . . Another way
In particular	Specifically
Like	

The following student essay, "Street Smart" by Kristin Whitehead, defines the term *street smart*. In the essay's introduction, Kristin defines her term briefly; in the essay's body paragraphs, she expands her definition. Notice that the topic sentences of Kristin's three body paragraphs repeat a key phrase to remind readers of her essay's subject.

Street Smart

I grew up in a big city, so I was practically born   1
street smart. I learned the hard way how to act and
what to do, and so did my friends. To us, street smart
meant having common sense. We wanted to be cool, but we
needed to be safe, too. Now I go to college in a big
city, and I realize that not everyone here grew up the
way I did. Lots of students are from suburbs or rural
areas, and they are either terrified of the city or
totally ignorant of city life. The few suburban or rural
kids who are willing to venture downtown are not street
smart--but they should be. Being street smart is a vital
survival skill, one that everyone should learn.

For me, being street smart means knowing how to   2
protect my possessions. Friends of mine who are not used
to city life insist on wearing all their jewelry when
they go downtown. I think this is asking for trouble,
and I know better. I always tuck my chain under my shirt
and leave my gold earrings home. Another thing that surprises me is how some of my friends wave their money

around. They always seem to be standing on the street, trying to count their change or stuff dollars into their wallets. Street-smart people make sure to put their money safely away in their pockets or purses before they leave a store. A street-smart person will also carry a backpack, a purse strapped across the chest, or no purse at all. A person who is not street smart carries a purse loosely over one shoulder or dangles it by its handle. Again, these people are asking for trouble.

Being street smart also means protecting myself. It   3
means being aware of my surroundings at all times and looking alert. A lot of times I have been downtown with people who kept stopping on the street to talk about where they should go next or walking up and down the same street over and over again. A street-smart person would never do this. It's important that I look as if I know where I am going at all times, even if I don't. Whenever possible, I decide on a destination in advance, and I make sure I know how to get there. Even if I am not completely sure where I am headed, I make sure my body language conveys my confidence in my ability to reach my destination.

Finally, being street smart means protecting my life. 4
A street-smart person does not walk alone, especially after dark, in an unfamiliar neighborhood. A street-smart person does not ask strangers for directions; when lost, he or she asks a shopkeeper for help. A street-smart person takes main streets instead of side streets. When faced with danger or the threat of danger, a street-smart person knows when to run, when to scream, and when to give up money or possessions to avoid violence.

So how does someone get to be street smart? Some   5
people think it is a gift, but I think it is something almost anyone can learn. Probably the best way to learn how to be street smart is to hang out with people who know where they are going.

◆ PRACTICE 14-22

1. Underline Kristin's thesis statement. Then, try to restate it in your own words.

2. In your own words, define the term *street smart*. Why does this term require more than a one-sentence definition?

3. Where does Kristin use examples to develop her definition? Where does she use comparison and contrast?

4. What phrase does Kristin repeat in the topic sentences to tie her three body paragraphs together?

5. Kristin's conclusion is quite a bit shorter than her other paragraphs. What, if anything, do you think she should add to this paragraph?

6. What is this essay's greatest strength? What is its greatest weakness?

◆ PRACTICE 14-23

Following the writing process outlined in Chapter 12, write a definition essay on one of the following topics.

Fear	Success	Surprise
Upward mobility	Responsibility	Happiness
Peer pressure	Procrastination	
Competition	Security	

◆ PRACTICE 14-24

▶ **Word Power**

nuclear family

a family unit made up of a mother and father and their children

On a separate sheet of paper, write an essay in which you define *family*. In what ways do the family groups shown below and on the following page fit or not fit into your definition?

✅ SELF-ASSESSMENT CHECKLIST:

Writing a Definition Essay

Does your introduction identify the term that your essay will define and provide a brief definition? If not, revise to make the scope of your essay clear.

Does your thesis statement indicate why you are defining the term? If not, revise to clarify your purpose.

(continued on the following page)

For more on the patterns of paragraph development, see Chapters 3–11.

14 I

(continued from the previous page)

- What pattern or patterns of development do you use to develop your definition? Try exploring other options.

- Do topic sentences clearly introduce the different aspects of your definition? If necessary, revise to clarify the relationships between paragraphs.

- Are all your ideas clearly related to the term you are defining? If not, revise to eliminate any irrelevant ideas.

- Do transitional words and phrases clearly link your ideas? If necessary, add transitions to help guide readers through your essay.

- Does your conclusion sum up your essay's main points? Does it remind readers why you are defining the term? If necessary, revise to make your conclusion consistent with the rest of your essay.

- What problems did you experience in writing your essay? What would you do differently next time?

I   Argument

For information on writing an argument paragraph, see Chapter 11.

Argument takes a stand on a debatable issue. An **argument essay** uses different kinds of evidence—facts, examples, and expert opinion—to persuade readers to accept a position.

FOCUS   Topics for Argument

The wording of your assignment may suggest argument. For example, you may be asked to *debate, argue, consider, give your opinion, take a position,* or *take a stand.*

For examples of argument essays by professional writers, see 35I.

Assignment	Thesis Statement
Composition Explain your position on a current social issue.	People who contribute to Social Security should be able to invest some of their money in the stock market.

(continued on the following page)

(continued from the previous page)

Assignment	Thesis Statement
American history Do you believe that General Lee was responsible for the South's defeat at the Battle of Gettysburg? Why or why not?	Because Lee refused to listen to the advice given to him by General Longstreet, he is largely responsible for the South's defeat at the Battle of Gettysburg.
Ethics In your opinion, should physician-assisted suicide be legalized?	Although many people think physician-assisted suicide should remain illegal, I believe it should be legal in certain situations.

An argument essay can be organized *inductively* or *deductively*. An **inductive argument** moves from the specific to the general—that is, from a group of specific observations to a general conclusion based on these observations. An inductive argument responding to the first topic in the Focus box above, for example, could begin with a series of facts, examples, and opinions about the benefits of investing in the stock market and end with the conclusion that people should be able to invest part of their Social Security money.

A **deductive argument** moves from the general to the specific. A deductive argument begins with a **major premise** (a general statement that the writer believes his or her audience will accept) and then moves to a **minor premise** (a specific instance of the belief stated in the major premise). It ends with a **conclusion** that follows from the two premises. For example, an essay that responds to the last topic in the Focus box above could begin with the major premise that all terminally ill patients who are in great pain should be given access to physician-assisted suicide. It could then go on to state and explain the minor premise that a particular patient is both terminally ill and in great pain, offering facts, examples, and the opinions of authorities to support this premise. The essay could conclude that this patient should, therefore, be allowed the option of physician-assisted suicide. In this way, the deductive argument goes through three steps.

MAJOR PREMISE All terminally ill patients who are in great pain should be allowed to choose physician-assisted suicide.

MINOR PREMISE John Lacca is a terminally ill patient who is in great pain.

CONCLUSION Therefore, John Lacca should be allowed to choose physician-assisted suicide.

Before you present your argument, think about whether your readers will be hostile to, neutral toward, or in agreement with your thesis. Once you understand your audience, you can decide which points to make in support of your argument.

As you write your argument essay, begin each paragraph with a topic sentence that clearly relates the discussion to the previous paragraph or to your thesis statement. Throughout your essay, try to include specific examples that will make your arguments persuasive. Keep in mind that arguments that rely just on generalizations are not as convincing as those that include vivid details and specific examples. Finally, strive for a balanced, moderate tone, and avoid name-calling or personal attacks.

In addition to presenting your case, you should also briefly identify arguments *against* your position and **refute** them (that is, prove them false) by identifying factual errors or errors in logic. If an opposing argument is particularly strong, concede its strength—but try to point out some weakness as well. Dealing with the opposing point of view in this manner will help you overcome any objections your audience might have and will establish you as a fair and reasonable person.

Options for Organizing Argument Essays

Induction	**Deduction**
¶1 Introduction	¶1 Introduction
¶2 First point (supported by facts, examples, and expert opinions)	¶2 Major premise stated and explained
¶3 Second point	¶3 Minor premise stated and explained
¶4 Third point	¶4 Evidence supporting minor premise presented
¶5 Identification and refutation of opposing arguments	¶5 Opposing arguments identified and refuted
¶6 Conclusion	¶6 Conclusion

Transitions are extremely important in argument essays because they not only signal the movement from one part of the argument to another but also relate specific points to one another and to the thesis statement.

FOCUS **Transitions for Argument**

Accordingly	However	On the one hand
Admittedly	In conclusion	. . . On the other
Although	Indeed	hand
Because	In fact	Since

(continued on the following page)

(continued from the previous page)

But	In summary	Therefore
Certainly	Meanwhile	Thus
Consequently	Moreover	To be sure
Despite	Nevertheless	Truly
Even so	Nonetheless	
Granted	Of course	

The following student essay, "Why Isn't Pete Rose in the Hall of Fame?" by John Fleeger, is an argument essay. John takes a strong stand, and he supports his thesis with specific facts and examples. The deductive argument that underlies John's essay moves from the major premise ("Qualified players who do not violate major-league rules should be inducted into the Hall of Fame") to the minor premise ("Pete Rose is a qualified player who did not violate major-league rules") to the conclusion ("Therefore, Pete Rose should be inducted into the Hall of Fame").

Why Isn't Pete Rose in the Hall of Fame?

The year 1992 was the first year Pete Rose would   1
have been eligible for the National Baseball Hall of
Fame. Not only was he not elected, his name did not
even appear on the ballot. Why? Has he not established
himself as the all-time best hitter in baseball? Was he
not a member of two championship teams with the Cincin-
nati Reds and one with the Philadelphia Phillies? Did he
not help build the foundation for the 1990 championship
Reds team? Has he not set or tied several major-league
and team records during his career? The answer to all
of these questions is yes. His dedication to and enthusiasm for the game of baseball earned him the nickname
"Charlie Hustle," but they did not earn him his rightful
place in the Hall of Fame. This situation is unfair and
should be changed.

In the late summer of 1989, Pete Rose was banned   2
from professional baseball. The legal agreement reached
between major-league officials and Pete Rose does not
offer any evidence that Rose bet on any baseball games,
and Rose himself does not say that he did. Despite the
lack of any confirmation, A. Bartlett Giamatti, Commis-

sioner of Baseball at that time, publicly stated that Rose bet not only on baseball but also on his own team. Betting on baseball is a violation of major-league rules and is punishable by lifetime banishment from baseball. This was the sentence Pete Rose received.

In 1991, the Hall of Fame Committee along with Fay Vincent, who was then Commissioner of Baseball, decided that as long as a player is banned from baseball, he is ineligible for Hall of Fame selection. This action was taken just a few weeks before Rose's name could have been placed on the ballot, and many believe that Vincent encouraged it specifically to make sure Rose could not be considered for selection. Several of the baseball writers who voted for the Hall of Fame candidates voiced their disapproval of this policy by writing in Rose's name on the ballot. Unfortunately, write-in votes are not counted.

Rose's only hope of making the Hall of Fame depends on his being readmitted to baseball. The commissioner would have to review Rose's application and approve his reinstatement. Chances are not good, however, that this will happen. In fact, in recent years, new charges have surfaced. Someone who calls himself a confidant of Rose's now accuses him not only of having bet on baseball but also of having people forge his signature on baseball memorabilia. However, at this time none of these charges has been proven.

Meanwhile, on the strength of circumstantial evidence and the testimony of convicted felons, baseball has convicted Pete Rose of betting on baseball. He has admitted to betting on horse races and football games but denies ever betting on the sport he loves. He has also admitted that his gambling was a problem and that he has spent time in counseling. Why is a player who once gambled any worse than the many players who have tested positive for drugs? Those players are suspended from the game for a period of time and are given one or more chances to recover and return to the major league. Why are gamblers not treated the same way as drug abusers?

Many people mistakenly believe that Pete Rose went 6 to prison for betting on baseball and that, for this reason, he should be kept out of the Hall of Fame. The fact is, however, that Rose went to prison for tax-law violations. He failed to pay income tax on his gambling winnings and on the money he made at baseball-card shows. Even so, when has the Hall of Fame ever been reserved for perfect people? Babe Ruth was an adulterer and a serious drinker, but he still holds a place in the Hall of Fame. Mickey Mantle and Willie Mays were barred from baseball for being employees of an Atlantic City casino (an obvious gambling connection), but even this decision was eventually overturned.

Granted, Pete Rose has made some serious mistakes 7 in his life, but this is no reason to keep him out of the Hall of Fame. His contributions to the game and his accomplishments as a player are all that should be considered, and these more than qualify him to occupy a place beside the greats of the game. Baseball should, in all fairness, let Pete Rose take his rightful place in the Hall of Fame.

◆ PRACTICE 14-25

1. What position does John take in his essay? Try to restate it in your own words.

2. On a separate sheet of paper, list the facts and examples John uses to support his thesis. Can you think of any that he doesn't mention?

3. Underline the transitional words and phrases John uses to move his argument along.

4. John's opening paragraph includes a series of questions he does not expect his readers to answer. Is this an effective opening strategy? Why or why not?

5. Throughout his essay, John acknowledges Pete Rose's problems and shortcomings. Do you think this is a good idea? Why or why not?

6. Where does John address opposing arguments? What other arguments should he have addressed?

7. What is this essay's greatest strength? What is its greatest weakness?

◆ PRACTICE 14-26

Following the writing process outlined in Chapter 12, write an argument essay on one of the following topics.

> The United States should (or should not) have an "open door" immigration policy, with no restrictions.
> Teenagers who commit serious crimes should (or should not) be tried as adults.
> All citizens without criminal records should (or should not) be permitted to carry concealed weapons.
> Welfare recipients with preschool children should (or should not) be required to work.
> Human beings should (or should not) be used in medical research experiments.
> Parents should (or should not) be permitted to use government vouchers to pay private school tuition.
> College financial aid should (or should not) be based solely on merit.
> Government funds should (or should not) be used to support the arts.
> Public high schools should (or should not) be permitted to distribute condoms to students.
> The minimim wage should (or should not) be raised to ten dollars an hour.

◆ PRACTICE 14-27

▶ **Word Power**
multitasking
doing several tasks at the same time

hazardous
dangerous

Many states are considering a ban on cell phone use by drivers in moving vehicles. Do you agree that this is a good idea, or do you believe that the convenience of cell phones outweighs the possible risk (which some consider remote) of accidents?

✔ SELF-ASSESSMENT CHECKLIST:

Writing an Argument Essay

- Does your introduction present the issue you will discuss and provide the background readers will need? If necessary, revise to clarify your focus.

- Is your topic debatable? Make sure you take a position on an issue that really has two sides.

- Does your thesis statement clearly express the stand you take on the issue? If necessary, revise to clarify your position.

- Are your readers likely to be hostile to, neutral toward, or in agreement with your position? Be sure you consider your audience's expectations when choosing the points you will make and deciding how you will present them.

- Is your essay an inductive argument or a deductive argument? If necessary, revise the structure of your argument so it conforms to the requirements of the option you have chosen.

- Have you addressed the major arguments against your position? Identify any additional opposing arguments, and refute them if you can.

- Do you have enough evidence to support your points? If not, add facts, examples, and the opinions of experts.

- Do all your points clearly support your position? Revise to eliminate any points that are not directly related to your argument.

- Do transitional words and phrases help readers follow the logic of your argument? Add transitions if necessary.

- Does your conclusion follow logically from the points you have made in your essay? If necessary, revise so that your concluding paragraph summarizes and reinforces your main points.

- What problems did you experience in writing your essay? What would you do differently next time?

UNIT FOUR

Writing Effective Sentences

Writing Simple Sentences

PREVIEW

In this chapter, you will learn
- to identify a sentence's subject (15A)
- to identify prepositions and prepositional phrases (15B)
- to distinguish a prepositional phrase from a subject (15B)
- to identify a sentence's verb (15C)

▶ **Word Power**

idol
someone who is admired or adored

role model
a person who serves as a model for other people to imitate

emulate
to strive to equal or excel, especially by imitating

■ SEEING AND WRITING

Look at the picture above, and then write about a person with whom you would like to trade places. What is this person like? What appeals to you about his or her life?

A **sentence** is a group of words that expresses a complete thought. Every sentence includes both a <u>subject</u> and a <u>verb</u>.

229

A   Identifying Subjects

Every sentence includes a subject. The **subject** of a sentence tells who or what is being talked about in the sentence. Without a subject, a sentence is not complete.

<u>Derek Walcott</u> won the 1992 Nobel Prize in literature.

<u>He</u> was born in the Caribbean.

<u>St. Lucia</u> is an island in the Caribbean.

For information on subject-verb agreement with compound subjects, see 23A.

The subject of a sentence can be a noun or a pronoun. A **noun** names a person, place, or thing—*Derek Walcott, St. Lucia.* A **pronoun** takes the place of a noun—*I, you, he, she, it, we, they.*

The subject of a sentence can be *singular* or *plural.* A **singular subject** is one person, place, or thing *(Derek Walcott, St. Lucia, he).*

A **plural subject** is more than one person, place, or thing *(poems, people, they).*

Walcott's <u>poems</u> are studied in college courses.

A plural subject that joins two or more subjects with *and* is called a **compound subject**.

<u>St. Lucia and Trinidad</u> are Caribbean islands.

FOCUS   **Simple and Complete Subjects**

A sentence's **simple subject** is just a noun or a pronoun.

    poems   he

A sentence's **complete subject** is the simple subject along with any words that describe it.

    Walcott's poems

A two-word name, such as *Derek Walcott,* is a simple subject.

ON THE WEB
For more practice, visit Exercise Central: www.bedford stmartins.com/ writingincontext

◆ PRACTICE 15-1

In the paragraph below, underline the complete subject of each sentence once. Then, place a check mark above the simple subject.

Example: The poet's <u>parents</u> were both teachers.

(1) Derek Walcott was born in 1930. (2) His ancestors came from Africa, the Netherlands, and England. (3) Walcott's early years were spent on the Caribbean island of St. Lucia. (4) Poetry occupied much of his time. (5) His early poems were published in Trinidad. (6) He later studied in Jamaica and in New York and founded the Trinidad Theatre Workshop. (7) Walcott eventually gained wide recognition as a poet. (8) He was a visiting lecturer at Harvard in 1981. (9) In 1990, the renowned poet published *Omeros*. (10) This long poem about classical Greek heroes is set in the West Indies. (11) In 1992, the sixty-two-year-old Caribbean poet was honored with a Nobel Prize. (12) Walcott later collaborated with songwriter Paul Simon on *The Capeman*, a Broadway musical.

◆ PRACTICE 15-2

Add a simple subject to each of the following sentences.

Example: *Pets* can reduce stress, high blood pressure, and depression.

1. For one thing, _____ allow us to express affection openly.

2. _____ can stroke, cuddle, and talk baby talk to a kitten or puppy.

3. _____ also love us unconditionally, no matter what our faults.

4. Our _____ do not care about our faults.

5. _____ now take pets into nursing homes and hospitals.

6. For some patients, their only _____ are these animals.

7. These _____ have better survival rates.

8. In addition, prison _____ sometimes train service dogs.

9. These _____ help disabled people.

10. Their _____ are making a positive contribution to society.

◆ PRACTICE 15-3

Underline the complete subject in each sentence. Then, write *S* above singular subjects and *P* above plural subjects. Remember, compound subjects are plural.

S

Example: An international space station is scheduled to be completed in 2004.

1. Sixteen nations are working together to build the station.

2. This million-pound satellite will contain six laboratories.

3. Living quarters will also be provided for seven people.

4. Scientists will use the laboratories to study how cells grow without gravity.

5. They will also study the effects of reduced gravity on humans.

6. The station is being constructed by manned space flights from the sixteen nations.

7. Russia and the United States made the first trips in 1998.

8. Other flight crews have delivered supplies and parts for the station since then.

9. An international crew will live and work on the completed station.

10. The crew's return vehicle will be attached to the station to ensure their safe return to Earth.

■ SEEING AND WRITING: Flashback

Look back at your response to the Seeing and Writing exercise on page 229. Underline the complete subject of each of your sentences once. Then, place a check mark above the simple subject. Finally, write *S* beside each singular subject and *P* beside each plural subject. (Remember that a compound subject is plural.)

B   Identifying Prepositional Phrases

A **phrase** is a group of words that lacks a subject or a verb or both and there-fore cannot stand alone as a sentence. A **prepositional phrase** consists of a **preposition** (a word such as *on, to, in,* or *with*) and its **object** (a noun or pronoun).

Preposition	+	Object	=	Prepositional phrase
on		the stage		on the stage
to		Nia's house		to Nia's house
in		my new car		in my new car
with		them		with them

A prepositional phrase **modifies** (describes, or limits) another word or word group in the sentence.

The girl <u>with long red hair</u> was first in line. *(With long red hair modifies the noun girl.)*

Ken met his future wife <u>at Ted's house</u>. *(At Ted's house modifies the verb met.)*

Because the object of a preposition is a noun or a pronoun, it may appear to be the subject of a sentence. However, the object of a preposition can never be the subject of a sentence. To identify a sentence's true subject, cross out each prepositional phrase.

The <u>cost</u> ~~of the repairs~~ was astronomical.

~~At the end of the novel,~~ ~~after an exciting chase,~~ the <u>lovers</u> flee ~~to Mexico~~.

Remember that every prepositional phrase is introduced by a preposition.

Frequently Used Prepositions

about	behind	except	off	toward
above	below	for	on	under
across	beneath	from	onto	underneath
after	beside	in	out	until
against	between	inside	outside	up
along	beyond	into	over	upon
among	by	like	through	with
around	despite	near	throughout	within
at	during	of	to	without
before				

◆ PRACTICE 15-4

Each of the following sentences includes at least one prepositional phrase. To identify each sentence's subject, begin by crossing out each prepositional phrase. Then, underline the simple subject of the sentence.

Example: ~~In twentieth-century presidential elections,~~ third-party <u>candidates</u> attracted many voters.

(1) With more than 27 percent of the vote, Theodore Roosevelt was the strongest third-party presidential candidate in history. (2) In the 1912 race with Democrat Woodrow Wilson and Republican William H. Taft, Roosevelt ran second to Wilson. (3) Until Roosevelt, no third-party candidate had won a significant number of votes. (4) After 1912, however, some candidates of other parties made strong showings. (5) For example, Robert M. LaFollette of the Progressive Party won about 16 percent of the vote in the 1924 race. (6) In 1968, with more than 13 percent of the popular vote, American Independent Party candidate George C. Wallace placed third behind Republican Richard M. Nixon and Democrat Hubert H. Humphrey. (7) In 1980, John B. Anderson, an Independent, challenged Republican Ronald Reagan and Democrat Jimmy Carter and got 6.6 percent of the vote. (8) With nearly 19 percent of the popular vote, Independent Ross Perot ran a strong race against Democrat Bill Clinton and Republican George Bush in 1992. (9) In 2000, with the support of many environmentalists, Ralph Nader challenged Al Gore and George W. Bush for the presidency. (10) To this day, the two-party system of the United States has remained intact despite many challenges by third-party candidates.

■ SEEING AND WRITING: Flashback

Look back at your response to the Seeing and Writing exercise on page 229. Have you used any prepositional phrases? Circle each one you find.

C   Identifying Verbs

In addition to its subject, every sentence also includes a verb. The **verb** tells what the subject does or connects the subject to words that describe or rename it. Without a verb, a sentence is not complete.

Action Verbs

An **action verb** tells what the subject does, did, or will do.

Nomar Garciaparra <u>plays</u> baseball.
Renee <u>will drive</u> to Tampa on Friday.
Amelia Earhart <u>flew</u> across the Atlantic.

Action verbs can also show mental and emotional actions.

Travis always <u>worries</u> about his job.

Sometimes, the subject of a sentence performs more than one action. In this case, the sentence includes two or more action verbs joined to form a **compound verb.**

He <u>hit</u> the ball, <u>threw</u> down his bat, and <u>ran</u> toward first base.

Linking Verbs

A **linking verb** does not show action. Instead, it connects the subject to a word or words that describe or rename it. The linking verb tells what the subject is (or what it was, will be, or seems to be).

A googolplex <u>is</u> an extremely large number.

Many linking verbs, like *is,* are forms of the verb *be.* Other linking verbs refer to the senses (*look, feel,* and so on).

Some students <u>feel</u> anxious about the future.
The photocopy <u>looks</u> blurry.

Note: Some linking verbs, such as *look, smell, turn,* and *taste,* can also function as action verbs: *I will <u>look</u> for a clearer photocopy.*

Frequently Used Linking Verbs		
act	feel	seem
appear	get	smell
be (am, is, are,	grow	sound
was, were)	look	taste
become	remain	turn

◆ **PRACTICE 15-5**

ON THE WEB
For more practice, visit Exercise Central:
www.bedford stmartins.com/ writingincontext

Underline the action verbs in the following sentences twice. Some sentences contain more than one action verb.

1. Many critics see one romance novel as just like another.

2. The plot usually involves a beautiful young woman, or heroine, in some kind of danger.

3. A handsome stranger offers to help the woman.

4. At first, she distrusts him.

5. Then, another man enters the story and wins the heroine's trust.

6. Readers, however, see this man as an evil villain.

7. Almost too late, the heroine too realizes the truth.

8. Luckily, the handsome hero returns and saves her from a nasty fate.

9. Many readers enjoy the predictable plots.

10. But critics dislike these books.

◆ **PRACTICE 15-6**

Underline the linking verbs in the following sentences twice. Some sentences contain more than one linking verb.

1. Urban legends are folk tales created in our own time to teach a lesson.

2. The most familiar urban legend is the story of Hookman.

3. According to this story, a young couple is alone in Lovers' Lane.

4. They are in a car in this secluded place, listening to a radio announcement.

5. An escaped murderer is nearby.

6. The murderer's left hand is a hook.

7. The young woman becomes hysterical.

8. Leaving Lovers' Lane, the car seems to scrape against something.

9. At home, they are stunned to see a hook hanging from the passenger door handle.

10. The purpose of this legend is to frighten young people into avoiding dangerous places.

◆ PRACTICE 15-7

Underline the verbs in each sentence twice. Remember that a verb can be an action verb or a linking verb.

Example: Some books <u>have</u> a great impact on their readers.

(1) Betty Smith wrote *A Tree Grows in Brooklyn,* a 1948 novel. (2) The novel tells the story of Francie Nolan. (3) Francie is very poor but seems determined to succeed. (4) She loves books and is an excellent student. (5) Francie lives with her parents and her younger brother, Neely. (6) She dreams of a better life for herself and her family. (7) Tragically, Francie's father dies. (8) Her mother supports her family and does her best for her children. (9) She works as a janitor in their apartment building. (10) Eventually, Francie graduates from high school, with a bright future ahead of her.

Helping Verbs

Many verbs consist of more than one word. The verb in the following sentence consists of two words.

Minh <u>must make</u> a decision about his future.

In this sentence, *make* is the **main verb**, and *must* is a **helping verb**.

FOCUS   **Helping Verbs**

Helping verbs include forms of *be, have,* and *do* as well as the words *must, will, can, could, may, might, should,* and *would.* Some helping verbs, like forms of *be* and *have,* combine with main verbs to give information about when the action occurs. Forms of *do* combine with main verbs to form questions and negative statements. Still other helping verbs indicate willingness *(can),* possibility *(may),* necessity *(should),* obligation *(must),* and so on.

A sentence's **complete verb** is made up of a main verb plus any helping verbs that accompany it. In the following sentences, the complete verb is underlined twice, and the helping verbs are checkmarked. (Note that sometimes other words can come between parts of a complete verb.)

Minh should have gone earlier.

Did Minh ask the right questions?

Minh will work hard.

Minh can really succeed.

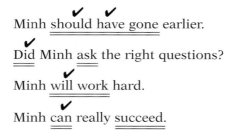

FOCUS **Helping Verbs with Participles**

For information on past participles, see Chapter 27.

Present participles, such as *thinking*, and many irregular **past participles**, such as *gone*, cannot stand alone as main verbs in a sentence. They need a helping verb to make them complete.

INCORRECT Minh going to the library.

CORRECT Minh is going to the library.

INCORRECT Minh gone to the library.

CORRECT Minh has gone to the library.

◆ PRACTICE 15-8

The verbs in the sentences that follow consist of a main verb and one or more helping verbs. In each sentence, underline the complete verb twice, and put a check mark above the helping verb(s).

Example: The Salk polio vaccine was given to more than a million schoolchildren in 1954.

(1) By the 1950s, parents had become terrified of polio. (2) For years, it had puzzled doctors and researchers. (3) Thousands had become ill each year in the United States alone. (4) Children should have been playing

happily. (5) Instead, they would get very sick. (6) Polio was sometimes called infantile paralysis. (7) In fact, it did cause paralysis in children and in adults as well. (8) Some patients could breathe only with the help of machines called iron lungs. (9) Others would remain in wheelchairs for life. (10) By 1960, Jonas Salk's vaccine had reduced the incidence of polio in the United States by more than 90 percent.

■ SEEING AND WRITING: Flashback

Look back at your response to the Seeing and Writing exercise on page 229. In each sentence, underline the complete verb twice, and put a check mark above each helping verb.

■ SEEING AND WRITING: Revising and Editing

Look back at your response to the Seeing and Writing exercise on page 229. Circle every action verb. Then, try to replace some of them with different action verbs that express more precisely what the subject of each sentence is, was, or will be doing. For example, you might replace *makes* with *builds* or *creates*.

CHAPTER REVIEW

◆ EDITING PRACTICE

Read the following student passage. Underline the complete subject of each sentence once, and underline the complete verb of each sentence twice. If you have trouble locating the subject, try crossing out the prepositional phrases. The first sentence has been done for you.

Escape to Freedom

~~On April 14, 1979,~~ ~~at 10 p.m.~~, <u>my family</u> <u>left</u> Vietnam. My mother had hidden gold and jewelry in water pipes. Now we could use these unconfiscated items. We could buy seats on a fishing boat. Then we could escape to freedom. The trip was extremely dangerous. Forty-two people drifted aimlessly on the water. We drifted for four days and five nights on the Pacific ocean. At last, on the 18th of April, we saw land. We stopped at Natuna Besar, Indonesia, for three days. Then, on the 21st, we came to Sedanau, another island of Indonesia. After a stay of one month, we traveled to Tanjungpinang, Indonesia. We stayed there for three and a half months. Life in the refugee camp was not luxurious. Our space was very cramped. Food was scarce. Luckily, my father had once been a captain in the army. As a result, our family was quickly resettled to the United States.

◆ COLLABORATIVE ACTIVITIES

1. Fold a sheet of paper in half vertically. Working in a group of three or four students, spend two minutes listing as many nouns as you can in the column to the left of the fold. When your time is up, exchange papers with another group of students. Limiting yourselves to five minutes, write an appropriate action verb beside each noun. Each noun will now be the subject of a short sentence.

2. Choose five short sentences from those you wrote for Collaborative Activity 1. Working in the same group, collaborate to create more fully developed sentences. First, expand each subject by adding words or prepositional phrases that give more information about the subject. (For example, you could expand *boat* to *the small, leaky boat with the red sail.*) Then, expand each sentence further, adding ideas after the verb. (For example, the sentence *The boat bounced* could become *The small, leaky boat with the red sail bounced helplessly on the water.*)

3. Collaborate in a group of three or four students to write one original sentence for each of the linking verbs listed on page 235. When you have finished, exchange papers with another group. Now, try to add words and phrases to the other group's sentences to make them more interesting.

16 *Writing Compound Sentences*

Word Power

innovation
something
newly
introduced

functional
designed for
a particular
need or
activity

■ SEEING AND WRITING

Look at the picture above. Imagine that you are the inventor of a familiar product—for example, Velcro, the zipper, or the rubber band—and that you are ready to introduce this product to the world. Begin by telling what this new invention is. Then, describe what it looks like, and give examples of its possible uses.

A Forming Compound Sentences with Coordinating Conjunctions

A **simple sentence** includes a subject and a verb.

European immigrants arrived at Ellis Island.

Asian immigrants arrived at Angel Island.

A **compound sentence** is made up of two or more simple sentences. One way to form a compound sentence is by joining two simple sentences with a **coordinating conjunction** preceded by a comma.

European immigrants arrived at Ellis Island, but Asian immigrants arrived at Angel Island.

Coordinating Conjunctions

and	for	or	yet
but	nor	so	

Coordinating conjunctions join ideas of equal importance. They describe the relationship between two ideas, showing how and why the ideas are connected. Different coordinating conjunctions have different meanings.

■ If you want to indicate addition, use *and*.

He acts like a child, and people think he is cute.

■ If you want to indicate contrast or contradiction, use *but* or *yet*.

He acts like a child, but he is an adult.

He acts like a child, yet he longs to be taken seriously.

■ If you want to indicate a cause-effect relationship, use *so* or *for*.

He acts like a child, so we treat him like one.

He acts like a child, for he craves attention.

■ If you want to present alternatives, use *or*.

He acts like a child, or he is ignored.

■ If you want to eliminate alternatives, use *nor*.

He does not act like a child, nor does he look like one.

FOCUS   **Punctuating with Coordinating Conjunctions**

When you use a coordinating conjunction to link two short sentences into a single compound sentence, always put a comma before the coordinating conjunction.

We can stand in line all night, or we can go home now.

Remember, though, not to use a comma before a coordinating conjunction unless it links two *complete sentences.*

INCORRECT   We can stand in line all night, or go home now.

CORRECT   We can stand in line all night or go home now.

◆ **PRACTICE 16-1**

ON THE WEB
For more practice, visit Exercise Central:
www.bedfordstmartins.com/writingincontext

Fill in the coordinating conjunction—*and, but, for, nor, or, so,* or *yet*— that most logically links the two parts of each compound sentence. Remember to insert a comma before each coordinating conjunction.

Example: Fairy tales have been told by many people around the world, _*but*_ the stories by two German brothers may be the most famous.

(1) Jakob and Wilhelm Grimm lived in the nineteenth century _____ they wrote many well-known fairy tales. (2) Most people think fondly of fairy tales _____ the Brothers Grimm wrote many unpleasant and violent stories. (3) In their best-known works, children are abused ____ endings are not always happy. (4) Either innocent children are brutally punished for no reason _____ they are neglected. (5) For example, in "Hansel and Gretel," the stepmother mistreats the children _____ their father abandons them in the woods. (6) In this story, the events are horrifying _____ the ending is still happy. (7) The children outwit the evil adults _____ they escape unharmed. (8) Apparently, they are not injured physically ____ are they harmed emotionally. (9) Nevertheless, their story can hardly be called pleasant ____ it remains a story of child abuse and neglect.

◆ PRACTICE 16-2

Join each of the following pairs of simple sentences with a coordinating conjunction. Be sure to place a comma before the coordinating conjunction.

Example: A computer can make drafting essays easier. It also lets
                                                              , and
you revise as often as possible.

1. Training a dog to heel is difficult. Dogs naturally resist strict control.

2. A bodhran is an Irish drum. It is played with a wooden stick.

3. Students should spend two hours of study time for each hour of class time. They may not pass the course.

4. Years ago, students wrote their lessons on slates. The teacher could correct each student's work.

5. Each state in the United States has two senators. The number of representatives depends on a state's population.

6. In 1973, only 2.5 percent of those in the U.S. military were women. By 1999, that percentage had increased to 14.1 percent.

7. A "small craft advisory" warns boaters of bad weather conditions. These conditions can be dangerous to small boats.

8. A digital video disc (DVD) looks like a compact disk. It can hold fifteen times as much information.

9. Hip-hop fashions include sneakers and baggy pants. These styles are very popular among today's young men.

10. People want to explore Mars. Sooner or later astronauts will land there.

◆ PRACTICE 16-3

Add coordinating conjunctions to combine simple sentences where necessary to relate one idea to another. Remember to put a comma before each coordinating conjunction you add.

Example: Years ago, few Americans lived to be one hundred. ~~Today,~~
                                                      , but today,
there are over 32,000 centenarians.

(1) Diet, exercise, and family history may account for centenarians' long lives. (2) This is not the whole story. (3) Recently, a study conducted in Georgia showed surprising common traits among centenarians. (4) They did not necessarily avoid tobacco and alcohol. (5) They did not eat low-fat diets. (6) In fact, they ate relatively large amounts of fat, cholesterol, and sugar. (7) Diet could not explain their long lives. (8) They did, however, share four key survival characteristics. (9) First, all of the centenarians were optimistic about life. (10) All of them were positive thinkers. (11) They were also involved in religious life and had deep religious faith. (12) In addition, all the centenarians had continued to lead physically active lives. (13) They remained mobile even as elderly people. (14) Finally, all were able to adapt to loss. (15) They had all experienced the deaths of friends, spouses, or children. (16) They were able to get on with their lives.

◆ PRACTICE 16-4

Write another simple sentence to follow each of the sentences below. Then, connect the sentences with a coordinating conjunction and the correct punctuation.

    Example: Many patients need organ transplants, *but there never seem to be enough available to meet the demand.*

1. Smoking in bed is dangerous. _____

_____

2. Many cars are equipped with front and side air bags. _____

_____

3. Diamonds can cut glass. _____

_____

4. Kangaroos carry their young in pouches. _____

_____

5. Dancing is good exercise. _____

_____

6. Taking driving lessons reduces the possibility of accidents. _____

_____

7. Some businesses sponsor bowling leagues for their employees. _____

_____

8. Pretzels are a healthier snack than potato chips. _____

_____

9. Many juice drinks actually contain very little real fruit juice. _____

_____

10. Human beings tend to resist change. _____

_____

■ SEEING AND WRITING: Flashback

Look back at your response to the Seeing and Writing exercise on page 242. If you see any compound sentences, bracket them. If you see any pairs of simple sentences that could be combined, try rewriting them and joining them with appropriate coordinating conjunctions to create compound sentences. Be sure each of your compound sentences includes a comma before the coordinating conjunction.

B Forming Compound Sentences with Semicolons

Another way to create a **compound sentence** is by joining two simple sentences with a *semicolon*.

The AIDS quilt contains thousands of panels; each panel is rectangular.

A semicolon generally connects simple sentences whose ideas are closely linked.

For information
on avoiding
sentence
fragments,
see Chapter 22.

FOCUS   **Using Semicolons to Join Sentences**

Remember that a semicolon can join only two *complete sentences.*
A semicolon cannot join a sentence and a fragment.

┌──────────────── FRAGMENT ────────────────┐
INCORRECT   Because thousands are dying of AIDS; more research is clearly needed.

CORRECT   Thousands are dying of AIDS; more research is clearly needed.

◆ PRACTICE 16-5

Combine each pair of simple sentences below by adding a semicolon in the appropriate place.

Example: People become famous for complicated reasons ; just being the first to accomplish something is no guarantee.

1. Sometimes runners-up are better remembered than winners the triumphant are forgotten.

2. The race to reach the South Pole is a perfect example it illustrates my point.

3. Robert Falcon Scott was a British naval officer Roald Amundsen was a Norwegian explorer.

4. Scott's men used Siberian ponies to drag equipment to the Pole Amundsen's men used dogs.

5. Amundsen's men buried food all along the trail Scott's men left food in only a few locations.

6. The Norwegian team skied to the Pole the British team tried to walk.

7. Amundsen's men made it to the Pole in December 1911 Scott's party arrived in January 1912.

8. The Norwegians found their supplies on the way back the men arrived back at their ship in good condition.

9. Scott's exhausted party could not get to their scarce provisions none of the men survived the trek to the Pole.

10. Nevertheless, Scott and his men are remembered for trying to get to the Pole the Norwegians—the "winners"—have been almost forgotten.

◆ PRACTICE 16-6

Each of the following simple sentences can be linked with a semicolon to another simple sentence to form a compound sentence. In each case, add a semicolon; then, complete the compound sentence with another simple sentence.

      Example: My brother is addicted to fast food *; he eats it every day.*

1. Fast-food restaurants are an American institution _____

_____

2. Families eat at these restaurants _____

_____

3. Many teenagers work there _____

_____

4. McDonald's is known for its hamburgers _____

_____

5. KFC is famous for its fried chicken _____

_____

6. Taco Bell serves Mexican-style food _____

_____

7. Pizza Hut specializes in pizza _____

_____

8. Many fast-food restaurants offer some low-fat menu items _____

_____

9. Some offer recyclable packaging _____

_____

10. Some even have playgrounds _____

_____

■ SEEING AND WRITING: Flashback

Look back at your response to the Seeing and Writing exercise on page 242. Do you see any pairs of simple sentences that you could connect with semicolons? Try linking such pairs with semicolons.

C **Forming Compound Sentences with Conjunctive Adverbs**

Another way to combine two simple sentences into one **compound sentence** is with a **conjunctive adverb**. When you use a conjunctive adverb to join two simple sentences, a semicolon always comes *before* the conjunctive adverb, and a comma always comes *after* it.

Some college students receive grants; <u>however</u>, others must take out loans.

Frequently Used Conjunctive Adverbs

also	instead	still
besides	later	subsequently
consequently	meanwhile	then
eventually	moreover	therefore
finally	nevertheless	thus
furthermore	now	
however	otherwise	

Adding a conjunctive adverb makes the connection between ideas in a sentence clearer and more precise than it would be if the ideas were linked with just a semicolon. Different conjunctive adverbs convey different meanings.

■ Some conjunctive adverbs signal addition (*also, besides, furthermore, moreover*).

I have a lot on my mind; <u>also</u>, I have a lot of things to do.

- Some conjunctive adverbs make causal connections *(therefore, consequently, thus)*.

    I have a lot on my mind; <u>therefore</u>, it is hard to concentrate.

- Some conjunctive adverbs indicate contradiction or contrast *(nevertheless, however, still)*.

    I have a lot on my mind; <u>still</u>, I must try to relax.

- Some conjunctive adverbs present alternatives *(instead, otherwise)*.

    I have a lot on my mind; <u>otherwise</u>, I could relax.
    I will try not to think; <u>instead</u>, I will relax.

- Some conjunctive adverbs indicate time sequence *(eventually, finally, later, meanwhile, now, subsequently, then)*.

    I have a lot on my mind; <u>meanwhile</u>, I still have work to do.

FOCUS **Transitional Expressions**

Transitional expressions can also link two simple sentences into one compound sentence.

He had a miserable time at the party; <u>in addition</u>, he drank too much.

The transitional expression is preceded by a semicolon and followed by a comma. *Note:* Do not forget to place a semicolon before every conjunctive adverb or transitional expression that joins two sentences. If you leave out the semicolon, you create a run-on sentence. (See 21B.)

Frequently Used Transitional Expressions

after all	in comparison
as a result	in contrast
at the same time	in fact
for example	in other words
for instance	of course
in addition	on the contrary

◆ PRACTICE 16-7

ON THE WEB
*For more
practice, visit
Exercise Central:*
www.bedford
stmartins.com/
writingincontext

Add semicolons and commas where required to set off conjunctive adverbs or transitional expressions that join two simple sentences.

> **Example:**   Ketchup is a popular condiment $\overset{;}{\underset{\wedge}{}}$ therefore $\overset{,}{\underset{\wedge}{}}$ it is available in almost every restaurant.

(1) Andrew F. Smith, a food historian, wrote a book about the tomato subsequently he wrote a book about ketchup. (2) The book, *Pure Ketchup,* was a big project in fact Smith worked on it for five years. (3) The word *ketchup* may have come from a Chinese word however Smith is not certain of the word's origins. (4) Ketchup has existed since ancient times in other words it is a very old product. (5) Ketchup has changed a lot over the years for example special dyes were developed in the nineteenth century to make it red. (6) Smith discusses many other changes for instance preservative-free ketchup was invented in 1907. (7) Ketchup is now used by people in many cultures still salsa is more popular than ketchup in the United States. (8) Today, designer ketchups are being developed meanwhile Heinz has introduced green and purple ketchup in squeeze bottles. (9) Some of today's ketchups are chunky in addition some ketchups are spicy. (10) Ketchup continues to evolve however Smith is now working on a book about the history of popcorn.

◆ PRACTICE 16-8

Consulting the list of conjunctive adverbs on page 250 and the list of transitional expressions on page 251, choose a word or expression that logically connects each pair of simple sentences below into one compound sentence. Be sure to punctuate appropriately.

> **Example:**   Every year since 1927, *Time* has designated a Man of the Year. $\overset{; \textit{however, the}}{\underset{\wedge}{\text{Year}_{/} \cancel{\text{The}} \text{ Man}}}$ of the Year has not always been a man.

(1) *Time* selects the Man of the Year to honor the person who has most influenced the previous year's events. The choice is often a prominent

politician. (2) In the 1920s and 1930s, world leaders were often chosen. Franklin Delano Roosevelt was chosen twice and Ethiopia's Haile Selassie once. (3) During the war years, Hitler, Stalin, Churchill, and Roosevelt were all chosen. Stalin was featured twice. (4) Occasionally, the Man of the Year was not an individual. In 1950, it was The American Fighting Man. (5) In 1956, The Hungarian Freedom Fighter was Man of the Year. In 1966, *Time* editors chose The Young Generation. (6) Only a few individual women have been selected. Queen Elizabeth II of England was featured in 1952 and Corazon Aquino, president of the Philippines, in 1986. (7) In 1975, American Women were honored as a group. The Man of the Year has nearly always been male. (8) Very few people of color have been designated Man of the Year. Martin Luther King Jr. was honored in 1963. (9) The Man of the Year has almost always been one or more human beings. The Computer was selected in 1982 and Endangered Earth in 1988. (10) More recently, prominent politicians have once again been chosen. In 2001, New York City mayor Rudy Giuliani was *Time*'s Man of the Year (now called Person of the Year).

◆ PRACTICE 16-9

Add the suggested conjunctive adverb or transitional expression to each of the following simple sentences. Then, add a new independent clause to follow it. Be sure to punctuate correctly.

Example: (however) Commuting students frequently miss out on the freedom of living on campus.

Students who commute to school frequently feel that they are missing

out on the freedom of living on campus; however, there are a lot of advan-

tages to being a commuter.

1. (in contrast) Living at home gives students access to free home-cooked meals.

    _____

    _____

2. (on the other hand) Commuters with cars have a wider choice of jobs.

_____

_____

3. (however) Commuters get to take part in family life.

_____

_____

4. (nonetheless) Commuters have a number of advantages over dorm residents.

_____

_____

5. (in fact) At most colleges, commuters have access to social activities such as dances, clubs, and games.

_____

_____

_____

6. (for instance) Unlike dorm students, most commuters have regular family responsibilities.

_____

_____

7. (for example) Commuter students might have to help take care of younger or older family members.

_____

_____

_____

8. (consequently) Commuters might have to pay rent to live at home.

_____

_____

9. (moreover) Commuters are always under the watchful eye of their parents.

_____

_____

10. (therefore) There are pros and cons to being a commuter.

_____

_____

◆ PRACTICE 16-10

Using the specified topics and conjunctive adverbs or transitional expressions, create five compound sentences on a separate sheet of paper. Be sure to punctuate appropriately.

Example:
Topic: fad diets
Transitional expression: for example

People are always falling for fad diets; for example, some people eat only pineapple to lose weight.

1. *Topic:* laws to protect people with disabilities
   Transitional expression: in addition

2. *Topic:* single men and women as adoptive parents
   Conjunctive adverb: however

3. *Topic:* prayer in public schools
   Conjunctive adverb: therefore

4. *Topic:* high school proms
   Conjunctive adverb: also

5. *Topic:* course requirements at your school
   Conjunctive adverb: instead

■ SEEING AND WRITING: Flashback

Look back at your response to the Seeing and Writing exercise on page 242. Have you used any conjunctive adverbs or transitional expressions to link sentences? If so, check to make sure that you have punctuated them correctly. Then, check to see that you have used the word or expression that best shows the relationship between the ideas in the two sentences. Revise your work if necessary.

■ SEEING AND WRITING: Revising and Editing

Look back at your response to the Seeing and Writing exercise on page 242. Now, try to incorporate one of the new compound sentences you created in the Flashback exercises on pages 247 and 250. Then, check each compound sentence to make sure you have used the coordinating conjunction, conjunctive adverb, or transitional expression that best conveys your meaning and that you have punctuated these sentences correctly. When you have finished, look over a piece of writing you have done in response to another assignment, and try combining some simple sentences into compound sentences.

CHAPTER REVIEW

◆ EDITING PRACTICE

Read the following student essay. Then, create compound sentences by linking pairs of simple sentences where appropriate with a coordinating conjunction, a semicolon, or a semicolon followed by either a conjunctive adverb or a transitional expression. Remember to put commas before coordinating conjunctions and to use semicolons and commas correctly with conjunctive adverbs and transitional expressions. The first two sentences have been combined for you.

My Father's Life

My grandparents were born in Ukraine, *but they* ~~They~~ raised my father in western Pennsylvania. The ninth of their ten children, he had a life I cannot begin to imagine. To me, he is my big, strong, powerful Daddy. In reality, he is a child of poverty.

My grandfather worked for the American Car Foundry. The family lived in a company house. They shopped at the company store. In 1934, my grandfather was laid off. He went to work digging sewer lines for the government. At that time, the family was on relief. Every week, they were entitled to get food rations. My father would go to pick up the food. They desperately needed the prunes, beans, flour, margarine, and other things.

For years, my father wore his brothers' hand-me-down clothes. He wore thrift-shop shoes with cardboard over the holes in the soles. He was often hungry. He would sometimes sit by the side of the railroad tracks, waiting for the engineer to throw him an orange. My father would do any job to earn a quarter. Once, for example, he weeded a mile-long row of tomato plants. For this work, he was paid twenty-five cents and a pack of Necco wafers.

My father saved his pennies. Eventually, he was able to buy a used bicycle for two dollars. He dropped out of school at fourteen and got a job. The family badly needed his income. He woke up every day at 4 a.m. He rode his bike to his job at a meatpacking plant. He worked for fifty cents a day.

In 1943, at the age of seventeen, my father joined the U.S. Navy. He discovered a new world. For the first time in his life, he had enough to eat. He was always first in line at the mess hall. He went back for seconds and thirds before anyone else. After the war ended in 1945, he was discharged from the Navy. He went to work in a meat market in New York City. The only trade he knew was the meat business. Three years later, he had saved enough to open his own store, Pete's Quality Meats.

16 C

◆ COLLABORATIVE ACTIVITIES

1. Working in a small group, pair each of the simple sentences in the left-hand column that follows with a sentence in the right-hand column to create ten compound sentences. Use as many different coordinating conjunctions as you can to connect ideas. Be sure each coordinating conjunction you choose conveys a logical relationship between ideas, and remember to put a comma before each one. You may use some of the listed sentences more than once. *Note:* Many different combinations—some serious and factually accurate, some humorous—are possible.

Some dogs wear little sweaters.	Many are named Hamlet.
Pit bulls are raised to fight.	They live in groups.
Bonobos are pygmy chimpanzees.	One even sings Christmas carols.
	They can wear bandanas.
Many people fear Dobermans.	They can play Frisbee.
Leopards have spots.	Many live in equatorial Zaire.
Dalmations can live in firehouses.	Some people think they are gentle.
Horses can wear blankets.	They don't get cold in winter.
All mules are sterile.	They are half horse and half donkey.
Great Danes are huge dogs.	
Parrots can often speak.	They can be unpredictable.

2. Work in a group of three or four students to create a cast of five characters for a movie, a television pilot, or a music video. Working individually, write five descriptive short sentences—one about each character. Then, exchange papers with another student. Add a coordinating conjunction to each sentence on the list, and create five new compound sentences.

Example

ORIGINAL SENTENCE   Mark is a handsome heartthrob.

NEW SENTENCE   Mark is a handsome heartthrob, but he has green dreadlocks.

Next, select the three characters who sound most interesting. Write additional descriptive sentences about those characters, using compound sentences whenever possible. Your new sentences can provide information about the characters' relationships with one another as well as about their personalities and physical traits.

Writing Complex Sentences

PREVIEW

In this chapter, you will learn
- to identify independent and dependent clauses (17A)
- to use subordinating conjunctions to form complex sentences (17B)
- to use relative pronouns to form complex sentences (17C)

Word Power

courtesy
polite behavior

infringe
(use with *on* or
upon) to go
beyond the
limits of

offend
to cause anger
or resentment

■ SEEING AND WRITING

Look at the picture above. Then, describe something that you believe needs to be changed—for example, a rule, a law, a policy, a situation, or a custom. First, identify what you think needs to be changed; then, explain why you think a change is necessary.

A   Identifying Independent and Dependent Clauses

A **clause** is a group of words that contains a subject and a verb. An **independent clause** can stand alone as a sentence. In this case, it is a **simple sentence**.

INDEPENDENT   The <u>exhibit</u> <u>was</u> controversial.
CLAUSE

A **dependent clause** cannot stand alone as a sentence because it needs other words to complete its meaning.

INCORRECT   Because the exhibit was controversial.

What happened because the exhibit was controversial? To answer this question, you need to add an independent clause that completes the idea begun in the dependent clause. The result is a **complex sentence**, a sentence that consists of one independent clause along with one or more dependent clauses.

————————— DEPENDENT CLAUSE ————————— ———— INDEPENDENT CLAUSE ————

Because the exhibit was controversial, many people came to see the paintings.

◆ PRACTICE 17-1

In the blank following each of the items below, indicate whether the group of words is an independent clause (*IC*) or a dependent clause (*DC*).

Example: Gymnastics became popular in the United States in the twentieth century. _*IC*_

1. Gymnastics exercises help develop all parts of the body. _____

2. The practice of gymnastics dates back to the athletes of ancient Greece. _____

3. Because a German named Frederick Jahn popularized gymnastics in the nineteenth century. _____

4. Although German immigrants to the United States engaged in gymnastics. _____

5. Gymnastics later became an event in the Olympic games. _____

6. Even though women's gymnastics once focused on physical grace rather than strength. _____

7. In the 1970s, women Olympic gymnasts began to dominate the games. _____

8. When Mary Lou Retton became the first American woman to win a gold medal for gymnastics in 1984. _____

9. Who was only sixteen years old at the time of her gold-medal win. _____

10. The first U.S. women's gymnastics team to win a gold medal competed in the 1996 games. _____

◆ PRACTICE 17-2

In the blank following each of the items below, indicate whether the group of words is an independent clause (*IC*) or a dependent clause (*DC*).

Example: When novelist Toni Morrison was born in Ohio in 1931. _DC_

1. As a young reader, Toni Morrison admired the classic Russian novelists. _____

2. After she graduated from Howard University with a bachelor's degree in English. _____

3. Morrison based her novel *The Bluest Eye* on a childhood friend's prayers to God for blue eyes. _____

4. While she raised two sons as a single mother and worked as an editor at Random House. _____

5. As her reputation as a novelist grew with the publication of *Song of Solomon* and *Tar Baby*. _____

6. Her picture appeared on the cover of Newsweek in 1981. _____

7. Before her novel *Beloved* won the 1988 Pulitzer Prize for fiction. _____

8. *Beloved* was later made into a film starring Oprah Winfrey. _____

9. In 1993, Morrison became the first black woman to win the Nobel Prize in literature. _____

10. Who published the novel *Paradise* in 1998 to mixed reviews. _____

<table>
<tr><td>**B**</td><td>**Forming Complex Sentences with Subordinating Conjunctions**</td></tr>
</table>

Subordinating conjunctions—words like *although* and *because*—can be used to join two simple sentences (independent clauses) by making one sentence a dependent clause. The result is a **complex sentence** in which the subordinating conjunction indicates the relationship between the ideas in the two clauses it links.

TWO SENTENCES	He was stripped of his title for refusing to be inducted into the army. Many people consider Muhammad Ali a hero.
COMPLEX SENTENCE	<u>Although he was stripped of his title for refusing to be inducted into the army</u>, many people consider Muhammad Ali a hero.

Frequently Used Subordinating Conjunctions

after	even though	since	whenever
although	if	so that	where
as	if only	than	whereas
as if	in order that	that	wherever
as though	now that	though	whether
because	once	unless	while
before	provided that	until	
even if	rather than	when	

Note: A clause introduced by a subordinating conjunction does not express a complete thought. Used by itself, it is a sentence fragment. See 22D.

Different subordinating conjunctions express different relationships between dependent and independent clauses.

Relationship between clauses	Subordinating conjunction	Example
Time	after, before, since, until, when, whenever, while	<u>When the whale surfaced</u>, Ahab threw his harpoon.
Reason or cause	as, because	Scientists scaled back the project <u>because the government cut funds</u>.

Relationship between clauses	Subordinating conjunction	Example
Result or effect	in order that, so that	So that students' math scores will improve, many schools have instituted special programs.
Condition	even if, if, unless	The rain forest could disappear unless steps are taken immediately.
Contrast	although, even though, though	Although Thomas Edison had almost no formal education, he was a productive inventor.
Location	where, wherever	Pittsburgh was built where the Allegheny and Monongahela Rivers meet.

FOCUS   **Punctuating with Subordinating Conjunctions**

Place a comma after the dependent clause when it comes *before* the independent clause in the sentence. Do not use a comma when the dependent clause comes *after* the independent clause in the sentence.

┌──────── DEPENDENT CLAUSE ────────┐ ┌──── INDEPENDENT CLAUSE ────┐
Although she wore the scarlet letter, Hester carried herself
proudly.

┌──────── INDEPENDENT CLAUSE ────────┐ ┌──── DEPENDENT CLAUSE ────┐
Hester carried herself proudly although she wore the scarlet
letter.

◆ **PRACTICE 17-3**

Write an appropriate subordinating conjunction in each blank in the sentences on page 264. Look at the list of subordinating conjunctions on page 262 to make sure you choose a conjunction that establishes a logical relationship between the two clauses it links. (The required punctuation has been provided.)

ON THE WEB
For more practice, visit Exercise Central: www.bedford stmartins.com/ writingincontext

Example: The World Wrestling Federation (WWF) is an empire of live events, pay-per-view matches, magazines, and Web sites _____*that*_____ presents the most famous wrestlers in the world.

(1) _____ wrestlers enter the ring, they are accompanied by bursts of flame, lightning, or the sound of a motorcycle engine. (2) _____ the fans roar in approval, Stone Cold Steve Austin may throw a chair. (3) _____ Ron Van Damme (RVD) may manage to do a full body slam on Chris Jericho, the match isn't over. (4) It doesn't end _____ the referee counts to three. (5) _____ Jericho lifts one shoulder from the floor before the final count, the match must go on. (6) _____ a match is over, the action shifts to the locker room. (7) _____ they do not wrestle themselves, the wrestlers' girlfriends play an important role in the WWF. (8) _____ the match begins, they pump up their men by serving them cookies and urging them to show no mercy in the ring. (9) These women go _____ they must to distract their man's opponents. (10) For most WWF fans, the fun does not end _____ the last match is finished.

◆ PRACTICE 17-4

Form one complex sentence by combining each of the following pairs of sentences. Use a subordinating conjunction from the list on page 262 to clarify the relationship between the dependent and independent clauses in each sentence. Make sure you include a comma where one is required.

Example: Orville and Wilbur Wright built the first powered plane/
although they
~~They~~ had no formal training as engineers.

1. Professional midwives are used widely in Europe. In the United States, they usually practice independently only in areas with few doctors.

2. John Deere constructed his first steel plow in 1837. A new era began in prairie agriculture.

3. Stephen Crane powerfully describes battles in *The Red Badge of Courage*. He never experienced a war.

4. Elvis Presley died suddenly in 1977. Thousands of his fans gathered in front of his mansion.

5. Jonas Salk developed the first polio vaccine in the 1950s. The incidence of polio began to decline rapidly in the United States.

6. The salaries of baseball players rose dramatically in the 1980s. Some sportswriters predicted a drop in attendance.

7. The Du Ponts arrived from France in 1800. American gunpowder was inferior to French gunpowder.

8. Margaret Sanger opened her first birth-control clinic in America in 1916. She was arrested and sentenced to thirty days in jail.

9. Thaddeus Stevens thought plantation land should be distributed to freed slaves. He disagreed with Lincoln's peace terms for the South.

10. Steven Spielberg directed some of the most popular movies of all time. He did not win an Academy Award until *Schindler's List*.

■ SEEING AND WRITING: Flashback

Look back at your response to the Seeing and Writing exercise on page 259. Identify two pairs of simple sentences that could be combined with subordinating conjunctions. On a separate sheet of paper, combine each pair into a complex sentence by making one sentence a dependent clause. Check to make sure you have punctuated your new sentences correctly.

C **Forming Complex Sentences with Relative Pronouns**

A **relative pronoun** (*who, that, which,* and so on) introduces a **dependent clause** that describes a noun or pronoun in the sentence.

Note: A clause introduced by a relative pronoun does not express a complete thought. Used by itself, it is a sentence fragment. See 22D.

Relative Pronouns

that	which	whoever	whomever
what	who	whom	whose

Relative pronouns can also join two simple sentences (independent clauses) to make a complex sentence. The relative pronoun shows the relationship between the ideas in the two sentences that it links.

TWO SENTENCES   Nadine Gordimer comes from South Africa. She won the Nobel Prize in literature in 1991.

COMPLEX SENTENCE   Nadine Gordimer, who won the Nobel Prize in literature in 1991, comes from South Africa.

TWO SENTENCES   Last week I had a job interview. It went very well.

COMPLEX SENTENCE   Last week I had a job interview that went very well.

TWO SENTENCES   Transistors have replaced vacuum tubes in radios and televisions. They were invented in 1948.

COMPLEX SENTENCE   Transistors, which were invented in 1948, have replaced vacuum tubes in radios and televisions.

Note: Who refers to people; *that* and *which* refer to things.

FOCUS   **Punctuating with Relative Pronouns**

In general, commas are used to set off a dependent clause introduced by *which.* Commas are not used to set off a dependent clause introduced by *that.* Depending on its meaning in a sentence, a dependent clause introduced by *who* is sometimes but not always set off by commas.

ON THE WEB
For more practice, visit Exercise Central: www.bedford stmartins.com/ writingincontext

◆ PRACTICE 17-5

Combine each of the following pairs of simple sentences into one complex sentence, using the relative pronoun that follows each pair.

Example: The United States is frightening to many Japanese. It is seen as a violent country. (which)

The United States, which is seen as a violent country, is frightening to

many Japanese.

1. Most Japanese learn English in high school by reading passages from text-books. The textbooks are designed to get them into universities. (that)

_____

_____

2. The English they learn is of little use in the real world. It is not enough to protect them from street hustlers. (which)

_____

_____

3. Some Japanese have been killed or injured in the United States. They could not understand spoken English. (who)

_____

_____

4. For example, a sixteen-year-old Japanese exchange student was shot. He did not understand the command *freeze*. (who)

_____

_____

5. This case has led many Japanese to learn "usable English." It will help them when they travel to the United States. (that)

_____

_____

◆ PRACTICE 17-6

Combine each of the following pairs of simple sentences into one complex sentence, using a relative pronoun (*who, which,* or *that*).

Example: MTV made its cable debut in August 1981. It was the first television network devoted to popular music videos.

MTV, which was the first television network devoted to popular music

videos, made its cable debut in August 1981.

1. MTV's very first music video was performed by a group called the Buggles. It made the claim "Video Killed the Radio Star."

   _____

   _____

2. Most of MTV's early videos were fairly simple productions. They basically recorded the artists in live or studio performances.

   _____

   _____

3. Recording executives soon realized the power of music videos in selling records. They had been suspicious of MTV at first.

   _____

   _____

4. Music videos became highly elaborate productions. They featured multiple settings, special effects, and large casts of dancers.

   _____

   _____

5. Today, MTV devotes less and less time to music videos. It produces many hours of original programming aimed at young people.

   _____

   _____

◆ PRACTICE 17-7

Fill in the blanks in the sentences that follow with a dependent clause that begins with a relative pronoun (*who, which,* or *that*). The new dependent clause should help complete the meaning of the original sentence.

> **Example:**   People _who are talking on cell phones_ may not be paying close attention to their driving.

1. People _____

   should have their driver's licenses revoked.

2. A speeding car is like a weapon _____.

3. Teenagers _____

   could be required to take driver's education first.

4. New drivers should be taught safety tips _____.

5. One activity _____

   is eating while one is driving.

6. A driver _____

   cannot possibly keep both hands on the steering wheel.

7. Putting on makeup while driving is another activity _____

   _____.

8. To encourage safe driving, the police should be allowed to pull over

   any driver _____.

9. For a first offense, a driver _____

   could be given only a warning.

10. A second offense, however, would result in a fine _____

    _____.

■ SEEING AND WRITING: Flashback

Look back at your response to the Seeing and Writing exercise on page
259. Identify two simple sentences that could be combined with a
relative pronoun. (If you cannot find two appropriate sentences, write
two new ones.) On a separate sheet of paper, write the new complex
sentence.

■ SEEING AND WRITING: Revising and Editing

Look back at your response to the Seeing and Writing exercise on page
259. Incorporating one of the new complex sentences you created in the
Flashback exercises on page 265 and above, revise your work. Then,
check to make sure there are no errors in your use of subordinating conjunctions and relative pronouns. When you have finished, look over a
piece of writing you have done in response to another assignment, and
try combining some simple sentences into complex sentences.

17 C

CHAPTER REVIEW

◆ EDITING PRACTICE

Read the following student essay. Then, revise it by combining pairs of simple sentences with subordinating conjunctions or relative pronouns that indicate the relationship between them. Be sure to punctuate correctly. The first sentence has been revised for you.

My Life in Haiti

My father and mother lived in Haiti, *although* I was born in the United States. My father and his brother opened a small business in Haiti. I was a baby. I grew up in Haiti. I experienced the culture as a native, not a foreigner. My friends were all Haitian. They wanted only to play soccer. I tried to teach them baseball and football. Before I learned to speak English, I spoke only the Haitian Creole dialect. I was a toddler. I went to New York to visit my grandmother. One day, I was thirsty. I asked her in Creole for a glass of water. At the same time, I pointed to the refrigerator. My grandmother had no idea what I meant. She spoke only English. I finally had to point to a glass so she would know what I wanted.

In Haiti, I developed close relationships with the neighbors. They lived on our street. They never shut their doors. I was constantly walking in and out of their houses. Whenever I opened my mouth, one of them fed me some candy or a bowl of curried goat stew. Dina was an elderly Cuban woman. She was like a grandmother to me. She encouraged me to eat. She thought I was too skinny. Lita, another neighbor, was an excellent storyteller. She would tell my

friends and me tales of voodoo. We were afraid to walk
home. Her stories terrified us. We could not wait to hear
more.

    When I was twelve, my life in Haiti ended. My father
died of cancer. He had been sick for a year. My mother and
I could have stayed in Haiti. She decided to return to her
parents in New York. She sold her share of the business to
my uncle. We needed the money. Sometimes, my mind wanders
back to those days. My life in Haiti is over. I will never
forget the people I knew and loved there.

◆ COLLABORATIVE ACTIVITIES

1. Working in a group of four students, make a list of three or four of your
   favorite television shows. Divide into pairs, and with your partner, write
   two simple sentences describing each show. Next, use subordinating
   conjunctions or relative pronouns to combine each pair of sentences
   into one complex sentence. With your group, discuss how the ideas
   in each complex sentence are related, and make sure you have used the
   subordinating conjunction or relative pronoun that best conveys this
   relationship.

   > EXAMPLE: *The Brady Bunch* portrays a 1970s family. It still appeals to
   >   many viewers.
   >
   >   Although *The Brady Bunch* portrays a 1970s family, it still
   >   appeals to many viewers.

2. Imagine that you and the members of your group live in a neighborhood
   where workers are repairing underground power lines. As they work, the
   workers talk loudly and use foul language. Write a letter of complaint to
   the power company in which you explain that the workers' behavior is
   offensive to you and to your children. Tell the company that you want the
   offensive behavior to end. Write the first draft of your letter in simple sentences. After you have written this draft, work as a group to combine as
   many sentences as you can with subordinating conjunctions and relative
   pronouns.

3. Assume you are in a competition to determine which collaborative group
   in your class is best at writing complex sentences. Working in a group, prepare a letter to your instructor in which you present the strengths of your

group. Be sure to use a subordinating conjunction or relative pronoun in each of the sentences in your letter. Finally, as a class, evaluate the letters from the groups and choose the letter that most successfully convinces you that its group is best.

Achieving Sentence Variety

PREVIEW

In this chapter, you will learn
- to vary sentence types (18A)
- to vary sentence openings (18B)
- to combine sentences (18C)
- to vary sentence length (18D)

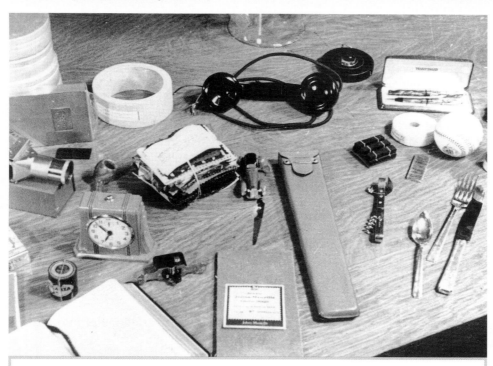

Word Power
capsule
a sealed container

memorabilia
things worthy of remembering

nostalgia
a longing for people or things that are no longer present

■ SEEING AND WRITING

Plan a time capsule that your children will open when they are adults. What items would you include? How would you expect each item to communicate to your children what you and your world were like? Look at the picture above, and then explain your decisions.

273

In Chapters 15 through 17, you learned to write simple, compound, and complex sentences. Now, you are ready to learn how to create more varied sentences. A passage of varied sentences flows more smoothly, is easier to read and understand, and is more interesting than one in which all the sentences are the same length and begin with the subject.

A   Varying Sentence Types

Most English sentences are **statements**. Others are **questions** or **exclamations**. One way to vary your sentences is to use an occasional question or exclamation where it is appropriate. *Note:* A statement ends with a period, a question ends with a question mark, and an exclamation ends with an exclamation point.

In the following paragraph, a question and an exclamation add variety.

Question

Exclamation

> In less than twenty years, the image of African Americans in television sitcoms seemed to change dramatically, reflecting the changing status of black men and women in American society. But had anything really changed? In *Beulah,* the 1950 sitcom that was the first to star an African-American woman, the title character was a maid. Her friends were portrayed as irresponsible and not very smart. *Amos 'n' Andy,* which also appeared in the 1950s, continued these negative stereotypes of black characters. In 1968, with the civil rights movement at its height, the NBC comedy hit *Julia* portrayed a black woman in a much more favorable light. A widowed nurse, raising a small boy on her own, Julia was a dedicated professional and a patient and devoted mother. The image of the African American was certainly more positive, but the character was no more balanced or three-dimensional than earlier black characters had been. Julia was not an object of ridicule; instead, she was a saint!

◆ PRACTICE 18-1

Revise the following passage by changing one of the statements into a question and one of the statements into an exclamation.

Example: Some people pursue two different careers at the same time. (statement)

Why do some people pursue two different careers at the same time? (question)

(1) Many working people have more than one job. (2) For example, a police officer might moonlight as a security guard, and a writer might also

teach. (3) These workers need their second jobs for survival. (4) In recent years, some professionals have decided to begin a second career without abandoning the first one. (5) The second career may seem very different from the first. (6) For example, a teacher might also work as a model. (7) Sometimes, however, the two careers have something in common. (8) For example, both teaching and modeling involve performing for an audience. (9) Similarly, a lawyer may be drawn to the ministry, another career dedicated to justice. (10) Many things motivate people to combine two seemingly different professions. (11) Those who do so are looking for professional satisfaction. (12) Obviously, these workers are very lucky people.

■ SEEING AND WRITING: Flashback

Look back at your response to the Seeing and Writing exercise on page 273. What questions does your writing answer? If you can, add one of these questions. (You may need to substitute it for a sentence that is already there.)

Now, try to think of an exclamation that would be an appropriate addition to your writing. Where could you add this exclamation? (Note that exclamations are widely used in informal, personal writing and in dialogue, but they are not often used in college writing.)

B Varying Sentence Openings

Varying the way you begin your sentences is another way of adding life to your writing. If you always begin your sentences with the subject, your writing is likely to seem dull and repetitive, as the writing in the paragraph below does.

> Scientists have been observing a disturbing phenomenon. The population of frogs, toads, and salamanders has been declining. This decline was first noticed in the mid-1980s. Some reports blamed chemical pollution. Some biologists began to suspect that a fungal disease was killing these amphibians. The most reasonable explanation seems to be that the amphibians' eggs are threatened by solar radiation. This radiation penetrates the thinned ozone layer, which used to shield them from the sun's rays.

COMPUTER TIP

To help you revise, use the Search or Find command to locate every use of *The, This,* and *It* at the beginning of a sentence.

Beginning with Adverbs

For more on adverbs, see Chapter 29.

Instead of opening every sentence with the subject, try beginning with one or more **adverbs**, as the following paragraph illustrates. (Always place a comma after an adverb, including a conjunctive adverb like *however,* when it opens a sentence.)

> Scientists have been observing a disturbing phenomenon. <u>Gradually but steadily</u>, the population of frogs, toads, and salamanders has been declining. This decline was first noticed in the mid-1980s. Some reports blamed chemical pollution. Some biologists began to suspect that a fungal disease was killing these amphibians. <u>However,</u> the most reasonable explanation seems to be that the amphibians' eggs are threatened by solar radiation. This radiation penetrates the thinned ozone layer, which used to shield them from the sun's rays.

Beginning with Prepositional Phrases

For more on prepositions, see 15B.

You can also begin some sentences with prepositional phrases. A **prepositional phrase** (such as *along the river* or *near the diner*) is made up of a preposition and its object. In general, place a comma after a prepositional phrase that opens a sentence. However, if an introductory prepositional phrase has fewer than three words, you can omit the comma.

> <u>In recent years</u>, scientists have been observing a disturbing phenomenon. Gradually but steadily, the population of frogs, toads, and salamanders has been declining. This decline was first noticed in the mid-1980s. <u>At first</u>, some reports blamed chemical pollution. <u>After a while</u>, some biologists began to suspect that a fungal disease was killing these amphibians. However, the most reasonable explanation seems to be that the amphibians' eggs are threatened by solar radiation. This radiation penetrates the thinned ozone layer, which used to shield them from the sun's rays.

FOCUS   **Sentence Openings**

Note that in addition to adding variety, adverbs and prepositional phrases at the beginnings of sentences can also function as transitions, joining the sentences smoothly into a paragraph. (See 2D.)

◆ PRACTICE 18-2

Underline the adverb in each of the following sentences, and then, on a separate piece of paper, rewrite the sentence so that the adverb appears at the beginning. Be sure to punctuate correctly.

ON THE WEB
For more practice, visit Exercise Central: www.bedford stmartins.com/ writingincontext

> **Example:** Applicants <u>often</u> become nervous when being interviewed for a job.
>
> *Often, applicants become nervous when being interviewed for a job.*

1. Applicants sometimes feel tongue-tied or even ill when asked questions.
2. There are, however, strategies that can control jitters during job interviews.
3. Applicants should realize first that interviewers expect nervousness.
4. They should then understand that one mistake does not ruin the interview.
5. Job applicants must ultimately trust their own abilities during interviews.

◆ PRACTICE 18-3

In each of the following sentences, fill in the blank with an appropriate adverb. Be sure to punctuate correctly.

> **Example:** ___*Slowly,*___ the sun crept over the horizon.

1. _____ the speeding car appeared from out of nowhere.
2. _____ it crashed into the guard rail.
3. _____ the car jackknifed across the highway.
4. _____ drivers behind the crashed car braked sharply.
5. _____ someone used a cell phone to call 911.
6. _____ a wailing siren could be heard.
7. _____ the ambulance arrived.
8. _____ emergency medical technicians went to work.
9. _____ a police officer was on hand to direct traffic.
10. _____ no one was badly hurt in the accident.

◆ **PRACTICE 18-4**

Underline the prepositional phrase in each of the following sentences, and then rewrite the sentence so that the prepositional phrase appears at the beginning. Be sure to punctuate correctly.

> **Example:** Few American women worked in factories <u>before the 1940s</u>.
>
> *Before the 1940s, few American women worked in factories.*

1. Many male factory workers became soldiers during World War II.

   _____

2. War-related industries faced a labor shortage as a result.

   _____

3. The U.S. government encouraged women to take factory jobs in the war's early years.

   _____

   _____

4. Women met this challenge with great eagerness and patriotic pride.

   _____

5. They entered the industrial workplace in unprecedented numbers.

   _____

◆ **PRACTICE 18-5**

In each of the following sentences, fill in the blank with an appropriate prepositional phrase. Be sure to punctuate correctly.

> **Example:** _By September,_ most college students are back in school.

1. _____ the first year of college can be a difficult experience.

2. _____ students must make many adjustments.

3. _____ they face a new and unfamiliar environment.

4. _____ they must learn to work independently.

5. _____ their classes may be large.

6. _____ they may feel lonely and even out of place.

7. _____ balancing a job with college can prove frustrating.

8. _____ being in college has become easier for many students.

9. _____ they are more comfortable in their new environment.

10. _____ they realize that the benefits of college are worth the challenges.

◆ PRACTICE 18-6

Several sentences in the following passage contain prepositional phrases and adverbs that could be moved to the beginnings of sentences. Revise the passage to vary the sentence openings by moving prepositional phrases to the beginnings of three sentences and moving adverbs to the beginnings of two other sentences. Be sure to place a comma after these prepositional phrases and adverbs.

Example: *Before the first day of school, some*
~~Some~~ students already know how to succeed ~~before the first day of school.~~

(1) Why are some college students more successful than others? (2) A study done at Harvard University recently provided some answers to this question and offered suggestions to students who want to get the most out of college. (3) According to the study, students should really get to know at least one professor each semester. (4) If they do this, they will have people to turn to for help when problems arise and will feel more connected to their school. (5) These professors can also write letters of recommendation for them after graduation. (6) Students should also take small classes whenever possible and take interesting electives as well as required courses. (7) The study recommends in addition that students study in groups and that they take courses that require writing, preferably several short papers rather than one long one. (8) Another recommendation is that students take foreign language courses, which are usually small and often require group work.

(9) Students should give themselves a chance to become involved in outside activities throughout their college careers. (10) Students must finally learn to manage their time and to set aside large blocks of time to study.

◆ PRACTICE 18-7

Listed below are two adverbs and four prepositional phrases. In the passage that follows, add each of these words or phrases to the beginning of a sentence in order to vary the sentence openings. Be sure your additions connect ideas clearly and logically. Remember to add commas where they are needed.

Occasionally	Sadly
For example	In fact
With their screams and chants	Of course

Example: ~~Pro~~ football players face great danger.

Sadly, pro

(1) Professional football is one of the most popular sports in the country; it is also one of the most dangerous. (2) Bob Utley and Darryl Stingley are now paraplegics because of injuries they suffered on the field, and the disabled list increases each season.

(3) The league has established new rules to make the game safer, and some of these have cut down on serious injuries. (4) A player cannot tackle a kicker after he has kicked the ball, and a player cannot tackle a quarterback after he has thrown the ball or a runner after he has gone out of bounds. (5) These precautions, however, do not always protect players. (6) Players still tackle other players in violation of the rules because they are angry and frustrated or even as a calculated strategy.

(7) The fans also share the blame for the violence of football. (8) They encourage players to hit harder or play with more intensity. (9) The unfortunate fact is that as football becomes more dangerous to players, it becomes more popular with fans.

■ SEEING AND WRITING: Flashback

Look back at your response to the Seeing and Writing exercise on page 273. Identify one sentence that you could revise by beginning it with an adverb and one that could open with a prepositional phrase. (Note that the adverb or prepositional phrase may already be somewhere in your sentence.) Write the revised sentences on a separate sheet of paper.

C Combining Sentences

For information on forming compound sentences, see Chapter 16. For information on forming complex sentences, see Chapter 17.

You can also create sentence variety by experimenting with different ways of combining sentences. You have already learned to combine simple sentences to create compound sentences (Chapter 16) and complex sentences (Chapter 17). Now, you will learn to combine sentences with *present participles, past participles, compounds,* or *appositives*. These different techniques will help you create varied, interesting sentences.

Using Present Participles

For more on present participles, see 25A.

The **present participle** is the *-ing* form of a verb: *using, carrying.* You can use a present participle to combine two sentences.

TWO SENTENCES Duke Ellington composed more than a thousand songs. He worked hard to establish his reputation as a musician.

COMBINED <u>Composing</u> more than a thousand songs, Duke Ellington worked hard to establish his reputation as a musician. (present participle)

When the sentences are combined, the present participle *(composing)* introduces a phrase that describes the sentence's subject *(Duke Ellington)*.

Using Past Participles

For more on past participles, see 25B; for a list of irregular past participles, see 27B.

Past participles of verbs are usually formed with *-ed (carried)* or *-d (used)*, but there are also many irregular past participle forms *(known, written)*. Two sentences can often be combined when one of them contains a past participle.

TWO SENTENCES Nogales is located on the border between Arizona and Mexico. It is a bilingual city.

COMBINED <u>Located</u> on the border between Arizona and Mexico, Nogales is a bilingual city. (past participle)

When the sentences are combined, the past participle *(located)* introduces a phrase that describes the sentence's subject *(Nogales)*. *Note:* Always place a comma after the phrase introduced by the present or past participle.

◆ PRACTICE 18-8

ON THE WEB
For more practice, visit Exercise Central: www.bedford stmartins.com/ writingincontext

Use a present participle to combine each of the following pairs of sentences into a single sentence. Eliminate any unnecessary words, and use a comma to set off each phrase introduced by a present participle. When you are finished, circle the present participle in each new sentence.

Example: Moviegoers accepted Chaplin enthusiastically. They identified with his characters.

(Accepting) Chaplin enthusiastically, moviegoers identified with his characters.

or

(Identifying) with his characters, moviegoers accepted Chaplin enthusiastically.

1. Charlie Chaplin grew up in the slums of London. He began his acting career in vaudeville shows.

2. Chaplin arrived in Hollywood in 1910. He was soon discovered by film director Mack Sennett.

3. Chaplin added writing and directing to acting. He made his first famous film, *The Tramp*, in 1915.

4. Chaplin wore baggy pants and a sad expression. He introduced his "little tramp" character.

_____

_____

5. Chaplin continued to play the little tramp in other silent films. He starred in *The Kid* (1921) and *The Gold Rush* (1925).

_____

_____

6. Chaplin moved from silent to talking movies. He made *City Lights* in 1931.

_____

_____

7. The little tramp charmed audiences in *City Lights*. He was last seen in *Modern Times* (1936).

_____

_____

8. Chaplin decided to make fun of Hitler. He directed and starred in *The Great Dictator* in 1940.

_____

_____

9. Chaplin departed from Hollywood in the 1950s. He settled in England.

_____

10. Charlie Chaplin died in 1977. He left behind many fans.

_____

◆ PRACTICE 18-9

For each of the first five sentences that follow, fill in the blank with an appropriate present participle modifier. For each of the final five sentences, fill in the blank with an appropriate independent clause. Be sure to punctuate correctly.

Examples: *Selling candy door to door,* _____ the team raised money for new uniforms.

Blasting its siren, *the fire truck raced through the busy streets.*

1. _____ the judge called for order in the courtroom.

2. _____ the miners found silver instead.

3. _____ migrating birds often travel long distances.

4. _____ fans waited patiently to buy tickets for the concert.

5. _____ the child seemed to be frightened.

6. Stepping up to home plate _____

7. Traveling at high speeds _____

8. Broiling in the ninety-degree weather _____

   _____

9. Looking both ways first _____

10. Talking to a group of news reporters _____

    _____

◆ PRACTICE 18-10

Use a past participle to combine each of the following pairs of sentences into a single sentence. Eliminate any unnecessary words, and use a comma to set off each phrase introduced by a past participle. When you are finished, circle the past participle in each new sentence.

Example: Sacajawea was born in about 1787. She lived among her Shoshone tribespeople until the age of eleven.

(Born) in about 1787, Sacajawea lived among her Shoshone tribespeople until the age of eleven.

1. She was captured as a young girl by a rival tribe. Sacajawea was later sold into slavery.

   _____

   _____

2. She was saved by a French Canadian fur trader named Charbonneau. Sacajawea became his wife.

_____

_____

3. The explorers Lewis and Clark hired Charbonneau in 1806. He brought his pregnant wife along on their westward expedition.

_____

_____

4. Sacajawea was skilled in several native languages. She helped Lewis and Clark trade for horses and other goods.

_____

_____

5. The expedition was guided by Sacajawea's knowledge of the rugged terrain. It also benefited from her familiarity with native food plants.

_____

_____

6. Clark's journals were rescued by Sacajawea when the party's boat overturned in whitewater. They would have been lost otherwise.

_____

_____

7. Lewis and Clark were protected by the presence of the Shoshone woman and her infant. They encountered little hostility from the tribes they met.

_____

_____

8. Clark was indebted to Sacajawea for the success of the journey. He wrote afterwards that she deserved much credit.

_____

_____

9. Sacajawea has been celebrated for many years as an American hero. She recently received an additional honor.

_____

_____

10. The U.S. dollar coin now bears her likeness. It was minted in 2000.

_____

◆ **PRACTICE 18-11**

For each of the first five sentences that follow, fill in the blank with an appropriate past participle modifier. For each of the final five sentences, fill in the blank with an appropriate independent clause. Be sure to punctuate correctly.

Examples: *Buried away for many years,* the treasure was discovered by accident.

Advertised as children's books, *the Harry Potter stories also appeal to adults.*

1. _____ the child started crying when the storm began.

2. _____ the hikers rested wearily at the top of the mountain.

3. _____ the small boat almost capsized.

4. _____ the balloons in the Macy's Thanksgiving Day parade soar above the crowds.

5. _____ family stories help families keep their traditions alive.

6. Annoyed by her parents _____

7. Lost in the woods for three days _____

8. Bored by the same old routine _____

9. Confronted with the evidence _____

10. Asked whether they supported the president _____

_____

Using Compound Subjects or Compound Verbs

A **compound subject** consists of two nouns or pronouns, usually joined by
and; a **compound verb** consists of two verbs, usually joined by *and.* You can
use a compound subject or a compound verb to combine two sentences.

TWO SENTENCES Elijah McCoy was an African-American inventor. Garrett Morgan was also an African-American inventor.

COMBINED <u>Elijah McCoy and Garrett Morgan</u> were African-
American inventors. (compound subject)

TWO SENTENCES Arundhati Roy's first novel, *The God of Small Things,*
appeared in 1997. It won the Pulitzer Prize.

COMBINED Arundhati Roy's first novel, *The God of Small Things,*
<u>appeared</u> in 1997 <u>and won</u> the Pulitzer Prize.

◆ PRACTICE 18-12

Creating a compound subject, combine each of the following pairs of sentences into a single sentence.

Example: The Magic Kingdom ~~is a popular Florida theme park.~~ Islands
    and ... *are*
of Adventure ~~is also a~~ popular Florida theme ~~park.~~ *parks*

ON THE WEB
*For more
practice, visit
Exercise Central:*
**www.bedford
stmartins.com/
writingincontext**

1. American tourists flock to Orlando's theme parks. Foreign visitors also
flock to Orlando's theme parks.

2. Dueling Dragons is a roller coaster at Islands of Adventure. The Incredible
Hulk is also a roller coaster there.

3. At the Magic Kingdom, the roller coaster Space Mountain draws large
crowds. The Pirates of the Caribbean ride draws large crowds as well.

4. Costumed characters appear throughout the park. Colorful street performers also appear throughout the park.

5. Children enjoy having their pictures taken with Mickey Mouse. Adults enjoy having their pictures taken with Mickey.

◆ PRACTICE 18-13

Creating a compound verb, combine each of the following pairs of sentences into a single sentence.

Example: The inventor Thomas Edison left school at an early age/ ~~He~~ *and* first made his living selling newspapers.

1. Despite his lack of formal education, Edison had a quick mind. He also showed a talent for problem solving.

2. His early work as a telegraph operator stimulated his interest in electricity. It also led him to experiment with inventions.

3. Edison patented the earliest phonograph in 1878. He created the first practical light bulb the following year.

4. Edison later developed an electric railroad. He also produced one of the first batteries to store long-term power.

5. Edison held many patents. He made a fortune from his inventions.

◆ PRACTICE 18-14

Combine each of the following pairs of sentences into one sentence by creating a compound subject or a compound verb. Remember that a compound subject is plural.

Example: The NCAA Presidents Commission wants to reform college athletic programs/ ~~It~~ *and* recommends a number of measures for doing so. (compound verb)

(1) These college presidents want to improve the academic performance of college athletes. Their supporters also want to improve the academic performance of college athletes. (2) Their first proposal raises the number

of required core courses for entering freshmen. It increases the SAT scores necessary for admission. (3) A second proposal requires athletes to earn a certain number of credits every year. It mandates a minimum grade point average for them. (4) Many athletic directors see the changes as unfair. They are resisting them. (5) Many Big East coaches believe standardized test scores are biased. They want their use in screening student athletes banned. (6) Some coaches also fear that the new rules will force many athletes to choose easy majors. Other opponents of these requirements fear the same thing. (7) According to supporters, however, many athletes under the current system fail to advance academically. They often finish their eligibility fifty or more hours short of graduation. (8) The new rules, they say, give student athletes a fair chance. They also keep them on the graduation track. (9) In the supporters' view, poor supervision by athletic directors is to be blamed for the poor performance of student athletes. Lack of support for academic excellence is also to blame.

Using Appositives

An **appositive** is a word or word group that identifies or renames a noun or pronoun. Using an appositive is often a good way to combine two sentences about the same subject. (When you combine sentences with an appositive, set off the appositive with commas.)

TWO SENTENCES C. J. Walker was the first American woman to become a self-made millionaire. She marketed a line of hair-care products for black women.

COMBINED C. J. Walker, the first American woman to become a self-made millionaire, marketed a line of hair-care products for black women. (appositive)

Notice that in addition to appearing in the middle of a sentence, an appositive can also come at the beginning or at the end of a sentence.

The first American woman to become a self-made millionaire, C. J. Walker marketed a line of hair-care products for black women.

Several books have been written about C. J. Walker, the first American woman to become a self-made millionaire.

18 C

◆ PRACTICE 18-15

ON THE WEB
*For more
practice, visit
Exercise Central:*
www.bedford
stmartins.com/
writingincontext

Use appositives to combine each of the following pairs of sentences into one sentence. Note that the appositive may appear at the beginning, in the middle, or at the end of the sentence. Be sure to use commas appropriately.

Example: Lorraine Hansberry's *A Raisin in the Sun* ~~was~~, one of the first American plays to focus on the experiences of African Americans, ~~It~~ was produced on Broadway in 1959.

(1) Lorraine Hansberry was born in Chicago in 1930. She was a playwright who wrote the prize-winning *A Raisin in the Sun*. (2) Hansberry's father was a successful businessman. He moved the family from the south side of Chicago to a predominately white neighborhood when Hansberry was eight. (3) Hostile neighbors there were responsible for throwing a brick through a window of their house. This was an act Hansberry never forgot. (4) Such experiences inspired *A Raisin in the Sun*. It is the story of a family's struggle to escape a cramped apartment in a poor Chicago neighborhood. (5) Lena Younger is the mother of the family. She is about to receive a ten-thousand-dollar insurance payment following her husband's death. (6) Her son wants to use the money to invest in a liquor store. This is an enterprise Lena finds unacceptable. (7) Her dream for the family is a house with a yard her grandson can play in. This dream leads her to purchase a home in a white neighborhood. (8) Her plans are almost shattered when Walter invests the rest of the insurance money in a scheme to obtain a liquor license illegally. This is a deal that quickly goes bad. (9) One of their new white neighbors has offered the Younger family a bribe not to move into the neighborhood. It is a deal Walter now decides to accept. (10) Lena is a woman who knows her son's heart. She makes Walter realize that to accept this money and give up their dream would be a betrayal of his father's memory.

■ SEEING AND WRITING: Flashback

Look back at your response to the Seeing and Writing exercise on page 273. Underline two or three pairs of sentences that you think could be combined. On a separate sheet of paper, combine each pair of sentences into a single sentence, using one of the methods discussed in 18C. Use a different method for each pair of sentences.

D   Varying Sentence Length

A paragraph of short, choppy sentences—or a paragraph of long, rambling sentences—can be very monotonous. By mixing long and short sentences, perhaps combining some simple sentences to create compound and complex sentences, you can create a more interesting paragraph.

Computer Tip

Some word-processing programs can tell you how long your average sentence is and how many words are in your shortest and longest sentences. Use this feature to help you vary sentence length.

In the following paragraph, the sentences are all quite short, and the result is a dull passage.

> The world's first drive-in movie theater opened on June 6, 1933, in Camden, New Jersey. Automobiles became more popular. Drive-ins did, too. By the 1950s, there were more than four thousand drive-ins in the United States. Over the years, the high cost of land led to the decline of drive-ins. So did the rising popularity of television. Now, the drive-in movie theater has been replaced by the multiplex. There are no drive-ins at all in Alaska. There are none in Rhode Island or Delaware, either. New Jersey's last drive-in closed in 1991.

The revised paragraph that appears below is more interesting because it mixes long and short sentences.

> The world's first drive-in movie theater opened on June 6, 1933, in Camden, New Jersey. As automobiles became more popular, drive-ins did too, and by the 1950s, there were more than four thousand drive-ins in the United States. Today, there are fewer than a thousand. Over the years, the high cost of land, along with the rising popularity of television, led to a

*For informa-
tion on creating
compound
and complex
sentences, see
Chapters 16
and 17.*

decline in the number of drive-ins. Now, the drive-in movie theater has been replaced by the multiplex and the VCR. There are no drive-ins at all in Alaska, Rhode Island, or Delaware, and New Jersey's last drive-in closed in 1991.

To increase sentence variety, the writer combined some of the original paragraph's short sentences, creating longer simple, compound, and complex sentences. He also added a new short sentence ("Today, there are fewer than a thousand") for emphasis after a long one.

◆ PRACTICE 18-16

ON THE WEB
*For more
practice, visit
Exercise Central:
www.bedford
stmartins.com/
writingincontext*

The following passage contains a series of short, choppy sentences that can be combined. Revise it so that it mixes long and short sentences. Be sure to use commas and other punctuation appropriately.

Example: Kente cloth has special significance for many African Americans/ *, but many* ~~Many~~ other people do not understand this significance.

(1) Kente cloth is made in western Africa. (2) It is produced primarily by the Ashanti people. (3) It has been worn for hundreds of years by African royalty. (4) They consider it a sign of power and status. (5) Many African Americans wear kente cloth. (6) They see it as a link to their heritage. (7) Each pattern on the cloth has a name. (8) Each color has a special significance. (9) For example, red and yellow suggest a long and healthy life. (10) Green and white suggest a good harvest. (11) African women may wear kente cloth as a dress or head wrap. (12) African-American women, like men, usually wear strips of cloth around their shoulders. (13) Men and women of African descent wear kente cloth as a sign of racial pride. (14) It often decorates college students' gowns at graduation.

■ SEEING AND WRITING: Flashback

Look back at your response to the Seeing and Writing exercise on page 273. Count the number of words in each sentence to determine which

(continued on the following page)

(continued from the previous page)
sentence is the longest. Then, write a new short sentence to follow your
longest sentence.

■ SEEING AND WRITING: Revising and Editing

Look back at your response to the Seeing and Writing exercise on page
273. Using any strategies from this chapter that seem appropriate, revise
your writing so that your sentences are varied, interesting, and smoothly
connected. (You may want to incorporate sentences you generated in
the Flashback exercises on pages 275, 281, 291, and above.) When you
are finished, revise the sentences in an assignment you have completed
for another course.

Computer Tip

Using the word-processing function that shows the average length of your sentences, compare
your first and final drafts to see if your sentences have become longer and more complex.

CHAPTER REVIEW

◆ EDITING PRACTICE

The following student essay lacks sentence variety. All of its sentences are
statements beginning with the subject, and it contains a number of short,
choppy sentences. Using the strategies discussed in this chapter, revise
the essay to achieve greater sentence variety. The first sentence has been
edited for you.

> A Wholesome Vegetarian Diet
>
> *Increasingly,*
> ^Young people who care about animal rights are ~~increas-~~
> ~~ingly~~ turning to a strict vegetarian diet. Such strict
> vegetarians are called vegans. They avoid eating all animal
> products including eggs, cow's milk, and dairy cheese.

Animal products do provide some essential nutrients, however. They cannot be dropped from one's diet without proper substitutes. Vegans must, therefore, be careful to substitute non-animal foods that provide the nutrition they need. They can be sure to do this in a variety of ways.

They can for a start learn how to get enough protein. Tofu is a versatile soybean product. It contains high levels of protein. It is widely available in its natural state. It is also found in prepared foods such as veggie burgers and soy dogs. Not everyone finds tofu appetizing, naturally. Peanut butter is a good source of protein for non-tofu eaters. Legumes (peas and beans) are also a good source of protein. Vegans snack on foods like sunflower seeds. They can get protein from between-meal treats as well.

Calcium and iron are also essential to health. Soy milk is made from non-dairy products. It is an excellent source of calcium. Fortified orange juice provides high levels of calcium as well. Dried figs provide high levels of calcium too. Calcium-rich broccoli, collard greens, and kale are often dietary staples for green vegetable lovers. Vegans who want a good source of iron may start the day with Grape Nuts. Grape Nuts is a breakfast cereal with a particularly high bran content. Any kind of bran flakes, in fact, can add iron to one's diet.

Beginning any kind of new diet requires people to adjust their eating habits carefully. Vegans eventually find they can fulfill their daily nutritional requirements with relative ease.

◆ COLLABORATIVE ACTIVITIES

Read the following list of sentences.

Many well-known African-American writers left the United States in the years following World War II.

Many went to Paris.

Richard Wright was a novelist.

He wrote *Native Son* and *Black Boy*.

He wrote *Uncle Tom's Children*.

He left the United States for Paris in 1947.

James Baldwin wrote *Another Country, The Fire Next Time,* and *Giovanni's Room.*

He also wrote essays.

He came to Paris in 1948.

Chester Himes was a detective story writer.

He arrived in Paris in 1953.

William Gardner Smith was a novelist and journalist.

He also left the United States for Paris.

These expatriates found Paris more hospitable than America.

They also found it less racist.

1. Working in a small group, add to the list one related sentence that is a question or an exclamation. Then, begin one or more of the sentences on the list with an appropriate adverb or prepositional phrase.

2. Continuing to work in your group, combine all the sentences on the list to create a varied and interesting paragraph. Use the strategies illustrated in 18C as a guide.

3. When your group's revisions are complete, trade paragraphs with another group and further edit the other group's paragraph to improve sentence variety.

19 *Using Parallelism*

Word Power

enlighten
to give insight
to; to educate

enrich
to make fuller
or more
rewarding

inspire
to stimulate to
action; to
motivate

■ SEEING AND WRITING

Look at the picture above, and then discuss three positive things about your school, neighborhood, or workplace. Support your statements with specific examples.

A   Recognizing Parallel Structure

Parallelism is the use of the same grammatical constructions to present comparable or equivalent ideas. For example, nouns are used with nouns, verbs with verbs, adjectives with adjectives, phrases with phrases, and clauses with clauses.

Parallel:

Casey is a <u>snowboarder</u>, not a <u>skier</u>. (two nouns)

We saw the ducks <u>fly</u>, <u>swim</u>, and <u>fish</u>. (three verbs)

The road of life is <u>long</u>, <u>bumpy</u>, and <u>steep</u>. (three adjectives)

<u>Making the team</u> was one thing; <u>staying on it</u> was another. (two phrases)

My, what big eyes you have, grandma! My, what big ears you have! My, what big teeth you have! (three independent clauses)

Faulty parallelism occurs when different grammatical constructions are used to present comparable or equivalent ideas. For example, notice how the sentences that follow fail to convey the links among related ideas.

Not Parallel:

Casey is a snowboarder, but skiing is not something that interests him.

We saw the ducks fly, and some swam, and others were fishing.

The road of life is long, has a lot of bumps, and climbs steeply.

Making the team was one thing, but she was worried about staying on the team.

My, what big eyes you have, Grandma! And you do have big ears. Your teeth are also quite large.

To correct faulty parallelism, reword the comparable ideas in your sentences so that they are expressed in matching grammatical constructions.

swim, and

We saw the ducks fly, ~~and some swam, and others were~~ fish~~ing~~.

◆ PRACTICE 19-1

In the following sentences, decide whether the underlined words are parallel. If so, write *P* in the blank. If not, rewrite the sentences so that the ideas they express are presented in parallel terms.

Examples: As a shopper, I <u>insist on quality</u>, <u>expect good service</u>, and <u>seek out value</u>. ___*P*___

ON THE WEB
For more practice, visit Exercise Central: www.bedford stmartins.com/ writingincontext

For me, getting an A on a math test is harder than ~~when I swim~~ ten
                                              ^swimming
miles. _____

1. People today are working more and playing less. _____

2. Some smokers say that they smoke cigarettes to help wake themselves
up, give themselves a break, and also so that they can keep themselves
going. _____

3. They also admit that cigarettes are expensive, smelly, and have dangers. _____

4. Surfing the Internet can be addictive and time-consuming. _____

5. Being happy in life is more important to me than that I make a lot of
money. _____

6. The team lost the game even though the quarterback played his best. _____

7. Judges must care about justice, uphold the laws, and they should treat
defendants fairly. _____

8. According to the newspaper, the economy is getting stronger. According to my wallet, the economy is getting weaker. _____

9. Love is blind, but the feeling of hate is blinder. _____

10. To succeed, set realistic goals, work toward them diligently, and you
must also believe in yourself. _____

■ **SEEING AND WRITING: Flashback**

Look back at your response to the Seeing and Writing exercise on page
296, and underline the parallel words, phrases, and clauses. Revise, if
necessary, to make sure that comparable ideas are presented in parallel
terms.

B   Using Parallel Structure

Parallel structure is especially important for emphasizing the relationships in *paired items, comparisons,* and *items in a series. Note:* Elements in an outline and items in a bulleted list should always be expressed in parallel terms.

Paired Items

Use parallel structure when you connect ideas with a coordinating conjunction—*and, but, for, nor, or, so,* and *yet.*

> George believes in <u>doing a good job</u> *and* <u>minding his own business</u>.

> You can <u>pay me now</u> *or* <u>pay me later</u>.

Also use parallel structure for paired items joined by correlative conjunctions, such as *both . . . and, not only . . . but also, either . . . or, neither . . . nor,* and *whether . . . or.*

> Jan is *both* <u>artistically talented</u> *and* <u>mechanically inclined</u>.

> The group's new recording *not only* <u>has a beat</u> *but also* <u>has thought-provoking lyrics</u>.

> I'd *rather* <u>eat one worm by itself</u> *than* <u>eat twenty with ice cream</u>.

Comparisons Formed with *Than* or *As*

Use parallel structure for comparisons formed with *than* or *as.*

> <u>Working hard</u> is more important than <u>being lucky</u>.

> <u>She cares about her patients</u> as much as <u>she cares about her family</u>.

Items in a Series

Use parallel structure for items in a series—words, phrases, or clauses.

> Every Wednesday I have <u>English</u>, <u>math</u>, and <u>psychology</u>.

> <u>Increased demand</u>, <u>high factory output</u>, and <u>a strong dollar</u> help the economy.

> She is a champion because she <u>stays in excellent physical condition</u>, <u>puts in long hours of practice</u>, and <u>has an intense desire to win</u>.

For information on punctuating items in a series, see 31A.

ON THE WEB
*For more
practice, visit
Exercise Central:*
www.bedford
stmartins.com/
writingincontext

◆ **PRACTICE 19-2**

Fill in the blanks in the following sentences with parallel words, phrases, or clauses of your own that make sense in context.

> **Example:** A good teacher ___*knows the subject*___ and ___*respects the students.*___

1. Before a test, I am both _____ and _____.

2. My ideal mate is _____, _____, and _____.

3. Next semester I will either _____

   or _____.

4. I define *success* more as _____

   than as _____.

5. Rich people _____, but poor people _____

   _____.

6. I have noticed that some _____,

   while other _____.

7. To advance in a job, you must _____, _____, and

   _____.

8. Three reasons to go to college are _____, _____,

   and _____.

9. _____ is more important to me than _____

   _____.

10. I enjoy _____ more than _____.

◆ **PRACTICE 19-3**

Edit the following sentences so that the ideas are presented in parallel terms. Add punctuation as needed.

> **Example:** California's San Gabriel Valley is close to mountains, ~~and~~
>
> beaches ‚and deserts ~~are nearby.~~

1. Pasadena and Claremont are major cities in the valley. So is Pomona.

2. Pasadena offers the famous Rose Bowl stadium, and the impressive Norton Simon Museum and the historic Wrigley house are also there.

3. Watching the big Tournament of Roses Parade is more exciting than it is to view the Macy's Thanksgiving Parade.

4. You can watch from the crowded parade route. The comfort of your living room is also a possibility.

5. Judges rate the rose-covered floats on their originality, what artistic merit they have, and the overall impact they make.

6. Some people enjoy going to the parade more than when they go to the Rose Bowl game.

7. The Rose Bowl game is not only America's oldest collegiate championship but also the bowl game that is the country's most popular.

8. Held every fall in Pomona, the Los Angeles County Fair offers carnival rides, popular performers, and there are agricultural shows included.

9. Visitors come to play challenging skill games, and they also can enjoy various ethnic foods.

10. The starting gate was introduced at the valley's Santa Anita Race Track, and so was electrical timing, as well as the photo finish.

■ SEEING AND WRITING: Flashback

Look back at your response to the Seeing and Writing exercise on page 296. On a separate sheet of paper, write three new sentences that you could add to your response, and then revise them as follows. (1) In one sentence, use a coordinating conjunction such as *and* or *but;* (2) in another sentence, create a comparison using *than* or *as;* (3) in a third sentence, present items in a series. When you have finished, check to make sure that you have used parallel structure in each sentence and that you have punctuated correctly.

> ■ **SEEING AND WRITING: Revising and Editing**
>
> Look back at your response to the Seeing and Writing exercise on page 296. Incorporating one or more sentences from the Flashback exercise on page 301, revise your work, correcting faulty parallelism and adding parallel constructions where necessary to emphasize a relationship or increase clarity. When you are finished, do the same for another assignment you are currently working on.

CHAPTER REVIEW

◆ EDITING PRACTICE

Read the following student essay, into which examples of faulty parallelism have been introduced. Identify the sentences you think need to be corrected, and make the changes required to achieve parallelism. Be sure to supply all words necessary for clarity, grammar, and sense, adding punctuation as needed. The first sentence has been edited for you.

Questionable Heroes

   Heroes are people who are looked up to for their out-
standing achievements, and their personal qualities *admirable* are also
admired. Earlier generations looked up to heroes who played
a part in their country's history, who contributed something to society, and they also liked people who showed
moral or intellectual superiority. These heroes included
the colonial Americans who established this country. The
abolitionists who brought an end to slavery, and the soldiers because they served their country in time of war,
were also included. Early American heroes like Johnny
Appleseed and Molly Pitcher were brave and also acted
generously. Most young people today, however, find

their heroes not in books or in history, but television is the place they look. Not only do they admire rock performers, but also athletes and movie stars are admired by them.

The heroes of today are recognized not for their honesty or leadership, but they are liked for the entertainment they provide. How can big-name celebrities like Arnold Schwarzenegger, Madonna, and Michael Jordan compare with genuine heroes like George Washington, Thomas Jefferson, or Martin Luther King Jr.? The answer is that they do not. Washington helped the thirteen colonies gain their independence from Great Britain, and the Declaration of Independence was drafted by Jefferson. In addition, Martin Luther King Jr. gave his life to achieve equal rights. By contrast, the people who are on the covers of magazines today are honored only because of their looks or they can toss a football. Sadly, many of today's heroes are admired not because of anything they have actually done, but people admire them because of the image they project.

◆ COLLABORATIVE ACTIVITIES

1. Working in a group, list three or four qualities that you associate with each word in the following pairs.

   Brothers/sisters
   Teachers/students
   Parents/children
   City/country
   Baseball/football
   The Internet/television
   Work/play

19 B

2. Write a compound sentence comparing each of the above pairs of words. Use a coordinating conjunction to join the clauses, and make sure each sentence uses clear parallel structure, mentions both words, and includes the qualities you listed for the words in Collaborative Activity 1.

3. Choose the three best sentences your group has written for Collaborative Activity 2. Assign one student from each group to write these sentences on the board so that the entire class can read them. The class can then decide which sentences use parallelism most effectively.

Using Words Effectively

PREVIEW

In this chapter, you will learn
- to use specific words (20A)
- to use concise language (20B)
- to avoid clichés (20C)
- to use similes and metaphors (20D)
- to avoid sexist language (20E)

■ SEEING AND WRITING

Look at the picture above, and then describe your dream house. What would it look like? What items would it contain? Be as specific as possible.

▶ **Word Power**

appealing
attractive or interesting

ideal
a model of perfection; the best of its kind

practical
useful

A   Using Specific Words

To write well, you need to use specific words that convey your ideas with precision and clarity.

Specific words refer to particular people, places, things, ideas, or qualities; **general** words refer to entire classes or groups. Statements that contain specific words are generally more vivid than ones that contain only generalities. All of the following sentences are grammatically correct, but they are not specific.

Sentences with General Words

While walking in the woods, I saw an <u>animal</u>.

<u>Someone</u> decided to run for Congress.

<u>Weapons</u> are responsible for many murders.

Denise bought new <u>clothes</u>.

I really enjoyed my <u>meal</u>.

Darrell had always wanted a <u>classic car</u>.

Specific words make the following revised sentences clearer and more precise.

Sentences with Specific Words

While walking in the woods, I saw a <u>baby skunk</u>.

<u>Rebecca</u> decided to run for Congress.

<u>Saturday night specials</u> are responsible for many murders.

Denise bought a new <u>blue vest</u>.

I really enjoyed my <u>pepperoni pizza</u>.

Darrell had always wanted a <u>black 1957 Chevy convertible</u>.

FOCUS   Using Specific Words

One way to strengthen your writing is to avoid **utility words**—general words like *good, nice,* or *great* that some writers use instead of taking the time to think of more specific words. For example, when you say the ocean looked *pretty,* do you really mean that it *sparkled, glistened, rippled, foamed, surged,* or *billowed?*

ON THE WEB
For more practice, visit Exercise Central: www.bedford stmartins.com/ writingincontext

◆ PRACTICE 20-1

In the following passage, the writer describes an old store in the town of Nameless, Tennessee. Underline the specific words in the passage that help you experience the scene the writer describes. The first sentence has been done for you.

(1) The old store, lighted only by three fifty-watt bulbs, smelled of coal oil and baking bread. (2) In the middle of the rectangular room, where the oak floor sagged a little, stood an iron stove. (3) To the right was a wooden table with an unfinished game of checkers and a stool made from an apple-tree stump. (4) On shelves around the walls sat earthen jugs with corncob stoppers, a few canned goods, and some of the two thousand old clocks and clockworks Thurmond Watts owned. (5) Only one was ticking; the others he just looked at.

William Least Heat-Moon, *Blue Highways*

◆ PRACTICE 20-2

For each of the five general words below, write a more specific word. Then, use the more specific word in a sentence of your own.

Example: talked _____*chattered*_____

All through dinner, my six-year-old chattered excitedly about his first day

of school.

1. car
2. walk *(verb)*
3. big
4. animal
5. clothing

◆ PRACTICE 20-3

The following letter of application for a job uses very general words. Choose a job that you might want to apply for. As you rewrite the paragraph on a separate page, substitute specific language for the general language of the original, and add details where necessary. Start by making the first sentence, which identifies the job, more specific: for example, "I would like to apply for the dental technician position you advertised in today's *Post*." Go on to include specific information about your background and qualifications, expanding the original paragraph into a three-paragraph letter.

I would like to apply for the position you advertised in today's paper. I graduated from high school and am currently attending college. I have taken several courses that have prepared me to fulfill the duties the position requires. I also have several personal qualities that I think you would find important in a person holding this position. In addition, I have had certain experiences that qualify me for such a job. I would appreciate the opportunity to meet with you to discuss your needs as an employer. Thank you.

■ SEEING AND WRITING: Flashback

Look back at your response to the Seeing and Writing exercise on page 305. Find several general words, and list those words on a separate sheet of paper. For each word, substitute another word that is more specific.

B Using Concise Language

Concise writing comes right to the point and says what it has to say in as few words as possible. Too often, however, writers use empty phrases that add nothing to a sentence's meaning. A good way to test a sentence for nonessential words is to see if crossing out the words changes its meaning.

~~It is a fact that~~ the United States was not prepared to fight World War II.

If the sentence's meaning does not change, you can assume the sentence is better off without the extra words.

WORDY Due to the fact that I was tired, I missed my first class.

CONCISE Because I was tired, I missed my first class.

WORDY In order to follow the plot, you must make an outline.

CONCISE To follow the plot, you must make an outline.

FOCUS Using Concise Language

The following phrases add nothing to a sentence. You can usually delete or condense them with no loss of meaning.

Wordy	Concise
It is clear that	(delete)
It is a fact that	(delete)
The reason is that	Because
It is my opinion that	I think/I believe

(continued on the following page)

(continued from the previous page)

Wordy	Concise
Due to the fact that	Because
Despite the fact that	Although
At the present time	Today/Currently
At that time	Then
In most cases	Usually
In order to	To
In the final analysis	Finally
Subsequent to	After

Repetition also adds words to your writing. Although repetition can be used effectively—for example, to emphasize important ideas—unnecessary repetition should be eliminated. Notice how easily these sentences can be edited to eliminate unnecessary repetition.

WORDY My instructor told me the book was <u>old-fashioned and outdated</u>. (An old-fashioned book *is* outdated.)

CONCISE My instructor told me the book was ~~old-fashioned and~~ outdated.

WORDY The <u>terrible tragedy</u> of the fire could have been avoided. (A tragedy is *always* terrible.)

CONCISE The ~~terrible~~ tragedy of the fire could have been avoided.

◆ PRACTICE 20-4

To make the following sentences more concise, eliminate any unnecessary repetition, and delete or condense wordy expressions.

Example: ~~It is a fact that many~~ _Many_ grown-up children have trouble getting their parents/~~their mother and father,~~ to treat them as adults.

(1) Adult children can become frustrated due to the fact that their parents seem to treat them as if they were not capable of making their own decisions by themselves. (2) For example, some parents constantly criticize all the time and offer unwanted advice that their children do not want to hear. (3) When this happens, the children may begin to whine childishly and in a juvenile manner or even throw a temper tantrum

despite the fact that such behavior only reinforces their parents' attitude. (4) In most cases, there are better ways to improve one's parents' behavior for the better. (5) In order to get parents to stop being critical, an adult child might turn the tables and encourage his or her parents to have a discussion and talk about their own childhoods. (6) The child can then point out any similarities between the parents' behavior then in the past and his or her behavior now in the present. (7) Another thing adult children might also do is to explain that while they value their parents' opinion, they are still going to make their own decisions for themselves. (8) Finally, an adult child should not sit by idly doing nothing when family stories are being told or related. (9) Despite the fact that parents may have been telling these stories the same way for years and years, the child may have a very different or contradictory perspective on the event. (10) Expressing and talking about this different perspective can help an adult child define his or her position in the family in a new way that is different from the old way.

■ SEEING AND WRITING: Flashback

Look back at your response to the Seeing and Writing exercise on page 305. Underline a sentence that contains unnecessary repetition. Then, try to edit the sentence to make it more concise.

C   Avoiding Clichés

One way of making your writing more effective is to avoid **clichés**, expressions that have been used so often they have lost their impact. Writers tend to plug in such ready-made phrases—for example, "easier said than done," "last but not least," and "work like a dog"—without giving them much thought, but these worn-out expressions deaden writing and do little to create interest.

When you identify a cliché in your writing, replace it with a direct statement—or, if possible, substitute a fresher expression.

CLICHÉ   When school was over, she felt <u>free as a bird</u>.

REVISED   When school was over, she felt free.

CLICHÉ   These days, you have to be <u>sick as a dog</u> before you are admitted to a hospital.

REVISED   These days, you have to be seriously ill before you are admitted to a hospital.

Computer Tip

Many grammar-checking programs flag clichés and wordy constructions. Remember, however, that although a grammar checker may highlight trouble spots, you, not the computer, must decide whether (and how) to revise.

◆ PRACTICE 20-5

Cross out any clichés in the following sentences, and either substitute a fresher expression or restate the idea in more direct language.

ON THE WEB
For more practice, visit Exercise Central:
www.bedford stmartins.com/ writingincontext

Example: Lottery winners often think they will be ~~on easy street~~ for
                                                    ^ *free of financial worries*
the rest of their lives.

(1) Many people think that a million-dollar lottery jackpot allows the winner to stop working like a dog and start living high on the hog. (2) All things considered, however, the reality for lottery winners is quite different. (3) For one thing, lottery winners who hit the jackpot do not receive their winnings all at once; instead, payments—for example, $50,000—are usually spread out over twenty years. (4) Of that $50,000 a year, close to $20,000 goes to taxes and anything else the lucky stiff owes the government, such as student loans. (5) Next come relatives and friends with their hands out, leaving winners between a rock and a hard place. (6) They can either cough up gifts and loans or wave bye-bye to many of their loved ones. (7) Adding insult to injury, many lottery winners have lost their jobs because employers thought that once they were "millionaires," they no

longer needed to draw a salary. (8) Many lottery winners wind up way over their heads in debt within a few years. (9) In their hour of need, many would like to sell their future payments to companies that offer lump-sum payments of forty to forty-five cents on the dollar. (10) This is easier said than done, however, because most state lotteries do not allow winners to sell their winnings.

■ SEEING AND WRITING: Flashback

Look back at your response to the Seeing and Writing exercise on page 305. If you have used any clichés, circle them. Then, either replace each cliché with a more direct statement, or think of a more original way of expressing the idea.

D   Using Similes and Metaphors

A **simile** is a comparison of two unlike things that uses *like* or *as*.

> His arm hung at his side <u>like</u> a broken branch.

> He was <u>as</u> content <u>as</u> a cat napping on a windowsill.

A **metaphor** is a comparison of two unlike things that does *not* use *like* or *as*.

> Invaders from another world, the dandelions conquered my garden.

> He was a beast of burden, hauling cement from the mixer to the building site.

The force of similes and metaphors comes from the surprise of seeing two seemingly unlike things being compared and, as a result, seeing a hidden or unnoticed similarity between them. Used in moderation, similes and metaphors can make your writing more lively and more interesting.

◆ PRACTICE 20-6

Use your imagination to complete each of the following by creating three appropriate similes.

Example: A boring class is like *toast without jam.*

a straitjacket.

a bedtime story.

1. A good friend is like _____

_____

_____

2. A thunderstorm is like _____

_____

_____

3. Falling in love is like _____

_____

_____

◆ PRACTICE 20-7

Think of a person you know well. Using that person as your subject, fill in each of the following blanks to create metaphors. Try to complete each metaphor with more than a single word, as in the example.

Example: If ___*my baby sister*___ were an animal, ___*she*___ would be *a curious little kitten.*

1. If _____ were an animal, _____ would be _____

_____

2. If _____ were a food, _____ would be _____

_____

3. If _____ were a means of transportation, _____ would be

_____

4. If _____ were a natural phenomenon, _____ would be _____

_____

5. If _____ were a toy, _____ would be _____

_____

■ SEEING AND WRITING: Flashback

Look back at your response to the Seeing and Writing exercise on page 305. Find two sentences that could be enriched with a simile or a metaphor. Add a simile to one sentence and a metaphor to the other.

E   Avoiding Sexist Language

For a discussion of subjects like everyone *(indefinite pronoun antecedents), see 28E.*

Sexist language refers to men and women in derogatory or insulting terms. Sexist language is not just words like *hunk, bimbo,* or *babe,* which many people find objectionable. It can also be words or phrases that unnecessarily call attention to gender or that suggest a job or profession is exclusively male or female when it actually is not.

You can avoid sexist usage by being sensitive and using a little common sense. There is always an acceptable nonsexist alternative for a sexist term.

Sexist	*Nonsexist*
man, mankind	humanity, humankind, human race
businessman	executive, businessperson
fireman, policeman, mailman	firefighter, police officer, letter carrier
male nurse, woman engineer	nurse, engineer
congressman	member of Congress, representative
stewardess, steward	flight attendant
man and wife	man and woman, husband and wife
manmade	synthetic
chairman	chair, chairperson
anchorwoman, anchorman	anchor

FOCUS   Avoiding Sexist Language

Do not use *he* when your subject could be either male or female.

■ Everyone should complete <u>his</u> assignment by next week.

You can correct this problem in three ways.

(continued on the following page)

(continued from the previous page)

- Use *he or she* or *his or her*.

  Everyone should complete his or her assignment by next week.

- Use plural forms. ——————

  Students should complete their assignment by next week.

- Eliminate the pronoun. ———

  Everyone should complete the assignment by next week.

Note: Use the Find or Search feature of your word processor to check the uses of *he*. If you have used *he* to refer to a subject that could be of either gender, revise to correct the problem.

◆ PRACTICE 20-8

Edit the following sentences to eliminate sexist language.

1. Many people today would like to see more policemen patrolling the streets.

2. A doctor should be honest with his patients.

3. The attorneys representing the plaintiff are Geraldo Diaz and Mrs. Barbara Wilkerson.

4. Chris Fox is the female mayor of Port London, Maine.

5. Travel to other planets will be a significant step for man.

ON THE WEB
For more practice, visit Exercise Central: www.bedford stmartins.com/ writingincontext

---

■ SEEING AND WRITING: Flashback

Look back at your response to the Seeing and Writing exercise on page 305. Have you used any words or phrases that unnecessarily call attention to gender? Have you used *he* when your subject could be either male or female? Cross out the sexist language, and try to substitute acceptable nonsexist alternatives.

■ SEEING AND WRITING: Revising and Editing

Look back at your response to the Seeing and Writing exercise on page 305. Revise the paragraph, making sure your language is as specific as possible, and avoids using clichés or sexist expressions. Be sure to incorporate the revisions you made in this chapter's Flashback exercises. When you have finished, revise another writing assignment you are currently working on.

CHAPTER REVIEW

◆ EDITING PRACTICE

Read the following student essay carefully, and then revise it, making sure your revision is as concise as possible and uses specific words and no sexist language or clichés. If you can, include an occasional simile or metaphor to add interest. Finally, underline any expressions that seem particularly fresh and original. The first sentence has been edited for you.

A Day at the Pool

It all begins on a ~~nice~~ *bright* summer day as we carry our neatly packed pool equipment from the car and head to the pool. We walk across the bumpy, gravel-covered parking lot with our arms piled high with a pretty beach bag, a gaily striped beach chair, colored beach towels, and an interesting drinking cup. We make it through the entrance and walk into the ladies' locker room. The walls are lined with lockers, and past the lockers is a metal door held open by a wooden wedge. Walking through the doorway, we proceed to our usual spot in the shaded grass area. This is where we spend our day socializing with other "pool princesses" and checking out the hunks.

As I sit, I hear the sounds of children crying and laughing and of parents yelling at them. Suddenly, the noises cease at the sound of a loud, high-pitched whistle. All eyes are on the female lifeguard. She is dressed in a nice bathing suit covered by a tank top with an unusual design on the front. She is wearing black Ray-Ban sunglasses, and she holds a silver whistle in her mouth. She sits on her high wooden platform and raises her hand, pointing her finger at the accused. Then, as quickly as the silence began, it ceases.

Due to the fact I am hungry, I go to the snack bar. I am enticed by the scent of freshly popped popcorn, the tantalizing aroma of spicy fries, and the equally tempting smell of hamburgers. The choice is difficult. I finally decide on a bright banana-yellow popsicle. It tastes good and takes care of my thirst. I turn and come face to face with a small child. His cheeks are red from overexposure to the burning rays of the sun. His nose is a white painted triangle, and his eyes are invisible due to the fact that he is wearing funny Superman sunglasses. Slithering around him, I head back to the safety of my towel.

Reaching my chair, I look down to see a strange toddler sitting as quiet as a mouse. He seems to have claimed my seat as his own. He looks up and smiles as drool slides out of the corner of his mouth. As he rises and waddles off, his wet diaper sags around his knees. When I look down, I discover that he has left his mark on my chair. At this point, I decide it is time to go home.

◆ COLLABORATIVE ACTIVITIES

1. Photocopy two or three paragraphs of description from a romance novel, a western novel, or a mystery novel, and bring your paragraphs to class. Working in a group, choose one paragraph that seems to need clearer, more specific language.

2. As a group, revise the paragraph you chose for Collaborative Activity 1, making it as clear and specific as possible and eliminating any clichés or sexist language.

3. Exchange your revised paragraph from Collaborative Activity 2 with the paragraph revised by another group, and check the other group's work. Make any additional changes you think your paragraph needs.

UNIT FIVE

Solving Common Sentence Problems

Run-Ons and Comma Splices

PREVIEW

In this chapter, you will learn
- to recognize run-ons and comma splices (21A)
- to correct run-ons and comma splices in five different ways (21B)

Word Power

lethargic
sluggishly
indifferent

obese
extremely
overweight

sedentary
accustomed to
sitting or to
engaging in
little exercise

■ SEEING AND WRITING

Why do you think so many American children are physically out of shape? What do you think can be done about this problem? Look at the picture above, and then write down your thoughts on this issue.

A   Recognizing Run-Ons and Comma Splices

A **run-on** is an error that occurs when two sentences (independent clauses) are joined without punctuation.

> RUN-ON   More and more students are earning high school equivalency diplomas the value of these diplomas is currently under debate.

A **comma splice** is an error that occurs when two sentences are joined with just a comma.

> COMMA SPLICE   More and more students are earning high school equivalency diplomas, the value of these diplomas is currently under debate.

Computer Tip

Grammar checkers sometimes mistakenly identify a sentence as a run-on or comma splice because it is long. However, a long sentence can be perfectly correct. Before you make changes, be sure your sentence actually contains an error (two independent clauses joined without punctuation or with just a comma). (See 21B.)

◆ PRACTICE 21-1

ON THE WEB
*For more
practice, visit
Exercise Central:*
www.bedford
stmartins.com/
writingincontext

Some of the sentences in the following passage are correct, but others are run-ons or comma splices. In the answer space after each sentence, write *C* if the sentence is correct, *RO* if it is a run-on, and *CS* if it is a comma splice.

Example: "Race movies" had all-black casts, they were intended for African-American audiences. _CS_

(1) In 1919, African-American director Oscar Micheaux filmed *Within Our Gates* this movie examined black life in Chicago. _RO_ (2) The film included scenes of violence, it even depicted two lynchings. _CS_ (3) It also treated interracial relationships white censors banned it. _RO_ (4) Race riots had occurred in Chicago that year, the censors feared violence. _CS_ (5) Micheaux appealed to the board they agreed to the film's release in Chicago. _RO_ (6) The movie was shown, twelve hundred feet of film were omitted. _CS_ (7) Micheaux later made many low-budget movies, few are socially conscious films like *Within Our Gates.* _C_ (8) One, *Body and Soul,*

was Paul Robeson's first film. _____ (9) Micheaux died in 1951. _____ (10) In 1990, an uncut version of *Within Our Gates* was discovered in Madrid, it was shown in Chicago for the first time in 1992.

■ SEEING AND WRITING: Flashback

Look back at your response to the Seeing and Writing exercise on page 321. Do you see any run-ons or comma splices? If so, put brackets around them.

B | **Correcting Run-Ons and Comma Splices**

You can correct a run-on or comma splice in five different ways.

1. Create two separate sentences.

INCORRECT Muslims fast during daylight for a period of thirty days this period is called Ramadan. (run-on)

INCORRECT Muslims fast during daylight for a period of thirty days, this period is called Ramadan. (comma splice)

CORRECT Muslims fast during daylight for a period of thirty days. This period is called Ramadan. (two separate sentences)

2. Use a coordinating conjunction. If you want to indicate a particular relationship between ideas—for example, cause and effect or contrast—you can connect two independent clauses with a coordinating conjunction (*and, but, or, nor, for, so,* or *yet*) that makes this relationship clear. Always place a comma before the coordinating conjunction.

For more on connecting ideas with a coordinating conjunction, see 16A.

INCORRECT The Emancipation Proclamation freed U.S. slaves in 1863 slaves in Texas were not officially freed until June 19, 1865 ("Juneteenth"). (run-on)

INCORRECT The Emancipation Proclamation freed U.S. slaves in 1863, slaves in Texas were not officially freed until June 19, 1865 ("Juneteenth"). (comma splice)

CORRECT The Emancipation Proclamation freed U.S. slaves in 1863, but slaves in Texas were not officially freed until June 19, 1865 ("Juneteenth"). (clauses connected with a comma followed by a coordinating conjunction)

3. Use a semicolon. If you want to indicate a particularly close connection—or a strong contrast—between two ideas, use a semicolon.

For more on connecting ideas with a semicolon, see 16B.

INCORRECT   The swastika was an ancient symbol of good luck it was also the official emblem of the Nazi Party. (run-on)

INCORRECT   The swastika was an ancient symbol of good luck, it was also the official emblem of the Nazi Party. (comma splice)

CORRECT   The swastika was an ancient symbol of good luck; it was also the official emblem of the Nazi Party. (clauses connected with a semicolon)

4. Use a semicolon followed by a conjunctive adverb or transitional expression. To clarify a specific relationship between two closely related ideas, add a conjunctive adverb or transitional expression after the semicolon.

INCORRECT   *Its* is a possessive pronoun *it's* is a contraction. (run-on)

INCORRECT   *Its* is a possessive pronoun, *it's* is a contraction. (comma splice)

CORRECT   *Its* is a possessive pronoun; however, *it's* is a contraction. (clauses connected with a semicolon followed by a conjunctive adverb)

FOCUS   **Run-Ons and Comma Splices with Conjunctive Adverbs or Transitional Expressions**

For a list of conjunctive adverbs, see 16C.

Run-ons and comma splices often occur when you use a conjunctive adverb or transitional expression to join two independent clauses *without also using a semicolon.*

INCORRECT   Some students have microwaves and refrigerators in their dorm rooms as a result, electrical circuits are overloaded. (run-on)

INCORRECT   Some students have microwaves and refrigerators in their dorm rooms, as a result, electrical circuits are overloaded. (comma splice)

To correct this kind of run-on or comma splice, simply add the missing semicolon.

CORRECT   Some students have microwaves and refrigerators in their dorm rooms; as a result, electrical circuits are overloaded.

For more on connecting ideas with a subordinating conjunction or relative pronoun, see Chapter 17.

5. Use a subordinating conjunction or relative pronoun. When one idea is dependent on another, you can turn the dependent idea into a dependent clause by adding a subordinating conjunction (such as *when, although,* or *because*) or a relative pronoun (such as *who, which,* or *that*). *Note:*

When you use a relative pronoun to correct a run-on or comma splice, the relative pronoun takes the place of another pronoun in the sentence.

INCORRECT   Horace Mann was the first president of Antioch College he encouraged the development of students' social consciences. (run-on)

INCORRECT   Horace Mann was the first president of Antioch College, he encouraged the development of students' social consciences. (comma splice)

CORRECT   <u>When</u> Horace Mann was the first president of Antioch College, he encouraged the development of students' social consciences. (clauses connected by a subordinating conjunction)

CORRECT   Horace Mann, <u>who</u> was the first president of Antioch College, encouraged the development of students' social consciences. (clauses connected by a relative pronoun)

◆ PRACTICE 21-2

Correct each of the run-ons and comma splices on the next page in one of the following four ways: by creating two separate sentences, by using a coordinating conjunction, by using a semicolon, or by using a semicolon followed by a conjunctive adverb or transitional expression. Be sure punctuation is correct. Remember to put a semicolon before, and a comma after, each conjunctive adverb or transitional expression.

ON THE WEB
For more practice, visit Exercise Central: www.bedford stmartins.com/ writingincontext

Example: Some people believe chronic sex offenders should be given therapy; however, others believe they should be jailed indefinitely.

1. Nursing offers job security and high pay; therefore, many people are choosing nursing as a career.

2. Anne Boleyn was the second wife of Henry VIII. her daughter was Elizabeth I.

3. The Democratic Republic of the Congo was previously known as Zaire; before that it was the Belgian Congo.

4. Housewife Jean Nidetch started Weight Watchers in 1961. she sold the company for $100 million in 1978.

5. Millions of Jews were killed during the Holocaust; in addition, Catholics, Gypsies, homosexuals, and other "undesirables" were killed.

6. Sojourner Truth was born a slave, she eventually became a leading abolitionist and feminist.

7. Japanese athletes play various positions on American baseball teams; however, until recently all the Japanese players were pitchers.

8. Oliver Wendell Holmes Jr. was a Supreme Court Justice, his father was a physician and writer.

9. Père Noel is the French name for Santa Claus, he is also known as Father Christmas and St. Nicholas.

10. Latin is one classical language; Greek is another.

◆ **PRACTICE 21-3**

Consulting the list of subordinating conjunctions on page 262 and the list of relative pronouns on page 266, correct the following run-ons and comma splices. Be sure to add correct punctuation where necessary.

Examples: Harlem was a rural area until the nineteenth century , when improved transportation linked it to lower Manhattan.

The community , which was soon home to people escaping the crowds of New York City, it became a fashionable suburb.

(1) Harlem was populated mostly by European immigrants at the turn of the last century, it saw an influx of African Americans beginning in 1910. (2) This migration from the South continued for several decades Harlem became one of the largest African-American communities in the United States. (3) Many African-American artists and writers created a community in Harlem during the 1920s, this led to a flowering of African-American art. (4) This "Harlem Renaissance" was an important era in American literary history it is not even mentioned in some textbooks. (5) Scholars of the era recognize the great works of the Harlem Renaissance, they point to the writers Langston Hughes and Countee Cullen and the artists Henry Tanner

and Sargent Johnson. (6) Zora Neale Hurston moved to Harlem from her native Florida in 1925, she began work there on a book of African-American folklore. (7) Harlem was an exciting place in the 1920s people from all over the city went there to listen to jazz and to dance. (8) The white playwright Eugene O'Neill went to Harlem to audition actors for his play *The Emperor Jones* it made an international star of the great Paul Robeson. (9) Contemporary African-American artists know about the Harlem Renaissance, it is still not familiar to many others. (10) The Great Depression occurred in the 1930s it led to the end of the Harlem Renaissance.

◆ PRACTICE 21-4

Correct each run-on and comma splice in the following passage in the way that best indicates the relationship between ideas. Be sure you use appropriate punctuation.

Example: Coney Island was once a bustling seaside resort, but it declined considerably over recent years.

In the late nineteenth century, Coney Island was famous, in fact, it was legendary. Every summer it was crowded, people mailed hundreds of thousands of postcards from the resort on some days. Then Coney Island was considered exotic and exciting, it even had a hotel shaped like an elephant. Some people saw Coney Island as seedy, but others thought it was a wonderful, magical place. It had beaches, hotels, racetracks, and a stadium; however, by the turn of the century, it was best known for three amusement parks. These parks were Luna Park, Steeplechase, and Dreamland. Gaslight was still the norm in New York, a million electric lights lit Luna Park. Steeplechase offered many rides; however, its main attraction was a two-mile ride on mechanical horses. At Dreamland, people could see a submarine, in addition, they could travel through an Eskimo village or visit Lilliputia, with its three hundred

midgets. Today, the old Coney Island no longer exists. Fire destroyed Dream-
land in 1911, Luna Park burned down in 1946. In 1964, Steeplechase closed.
The once-grand Coney Island is gone, still its beach and its boardwalk endure.
Its famous roller coaster, the Cyclone, still exists, its giant Ferris wheel, the
Wonder Wheel, keeps on turning. Now, a ballpark has been built for a new
minor league baseball team the new team is called the Brooklyn Cyclones.

■ SEEING AND WRITING: Flashback

For each run-on or comma splice you identified in the Flashback exercise on page 323, write two possible corrected versions on a separate
sheet of paper.

■ SEEING AND WRITING: Revising and Editing

Look back at your responses to the Seeing and Writing exercise on page
321 and the Flashback exercises on page 323 and above. For each run-
on and comma splice you found, choose the revision that best conveys
your meaning, and revise your Seeing and Writing exercise accordingly.
If you do not find any run-ons or comma splices in your own writing,
work with a classmate to correct his or her writing, or edit the work you
did for another assignment.

CHAPTER REVIEW

◆ EDITING PRACTICE

Read the following student essay, into which sentence errors have been
introduced. Then, revise it by eliminating run-ons and comma splices and

carefully correcting them to indicate the relationships between ideas. Be sure punctuation is correct. The first error has been corrected for you.

Blood Sports

Since the time of ancient Rome, citizens have rushed to the stadium to see battles. *While* Christians fought lions in ancient times, athletes now fight each other. Society may have evolved morally to some degree, I believe only our laws keep us from behaving like the ancient Romans.

I played "barbaric" sports for ten years. My parents encouraged my athletic career, *and* they got me started in sports early on. Between the ages of ten and seventeen, I was very active in martial arts, for four years, I played high school football. As a young child, I competed in karate tournaments, I was injured frequently. I broke my nose three times, I also broke my hand twice, and my foot once. As a competitor, I enjoyed the thrill of battle, however, I *and* feared serious injury. Eventually, I gave up karate, instead I concentrated on football.

Extreme force was very important in high school football. I played defense, *and* I often hurt my opponents. Once, I hit a quarterback in his hip with my helmet, the blow knocked him to the ground. They carried him off the field, *however,* my team's fans went berserk. For weeks, people congratulated me, *but* still I felt uncomfortable. I now understand that playing sports requires a great deal of physical aggressiveness and pain. I accept this as part of the game, *and* I just don't want to play anymore.

◆ COLLABORATIVE ACTIVITIES

1. Find an interesting paragraph from a newspaper or magazine article. Working in a small group, recopy it onto a separate sheet of paper, creating run-ons and comma splices. Exchange exercises with another group.

2. Work in a small group to correct each run-on and comma splice in an exercise prepared by another group of students. When you have finished, return the exercise to the group that created it.

3. Continuing to work with members of your group, evaluate the other group's work on your exercise, comparing it to the original newspaper or magazine paragraph. Pay particular attention to punctuation. Where the students' version differs from the original, decide whether their version is incorrect or whether it represents an acceptable (or even superior) alternative to the original.

Sentence Fragments

PREVIEW

In this chapter, you will learn
- to recognize sentence fragments (22A)
- to correct sentence fragments created when phrases are punctuated as sentences (22B)
- to correct sentence fragments created when verbs are incomplete (22C)
- to correct sentence fragments created when dependent clauses are punctuated as sentences (22D)

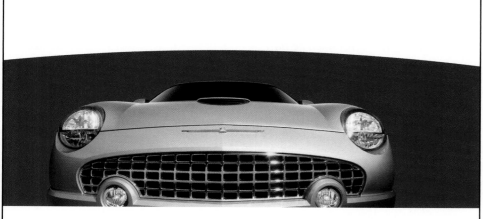

Is your tank half empty or half full?

■ SEEING AND WRITING

Look at the advertisement above, and then write several lines of copy for a magazine ad for your favorite beverage, footwear, or health or beauty product.

▶ **Word Power**

unique
unlike
anything else

transform
to change
completely

empower
to give strength
or power to

A   Recognizing Sentence Fragments

A **sentence fragment** is an incomplete sentence. Every sentence must include at least one subject and one verb, and every sentence must express a complete thought. If a group of words does not do *all* these things, it is a fragment and not a sentence—even if it begins with a capital letter and ends with a period.

> SENTENCE   The <u>actors</u> in the play *Into the Woods* <u>were</u> ethnically diverse. (includes both a subject and a verb and expresses a complete thought)

Because a sentence must have both a subject and a verb and express a complete thought, the following groups of words are not complete sentences but fragments.

> FRAGMENT (NO VERB)   The actors in the play *Into the Woods*. (What point is being made about the actors?)

> FRAGMENT (NO SUBJECT)   Were ethnically diverse. (What was ethnically diverse?)

Note: You may see sentence fragments used in advertisements and other informal writing *(A full head of hair in just 30 minutes!),* but fragments are not acceptable in college writing.

FOCUS   Identifying Sentence Fragments

Sentence fragments almost always appear in paragraphs and longer passages, right beside complete sentences.

┌─── COMPLETE SENTENCE ───┐ ┌─── FRAGMENT ───┐
Celia took two electives. Physics 320 and Spanish 101.

The fragment above does not have a verb. The complete sentence that precedes it, however, has both a subject *(Celia)* and a verb *(took).*

Often, as in this case, you can correct a sentence fragment by attaching it to an adjacent sentence that supplies the missing words.

Celia took two electives, Physics 320 and Spanish 101.

ON THE WEB
For more practice, visit Exercise Central:
www.bedford stmartins.com/ writingincontext

◆ PRACTICE 22-1

Each of the following items is a fragment. On the line following each fragment, indicate what is missing and what needs to be changed to make it a complete sentence. There are four possible ways to correct these sentence fragments: (1) add a subject; (2) add a verb; (3) add a subject and a verb; or (if the fragment has a subject and a verb) (4) revise to express a complete thought.

Example: At the beginning of the test. _add a subject and a verb_

1. The students in the classroom. _____

2. Before the teacher handed out the answer sheets. _____

   _____

3. With a number-two pencil. _____

4. Opened their test booklets. _____

5. After twenty-five minutes. _____

6. Began the second part of the test. _____

7. The last set of questions. _____

8. When the teacher called "Time." _____

9. Breathed a sigh of relief. _____

10. Quickly out into the hallway. _____

◆ PRACTICE 22-2

In the following passage, some of the numbered groups of words are missing a subject, a verb, or both. Identify each fragment by labeling it *F.* Then, attach each fragment to a nearby word group to create a complete new sentence. Finally, on a separate sheet of paper, rewrite the entire passage, using complete sentences.

Example: Martha Grimes, Ruth Rendell, and Deborah Crombie write

detective novels. _____ Set in England. __*F*__

Martha Grimes, Ruth Rendell, and Deborah Crombie write detective novels

set in England.

   (1) Sara Paretsky writes detective novels. _____ (2) Such as *Burn Marks*

and *Guardian Angel.* _____ (3) These novels are about V. I. Warshawski. _____

(4) A private detective. _____ (5) V. I. lives and works in Chicago. _____

(6) The Windy City _____ (7) Every day as a detective. _____ (8) V. I. takes

risks. _____ (9) V. I. is tough. _____ (10) She is also a woman. _____

■ SEEING AND WRITING: Flashback

Look back at your response to the Seeing and Writing exercise on page 331. Do all your sentences seem complete? If you think any are not complete, copy them on a separate sheet of paper.

B   Correcting Phrase Fragments

Every sentence must include a subject and a verb. A **phrase** is a group of words that is missing a subject or a verb or both. When you punctuate a phrase as if it is a sentence, you create a fragment.

Two kinds of phrases that are often written as sentence fragments are *appositives* and *prepositional phrases*.

Appositive Fragments

For more on appositives, see 18C. For information on punctuating appositives, see 31C.

An **appositive** is a phrase that identifies or renames a noun or a pronoun. An appositive cannot stand alone as a sentence. To correct an appositive fragment, add the words needed to make it a complete sentence: the nouns or pronouns that the appositive identifies. (You will often find these words in an adjacent sentence.)

APPOSITIVE
FRAG

INCORRECT   He decorated the room in his favorite colors. Brown and black.

CORRECT   He decorated the room in his favorite colors, brown and black.

Sometimes an expression like *such as, for example,* or *for instance* introduces an appositive. Even if an appositive is introduced by one of these expressions, it is still a fragment.

APPOSITIVE
FRAG

INCORRECT   A good diet should include high-fiber foods. Such as leafy vegetables, fruits, beans, and whole-grain bread.

CORRECT A good diet should include high-fiber foods, such as leafy vegetables, fruits, beans, and whole-grain bread.

Prepositional Phrase Fragments

A **prepositional phrase** consists of a preposition and its object. A prepositional phrase cannot stand alone as a sentence. To correct a prepositional phrase fragment, add the words needed to make it a complete sentence. (You will often find these words in an adjacent sentence.)

For more on prepositional phrases, see 15B.

```
                       PREPOSITIONAL PHRASE
                     ┌─────── FRAG ───────┐
```

INCORRECT She promised to stand by him. In sickness and in health.

CORRECT She promised to stand by him in sickness and in health.

◆ PRACTICE 22-3

Each of the following items includes an appositive fragment. In each case, revise to correct the appositive fragment.

ON THE WEB
For more practice, visit Exercise Central: www.bedfordstmartins.com/ writingincontext

> **Example:** The Pledge of Allegiance was written in 1892 by Francis Bellamy. A Baptist minister.
>
> *The Pledge of Allegiance was written in 1892 by Francis Bellamy, a Baptist*
>
> *minister.*

1. Most scholars agree that the U.S. flag was designed by Francis Hopkinson. A New Jersey delegate to the Continental Congress.

   _____

   _____

2. For the new flag, the Continental Congress required certain design features. Such as the original thirteen stars and thirteen stripes.

   _____

   _____

3. The United States has adopted a number of other patriotic symbols. Such as the Pledge of Allegiance.

   _____

   _____

4. The Pledge of Allegiance was first recited during a ceremony in 1892. The four-hundredth anniversary of Columbus's arrival in the New World.

_____

_____

5. Congress officially recognized the pledge in 1942. The first year the United States participated in World War II.

_____

_____

◆ PRACTICE 22-4

Each of the following items includes a prepositional phrase fragment. In each case, revise to correct the prepositional phrase fragment.

Example: Birth order has a strong influence. On one's personality.

Birth order has a strong influence on one's personality.

1. First-borns and only children often display distinct leadership qualities. As children and later as adults.

_____

_____

2. Second-born children may compete with their older sibling but more often pursue different interests. In terms of academics and other activities.

_____

_____

3. In large families, middle-born children often form close personal relationships. Among themselves or with friends outside of the family.

_____

_____

4. The youngest child in a family is always seeking ways to get attention. From the older members of the family.

_____

_____

5. Youngest children can be charming and funny but sometimes manipulative. In their relationships with other family members.

_____

_____

◆ PRACTICE 22-5

Each of the following items is a phrase fragment, not a sentence, because it lacks a subject or a verb or both. On a separate sheet of paper, correct each fragment by adding any words needed to turn the fragment into a complete sentence.

Example: During World War I. _A flu epidemic killed millions of people_

during World War I.

1. The best player on the Yankees.

2. From a developing nation in Africa.

3. Such as tulips or roses.

4. Behind door number 3.

5. The worst week of my life.

6. With a new car in the driveway.

7. A very small animal.

8. For a long time.

9. Turkey, stuffing, potatoes, and cranberry sauce.

10. In less than a year.

■ SEEING AND WRITING: Flashback

Look back at your response to the Seeing and Writing exercise on page 331. Are any phrases incorrectly punctuated as sentences? On a separate sheet of paper, correct each fragment you find by adding any words necessary to create complete sentences. (Hint: You may find these words in a sentence that comes before or after the fragment.)

C   Correcting Incomplete Verbs

Every sentence must include a **complete verb**. Present participles and past participles are not complete verbs. They need helping verbs to complete them.

For more on helping verbs, see 15C.

A **present participle**, such as *looking*, is not a complete verb because it cannot stand alone in a sentence without a **helping verb** (*is looking*, *was looking*, *were looking*, and so on). When you use a present participle without a helping verb, you create a fragment.

FRAGMENT   The twins always looking for trouble.

To correct the fragment, add a helping verb.

CORRECT   The twins <u>are</u> always looking for trouble.

For a list of irregular past participles, see 27B.

An irregular **past participle**, such as *hidden*, is not a complete verb because it cannot stand alone in a sentence without a helping verb (*is hidden*, *was hidden*, *has hidden*, and so on). When you use one of these past participles without a helping verb, you create a fragment.

FRAGMENT   The letter hidden behind the sofa pillow.

To correct the fragment, add a helping verb.

CORRECT   The letter <u>was</u> hidden behind the sofa pillow.

FOCUS   Correcting Participle Fragments

Sometimes you need to add a subject as well as a helping verb to correct a participle fragment. In most cases, you will find the missing subject and verb in an adjacent sentence.

INCORRECT   The twins spent most of the day outside. <u>Looking for trouble</u>.

CORRECT   The twins spent most of the day outside, looking for trouble.

INCORRECT   We finally found the letter. <u>Hidden behind the sofa pillow</u>.

CORRECT   We finally found the letter, hidden behind the sofa pillow.

An **infinitive** (*to be, to go, to write*) is not a complete verb. An infinitive phrase (*to be free, to go home, to write a novel*) cannot stand alone as a sentence because it does not include a subject or a complete verb.

INCORRECT   Eric considered dropping out of school. <u>To start his own business</u>.

To correct an infinitive phrase fragment, you can add the words necessary to complete the sentence.

> CORRECT Eric considered dropping out of school. He thought he might
> like to start his own business.

Often, however, the easiest way to correct an infinitive phrase fragment is to attach it to an adjacent sentence.

> CORRECT Eric considered dropping out of school to start his own
> business.

◆ PRACTICE 22-6

Each of the following items is a fragment because it does not have a complete verb. On a separate sheet of paper, correct each fragment by adding a helping verb.

> **Example:** The sun setting behind the clouds. *The sun was setting*
> *behind the clouds.*

1. The family been worried about money for a long time.
2. The Huangs trying to decide where to live.
3. Both Luz and Kate chosen to receive a fellowship.
4. Janis always complaining about the lab manual.
5. Asbestos fallen from the heating ducts.

◆ PRACTICE 22-7

Each of the following items is a fragment because it is missing a subject and its verb is not complete. On a separate sheet of paper, correct each fragment by attaching it to a new sentence that contains a subject and a complete verb.

> **Example:** Running for his life.
> *Running for his life, he dashed out the door.*

1. Speeding down the freeway.
2. Taken to the cleaner's.
3. To major in biology.
4. Becoming a better athlete.
5. Enlisting in the air force.

6. Been out of town for three weeks.

7. Really feeling optimistic about the future.

8. To play the lead in the musical.

9. To get away with murder.

10. Trying hard to be helpful.

◆ **PRACTICE 22-8**

Each of the following items includes a participle fragment. In each case, correct the participle fragment by attaching it to the adjacent sentence.

> **Example:**   Today, animated films are quite popular. Appealing to children and adults alike.
>
> *Today, animated films are quite popular, appealing to children and adults alike.*

1. Prior to the 1990s, most animated films were hand-drawn. Requiring painstaking skill.

   _____

   _____

2. In recent years, this process has been changed. Replaced by computerized graphics.

   _____

   _____

3. Computer animation has gained a wide audience. Impressed by its range of visual possibilities.

   _____

   _____

4. The first full-length animated film was Walt Disney's *Snow White and the Seven Dwarfs*. Released originally in 1937.

   _____

   _____

5. For decades after that, the Disney studios provided the very best in animated storytelling. Focusing on fairy tales and classics of children's literature.

   _____

   _____

◆ PRACTICE 22-9

Each of the following items includes an infinitive phrase fragment. Correct the first five by adding the words necessary to make the infinitive fragment a complete sentence.

Example: Most milk we drink today is pasteurized. To destroy disease-causing organisms.

Most milk we drink today is pasteurized. This process is used to destroy

disease-causing organisms.

Correct the final five by attaching the infinitive fragment to the adjacent sentence.

Example: Many wetlands have been destroyed. To create new housing developments.

Many wetlands have been destroyed to create new housing developments.

1. Emergency medical technicians receive intensive training. To prepare them for saving lives.

   _____

   _____

2. Many states have adopted standardized testing of students. To rank local school districts.

   _____

   _____

3. Retailers often locate frequently purchased items at the back of their stores. To increase customer traffic.

   _____

   _____

4. The handshake originated as an act between suspicious strangers. To show that they were unarmed.

   _____

   _____

5. Japan's Tokyo Zoo is closed for two months each year. To give the animals a vacation from visitors.

   _____

   _____

6. Chimpanzees have been observed picking the leaves off twigs. To create a tool for scooping honey.

_____

_____

7. More and more, people rely on e-mail. To keep in touch with family and friends.

_____

_____

8. Some student writers are taught the technique of freewriting. To help them overcome writer's block.

_____

_____

9. Early telephone users said "Ahoy" instead of "Hello." To greet incoming callers.

_____

_____

10. The public bus system is being expanded. To provide service for more commuters.

_____

_____

■ SEEING AND WRITING: Flashback

Look back at your response to the Seeing and Writing exercise on page 331. Underline any present or past participles or infinitives. Are the sentences in which they appear complete? Correct each fragment you find by adding the words necessary to complete them.

D   Correcting Dependent Clause Fragments

Every sentence must express a complete thought. A **dependent clause** is a group of words that includes a subject and a verb but does not express a complete thought. Therefore, it cannot stand alone as a sentence. To correct a dependent clause fragment, you must complete the thought.

The following dependent clause is punctuated as if it were a sentence.

After Simon won the lottery.

This sentence fragment includes both a subject *(Simon)* and a complete verb *(won),* but it does not express a complete thought. What happened after Simon won the lottery? To turn this fragment into a sentence, you need to complete the thought.

After Simon won the lottery, he quit his night job.

Dependent Clauses Introduced by Subordinating Conjunctions

Some dependent clauses are introduced by **subordinating conjunctions**.

FRAGMENT Although Marisol had always dreamed of coming to America.

This sentence fragment includes a subject *(Marisol)* and a complete verb *(had dreamed),* but it is not a sentence; it is a dependent clause introduced by the subordinating conjunction *although.*

One way to correct this fragment is to add an **independent clause** (a complete sentence) to complete the idea and finish the sentence.

SENTENCE Although Marisol had always dreamed of coming to America, she did not have enough money for the trip until 1985.

Another way to correct the fragment is to delete the subordinating conjunction *although,* the word that makes the idea incomplete.

SENTENCE Marisol had always dreamed of coming to America.

For more on subordinating conjunctions, see 17B.

Dependent Clauses Introduced by Relative Pronouns

Other dependent clauses are introduced by **relative pronouns** (*who, which, that,* and so on).

FRAGMENT Novelist Richard Wright, who came to Paris in 1947.

FRAGMENT A quinceañera, which celebrates a Latina's fifteenth birthday.

FRAGMENT A key World War II battle that was fought on the Pacific island of Guadalcanal.

For more on relative pronouns, see 17C.

Each of the above sentence fragments includes a subject *(Richard Wright, quinceañera, battle)* and a complete verb *(came, celebrates, was fought).* However, they are not sentences because they do not express complete thoughts. In each case, a relative pronoun creates a dependent clause.

One way to correct each fragment is to add the words needed to complete the idea.

SENTENCE   Novelist Richard Wright, who came to Paris in 1947, spent the rest of his life there.

SENTENCE   A quinceañera, which celebrates a Latina's fifteenth birthday, signifies her entrance into womanhood.

SENTENCE   A key World War II battle that was fought on the Pacific island of Guadalcanal took place in 1943.

Another way to correct the fragments is to delete the relative pronouns that make the ideas incomplete.

SENTENCE   Novelist Richard Wright came to Paris in 1947.

SENTENCE   A quinceañera celebrates a Latina's fifteenth birthday.

SENTENCE   A key World War II battle was fought on the Pacific island of Guadalcanal.

◆ PRACTICE 22-10

ON THE WEB
For more practice, visit Exercise Central:
www.bedford stmartins.com/ writingincontext

Correct each of these dependent clause fragments in two ways. First, make the fragment a complete sentence by adding a group of words that completes the idea. Second, delete the subordinating conjunction or relative pronoun that makes the idea incomplete.

Example: Before it became a state.

Revised: *Before it became a state, West Virginia was part of Virginia.*

Revised: *It became a state.*

1. Because many homeless people are mentally ill.

   Revised: _____

   Revised: _____

2. The film that frightened me.

   Revised: _____

   Revised: _____

3. Although people disagree about the effects of violent video games.

   Revised: _____

   Revised: _____

4. People who drink and drive.

Revised: _____

Revised: _____

5. As competition for athletic scholarships increased.

Revised: _____

Revised: _____

◆ **PRACTICE 22-11**

All of the following are fragments. Turn each fragment into a complete sentence, and write the revised sentence on the line below the fragment.

Example: Waiting in the dugout.

Revised: *Waiting in the dugout, the players chewed tobacco.*

1. Because three-year-olds are still very attached to their parents.

Revised: _____

_____

2. Going around in circles.

Revised: _____

_____

3. To win the prize for the most unusual costume.

Revised: _____

_____

4. Students who thought they could not afford to go to college.

Revised: _____

_____

5. On an important secret mission.

Revised: _____

_____

■ SEEING AND WRITING: Flashback

Look back at your response to the Seeing and Writing exercise on page 331. Underline every subordinating conjunction you find (first, consult the list on page 262), and underline *which, that,* and *who* wherever you find them. Do any of these words create a dependent clause that is punctuated as if it is a sentence? If so, either cross out the subordinating conjunction or relative pronoun, or attach the fragment to another word group to create a complete sentence.

■ SEEING AND WRITING: Revising and Editing

Look back at your response to the Seeing and Writing exercise on page 331, and check one more time to make sure every sentence is complete. If you find a fragment, revise it by adding whatever is necessary to complete it or by attaching it to a nearby sentence. If you do not find any fragments, work with a classmate to correct his or her writing, or edit the work you did in response to another assignment.

CHAPTER REVIEW

◆ **EDITING PRACTICE**

Read the following student essay, into which incomplete sentences have been introduced. Underline each fragment. Then, correct it by adding the words necessary to complete it or attaching it to an adjacent sentence that completes the idea. The first fragment has been underlined and corrected for you.

                        My First Job

      Like many other teenagers, I got my first job when
                                                      in
I was in high school. I worked as a salesperson/ ~~In~~ a
retail clothing chain. At first, I was really excited.
Learning about pricing procedures, arranging displays,
and getting to see all the new styles. I also got to use

my employee discount. A benefit that saved me a lot of money.

People always coming into the store, asking for help in finding things. They would have requests like "Could you tell me where to find a blue and purple lambswool sweater?" and "You're about the same size as my niece. Could you try this on for me?" Sometimes, the customers were annoying. Still, I felt useful and important. When I was able to help them.

The job had its bad side, though. I always seemed to be running. Constantly straightening the same racks over and over. Also rearranging displays several times every night. When the store was busy, it was very hectic. Not all the customers were patient or polite. Some lost their tempers. Because they could not find a particular size or color. Then, they took out their anger on me. On slow nights, when the store was almost empty. I was restless and bored. Eventually, I found a more stimulating position. At a preschool for developmentally delayed children.

◆ COLLABORATIVE ACTIVITIES

1. Exchange papers with another student, and read each other's responses to the Seeing and Writing exercise on page 331. On a separate sheet of paper, list five fragments that describe the product your partner has written about. When your own exercise is returned to you, revise each fragment written by your partner, creating a complete sentence for each one. Finally, add one of these new sentences to your own Seeing and Writing exercise.

2. Working in a group of three or four students, add different subordinating conjunctions to sentences *a* through *d* on the next page to create several different fragments. (See 17B for a list of subordinating conjunctions.)

Then, turn each of the resulting fragments into a complete sentence by adding a word group that completes the idea.

Example:

SENTENCE	FRAGMENT	NEW SENTENCE
I left the party.	As I left the party	As I left the party, I fell.
	After I left the party	After I left the party, the fun stopped.
	Until I left the party	Until I left the party, I had no idea it was so late.

SENTENCES

a. My mind wanders.
b. She caught the ball.
c. He made a wish.
d. Disaster struck.

3. Working in a group of three or four students, build as many sentences as you can from the fragments listed below, each of which is introduced by a past or present participle. Use your imagination to create as many creative, comical, or even silly sentences as you can.

Example:

FRAGMENT Known for his incredible memory

SENTENCES Zack, known for his incredible memory, has somehow managed to forget everything he learned about chemistry.

Known for his incredible memory, Monty the Magnificent mesmerized audiences.

FRAGMENTS

a. wandering in the desert
b. stranded in the jungle
c. looking for his ideal mate
d. always using as much ketchup as possible
e. folded, stapled, and mutilated

Subject-Verb Agreement

PREVIEW

In this chapter, you will learn
- to understand subject-verb agreement (23A)
- to avoid agreement problems with *be, have,* and *do* (23B)
- to avoid agreement problems when a prepositional phrase comes between the subject and the verb (23C)
- to avoid agreement problems with indefinite pronouns as subjects (23D)
- to avoid agreement problems when the verb comes before the subject (23E)
- to avoid agreement problems with dependent clauses (23F)

■ SEEING AND WRITING

Look at the painting above. Then, using present tense verbs, describe what you think the artist is trying to convey. For example, what might this woman be thinking?

▶ **Word Power**

composition
the arrangement of parts to make a whole

pensive
thoughtful

realistic
presented or depicted as something really is

349

A · Understanding Subject-Verb Agreement

A sentence's subject (a noun or pronoun) and its verb must **agree** in number. Singular subjects must have singular verbs, and plural subjects must have plural verbs.

> $\overset{\text{s}}{\underline{\text{The museum}}}$ $\overset{\text{v}}{\underline{\underline{\text{opens}}}}$ at ten o'clock. (singular noun subject *museum* takes singular verb *opens*)

> $\overset{\text{s}}{\underline{\text{The museums}}}$ $\overset{\text{v}}{\underline{\underline{\text{open}}}}$ at ten o'clock. (plural noun subject *museums* takes plural verb *open*)

> $\overset{\text{s}}{\underline{\text{She}}}$ always $\overset{\text{v}}{\underline{\underline{\text{watches}}}}$ the eleven o'clock news. (singular pronoun subject *she* takes singular verb *watches*)

For more on identifying plural noun and pronoun subjects, see 28B and 28C.

> $\overset{\text{s}}{\underline{\text{They}}}$ always $\overset{\text{v}}{\underline{\underline{\text{watch}}}}$ the eleven o'clock news. (plural pronoun subject *they* takes plural verb *watch*)

Most subject-verb agreement problems occur in the present tense, where third-person singular subjects require special verb forms. Regular verbs form the third-person singular by adding *-s* or *-es* to the base form (the form of the verb used with *I*).

For information about subject-verb agreement with the irregular verb be, see 23B.

Subject-Verb Agreement with Regular Verbs

	Singular	**Plural**
First person	I play	Molly and I/we play
Second person	you play	you play
Third person	he/she/it plays	they play
	the man plays	the men play
	Molly plays	Molly and Sam play

In verb tenses other than the present, the same form of the regular verb is used with every subject: *I played, he played, they played; I will play, she will play, they will play.*

FOCUS **Subject-Verb Agreement with Compound Subjects**

The subject of a sentence is not always a single word. It can also be a **compound subject**, consisting of two or more words. Special rules govern subject-verb agreement with compound subjects.

(continued on the following page)

(continued from the previous page)

■ When the parts of a compound subject are connected by *and,* the compound subject takes a plural verb.

     S   V

John and Marsha <u>share</u> an office.

■ If both parts of a compound subject connected by *or* are singular, the compound subject takes a singular verb.

     S   V

John or Marsha <u>locks</u> up at the end of the day.

■ If both parts of a compound subject connected by *or* are plural, the compound subject takes a plural verb.

     S   V

Buses or trains <u>take</u> you to the center of the city.

■ If one part of a compound subject connected by *or* is singular and the other part is plural, the verb agrees with the word that is closer to it.

     S   V

The mayor or the council members <u>meet</u> with community groups.

     S   V

The council members or the mayor <u>meets</u> with community groups.

◆ PRACTICE 23-1

Underline the correct form of the verb in each of the following sentences. Make sure the verb agrees with its subject.

    Example: Radio stations (<u>broadcast</u>/broadcasts) many kinds of music.

(1) Most music fans (know/knows) about salsa, a popular style of Latin music. (2) However, they probably (need/needs) a little education when it comes to ranchera, a blend of traditional forms of regional Mexican music. (3) These forms (include/includes) mariachi music as well as rural-influenced ballads and waltz-like tunes. (4) The ranchera style (appeal/appeals) particularly to a wide number of Americans of Mexican descent. (5) Its performers (sell/sells) millions of records a year, and they often

ON THE WEB
For more practice, visit Exercise Central: www.bedford stmartins.com/ writingincontext

(top/tops) *Billboard*'s Latin charts. (6) In fact, regional Mexican recordings (outsell/outsells) any other form of Latin music in the United States. (7) This popularity (surprise/surprises) many people because the mainstream music industry (give/gives) most of its attention to Latin pop stars who sing in English. (8) Older ranchera lovers (tend/tends) to be first-generation, working-class immigrants, but more and more young listeners (seem/seems) drawn to ranchera because of their pride in their Mexican heritage. (9) When one Los Angeles nightclub (host/hosts) a ranchera night, it (draw/draws) a large crowd of English-speaking fans in their twenties. (10) Clearly, ranchera stars (deserve/deserves) more attention from the music industry.

◆ PRACTICE 23-2

Fill in the blank with the correct present tense form of the verb.

> **Example:**   Every day, she ___*visits*___ the computer lab in the basement of Reinhold Hall. (visit)

(1) I _____ with a computer. (write) (2) It _____ my work easier. (make) (3) Our instructors _____ our work. (supervise) (4) They _____ our computer disks. (collect) (5) Each week, Ms. Keane and Mr. Marlowe _____ back the disks. (give) (6) The disks _____ our instructors' comments. (contain) (7) I _____ my disk into the computer (put) and _____ Mr. Marlowe's comments as I revise. (read) (8) We _____ this technique for marking papers. (like) (9) One student says he _____ the computer, however. (hate) (10) The screen _____ him headaches. (give)

◆ PRACTICE 23-3

Underline the correct form of the verb in each of the following sentences. Make sure that the verb agrees with its compound subject.

> **Example:**   Gloves or a scarf (make/<u>makes</u>) a good wintertime gift.

1. Cars and trucks (fill/fills) the municipal parking lot each day.

2. Grapes or an apple (provide/provides) a nutritious addition to a lunch.

3. A security officer and a video monitoring system (survey/surveys) the bank's lobby during business hours.

4. A vegetable dish or french fries (come/comes) with the entrée.

5. A pianist or a guitarist (play/plays) at the club every weekend.

6. Nurses or nurse practitioners (offer/offers) round-the-clock care.

7. According to the old saying, fish and houseguests (smell/smells) after three days.

8. Flowers or a get-well balloon (cheer/cheers) people up when they are ill.

9. The restaurant owner or her daughter always (greet/greets) customers.

10. A sliding glass door or French windows (allow/allows) the greatest amount of light into a room.

■ SEEING AND WRITING: Flashback

Look back at your response to the Seeing and Writing exercise on page 349. Choose two sentences that contain present tense verbs, and rewrite them on a separate sheet of paper. Underline the subject of each sentence once and the verb twice. If the subject and verb of each sentence do not agree, correct them.

B   Avoiding Agreement Problems with *Be*, *Have*, and *Do*

The irregular verbs *be*, *have*, and *do* often present problems with subject-verb agreement in the present tense. Memorizing their forms is the only sure way to avoid such problems.

Subject-Verb Agreement with Be

	Singular	**Plural**
First person	I am	we are
Second person	you are	you are
Third person	he/she/it is	they are
	Tran is	Tran and Ryan are
	the boy is	the boys are

For more on regular and irregular verbs, see 26A and 26B.

Subject-Verb Agreement with Have

	Singular	**Plural**
First person	I have	we have
Second person	you have	you have
Third person	he/she/it has	they have
	Shana has	Shana and Robert have
	the student has	the students have

Subject-Verb Agreement with Do

	Singular	**Plural**
First person	I do	we do
Second person	you do	you do
Third person	he/she/it does	they do
	Ken does	Ken and Mia do
	the book does	the books do

◆ PRACTICE 23-4

ON THE WEB
*For more
practice, visit
Exercise Central:*
www.bedford
stmartins.com/
writingincontext

Fill in the blank with the correct present tense form of the verb.

Example: Sometimes, people ___*do*___ damage without meaning to. (do)

(1) Biologists _____ serious worries about the damage that exotic ani-mals can cause when they move into places where native species have devel-oped few defenses against them. (have) (2) The English sparrow _____ one example. (be) (3) It _____ a role in the decline in the number of bluebirds. (have) (4) On the Galapagos Islands, cats _____ another example. (be) (5) Introduced by early explorers, they currently _____ much damage to the eggs of the giant tortoises that live on the islands. (do) (6) Scientists today _____ worried about a new problem. (be) (7) This _____ a situation caused by fish and wildlife agencies that deliberately introduce exotic fish into lakes and streams. (be) (8) They _____ this to please those who enjoy fishing. (do) (9) Although popular with people who fish, this policy _____ major draw-backs. (have) (10) It _____ one drawback in particular: many species of fish have been pushed close to extinction. (have)

■ SEEING AND WRITING: Flashback

Look back at your response to the Seeing and Writing exercise on page 349. Have you used a form of *be, have,* or *do* in any of your sentences? Have you used the correct forms of *be, have,* and *do*? If not, rewrite the sentences on a separate sheet of paper, and correct any agreement errors.

C   Avoiding Agreement Problems When a Prepositional Phrase Comes between the Subject and the Verb

Sometimes, a subject-verb agreement problem occurs when a prepositional phrase (a phrase that begins with *of, in, between,* and so on) comes between the subject and the verb. In such cases, the object of the preposition appears to be the subject of the sentence when really it is not. This error can lead to an incorrect verb choice, as in the three incorrect sentences below.

For more on prepositional phrases, see 15B. For a list of prepositions, see 30L.

> INCORRECT High levels of mercury occurs in some fish.
>
> CORRECT High <u>levels</u> of mercury <u>occur</u> in some fish.
>
> INCORRECT Water in the fuel lines cause an engine to stall.
>
> CORRECT <u>Water</u> in the fuel lines <u>causes</u> an engine to stall.
>
> INCORRECT Food between the teeth result in decay.
>
> CORRECT <u>Food</u> between the teeth <u>results</u> in decay.

By crossing out the prepositional phrase, you can easily see if there are any agreement errors.

> High levels ~~of mercury~~ occur in some fish.
>
> Water ~~in the fuel lines~~ causes an engine to stall.
>
> Food ~~between the teeth~~ results in decay.

FOCUS   Words That Come between Subject and Verb

Prepositional phrases introduced by *in addition to, along with, together with, as well as, except,* and *including* can be especially confusing.

(continued on the following page)

(continued from the previous page)

A noun or pronoun that follows such a phrase is an object of the preposition; therefore, it cannot be the subject of the sentence.

$\overset{s}{\text{St. Thomas}}$, ~~along with St. Croix and St. John~~, $\overset{v}{\underline{\underline{\text{is}}}}$ part of the United States Virgin Islands.

◆ PRACTICE 23-5

ON THE WEB

For more practice, visit Exercise Central: www.bedford stmartins.com/ writingincontext

In each of the following sentences, cross out the prepositional phrase that separates the subject and the verb. Then, underline the subject of the sentence once and the verb that agrees with the subject twice.

Example: The <u>mustard stains</u> ~~on the carpet~~ (suggest/<u><u>suggests</u></u>) that Hiro and Mika had a party.

1. The cupids in the painting (symbolize/symbolizes) lost innocence.

2. Fans at a concert (get/gets) angry if the band is late.

3. The appliances in the kitchen (make/makes) strange noises.

4. The United States, along with Germany and Japan, (produce/produces) most of the world's cars.

5. A good set of skis and poles (cost/costs) a lot.

6. Unfortunately, one out of ten men (gets/get) prostate cancer.

7. Workers in the city (pays/pay) a high wage tax.

8. Each summer, fires from lightning (cause/causes) hundreds of millions of dollars in property damage.

9. Volunteers, including people like my father, (help/helps) paramedics in my community.

10. A doctor, together with two nurses, (staff/staffs) the clinic at the health center.

■ SEEING AND WRITING: Flashback

Look back at your response to the Seeing and Writing exercise on page 349. Can you find any sentences in which a prepositional phrase

(continued on the following page)

(continued from the previous page)
comes between the subject and the verb? If so, lightly cross out the prepositional phrase, and then correct any subject-verb agreement errors.

D Avoiding Agreement Problems with Indefinite Pronouns as Subjects

An **indefinite pronoun** is a pronoun that does not refer to a particular person, place, or idea. When an indefinite pronoun is the subject of a sentence,
the verb must agree with it. Most indefinite pronouns, such as *no one* and
everyone, are singular and take a singular verb.

For information on pronoun-antecedent agreement with indefinite pronouns, see 28E.

$$\overset{S}{\text{No one}}\ \underline{\underline{\overset{V}{\text{likes}}}}\ \text{getting up early.}$$

$$\underline{\overset{S}{\text{Everyone}}}\ \underline{\underline{\overset{V}{\text{likes}}}}\ \text{to sleep late.}$$

$$\underline{\overset{S}{\text{Somebody}}}\ \underline{\underline{\overset{V}{\text{likes}}}}\ \text{beets.}$$

Singular Indefinite Pronouns

another	either	neither	one
anybody	everybody	nobody	somebody
anyone	everyone	no one	someone
anything	everything	nothing	something
each	much		

A few indefinite pronouns are plural *(both, many, several, few, others)* and
take a plural verb.

$$\underline{\overset{S}{\text{Many}}}\ \underline{\underline{\overset{V}{\text{were}}}}\ \text{left homeless by the storm.}$$

FOCUS Indefinite Pronouns as Subjects

If a prepositional phrase comes between the indefinite pronoun and the
verb, cross out the prepositional phrase to help you identify the sentence's subject.

(continued on the following page)

> *(continued from the previous page)*
>
>   s   v
> Each ~~of the boys~~ has a bike.
>
>   s   v
> Many ~~of the boys~~ have bikes.

◆ PRACTICE 23-6

ON THE WEB
For more practice, visit Exercise Central: www.bedford stmartins.com/ writingincontext

Circle the correct verb in each sentence.

Example: Each of the three streams in our area (is/are) polluted.

1. One of the streams no longer (have/has) any fish.

2. Another (contain/contains) a lot of algae.

3. Everybody (want/wants) to improve the situation.

4. No one (are/is) willing to do anything.

5. Somebody always (take/takes) control.

6. Everyone (know/knows) that pollution is difficult to control.

7. Neither of the candidates (seem/seems) willing to act.

8. Whenever anyone (ask/asks) for suggestions, neither (have, has) any.

9. According to the candidates, everything (is/are) being done that can be done.

10. One of my friends (say/says) that she will not vote for either candidate.

■ SEEING AND WRITING: Flashback

Look back at your response to the Seeing and Writing exercise on page 349. Do any of the sentences contain indefinite pronouns that act as subjects? If so, circle each indefinite pronoun subject. Do the verbs in these sentences agree with the indefinite pronoun subjects? If you find any that do not, rewrite the correct form of the verb above the line, and cross out the incorrect verb form.

E   Avoiding Agreement Problems When the Verb Comes before the Subject

A verb always agrees with its subject, even if the verb comes *before* the subject. In questions, for example, word order is reversed, with the verb coming before the subject or with the subject coming between two parts of the verb.

         V   S
Where <u>is</u> the <u>telephone booth</u>?

   V   S   V
<u>Are</u> <u>you</u> <u>going</u> to the party?

If you have trouble identifying the subject of a question, answer the question.

         V   S
Where <u>is</u> the <u>telephone booth</u>?

           S   V
The <u>telephone booth</u> <u>is</u> outside.

FOCUS   *There Is and There Are*

In a sentence that begins with *there is* or *there are*, the subject comes after the form of the verb *be*. (*There* can never be the subject.)

        V   S
There <u>are</u> nine <u>justices</u> on the Supreme Court.

       V   S
There <u>is</u> one <u>chief justice</u> on the Court.

◆ PRACTICE 23-7

Underline the subject of each sentence, and circle the correct form of the verb.

    Example: Who (is)/are) <u>the writer</u> who won the 1992 Nobel Prize in literature?

1. Where (is/are) the Bering Straits?

2. Why (do/does) the compound change color after being exposed to light?

ON THE WEB
For more practice, visit Exercise Central: **www.bedford stmartins.com/ writingincontext**

3. (Is/Are) the twins identical or fraternal?

4. How (do/does) Congress override a presidential veto?

5. What (have/has) this got to do with me?

6. There (is/are) ten computers in the writing center.

7. There (is/are) more than nine million people living in Mexico City.

8. There (is/are) several reference books in this library that can help you with your research.

9. There (is/are) four reasons that we should save the spotted owl from extinction.

10. There (is/are) only one right answer to the question.

■ **SEEING AND WRITING: Flashback**

Look back at your response to the Seeing and Writing exercise on page 349. Do you have any sentences in which the verb comes before the subject? If so, check carefully to make sure the subjects and verbs agree. If they do not, revise the incorrect sentence.

F   Avoiding Agreement Problems with Dependent Clauses

For more on who, which, that, and other relative pronouns, see 17C.

The verb in a dependent clause introduced by the relative pronoun *who, which,* or *that* must agree with the word to which the relative pronoun refers. The relative pronouns are singular when they refer to a singular word and plural when they refer to a plural word.

The author, who writes about Chinese immigrants, spoke at our college. (The verb *writes* is singular because the relative pronoun *who* refers to *author.*)

This course, which has a waiting list, is open only to juniors and seniors. (The verb *has* is singular because the relative pronoun *which* refers to *course,* which is singular.)

Computers that have flat-screen monitors are expensive. (The verb *have* is plural because the relative pronoun *that* refers to *computers,* which is plural.)

◆ PRACTICE 23-8

Draw an arrow from *who, which,* or *that* to the word that it refers to. Then, circle the correct form of the verb.

Example: Edgar Allan Poe, who (tell/(tells)) tales of horror, was born in 1809.

ON THE WEB
For more practice, visit Exercise Central:
www.bedford stmartins.com/ writingincontext

(1) Poe's "The Fall of the House of Usher" is a story that (have/has) entertained many readers. (2) The story, which (contain/contains) the poem "The Haunted Palace," was published in 1839. (3) The narrator, who (have/has) not seen Roderick Usher for many years, is summoned to the House of Usher. (4) The decaying mansion, which (is/are) dark and dreary, stands at the edge of a swamp. (5) Roderick's twin sister, Madeline, who (live/lives) in the house, is very ill. (6) At one point in the story, Roderick's sister, who (is/are) in a trance, is thought to be dead. (7) Roderick buries her in the family vault that (is/are) under the house. (8) Later, Madeline, who (is/are) dressed in her shroud, walks into the room. (9) Roderick, who (is/are) terrified, falls down dead. (10) Running outside, the narrator sees the house, which (have/has) split apart, sink into the swamp.

■ SEEING AND WRITING: Flashback

Look back at your response to the Seeing and Writing exercise on page 349. Can you find any sentences that include the relative pronoun *who, which,* or *that?* Revise if necessary to make sure you use a singular verb when *who, which,* or *that* refers to a singular word, and a plural verb when the reference is to a plural word.

■ SEEING AND WRITING: Revising and Editing

Look back at your response to the Seeing and Writing exercise on page 349 and check one more time to make sure all your verbs agree with

(continued on the following page)

> *(continued from the previous page)*
> their subjects. Cross out any incorrect verb forms, and write the correct forms above them. When you have finished, rewrite the entire paragraph on a separate sheet of paper, changing all the singular subjects to plural subjects and the plural subjects to singular ones. (For example, *picture* would become *pictures*, and *he* or *she* would become *they*.) Then, change the verbs so that they agree with their new subjects.

CHAPTER REVIEW

◆ EDITING PRACTICE

Read the following student essay, into which errors of subject-verb agreement have been introduced. Decide whether each of the underlined verbs agrees with its subject. If it does not, cross out the verb and write in the correct form. If it does, write *C* above the verb. The first sentence has been done for you.

Watching Movies

                          C   *have*

I <u>believe</u> that to be appreciated fully, movies <u>has</u> to be seen in a theater on a big screen. There <u>is</u> many reasons that I and other moviegoers <u>feels</u> this way. In many cases, a blockbuster movie's sound or its other special effects <u>requires</u> a theater screening if the movie <u>is</u> to achieve its full impact for viewers. Even movies that <u>has</u> no special effects <u>benefits</u> from being seen on a large screen. There <u>is</u> something about sitting with other people in a darkened theater that audiences <u>responds</u> to in a special way.

    I <u>has</u> a good friend who <u>disagree</u> with me. He, along with others, <u>argue</u> that the price of movies <u>are</u> too high. Too often, people in the audience <u>makes</u> noise and <u>have</u> conversations during the screening. Even worse, my friend say, viewers <u>feel</u> that it <u>be</u> acceptable to go in and out of the theater whenever they <u>chooses</u>. These distractions <u>makes</u> it hard to concentrate on the movie. Movie fans like my friend who <u>do</u> not appreciate such interruptions <u>prefers</u> to wait until a film <u>come</u> out on video. Then they <u>are</u> able to watch it in private, and there <u>are</u> nobody to disturb them.

It is true that members of a theater audience <u>does</u> sometimes cause disruptions. I, however, <u>see</u> these as minor disturbances that <u>has</u> little effect on my enjoyment of a movie. The spectacle of big-screen movies <u>fascinate</u> me, so I hardly <u>notices</u> what is going on around me. Anyone who <u>think</u> watching videos on television is better than seeing movies in theaters cannot truly love the art of film.

◆ COLLABORATIVE ACTIVITIES

1. Working in a group of four students, list ten nouns (five singular and five plural)—people, places, or things—on the left-hand side of a sheet of paper. Beside each noun, write the present tense form of a verb that could logically go with the noun. Exchange papers with another group, and check to see that singular nouns have singular verbs and plural nouns have plural verbs.

2. Working with your group, expand each noun-and-verb combination you listed in Collaborative Activity 1 into a complete sentence. (If a combination makes a complete sentence, expand it into a longer sentence.) Next, write a sentence that could logically follow each of these sentences, using a pronoun as the subject of the new sentence. Make sure the pronoun you choose refers to the noun in the previous sentence, as in the following example: *Alan watches three movies a week. He is addicted to films.* Check to be certain the subjects in your new sentences agree with the verbs.

3. Exchange the final version of your edited Seeing and Writing exercise with another student in your group. Answer the following questions about each sentence in your partner's exercise.

- Does the sentence contain a prepositional phrase that comes between the subject and the verb?
- Does the sentence contain an indefinite pronoun used as a subject?
- Does the verb come before the subject?
- Does the sentence include a dependent clause introduced by a relative pronoun (*who, which,* or *that*)?

As you answer these questions, check to make sure all the verbs agree with their subjects. When your own exercise is returned to you, make any necessary corrections.

Illogical Shifts

PREVIEW

In this chapter, you will learn
- to avoid illogical shifts in tense (24A)
- to avoid illogical shifts in person (24B)
- to avoid illogical shifts in number (24C)
- to avoid illogical shifts in voice (24D)

▶ **Word Power**

aspire
to strive
toward a goal

encourage
to inspire
with hope or
confidence

nurture
to nourish;
to educate
or train

■ SEEING AND WRITING

Look at the picture above, and write about what parents can do to help their children succeed in life. How can parents motivate their children to set appropriate goals and work to achieve them?

A **shift** occurs anytime a writer changes *tense, person, number,* or *voice.* As you write and revise, be sure that any shifts you make are logical. An **illogical shift** occurs when a writer changes tense, person, number, or voice for no good reason.

A   Avoiding Illogical Shifts in Tense

For more on tense, see Chapters 26 and 27.

The three basic tenses are past, present, and future. An **illogical shift in tense** occurs when a writer shifts from one tense to another for no apparent reason.

> ILLOGICAL SHIFT IN TENSE   The dog <u>walked</u> to the fireplace. Then, he <u>circles</u> twice and <u>lies</u> down in front of the fire. (past to present)

> REVISED   The dog <u>walked</u> to the fireplace. Then, he <u>circled</u> twice and <u>lay</u> down in front of the fire. (consistent past)

> REVISED   The dog <u>walks</u> to the fireplace. Then, he <u>circles</u> twice and <u>lies</u> down in front of the fire. (consistent present)

◆ PRACTICE 24-1

ON THE WEB
For more practice, visit Exercise Central:
www.bedford
stmartins.com/
writingincontext

Edit the following sentences for illogical shifts in tense. If a sentence is correct, write *C* in the blank.

Examples:

She was surprised when she ~~receives~~ ^{*received*} the news. _____ (illogical shift)

Last year, she was a captain on the force. Now, she is chief of police. __*C*__ (logical shift)

(1) When Beverly Harvard became the chief of the Atlanta police force, she is the first African-American woman ever to hold that title in a major U.S. city. _____ (2) She started on the police force when she was twenty-two, at a time when Atlanta employs mostly white men as police officers. _____ (3) Now, more than half the department is African American, and women made up about a quarter of the force. _____ (4) Harvard first thought about joining the force because her husband and a male friend said they do not believe women are capable of doing police work. _____ (5) Her husband even agrees to pay her $100 if she made it onto the force. _____ (6) She accepted

the challenge, and today she looks back on her first years of training with amazement at how little she knew then. _____ (7) In fact, when she entered the police academy, she did not really plan to be a police officer; she just wants to prove her husband wrong and to win the $100 bet. _____ (8) One thing that helped her to advance was her administrative ability; another is her talent for effective management. _____ (9) When her promotion was announced, some veteran officers criticize her appointment as police chief, but most younger officers praised the choice. _____ (10) Eventually, most members of the force came to appreciate her accessibility and are happy about her willingness to listen to new ideas and approaches. _____

■ SEEING AND WRITING: Flashback

Look back at your response to the Seeing and Writing exercise on page 365. Check each sentence to make sure you have no illogical shifts from one tense to another. If you find an incorrect sentence, correct the illogical shift in tense.

B Avoiding Illogical Shifts in Person

Person is the form a pronoun takes to indicate who is speaking, spoken about, or spoken to.

Person	Singular	Plural
First person	I	we
Second person	you	you
Third person	he, she, it	they

An **illogical shift in person** occurs when a writer shifts from one person to another for no apparent reason. Most errors occur in the second and third person.

ILLOGICAL SHIFT The <u>hikers</u> were told that <u>you</u> had to stay on the trail. (third to second person)

REVISED   The <u>hikers</u> were told that <u>they</u> had to stay on the trail. (consistent use of third person)

ILLOGICAL SHIFT   <u>Anyone</u> can learn to cook if <u>you</u> practice. (third to second person)

REVISED   <u>You</u> can learn to cook if <u>you</u> practice. (consistent use of second person)

REVISED   <u>Anyone</u> can learn to cook if <u>he or she</u> practices. (consistent use of third person)

Note: Be careful not to use the pronoun *he* to refer to an indefinite pronoun antecedent, such as *anyone,* that could be either masculine or feminine. (See 28E.)

◆ **PRACTICE 24-2**

For more on subject-verb agreement, see Chapter 23.

The following sentences contain illogical shifts between the second person and the third person. Edit each sentence so that it uses third-person pronouns consistently. Be sure to change the verb if necessary to make it agree with the new subject.

> **Example:**   Before a person finds a job in the fashion industry, ~~you have~~
> *he or she has*
> to have some experience.

ON THE WEB
For more practice, visit Exercise Central: www.bedford stmartins.com/ writingincontext

(1) Young people who want a career in the fashion industry do not always realize how hard you will have to work. (2) They think that working in the world of fashion will be glamorous and that you will quickly make a fortune. (3) In reality, no matter how talented you are, a recent college graduate entering the industry is paid only about $22,000 a year. (4) The manufacturers and retailers who employ new graduates expect you to work for three years or more at this salary before you are promoted. (5) A young designer may receive a big raise if you are very talented, but this is unusual. (6) New employees have to pay their dues, and you soon realize that most of your duties are tedious. (7) Employees may be excited to land a job as an assistant designer but then find that you color in designs that have already been drawn. (8) Other beginners in fashion houses discover that you spend

most of your time sewing or typing up orders. (9) If a person is serious about working in the fashion industry, you have to be realistic. (10) For most newcomers to the industry, the ability to do what you are told to do is more important than your artistic talent or fashion sense.

■ SEEING AND WRITING: Flashback

Look back at your response to the Seeing and Writing exercise on page 365. Check each sentence to make sure there are no illogical shifts in person. If you find an incorrect sentence, correct the illogical shift in person.

C   Avoiding Illogical Shifts in Number

Number is the form a noun, pronoun, or verb takes to indicate whether it is singular (one) or plural (more than one).

Number	
Singular	**Plural**
I	we
he, she	they
Fred	Fred and Ethel
man	men
an encyclopedia	encyclopedias
his, her	their
am, is, was	are, were

An **illogical shift in number** occurs when a writer shifts from singular to plural (or the other way around) for no apparent reason.

ILLOGICAL SHIFT IN NUMBER   Each <u>visitor</u> to the museum must check <u>their</u> cameras at the entrance. (singular to plural)

REVISED   Each <u>visitor</u> to the museum must check <u>his or her</u> camera at the entrance. (consistent singular)

REVISED   <u>Visitors</u> to the museum must check <u>their</u> cameras at the entrance. (consistent plural)

◆ **PRACTICE 24-3**

Edit the following sentences for illogical shifts from singular to plural. You
can either change the singular element to the plural or change the plural element to the singular. Be sure to change the verb so it agrees with the new subject. If the sentence is correct, write *C* in the blank.

Examples:

his or her
Each attorney first makes ~~their~~ opening speech. _____

Good jurors
~~A good juror~~ takes their time in making their decision. _____

(1) According to recent studies, a juror may have their mind made up
before the trial even begins. _____ (2) As attorneys offer their opening arguments, a juror may immediately decide whether they think the defendant is
innocent or guilty. _____ (3) This unfounded conclusion often depends on
which attorney makes their initial description of the case the most dramatic.
_____ (4) During the trial, that juror will pay attention only to evidence that
corresponds to the decision they have already made. _____ (5) A juror with
poor decision-making skills is also not likely to listen to challenges to their
opinions during the deliberation phase of the trial. _____ (6) No matter how
wrong they are, such a juror argues their positions strongly and urges the
strictest sentencing or the highest damage payments. _____ (7) These jurors
believe their responsibility is to argue for their version of the truth rather
than to weigh all the evidence and alternative possibilities. _____ (8) Such
a juror will even make up their own evidence to support their case. _____
(9) For example, one juror argued that a man being tried for murder was
acting in their own defense because the victim was probably carrying a
knife, but no knife was mentioned during the trial. _____ (10) Studies
suggest that a person who jumps to conclusions on a jury probably will
not take their time when making other important decisions in life. _____

■ SEEING AND WRITING: Flashback

Look back at your response to the Seeing and Writing exercise on page 365. Find all the sentences in which you use the pronoun *they* or *their*. Check every sentence to make sure each of these pronouns refers to a plural noun or pronoun. If you find an incorrect sentence, correct the illogical shift in number.

D   Avoiding Illogical Shifts in Voice

When the subject of a sentence *performs* the action, the sentence is in the **active voice**. When the subject of a sentence *receives* the action, the sentence is in the **passive voice**.

ACTIVE VOICE   Nat Turner organized a slave rebellion in August 1831. (Subject *Nat Turner* performs the action.)

PASSIVE VOICE   A slave rebellion was organized by Nat Turner in 1831. (Subject *rebellion* receives the action.)

An **illogical shift in voice** occurs when a writer shifts from active to passive voice or from passive to active voice for no apparent reason.

ILLOGICAL SHIFT IN VOICE   J. D. Salinger wrote *The Catcher in the Rye,* and *Franny and Zooey* was also written by him. (active to passive)

REVISED   J. D. Salinger wrote *The Catcher in the Rye,* and he also wrote *Franny and Zooey.* (consistent voice)

ILLOGICAL SHIFT IN VOICE   Radium was discovered by Marie Curie, and Watson and Crick described the structure of DNA. (passive to active)

REVISED   Marie Curie discovered radium, and Watson and Crick described the structure of DNA. (consistent voice)

FOCUS   **Correcting Illogical Shifts in Voice**

The active voice is stronger and more direct than the passive voice. For this reason, you should usually use the active voice in your college writing. To change a sentence from the passive to the active voice, determine

(continued on the following page)

(continued from the previous page)
who or what performs the action, and make this noun the subject of a
new active-voice sentence.

> PASSIVE VOICE The campus escort service <u>is used</u> by some of my
> friends. (*Some of my friends* performs the action.)
>
> ACTIVE VOICE Some of my friends <u>use</u> the campus escort service.

Use the passive voice in your college writing only when the action being
performed is more important than the person performing it. To change
a sentence from the active to the passive voice, determine who or what
receives the action, and make this noun the subject of a new passive-
voice sentence.

> ACTIVE VOICE I <u>completed</u> the report on schedule. (*Report* receives
> the action.)
>
> PASSIVE VOICE The report <u>was completed</u> on schedule.

 Computer Tip

To see if your writing overuses the passive voice, use the Search or Find command to look
for *is, are, was,* and *were,* which often appear as part of passive-voice verbs.

◆ PRACTICE 24-4

ON THE WEB
*For more
practice, visit
Exercise Central:*
www.bedford
stmartins.com/
writingincontext

The following sentences contain illogical shifts in voice. Revise each sentence
by changing the underlined passive-voice verb to the active voice.

Example:
Several researchers are interested in leadership qualities, and a study of
decision making <u>was conducted</u> by them recently.

Several researchers are interested in leadership qualities, *and they*
recently conducted a study of decision making.

1. A local university funded the study, and the research team <u>was led</u> by
   Dr. Alicia Flynn.

   A local university funded the study, _____

   _____

2. The researchers developed a series of questions about decision making,
   and then a hundred subjects <u>were interviewed</u> by them.

The researchers developed a series of questions about decision making,

_____

3. Instinct alone <u>was relied on</u> by two-thirds of the subjects, and only one-third used logical <u>analysis</u>.

_____ and only one-third

used logical analysis.

4. After the researchers completed the study, a report <u>was written</u> about their findings.

After the researchers completed the study, _____

_____

5. The report <u>was read</u> by many experts, and most of them found the results surprising.

_____ , and most

of them found the results surprising.

■ SEEING AND WRITING: Flashback

Look back at your response to the Seeing and Writing exercise on page 365. Check each sentence to make sure there are no illogical shifts in voice. If you find an incorrect sentence, correct the illogical shift in voice.

■ SEEING AND WRITING: Revising and Editing

Look back at your response to the Seeing and Writing exercise on page 365. Check carefully to make sure no illogical shifts in tense, person, number, or voice remain. When you have finished, do the same for another assignment you are currently working on.

CHAPTER REVIEW

◆ **EDITING PRACTICE**

Read the following student essay, into which illogical shifts in tense, person, number, and voice have been introduced. Edit the passage to eliminate the unnecessary shifts, making sure subjects and verbs agree. The first sentence has been edited for you.

The Mixing of Cultures

Because the United States is the melting pot of the world, it ~~drew~~ *draws* thousands of immigrants from Europe, Asia, and Africa. Many of them come to the United States because they wanted to become Americans. At the same time, they also want to preserve parts of their original cultures. This conflict confuses many immigrants. Some immigrants think that in order to become American, you have to give up your ethnic identity. Others, however, realize that it is possible to become an American without losing your ethnic identity. To me, in fact, this is the strength of the United States: as a Filipino American, I am able to be both Filipino and American. I know of no other country in the world where this was true.

Many Filipino Americans are able to maintain their Filipino culture in the United States. For example, they decorate their houses to remind themselves of traditional houses in the Philippines. Filipinos also try to preserve their native language. Although every Filipino speaks English, Tagalog is also spoken by them--usually at home. On holidays, Filipinos observe the traditions of the Philippines. They sing Filipino folk songs, do traditional dances, and cook Filipino foods. Everyone tries to visit their relatives in the Philippines as often as they can. In this way, a Filipino child can often experience their ethnic culture firsthand.

A person who wants to hold on to their ethnic background can enjoy life in America. Here, cultures mix and enrich one another. Each culture has something to offer America--their food, language, and traditions. At the same time, America had something to offer each culture--economic opportunity, education, and freedom.

◆ COLLABORATIVE ACTIVITIES

1. On a separate sheet of paper, write five sentences that include shifts from present to past tense, some logical and some illogical. Exchange papers with another person in your group, and revise any incorrect sentences.

2. As a group, compose a test made up of five sentences containing illogical shifts in tense, person, number, and voice. Exchange tests with another group in the class. After you have taken their test, compare your answers with theirs.

3. As a group, choose five words from the list that follows, and use each as the subject of a sentence. Make sure each sentence includes a pronoun that refers to the subject.

Example: Doctors must know their patients.

doctors	anything	a parent	everybody
someone	raccoons	anyone	a woman
workers	no one	children	everyone
something	a book	anybody	people

Make sure the sentences you have written do not include any illogical shifts in person or number.

25 *Dangling and Misplaced Modifiers*

PREVIEW

In this chapter, you will learn

- to identify present participle modifiers (25A)
- to identify past participle modifiers (25B)
- to recognize and correct dangling modifiers (25C)
- to recognize and correct misplaced modifiers (25D)

Word Power

assemble
to put together
into a whole

ingredient
something
required to
form a mixture

■ SEEING AND WRITING

Look at the picture above, and then explain the process that is taking place.

A **modifier** is a word or word group that functions as an adjective or an adverb. Thus, a modifier describes or limits other words in a sentence. In order to avoid confusion, a modifier should be placed as close as possible to the word or words it modifies—ideally, directly before or directly after them. Many word groups that act as modifiers are introduced by present or past participles.

For more on using adjectives and adverbs to modify other words, see Chapter 29.

A Identifying Present Participle Modifiers

A **present participle modifier** consists of the present participle form of the verb (the *-ing* form) along with the words it introduces. A present participle modifier provides information about a noun or pronoun that appears right before or right after it in the sentence.

For more on present participles, see 18C.

PRESENT PARTICIPLE MODIFIER

Running through the streets, Archimedes could not wait to tell people what he had discovered.

PRESENT PARTICIPLE MODIFIER

Steve Jobs, using his garage as a workshop, invented the personal computer.

FOCUS **Punctuating Sentences with Present Participle Modifiers**

Use commas to set off a present participle modifier from the rest of the sentence.

PRESENT PARTICIPLE MODIFIER

Remembering his working-class roots, Paul McCartney returned to Liverpool to give a concert.

PRESENT PARTICIPLE MODIFIER

Paul McCartney, remembering his working-class roots, returned to Liverpool to give a concert.

◆ PRACTICE 25-1

Underline the present participle modifier in each of the following sentences. Draw an arrow from the modifier to the word or word group it modifies.

Example: Seeking social acceptance, some college students join fraternities or sororities.

(1) Tracing their origins to the late 1700s, social organizations for college students have a long history on many campuses. (2) Naming themselves with two or three Greek letters, these organizations are now generally called fraternities or sororities. (3) The earliest fraternities, focusing on academics, were essentially honor societies. (4) Recognizing scholarship in various fields, they provided an intellectual gathering place. (5) Evolving out of these, modern fraternities and sororities now are mainly social clubs. (6) Providing a variety of activities, many clubs encourage members to perform community service and raise money for worthwhile causes. (7) Reflecting members' interests, fraternities and sororities also sponsor parties and opportunities for members to network with former graduates. (8) Potential members, wanting to get into such clubs, subject themselves to a period of hazing. (9) Taking various forms, such hazing may involve serious humiliation and even dangerous stunts. (10) Responding to abusive and violent hazing, many colleges have limited the fraternities and sororities allowed on campus.

■ SEEING AND WRITING: Flashback

Look back at your response to the Seeing and Writing exercise on page 376. Underline any sentences that contain present participle modifiers. (If you cannot find any, write two new sentences on a separate sheet of paper.) Check to make sure you have punctuated your sentences correctly.

B   Identifying Past Participle Modifiers

A **past participle modifier** consists of the past participle form of the verb (usually ending in -d or -ed) along with the words it introduces. A past participle modifier provides information about a noun or a pronoun that is located next to it in the sentence.

PAST PARTICIPLE MODIFIER

Rejected by Hamlet, Ophelia goes mad and drowns herself.

PAST PARTICIPLE MODIFIER

Hamlet, written by William Shakespeare, is a tragedy.

FOCUS **Punctuating Sentences
with Past Participle Modifiers**

Use commas to set off a past participle modifier from the rest of the
sentence.

PAST PARTICIPLE MODIFIER

Terrorized by bandits, the villagers decided to fight back.

PAST PARTICIPLE MODIFIER

The villagers, terrorized by bandits, decided to fight back.

*For more on
irregular past
participles,
see 27B.*

◆ **PRACTICE 25-2**

Underline the past participle modifier in each of the following sentences.
Draw an arrow from each past participle modifier to the word or word group
it modifies.

   Example: Seized by the F.B.I., a fossilized *Tyrannosaurus rex* caused a
great deal of controversy.

   (1) The best-preserved fossil ever found, it was claimed by a South
Dakota dealer. (2) Uncovered several years ago, the fossil was found on government land. (3) The fossil hunters, excited by the find, paid the Indian
owner of the land $5,000. (4) Known as "Sue," the fossil was stored at a
private museum in Hill City, South Dakota. (5) Supported by previous
rulings, a judge ordered the fossil turned over to the government. (6) Accompanied by federal agents, local law enforcement officials impounded the
fossil. (7) Questioned by the press, some fossil hunters praised the verdict.
(8) Others said that commercial dealers, hindered by the verdict, would

stop collecting fossils. (9) Shocked by the ruling, the dealer appealed.

(10) Believed to be the first legal civil action involving a *Tyrannosaurus rex,* the case was settled in favor of the dealer.

■ SEEING AND WRITING: Flashback

Look back at your response to the Seeing and Writing exercise on page 376. Underline any sentences that contain past participle modifiers. (If you cannot find any, write two new sentences on a separate sheet of paper.) Check to make sure you have punctuated your sentences correctly.

C   Correcting Dangling Modifiers

A **dangling modifier** "dangles" when it cannot logically describe any word or word group in the sentence.

> Using my computer, the report was finished in two days.

In the sentence above, the present participle modifier *Using my computer* appears to refer to *the report,* but this makes no sense. (How can the report use a computer?) The word to which the modifier should logically refer is not included in the sentence. To correct this sentence, you need to supply the missing word.

> Using my computer, I finished the report in two days.

As in the example above, the easiest way to correct a dangling modifier is to supply a word or word group to which the dangling modifier can logically refer.

> INCORRECT Moving the microscope's mirror, the light can be directed onto the slide. (Did the light move the mirror?)
>
> CORRECT Moving the microscope's mirror, you can direct the light onto the slide.
>
> INCORRECT Paid in advance, the furniture was delivered. (Was the furniture paid in advance?)
>
> CORRECT Paid in advance, the movers delivered the furniture.

◆ PRACTICE 25-3

Rewrite the following sentences, which contain dangling modifiers, so that each modifier refers to a word or word group it can logically modify.

ON THE WEB

For more practice, visit Exercise Central: www.bedford stmartins.com/ writingincontext

> **Example:** Waiting inside, my bus passed by.
>
> *Waiting inside, I missed my bus.*

1. Paid by the school, the books were sorted in the library.

   _____

2. Pushing on the brakes, my car would not stop for the red light.

   _____

3. Short of money, the trip was canceled.

   _____

4. Working overtime, his salary almost doubled.

   _____

5. Angered by the noise, the concert was called off.

   _____

6. Using the proper formula, the problem was easily solved.

   _____

7. Tired and hungry, the assignment was finished by midnight.

   _____

8. Sitting in the park, the pigeons were fed.

   _____

9. Staying in bed on Sunday, the newspaper was read from beginning to end.

   _____

10. Driving for a long time, my leg began to hurt.

    _____

◆ PRACTICE 25-4

Complete the following sentences by supplying words to which the modifiers can logically refer.

Example: Dancing with the man of her dreams, *she decided that it*
was time to wake up.

1. Tired of studying, _____

   _____

2. Sleeping late this morning, _____

   _____

3. Seeing a strange light in the sky, _____

   _____

4. Warned about driving in the snow, _____

   _____

5. Alerted by a sound from outside, _____

   _____

6. Sent to fight in a foreign land, _____

   _____

7. Jumping over the rail and grabbing the chandelier, _____

   _____

8. Told by her instructor to study more, _____

   _____

9. Wanting desperately to go to the concert, _____

   _____

10. Distrusting the advice he got from his friends, _____

   _____

■ SEEING AND WRITING: Flashback

Look back at your response to the Seeing and Writing exercise on
page 376. Do any of your sentences contain dangling modifiers?
On a separate sheet of paper, rewrite any sentence that contains a

(continued on the following page)

(continued from the previous page)
dangling modifier, and correct it by supplying a word or word group
to which the modifier can logically refer.

D   Correcting Misplaced Modifiers

A **misplaced modifier** is a modifier (often introduced by a present or past
participle) that has no clear relationship to the word it modifies because it is
too far from it. As a result, it appears to modify the wrong word. Frequently,
the result is confusing, illogical, or even silly. To correct this problem, you
need to place the modifier as close as possible to the word or words it modifies—usually directly before or directly after it.

> INCORRECT   Sarah fed the dog wearing her pajamas. (Was the dog wear-
> ing Sarah's pajamas?)
>
> CORRECT   Wearing her pajamas, Sarah fed the dog.
>
> INCORRECT   Dressed in a raincoat and boots, I thought my son was pre-
> pared for the storm. (Who was dressed in a raincoat and
> boots?)
>
> CORRECT   I thought my son, dressed in a raincoat and boots, was pre-
> pared for the storm.

Not all misplaced modifiers are participles. Prepositional phrases, too, can
modify other words in the sentence, and they must be placed carefully.

*For more on
prepositional
phrases,
see 15B.*

> INCORRECT   At the wedding, she danced with the groom in a beautiful
> white gown. (Was the groom wearing a white gown?)
>
> CORRECT   At the wedding, she danced in a beautiful white gown with
> the groom.

FOCUS   Misplaced Modifiers

Be especially careful when placing **limiting modifiers** such as *almost,
even, hardly, just, nearly, only,* and *simply.* Notice how the meaning of
the following sentences changes when the modifier *only* is placed in different positions.

> Only David could go to the movies yesterday.
>
> David could only go to the movies yesterday.

(continued on the following page)

> *(continued from the previous page)*
> David could go <u>only</u> to the movies yesterday.
>
> David could go to the movies <u>only</u> yesterday.

◆ PRACTICE 25-5

ON THE WEB
*For more
practice, visit
Exercise Central:*
www.bedford
stmartins.com/
writingincontext

Rewrite the following sentences, which contain misplaced modifiers, so that each modifier clearly refers to the word it logically modifies.

Example: Mark ate a pizza standing in front of the refrigerator.

Standing in front of the refrigerator, Mark ate a pizza.

1. The cat broke the vase frightened by a noise.

2. Running across my bathroom ceiling, I saw two large, hairy bugs.

3. Lori looked at the man sitting in the chair with red hair.

4. *Titanic* is a film about a love affair directed by James Cameron.

5. With their deadly venom, people are sometimes killed by snakes.

6. *Pudd'nhead Wilson* is a book about an exchange of identities by Mark Twain.

7. I ran outside and saw eight tiny reindeer in my bathrobe.

8. Barking all night, I listened to my neighbor's dog.

9. The exterminator sprayed the insect wearing a mask.

10. With a mysterious smile, Leonardo da Vinci painted the *Mona Lisa*.

■ SEEING AND WRITING: Flashback

Look back at your response to the Seeing and Writing exercise on page 376. Do any sentences contain misplaced modifiers? On a separate sheet of paper, rewrite any such sentences by placing the modifiers as close as possible to a word or word group they can logically modify.

■ SEEING AND WRITING: Revising and Editing

Look back at your response to the Seeing and Writing exercise on page 376. Incorporating changes and corrections from this chapter's Flashback exercises, revise your work. Then, add two sentences, one with a present participle modifier and one with a past participle modifier. Finally, check your work one more time to make sure you have no dangling or misplaced modifiers.

CHAPTER REVIEW

◆ EDITING PRACTICE

Read the following student essay, into which modification errors have been introduced. Rewrite sentences to correct dangling and misplaced modifiers. In some cases, you may have to supply a word or word group to which the modifier can logically refer. The first incorrect sentence has been corrected for you.

<pre>
              The ABCs of My Education
                      I spent
     Born in New York City, my early years <s>were spent</s> in
                           ^
the South Bronx. My parents worked hard but made just

enough money to get by. Raised in this environment, there

was violence everywhere. I watched my friends get involved
</pre>

with gangs and drugs and ruin their lives. Concerned about me, I walked to school every day with one of my parents. They took a lot of time out of their lives to see that I got an education, believing that school was a safe place for me. Getting older, school was the place where I stayed longer and longer. After a while, I started getting good grades, and my guidance counselor recommended me to the A Better Chance (A.B.C.) program, seeing my potential.

The A.B.C. program is nationally acclaimed. Participating in the program, the classes help children with limited opportunities receive better academic support. I was able to go to Strath Haven High School in Pennsylvania, based on my record. Arriving at my new school, it was difficult for me to adjust. My teachers encouraged every student to aim for college in the program, and I was no exception. With the help of my teachers, my friends, and especially my parents, I began to excel. Graduating in the top 20 percent of my class, my dreams had come true.

The A.B.C. program helped me realize the importance of a good education. I hope to return to the South Bronx, finished with my schooling, to become a teacher. Teaching in the Bronx, my students will be shown the value of education. I will also tell them that they themselves can only choose to make something positive of their lives.

◆ COLLABORATIVE ACTIVITIES

1. Working in a group of five or six students, make a list of five present participle modifiers and five past participle modifiers. Exchange your list with another group, and complete one another's sentences.

Examples:

Typing as fast as he could, _____

Typing as fast as he could, <u>John could not wait to finish writing his screen-

play</u>, *The Tomato That Ate Cleveland*.

2. Working in a team of three students, compete with other teams to compose sentences that contain outrageous and confusing dangling or misplaced modifiers. As a class, correct the sentences. Then, vote on which group developed the most challenging sentences.

3. In a group of four or five students, find examples of confusing dangling and misplaced modifiers in magazines and newspapers. Rewrite the sentences, making sure each modifier is placed as close as possible to the word or word group it describes.

UNIT SIX
Understanding Basic Grammar

Verbs: Past Tense

PREVIEW

In this chapter, you will learn
- to understand regular verbs in the past tense (26A)
- to understand irregular verbs in the past tense (26B)
- to deal with problem verbs in the past tense (26C and 26D)

Obituaries

June 23, 1988   *The St. James Times*

Edward J. DeRoo dies—writer, scholar, naturalist

Edward John DeRoo

Author and professor emeritus Edward John DeRoo of Head of the Harbor, Saint James, died of heart failure Monday, June 20, at University Hospital at Stony Brook. He was 65. Dr. DeRoo was a professor of communications at Nassau Community College until he retired two years ago following open heart surgery.

During his 23 years at the college, he taught TV and film production, mass media, and interpersonal communications, and was recipient of a state university fellowship grant for filmmaking.

He wrote five novels, which were published in the United States and England. They included *The Fires of Youth, The Young Wolves,* and *The Little Caesars.* In the 1960s he was also the weekly drama columnist for the *Long Island Post* and *The West Side News.*

Before coming to Long Island, he had taught at the University of New Mexico, Texas at El Paso, and the University of Southern California. While in California in the 1950s he had his own TV program, *The Halls of Science,* for five years, and also several small roles as an actor in Hollywood films.

In the late 1940s he had been a playwright, director and actor with The Cleveland Playhouse. Four of his comedies saw local productions by the Salisbury Players in libraries in Nassau.

His degrees include a doctorate in education from Columbia, a master of fine arts from the Yale Drama School, master of arts from the University of Denver and bachelor of arts from the University of Rochester. He was a World War II veteran.

Since retirement he had returned to writing and was active in the Smithtown Writers Guild and Suffolk County's Taproots writing group. One of his short stories was recently purchased by the PEN syndicate affiliated with the National Endowment for the Arts. He was a Friend of the Arts at the State University at Stony Brook, and for many years was a linesman with the National Lawn Tennis Umpires Association. Under the auspices of the National Wildlife Federation, Dr. DeRoo and his wife created a certified wildlife habitat at their Head of the Harbor home.

Dr. DeRoo leaves his wife R. Deborah DeRoo, a son, Adrian of Riverdale, a daughter, Deborah of Montreal, and a stepdaughter, Andrea Kovacs of Manhattan.

Services were held at the St. James Funeral Home on Wednesday, June 22.

■ SEEING AND WRITING

Look at the newspaper obituary that is reproduced above, and then write your own obituary. (Refer to yourself by name or by *he* or *she*.) As

(continued on the following page)

▶ **Word Power**
accomplishment
something completed successfully; an achievement

longevity
long life

objective
a goal

> *(continued from the previous page)*
> you write, assume that you have led a long life and have achieved almost everything you hoped you would, and be sure to include the accomplishments for which you would most like to be remembered. Remember to use transitional words and phrases that clearly show the relationship of one event in your life to another.

A Understanding Regular Verbs in the Past Tense

Tense is the form a verb takes to show when an action or situation took place. The **past tense** is the form a verb takes to show that an action occurred in the past. **Regular verbs** form the past tense by adding either *-ed* or *-d* to the **base form** of the verb (the present tense form of the verb that is used with the pronoun *I*).

   Note: Not all verb forms ending in *-ed* or *-d* are in the past tense. Some are past participles. (See 27A.)

FOCUS   Regular Verbs in the Past Tense

■ Most regular verbs form the past tense by adding *-ed* to the base form of the verb.

  I <u>registered</u> for classes yesterday.
  Juan <u>walked</u> to the concert.

■ Regular verbs that end in *-e* form the past tense by adding *-d*.

  Walt Disney <u>produced</u> short cartoons in 1928.
  Tisha <u>liked</u> to read romance novels.

■ Regular verbs that end in *-y* form the past tense by changing the *y* to *i* and adding *-ed*.

  tr<u>y</u>   tr<u>ied</u>
  appl<u>y</u>   appl<u>ied</u>

  Note: All regular verbs use the same form for singular and plural in the past tense: *I cheered. They cheered.*

◆ PRACTICE 26-1

Change the verbs in the following sentences to the past tense. Cross out the present tense form of each underlined verb, and write the past tense form above it.

ON THE WEB
For more practice, visit Exercise Central: www.bedford stmartins.com/ writingincontext

Example: My grandparents ~~live~~ *lived* in a small town.

(1) My grandparents <u>own</u> a combination magazine stand and candy store in downtown Madison. (2) They <u>stock</u> about three hundred different magazines that <u>range</u> in subject matter from health and fitness to guns and ammo to angels and flying saucers. (3) Customers sometimes <u>browse</u> for an hour or more. (4) As they <u>look</u> through the magazines, they often <u>munch</u> on candy bars or <u>try</u> a soda. (5) When the candy bar or soda <u>turns</u> out to be a customer's only purchase, my grandfather <u>wants</u> to throw out the "library patron." (6) My grandmother, however, <u>recognizes</u> the importance of customer satisfaction. (7) She always <u>insists</u> that my grandfather be more patient. (8) My grandfather sometimes <u>refuses</u> to listen to her. (9) He never actually <u>kicks</u> out a customer. (10) Sometimes, though, he noisily <u>storms</u> out of the store, leaving my grandmother to deal with the startled customer.

■ SEEING AND WRITING: Flashback

Look back at your response to the Seeing and Writing exercise on page 391. Underline the past tense verbs that end in -*ed* and -*d*.

| B | Understanding Irregular Verbs in the Past Tense |

Unlike regular verbs, whose past tense forms end in -*ed* or -*d*, **irregular verbs** have irregular forms in the past tense. In fact, their past tense forms may look very different from their present tense forms.

The following chart lists the base form and past tense form of many of the most commonly used irregular verbs.

Irregular Verbs in the Past Tense

Base Form	Past	Base Form	Past
awake	awoke	leave	left
be	was, were	let	let
beat	beat	lie (to recline)	lay
become	became	light	lit
begin	began	lose	lost
bet	bet	make	made
bite	bit	meet	met
blow	blew	pay	paid
break	broke	quit	quit
bring	brought	read	read
build	built	ride	rode
buy	bought	ring	rang
catch	caught	rise	rose
choose	chose	run	ran
come	came	say	said
cost	cost	see	saw
cut	cut	sell	sold
dive	dove (dived)	send	sent
do	did	set	set
draw	drew	shake	shook
drink	drank	shine	shone (shined)
drive	drove	sing	sang
eat	ate	sit	sat
fall	fell	sleep	slept
feed	fed	speak	spoke
feel	felt	spend	spent
fight	fought	spring	sprang
find	found	stand	stood
fly	flew	steal	stole
forgive	forgave	stick	stuck
freeze	froze	sting	stung
get	got	swear	swore
give	gave	swim	swam
go (goes)	went	take	took
grow	grew	teach	taught
have	had	tear	tore
hear	heard	tell	told
hide	hid	think	thought
hold	held	throw	threw
hurt	hurt	understand	understood
keep	kept	wake	woke
know	knew	wear	wore
lay (to place)	laid	win	won
lead	led	write	wrote

◆ PRACTICE 26-2

In the following sentences, fill in the correct past tense form of the irregular verb in parentheses. Use the chart that begins on the preceding page to help you find the correct irregular verb form. If you do not find a verb on the chart, look it up in the dictionary.

ON THE WEB
For more practice, visit Exercise Central: www.bedford stmartins.com/ writingincontext

Example: They ___*said*___ (say) it couldn't be done.

(1) At the world championship games played in Tokyo in 1991, long-jumper Mike Powell _____ (break) the longest-standing record in track and field. (2) His leap of twenty-nine feet, four and one-half inches _____ (bring) him worldwide attention. (3) He also _____ (beat) his great rival, Olympic gold-medalist Carl Lewis. (4) The next year, competing against Lewis in the 1992 Olympics, Powell _____ (swear) to himself that he would take the gold. (5) Lewis, however, _____ (let) it be known that he _____ (feel) he could overtake Powell's record during the games. (6) Lewis _____ (make) a valiant attempt, but he still _____ (fall) short of Powell's record. (7) Even so, Lewis's winning jump _____ (keep) Powell from achieving a gold medal; he _____ (take) home a silver medal instead. (8) At the Atlanta Olympics in 1996, things _____ (go) even worse for Powell when he _____ (hurt) his groin and then in his final jump _____ (lose) his balance and ended up flat on his face. (9) Again, Carl Lewis _____ (win) the gold medal, his fourth in the long-jump. (10) Mike Powell _____ (leave) the Atlanta Olympics without a single medal; still, he _____ (come) away with his world record intact.

■ SEEING AND WRITING: Flashback

Look back at your response to the Seeing and Writing exercise on page 391. Circle each irregular past tense verb you find. Then, list all the irregular past tense verbs on a separate sheet of paper. Beside each past tense verb write its base form. (If necessary, consult the list of irregular verbs on page 394 or a dictionary.)

C Problem Verbs in the Past Tense: *Be*

For detailed information about subject-verb agreement with the irregular verb be, *see 23B.*

The irregular verb *be* can be especially troublesome because it has two different past tense forms—*was* and *were*.

Carlo <u>was</u> interested in becoming a city planner. (singular)

They <u>were</u> happy to help out at the school. (plural)

Past Tense Forms of the Verb *Be*

	Singular	Plural
First person	I <u>was</u> tired.	We <u>were</u> tired.
Second person	You <u>were</u> tired.	You <u>were</u> tired.
Third person	He <u>was</u> tired.	
	She <u>was</u> tired.	They <u>were</u> tired.
	It <u>was</u> tired.	
	The man <u>was</u> tired.	Frank and Billy <u>were</u> tired.

ON THE WEB
For more practice, visit Exercise Central: www.bedfordstmartins.com/writingincontext

◆ PRACTICE 26-3

Edit the following passage for errors in the use of the verb *be*. Cross out any underlined verbs that are incorrect, and write the correct forms above them. If a verb form is correct, label it *C*.

Example: Korean-American comic Margaret Cho <u>was</u> *(C)* one of the first people of Asian descent to achieve success in stand-up comedy.

(1) She <u>were</u> only sixteen when she began to perform her act. (2) Her parents <u>was</u> quite conservative, and they <u>were</u> opposed to her career choice. (3) Cho <u>was</u> not to be stopped, though. (4) Even when an agent refused to sign her as a client because he said no Asians <u>was</u> going to make it in stand-up comedy, Cho did not back down. (5) She <u>were</u> an immediate hit on college campuses. (6) Variety show hosts <u>were</u> quick to book her, and she <u>was</u> soon cast in her own television series, *All-American Girl*. (7) The program <u>were</u> canceled after only one season, but Cho's fans <u>was</u> still eager to see

her. (8) Her one-woman show, called "I'm the One That I Want," <u>were</u> a

sell-out all over the country. (9) A filmed version of this performance <u>was</u>

also released. (10) "Notorious C.H.O.," her most recent show, <u>were</u> similarly

successful.

■ SEEING AND WRITING: Flashback

Look back at your response to the Seeing and Writing exercise on page 391. Find all the sentences in which you use the past tense of *be*, and underline each subject of the verb *be* in each sentence. Make sure you have used the correct form of the verb in each case, and correct any errors you find.

| D | **Problem Verbs in the Past Tense: *Can/Could* and *Will/Would*** |

The helping verbs *can/could* and *will/would* present problems because their past tense forms are sometimes confused with their present tense forms.

For more on helping verbs, see 15C.

Can/Could

Can, a present tense verb, means "is able to" or "are able to."

First-year students <u>can</u> apply for financial aid.

Could, the past tense of *can,* means "was able to" or "were able to."

Escape artist Harry Houdini claimed that he <u>could</u> escape from any prison.

Will/Would

Will, a present tense verb, talks about the future from a point in the present.

A solar eclipse <u>will</u> occur in ten months.

Would, the past tense of *will,* talks about the future from a point in the past.

I told him yesterday that I <u>would</u> think about it.

> **FOCUS** *Will* and *Would*
>
> Note that *will* is used with *can,* and *would* is used with *could.*
>
> I <u>will</u> feed the cats if I <u>can</u> find their food.
>
> I <u>would</u> feed the cats if I <u>could</u> find their food.

◆ **PRACTICE 26-4**

ON THE WEB
*For more
practice, visit
Exercise Central:*
www.bedford
stmartins.com/
writingincontext

Circle the appropriate helping verb from the choices in parentheses.

Example: Years ago, travel took so long that my grandfather (will/ (would)) rarely drive more than ten miles from home.

(1) Twenty years ago, it (can/could) take hours to travel across the state. (2) With the new highway, the trip now (can/could) take as little as an hour. (3) As people make the drive, they (will/would) be surprised. (4) Before I made the trip, I (will/would) not have believed the difference. (5) On the old highway, I (can/could) get stuck behind a truck on those winding, two-lane roads. (6) With the new highway, I (can/could) zip along on four lanes in each direction. (7) Because they were so low, those old roads (will/would) often be flooded. (8) The new highway (will/would) never flood because it is elevated. (9) If they (can/could) go back to the old ways, some people would do so. (10) However, I (will/would) always try to adapt to progress and to change if I can.

■ SEEING AND WRITING: Flashback

Look back at your response to the Seeing and Writing exercise on page 391. On a separate sheet of paper, write a few sentences that describe what else you would have accomplished if you had had the chance. Be sure to use *could* and *would* in your sentences.

■ SEEING AND WRITING: Revising and Editing

Look back at your response to the Seeing and Writing exercise on page 391. Check your work once again to make sure you have used the correct past tense form for each of your verbs. If you have not, cross out the incorrect form, and write the proper past tense form of the verb above the line.

CHAPTER REVIEW

◆ EDITING PRACTICE

Read the following student essay, into which errors in past tense verb forms have been introduced. Decide whether each of the underlined past tense verbs is correct. If the verb is correct, write *C* above it. If it is not, cross out the verb, and write in the correct past tense form. The first sentence has been corrected for you. (If necessary, consult the list of irregular verbs on page 394.)

Healing

was

The window seat ~~were~~ our favorite place to sit. I

piled comfortable pillows on the ledge and spended several

minutes rearranging them. My friend and I lied on our backs

and propped our feet on the wall. We sat with our arms

around our legs and thinked about the mysteries of life.

We also stared at the people on the street below and

wonder who they was and where they was going. We imagined

that they can be millionaires, foreign spies, or ruthless

drug smugglers. We believed that everyone except us leaded

wonderful and exciting lives.

I heard a voice call my name. Reluctantly, I standed

up, tearing myself away from my imaginary world. My dearest

For more on using lie *and* lay, *see 34E.*

and oldest friend--my teddy bear--and I reentered the real world. I grabbed Teddy and brung him close to my chest. Together we go into the cold sitting room, where twelve other girls sit around a table eating breakfast. None of them looked happy. In the unit for eating disorders, meals was always tense. Nobody wants to eat, but the nurses watched us until we eated every crumb. I set Teddy on the chair beside me and stared gloomily at the food on our plate. I closed my eyes and taked the first bite. I feeled the calories adding inches of ugly fat. Each swallow were like a nail being ripped from my finger. At last, it was over. I had survived breakfast.

    Days passed slowly; each passing minute was a triumph. I learned how to eat properly. I learned about other people's problems. I also learned that people loved me. Eventually, even Teddy stopped feeling sorry for me. I begun to smile--and laugh. Sometimes, I even considered myself happy. My doctors challenged me--and, surprisingly, I rised to the occasion.

◆ COLLABORATIVE ACTIVITIES

1. Working in a group of three or four students, choose a famous living figure—an actor, a sports star, or a musician, for example—and brainstorm together to list details about this person's life. Then, working on your own, use the details to write a profile of the famous person.
2. Working in a group, list several contemporary problems that you think will be solved within ten or fifteen years. Each member of the group should then select a problem from the list and write a paragraph or two describing how the problem could be solved. As a group, arrange the paragraphs so that they form the body of an essay. Develop a thesis statement, write an introduction and a conclusion, and then revise the body paragraphs of the essay.

3. Form a group with three other students. What national or world events do you remember most vividly? Take ten minutes to list news events that you think have defined the last five years. On your own, write a short essay in which you discuss the significance of the three or four events that the members of your group agree were the most important.

27 *Verbs: Past Participles*

PREVIEW

In this chapter, you will learn
- to identify regular past participles (27A)
- to identify irregular past participles (27B)
- to use the present perfect tense (27C)
- to use the past perfect tense (27D)
- to use past participles as adjectives (27E)

■ SEEING AND WRITING

Look at the picture above. Then, write about an activity—a hobby or a sport, for example—that you have been involved in for a relatively long time. Begin by identifying the activity and stating why it has been important to you. Then, describe the activity, paying particular attention to what you have gained from it over the years.

A   Identifying Regular Past Participles

Every verb has a past participle form. The **past participle** form of a regular verb is identical to its past tense form. Both are formed by adding *-d* or *-ed* to the **base form** of the verb (the present tense form of the verb used with *I*).

> PAST TENSE
> He earned.

> PAST PARTICIPLE
> He has earned.

Together with a **helping verb** (a form of the verb *have*), past participles form the present perfect and past perfect tenses.

>   HELPING VERB   PAST PARTICIPLE
> PRESENT PERFECT The government **has changed** its policy on illegal
>   TENSE immigration.

>   HELPING VERB   PAST PARTICIPLE
> PAST PERFECT I **had finished** studying for the test by Tuesday.
>   TENSE

Note that the helping verb changes its form to agree with the subject, but the past participle always has the same form: *I have earned. She has earned.*

◆ PRACTICE 27-1

Fill in the correct past participle form of each verb in parentheses.

Example: Coffee prices have _____*dropped*_____ (drop) recently.

(1) Americans have _____ (start) a coffee craze in the last fifteen years. (2) Since the early 1980s, more than ten thousand coffee bars have _____ (open) in the United States. (3) Many of these bars have _____ (appear) in metropolitan areas. (4) However, they have _____ (sprout) in suburban malls and small college towns, too. (5) One chain alone has _____ (expand) to more than four hundred outlets. (6) Americans have always _____ (enjoy) coffee. (7) In fact, Americans have traditionally _____ (consume) one-third of the world's yearly coffee production. (8) One survey has _____

(estimate) that Americans drink 130 million cups a day. (9) Tastes have

_____ (change), though. (10) Today's market has _____

(broaden) to include cappuccino and latte.

■ SEEING AND WRITING: Flashback

Look back at your response to the Seeing and Writing exercise on page 402. Circle each helping verb (a form of the verb *have*) that is followed by a regular past participle (ending in *-ed* or *-d*). Then, underline both the helping verb and the past participle.

B Identifying Irregular Past Participles

Irregular verbs nearly always have irregular past participles. They do not form the past participle by adding *-ed* or *-d* to the base form of the verb.

Base Form	Past Tense	Past Participle
choose	chose	chosen
buy	bought	bought
ride	rode	ridden

The following chart lists the base form, the past tense form, and the past participle of the most commonly used irregular verbs.

 Computer Tip

You can use the Find or Search command to find all uses of *have, has,* and *had* in a piece of your own writing. Then, you can check to make sure the correct past participle form follows each helping verb.

Irregular Past Participles

Base Form	Past Tense	Past Participle
awake	awoke	awoken
be (am, are)	was (were)	been
beat	beat	beaten
become	became	become
begin	began	begun
bet	bet	bet

(continued on the following page)

(continued from the previous page)

Base Form	Past Tense	Past Participle
bite	bit	bitten
blow	blew	blown
break	broke	broken
bring	brought	brought
build	built	built
buy	bought	bought
catch	caught	caught
choose	chose	chosen
come	came	come
cost	cost	cost
cut	cut	cut
dive	dove, dived	dived
do	did	done
draw	drew	drawn
drink	drank	drunk
drive	drove	driven
eat	ate	eaten
fall	fell	fallen
feed	fed	fed
feel	felt	felt
fight	fought	fought
find	found	found
fly	flew	flown
forgive	forgave	forgiven
freeze	froze	frozen
get	got	got, gotten
give	gave	given
go	went	gone
grow	grew	grown
have	had	had
hear	heard	heard
hide	hid	hidden
hold	held	held
hurt	hurt	hurt
keep	kept	kept
know	knew	known
lay (to place)	laid	laid
lead	led	led
leave	left	left
let	let	let
lie (to recline)	lay	lain
light	lit	lit

(continued on the following page)

(continued from the previous page)

Base Form	Past Tense	Past Participle
lose	lost	lost
make	made	made
meet	met	met
pay	paid	paid
quit	quit	quit
read	read	read
ride	rode	ridden
ring	rang	rung
rise	rose	risen
run	ran	run
say	said	said
see	saw	seen
sell	sold	sold
send	sent	sent
set	set	set
shake	shook	shaken
shine	shone, shined	shone, shined
sing	sang	sung
sit	sat	sat
sleep	slept	slept
speak	spoke	spoken
spend	spent	spent
spring	sprang	sprung
stand	stood	stood
steal	stole	stolen
stick	stuck	stuck
sting	stung	stung
swear	swore	sworn
swim	swam	swum
take	took	taken
teach	taught	taught
tear	tore	torn
tell	told	told
think	thought	thought
throw	threw	thrown
understand	understood	understood
wake	woke, waked	woken, waked
wear	wore	worn
win	won	won
write	wrote	written

◆ PRACTICE 27-2

Fill in the correct past participle of the verb in parentheses. Refer to the chart on pages 404–406 as needed. If you cannot find a particular verb on the chart, look it up in the dictionary.

ON THE WEB
For more practice, visit Exercise Central: www.bedford stmartins.com/ writingincontext

Example: The network has _____*won*_____ (win) a loyal audience.

(1) Nick at Nite has _____ (find) a receptive audience for old television programs. (2) The cable network Nickelodeon, which broadcasts children's programs during the day, has _____ (catch) on with adults at night. (3) It has _____ (draw) viewers away from current network sitcoms to ones from the 1980s and earlier. (4) Many viewers have _____ (know) and loved these shows since they were children. (5) They feel this affection even if they have not _____ (see) the shows for years. (6) They have _____ (run) the candy-making machine with Lucy, _____ (see) Archie Bunker yell at his son-in-law, and _____ (keep) up with the antics of the Brady children. (7) As they have _____ (get) older, viewers have _____ (grow) nostalgic for these familiar characters. (8) Young viewers have _____ (have) a chance to discover them for the first time. (9) Both older and younger viewers have _____ (begin) to appreciate the shows for their old-fashioned humor. (10) Nick has also _____ (make) a name for itself with its clever commercials and station breaks, which imitate 1950s style.

◆ PRACTICE 27-3

Edit the following passage for errors in irregular past participles. Cross out any underlined past participles that are incorrect, and write in the correct form above them. If the verb form is correct, label it *C*. Notice that sometimes words (such as *not, also, even, always, never,* and *hardly*) can come between the helping verb and the past participle.

Example: In recent years, some people have ~~standed~~ *stood* up against overseas sweatshops.

(1) The problem of U.S. manufacturers using overseas sweatshops has became controversial over the last few decades. (2) Manufacturers have sended their goods to developing countries where employees work under terrible conditions for very low wages. (3) Some companies, such as Nike, have came under fire for such practices, and celebrities who lend their names to lines of clothing manufactured in sweatshops have finded themselves severely criticized. (4) Many people have went as far as to boycott products manufactured in overseas sweatshops. (5) Recently, colleges have taken heat for using overseas sweatshops that have maked clothing and other items featuring school names. (6) Student protestors have sprang into action upon learning that their colleges have selled goods manufactured in overseas sweatshops. (7) They have spoke out against such practices, and schools have had to respond. (8) While manufacturers may have losed money by increasing wages for overseas workers, they have understanded that this is the right thing to do. (9) They have made a promise to their customers that they will not employ sweatshop labor. (10) Still, customers have not always forgave the manufacturers' history of such practices.

■ **SEEING AND WRITING: Flashback**

Look back at your response to the Seeing and Writing exercise on page 402, and place a checkmark above each form of the helping verb *have* that is followed by an irregular past participle. Then, underline both the helping verb and the irregular past participle.

C   Using the Present Perfect Tense

The past participle can be used to form different verb tenses. For example, the past participle can be combined with the present tense forms of *have* to form the **present perfect tense**.

The Present Perfect Tense
(have *or* has + *past participle*)

Singular	**Plural**
I have gained.	We have gained.
You have gained.	You have gained.
He has gained.	They have gained.
She has gained.	
It has gained.	

As you have already learned, the past tense is used to indicate an action that occurred in the past. The present perfect tense has different uses.

Use the present perfect tense to indicate an action that began in the past and continues into the present.

> PRESENT PERFECT   The nurse has worked at the Welsh Mountain clinic for two years. (The working began in the past and continues into the present.)

Also use the present perfect tense to indicate that an action has just occurred.

> PRESENT PERFECT   I have just eaten. (The eating has just occurred.)

In the sentence above, the word *just* indicates that the action has just now occurred. (The words *now, already,* and *recently* can also be used with the present perfect tense to indicate a recent action.)

◆ PRACTICE 27-4

Circle the appropriate verb tense (past tense or present perfect) from the choices in parentheses.

> **Example:**   My new kitten (began/has begun) to dominate the household already.

ON THE WEB
For more practice, visit Exercise Central: www.bedford stmartins.com/ writingincontext

(1) I (was/have been) a cat addict all my life. (2) I (got/have gotten) my first cat when I was seven years old. (3) I (named/have named) him Tweetie after the little bird in the cartoons. (4) Since then, I (owned/have owned) many more felines. (5) At one point, I (had/have had) five cats at once. (6) Last year, one (died/has died). (7) My sister (adopted/has adopted) another when she got married. (8) Since then, I (took/have taken) care of the other three cats. (9) Through the years, my cats (gave/have given) me much pleasure but also a lot of aggravation. (10) Anyone who (raised/has raised) cats will understand what I mean.

◆ PRACTICE 27-5

Fill in the appropriate verb tense (past tense or present perfect) of the verb in parentheses.

Example: In 2000, many polls ___*predicted*___ (predict) the presidential election results inaccurately.

(1) Newspapers and magazines in America _____ (present) the results of public opinion polls since the mid-1900s. (2) Until the early twentieth century, these polls _____ (be) unscientific and their results far from accurate. (3) In the 1930s, however, George Horace Gallup _____ (develop) original techniques for polling. (4) Over the last sixty years, these methods _____ (achieve) considerable success in predicting elections. (5) Since its development, the Gallup poll _____ (become) the best known of all public opinion polls. (6) Such polls _____ (occupy) a larger and larger place in our public lives. (7) In recent years, however, some critics _____ (begin) to argue against the extensive use of polls to measure public opinion.

■ SEEING AND WRITING: Flashback

Look back at your response to the Seeing and Writing exercise on page 402. Choose three sentences with past tense verbs and rewrite them on a separate sheet of paper, changing past tense to present perfect tense. How does your revision change the meaning of each sentence?

D   Using the Past Perfect Tense

The past participle can also be used to form the **past perfect tense**, which consists of the past tense of *have* plus the past participle.

The Past Perfect Tense
(had + past participle)

Singular	**Plural**
I had returned.	We had returned.
You had returned.	You had returned.
He had returned.	They had returned.
She had returned.	
It had returned.	

Use the past perfect tense to show that an action occurred before another past action.

PAST PERFECT TENSE   PAST TENSE

Chief Sitting Bull had fought many other battles before he defeated General Custer.

This sentence identifies two actions that happened in the past—the other fighting done by Sitting Bull, and his defeat of Custer. The verb in the first part of the sentence *(had fought)* is in the past perfect tense. The verb in the second part of the sentence *(defeated)* is in the past tense. The use of the past perfect tense indicates that Sitting Bull's other battles took place *before* he defeated Custer.

◆ **PRACTICE 27-6**

Circle the appropriate verb tense (present perfect or past perfect) from the choices in parentheses.

ON THE WEB
For more practice, visit Exercise Central: www.bedford stmartins.com/ writingincontext

Example: Although the children (have eaten/(had eaten)) dinner, they still had room for ice cream.

1. Ren wondered where he (has left/had left) his keys.

2. He now believes he (has lost/had lost) them.

3. The receptionist told the interviewer that the applicant (has arrived/ had arrived).

4. The interviewer says that she (has waited/had waited) for an hour.

5. The jury decided that the defendant (has lied/had lied) on the witness stand.

6. The jury members are still deliberating although they (have been/had been) in the jury room for three days.

7. By the time I reached the restaurant, I (have decided/had decided) to order a pepperoni pizza.

8. By the time my pizza is ready, I usually (have finished/had finished) my pinball game.

9. The movie (has been/had been) on only ten minutes when I turned it off.

10. This movie is excellent; I (have seen/had seen) it at least five times.

■ SEEING AND WRITING: Flashback

Look back at your response to the Seeing and Writing exercise on page 402. Rewrite any present perfect tense sentences on a separate sheet of paper, this time changing them to the past perfect tense. How do your revisions change the meaning of each sentence?

E   Using Past Participles as Adjectives

See 29A for more on adjectives.

In addition to functioning as a verb form, the past participle can function as an adjective after a **linking verb**, as it does in the following sentences, where the past participle describes the subject. (A linking verb connects a subject to the word that describes it.)

Jason seemed surprised.

He looked shocked.

The past participle can also function as an adjective before a noun.

I cleaned up the broken glass.

The exhausted runner finally crossed the finish line.

◆ PRACTICE 27-7

Edit the following passage for errors in past participle forms used as adjectives. Cross out any underlined participles that are incorrect, and write the correct form above them. If the participle form is correct, label it *C*.

> **Example:**   College students are often <u>strapped</u> for cash. *C*

(1) College students are often <u>surprise</u> when they find <u>preapprove</u> applications for credit cards turning up in their mail. (2) Credit-card companies also recruit <u>targeted</u> students through booths near student unions and libraries. (3) The booths attract new customers with offers of <u>inscribe</u> coffee mugs and tote bags. (4) Why have companies gone to all this effort to attract <u>qualified</u> students? (5) Most older Americans already have at least five credit cards <u>stuffed</u> in their billfolds. (6) Banks and credit-card companies see younger college students as their major <u>untapped</u> market. (7) According to experts, students are also a good credit risk because <u>concern</u> parents may bail them out when they are not able to pay a bill. (8) Finally, people tend to feel <u>tie</u> to their first credit card. (9) Some people consider their first card a <u>cherish</u> item. (10) For this reason, it is a <u>known</u> fact that credit-card companies target <u>uninform</u> college students.

■ SEEING AND WRITING: Flashback

Look back at your response to the Seeing and Writing exercise on page 402. Choose three nouns you used in your writing, and list them on a separate sheet of paper. Then, think of a past participle that can modify each noun, and write the modifier before each noun. Now, use each of these nouns and its past participle modifier in an original sentence.

> ### ■ SEEING AND WRITING: Revising and Editing
>
> Look back at your response to the Seeing and Writing exercise on page 402. Do you need to revise any sentences to add the correct present perfect and past perfect tense verb forms? If so, cross out the incorrect verb forms, and write your corrections above them. When you have finished, check the past participles and perfect tenses in another writing assignment on which you are currently working.

CHAPTER REVIEW

◆ EDITING PRACTICE

Read the following student essay, into which errors in the use of past participles and the perfect tenses have been introduced. Decide whether each of the underlined verbs or participles is correct. If it is correct, write *C* above it. If it is not, write in the correct verb form. The first error has been corrected for you.

Drug Testing in High Schools

In recent years, some high schools in the United States have ~~began~~ *begun* to test their students for illegal drug use. For a decade or more, student athletes <u>have took</u> drug tests in order to participate in sporting events. In some schools, however, the number of students now being tested <u>has growed</u> to include anyone who participates in extracurricular activities, such as drama, choir, or band. Some schools <u>have</u> even <u>feel</u> the need to test their entire student bodies. They <u>have use</u> such tests to suspend students who <u>have test</u> positive as well as any student who <u>has refused</u> to take the test. This practice <u>has cause</u> concern on the part of some students, parents, and proponents of civil liberties and <u>has lead</u> to significant controversy.

People who protest such universal student drug testing have fighted the issue in court. They have argue that testing all students, even those who have did nothing to indicate drug use and who have chose not to participate in after-school activities, is unfair. The courts have tended to agree. In the case of a Texas school that had setted up a policy of testing all students for drug use, a federal judge decided the school has violated students' right to privacy. Courts have make similar decisions in other cases. Some school administrators have express disappointment with these legal decisions. They have sended out the message that drug testing at school is an effective deterrent to drug use among teenagers. In addition, many parents have sayed that they want their children to be tested for drugs at school. In general, however, students have been less supportive of school drug testing. This issue will probably continue to provoke debate for years to come.

◆ COLLABORATIVE ACTIVITIES

1. Exchange Seeing and Writing exercises with another student. Read each other's work, making sure that present perfect and past perfect tenses are used correctly.

2. Assume that you are a restaurant employee who has been nominated for the prestigious Employee of the Year Award. To win this award (along with a thousand-dollar prize), you have to explain in writing what you have done during the past year to deserve this honor. Write a letter to your supervisor and the awards committee. When you have finished, trade papers with another student, and edit his or her letter. Read your letter to the class; after all your classmates have shared their letters, your class will discuss which is the most convincing.

28 *Nouns and Pronouns*

PREVIEW

In this chapter, you will learn
- to identify nouns (28A)
- to form plural nouns (28B)
- to identify pronouns (28C)
- to understand pronoun-antecedent agreement (28D)
- to solve special problems with pronoun-antecedent agreement (28E)
- to understand pronoun case (28F)
- to solve special problems with pronoun case (28G)
- to identify reflexive and intensive pronouns (28H)

▶ **Word Power**

compelling
extremely forceful

mesmerizing
hypnotic

■ SEEING AND WRITING

Look at the picture above, and then explain why you like a particular musician or group, television show, or movie. Assume your readers are not familiar with your subject.

A   Identifying Nouns

A **noun** is a word that names a person *(singer, Jennifer Lopez)*, an animal *(dolphin, Flipper)*, a place *(downtown, Houston)*, an object *(game, Scrabble)*, or an idea *(happiness, Darwinism)*.

A **singular noun** names one thing. A **plural noun** names more than one thing.

FOCUS   Common and Proper Nouns

Most nouns, called **common nouns**, begin with lowercase letters.

character   holiday

Some nouns, called **proper nouns**, name particular people, animals, places, objects, or ideas. A proper noun always begins with a capital letter.

Homer Simpson   Labor Day

For information on capitalizing proper nouns, see 33A.

B   Forming Plural Nouns

Most nouns add *-s* to form plurals. Other nouns, whose singular forms end in *-s, -ss, -sh, -ch, -x,* or *-z,* add *-es* to form plurals. Some nouns that end in *-s* or *-z* double the *s* or *z* before adding *-es.*

Singular	Plural
street	streets
gas	gases
class	classes
bush	bushes
church	churches
fox	foxes
quiz	quizzes

Irregular Noun Plurals

Some nouns form plurals in unusual ways. (Note that when a noun has an irregular plural, the dictionary will list its plural form.)

(continued on the following page)

(continued from the previous page)

■ Nouns whose plural forms are the same as their singular forms

Singular	Plural
a deer	a few deer
this species	these species
a television series	two television series

■ Nouns ending in *-f* or *-fe*

Singular	Plural
each half	both halves
my life	our lives
a lone thief	a gang of thieves
one loaf	two loaves
the third shelf	several shelves

Familiar exceptions: roof (plural *roofs*), proof (plural *proofs*), belief (plural *beliefs*)

■ Nouns ending in *-y*

Singular	Plural
another baby	more babies
every worry	many worries

Note that when a vowel (*a, e, i, o, u*) comes before the *y*, the noun has a regular plural form: monkey (plural *monkeys*), day (plural *days*).

■ Hyphenated compound nouns

Singular	Plural
Lucia's sister-in-law	Lucia's two favorite sisters-in-law
a mother-to-be	twin mothers-to-be
the first runner-up	all the runners-up

■ Miscellaneous irregular plurals

Singular	Plural
that child	all children
a good man	a few good men
the woman	lots of women
my left foot	both feet
a wisdom tooth	my two front teeth
this bacterium	some bacteria

◆ PRACTICE 28-1

Next to each of the following singular nouns, write the plural form of the noun. Then, circle the plural forms of irregular nouns.

Examples: bottle _____*bottles*_____   child _____(*children*)_____

1. life _____

2. foot _____

3. chain _____

4. deer _____

5. honey _____

6. bride-to-be _____

7. loaf _____

8. kiss _____

9. beach _____

10. duty _____

◆ PRACTICE 28-2

Proofread the underlined nouns in the following paragraph, checking for correct singular or plural forms. If a correction needs to be made, cross out the noun and write the correct form above it. If the noun is correct, write *C* above it.

Example: Many ~~studys~~ *studies* prove this.

(1) I recently talked to some unmarried <u>friend</u> about what they look for in a person of the opposite sex. (2) Most of the <u>woman</u> said that their <u>standardes</u> were the same whether they just wanted to date a <u>men</u> for fun or to consider him as a potential mate. (3) Both just-for-fun dates and potential <u>husband-to-bes</u> were considered real <u>catchs</u> if they had decent jobs, if they were considerate and honest, and if they had good <u>sensess</u> of humor. (4) My male <u>buddies</u>, however, had different <u>ideaes</u>. (5) They wanted <u>dates</u> to be good-looking, to have outgoing <u>personalitys</u>, and to have independent <u>lifes</u> of their own. (6) Potential <u>wifes</u>, on the other hand, should not be too attractive to other <u>mens</u>, should be <u>homebodies</u>, and should see themselves not as independent but as <u>halfes</u> of a whole. (7) Sometimes I think the two <u>sexs</u> are different <u>specieses</u>.

> ■ **SEEING AND WRITING: Flashback**
>
> Look back at your response to the Seeing and Writing exercise on page 416. Underline each noun. Write *P* above any plural nouns, and circle any irregular plurals.

C Identifying Pronouns

A **pronoun** is a word that refers to or takes the place of a noun or another pronoun.

> Michelle was really excited. She had finally found a job that made her happy. *(She refers to Michelle; her refers to she.)*

Without pronouns, your sentences would be tedious because you would have to repeat the same nouns over and over again.

> Michelle was really excited. Michelle had finally found a job that made Michelle happy.

Pronouns, like nouns, can be singular or plural. The pronouns *I, he, she,* and *it* are always singular and take the place of singular nouns or pronouns.

> Geoff left his jacket at work, so he went back to get it before it could be stolen. *(He refers to Geoff; it refers to it.)*

The pronouns *we* and *they* are always plural and take the place of plural nouns or pronouns.

> Jessie and Dan got up early, but they still missed their train. *(They refers to Jessie and Dan; their refers to they.)*

The pronoun *you* can be either singular or plural.

> When the volunteers met the mayor, they said, "We really admire you." The mayor replied, "I admire you, too."

◆ PRACTICE 28-3

In the following sentences, fill in each blank with an appropriate pronoun.

Example: ___I___ like to be direct with my friends.

(1) _____ pride myself on always being honest. (2) My father used to tell me that honesty is the best policy, and _____ was right. (3) Sometimes my honesty hurts my friends' feelings, and _____ tell me that _____ am being

rude to them. (4) _____ answer them by saying that _____ all need to hear the honest truth about ourselves sometimes. (5) My friend Linda understands my point, and _____ is always eager to let me hear the honest truth about myself whenever _____ have made a comment about her. (6) She tells me, "If _____ are going to dish _____ out, then _____ had better learn to take _____ yourself." (7) It's true that if her comment is really strong, _____ can upset me for a day or two. (8) But then _____ remember that it's only Linda's opinion, and _____ is never right about anything.

■ SEEING AND WRITING: Flashback

Look back at your response to the Seeing and Writing exercise on page 416. On a separate sheet of paper, list all the pronouns *(I, he, she, it, we, you, they)* you used. Then, list the noun or pronoun each pronoun replaces.

D   Understanding Pronoun-Antecedent Agreement

The word that a pronoun refers to is called the pronoun's **antecedent**. In the following sentence, the noun *leaf* is the antecedent of the pronoun *it*.

The leaf turned yellow, but it did not fall.

A pronoun must always agree in **number** with its antecedent. If an antecedent is singular, as it is in the sentence above, the pronoun must be singular. If the antecedent is plural, as it is in the sentence below, the pronoun must also be plural.

The leaves turned yellow, but they did not fall.

Pronouns must also agree with their antecedents in **gender**. If an antecedent is feminine, the pronoun that refers to it must also be feminine.

Melissa passed her driver's exam with flying colors.

If an antecedent is masculine, the pronoun that refers to it must be masculine.

Matt wondered what courses he should take.

If an antecedent is neuter (that is, neither masculine nor feminine), the pronoun that refers to it must also be neuter.

Lee's car broke down, but she refused to fix it again.

> **FOCUS** Vague Pronoun References
>
> A pronoun should always refer to a specific antecedent.
>
> VAGUE On the evening news, they said a baseball strike was inevitable.
>
> REVISED On the evening news, the sportscaster said a baseball strike was inevitable.

◆ PRACTICE 28-4

ON THE WEB
For more practice, visit Exercise Central: www.bedford stmartins.com/ writingincontext

In the following sentences, circle the antecedent of each underlined pronoun. Then, draw an arrow from the pronoun to the antecedent.

Example: College students today often fear they will be the victims of crime on campus.

(1) Few campuses are as safe as they should be, experts say. (2) However, crime on most campuses is probably no worse that it is in any other community. (3) Still, students have a right to know how safe their campuses are. (4) My friend Joyce never sets foot on campus without her can of Mace. (5) Joyce believes she must be prepared for the worst. (6) Her boyfriend attended a self-defense program that he said was very helpful. (7) My friends do not let fear of crime keep them from enjoying the college experience. (8) We know that our school is doing all it can to provide a safe environment.

◆ PRACTICE 28-5

Fill in each blank in the following passage with an appropriate pronoun.

Example: Multiplexes are springing up everywhere; sometimes *they* are replacing drive-ins.

(1) Drive-in movie theaters used to be common in the United States, but now _____ are fairly rare. (2) In 1958, there were more than four thousand

drive-ins across the country, but _____ have been reduced to fewer than nine hundred today. (3) One of the most amazing is the Thunderbird Drive-In in Ft. Lauderdale, Florida; _____ has twelve different screens. (4) Owner Preston Henn says _____ is the largest drive-in theater in the world. (5) _____ opened the theater with only one screen in 1963. (6) _____ also opened a flea market on the property. (7) _____ is now one of the largest flea markets in the state, with over two thousand vendors. (8) The vendors think _____ are getting a good deal, and so do moviegoers.

■ SEEING AND WRITING: Flashback

Look back at your response to the Seeing and Writing exercise on page 416. Underline each pronoun in your paragraph, circle its antecedent, and draw an arrow from each pronoun to its antecedent. Do all your pronouns agree with their antecedents? If not, correct your pronouns.

E Solving Special Problems with Pronoun-Antecedent Agreement

Certain situations present special problems with pronoun-antecedent agreement.

Compound Antecedents

A **compound antecedent** consists of two or more words connected by *and* or *or*. Compound antecedents connected by *and* are plural, and they are used with plural pronouns.

   During World War II, Belgium and France tried to protect their borders.

Compound antecedents connected by *or* may take a singular or a plural pronoun. When both elements of a compound antecedent connected by *or* are singular, use a singular pronoun to refer to the compound antecedent.

   Either a dog or a cat must have put its paw in the frosting.

When both elements are plural, use a plural pronoun.

   Are dogs or cats more loyal to their owners?

For information on subject-verb agreement with compound subjects, see 23A.

When one element of a compound antecedent connected by *or* is singular and one is plural, use the pronoun that agrees with the word closer to it.

> Is it possible that European nations or Russia may send <u>its</u> [not *their*] troops?

> Is it possible that Russia or European nations may send <u>their</u> [not *its*] troops?

◆ PRACTICE 28-6

In each of the following sentences, underline the compound antecedent and circle the connecting word *(and* or *or)*. Then, circle the appropriate pronoun in parentheses.

> **Example:**   Groucho (and) Harpo were younger than (his/their) brother Chico.

1. Larry and Curly were younger than (his/their) partner Moe.

2. Either Chip or Dale has a stripe down (his/their) back.

3. Most critics believe Laurel and Hardy did (his/their) best work in silent comedies.

4. Lucy and Ethel never seem to learn (her/their) lesson.

5. Either *MASH* or *The Fugitive* had the highest ratings for any television show in (its/their) final episode.

6. Was it Francis Ford Coppola or Martin Scorcese who achieved the triumph of (his/their) career with *The Godfather*?

7. Either film or videotapes lose (its/their) clarity over time.

8. Either Tower or Blockbuster is having (its/their) grand opening today.

9. The popcorn and soft drinks here are expensive for (its/their) size.

10. Do comedies or dramas have a greater impact on (its/their) audiences?

Indefinite Pronoun Antecedents

Some pronouns are called **indefinite pronouns** because they do not refer to any particular person or thing.

Most indefinite pronouns are singular.

Singular Indefinite Pronouns

another	everybody	no one
anybody	everyone	nothing
anyone	everything	one
anything	much	somebody
each	neither	someone
either	nobody	something

When an indefinite pronoun antecedent is singular, use a singular pronoun to refer to it.

> Everything was in its place. (*Everything* is singular, so it is used with the singular pronoun *its*.)

Some indefinite pronouns are plural.

For information on subject-verb agreement with indefinite pronouns, see 23D.

Plural Indefinite Pronouns

both

few

many

others

several

When an indefinite pronoun antecedent is plural, use a plural pronoun to refer to it.

> They all wanted to graduate early, but few received their diplomas in January. (*Few* is plural, so it is used with the plural pronoun *their.*)

Note: Some indefinite pronouns (such as *all, any, more, most, none,* and *some*) can be either singular or plural: *All* is quiet. *All* were qualified.

FOCUS **His or Her with Singular Indefinite Pronouns**

Even though the indefinite pronouns *anybody, anyone, everybody, everyone, somebody, someone,* and so on are singular, many people use plural pronouns to refer to them.

(continued on the following page)

(continued from the previous page)

Everyone must hand in their completed work before 2 P.M.

This usage is widely accepted in spoken English. Nevertheless, indefinite pronouns like *everyone* are singular, and written English requires a singular pronoun.

Although using the singular pronoun *his* to refer to *everyone* is technically correct, doing so assumes that *everyone* refers to an individual who is male. Using *his or her* allows for the possibility that the indefinite pronoun may refer to either a male or a female.

Everyone must hand in his or her completed work before 2 P.M.

When used repeatedly, however, *he or she, him or her,* and *his or her* can create wordy or awkward sentences. Whenever possible, use plural forms.

All students must hand in their completed work before 2 P.M.

FOCUS **Indefinite Pronouns with *Of***

Some singular indefinite pronouns may be used in phrases with *of*— *each of, either of, neither of,* or *one of,* for example. Even in such phrases, these indefinite pronoun antecedents are always singular and take singular pronouns.

Each of the routes has its [not *their*] own special challenges.

◆ **PRACTICE 28-7**

In the following sentences, first circle the indefinite pronoun. Then, circle the pronoun in parentheses that refers to the indefinite pronoun antecedent.

Example: (Each) of the artists will have (his or her/their) own exhibit.

1. Either of those paintings will be sold with (its/their) frame.

2. Each of the artist's brushes has (its/their) own use.

3. Everything in the room made (its/their) contribution to the whole design.

4. Everyone must remember to take (his or her/their) paint box.

5. Neither of my sisters wanted (her/their) picture displayed.

6. Many of the men brought (his/their) children to the exhibit.

7. Several of the colors must be mixed with (its/their) contrasting colors.

8. When someone compliments your work, be sure to tell (him or her/them) that it's for sale.

9. Anyone can improve (his or her/their) skills as an artist.

10. Both of these workrooms have (its/their) own advantages.

◆ PRACTICE 28-8

Edit the following sentences for errors in pronoun-antecedent agreement. In some sentences, substitute *his or her* for *their* when the antecedent is singular. In other sentences, replace the antecedent with a plural word.

Examples:

Everyone will be responsible for ~~their~~ *his or her* own transportation.

~~Each of~~ *All* the children took their books out of their backpacks.

1. Everyone has the right to their own opinion.

2. Everyone can eat their lunch in the cafeteria.

3. Somebody forgot their backpack.

4. Each of the patients had their own rooms, with their own televisions and their own private baths.

5. Someone in the store has left their car's lights on.

6. Simone keeps everything in her kitchen in their own little container.

7. Each of the applicants must have their driver's license.

8. Anybody who has ever juggled a job and children knows how valuable their free time can be.

9. Either of the coffeemakers comes with their own filter.

10. Almost everyone waits until the last minute to file their income tax returns.

Collective Noun Antecedents

Collective nouns are words (like *band* and *team*) that name a group of people or things but are singular. Because they are singular, collective noun antecedents are used with singular pronouns.

The band played on, but <u>it</u> never played our song.

Frequently Used Collective Nouns			
army	club	gang	mob
association	committee	government	posse
band	company	group	team
class	family	jury	union

◆ PRACTICE 28-9

Circle the collective noun antecedent in the following sentences. Then, circle the correct pronoun in parentheses.

Example: The (jury) returned with ((its)/their) verdict.

1. The company provides (its/their) employees with very generous benefits.
2. Each study group is supposed to hand in (its/their) project by the end of the week.
3. Any government should be concerned for the welfare of (its/their) citizens.
4. Every family has (its/their) share of troubles.
5. An army is only as strong as the loyalty of (its/their) soldiers.

◆ PRACTICE 28-10

Edit the following passage for correct pronoun-antecedent agreement. First, identify the antecedent of each underlined pronoun. Then, cross out any pronoun that does not agree with its antecedent, and write the correct form above it. If the pronoun is correct, write *C* above it.

Example: Diversity is an important goal for the American corporation and ~~their~~ *its* workers.

(1) Diversity has come to corporate America. (2) Today, the average company counts among <u>their</u> employees many more women and members of minority groups than at any other time in our history. (3) The U.S. government has established laws to protect <u>its</u> citizens from discrimination in employment. (4) Anyone who can prove discrimination can usually see

their company fined. (5) For this reason, a corporation and <u>their</u> board
will usually set diversity as one of <u>its</u> goals. (6) Having a diverse work force,
however, does not mean that an organization has truly met the needs of
<u>its</u> employees. (7) While a Hispanic employee or a female employee may
now find that <u>their</u> opportunities are greater, issues remain to be resolved.
(8) Employees and management must first understand <u>its</u> common goals.
(9) Only then will a company be able to implement the kinds of policies that
will make it possible for each of <u>their</u> employees to work at <u>his or her</u> best.
(10) For example, company policy should allow leave time to anyone in the
company, regardless of <u>their</u> position.

■ SEEING AND WRITING: Flashback

Look back at your response to the Seeing and Writing exercise on page
416. Does your paragraph contain any antecedents that are compounds,
indefinite pronouns, or collective nouns? Have you used the correct pronoun to refer to each of these antecedents? If not, correct your pronouns.

F   Understanding Pronoun Case

A **personal pronoun** refers to a particular person or thing. Personal pronouns
change form according to the way they function in a sentence. Personal pronouns can be *subjective, objective,* or *possessive.*

Personal Pronouns

Subjective Case	Objective Case	Possessive Case
I	me	my, mine
he	him	his
she	her	her, hers
it	it	its

(continued on the following page)

(continued from the previous page)

we	us	our, ours
you	you	your, yours
they	them	their, theirs
who	whom	whose
whoever	whomever	

When a pronoun functions as a sentence's subject, it is in the **subjective case**.

Finally, <u>she</u> realized that dreams could come true.

When a pronoun functions as an object, it is in the **objective case**.

If Joanna hurries, she can stop <u>him</u>. (The pronoun *him* is the direct object of the verb *can stop*.)

Professor Miller sent <u>us</u> information about his research. (The pronoun *us* is the indirect object of the verb *sent*.)

Marc threw the ball to <u>them</u>. (The pronoun *them* is the object of the preposition *to*.)

FOCUS   Objects

A **direct object** is a noun or pronoun that receives the action of the verb.

DIRECT OBJECT
What did I send yesterday? I sent a <u>fax</u> yesterday.

DIRECT OBJECT
Whom will I call today? I'll call <u>him</u> today.

An **indirect object** is the noun or pronoun that tells to whom or for whom the verb's action was done.

INDIRECT OBJECT
To whom did I send a fax? I sent <u>Adam</u> a fax.

INDIRECT OBJECT
To whom did I give money? I gave <u>her</u> money.

A word or word group introduced by a preposition is called the **object of the preposition**. (See 15B.)

OBJECT OF PREPOSITION
From what did she run? She ran from the <u>fire</u>.

(continued on the following page)

(continued from the previous page)

OBJECT OF PREPOSITION

For whom did Kelly work? Kelly worked for <u>them</u>.

When a pronoun shows ownership, it is in the **possessive case**.

> Hieu took <u>his</u> lunch to the meeting. (The pronoun *his* indicates that the lunch belongs to Hieu.)

> Debbie and Kim decided to take <u>their</u> lunches, too. (The pronoun *their* indicates that the lunches belong to Debbie and Kim.)

◆ PRACTICE 28-11

In the following passage, fill in the blank after each pronoun to indicate whether the pronoun is subjective (*S*), objective (*O*), or possessive (*P*).

Example: We __*S*__ voted for her __*O*__ in the election.

(1) I _____ was never much interested in politics until last year when my _____ older sister, Nadia, decided to run for a seat on the school board. (2) Nadia's decision surprised me _____ because she _____ had never shown much interest in politics either. (3) However, public education had become important to her _____ because her _____ son was in his _____ second year of school. (4) Other family members supported Nadia's decision when they _____ realized its _____ importance to our _____ community. (5) We _____ all said to Nadia, "You _____ go for your _____ dream," and all of us _____ were eager to join the campaign. (6) Nadia's opponent was a man who _____ had served on the school board for two terms. (7) When Nadia challenged him _____ to a debate, he _____ declined, saying that my _____ sister was no real competition. (8) After that, many people switched their _____ support to Nadia because it _____ seemed to them _____ that whoever _____ chose to run for election should be prepared to debate. (9) People whose _____ minds were changed by this event were crucial to the outcome of the

vote. (10) It was Nadia for whom _____ the majority voted, and the victory was hers _____.

■ SEEING AND WRITING: Flashback

Look back at your response to the Seeing and Writing exercise on page 416. On a separate sheet of paper, list all the personal pronouns you have used, classifying them as subjective, objective, or possessive. Have you used correct pronoun case in every sentence? Make any necessary corrections.

G   Solving Special Problems with Pronoun Case

Three special situations can cause problems when you are trying to determine which pronoun case to use. One problem occurs with pronouns *in compounds*, another occurs with pronouns *in comparisons*, and the third occurs with the pronouns *who* and *whom*.

Pronouns in Compounds

Sometimes a pronoun is linked to a noun or to another pronoun with *and* or *or* to form a **compound**.

> The teacher and I met for an hour.

> She and I had a good meeting.

To determine whether to use the subjective or objective case for a pronoun in a compound, follow the same rules that apply for a pronoun that is not part of a compound.

If the compound in which the pronoun appears is the sentence's subject, use the subjective case.

> Toby and I [not *me*] like jazz.

> He and I [not *me*] went to the movies.

If the compound in which the pronoun appears is the object of the verb or the object of a preposition, use the objective case.

> The school sent my father and me [not *I*] the financial aid forms.

> This fight is between her and me [not *I*].

FOCUS **Choosing Pronouns in Compounds**

To determine which pronoun case to use in a compound that joins a noun and a pronoun, rewrite the sentence with just the pronoun.

Toby and [*I* or *me*?] like jazz.

I like jazz. (not *Me like jazz.*)

Toby and I like jazz.

Pronouns in Comparisons

Sometimes a pronoun appears after the word *than* or *as* in a **comparison**.

John is luckier than I.

The inheritance changed Raymond as much as her.

If the pronoun is a subject, use the subjective case.

John is luckier than I [am].

If the pronoun is an object, use the objective case.

The inheritance changed Raymond as much as [it changed] her.

FOCUS **Choosing Pronouns in Comparisons**

Sometimes the pronoun you use can change your sentence's meaning. For example, if you say, "I like Cheerios more than he," you mean that you like Cheerios more than the other person likes them.

I like Cheerios more than he [does].

If, however, you say, "I like Cheerios more than him," you mean that you like Cheerios more than you like the other person.

I like Cheerios more than [I like] him.

The Pronouns *Who* and *Whom*, *Whoever* and *Whomever*

To determine whether to use *who* or *whom* (or *whoever* or *whomever*), you need to know how the pronoun functions within the clause in which it appears.

When the pronoun is the subject of the clause, use *who* or *whoever*.

I wonder <u>who</u> wrote that song. (*Who* is the subject of the clause *who wrote that song.*)

I will vote for <u>whoever</u> supports the youth center. (*Whoever* is the subject of the clause *whoever supports the youth center.*)

When the pronoun is the object, use *whom* or *whomever*.

<u>Whom</u> do the police suspect? *(Whom* is the direct object of the verb *suspect.)*

I wonder <u>whom</u> the song is about. *(Whom* is the object of the preposition *about* in the clause *whom the song is about.)*

Vote for <u>whomever</u> you prefer. *(Whomever* is the object of the verb *prefer* in the clause *whomever you prefer.)*

FOCUS   *Who* and *Whom*

To determine whether to use *who* or *whom,* try substituting another pronoun for *who* or *whom* in the clause. If you can substitute *he* or *she,* use *who;* if you can substitute *him* or *her,* use *whom.*

[<u>Who</u>/Whom] wrote a love song? <u>He</u> wrote a love song.

[Who/<u>Whom</u>] was the song about? The song was about <u>her</u>.

The same test will work for *whoever* and *whomever*.

◆ PRACTICE 28-12

ON THE WEB
For more practice, visit Exercise Central: www.bedford stmartins.com/ writingincontext

In the following sentences, check the underlined pronouns, which are part of compound constructions, for correct subjective or objective case. If a correction needs to be made, cross out the pronoun and write the correct form above it. If the pronoun is correct, write *C* above it.

Example: The reward was divided between my friend and <u>me</u>.   *C*

(1) The deejay at the wedding reception asked Dionne and <u>I</u> to do an encore. (2) <u>Her</u> and <u>I</u> enjoy singing together. (3) The first time we sang, we really played up to <u>he</u> and the crowd. (4) <u>Her</u> and <u>me</u> talked with him for a few minutes about what we should sing for the encore. (5) Dionne and <u>me</u> couldn't agree. (6) Dionne and <u>I</u> always have trouble deciding on a song.

(7) Finally, the deejay made the decision for <u>her</u> and <u>I</u>. (8) After <u>she</u> and <u>I</u> finished, the guests went wild. (9) <u>Them</u> and the servers started chanting, "More, more, more." (10) It was too much for Dionne and <u>I</u> to believe.

◆ PRACTICE 28-13

Each of the following sentences includes a comparison with a pronoun following *than* or *as*. Write in each blank the correct form (subjective or objective) of the pronouns in parentheses. In brackets, add the word or words needed to complete the comparison.

> **Example:** He's a better poker player than _____*I [am]*_____ (I/me).

1. Denzel Washington is a better actor than _____ (she/her).

2. They are such a mismatched couple. Most people like her much more than _____ (he/him).

3. No one enjoys shopping more than _____ (she/her).

4. My brother and our Aunt Cecile were very close. Her death affected him more than _____ (I/me).

5. Could any two people have a better relationship than _____ (we/us)?

6. I'll admit my roommate drives better than _____ (I/me).

7. We at Steer Hut serve juicier steaks than _____ (they/them).

8. Even if you are as old as _____ (I/me), you're not as smart.

9. That jacket fits you better than _____ (I/me).

10. The Trumps may be richer than _____ (we/us), but I'll bet they don't have as much fun.

◆ PRACTICE 28-14

Circle the correct form of *who* or *whom* (or *whoever* or *whomever*) in parentheses in each sentence.

> **Example:** With (who/whom) did Rob collaborate?

1. The defense team learned (who/whom) was going to testify for the prosecution.

2. (Who/Whom) does she think she can find to be a witness?

3. I think the runner (who/whom) crosses the finish line first will be the winner.

4. They will argue their case to (whoever/whomever) will listen.

5. It will take time to decide (who/whom) the record holder is.

6. Take these forms to the clerk (who/whom) is at the front desk.

7. We will have to penalize (whoever/whomever) misses the first training session.

8. (Who/Whom) did Kobe take to the prom?

9. We saw the man (who/whom) fired the shots.

10. To (who/whom) am I speaking?

■ SEEING AND WRITING: Flashback

Look back at your response to the Seeing and Writing exercise on page 416. Can you find any sentences that contain a pronoun used in a compound or a comparison? If so, make sure you have used the appropriate pronoun case. When you have finished, check to make sure you have used the pronouns *who* and *whom* correctly.

H   **Identifying Reflexive and Intensive Pronouns**

Two special kinds of pronouns, *reflexive pronouns* and *intensive pronouns,* also always agree with their antecedents in person and number. Although the functions of the two kinds of pronouns are different, their forms are identical.

Reflexive and Intensive Pronouns

Singular Forms

Antecedent	*Reflexive or Intensive Pronoun*
I	myself
you	yourself
he	himself
she	herself
it	itself

(continued on the following page)

(continued from the previous page)

Plural Forms

Antecedent	*Reflexive or Intensive Pronoun*
we	ourselves
you	yourselves
they	themselves

Reflexive Pronouns

Reflexive pronouns always end in *-self* (singular) or *-selves* (plural). They indicate that people or things did something to themselves or for themselves.

Rosanna lost herself in the novel.

You need to watch yourself when you mix those solutions.

Mehul and Paul made themselves cold drinks.

Intensive Pronouns

Intensive pronouns also end in *-self* or *-selves*. However, they always appear directly after their antecedents, and they are used for emphasis.

I myself have had some experience in sales and marketing.

The victim himself collected the reward.

They themselves were uncertain of the significance of their findings.

◆ PRACTICE 28-15

Fill in the correct reflexive or intensive pronoun in each of the following sentences.

ON THE WEB
For more practice, visit Exercise Central: www.bedford stmartins.com/ writingincontext

Example: Sometimes I find _____*myself*_____ daydreaming in class.

1. The leaders gave _____ more credit than they deserved.

2. That woman takes _____ too seriously.

3. The president _____ visited the AIDS patients.

4. I don't see _____ as a particularly funny person.

5. Have you _____ ever actually seen an extraterrestrial?

6. We Americans pride _____ on our tolerance of diversity, but we can still be narrow-minded.

7. The bird settled _____ on my window ledge.

8. You should all give _____ a big pat on the back for a job well done.

9. Dorothy and the others hardly recognized _____ after their makeovers.

10. I _____ am opposed to the legislation, but I know that others support it.

■ SEEING AND WRITING: Flashback

Look back at your response to the Seeing and Writing exercise on page 416. Have you used any reflexive or intensive pronouns? If so, check to make sure you have used the correct forms. If not, write two new sentences, one using a reflexive pronoun and one using an intensive pronoun.

■ SEEING AND WRITING: Revising and Editing

Look back at your response to the Seeing and Writing exercise on page 416. Recopy your work on a separate sheet of paper, changing every singular noun to a plural noun and every plural noun to a singular noun. Then, edit your pronouns so singular pronouns refer to singular nouns and plural pronouns refer to plural nouns. You might also do this exercise with a piece of writing you did for another class.

CHAPTER REVIEW

◆ EDITING PRACTICE

Read the following student essay, into which noun and pronoun errors have been introduced. Check for errors in plural noun forms, pronoun case, and pronoun-antecedent agreement. Make any editing changes you think are necessary. The first sentence has been edited for you.

Going beyond Books

Extracurricular ~~activitys~~ *activities* can be just as important for
~~a~~ college student*s* as their coursework. Two students I
myself have met illustrate the truth of this statement. For
each of them, their extracurricular activities made a real
difference.

Julia joined our school's rifle team and soon began to
feel comfortable with the group and their routine. In her
first year, her team won the state Junior Varsity championship, and judges ranked them third in the region. In her
second year, her and the team placed sixth in the championship match. Julia found that intercollegiate competition
gave she and her teammates a much-needed escape from her
studies. Most important, Julia had the opportunity to
visit other campuses and to meet other competitors, some of
who were also woman.

Chris, a chemistry major, received similar benefits from
his participation in the student chapter of the American
Chemical Society (ACS). By the time he was a sophomore, he
was president of our school's chapter. Serving in this office
taught him how to handle leadership and responsibility. The
organization's goal was to educate their members about chemistry through seminars and visits to industry sites. They
also encouraged members to attend social functions with
other chemistry majors and faculty. Chris was active in
organizing all these events. Through the school's ACS chapter, a student like Chris could increase their knowledge
of chemistry beyond what their textbooks offered.

```
        Many students believe courses are what school is all

about, but Julia and Chris would disagree. For students

like they, time spent on extracurricular activities can be

as valuable as time spent in a classroom or library. Study-

ing and extracurricular activities are two halfs of a whole

educational experience.
```

◆ COLLABORATIVE ACTIVITIES

1. Working in a group, prepare a chart with the following five column headings. Write four nouns under each heading. If any noun is a proper noun, be sure to capitalize it.

Cars	Trees	Foods	Famous Couples	Cities

   Now, using as many of your nouns as possible, write a one-paragraph news article that describes an imaginary event. Exchange your work with another group, and check the other group's news article to be sure the correct pronoun form refers to each noun. Return the articles to their original groups for editing.

2. Working in a group, write a silly story that uses each of these nouns at least once: *Martians, eggplant, MTV, toupee, kangaroo, Iceland, bat, herd,* and *kayak.* Then, exchange stories with another group. After you have read the other group's story, edit it so that it includes all of the following pronouns: *it, its, itself, they, their, them,* and *themselves.* Return the edited story to its authors. Finally, reread your group's story, and check to make sure pronoun-antecedent agreement is clear and correct.

Adjectives and Adverbs

PREVIEW

In this chapter, you will learn
- to understand the difference between adjectives and adverbs (29A)
- to identify demonstrative adjectives (29A)
- to form comparatives and superlatives of adjectives and adverbs (29B)

Word Power

tutor
a private instructor

extra-curricular
outside the regular course of study

socialize
to make fit for companionship with others

cohort
a group united by common experiences

■ SEEING AND WRITING

What are the advantages and disadvantages of being educated at home by parents or other relatives instead of at school by professional teachers? Look at the picture above, and then discuss your opinions on this topic.

A　Identifying Adjectives and Adverbs

Adjectives and adverbs are words that modify—that is, describe or limit—other words. They help make sentences more specific and more interesting.

An **adjective** answers the question *What kind? Which one?* or *How many?* Adjectives modify nouns or pronouns.

> The Turkish city of Istanbul spans two continents. *(Turkish modifies the noun city, and two modifies the noun continents.)*

> It is fascinating because of its location and history. *(Fascinating modifies the pronoun it.)*

FOCUS　**Demonstrative Adjectives**

Demonstrative adjectives—*this, that, these,* and *those*—do not describe other words. They simply identify particular nouns.

This and *that* identify singular nouns and pronouns.

> This encyclopedia is much more thorough and up-to-date than that one.

These and *those* identify plural nouns.

> These words and phrases are French, but those expressions are Creole.

An **adverb** answers the question *How? Why? When? Where?* or *To what extent?* Adverbs modify verbs, adjectives, or other adverbs.

> Traffic moved steadily. *(Steadily modifies the verb moved.)*

> Still, we were quite impatient. *(Quite modifies the adjective impatient.)*

> Very slowly, we inched into the center lane. *(Very modifies the adverb slowly.)*

FOCUS　**Distinguishing Adjectives from Adverbs**

Many adverbs are formed when *-ly* is added to an adjective form.

(continued on the following page)

(continued from the previous page)

Adjective	Adverb
slow	slowly
nice	nicely
quick	quickly
real	really

ADJECTIVE Let me give you one <u>quick</u> reminder. *(Quick modifies the noun reminder.)*

ADVERB He <u>quickly</u> changed the subject. *(Quickly modifies the verb changed.)*

ADJECTIVE Tell me your <u>real</u> name. *(Real modifies the noun name.)*

ADVERB It was <u>really</u> rude of her to ignore me. *(Really modifies the adjective rude.)*

Note: Some adjectives—*lovely, friendly,* and *lively,* for instance—end in *-ly.* Be careful not to confuse these words with adverbs.

◆ PRACTICE 29-1

In the following sentences, circle the correct form (adjective or adverb) from the choices in parentheses.

ON THE WEB
For more practice, visit Exercise Central: www.bedford stmartins.com/ writingincontext

Example: Women who are (serious)/seriously) walkers or runners need to wear athletic shoes that fit.

(1) Doctors have found that many athletic shoes are (poor/poorly) designed for women. (2) Women's athletic shoes are actual/actually) just smaller versions of men's shoes. (3) Consequently, they cannot provide a (true/truly) comfortable fit. (4) Studies have shown that to get a shoe that fits (comfortable/comfortably) in the heel, most women must buy one that is too (tight/tightly) for the front of the foot. (5) This can have a (real/really) negative impact on athletic performance. (6) It can also cause (serious/ seriously) pain and even physical deformity. (7) Some athletic shoe manufacturers have begun to market athletic shoes that are designed (specific/ specifically) for women. (8) Experts say that women must become informed consumers and choose (careful/carefully) when they shop for athletic

shoes. (9) One (important/importantly) piece of advice is to shop for shoes (immediate/immediately) after exercising or at the end of a work day, when the foot is at its largest. (10) Experts advise that athletic shoes should feel (comfortable/comfortably) from the moment they are tried on—or else be returned to the box.

FOCUS   *Good and Well*

Be careful not to confuse *good* and *well*. Unlike regular adjectives, whose adverb form adds *-ly*, the adjective *good* is irregular. Its adverb form is *well*.

> ADJECTIVE   Fred Astaire was a good dancer. *(Good* modifies the noun *dancer.)*

> ADVERB   He danced especially well with Ginger Rogers. *(Well* modifies the verb *danced.)*

Always use *well* when you are describing a person's health.

> He really didn't feel well [not *good*] after eating an entire pizza.

Use *good* when you are describing a person's emotional state.

> He felt good [not *well*] about his high score on the test.

◆ PRACTICE 29-2

Circle the correct form *(good* or *well)* in the sentences below.

Example: Eating (good/well) is part of (good/well) living.

(1) A particular food can sometimes be (good/well) for you in ways you might not expect. (2) For example, if you are feeling down and just not doing (good/well) emotionally, you might need a carbohydrate pick-me-up. (3) Some doctors recommend pasta, rice cakes, or pretzels as (good/well) sources of carbohydrates. (4) If you need to perform (good/well) mentally—on a test, for example—protein-rich foods may be helpful. (5) Three to four ounces of fish or chicken can be especially (good/well) for helping you remain alert. (6) Carbohydrates can be eaten with the protein, but you

would do (good/well) to avoid overeating, which can make you drowsy.
(7) Most people know that caffeine works (good/well) to help overcome
drowsiness. (8) Caffeine can also be a (good/well) stimulant for helping one
stay alert. (9) High-fat foods are also useful because they encourage the
brain to produce endorphins, the same substances that make us feel so
(good/well) when we are with someone we love. (10) However, the greatest
supply of endorphins is produced in people who exercise regularly and eat
(good/well).

■ SEEING AND WRITING: Flashback

Look back at your response to the Seeing and Writing exercise on page
441. Underline each adjective and adverb, and draw an arrow from each
to the word it describes or limits. Do all adjectives modify nouns or pronouns? Do all adverbs modify verbs, adjectives, or other adverbs? Have
you used *good* and *well* correctly? Revise any sentences that use adjectives or adverbs incorrectly.

B   Understanding Comparatives and Superlatives

Sometimes an adjective or adverb describes something by comparing it to
something else. The **comparative** form of an adjective or adverb compares
two people or things. Adjectives and adverbs form the comparative with *-er* or
more. The **superlative** form of an adjective or adverb compares more than
two things. Adjectives and adverbs form the superlative with *-est* or *most*.

ADJECTIVES This film is <u>dull</u> and <u>predictable</u>.

COMPARATIVE The film I saw last week was even <u>duller</u> and <u>more</u>
<u>predictable</u> than this one.

SUPERLATIVE The film I saw last night was the <u>dullest</u> and <u>most</u>
<u>predictable</u> one I've ever seen.

ADVERB For a beginner, Jane did needlepoint <u>skillfully</u>.

COMPARATIVE After she had watched the demonstration, Jane did needlepoint <u>more skillfully</u> than Rosie.

SUPERLATIVE Of the twelve beginners, Jane did needlepoint the <u>most</u>
<u>skillfully</u>.

Forming Comparatives and Superlatives

Adjectives

- One-syllable adjectives generally form the comparative with -*er* and the superlative with -*est*.

    great   greater   greatest

- Adjectives with two or more syllables form the comparative with *more* and the superlative with *most*.

    wonderful   more wonderful   most wonderful

    Exception: Two-syllable adjectives ending in -*y* add -*er* or -*est* after changing the *y* to an *i*.

    funny   funnier   funniest

Adverbs

- All adverbs ending in -*ly* form the comparative with *more* and the superlative with *most*.

    efficiently   more efficiently   most efficiently

- Some other adverbs form the comparative with -*er* and the superlative with -*est*.

    soon   sooner   soonest

FOCUS   **Special Problems with Comparatives and Superlatives**

- Never use both -*er* and *more* to form the comparative or both -*est* and *most* to form the superlative.

    Nothing could have been <u>more awful</u>. (not *more awfuller*)

    Space Mountain is the <u>most frightening</u> (not *most frighteningest*) ride at Disney World.

(continued on the following page)

(continued from the previous page)

■ Never use the superlative when you are comparing only two things.

This is the <u>more serious</u> (not *most serious*) of the two problems.

■ Never use the comparative when you are comparing more than two things.

This is the <u>worst</u> (not *worse*) day of my life.

FOCUS   **Adjectives and Adverbs with No Comparative and Superlative Forms**

■ Some adverbs—such as *very, somewhat, quite, extremely,* and *rather*—do not have comparative and superlative forms.

■ Demonstrative adjectives *(this, that, these,* and *those)* do not have comparative superlative forms.

■ The adjective *unique* means "one of a kind." For this reason, it has no comparative or superlative form (*more unique* and *most unique* are incorrect).

◆ **PRACTICE 29-3**

Fill in the correct comparative form of the word supplied in parentheses.

Example: Children tend to be _____*noisier*_____ (noisy) than adults.

1. Traffic always moves _____ (slow) during rush hour than late at night.

2. The weather report says temperatures will be _____ (cold) tomorrow.

3. Some elderly people are _____ (healthy) than younger people.

4. It has been proven that pigs are _____ (intelligent) than dogs.

ON THE WEB
For more practice, visit Exercise Central: www.bedford stmartins.com/ writingincontext

5. When someone asks you to repeat yourself, you usually answer
   _____ (loud).

6. The _____ (tall) the building, the more damage the earth-
   quake caused.

7. They want to teach their son to be _____ (respectful) of
   women than many other young men are.

8. Las Vegas is _____ (famous) for its casinos than for its natural
   resources.

9. The WaterDrop is _____ (wild) than any other ride in the park.

10. You must move _____ (quick) if you expect to catch the ball.

◆ PRACTICE 29-4

Fill in the correct superlative form of the word supplied in parentheses.

   Example: Consumers now pay the ___*highest*___ (high) surcharge
   ever when they buy tickets for arena events.

   (1) Ticketmaster is the _____ (large) seller of sports
and entertainment tickets in the country. (2) The company was the
_____ (early) to sell concert and sporting event tickets both by
phone and through retail outlets. (3) It has also been the _____
(successful) at making deals to keep rival ticket agencies from carrying
tickets for large arenas and stadiums. (4) Its markup on tickets adds at least
20 percent to the cost of each ticket sold and is by far the _____
(great) in the business. (5) Because Ticketmaster is the _____
(powerful) ticket outlet in the country, however, fans have no choice but to
pay the price. (6) Critics have argued that Ticketmaster's control of the market
is the _____ (strong) monopoly in the country. (7) In 1994,
the rock group Pearl Jam launched the _____ (serious) offensive
to date against the ticket giant. (8) Wanting its fans to be able to buy the

_____ (cheap) tickets possible, Pearl Jam proposed to lower its own profits as well as Ticketmaster's for its 1994 summer tour. Ticketmaster refused. (9) Still one of the _____ (popular) groups in the country, Pearl Jam has tried to use arenas that are not controlled by Ticketmaster for its more recent tours. (10) Ticketmaster's president argues that it has succeeded not because of unfairness but because it has worked the _____ (hard) and is the _____ (aggressive) company in the business.

FOCUS *Good/Well and Bad/Badly*

Most adjectives and adverbs form the comparative with *-er* or *more* and the superlative with *-est* or *most*. The adjectives *good* and *bad* and their adverb forms *well* and *badly* are exceptions.

Adjective	Comparative Form	Superlative Form
good	better	best
bad	worse	worst

Adverb	Comparative Form	Superlative Form
well	better	best
badly	worse	worst

◆ PRACTICE 29-5

Fill in the correct comparative or superlative form of *good, well, bad,* or *badly.*

Example: She is at her ___*best*___ (good) when she is under pressure.

1. Today in track practice, Luisa performed _____ (well) than she has in weeks.

2. In fact, she ran her _____ (good) time ever in the fifty meter.

3. When things are bad, we wonder whether they will get _____ (good) or _____ (bad).

4. I've had some bad meals before, but this is the _____ (bad).

5. The world always looks _____ (good) when you're in love than when you're not.

6. Athletes generally play their _____ (badly) when their concentration is poorest.

7. The Sport Shop's prices may be good, but Athletic Attic's are the _____ (good) in town.

8. There are _____ (good) ways to solve conflicts than by fighting.

9. People seem to hear _____ (well) when they agree with what you're saying than when they don't agree with you.

10. Of all the children, Manda took the _____ (good) care of her toys.

■ SEEING AND WRITING: Flashback

Look back at your response to the Seeing and Writing exercise on page 441. On a separate sheet of paper, copy the adjectives and adverbs from your paragraph. Then, write the comparative and superlative forms beside each adjective or adverb.

■ SEEING AND WRITING: Revising and Editing

Look back at your response to the Seeing and Writing exercise on page 441. Have you used adjectives and adverbs that effectively communicate the situation you describe? Have you used enough adjectives and adverbs to explain your ideas to readers? Add or substitute modifying words as needed to make your writing more precise and more interesting. Delete any unnecessary adjectives and adverbs.

CHAPTER REVIEW

◆ EDITING PRACTICE

Read the following student essay, into which errors in the use of adjectives and adverbs have been introduced. Make any changes necessary to correct adjectives incorrectly used for adverbs and adverbs incorrectly used for adjectives. Also correct any errors in the use of comparatives and superlatives and in the use of demonstrative adjectives. If you like, you may add adjectives and adverbs that you feel would make the writer's ideas clearer or more specific. The first sentence has been edited for you.

Starting Over

A wedding can be the ~~joyfullest~~ *most joyful* occasion in two people's lives, the beginning of a couple's ~~most~~ happiest years. For some unlucky women, however, a wedding can be the worse thing that ever happens; it is the beginning not of their happiness but of their battered lives. As I went through the joyful day of my wedding, I wanted bad to find happiness for the rest of my life, but what I hoped and wished for did not come true.

I was married in the savannah belt of the Sudan in the eastern part of Africa, where I grew up. I was barely twenty-two years old. The first two years of my marriage progressed peaceful, but problems started as soon as our first child was born.

Many American women say, "If my husband gave me just one beating, that would be it. I'd leave." But those attitude does not work in cultures where tradition has overshadowed women's rights and divorce is not accepted. All women can do is accept their sadly fate. Battered women give many reasons for staying in their marriages, but fear is the commonest. Fear immobilizes these women, ruling their decisions, their actions, and their very lives. This is how it was for me.

Of course, I was real afraid whenever my husband hit me. I would run to my mother's house and cry, but she would always talk me into going back and being more patiently with my husband. Our tradition discourages divorce, and wife-beating is taken for granted. The situation is really quite ironic: Islam, the religion I practice, sets harsh punishments for abusive husbands, but tradition has so overpowered religion that the laws do not really work very good.

One night, after nine years of torture, I asked myself whether life had treated me fair. True, I had a high school diploma and two of the beautifullest children in the world, but all this was not enough. I realized that to stand up to the husband who treated me so bad, I would have to achieve a more better education than he had. That night, I decided to get a college education in the United States. My husband opposed my decision, but with the support of my father and mother, I was able to begin to make a new life for myself and my children in America.

◆ COLLABORATIVE ACTIVITIES

1. Working in a small group, write a plot summary for an imaginary film. Begin with one of the following three sentences.

   ■ Dirk and Clive were sworn enemies, but that night on Boulder Ridge they vowed to work together just this once, for the good of their country.
   ■ Genevieve entered the room in a cloud of perfume, and when she spoke, her voice was like velvet.
   ■ The desert sun beat down on her head, but Susanna was determined to protect what was hers, no matter what the cost.

2. Trade summaries with another group. Add as many adjectives and adverbs as you can to the other group's summary. Make sure each modifier is appropriate.
3. Reread your group's plot summary and edit it carefully, paying special attention to the way adjectives and adverbs are used.

Grammar and Usage Issues for ESL Writers

PREVIEW

In this chapter, you will learn
- to include subjects in sentences (30A)
- to avoid special problems with subjects (30B)
- to identify plural nouns (30C)
- to understand count and noncount nouns (30D)
- to use determiners with count and noncount nouns (30E)
- to understand articles (30F)

- to form negative statements and questions (30G)
- to indicate verb tense (30H)
- to recognize stative verbs (30I)
- to place modifiers in order (30J)
- to choose correct prepositions (30K)
- to use prepositions in familiar expressions (30L)
- to use prepositions in two-word verbs (30M)

▶ **Word Power**
ritual
a procedure that is followed faithfully

tradition
the passing down of parts of a culture from generation to generation

■ SEEING AND WRITING

Look at the painting above, and then explain how you and your family celebrate a holiday that is important to you.

Learning English as a second language involves more than just learning grammar. In fact, if you have been studying English as a second language, you may know as much about English grammar as many native speakers do—or even more. However, you will still need to learn the conventions and rules that are second nature to most (though by no means all) native speakers. This chapter covers the grammar and usage issues that give nonnative speakers the most trouble.

A Including Subjects in Sentences

English requires that every sentence state its subject. In fact, every dependent clause must also have a subject.

> INCORRECT Elvis Presley was only 42 years old when died.
>
> CORRECT Elvis Presley was only 42 years old when <u>he</u> died.

English even requires a false or "dummy" subject to fill the subject position in sentences like the following one.

> <u>It</u> is hot in this room.

It is not correct to write just *Hot in this room* or *Is hot in this room.*

◆ PRACTICE 30-1

ON THE WEB
For more practice, visit Exercise Central: www.bedford stmartins.com/ writingincontext

Each of the following sentences is missing the subject of a dependent or an independent clause. Add an appropriate subject to each sentence.

Example: Reality TV programs are very popular, but critics say ⌄*they* are going too far.

1. When the first season of the reality show *Survivor* aired, was an immediate hit.

2. At first, media experts thought was strange that a show like *Survivor* would be so successful.

3. For a while, *Survivor* became a cultural phenomenon—probably because was seldom in bad taste.

4. Millions of Americans planned their evening so that could be sure not to miss the next episode.

5. Was surprising to see the controversial shows that suddenly appeared on the air.

6. Many people refused to watch shows that felt were "morally corrupt."

7. A recent poll asked viewers: "Do enjoy reality TV, or has it gone too far?"

8. Most viewers thought that reality TV had gone too far even though enjoyed *Survivor* and similar shows.

9. Turns out that reality TV is nothing new.

10. In 1973, the documentary *An American Family* showed members of the Loud family as went about their daily lives.

B Avoiding Special Problems with Subjects

Some languages commonly begin a sentence with a word or phrase that has no grammatical link to the sentence but that states clearly what the sentence is about. If you speak such a language, you might write a sentence like this one.

> INCORRECT Career plan I am studying to be a computer scientist.

A sentence like this cannot occur in English. The phrase *career plan* cannot be a subject because the sentence already includes one: the pronoun *I*, which agrees with the verb *am studying*. In addition, *career plan* is not connected to the rest of the sentence in any other way. One way to revise this sentence is to rewrite it so that *career plan* is the subject.

For more on subjects, see 15A.

> CORRECT My career plan is to be a computer scientist.

Another way to revise the sentence is to make *career plan* the object of a preposition.

> CORRECT In terms of my career plan, I am studying to be a computer scientist.

Standard English also does not permit a two-part subject in which the second part is a pronoun referring to the same person or thing as the first part.

> INCORRECT The Caspian Sea it is the largest lake in the world.

> CORRECT The Caspian Sea is the largest lake in the world.

When the real subject follows the verb, and the normal subject position before the verb is empty, it must be filled by a "dummy" subject, such as *there*.

INCORRECT   Are many rivers in my country.

CORRECT   <u>There</u> are many rivers in my country.

◆ PRACTICE 30-2

ON THE WEB
*For more
practice, visit
Exercise Central:*
www.bedford
stmartins.com/
writingincontext

Revise each sentence by either adding or deleting words to correct the problem with the subject. (Some of the sentences can be corrected in more than one way.)

Example: *In*
My opinion the birth of the United States is an interesting
subject.

1. By the 1700s, were thirteen British colonies in North America.

2. On July 4, 1776, the colonies they declared their independence from England.

3. The Revolutionary War it went on for eight years.

4. Was a bit of confusion over how to set up a government.

5. The first Congress the colonies sent representatives to Philadelphia in 1787.

6. These men they are called "the founding fathers."

7. One of their goals they wanted to protect the rights of individuals.

8. The Constitution it is the formal statement of the U.S. system of government.

9. The effectiveness of the Constitution the Constitution works because it was written to allow additions or amendments.

10. Today, are twenty-six amendments to the U.S. Constitution.

■ SEEING AND WRITING: Flashback

Look back at your response to the Seeing and Writing exercise on page 453. Does every sentence state its subject? Underline the subject of each sentence. If a sentence does not have a subject, add one. If any sentence has a two-part subject, cross out the extra word or words.

C   Identifying Plural Nouns

In English, most nouns add *-s* to form plurals. Every time you use a noun, ask yourself whether you are talking about one item or more than one, and choose a singular or plural form accordingly. Consider this sentence.

CORRECT   The <u>books</u> in both <u>branches</u> of the <u>library</u> are deteriorating.

The three nouns in this sentence are underlined: one is singular *(library)*, and the other two are plural *(books, branches)*. You might think that the word *both* is enough to indicate that *branch* is plural, and that it is obvious that there would have to be more than one book in any branch of a library. But even if a sentence includes information that tells you that a noun is plural, you must always use a form that shows explicitly that a noun is plural.

For more on singular and plural nouns, see 28A and 28B.

◆ PRACTICE 30-3

Underline the plural nouns in the following sentences. (Not all the sentences contain plural nouns.)

ON THE WEB
For more practice, visit Exercise Central: www.bedford stmartins.com/ writingincontext

Example: The shark is one of the earth's most feared <u>animals</u>.

1. There are about 360 species of sharks.

2. These fish live in oceans and seas throughout the world but are most commonly found in warm water.

3. Sharks vary greatly in size and behavior.

4. Whale sharks are the largest, growing up to 40 feet long and weighing over 15 tons.

5. The smallest shark measures as little as half a foot and weighs less than an ounce.

6. Some sharks live in the deepest areas of the ocean, while other sharks stay near the water's surface.

7. Although all sharks are meat-eaters, only a few species are a danger to people.

8. Most sharks eat live fish, including their fellow sharks.

9. Since the 1950s, sharks have been used more and more in scientific research.

10. Few sharks have ever been found with cancer, and scientists hope to find out what protects these creatures from this disease.

> ■ SEEING AND WRITING: Flashback
>
> Look back at your response to the Seeing and Writing exercise on page 453. On a separate sheet of paper, list all the plural nouns. Check carefully to make sure each plural noun has a form that shows the noun is plural. Correct any errors you find.

D   Understanding Count and Noncount Nouns

A **count noun** names one particular thing or a group of particular things: *a teacher, a panther, a bed, an ocean, a cloud; two teachers, many panthers, three beds, two oceans, several clouds.* A **noncount noun**, however, names things that cannot be counted: *gold, cream, sand, blood, smoke.*

Count nouns usually have a singular form and a plural form: *cloud, clouds.* Noncount nouns usually have only a singular form: *smoke.* Note how the nouns *cloud* and *smoke* differ in the way they are used in sentences.

CORRECT The sky is full of clouds.

CORRECT The sky is full of smoke.

INCORRECT The sky is full of smokes.

CORRECT I see ten clouds.

INCORRECT I see ten smokes.

Often, the same idea can be represented with either a count noun or a noncount noun.

Count	Noncount
people (plural of *person*)	humanity [*not* humanities]
tables, chairs, beds	furniture [*not* furnitures]
letters	mail [*not* mails]
tools	equipment [*not* equipments]
facts	information [*not* informations]

Some words can be either count or noncount, depending on the meaning intended.

COUNT He had many interesting experiences at his first job.

NONCOUNT It is often difficult to get a job if you do not have experience.

FOCUS   **Count and Noncount Nouns**

Here are some general guidelines for using count and noncount nouns.

■ Use a count noun to refer to a living animal, but use a noncount noun to refer to the food that comes from that animal.

> COUNT There are three live <u>lobsters</u> in the tank.
>
> NONCOUNT This restaurant specializes in <u>lobster</u>.

■ If you use a noncount noun for a substance or class of things that can come in different varieties, you can often make that noun plural if you want to talk about those varieties.

> NONCOUNT <u>Cheese</u> is a rich source of calcium.
>
> COUNT Many different <u>cheeses</u> come from Italy.

■ If you want to shift attention from a concept in general to specific examples of it, you can often use a noncount noun as a count noun.

> NONCOUNT You have a great deal of <u>talent</u>.
>
> COUNT My <u>talents</u> do not include singing.

◆ PRACTICE 30-4

In each of the following sentences, identify the underlined word as a count or noncount noun. If it is a noncount noun, circle the *N* following the sentence, but do not write in the blank. If it is a count noun, circle the *C*, and then write the plural form of the noun in the blank.

ON THE WEB
For more practice, visit Exercise Central: www.bedford stmartins.com/ writingincontext

Examples: Psychologists, sociologists, and anthropologists work in the

field of behavioral <u>science</u>. (N) C _____

They all have the same <u>goal</u>: to understand human behavior. N (C)

____goals____

1. Each type of scientist has a different <u>approach</u> to solving a problem

   N   C   _____

2. An <u>example</u> is the problem of homeless people on our cities' streets.

    N   C   _____

3. Sociologists concentrate on the social causes of <u>homelessness</u>. N   C

    _____

4. They might study how <u>unemployment</u> contributes to a rise in the number

    of homeless people. N   C   _____

5. A <u>shortage</u> of inexpensive housing can also cause someone to lose his or

    her home. N   C   _____

6. A sociologist's next question could be: How does <u>society</u> deal with home-

    less people? N   C   _____

7. Psychologists, on the other hand, are interested in the <u>individual</u>.

    N   C   _____

8. Their focus would be on how a homeless <u>person</u> feels and thinks.

    N   C   _____

9. Anthropologists are interested in studying culture, a society's <u>system</u> of

    beliefs and its ways of doing things. N   C   _____

10. An anthropologist might focus on how the <u>homeless</u> find food and shelter

    and on how they raise their children. N   C   _____

E   Using Determiners with Count and Noncount Nouns

Determiners are adjectives that *identify* rather than describe the nouns they modify. Determiners may also *quantify* nouns (that is, indicate an amount or a number).

Determiners include the following words.

- Articles: *a, an, the*
- *This, these, that, those*
- Possessive pronouns: *my, our, your, his, her, its, their*
- Possessive nouns: *Sheila's, my friend's,* and so on
- *Whose, which, what*
- *All, both, each, every, some, any, either, no, neither, many, most, much, a few, a little, few, little, several, enough*
- All numerals: *one, two,* and so on

When a determiner is accompanied by one or more other adjectives, the determiner always comes first. For example, in the phrase *my expensive new digital watch, my* is a determiner; you cannot put *expensive, new, digital,* or any other adjective before *my.*

A singular count noun must be accompanied by a determiner—for example, *my watch* or *the new digital watch,* not just *watch* or *new digital watch.* Noncount nouns and plural count nouns, however, sometimes have determiners but sometimes do not. *This honey is sweet* and *Honey is sweet* are both acceptable, as are *These berries are juicy* and *Berries are juicy.* (In each case, the meaning is different.) You cannot say *Berry is juicy,* however; say instead *This berry is juicy, Every berry is juicy,* or *A berry is juicy.*

FOCUS **Determiners**

Some determiners can be used only with certain types of nouns.

■ *This* and *that* can be used only with singular nouns (count or noncount): *this berry, that honey.*
■ *These, those, a few, few, many, both,* and *several* can be used only with plural count nouns: *these berries, those apples, a few ideas, few people, many students, both sides, several directions.*
■ *Much* and *a little* can be used only with noncount nouns: *much affection, a little honey.*
■ *Some* and *enough* can be used only with noncount or plural count nouns: *some honey, some berries, enough trouble, enough problems.*
■ *A, an, every,* and *each* can be used only with singular count nouns: *a berry, an elephant, every possibility, each citizen.*

◆ **PRACTICE 30-5**

In each of the following sentences, circle the more appropriate choice from each pair of words or phrases in parentheses.

ON THE WEB
For more practice, visit Exercise Central: www.bedford stmartins.com/ writingincontext

Examples:
Volcanoes are among the most destructive of (all/every) natural forces on Earth.

People have always been fascinated and terrified by (this/these) force of nature.

1. Not (all/every) volcano is considered a danger.

2. In (major some/some major) volcanic eruptions, huge clouds rise over the mountain.

3. (A few violent/Violent a few) eruptions are so dramatic that they blow the mountain apart.

4. (Most/Much) volcanic eruptions cannot be predicted.

5. Since the 1400s, almost 200,000 people have lost (his/their) lives in volcanic eruptions.

6. When a volcano erupts, (little/a little) can be done to prevent property damage.

7. (Many/Much) lives can be saved, however, if people in the area are evacuated in time.

8. Unfortunately, when people realize an eruption is about to take place, there rarely is (every/enough) time to escape.

9. Volcanoes can be dangerous, but they also produce (a little/some) benefits.

10. For example, (a few/a little) countries around the world use geothermal energy—from underground steam in volcanic areas—to produce electric power.

■ SEEING AND WRITING: Flashback

Look back at your response to the Seeing and Writing exercise on page 453. On a separate sheet of paper, list all the count nouns in one column and all the noncount nouns in another column. Check carefully to make sure you have used count and noncount nouns correctly, and correct any errors you find.

F   Understanding Articles

The definite article *the* and the indefinite articles *a* and *an* are determiners that tell readers whether the noun that follows is one they can identify *(the book)* or one they cannot yet identify *(a book).*

Definite Articles

When the definite article *the* is used with a noun, the writer is saying to readers, "You can identify which particular thing or things I have in mind. The information you need to make that identification is available to you. Either you have it already, or I am about to supply it to you."

Readers can find the necessary information in the following ways.

■ By looking at other information in the sentence.

> Meet me at <u>the</u> corner of Main Street and Lafayette Road.

In this example, *the* is used with the noun *corner* because other words in the sentence tell readers which particular corner the writer has in mind: the one located at Main and Lafayette.

■ By looking at information in other sentences.

> Aisha ordered a slice of pie and a cup of coffee. <u>The</u> pie was delicious. She asked for a second slice.

Here, *the* is used before the word *pie* in the second sentence to indicate that it is the same pie identified in the first sentence. Notice, however, that the noun *slice* in the third sentence is preceded by an indefinite article *(a)* because it is not the same slice referred to in the first sentence.

■ By drawing on general knowledge.

> <u>The</u> planet revolves around <u>the</u> sun.

Here, *the* is used with the nouns *planet* and *sun* because readers are expected to know which particular things the writer is referring to.

FOCUS   **Definite Articles**

Always use *the* (rather than *a* or *an*) in the following situations.

■ Before the word *same: the same day*
■ Before the superlative form of an adjective: *the youngest son*
■ Before a number indicating order or sequence: *the third time*

For information on the superlative forms of adjectives and adverbs, see 29B.

Indefinite Articles

When an indefinite article is used with a noun, the writer is saying to readers, "I don't expect you to have enough information right now to identify a particular thing that I have in mind. I do expect you to recognize that I'm referring to only one item."

Consider the following sentences.

We need a table for our computer.

I have a folding table; maybe you can use that.

In the first sentence, the writer is referring to a hypothetical table, not an actual one. Because the table is indefinite to the writer, it is clearly indefinite to the reader, so *a* is used, not *the*. The second sentence refers to an actual table, but because the writer does not expect the reader to be able to identify the table specifically, it is also used with *a* rather than *the*.

FOCUS   **Indefinite Articles**

Unlike the definite article, the indefinite articles *a* and *an* occur only with singular count nouns. *A* is used when the next sound is a consonant, and *an* is used when the next sound is a vowel. In choosing *a* or *an*, pay attention to sounds rather than to spelling: *a house, a year, a union,* but *an hour, an uncle.*

No Article

For more on
count and
noncount
nouns,
see 30D.

Only noncount and plural count nouns can stand without articles: *butter, chocolate, cookies, strawberries* (but *a cookie* or *the strawberry*).

Nouns without articles can be used to make generalizations.

Infants need affection as well as food.

Here, the absence of articles before the nouns *infants, affection,* and *food* indicates that the statement is not about particular infants, affection, or food but about infants, affection, and food in general. Remember not to use *the* in such sentences; in English, a sentence like *The infants need affection as well as food* can only refer to particular, identifiable infants, not to infants in general.

Articles with Proper Nouns

For more
on proper
nouns, see
28A and 33A.

Proper nouns can be divided into two classes: names that take *the* and names that take no article.

■ Names of people usually take no article unless they are used in the plural to refer to members of a family, in which case they take *the: Napoleon, Mahatma Gandhi,* but *the Parkers.*

■ Names of places that are plural in form usually take *the: the Andes, the United States.*

- The names of most places on land (cities, states, provinces, and countries) take no article: *Salt Lake City, Mississippi, Alberta, Japan.* The names of most bodies of water (rivers, seas, and oceans, although not lakes or bays) take *the: the Mississippi, the Mediterranean, the Pacific,* but *Lake Erie* and *San Francisco Bay.*
- Names of streets take no article: *Main Street.* Names of highways take *the: the Belt Parkway.*

◆ PRACTICE 30-6

In the following passage, decide whether each blank needs a definite article (*the*), an indefinite article (*a* or *an*), or no article. If a definite or indefinite article is needed, write it in the space provided. If no article is needed, leave the space blank.

ON THE WEB
For more practice, visit Exercise Central: www.bedford stmartins.com/ writingincontext

Example:　Vicente Fox was born on _____ July 2, 1942, in _the_ Mexican capital of Mexico City.

(1) Vicente was _____ second of nine children born to José Luis Fox, _____ wealthy farmer, and Mercedes Quesada. (2) When Vicente was only four days old, _____ Fox family went to live in San Francisco del Rincón, in _____ state of Guanajuato. (3) Vicente Fox studied _____ business administration at the Universidad Iberoamericana in Mexico City. (4) He then traveled to _____ United States, where he received _____ degree in management at _____ Harvard University. (5) When he returned to Mexico, he went to work for Coca-Cola, and over _____ next fifteen years, he climbed _____ corporate ladder and became _____ company's youngest manager and eventually Coca-Cola's president for Mexico and _____ Latin America. (6) Fox entered _____ politics by joining _____ National Action Party during _____ 1980s. (7) In 1988, he was elected to _____ Congress. (8) _____ few years later, in 1991, he ran for _____ post of governor of Guanajuato but lost. (9) Four years later, he won by _____ landslide. (10) In 1999, Fox took _____ leave of absence as governor to run in _____ presidential elections. (11) In one interview during his campaign, he said he wanted to rebuild Mexico into _____ country "where _____ security and _____ justice prevail, where no one

is above _____ law." (12) After promoting himself as _____ "down-to-earth man of _____ people," on July 2, 2000, Vicente Fox became _____ first opposition candidate to reach _____ presidency of _____ Republic of Mexico.

> ■ **SEEING AND WRITING: Flashback**
>
> Look back at your response to the Seeing and Writing exercise on page 453. Circle each definite article (*the*) and indefinite article (*a* or *an*) you have used. Have you used articles correctly? Correct any errors you find.

G Forming Negative Statements and Questions

Negative Statements

For more on helping verbs, see 15C.

To form a negative statement, add the word *not* directly after the first helping verb of the complete verb.

Global warming has been getting worse.

Global warming has <u>not</u> been getting worse.

When there is no helping verb, a form of the verb *do* must be inserted before *not*.

Automobile traffic contributes to pollution.

Automobile traffic <u>does not</u> contribute to pollution.

For information on subject-verb agreement with the verb do, *see 23B.*

Remember that when *do* is used as a helping verb, the form of *do* used must match the tense and number of the original main verb. Note that in the negative statement above, the main verb loses its tense and appears in the base form (*contribute,* not *contributes*).

Exception: It is not necessary to use a form of *do* when forming negative statements with the verb *be.*

I am happy.

I am <u>not</u> happy.

Questions

To form a question, move the helping verb that follows the subject to the position directly before the subject.

The governor <u>is</u> trying to compromise.

<u>Is</u> the governor trying to compromise?

The governor <u>is</u> working on the budget.

<u>Is</u> the governor working on the budget?

The same rule stated above applies even when the verb is in the past or future tense.

The governor <u>was</u> trying to lower state taxes.

<u>Was</u> the governor trying to lower state taxes?

The governor <u>will</u> try to get re-elected.

<u>Will</u> the governor try to get re-elected?

Note: If a statement includes more than one helping verb, move only the *first* helping verb when you form a question: *The governor <u>will</u> be working on the budget; <u>Will</u> the governor <u>be</u> working on the budget?*

When the verb does not include a helping verb, you must supply a form of *do.* To form a question, put *do* directly before the subject.

The governor <u>works</u> hard.

<u>Does</u> the governor <u>work</u> hard?

The governor <u>improved</u> life in his state.

<u>Did</u> the governor <u>improve</u> life in his state?

Exception: It is not necessary to use a form of *do* when forming questions with the verb *be.*

The governor <u>is</u> a Republican.

<u>Is</u> the governor a Republican?

Note: The helping verb never comes before the subject in a question that begins with a subject like *who* or *which.*

<u>Who</u> is talking to the governor?

<u>Which</u> bills have been vetoed by the governor?

◆ PRACTICE 30-7

Edit sentences 1–5 to turn each into a question beginning with a helping verb. Edit sentences 6–10 to turn each into a negative statement.

ON THE WEB

For more practice, visit Exercise Central: www.bedford stmartins.com/ writingincontext

Examples: Her newest album ~~is~~ selling as well as her first one. *Is ... ?*

Her newest album will surely *not* win an award.

1. Converting metric measurements to English measurements is difficult.

2. The early frost damaged many crops.

3. That family was very influential in the early 1900s.

4. Most stores in downtown areas open on Sundays.

5. The winner of the presidential election has always been the candidate who got the most votes.

6. Many great artists attain recognition and success during their lifetimes.

7. The prosecutor can verify the accuracy of the witness's story.

8. The next Olympic Games will be held in the United States.

9. Customs officers at the border have been requiring motorists to show proof of citizenship.

10. The policy of segregation of blacks and whites in the American South ended with the Civil War.

■ SEEING AND WRITING: Flashback

Look back at your response to the Seeing and Writing exercise on page 453. Do you see any negative statements? If so, check to make sure you have formed them correctly. Then, on a separate sheet of paper, write a question that you could add to your Seeing and Writing exercise. Check carefully to make sure you have formed the question correctly.

H Indicating Verb Tense

For more on verb tense, see Chapters 26 and 27.

In English, a verb's form must always indicate when an action took place (for instance, in the past or in the present). Use the appropriate tense of the verb, even if the time is obvious or if the sentence includes other indications of time (such as *two years ago* or *at present*).

CORRECT Albert Einstein <u>emigrated</u> from Germany in 1933.

INCORRECT Albert Einstein <u>emigrate</u> from Germany in 1933.

■ SEEING AND WRITING: Flashback

Look back at your response to the Seeing and Writing exercise on page 453. Are all your verbs in the present tense? Correct any errors you find.

I Recognizing Stative Verbs

Stative verbs usually tell us that someone or something is in a state that will not change, at least for a while.

Hiro <u>knows</u> American history very well.

The **present progressive** tense consists of the present tense of *be* plus the present participle *(I am going)*. The **past progressive** tense consists of the past tense of *be* plus the present participle *(I was going)*. Most English verbs show action, and these action verbs can be used in the progressive tenses. Stative verbs, however, are rarely used in the progressive tenses.

INCORRECT Hiro <u>is knowing</u> American history very well.

FOCUS Stative Verbs

Verbs that are stative often refer to mental states like *know, understand, think, believe, want, like, love,* and *hate.* Other stative verbs include *be, have, need, own, belong, weigh, cost,* and *mean.* Certain verbs of sense perception, like *see* and *hear,* are also stative even though they can refer to momentary events rather than unchanging states.

Many verbs have more than one meaning, and some of these verbs are active with one meaning but stative with another. An example is the verb *weigh.*

ACTIVE The butcher <u>weighs</u> the meat.

STATIVE The meat <u>weighs</u> three pounds.

In the first sentence above, the verb *weigh* means "to put on a scale"; it is active, not stative. In the second sentence, however, the same verb means "to have weight," so it is stative, not active. It would be unacceptable to say, "The meat is weighing three pounds," but "The butcher is weighing the meat" would be correct.

◆ **PRACTICE 30-8**

ON THE WEB
*For more
practice, visit
Exercise Central:*
www.bedford
stmartins.com/
writingincontext

In each of the following sentences, circle the verb or verbs. Then, correct any problems with stative verbs by crossing out the incorrect verb tense and writing the correct verb tense above the line. If the verb is correct, write *C* above it.

> **Example:**   Many people ~~are thinking~~ *think* that the typical American does not *C*
> follow a healthy diet.

1. Unfortunately, this view is being close to the truth.

2. A diet that is including high levels of sugar, salt, fat, and cholesterol is often causing serious health problems.

3. We are knowing that nutrition is an important part of health.

4. Busy families are wanting food that is inexpensive and easy to prepare.

5. Many convenience foods, frozen or canned, are having very little food value.

6. Too many Americans are weighing much more than they should.

7. Some people's eating habits are changing, however, and more and more Americans are becoming more concerned about nutrition.

8. Some experts believe that Americans are trying to eat better.

9. Unfortunately, a recent survey was showing that too many Americans are still couch potatoes.

10. Health experts are agreeing that Americans of all ages are needing to get more exercise.

■ **SEEING AND WRITING: Flashback**

Look back at your response to the Seeing and Writing exercise on page 453. Can you identify any stative verbs? If so, list them on a separate sheet of paper. Check carefully to be sure you have not used any of these verbs in a progressive tense. Correct any errors you find.

J   Placing Modifiers in Order

Adjectives and other modifiers that come before a noun usually follow a set order.

Required Order

- Determiners always come first in a series of modifiers: *these fragile glasses.* The determiners *all* or *both* always precede any other determiners: *all these glasses.*
- If one of the modifiers is a noun, that modifier must come directly before the noun it modifies: *these wine glasses.*
- Descriptive adjectives are placed between the determiners and the noun modifiers: *these fragile wine glasses.* If there are two or more of these adjectives, the following order is preferred.

For more on determiners, see 30E.

Preferred Order

- Adjectives that show the writer's attitude generally precede adjectives that merely describe: *these lovely fragile wine glasses.*
- Adjectives that indicate size generally come early: *these lovely large fragile wine glasses.*

◆ PRACTICE 30-9

Arrange each group of adjectives in the correct order, and rewrite the complete phrase in the blank.

ON THE WEB
For more practice, visit Exercise Central: www.bedford stmartins.com/ writingincontext

Example: (annual, impressive, the, publisher's) report

the publisher's impressive annual report

1. (brand-new, a, apartment, high-rise) building

_____

2. (gifted, twenty-five-year-old, Venezuelan, this) author

_____

3. (successful, short-story, numerous) collections

_____

4. (her, all, intriguing, suspense) novels

_____

5. (publisher's, best-selling, the, three) works

_____

6. (main, story's, two, this) characters

_____

7. (young, a, strong-willed) woman

_____

8. (middle-aged, attractive, the, British) poet

_____

9. (exquisite, wedding, an, white) gown

_____

10. (elaborate, wedding, an, million-dollar) reception

_____

■ SEEING AND WRITING: Flashback

Look back at your response to the Seeing and Writing exercise on page 453. Have you used several modifiers before a single noun? If so, list all the modifiers and the noun that follows them on a separate sheet of paper. Check carefully to make sure you have arranged the modifiers in the correct order. Make any necessary corrections.

K   Choosing Correct Prepositions

A **preposition** links a noun (or a word or word group that functions as a noun) to a verb, an adjective, or another noun in the sentence. Thus, prepositions show the precise relationships between words—for example, whether a book is *on, near,* or *under* a table.

> I thought I had left the book <u>on</u> the table or somewhere <u>near</u> the table, but I found it <u>under</u> the table.

The prepositions *at, in,* and *on* sometimes cause problems for nonnative speakers of English. For example, to identify the location of a place or an event, you can use *at, in,* or *on.*

- The preposition *at* specifies an exact point in space or time.

  The museum is <u>at</u> 1000 Fifth Avenue. Let's meet there <u>at</u> 10:00 tomorrow morning.

- Expanses of space or time are treated as containers and therefore require *in*.

  Jean-Pierre went to school <u>in</u> the 1970s.

- *On* must be used in two cases: with names of streets (but not with exact addresses) and with days of the week or month.

  We will move into our new office <u>on</u> 18th Street either <u>on</u> Monday or <u>on</u> March 12.

L Using Prepositions in Familiar Expressions

Many familiar expressions end with prepositions. Learning to write clearly and *idiomatically*—in keeping with the conventions of written English— means learning which preposition is used in such expressions. Even native speakers of English sometimes have trouble choosing the correct preposition.

The sentences that follow illustrate idiomatic use of prepositions in various expressions. Note that sometimes different prepositions are used with the same word. For example, both *on* and *for* can be used with *wait* to form two different expressions with two different meanings *(He waited on their table; She waited for the bus)*. Which preposition you choose depends on your meaning. (In the list that follows, pairs of similar expressions that end with different prepositions are bracketed.)

Expression with Preposition	Sample Sentence
acquainted with	During orientation, the university offers workshops to make sure that students are <u>acquainted with</u> its rules and regulations.
addicted to	I think Abby is becoming <u>addicted to</u> pretzels.
agree on (a plan or objective)	It is vital that all members of the school board <u>agree on</u> goals for the coming year.
agree to (a proposal)	Striking workers finally <u>agreed to</u> the terms of management's offer.
angry about or at (a situation)	Taxpayers are understandably <u>angry about</u> (or <u>at</u>) the deterioration of city recreation facilities.
angry with (a person)	When the mayor refused to hire more police officers, his constituents became <u>angry with</u> him.

approve of	Amy's adviser <u>approved of</u> her decision to study in Guatemala.
bored with	Salah got <u>bored with</u> economics, so he changed his major to psychology.
capable of	Hannah is a good talker, but she is not <u>capable of</u> acting as her own lawyer.
consist of	The deluxe fruit basket <u>consisted of</u> five pathetic pears, two tiny apples, a few limp bunches of grapes, and one lonely kiwi.
contrast with	Coach Headley's relaxed style <u>contrasts</u> sharply <u>with</u> the previous coach's more formal approach.
convenient for	The proposed location of the new day-care center is <u>convenient for</u> many families.
deal with	Many parents and educators believe it is possible to <u>deal with</u> the special needs of autistic children in a regular classroom.
depend on	Children <u>depend on</u> their parents for emotional as well as financial support.
differ from (something else)	A capitalist system <u>differs from</u> a socialist system in its view of private ownership.
differ with (someone else)	When Miles realized that he <u>differed with</u> his boss on most important issues, he handed in his resignation.
emigrate from	My grandfather and his brother <u>emigrated from</u> the part of Russia that is now Ukraine.
grateful for (a favor)	If you can arrange an interview next week, I will be very <u>grateful for</u> your time and trouble.
grateful to (someone)	Jerry Garcia was always <u>grateful to</u> his loyal fans.
immigrate to	Many Cubans want to leave their country and <u>immigrate to</u> the United States.
impatient with	Keshia often gets <u>impatient with</u> her four younger brothers.
interested in	Tomiko had always been <u>interested in</u> computers, so no one was surprised when she became a Web designer.
interfere with	College athletes often find that their dedication to sports <u>interferes with</u> their schoolwork.
meet with	I hope I can <u>meet with</u> you soon to discuss my research paper.
object to	The defense attorney <u>objected to</u> the prosecutor's treatment of the witness.

pleased with	Most of the residents are <u>pleased with</u> the mayor's crackdown on crime.
protect against	Nobel Prize winner Linus Pauling believed that large doses of vitamin C could <u>protect</u> people <u>against</u> the common cold.
reason with	When two-year-olds are having tantrums, it is nearly impossible to <u>reason with</u> them.
reply to	If no one <u>replies to</u> our ad within two weeks, we will advertise again.
responsible for	Should teachers be held <u>responsible for</u> their students' low test scores?
similar to	The blood sample found at the crime scene was remarkably <u>similar to</u> one found in the suspect's residence.
specialize in	Dr. Casullo is a dentist who <u>specializes in</u> periodontal surgery.
succeed in	Lisa hoped her M.B.A. would help her <u>succeed in</u> a business career.
take advantage of	Some consumer laws are designed to prevent door-to-door salespeople from <u>taking advantage of</u> buyers.
wait for (something to happen)	Many parents of teenagers experience tremendous anxiety while <u>waiting for</u> their children to come home at night.
wait on (in a restaurant)	We sat at the table for twenty minutes before someone <u>waited on</u> us.
worry about	Why <u>worry about</u> things you cannot change?

◆ PRACTICE 30-10

In the following passage, fill in each blank with the correct preposition.

Example: Tony Bartoli is ___*in*___ his second year ___*at*___ a large state college.

ON THE WEB
For more practice, visit Exercise Central:
www.bedford stmartins.com/ writingincontext

(1) There have been many changes _____ Tony's life _____ the past few years. (2) _____ 1997, Tony's family emigrated _____ Argentina. (3) Although Tony had studied English _____ Argentina, he was amazed _____ how little he seemed to know when he got _____ the States. (4) _____ his first day _____ high school, he

met _____ a guidance counselor who convinced him to take advantage _____ the special English classes that were being offered _____ the vocational-technical school. (5) Since Tony was very interested _____ improving his English (and knew he would have to do that if he wanted to succeed _____ his new world), he enrolled _____ the class. (6) Now, Tony is grateful not only _____ his guidance counselor but also _____ all the teachers who supported him and showed him that he was capable _____ succeeding. (7) Adjusting _____ a new life _____ a new country and getting acquainted _____ a culture that differs greatly _____ the one that he was used _____ were challenges that he met _____ enthusiasm and _____ success. (8) Last year, when he first arrived _____ Florida University, he was worried _____ taking regular college courses_____ his second language, English. (9) Some of the first-year classes were difficult, but he was pleased _____ his grades _____ the end _____ the year. (10) This year is going to be great, and Tony is looking forward _____ it.

■ **SEEING AND WRITING: Flashback**

Look back at your response to the Seeing and Writing exercise on page 453. Have you used any of the idiomatic expressions listed on pages 473–475? If so, bracket each expression. Check carefully to make sure you have used the correct prepositions. Make any necessary corrections.

M **Using Prepositions in Two-Word Verbs**

Some verbs consist of two words, a verb and a preposition. If the preposition introduces a prepositional phrase, the preposition always comes right after the verb. In the following sentence, *over* introduces the prepositional phrase *over the manual*; therefore, *over* must come right after the verb *(go)*.

CORRECT Please <u>go over</u> the manual carefully.

INCORRECT Please <u>go</u> the manual <u>over</u> carefully.

In other two-word verbs, words that look like prepositions do not always function as prepositions. For example, in the sentence below, the second word of the verb *(up)* does not introduce a prepositional phrase; instead, it combines with the first word of the verb to form a two-word verb with its own meaning. Verbs like these are also not usually separated.

CORRECT   The student <u>spoke up</u> without hesitation.

INCORRECT   The student <u>spoke</u> without hesitation <u>up</u>.

Some Common Inseparable Two-Word Verbs

come across	grow up
get along	run into
go over	stay away
give in	speak up

In some cases, however, a two-word verb may be split. For example, two-word verbs that are *transitive* may be split. **Transitive verbs** express an action toward an object. When the object of a transitive verb is a noun, the second word of the verb can come either before or after the object. In the sentence below, *turn off* is a transitive verb. Because the object of the verb *turn off* is a noun *(printer)*, the second word of the verb can come either before or after the verb's object.

CORRECT   Please <u>turn off</u> the printer.

CORRECT   Please <u>turn</u> the printer <u>off</u>.

When the object of a transitive verb is a pronoun, however, these two-word verbs *must* be split, and the pronoun must come between the two parts.

CORRECT   Please <u>turn</u> it <u>off</u>.

INCORRECT   Please <u>turn off</u> it.

Some Common Separable Two-Word Verbs

ask out	give away	put back	throw away
bring up	hang up	put on	try out
call up	let out	shut off	turn down
drop off	make up	take down	turn off
fill out	put away	think over	wake up

Remember, when the object of the verb is a pronoun, these two-word verbs must be split and the pronoun must come between the two parts (e.g., *take (it) down, put (it) on, let (it) out,* and *make (it) up*).

◆ **PRACTICE 30-11**

ON THE WEB
*For more
practice, visit
Exercise Central:*
**www.bedford
stmartins.com/
writingincontext**

In each of the following sentences, look closely at the two-word verb, and decide whether the preposition is correctly placed in the sentence. If it is, write *C* in the blank after the sentence. If the preposition needs to be moved, edit the sentence.

Example: How many timid students sit in the back of the classroom
and hope that the professor will not call them ~~on~~? _____
                                                          on   *?*

1. Some people who have dreams of going to college have to set aside them for a variety of reasons. _____

2. Many colleges and universities recognize the difficulty some people face and have found a way to deal it with. _____

3. Students are no longer obligated to put in hours and hours sitting in classrooms. _____

4. Thanks to the Internet and other technology, the education system has developed "distance education" and is constantly working it on in order to improve it. _____

5. "Distance learning" takes place when a teacher and student are separated by physical distance, and technology hooks up them. _____

6. A distance-education program involves several people, and any program's success depends their efforts on. _____

7. Several technological options are available—including telephone, video, and computer—but distance educators should remember that different students have different needs and that it is important to focus on those needs. _____

8. Although some online courses are free, most students must pay for them. _____

9. Teachers can distribute assignments, and students can hand in them by fax or e-mail. _____

10. If the subject of distance learning interests you, you can look it into at

    <www.askjeeves.com>. _____

■ SEEING AND WRITING: Flashback

Look back at your response to the Seeing and Writing exercise on page 453. Have you used any two-word verbs? If so, list them on a separate sheet of paper. Check carefully to make sure you have placed the preposition correctly in each case. Make any necessary corrections.

■ SEEING AND WRITING: Revising and Editing

Look back at your response to the Seeing and Writing exercise on page 453. Then, review all your Flashback exercises, and be sure you have made all necessary corrections in grammar and usage. When you have finished, add any additional transitional words and phrases you need to make the celebration you have described clear to your readers.

CHAPTER REVIEW

◆ EDITING PRACTICE

Read the following student essay, which contains errors in the use of subjects, articles and determiners, stative verbs, and idiomatic expressions. Check each underlined word or phrase. If it is not used correctly, cross it out and write the correct word or phrase above the line. If the underlined word or phrase is correct, write *C* above it. The title of the essay has been edited for you.

```
                              in
    How to Succeed on Multinational Business
                        ^
    Success in multinational business often depends in

people's ability to understand other countries' cultures.

Understanding how cultures differ with our own is not, how-

ever, an only key to multinational these enterprises. Is

also crucial that people doing business internationally
```

they learn to adapt to this cultures. One cause of the problems that can arise is ethnocentrism. The ethnocentrism is the belief that one's own culture's way of doing something is a best way. When a company uses the same methods overseas that it uses in home, does not adapt a product to fit the cultural needs of another country, and sends representatives without international experiences, could be problems.

To avoid the ethnocentrism, a company wanting to sell its product internationally it should do a few market research. For example, if an American company goes into a new market and looks it at without considering language, religion, values, customs, and other element, the results can often be disastrous.

A knowledge of the local language is important for an international businessperson for a little reasons. If the person he or she knows the language, is possible to communicate directly, without an interpreter. In addition, people are usually more comfortable when they meet with people who speak their language. Most important, it is easier for a person who is knowing the local language to become better acquainted to the culture.

An understanding of other countries' customs and manners is also crucial to an international business's success--and the same is true for individual businesspeople. Although businesspeople often call one another by their first names in United States, addressing someone by his or her first name can be extremely offensive in some cultures.

Although arriving on time for a business appointment is normal practice in much places, the punctuality is considered less important in other country. Even the type of clothing that people wear can determine whether or not will establish a business healthy relationship with someone from the culture different from their own.

As a world becomes smaller, the marketplace is becoming global. In those setting, individuals from numerous cultures will come together. Not only the individuals but also the multinational companies within today's global market must show the highest respects for other cultures.

◆ COLLABORATIVE ACTIVITIES

1. Working in a small group, make a list of ten prepositional phrases that include the prepositions *above, around, at, between, from, in, on, over, under,* and *with.* Use specific nouns as objects of these prepositions, and use as many modifying words as you wish. (Try, for example, to write something like *above their hideous wedding portrait,* not just *above the picture.*)
2. Exchange lists with another group. Still working collaboratively, compose a list of ten sentences, each including one of the other group's ten prepositional phrases. Give your list of ten sentences to another group.
3. Working with this new list of ten sentences, substitute a different prepositional phrase for each one that appears in a sentence. Make sure each sentence still makes sense.

UNIT SEVEN

Understanding Punctuation, Mechanics, and Spelling

Using Commas

PREVIEW

In this chapter, you will learn
- to use commas in a series (31A)
- to use commas to set off introductory phrases, conjunctive adverbs, and transitional expressions (31B)
- to use commas with appositives (31C)

- to use commas to set off nonrestrictive clauses (31D)
- to use commas in dates and addresses (31E)
- to avoid unnecessary commas (31F)

■ SEEING AND WRITING

Look at the picture above, and then describe an ideal public housing complex for low-income families. Where should it be located? What kinds of buildings should be constructed? What facilities and services should be offered to residents?

▶ **Word Power**
subsidized
assisted or
supported
financially

low-density
sparsely
settled; not
crowded

485

A **comma** is a punctuation mark that separates words or groups of words within sentences. Thus, commas keep ideas distinct from one another. In earlier chapters, you learned to use a comma between two independent clauses linked by a coordinating conjunction (16A) and to use a comma after a dependent clause that comes before an independent clause (17B). Commas have several other uses, as you will learn in this chapter.

A Using Commas in a Series

Use commas to separate all elements in a **series** of three or more words or word groups.

> Leyla, Zack, and Kathleen campaigned for Representative Fattah.
> Leyla, Zack, or Kathleen will be elected president of Students for Fattah.
> Leyla made phone calls, licked envelopes, and ran errands for the campaign.
> Leyla is president, Zack is vice-president, and Kathleen is treasurer.

FOCUS Using Commas in a Series

Newspapers and magazines usually omit the comma before the coordinating conjunction in a series. However, your writing will be clearer if you use a comma before the coordinating conjunction.

> Leyla, Zack, and Kathleen worked on the campaign.

Exception: Do not use *any* commas if all the items in a series are separated by coordinating conjunctions.

> Leyla or Zack or Kathleen will be elected president of Students for Fattah.

◆ PRACTICE 31-1

ON THE WEB
For more practice, visit Exercise Central: www.bedford stmartins.com/ writingincontext

Edit the following sentences for the use of commas in a series. If the sentence is correct, write *C* in the blank.

Examples:

Costa Rica produces bananas, cocoa, and sugar cane. ___C___

The pool rules state that there is no running/or jumping/or diving. _____

1. A talented musician, he plays guitar bass and drums. _____

2. The organization's goals are feeding the hungry, housing the homeless and helping the unemployed find work. _____

3. *The Price Is Right, Let's Make a Deal,* and *Jeopardy!* are three of the longest-running game shows in television history. _____

4. In native Hawaiian culture, yellow was the color worn by the royalty red was worn by priests and a mixture of the two colors was worn by others of high rank. _____

5. The remarkable diary kept by young Anne Frank while her family hid from the Nazis is insightful, touching and sometimes humorous. _____

6. A standard bookcase is sixty inches tall forty-eight inches wide and twelve inches deep. _____

7. Most coffins manufactured in the United States are lined with bronze, or copper, or lead. _____

8. Young handsome and sensitive, Leonardo DiCaprio was the 1990s answer to the 1950s actor James Dean. _____

9. California's capital is Sacramento, its largest city is Los Angeles and its oldest settlement is San Diego. _____

10. Watching television, playing video games, and riding his bicycle are the average ten-year-old boy's favorite pastimes. _____

■ SEEING AND WRITING: Flashback

Look back at your response to the Seeing and Writing exercise on page 485. If you have included a series of three or more words or word groups in any of your sentences, check carefully to make sure you have used

(continued on the following page)

> *(continued from the previous page)*
> commas correctly to separate elements in the series. If not, correct your punctuation. If no sentence includes a series, write a new sentence that does on a separate sheet of paper.

B — Using Commas to Set Off Introductory Phrases, Conjunctive Adverbs, and Transitional Expressions

For lists of frequently used conjunctive adverbs and transitional expressions, see 16C.

Use a comma to set off an introductory phrase from the rest of the sentence.

In the event of a fire, proceed to the nearest exit.

Walking home, Nelida decided to change her major.

To keep fit, people should try to exercise regularly.

Also use commas to set off conjunctive adverbs or transitional expressions whether they appear at the beginning, in the middle, or at the end of a sentence.

In fact, Thoreau spent only one night in jail.

He was, of course, bailed out by a friend.

He did spend more than two years at Walden Pond, however.

FOCUS **Using Commas in Direct Address**

Always use commas to set off the name of someone whom you are addressing (speaking to) directly, whether the name appears at the beginning, in the middle, or at the end of a sentence.

Molly, come here and look at this.

Come here, Molly, and look at this.

Come here and look at this, Molly.

ON THE WEB
For more practice, visit Exercise Central: www.bedfordstmartins.com/writingincontext

◆ PRACTICE 31-2

Edit the following sentences for the use of commas with introductory phrases. If the sentence is correct, write *C* in the blank.

Example: From professional athletes to teenagers͵ people have begun to find alternatives to steroids. _____

(1) In recent years many Olympic athletes have been disqualified because they tested positive for banned drugs. _____ (2) To the surprise of many fans these drugs are not always steroids. _____ (3) For example, some athletes have been accused of taking a drug called clenabutal, which is meant for animals. _____ (4) In addition to clenabutal the poison strychnine has also been detected. _____ (5) Banned by the rules of the Olympics these drugs still appeal to athletes because they supposedly enhance performance. _____ (6) Because of the laws prohibiting steroids many athletes have turned to these and other unregulated substances. _____ (7) Often called dietary supplements these alternative chemicals are supposed to enhance athletic performance in the same way steroids supposedly do. _____ (8) According to the *Journal of the American Medical Association* these dietary supplements do no such thing. _____ (9) Instead of enhancing performance they often cause considerable damage to the body. _____ (10) Over the course of the last few years investigators have collected more than three thousand samples of such products sold on the black market. _____

◆ PRACTICE 31-3

Edit the following sentences for the use of commas with conjunctive adverbs and transitional expressions. If the sentence is correct, write *C* in the blank.

Example: Some holidays͵ of course͵ are fairly new.

(1) For example the African-American celebration of Kwanzaa is less than forty years old. _____ (2) This holiday to remind us of important African traditions has, however attracted many celebrants over its short life. _____ (3) By the way the word *Kwanzaa* means "first fruits" in Swahili.

_____ (4) In other words, Kwanzaa stands for renewal. _____ (5) This can in fact be demonstrated in some of the seven principles of Kwanzaa. _____ (6) Kwanzaa is, after all celebrated over seven days to focus on each of these seven principles. _____ (7) The focus first of all is on unity *(umoja).* _____ (8) Also Kwanzaa focuses on personal self-determination *(kujichagulia).* _____ (9) In addition Kwanzaa celebrations emphasize three kinds of community responsibility *(ujima, ujamaa,* and *nia).* _____ (10) The other principles of Kwanzaa are creativity *(kuumba)* and finally, faith *(imani).* _____

■ SEEING AND WRITING: Flashback

Look back at your response to the Seeing and Writing exercise on page 485. Underline any introductory phrases, conjunctive adverbs, or transitional expressions. Have you set off each of these with commas where appropriate? Revise any incorrect sentences by adding commas where needed.

C   Using Commas with Appositives

Use commas to set off an **appositive**—a word or word group that identifies or renames a noun or pronoun.

> I have visited only one country, <u>Canada</u>, outside the United States.
>
> Carlos Santana, <u>leader of the group Santana</u>, played at Woodstock in 1969.

FOCUS   Using Commas with Appositives

Most appositives are set off by commas, whether they fall at the beginning, in the middle, or at the end of a sentence.

> <u>A dreamer</u>, he spent his life thinking about what he could not have.

(continued on the following page)

(continued from the previous page)

> He always wanted to build a house, <u>a big white one</u>, overlooking the ocean.
>
> He finally built his dream house, <u>a log cabin</u>.

◆ PRACTICE 31-4

Edit the following sentences for the correct use of commas to set off appositives. If the sentence is correct, write *C* in the blank.

ON THE WEB
For more practice, visit Exercise Central: www.bedford stmartins.com/ writingincontext

> **Example:** The Buccaneers have not joined the Cheese League, the group of NFL teams that holds summer training in Wisconsin. _____

1. Traditional Chinese medicine is based on meridians channels of energy believed to run in regular patterns through the body. _____

2. Acupuncture the insertion of thin needles at precise points in the body, stimulates these meridians. _____

3. Herbal medicine the basis of many Chinese healing techniques requires twelve years of study. _____

4. Gary Larson, creator of the popular *Far Side* cartoons ended the series in 1995. _____

5. A musician at heart, Larson said he wanted to spend more time practicing the guitar. _____

6. *Far Side* calendars and other product tie-ins earned Larson over $500 million a lot of money for guitar lessons. _____

7. Nigeria the most populous country in Africa is also one of the fastest-growing nations in the world. _____

8. On the southwest coast of Nigeria lies Lagos a major port. _____

9. The Yoruban people the Nigerian settlers of Lagos, are unusual in Africa because they tend to form large urban communities. _____

10. A predominantly Christian people the Yoruba have incorporated many native religious rituals into their practice of Christianity. _____

■ SEEING AND WRITING: Flashback

Look back at your response to the Seeing and Writing exercise on page 485. Have you used any appositives? Underline each one. Check carefully to make sure you have set off appositives with commas. Revise any incorrect sentences.

D   Using Commas to Set Off Nonrestrictive Clauses

Use commas to set off **nonrestrictive clauses**, clauses that are not essential to a sentence's meaning. Do not use commas to set off **restrictive clauses**.

A **restrictive** clause contains essential information; therefore, it is *not* set off from the rest of the sentence by commas.

Many rock stars <u>who recorded hits in the 1950s</u> made little money from their songs.

In the sentence above, the clause *who recorded hits in the 1950s* supplies specific information that is essential to the idea the sentence is communicating: it tells readers which group of rock stars made little money. Without the clause, the sentence does not communicate the same idea because it does not tell which rock stars made little money.

Many rock stars made little money from their songs.

A **nonrestrictive** clause does *not* contain essential information; therefore, a nonrestrictive clause *is* set off from the rest of the sentence by commas.

Telephone calling-card fraud, <u>which cost consumers and phone companies four billion dollars last year</u>, is increasing.

Here, the underlined clause provides extra information to help readers understand the sentence, but the sentence communicates the same idea without this information.

Telephone calling-card fraud is increasing.

FOCUS *Who, Which, and That*

■ *Who* can introduce either a restrictive or a nonrestrictive clause.

> RESTRICTIVE Many parents <u>who work</u> feel a lot of stress. (no commas)

> NONRESTRICTIVE Both of my parents, <u>who have always wanted the best for their children</u>, have worked two jobs for years. (clause set off by commas)

■ *Which* always introduces a nonrestrictive clause.

> The job, <u>which had excellent benefits</u>, did not pay well. (clause set off by commas)

■ *That* always introduces a restrictive clause.

> He accepted the job <u>that had the best benefits</u>. (no commas)

Note: Never use *that* to refer to a person.

◆ **PRACTICE 31-5**

Edit the following sentences so that commas set off all nonrestrictive clauses. (Remember, commas are *not* used to set off restrictive clauses.) If a sentence is correct, write *C* in the blank.

ON THE WEB
For more practice, visit Exercise Central: www.bedford stmartins.com/ writingincontext

Example: An Alaska museum exhibition that celebrates the Alaska high-

way has rescued the story of its construction. __*C*__

(1) During the 1940s, a group of African-American soldiers who defied the forces of nature and human prejudice were shipped to Alaska. _____ (2) They built the Alaska highway which stretches twelve hundred miles across Alaska. _____ (3) The African-American troops who worked on the highway have received little attention in most historical accounts. _____

(4) The highway which cut through some of the roughest terrain in the world was begun in 1942. _____ (5) The Japanese had just landed in the Aleutian Islands which lay west of the tip of the Alaska Peninsula. _____ (6) Military officials, who oversaw the project, doubted the ability of the African-American troops. _____ (7) As a result, they made them work under conditions, that made construction difficult. _____ (8) The African-American troops who worked on the road proved their commanders wrong by finishing the highway months ahead of schedule. _____ (9) In one case, white engineers, who surveyed a river, said it would take two weeks to bridge. _____ (10) To the engineers' surprise, the African-American soldiers who worked on the project beat the estimate by half a day. _____

■ SEEING AND WRITING: Flashback

Look back at your response to the Seeing and Writing exercise on page 485. Make sure you have included commas to set off nonrestrictive clauses and have *not* set off restrictive elements with commas. Make any necessary corrections.

E   Using Commas in Dates and Addresses

Dates

Use commas in dates to separate the day of the week from the month and the day of the month from the year.

> The first Cinco de Mayo we celebrated in the United States was Tuesday, May 5, 1998.

When a date that includes commas does not fall at the end of a sentence, place a comma after the date.

> Tuesday, May 5, 1998, was the first Cinco de Mayo we celebrated in the United States.

Note: Do not use commas between a month and the number of the day (*May 5*) or year (*May 1998*).

Addresses

Use commas in addresses to separate the street address from the city and the city from the state or country.

> The office of the famous fictional detective Sherlock Holmes was located at 221b Baker Street, London, England.

When an address that includes commas does not fall at the end of a sentence, place a comma after the state or country.

> The office at 221b Baker Street, London, England, belonged to the famous fictional detective Sherlock Holmes.

Note: In addresses, do not use a comma between the building numbers and the street name.

◆ PRACTICE 31-6

Edit the following sentences for the correct use of commas in dates and addresses. Add any missing commas, and cross out any unnecessary commas. If the sentence is correct, write *C* in the blank.

ON THE WEB
For more practice, visit Exercise Central: www.bedford stmartins.com/ writingincontext

Examples:

June 3, 1968, is the day my parents were married. _____

Their wedding took place in Santiago, Chile. _____

1. The American Declaration of Independence was approved on July 4 1776. _____

2. The Pelican Man's Bird Sanctuary is located at 1705 Ken Thompson Parkway, Sarasota Florida. _____

3. At 175 Carlton Avenue Brooklyn New York is the house where Richard Wright began writing *Native Son*. _____

4. I found this information in the February 12, 1994 issue of the *New York Times*. _____

5. The Mexican hero Father Miguel Hidalgo y Costilla was shot by a firing squad on June 30, 1811. _____

6. The Palacio de Gobierno at Plaza de Armas, Guadalajara, Mexico houses a mural of the famous revolutionary. _____

7. The Pueblo Grande Museum is located at 1469 East Washington Street Phoenix Arizona. _____

8. Brigham Young led the first white settlers into the valley that is now Salt Lake City, Utah, in July, 1847. _____

9. St. Louis Missouri was the birthplace of writer Maya Angelou, but she spent most of her childhood in Stamps Arkansas. _____

10. Some records list the actress's birthday as May 19 1928 while others indicate she was born on May 20 1924. _____

F   Avoiding Unnecessary Commas

In addition to knowing where commas are required, it is also important to know when *not* to use commas.

Do not use a comma before the first item in a series.

INCORRECT *Duck Soup* starred, Groucho, Chico, and Harpo Marx.

CORRECT *Duck Soup* starred Groucho, Chico, and Harpo Marx.

Do not use a comma after the last item in a series.

INCORRECT Groucho, Chico, and Harpo Marx, starred in *Duck Soup*.

CORRECT Groucho, Chico, and Harpo Marx starred in *Duck Soup*.

Do not use a comma between a subject and a verb.

INCORRECT Students and their teachers, should try to respect one another.

CORRECT Students and their teachers should try to respect one another.

Do not use a comma before the coordinating conjunction that separates the two parts of a compound verb.

INCORRECT The transit workers voted to strike, and walked off the job.

CORRECT The transit workers voted to strike and walked off the job.

Do not use a comma before the coordinating conjunction that separates the two parts of a compound subject.

INCORRECT The transit workers, and the sanitation workers voted to strike.

CORRECT The transit workers and the sanitation workers voted to strike.

Do not use a comma to set off a restrictive clause.

INCORRECT People, who live in glass houses, should not throw stones.

CORRECT People who live in glass houses should not throw stones.

Finally, do not use a comma before a dependent clause that follows an independent clause.

INCORRECT He was exhausted, because he had driven all night.

CORRECT He was exhausted because he had driven all night.

◆ PRACTICE 31-7

Some of the following sentences contain unnecessary commas. Edit to correct for unnecessary commas. If the sentence is correct, write *C* in the blank following it.

Example: Both the Dominican Republic/ and the republic of Haiti occupy the West Indian island of Hispaniola. _____

1. The capital of the Dominican Republic, is Santo Domingo. _____

2. The country's tropical climate, generous rainfall, and fertile soil, make the Dominican Republic suitable for many kinds of crops. _____

3. Chief among these are, sugarcane, coffee, cocoa, and rice. _____

4. Mining is also important to the country's economy, because the land is rich in many ores. _____

5. Spanish is the official language of the Dominican Republic, and Roman Catholicism is the state religion. _____

6. In recent years, resort areas have opened, and brought many tourists to the country. _____

7. Tourists who visit the Dominican Republic, remark on its tropical beauty.

_____

8. Military attacks from abroad, and internal political unrest have marked much of the Dominican Republic's history. _____

9. Because the republic's economy has not always been strong, many Dominicans have immigrated to the United States. _____

10. Most Dominican immigrants maintain close ties to their home country, and return often to visit. _____

■ SEEING AND WRITING: Flashback

Look back at your response to the Seeing and Writing exercise on page 485. Check your work carefully to make sure you have not used commas in any of the situations listed in 31F. Make any necessary corrections.

■ SEEING AND WRITING: Revising and Editing

Look back at your response to the Seeing and Writing exercise on page 485. Then, make the following additions.

1. Add a sentence that includes a series of three or more words or word groups.
2. Add introductory phrases to two of your sentences.
3. Add an appositive to one of your sentences.
4. Add a conjunctive adverb or transitional expression to one of your sentences.
5. Add a nonrestrictive clause to one of your sentences.

When you have made all the additions, reread your work to check your use of commas in the new material.

 Computer Tip

Use the Find or Search command to highlight all the commas in your writing. Check to see if you have used the commas correctly.

CHAPTER REVIEW

◆ EDITING PRACTICE

Read the following student essay, from which some commas have been intentionally deleted. Add commas where necessary between items in a series and with introductory phrases, conjunctive adverbs or transitional expressions, appositives, and nonrestrictive clauses. Cross out any unnecessary commas. The first sentence has been edited for you.

Brave Orchid

One of the most important characters in <u>The Woman Warrior</u>, Maxine Hong Kingston's autobiographical work, is Brave Orchid, Kingston's mother. Brave Orchid, a complex character is an imaginative storyteller, who tells vivid tales of China. A quiet woman she still impresses her school classmates with her intelligence. She is also a traditional woman. However she will stop at nothing to make her family exactly what she wants it to be. Brave Orchid strongly believes in herself; even so, she sees herself as a failure.

In her native China Brave Orchid trains to be a midwife. The other women in her class envy her independence brilliance and courage. At one point Brave Orchid proves her courageousness by confronting the Fox Spirit, and telling him he will not win. First of all she tells him she can endure any pain that he inflicts on her. Next she gathers together the women in the dormitory to burn the ghost away. After this event the other women admire her even more.

Working hard Brave Orchid becomes a midwife in China. After coming to America however she cannot work as a midwife. Instead she works in a Chinese laundry, and picks tomatoes. None of her classmates in China could have imagined this outcome. During her later years in America Brave Orchid becomes a woman, who is overbearing and domineering. We see another side of her at this point in the book. She bosses her children around, she tries to ruin her sister's life and she criticizes everyone and everything around her. Her daughter, a straight-A student is the object of her worst criticism.

Brave Orchid's intentions are good. Nevertheless she devotes her energy to the wrong things. She wants the people, around her, to be as strong as she is. Because she bullies them however she eventually loses them. In addition she is too busy noticing her daughter's faults to see all her accomplishments. Brave Orchid an independent woman and a brilliant student never reaches her goals. She is hard on the people around her, because she is disappointed in herself.

◆ COLLABORATIVE ACTIVITIES

1. Bring a homemaking, sports, or fashion magazine to class. Working in a small group, look at the people pictured in the ads. In what roles are men most often depicted? In what roles are women most often presented? Identify the three or four most common roles for each sex, and give each kind of character a descriptive name—*jock* or *mother*, for example.

2. Working on your own, choose one type of character from the list your group made in the preceding activity. Then, write a paragraph in which you describe this character's typical appearance and habits. Refer to the appropriate magazine pictures to support your characterization.

3. Collaborating with other members of your group, write two paragraphs, one discussing how men are portrayed in ads and one discussing how women are portrayed.

4. Circle every comma in the paragraph you wrote for Collaborative Activity 2. Work with your group to explain why each comma is used. If no one in your group can justify a particular comma's use, cross it out.

Using Apostrophes

PREVIEW

In this chapter, you will learn
- to use apostrophes to form contractions (32A)
- to use apostrophes to form possessives (32B)
- to revise incorrect use of apostrophes (32C)

▶ **Word Power**
gender
sexual identity (male or female)

stereotype
(n) a conventional, usually oversimplified, opinion or belief; (v) to develop a fixed opinion

■ SEEING AND WRITING

Certain household tasks have traditionally been considered "men's work," and others have been viewed as "women's work." Although the family, like the workplace, has changed considerably in recent years, some habits and behavior patterns have remained the same. Look at the picture above, and then discuss the tasks that are considered "men's work" and "women's work" in your current household (or in the household in which you grew up). Be sure to give examples of the responsibilities of different people in your household.

An **apostrophe** is a punctuation mark that is used in two situations: to form a contraction and to form the possessive of a noun or an indefinite pronoun.

A   Using Apostrophes to Form Contractions

A **contraction** is a word that uses an apostrophe to combine two words. The apostrophe takes the place of the omitted letters.

> I <u>didn't</u> *(did not)* realize how late it was.
>
> <u>It's</u> *(it is)* not right for cheaters to go unpunished.

Frequently Used Contractions

I + am = I'm	are + not = aren't
we + are = we're	can + not = can't
you + are = you're	do + not = don't
it + is = it's	will + not = won't
I + have = I've	should + not = shouldn't
I + will = I'll	let + us = let's
there + is = there's	that + is = that's
is + not = isn't	who + is = who's

Note: Even though contractions are used in speech and informal writing, they are not acceptable in most business or college writing situations.

◆ PRACTICE 32-1

ON THE WEB
For more practice, visit Exercise Central: www.bedfordstmartins.com/ writingincontext

In the following sentences, add apostrophes to contractions if needed. If the sentence is correct, write *C* in the blank.

Example: If you <s>dont</s> don't eat healthy foods, you <s>are'nt</s> aren't going to feel your best. _____

(1) Were all trying hard to watch our diets, but its not easy. _____ (2) Have you ever noticed how wer'e bombarded by images of high-calorie, high-fat foods? _____ (3) Maybe we shouldnt be so tempted, but it's hard to resist the lure of the fast-food chains and their commercials. _____ (4) Of course, the actual sandwich doesnt look much like the one on television, but that isnt

the point. _____ (5) When wer'e away from home and hungry, its the picture

of that burger that pops into our minds. _____ (6) Well be likely to rush to a

fast-food place for lunch instead of looking for a meal thats healthier. _____

(7) It should'nt be so hard to find a fast, healthy meal. _____ (8) For example,

a grilled chicken sandwich doesn't have nearly as much fat or as many

calories as a burger has. _____ (9) Its still not the perfect meal for a dieter,

but it isnt too bad. _____ (10) When we dont have many options, wev'e got

to make the best of the situation. _____

■ SEEING AND WRITING: Flashback

Look back at your response to the Seeing and Writing exercise on page
501, and underline any contractions. Have you used apostrophes correctly to replace the missing letters? Recopy all the contractions correctly on a separate sheet of paper. Then, rewrite the contractions as two
separate words.

B   Using Apostrophes to Form Possessives

Possessive forms indicate ownership. Nouns and indefinite pronouns do
not have special possessive forms. Instead, they use apostrophes to indicate
ownership.

*For information
on possessive
pronouns,
see 28F.*

Singular Nouns and Indefinite Pronouns

To form the possessive of singular nouns (including names) and indefinite
pronouns, add an apostrophe plus an -*s*.

*For more on
indefinite
pronouns, see
23D and 28E.*

Cesar Chavez's goal *(the goal of Cesar Chavez)* was justice for American
farm workers.

The strike's outcome *(the outcome of the strike)* was uncertain.

Whether it would succeed was anyone's guess *(the guess of anyone)*.

> **FOCUS** **Singular Nouns Ending in -s**
>
> Even if a singular noun already ends in -s, add an apostrophe plus an -s to form the possessive.
>
> > The class's next assignment was a research paper.
> >
> > Dr. Ramos's patients are participating in a double-blind study.

Plural Nouns

To form the possessive of plural nouns ending in -s (including names), add just an apostrophe (not an apostrophe plus -s).

> The two drugs' side effects *(the side effects of the two drugs)* were quite different.
>
> The Johnsons' front door *(the front door of the Johnsons)* is red.

For a list of frequently used irregular noun plurals, see 28B.

Some irregular noun plurals do not end in -s. If a plural noun does not end in -s, add an apostrophe plus an -s to form the possessive.

> The men's room is right next to the women's room.

◆ PRACTICE 32-2

ON THE WEB
For more practice, visit Exercise Central: www.bedford stmartins.com/ writingincontext

Rewrite the following phrases, changing the noun or indefinite pronoun that follows *of* to the possessive form. Be sure to distinguish between singular and plural nouns.

Examples:

the mayor of the city *the city's mayor* _____

the uniforms of the players *the players' uniforms* _____

1. the video of the singer _____

2. the scores of the students _____

3. the first novel of the writer _____

4. the office of the boss _____

5. the union of the players _____

6. the specialty of the restaurant _____

7. the bedroom of the children _____

8. the high cost of the tickets _____

9. the dreams of everyone _____

10. the owner of the dogs _____

■ SEEING AND WRITING: Flashback

Look back at your response to the Seeing and Writing First exercise on
page 501. Circle any possessive forms of nouns or indefinite pronouns,
and then check to make sure you have used apostrophes correctly to
form these possessives.

C   Revising Incorrect Use of Apostrophes

Be careful not to confuse a plural noun *(boys)* with the singular possessive
form of the noun *(boy's)*. Never use an apostrophe with a plural noun unless
the noun is possessive.

   Termites can be dangerous <u>pests</u> [not *pest's*].

   The <u>Velezes</u> [not *Velez's*] live on Maple Drive.

   Also, be careful not to use apostrophes with possessive pronouns that end
in *-s: theirs* (not *their's*), *hers* (not *her's*), *its* (not *it's*), *ours* (not *our's*), and *yours*
(not *your's*).

Computer Tip

Your computer's spell checker will not tell you when you have used a contraction for a possessive form—*it's* for *its*, for example. If you are not sure you have used the correct form,
consult a dictionary.

FOCUS   Possessive Pronouns

Be especially careful not to confuse possessive pronouns with sound-
alike contractions. Possessive pronouns never include apostrophes.

(continued on the following page)

(continued from the previous page)

Possessive Pronoun	Contraction
The dog bit <u>its</u> master.	<u>It's</u> *(it is)* time for breakfast.
The choice is <u>theirs</u>.	<u>There's</u> *(there is)* no place like home.
<u>Whose</u> house is this?	<u>Who's</u> *(who is)* on first?
Is this <u>your</u> house?	<u>You're</u> *(you are)* late again.

◆ PRACTICE 32-3

ON THE WEB
For more practice, visit Exercise Central:
www.bedford
stmartins.com/
writingincontext

Check the underlined words in the following sentences for correct use of apostrophes. If a correction needs to be made, cross out the word, and write the correct version above it. If the noun or pronoun is correct, write *C* above it.

> **Example:**   The secretary presented the <u>president's</u> views after several other
> *speakers*   *theirs.*
> ~~speaker's~~ first presented ~~their's~~.

1. <u>Parent's</u> should realize that when it comes to disciplining children, the responsibility is <u>their's</u>.

2. <u>It's</u> also important that parents offer praise for a <u>child's</u> good behavior.

3. In <u>it's</u> first few <u>week's</u> of life, a child is already developing a personality.

4. His and <u>her's</u> towels used to be popular with <u>couple's</u>, but <u>it's</u> not so common to see them today.

5. All the <u>Ryan's</u> spent four <u>year's</u> in college and then went on to graduate school.

6. From the radio came the lyrics "<u>You're</u> the one <u>who's</u> love I've been waiting for."

7. If you expect to miss any <u>classes'</u>, you will have to make arrangements with someone <u>who's</u> willing to tell you <u>you're</u> assignment.

8. No other <u>school's</u> cheerleading squad ever tried as many tricky stunts as <u>our's</u> did.

9. Surprise <u>test's</u> are a regular feature of my economics <u>teacher's</u> class.

10. <u>Jazz's</u> influence on many mainstream <u>musician's</u> is one of the <u>book's</u> main

<u>subject's</u>.

■ SEEING AND WRITING: Flashback

Look back at your response to the Seeing and Writing exercise on page
501. Circle each plural noun. Then, circle each possessive pronoun that
ends in -*s*. Have you incorrectly used an apostrophe with any of the circled words? If so, revise your work.

■ SEEING AND WRITING: Revising and Editing

Look back at your response to the Seeing and Writing exercise on page
501. Because this is an informal exercise, contractions are acceptable; in
fact, they may be preferable because they give your writing a conversa-
tional tone. Edit your writing so that you have used contractions in all
possible situations.

   Now, add two sentences—one that includes a singular possessive
noun and one that includes a plural possessive noun. Make sure these
two new sentences fit smoothly into your writing and that they, too, use
contractions wherever possible.

CHAPTER REVIEW

◆ **EDITING PRACTICE**

Read the following student essay, into which errors in the use of apostrophes
have been introduced. Edit it to eliminate errors by crossing out incorrect
words and writing corrections above them. (Note that this is an informal
response paper, so contractions are acceptable.) The first sentence has been
edited for you.

                    The Women of Messina
                Shakespeare's
    In William ~~Shakespeares'~~ play <u>Much Ado about Nothing</u>,

the women of Messina, whether they are seen as love objects

or ~~shrew's,~~ *shrews,* have very few options. A womans role is to
please a man. She can try to resist, but she will probably
wind up giving in. The plays two women, Hero and Beatrice,
are very different. Hero is the obedient one. Heros'
cousin, Beatrice, tries to challenge the rules of the mans
world in which she lives. However, in a place like Messina,
even women like Beatrice find it hard to get the respect
that should be their's.

Right from the start, we are drawn to Beatrice. Shes
funny, she has a clever comment for most situation's, and
she always speaks her mind about other peoples behavior.
Unlike Hero, she tries to stand up to the men in her life,
as we see in her and Benedicks conversations. But even
though Beatrice's intelligence is obvious, she often mocks
herself. Its obvious that she doesn't have much self-
esteem. In fact, Beatrice is'nt the strong woman she seems
to be.

Ultimately, Beatrice does get her man, and she will
be happy--but at what cost? Benedicks' last words to her
are "Peace! I will stop your mouth." Then, he kisses her.
The kiss is a symbolic end to their bickering. It is also
the mark of Beatrices' defeat. She has lost. Benedick has
shut her up. Now, she will be Benedick's wife and do what
he wants her to do. Granted, she will have more say in her
marriage than Hero will have in her's, but she is still
defeated. Even Beatrice, the most rebellious of Messinas
women, finds it impossible to achieve anything of importance in Messinas' male-dominated society.

◆ COLLABORATIVE ACTIVITIES

1. Working in a group of four and building on your individual responses to the Seeing and Writing exercise at the beginning of the chapter, consider which specific occupational and professional roles are still associated largely with men and which are associated primarily with women. Make two lists, heading one "women's jobs" and one "men's jobs."

2. Now, work in pairs, with one pair of students in each group concentrating on men and the other pair on women. Write a paragraph that attempts to justify why the particular jobs you listed should or should not be restricted to one gender. In your discussion, list the various qualities men or women possess that qualify (or disqualify) them for particular jobs. Use possessive forms whenever possible—for example, *women's energy* (not *women have energy*).

3. Bring to class a book, magazine, or newspaper whose style is informal—for example, a romance novel, *TV Guide,* your school newspaper, or even a comic book. Working in a group, circle every contraction you can find on one page of each publication, and substitute for each contraction the words it combines. Are your substitutions an improvement? (You may want to read a few paragraphs aloud before you reach a conclusion.)

33 *Understanding Mechanics*

PREVIEW

In this chapter, you will learn
- to capitalize proper nouns (33A)
- to punctuate direct quotations (33B)
- to set off titles of books, stories, and other works (33C)
- to use minor punctuation marks (33D)

▶ **Word Power**

compelling
forceful

empathize
to identify with

plot
a series of
events in a
narrative or
drama

■ SEEING AND WRITING

Look at the picture above, and then describe a memorable scene from your favorite movie. Begin by giving the film's title and listing the names of the major stars and the characters they play. Then, tell what happens in the scene, quoting a few lines of dialogue if possible.

A   Capitalizing Proper Nouns

A **proper noun** names a particular person, animal, place, object, or idea. Proper nouns are always capitalized. The list that follows explains and illustrates specific rules for capitalizing proper nouns and also includes some important exceptions to those rules.

For more on proper nouns, see 28A.

1. Always capitalize names of races, ethnic groups, tribes, nationalities, languages, and religions.

   The census data revealed a diverse community of Caucasians, African Americans, and Asian Americans, with a few Latino and Navajo residents. Native languages include English, Korean, and Spanish. Most people identified themselves as Catholic, Protestant, or Muslim.

   Note: The words *black* and *white* are generally not capitalized when they name racial groups. However, *African American* and *Caucasian* are always capitalized.

2. Capitalize names of specific people and the titles that precede them. In general, do not capitalize titles used without a name or titles that follow names.

   In 1994, President Nelson Mandela was elected to lead South Africa.

   The newly elected fraternity president addressed the crowd.

3. Capitalize names of specific family members and their titles. Do not capitalize words that identify family relationships, including those introduced by possessive pronouns.

   The twins, Aunt Edna and Aunt Evelyn, are Dad's sisters.

   My aunts, my father's sisters, are twins.

4. Capitalize names of specific countries, cities, towns, bodies of water, streets, and so forth. Do not capitalize words that do not name particular places.

   The Seine runs through Paris, France.

   The river runs through the city.

5. Capitalize names of specific geographical regions. Do not capitalize such words when they specify direction.

   William Faulkner's novels are set in the American South.

   Turn right at the golf course, and go south for about a mile.

6. Capitalize names of specific buildings and monuments. Do not capitalize general references to buildings and monuments.

   He drove past the Liberty Bell and looked for a parking space near City Hall.

   He drove past the monument and looked for a parking space near the building.

7. Capitalize names of specific groups, clubs, teams, and associations. Do not capitalize general references to such groups.

The Teamsters Union represents workers who were at the stadium for the Republican Party convention, the Rolling Stones concert, and the Phillies–Astros game.

The union represents workers who were at the stadium for the political party's convention, the rock group's concert, and the baseball teams' game.

8. Capitalize names of specific historical periods, events, and documents. Do not capitalize nonspecific references to periods, events, or documents.

The Emancipation Proclamation was signed during the Civil War, not during Reconstruction.

The document was signed during the war, not during the postwar period.

9. Capitalize names of businesses, government agencies, schools, and other institutions. Do not capitalize nonspecific references to such institutions.

The Department of Education and Apple Computer have launched a partnership project with Central High School.

A government agency and a computer company have launched a partnership project with a high school.

10. Capitalize brand names. Do not capitalize general references to kinds of products.

While Jeff waited for his turn at the Xerox machine, he drank a can of Coke.

While Jeff waited for his turn at the copier, he drank a can of soda.

Note: Trade names that have become part of the language—*nylon* and *aspirin,* for example—are no longer capitalized.

11. Capitalize titles of specific academic courses. Do not capitalize names of general academic subject areas, except for proper nouns—for example, a language or a country.

Are Introduction to American Government and Biology 200 closed yet?

Are the introductory American government course and the biology course closed yet?

12. Capitalize days of the week, months of the year, and holidays. Do not capitalize the names of seasons.

The Jewish holiday of Passover usually falls in April.

The Jewish holiday of Passover falls in the spring.

◆ PRACTICE 33-1

Edit the following sentences, capitalizing letters or changing capitals to low-ercase where necessary.

ON THE WEB
For more practice, visit Exercise Central: **www.bedford stmartins.com/** writingincontext

Example: The third largest C̲ity in the U̲nited S̲tates is C̲hicago, I̲llinois.

(1) Located in the midwest on lake Michigan, chicago is an impor-tant port city, a rail and highway hub, and the site of o'hare international airport, the Nation's busiest. (2) The financial center of the city is Lasalle street, and the lakefront is home to Grant park, where there are many Museums and monuments. (3) In the North of the city, soldier field is home to the chicago bears, the city's football team, and wrigley field is home to the chicago cubs, a national league Baseball Team.

(4) In the mid-1600s, the site of what is now Chicago was visited by father jacques marquette, a catholic missionary to the ottawa and huron tribes, who were native to the area. (5) By the 1700s, the city was a trading post run by john kinzie. (6) The city grew rapidly in the 1800s, and immi-grants included germans, irish, italians, poles, greeks, and chinese, along with african americans who migrated from the south. (7) In 1871, much of the city was destroyed in one of the worst fires in united states history; the fire started when, according to legend, mrs. O'Leary's Cow kicked over a burning lantern.

(8) Today, Chicago's skyline is marked by many Skyscrapers, built by businesses like the john hancock company, sears, and amoco. (9) I know Chicago well because my Mother grew up there and my aunt jean and uncle amos still live there. (10) I also got information from the Chicago Chamber of Commerce when I wrote a paper for introductory research writing, a course I took at Graystone high school.

> ■ **SEEING AND WRITING: Flashback**
>
> Look back at your response to the Seeing and Writing exercise on page 510. Underline every proper noun. Check carefully to make sure each begins with a capital letter.

B Punctuating Direct Quotations

A **direct quotation** reproduces the *exact* words of a speaker or writer. Direct quotations are always placed within quotation marks.

> Lauren said, "My brother and Tina have gotten engaged."
>
> A famous advertiser wrote, "Don't sell the steak; sell the sizzle."

When a quotation is a complete sentence, it begins with a capital letter. When a quotation falls at the end of a sentence, as in the last two examples, the period is placed inside the quotation marks. If the quotation is a question or exclamation, the question mark or exclamation point is also placed inside the quotation marks.

> The instructor asked, "Has anyone read *Sula*?"
>
> Officer Warren shouted, "Hold it right there!"

If the quotation itself is not a question or an exclamation, the question mark or exclamation point goes *outside* the quotation marks.

> Did Joe really say, "I quit"?
>
> I can't believe he really said, "I quit"!

FOCUS **Indirect Quotations**

Be careful not to confuse direct and indirect quotations. A direct quotation reproduces someone's *exact* words, but an **indirect quotation** simply summarizes what was said or written.

Indirect quotations are not placed within quotation marks.

> DIRECT QUOTATION Martin Luther King Jr. said, "I have a dream."
>
> INDIRECT QUOTATION Martin Luther King Jr. said that he had a dream.

Note: An indirect quotation is usually introduced by the word *that*.

FOCUS Identifying Tags

A direct quotation is usually accompanied by an **identifying tag**, a phrase that names the person or work being quoted.

Identifying Tag at the Beginning

When the identifying tag comes *before* the quotation, it is followed by a comma.

> Alexandre Dumas wrote, "Nothing succeeds like success."

Identifying Tag at the End

When the identifying tag comes at the *end* of the sentence, it is followed by a period. A comma (or, sometimes, a question mark or exclamation point) inside the closing quotation marks separates the quotation from the identifying tag.

> "Life is like a box of chocolates," stated Forrest Gump.

> "Is that so?" his friends wondered.

Identifying Tag in the Middle

When the identifying tag comes in the *middle* of the quoted sentence, it is followed by a comma. The first part of the quotation is also followed by a comma, placed inside the quotation marks. Because the part of the quotation that follows the tag is not a new sentence, it does not begin with a capital letter.

> "This is my life," Bette insisted, "and I'll live it as I please."

Identifying Tag between Two Sentences

When the identifying tag comes *between* two quoted sentences, it is followed by a period, and the second quoted sentence begins with a capital letter.

> "Producer Berry Gordy is an important figure in the history of music," Tony explained. "He was the creative force behind Motown records."

◆ PRACTICE 33-2

In the following sentences containing direct quotations, first underline the identifying tag. Then, punctuate the quotation correctly, adding capital letters as necessary.

ON THE WEB

For more practice, visit Exercise Central: www.bedford stmartins.com/ writingincontext

Example: "Why, Darryl asked, are teachers so strict about deadlines?"

1. We who are about to die salute you said the gladiators to the emperor.

2. When we turned on the television, the newscaster was saying ladies and gentlemen, we have a new president-elect.

3. The bigger they are said boxer John L. Sullivan the harder they fall.

4. Do you take Michael to be your lawfully wedded husband asked the minister.

5. Lisa Marie replied I do.

6. If you believe the *National Enquirer* my friend always says then you'll believe anything.

7. When asked for the jury's verdict, the foreman replied we find the defendant not guilty.

8. I had felt for a long time that if I was ever told to get up so a white person could sit Rosa Parks recalled I would refuse to do so.

9. Yabba dabba doo Fred exclaimed this brontoburger looks great.

10. Where's my money Addie Pray asked you give me my money.

◆ **PRACTICE 33-3**

These quotations are followed in parentheses by the names of the people who wrote or spoke them. On the blank lines, write a sentence that includes the quotation and places the identifying tag in the position that the directions specify. Be sure to punctuate and capitalize correctly.

Example: Nothing endures but change. (written by the Greek philosopher Heraclitus)

Identifying tag in the middle *"Nothing endures," wrote the Greek philosopher Heraclitus, "but change."*

1. One is not born a woman; one becomes one. (written by essayist Simone de Beauvoir)

   Identifying tag at the beginning _____

   _____

2. Tribe follows tribe, and nation follows nation. (spoken by Suquamish Chief Seattle in 1854)

   Identifying tag in the middle _____

   _____

3. When I'm good, I'm very good. When I'm bad, I'm better. (spoken by actress Mae West in the classic film *I'm No Angel*)

   Identifying tag in the middle _____

   _____

4. The rich rob the poor, and the poor rob one another. (spoken by abolitionist Sojourner Truth)

   Identifying tag at the beginning _____

   _____

5. If a man hasn't discovered something he will die for, then he isn't fit to live. (spoken by Martin Luther King Jr.)

   Identifying tag at the end _____

   _____

■ SEEING AND WRITING: Flashback

Look back at your response to the Seeing and Writing exercise on page 510. Make sure you have enclosed any direct quotations in quotation marks, placed other punctuation correctly, and capitalized where necessary. Revise any incorrectly punctuated quotations.

C **Setting Off Titles of Books, Stories, and Other Works**

Some titles are typed in *italics* (or underlined to indicate italics). Others are enclosed in quotation marks. The following box shows how to set off different kinds of titles.

Italicized Titles	**Titles in Quotation Marks**
Books: *How the García Girls Lost Their Accents*	Book chapters: "Understanding Mechanics"

(continued on the following page)

(continued from the previous page)

Newspapers: the *Miami Herald*

Magazines: *People*

Long poems: *John Brown's Body*

Plays: *Death of a Salesman*

Films: *The Rocky Horror Picture Show*

Television or radio series: *Star Trek: The Next Generation*

Short stories: "The Tell-Tale Heart"

Essays and articles: "The Suspected Shopper"

Short poems: "Richard Cory"

Songs: "America the Beautiful"

Individual episodes of television or radio series: "The Montgomery Bus Boycott," an episode of the PBS series *Eyes on the Prize*

Note: When you type one of your own papers, do not underline your title or enclose it in quotation marks. (Only titles of *published* works are set off in this way.)

FOCUS **Capital Letters in Titles**

The first letters of all important words in a title are capitalized. Do not capitalize an article *(a, an, the)*, a preposition *(to, of, around,* and so on*)*, or a coordinating conjunction *(and, but,* and so on*)* unless it is the first or last word of the title or subtitle *(On the Road;* "To an Athlete Dying Young"; *No Way Out; And Quiet Flows the Don).*

◆ **PRACTICE 33-4**

ON THE WEB
For more practice, visit Exercise Central:
www.bedford stmartins.com/ writingincontext

Edit the following sentences, capitalizing letters as necessary in titles.

Example: Eudora Welty's "a worn path" is a very moving short story.

1. Directed by the wacky Ed Wood, the 1959 movie *plan nine from outer space* has been called the worst picture of all time.

2. Gary Larson's cartoon collections include the books *in search of the far side, it came from the far side,* and *valley of the far side.*

3. En Vogue's first hit album, *born to sing,* included the songs "you don't have to worry," "time goes on," and "just can't stay away."

4. Everyone should read Martin Luther King Jr.'s "i have a dream" and "letter from birmingham jail."

5. NBC has had hits with shows like *the weakest link, friends,* and *law and order.*

◆ **PRACTICE 33-5**

In the following sentences, underline or insert quotation marks around titles. (Remember that titles of books and other long works are underlined, and titles of stories, essays, and other shorter works are enclosed in quotation marks.)

> **Example:** An article in the New York Times called "It's Not Easy Being Green" is a profile of former Chicago Bulls player Dennis Rodman, who once had green hair.

1. Sui Sin Far's short story The Wisdom of the New, from her book Mrs. Spring Fragrance, is about the clash between Chinese and American cultures in the early twentieth century.

2. Major league baseball games traditionally open with fans singing The Star-Spangled Banner.

3. Interesting information about fighting skin cancer can be found in the article Putting Sunscreens to the Test, which appeared in the magazine Consumer Reports.

4. One of the best-known poems of the twentieth century is Robert Frost's The Road Not Taken.

5. Ang Lee has directed several well-received films, including Crouching Tiger, Hidden Dragon.

6. It is surprising how many people enjoy reruns of the 1960s television series Bewitched and I Dream of Jeannie.

7. The title of Lorraine Hansberry's play A Raisin in the Sun comes from Langston Hughes's poem Harlem.

8. In his autobiography, Breaking the Surface, Olympic diving champion Greg Louganis wrote about his struggle with AIDS.

■ **SEEING AND WRITING: Flashback**

Look back at your response to the Seeing and Writing exercise on page 510. Circle the film's title. Have you underlined it? Are capital letters used where necessary? Make any necessary corrections.

D   **Using Minor Punctuation Marks**

For information on sentence types, see 18A.

A statement ends with a **period**, a question ends with a **question mark**, and an exclamation ends with an **exclamation point**. Other important punctuation marks are the **comma** (Chapter 31), the **apostrophe** (Chapter 32), and the **semicolon** (16B). Three additional punctuation marks—*colons, dashes,* and *parentheses*—are used to set off material from the rest of the sentence.

The Colon

A **colon** can be used to introduce a quotation.

Our family motto is a simple one: "Accept no substitutes."

A colon can be used to introduce an explanation, a clarification, or an example.

Only one thing kept him from climbing Mt. Everest: fear of heights.

A colon is also used to introduce a list.

I left my job for four reasons: boring work, poor working conditions, low pay, and a terrible supervisor.

Note: When a colon introduces a quotation, example, or list, it must follow a complete sentence.

The Dash

Use **dashes** to emphasize information by setting it off from the rest of the sentence.

I parked my car—a red Firebird—in a towaway zone.

Note: Dashes give writing an informal tone; use them sparingly in college and professional writing.

Parentheses

Use **parentheses** to present material that is not an essential part of the sentence.

The weather in Portland (a city in Oregon) was overcast.

◆ PRACTICE 33-6

Add colons, dashes, and parentheses to the following sentences where necessary.

ON THE WEB
For more practice, visit Exercise Central: www.bedford stmartins.com/ writingincontext

Example: New Orleans (population 465,000) is the largest city in Louisiana.

1. New Orleans has three nicknames "The Big Easy," the "Crescent City," and the "City that Care Forgot."

2. The oldest part of the city known as the French Quarter dates to the early 1700s.

3. The French Quarter is famous for several attractions its unique buildings, its fine food, its street musicians, and its wild nightlife.

4. Jackson Square called Place d'Armes by the original French settlers lies at the heart of the French Quarter.

5. The square a gathering place for artists and other merchants centers on a monument to Andrew Jackson.

6. Located next to Jackson Square is a famous coffee house the Café du Monde.

7. Its popular beignets pronounced ben-*yeas* are deep-fried pastries covered with sugar.

8. Visitors to New Orleans can try many traditional foods crayfish, gumbo, blackened fish, and "dirty" rice.

9. New Orleans visitors people from all over the world particularly enjoy the laid-back atmosphere of the city.

10. This atmosphere is summed up in the city's unofficial motto "Let the good times roll."

■ **SEEING AND WRITING: Flashback**

Look back at your response to the Seeing and Writing exercise on page 510. Do you see places where you might add a quotation, an example, or a list that could be introduced by a colon? Write your possible additions on a separate sheet of paper.

■ **SEEING AND WRITING: Revising and Editing**

Look back at your response to the Seeing and Writing exercise on page 510. If you have quoted specific lines of dialogue from the film, try varying the placement of the identifying tags you have used. If you did not include quotations, try adding one or two. Then, add the quotation, example, or list from the Flashback above to your Seeing and Writing exercise, introducing it with a colon. Finally, edit for proper use of capital letters, quotation marks, and underlining.

CHAPTER REVIEW

◆ **EDITING PRACTICE**

Read the following student essay, into which errors in capitalization and punctuation and in the use of direct quotations and titles have been introduced. Edit the passage to correct any such errors. The first sentence has been edited for you.

The World of Gary Soto

My favorite Author is Gary Soto, a mexican-american poet and fiction writer whose first book of poetry, The Elements of San Joaquin, was published in 1977. Soto was born in 1952 in fresno, california, and grew up in a large

spanish-speaking family. His Father he died when Soto was
five worked in a factory, and his Mother picked grapes and
other crops in the farms of the san joaquin valley. Much
of Soto's writing is influenced by childhood memories.
"These are the pictures I take with me when I write", he
once said. "they stir the past, the memories that are so
vivid."

Soto attended fresno city college and later studied at
the university of California at fresno, where he originally
majored in Geology. There, according to Soto: "One day I
came across a book of poetry on a shelf in the college
library. I read it, liked it, and began to write poems of
my own".

One of Soto's best poems is Oranges from his 1985
book, "Black Hair." In this poem, he describes the events
of a cold december afternoon when a boy takes his Girlfriend into a drugstore to buy her a treat. She wants a
chocolate that costs a Dime, but he only has a Nickel. He
gives the Saleslady the coin plus an orange he has in his
pocket, and, knowing what is going on, she lets him pay
for the candy this way. In another poem, "How things Work,"
Soto also writes about money. This poem is about how People
are connected by one important thing the money they spend.

This theme of money is picked up again in the Title
of one of Soto's books of stories, "Nickel And Dime." The
first story is called "We Ain't Asking Much and is about
Roberto, who loses his job, cannot pay his rent, and ends
up on the Street, trying to sell christmas ornaments made

of twigs to rich people. Silver, a Character in another
story, has something in common with Soto he is a poet but
he also has trouble making enough money to live on. It
is interesting that Silver lives in Oakland near San
Francisco, where Soto himself lives.

 Does Soto write from Personal Experience? He says that
this is only partly true "Although the experiences in my
stories, poems, and novels may seem autobiographical, much
of what I write is the stuff of imagination."

◆ COLLABORATIVE ACTIVITIES

1. Imagine that you and the other members of your group are the nominations committee for this year's Emmy, Oscar, or Grammy Awards. Work together to compile a list of categories and several nominees for each category.

   Trade lists with another group. From each category, select the individual artist or work you believe deserves to win the award. Write a sentence about each winner, explaining why each is the best in its category.

   When you have finished, exchange papers with another group. Check one another's papers for correct use of capitals, quotation marks, and underlining.

2. Using a separate sheet of paper, work in groups to list as many items in each of the following five categories as you can: planets, islands, musicians or bands, automobile models, sports teams. Be sure all your items are proper nouns. When you have finished, work together to generate five original sentences using one proper noun from each category in each sentence.

3. Working in pairs, write a conversation between two characters, real or fictional, who have very different positions on a particular issue. Place all direct quotations within quotation marks, and include identifying tags that clearly indicate which character is speaking. (Begin a new paragraph each time a new person speaks.)

   Exchange your conversations with another pair of students, and check their work to see that all directly quoted speech is set within quotation marks and that capital letters and all other punctuation are used correctly.

Understanding Spelling

PREVIEW

In this chapter, you will learn
- to become a better speller (34A)
- to know when to use *ie* and *ei* (34B)
- to understand prefixes (34C)
- to understand suffixes (34D)
- to identify commonly confused words (34E)

▶ **Word Power**

conducive to
leading to;
contributing to

economical
thrifty

individuality
the quality of
being distinct
from others

■ SEEING AND WRITING

Look at the picture above. Then, write about whether or not you think elementary school students should be required to wear uniforms.

A   Becoming a Better Speller

Improving your spelling may take time, but the following steps can make this task a lot easier.

1. *Use a dictionary.* As you proofread your papers, circle words whose spellings you are unsure of. After you have finished your draft, look up these words in the dictionary to make sure they are spelled correctly. (Note that the dictionary will also tell you how to pronounce a word and which syllables to stress.)

2. *Use a spell checker.* When you write on a computer, use your spell checker. It will correct most misspelled words and also identify many typos, such as transposed or omitted letters.

3. *Proofread carefully.* Even if you have used a spell checker, always proofread your papers for spelling before you hand them in.

 Computer Tip

Keep in mind that spell checkers have limitations. They do not identify typos that create other words (*then/than*, *form/from*, or *big/beg*, for example) or words that you have used incorrectly (*their/there* or *its/it's*, for example).

---

4. *Keep a personal spelling list.* Write down all the words you misspell. If you keep a writing journal, set aside a few pages in the back for your personal spelling list. Whenever your instructor hands back one of your papers, look for misspelled words—usually circled and marked *sp.* Add these to your personal spelling list.

5. *Look for patterns in your misspelling.* Do you consistently misspell words with *ei* combinations? Do you have trouble forming plurals? Once you figure out which errors you make most frequently, you can take steps to eliminate them.

6. *Learn the basic spelling rules.* Memorize the spelling rules in this chapter, especially those that apply to areas in which you are weak. Remember that each rule can help you spell many words correctly.

7. *Review the list of commonly confused words on pages 533 to 541.* If you have problems with any of these word pairs, add them to your personal spelling list.

Computer Tip

Use the Search or Find command to look for words you frequently misspell.

---

8. *Make flash cards.* If you consistently have trouble with spelling, put individual words on 3 × 5 cards. You can use them to test yourself periodically.

9. *Use memory cues.* Memory cues help you remember how to spell certain words. For example, remembering that *definite* contains the word *finite* will help you remember that *definite* is spelled with an *i*, not an *a*.

10. *Learn to spell some of the most frequently misspelled words.* Identify those on the list below that give you trouble, and add them to your personal spelling list.

Frequently Misspelled Words

across	disappoint	loneliness	reference
all right	early	medicine	restaurant
a lot	embarrass	minute	roommate
already	entrance	necessary	secretary
argument	environment	noticeable	sentence
beautiful	everything	occasion	separate
becoming	exercise	occur	speech
beginning	experience	occurred	studying
believe	finally	occurrences	surprise
benefit	forty	occurring	tomato
calendar	fulfill	occurs	tomatoes
cannot	generally	personnel	truly
careful	government	possible	until
careless	grammar	potato	usually
cemetery	harass	potatoes	Wednesday
certain	height	prejudice	weird
conscience	holiday	prescription	window
definite	integration	privilege	withhold
definitely	intelligence	probably	woman
dependent	interest	professor	women
describe	interfere	receive	writing
develop	judgment	recognize	written

Because English pronunciation is not always a reliable guide for spelling, most people find it useful to memorize some spelling rules.

FOCUS   **Vowels and Consonants**

Knowing which letters are vowels and which are consonants will help you understand the spelling rules presented in this chapter.

> ***Vowels:*** *a, e, i, o, u*
>
> ***Consonants:*** *b, c, d, f, g, h, j, k, l, m, n, p, q, r, s, t, v, w, x, z*

(continued on the following page)

(continued from the previous page)

The letter *y* may be considered either a vowel or a consonant, depending on how it is pronounced. In *young, y* acts as a consonant because it has the sound of *y;* in *truly,* it acts as a vowel because it has the sound of *ee.*

B   Deciding between *ie* and *ei*

Memorize this rule: *i* comes before *e* except after *c,* or when the *ei* sound is pronounced *ay* (as in *neighbor*).

i before *e*	except after *c*	or when *ei* is pronounced *ay*
achieve	ceiling	eight
believe	conceive	freight
friend	deceive	neighbor
		weigh

FOCUS   **Exceptions to the "*i* before *e*" Rule**

There are some exceptions to the "*i* before *e*" rule. The exceptions follow no pattern, so you must memorize them.

ancient	either	leisure	seize
caffeine	foreign	neither	species
conscience	height	science	weird

Note that when the *i* and *e* in a word are not pronounced as a unit (as they are not in *science*), the *i* before *e* rule does not apply.

ON THE WEB

For more practice, visit Exercise Central: www.bedford stmartins.com/ writingincontext

◆ PRACTICE 34-1

Proofread the underlined words in the following sentences for correct spelling. If a correction needs to be made, cross out the incorrect word, and write the correct spelling above it. If the word is spelled correctly, write *C* above it.

                                              C   *receive*
Example: It was a <u>relief</u> to <s>recieve</s> the good news.

1. Be sure to <u>wiegh</u> the pros and cons before making important decisions, particularly those involving <u>friends</u>.

2. When your <u>beliefs</u> are tested, you may be able to <u>acheive</u> a better understanding of yourself.

3. In our <u>society</u>, many people <u>decieve</u> themselves into <u>beleiving</u> that they are better than everyone else.

4. <u>Cheifly</u> because they have been lucky, they have reached a certain <u>height</u> in the world.

5. They think that the blood running through <u>their</u> <u>viens</u> makes them belong to a higher <u>species</u> than the average person.

6. In fact, they are probably <u>niether</u> smarter nor more talented than others, but they are certainly <u>deficient</u> in humility.

7. <u>Thier</u> <u>impatient</u> attitude can cause others a lot of <u>greif</u>.

8. I have always <u>percieved</u> myself as thoughtful of others, and my <u>conscience</u> leads me to treat everyone with respect.

9. There are a <u>vareity</u> of ways to learn a <u>foriegn</u> language.

10. *Dark City* is a really <u>weird</u> movie, even for <u>science</u> fiction.

■ SEEING AND WRITING: Flashback

Look back at your response to the Seeing and Writing exercise on page 525. Underline any words that have *ie* or *ei* combinations, and check a dictionary to make sure they are spelled correctly. Correct any spelling errors you find.

C   Understanding Prefixes

A **prefix** is a group of letters added at the beginning of a word that changes the word's meaning. Adding a prefix to a word never affects the spelling of the original word.

dis + service = disservice   pre + heat = preheat
un + able = unable   un + natural = unnatural
co + operate = cooperate   over + rate = overrate

◆ PRACTICE 34-2

ON THE WEB
*For more
practice, visit
Exercise Central:*
www.bedford
stmartins.com/
writingincontext

Write in the blank the new word that results when the specified prefix is added
to each of the following words.

Example: dis + respect = _____*disrespect*_____

1. un + happy = _____   6. non + negotiable = _____

2. tele + vision = _____   7. im + patient = _____

3. pre + existing = _____   8. out + think = _____

4. dis + satisfied = _____   9. over + react = _____

5. un + necessary = _____   10. dis + solve = _____

■ SEEING AND WRITING: Flashback

Look back at your response to the Seeing and Writing exercise on page
525. Underline words that have prefixes, and check a dictionary to make
sure each word is spelled correctly. Correct any spelling errors you find.

D   Understanding Suffixes

A **suffix** is a group of letters attached to the end of a word that changes the
word's meaning or its part of speech. Adding a suffix to a word can change the
spelling of the original word.

Words Ending in Silent *e*

If a word ends with a silent (unpronounced) *e,* drop the *e* if the suffix begins
with a vowel.

DROP THE *E*

hope + ing = hoping   dance + er = dancer
continue + ous = continuous   insure + able = insurable

EXCEPTIONS

change + able = changeable	courage + ous = courageous
notice + able = noticeable	replace + able = replaceable

Keep the *e* if the suffix begins with a consonant.

KEEP THE *E*

hope + ful = hopeful	bore + dom = boredom
excite + ment = excitement	same + ness = sameness

EXCEPTIONS

argue + ment = argument	true + ly = truly
judge + ment = judgment	nine + th = ninth

◆ PRACTICE 34-3

Write in the blank the new word that results from adding the specified suffix to each of the following words.

ON THE WEB
For more practice, visit Exercise Central: www.bedford stmartins.com/ writingincontext

Examples:

insure + ance = ___*insurance*___

love + ly = ___*lovely*___

1. lone + ly = _____   6. true + ly = _____

2. use + ful = _____   7. microscope + ic = _____

3. revise + ing = _____   8. prepare + ation = _____

4. base + ment = _____   9. nine + th = _____

5. desire + able = _____   10. indicate + ion = _____

Words Ending in -y

When you add a suffix to a word that ends in *-y,* change the *y* to an *i* if the letter before the *y* is a consonant.

CHANGE *Y* TO *I*

beauty + ful = beautiful	busy + ly = busily
try + ed = tried	friendly + er = friendlier

EXCEPTIONS

■   Keep the *y* if the suffix starts with an *i.*

cry + ing = crying   baby + ish = babyish

■ Keep the *y* when you add a suffix to some one-syllable words.

shy + er = shyer   dry + ness = dryness

Keep the *y* if the letter before the *y* is a vowel.

KEEP THE *Y*

annoy + ance = annoyance   enjoy + ment = enjoyment
play + ful = playful   display + ed = displayed

EXCEPTIONS

day + ly = daily   say + ed = said
gay + ly = gaily   pay + ed = paid

◆ PRACTICE 34-4

Write in the blank the new word that results from adding the specified suffix to each of the following words.

Examples:

study + ed = ____studied____

employ + ment = ____employment____

1. happy + ness = _____   6. annoy + ing = _____

2. convey + or = _____   7. destroy + er = _____

3. deny + ing = _____   8. twenty + eth = _____

4. carry + ed = _____   9. forty + ish = _____

5. ready + ness = _____   10. day + ly = _____

Doubling the Final Consonant

For more information on vowels and consonants, see the Focus box in 34A.

When you add a suffix that begins with a vowel—for example, *-ed*, *-er*, or *-ing*—double the final consonant in the original word if (1) the last three letters of the word have a consonant-vowel-consonant pattern (cvc), *and* (2) the word has one syllable, or the last syllable is stressed.

FINAL CONSONANT DOUBLED

cut   + ing = cutting (cvc—one syllable)
bat   + er   = batter (cvc—one syllable)

pet	+	ed	=	petted (cvc—one syllable)
commit	+	ed	=	committed (cvc—stress is on last syllable)
occur	+	ing	=	occurring (cvc—stress is on last syllable)

FINAL CONSONANT NOT DOUBLED

answer	+	ed	=	answered (cvc—stress is not on last syllable)
happen	+	ing	=	happening (cvc—stress is not on last syllable)
act	+	ing	=	acting (no cvc)

◆ PRACTICE 34-5

Write in the blank the new word that results from adding the specified suffix to each of the following words.

Examples:

rot + ing = _____*rotting*_____

narrow + er = _____*narrower*_____

1. hope + ed = _____

2. rest + ing =_____

3. reveal + ing =_____

4. unzip + ed =_____

5. cram + ing = _____

6. appeal + ing = _____

7. refer + ing = _____

8. omit + ed = _____

9. fat + er = _____

10. repel + ed =_____

■ SEEING AND WRITING: Flashback

Look back at your response to the Seeing and Writing exercise on page 525. Underline words that have suffixes, and check a dictionary to make sure each word is spelled correctly. Correct any spelling errors you find.

| **E** | **Learning Commonly Confused Words** |

Computer Tip

Delete commonly confused words from your computer's spell checker so that they will always be flagged as possible errors.

Accept/Except   *Accept* means "to receive something." *Except* means "with the exception of" or "to leave out or exclude."

"I <u>accept</u> your challenge," said Alexander Hamilton to Aaron Burr.

Everyone <u>except</u> Darryl visited the museum.

Affect/Effect   *Affect* is a verb meaning "to influence." *Effect* is a noun meaning "result" and sometimes a verb meaning "to bring about."

Carmen's job could <u>affect</u> her grades.

Overexposure to sun can have a long-term <u>effect</u> on skin.

Commissioner Williams tried to <u>effect</u> changes in police procedure.

All ready/Already   *All ready* means "completely prepared." *Already* means "previously, before."

Serge was <u>all ready</u> to take the history test.

Gina had <u>already</u> been to Italy.

Brake/Break   *Brake* is a noun that means "a device to slow or stop a vehicle." *Break* is a verb meaning "to smash" or "to detach" and sometimes a noun meaning either "a gap" or "an interruption" or "a stroke of luck."

Peter got into an accident because his foot slipped off the <u>brake</u>.

Babe Ruth thought no one would ever <u>break</u> his home run record.

The baseball game was postponed until there was a <u>break</u> in the bad weather.

Buy/By   *Buy* means "to purchase." *By* is a preposition meaning "close to" or "next to" or "by means of."

The Stamp Act forced colonists to <u>buy</u> stamps for many public documents.

He drove <u>by</u> but did not stop.

He stayed <u>by</u> her side all the way to the hospital.

Malcolm X wanted "freedom <u>by</u> any means necessary."

◆ PRACTICE 34-6

ON THE WEB
For more practice, visit Exercise Central: www.bedford stmartins.com/ writingincontext

Proofread the underlined words in the following sentences for correct spelling. If a correction needs to be made, cross out the incorrect word, and write the correct spelling above it. If the word is spelled correctly, write *C* above it.

                        accept   *C*

Example: We must <s>except</s> the fact that the human heart can <u>break</u>.

  1. The <u>affects</u> of several new AIDS drugs have <u>all ready</u> been reported.

2. *Consumer Reports* gave high ratings to the breaks on all the new cars tested accept one.

3. Advertisements urge us to by a new product even if we already own a comparable item.

4. If you except the charges for a collect telephone call through the ITC network, you will probably have to brake your piggy bank to pay their bill.

5. Cigarette smoking affects the lungs by creating deposits of tar that inhibit breathing.

Conscience/Conscious   *Conscience* is a noun that refers to the part of the mind that urges a person to choose right over wrong. *Conscious* is an adjective that means "aware" or "deliberate."

After he cheated at cards, his conscience started to bother him.

As she walked through the woods, she became conscious of the hum of insects.

Elliott made a conscious decision to stop smoking.

Everyday/Every day   *Everyday* is a single word that means "ordinary" or "common." *Every day* is two words that mean "occurring daily."

I Love Lucy was a successful comedy show because it appealed to everyday people.

Every day, Lucy and Ethel would find a new way to get into trouble.

Find/Fine   *Find* means "to locate." *Fine* means "superior quality" or "a sum of money paid as a penalty."

Some people still use a willow rod to find water.

He sang a fine solo at church last Sunday.

Demi had to pay a fine for speeding.

Hear/Here   *Hear* means "to perceive sound by ear." *Here* means "at or in this place."

I moved to the front so I could hear the speaker.

My great-grandfather came here in 1883.

Its/It's   *Its* is the possessive form of *it*. *It's* is the contraction of *it is* or *it has*.

The airline canceled its flights because of the snow.

It's twelve o'clock, and we are late.

Ever since it's been in the accident, the car has rattled.

◆ **PRACTICE 34-7**

Proofread the underlined words in the following sentences for correct spelling. If a correction needs to be made, cross out the incorrect word, and write the correct spelling above it. If the word is spelled correctly, write *C* above it.

>   *C*   *everyday*
> **Example:**   <u>It's</u> often difficult for celebrities to adjust to ~~every day~~ life.

1. <u>Hear</u> at Simonson's Fashions, we try to make our customers feel that <u>everyday</u> is a sale day.

2. The minister was a <u>find</u> person, and <u>its</u> a shame that he died so young.

3. That inner voice you <u>hear</u> is your <u>conscious</u> telling you how you should behave.

4. In the <u>every day</u> world of work and school, it can be hard to <u>fine</u> the time to relax and appreciate life.

5. By the time I became <u>conscience</u> of the leaking pipe, <u>it's</u> damage had run to more than a hundred dollars.

Knew/Know/New/No   *Knew* is the past tense form of the verb *know*. *Know* means "to have an understanding of" or "to have fixed in the mind." *New* means "recent or never used." *No* means "not any," "not at all," or "not one."

> He <u>knew</u> how to install a <u>new</u> light switch.
> I <u>know</u> there will be a lunar eclipse tonight.
> You have <u>no</u> right to say that.

Lay/Lie   *Lay* means "to put or place something down." The past tense of *lay* is *laid*. *Lie* means "to rest or recline." The past tense of *lie* is *lay*.

> Tammy told Carl to <u>lay</u> his cards on the table.
> Brooke and Cassia finally <u>laid</u> down their hockey sticks.
> Every Sunday I <u>lie</u> in bed until noon.
> They <u>lay</u> on the grass until it began to rain, and then they went home.

Loose/Lose   *Loose* means "not fixed or rigid" or "not attached securely." *Lose* means "to mislay" or "to misplace."

> In the 1940s, many women wore <u>loose</u>-fitting pants.
> I don't gamble because I hate to <u>lose</u>.

Mind/Mine *Mind* can be a noun meaning "human consciousness" or "intelligence" or a verb meaning "to obey" or "to attend to." *Mine* is a possessive pronoun that indicates ownership.

A mind is a terrible thing to waste.

"Mind your manners when you visit your grandmother," Dad said.

That red mountain bike is mine.

Passed/Past *Passed* is the past tense of the verb *pass*. It means "moved by" or "succeeded in." *Past* is a noun meaning "earlier than the present time."

The car that passed me must have been doing more than eighty miles an hour.

David finally passed his driving test.

The novel was set in the past.

Peace/Piece *Peace* means "the absence of war" or "calm." *Piece* means "a part of something."

The British prime minister thought he had achieved peace with honor.

My peace of mind was destroyed when the flying saucer landed.

"Have a piece of cake," said Marie.

◆ PRACTICE 34-8

Proofread the underlined words in the following sentences for correct spelling. If a correction needs to be made, cross out the incorrect word, and write the correct spelling above it. If the word is spelled correctly, write *C* above it.

Example: I thought I would ~~loose~~ *lose* my mind. *C*

1. In the passed, many people new their neighbors well.

2. Today, however, we often loose touch with our neighbors or do not know them at all.

3. In a search for inner piece and serenity, we may use relaxation techniques to get in touch with our unconscious minds.

4. We may want to loose ourselves in a place where no other person can reach us.

5. She lay in bed reading for an hour and then lay the book on the table.

Plain/Plane   *Plain* means "simple, not elaborate." *Plane* is the shortened form of *airplane.*

> Sometimes the Amish are referred to as the <u>plain</u> people.
>
> Chuck Yeager was the first person to fly a <u>plane</u> faster than the speed of sound.

Principal/Principle   *Principal* means "first" or "highest" or "the head of a school." *Principle* means "a law or basic assumption."

> She had the <u>principal</u> role in the movie.
>
> I'll never forget the day the <u>principal</u> called me into his office.
>
> It was against his <u>principles</u> to lie.

Quiet/Quit/Quite   *Quiet* means "free of noise" or "still." *Quit* means "to leave a job" or "to give up." *Quite* means "actually" or "very."

> Jane looked forward to the <u>quiet</u> evenings at the lake.
>
> Sammy <u>quit</u> his job and followed the girls into the parking lot.
>
> "You haven't <u>quite</u> got the hang of it yet," she said.
>
> After practicing all summer, Tamika got <u>quite</u> good at handball.

Raise/Rise   *Raise* means "to elevate" or "to increase in size, quantity, or worth." The past tense of *raise* is *raised. Rise* means "to stand up" or "to move from a lower position to a higher position." The past tense of *rise* is *rose.*

> Carlos <u>raises</u> his hand whenever the teacher asks for volunteers.
>
> They finally <u>raised</u> the money for the down payment.
>
> The crowd <u>rises</u> every time their team scores a touchdown.
>
> Sarah <u>rose</u> before dawn so that she could see the eclipse.

Right/Write   *Right* means "correct" or "the opposite of left." *Write* means "to form letters with a writing instrument."

> If you turn <u>right</u> at the corner, you will be going in the <u>right</u> direction.
>
> All students are required to <u>write</u> three short papers.

Set/Sit   *Set* means "to put down or place" or "to adjust something to a desired position." The past tense of *set* is *set. Sit* means "to assume a sitting position." The past tense of *sit* is *sat.*

> Elizabeth <u>set</u> the mail on the kitchen table and left for work.
>
> Every semester I <u>set</u> goals for myself.
>
> I usually <u>sit</u> in the front row at the movies.
>
> They <u>sat</u> at the clinic waiting for their names to be called.

Suppose/Supposed   *Suppose* means "to consider" or "to assume." *Supposed* is both the past tense and the past participle of *suppose. Supposed* also means "expected" or "required." (Note that when *supposed* has this meaning, it is followed by *to*.)

> <u>Suppose</u> researchers were to find a cure for AIDS.
>
> We <u>supposed</u> the movie would be over by ten o'clock.
>
> You were <u>supposed</u> to finish a draft of the report by today.

Note: Be careful not to drop the *d* of *supposed* before *to: He is <u>supposed</u> to study*, not *He is <u>suppose</u> to study.*

◆ PRACTICE 34-9

Proofread the underlined words in the following sentences for correct spelling. If a correction needs to be made, cross out the incorrect word, and write the correct spelling above it. If the word is spelled correctly, write *C* above it.

>   *C*   *supposed*
>
> **Example:** A <u>principal</u> is ~~suppose~~ to care about his or her students' welfare.

1. Last week I flew in a <u>plain</u> that made <u>quit</u> a rough landing.

2. It is not <u>write</u> to expect everyone to agree with your personal <u>principals</u> of morality in every case.

3. In earlier times, children were always <u>suppose</u> to be <u>quite</u> and not speak when their elders were talking.

4. My favorite teacher never <u>raised</u> his voice in anger, and this <u>set</u> a good example for students.

5. Surveys have shown that many college students' <u>principle</u> goal in life is to become <u>quite</u> wealthy.

Than/Then   *Than* is used to introduce the second element in a comparison. *Then* means "at that time" or "next in time."

> My dog is smarter <u>than</u> your dog.
>
> He was young and naive <u>then</u>.
>
> I went to the job interview and <u>then</u> stopped off for a chocolate shake.

Their/There/They're   *Their* is the possessive form of the pronoun *they*. *There* means "at or in that place." *There* is also used in the phrases *there is* and *there are*. *They're* is the contraction of "they are."

Jane Addams wanted poor people to improve <u>their</u> living conditions.

I put the book over <u>there</u>.

<u>There</u> are three reasons I will not eat meat.

<u>They're</u> the best volunteer firefighters I've ever seen.

Threw/Through   *Threw* is the past tense of *throw*. *Through* means "in one side and out the opposite side" or "finished."

Satchel Paige <u>threw</u> a baseball more than ninety-five miles an hour.

It takes almost thirty minutes to go <u>through</u> the tunnel.

"I'm <u>through</u>," said Clark Kent, storming out of Perry White's office.

To/Too/Two   *To* means "in the direction of." *Too* means "also" or "more than enough." *Two* denotes the numeral *2*.

During spring break, I am going <u>to</u> Disney World.

My roommates are coming <u>too</u>.

The microwave popcorn is <u>too</u> hot to eat.

"If we get rid of the Tin Man and the Cowardly Lion, the <u>two</u> of us can go to Oz," said the Scarecrow to Dorothy.

Use/Used   *Use* means "to put into service" or "to consume." *Used* is both the past tense and past participle of *use*. *Used* also means "accustomed." (Note that when *used* has this meaning, it is followed by *to*.)

I <u>use</u> a soft cloth to clean my glasses.

"Hey! Who <u>used</u> all the hot water?" he yelled from the shower.

Mary had <u>used</u> all the firewood during the storm.

After two years in Alaska, they got <u>used</u> to the short winter days.

◆ PRACTICE 34-10

Proofread the underlined words in the following sentences for correct spelling. If a correction needs to be made, cross out the incorrect word, and write the correct spelling above it. If the word is spelled correctly, write *C* above it.

Example: Most chemicals are not dangerous when ~~their~~ *they're* <u>used</u> *C* properly.

1. <u>Their</u> is more <u>than</u> one way to get ahead in this world.

2. Critics charge that in preventing crime our country's criminal justice system often does <u>two</u> little <u>to</u> late.

3. An appeals judge <u>through</u> out the evidence that the jury had <u>used</u>.

4. When they think of <u>there</u> past, people often wonder whether they were

better off earlier <u>then</u> they are now.

5. Eighty percent of the students who responded <u>too</u> the survey said that

<u>their</u> in favor of a moment of silence, but they aren't in favor of school prayer.

Weather/Whether   *Weather* refers to the state of the atmosphere with respect to temperature, humidity, precipitation, and so on. *Whether* is used to introduce alternative possibilities.

The *Farmer's Almanac* says that the <u>weather</u> this winter will be severe.

<u>Whether</u> or not this prediction will be correct is anyone's guess.

Were/We're/Where   *Were* is the past tense of *are*. *We're* is the contraction of "we are." *Where* means "at or in what place."

Charlie Chaplin and Mary Pickford <u>were</u> popular stars of silent movies.

<u>We're</u> doing our back-to-school shopping early this year.

<u>Where</u> are you going, and <u>where</u> have you been?

Who's/Whose   *Who's* is the contraction of either "who is" or "who has." *Whose* is the possessive form of *who*.

"<u>Who's</u> there?" squealed the second little pig as he leaned against the door.

<u>Who's</u> left a yellow 1957 Chevrolet blocking the driveway?

My roommate asked, "<u>Whose</u> book is this?"

Your/You're   *Your* is the possessive form of *you*. *You're* is the contraction of "you are."

"You should have worn <u>your</u> running shoes," said the hare as he passed the tortoise.

"<u>You're</u> too kind," said the tortoise sarcastically.

◆ PRACTICE 34-11

Proofread the underlined words in the following sentences for correct spelling. If a correction needs to be made, cross out the incorrect word, and write the correct spelling above it. If the word is spelled correctly, write *C* above it.

                            we're   *C*

Example: As citizens, ~~were~~ all concerned with <u>where</u> our country is going.

1. Authorities are attempting to discover <u>who's</u> fingerprints <u>were</u> left at the

scene of the crime.

2. Cancer does not care <u>weather</u> <u>your</u> rich or poor, young or old, black or white; it can strike anyone.

3. Santa Fe, <u>were</u> I lived for many years, has better <u>weather</u> than New Jersey has.

4. Whenever we listen to politicians debate, <u>were</u> likely to be wondering <u>whose</u> telling the truth.

5. You should take <u>your</u> time before deciding <u>weather</u> to focus <u>your</u> energy on school or on work.

■ **SEEING AND WRITING: Flashback**

Look back at your response to the Seeing and Writing exercise on page 525. Identify any words that appear on the lists of commonly confused words (pages 533–541), and check to make sure you have spelled them correctly. Correct any misspelled words you find.

■ **SEEING AND WRITING: Revising and Editing**

Type your response to the Seeing and Writing exercise on page 525 if you have not already done so. Now, run a spell check. Did the computer pick up all the errors? Which did it identify? Which did it miss? Correct the spelling errors the computer identified as well as the ones that you found while proofreading. (You can also check spelling in this way in a longer writing assignment you are currently working on.)

CHAPTER REVIEW

◆ EDITING PRACTICE

Read the following student essay, into which spelling errors have been introduced. Identify the words you think are misspelled; then, look them up in a dictionary. Finally, cross out each incorrectly spelled word, and write the correct spelling above the line. The first sentence has been edited for you.

Fudging

The origin of the word <u>fudge</u> is ~~unnown.~~ *unknown.* It's meaning
seems to have been adopted from many diffrent sources. At
present, it has too meanings. The first is "a rich candy
made of sugar, butter, milk, and chocolate." The second--
and more intresting--definition is "to fake or falsify."

Everone can remember fudging on an essay test during
his or her academic career. A good freind of mine, for
example, could not answer a question on a history test
because he did not know all the causes of World War II.
What did he do? He made some causes up and got a B. Some
people, like my friend, have had great sucess and become
expert fudgers. Those students who were able to get away
with fudging in high school continue to fudge in college
and beyond. Many politicians, for example, feel comfortible
fudging there campain speeches to attract voters. They
promise to fight corruption, find homes for the homeless,
and put an end to crime. Of course, these are empty
promises. How are voters suppose to judge a canidate if he
or she does not tell them the truth?

Fudging takes place not only in politics but also in
many other professions. In sceince, people fudge to save
time and money. Many products on the market are the result
of sceintific fudging. Some researchers manufacture data
so that there research projects can be finished quickly and
cheaply. For example, in the 1980s, a firm fudged data to
get the Food and Drug Aministration to approve one of it's
products: a pill to help people loose wieght. When consumers complained they were getting sick, the FDA puled the

pill off the market. Of course, weather or not the researcher was fired makes no difference. The damage was all ready done.

◆ COLLABORATIVE ACTIVITIES

1. Working in pairs, compare responses to the Seeing and Writing: Revising and Editing exercise on page 542. How many misspelled words did both you and your partner find? How many errors did you and your partner have in common?

2. Are there any patterns of misspelling in your Seeing and Writing exercises? What types of spelling errors seem most common?

3. Collaborate with your partner to make a spelling list for the two of you, and then work with other groups to create a spelling list for the whole class. When you have finished, determine which types of errors are most common.

UNIT EIGHT

Reading Essays

35 *Readings for Writers* 547

Readings for Writers

PREVIEW

In this chapter, you will learn to react critically to essays by professional writers.

The following nineteen essays by professional writers offer interesting material to read, react to, think critically about, discuss, and write about. In addition, these essays illustrate some of the ways you can organize ideas in your own writing.

The essays in this chapter use the nine patterns of development you learned about in Units 1 to 3 of this book: exemplification, narration, description, process, cause and effect, comparison and contrast, classification, definition, and argument. These patterns are not your only options for arranging ideas in essays; in fact, many essays combine several patterns of development. Still, understanding how each of these nine patterns works will help you choose the most effective organization strategy when you are writing for a particular purpose and audience.

See Chapters 3–11 for information on using various patterns for developing paragraphs; see Chapter 14 for information on writing essays that use these patterns of development.

In this chapter, two essays by professional writers illustrate each pattern of development. (For argument, three model essays are included.) Each essay is preceded by a short introduction that tells you something about the writer and suggests what to look for as you read. Following each selection are four sets of questions. Questions that you can work on in collaboration with other students are marked with an asterisk (*).

- ■ **Reacting to the Reading** questions suggest guidelines for highlighting and annotating the essay.
- ■ **Reacting to Words** questions focus on the writer's word choice.
- ■ **Reacting to Ideas** questions encourage you to respond critically to the writer's ideas and perhaps to consider his or her audience or purpose.
- ■ **Reacting to the Pattern** questions ask you to consider how ideas are arranged within the essay and how they are connected to one another.

For more on highlighting and annotating, see the Introduction.

Each selection also concludes with **Writing Practice** suggestions that give you opportunities to explore in writing some ideas related to the reading.

A   Exemplification

*For more on
how to write an
exemplification
essay, see 14A.*

An **exemplification** essay uses one or more specific examples to support a thesis statement. The two selections that follow, "Don't Call Me a Hot Tamale" by Judith Ortiz Cofer and "The Suspected Shopper" by Ellen Goodman, are exemplification essays. The first uses a series of short examples to support a thesis; the second uses a single extended example.

DON'T CALL ME A HOT TAMALE

Judith Ortiz Cofer

Award-winning poet, novelist, and essayist Judith Ortiz Cofer often writes about her experiences as a Latina—a Hispanic woman—living in a non-Hispanic culture. In "Don't Call Me a Hot Tamale" (1993), she discusses how being Puerto Rican has affected her in the world beyond Puerto Rico. Note that all her examples illustrate the stereotypes she encounters not simply in reaction to her heritage but also in reaction to her gender.

On a bus to London from Oxford University, where I was earning some graduate credits one summer, a young man, obviously fresh from a pub, approached my seat. With both hands over his heart, he went down on his knees in the aisle and broke into an Irish tenor's rendition of "Maria" from *West Side Story*. I was not amused. "Maria" had followed me to London, reminding me of a prime fact of my life: You can leave the island of Puerto Rico, master the English language, and travel as far as you can, but if you're a Latina, especially one who so clearly belongs to Rita Moreno's[1] gene pool, the island travels with you.   1

Growing up in New Jersey and wanting most of all to belong, I lived in two completely different worlds. My parents designed our life as a microcosm of their *casas* on the island—we spoke in Spanish, ate Puerto Rican food bought at the *bodega*, and practiced strict Catholicism complete with Sunday mass in Spanish.   2

I was kept under tight surveillance by my parents, since my virtue and modesty were, by their cultural equation, the same as their honor. As teenagers, my friends and I were lectured constantly on how to behave as proper *señoritas*. But it was a conflicting message we received, since our Puerto Rican mothers also encouraged us to look and act like women by dressing us in clothes our Anglo schoolmates and their mothers found too "mature" and flashy. I often felt humiliated when I appeared at an American friend's birthday party wearing a dress more suitable for a semiformal. At Puerto Rican festivities, neither the music nor the colors we wore could be too loud.   3

---

1. A Puerto Rican actress, dancer, and singer. She is well known for her role in the movie musical *West Side Story*, a version of Shakespeare's *Romeo and Juliet* featuring Anglos and Puerto Ricans in New York City.

I remember Career Day in high school, when our teachers told us to come   4
dressed as if for a job interview. That morning, I agonized in front of my
closet, trying to figure out what a "career girl" would wear, because the only
model I had was Marlo Thomas[2] on TV. To me and my Puerto Rican girlfriends, dressing up meant wearing our mother's ornate jewelry and clothing.

At school that day, the teachers assailed us for wearing "everything at   5
once"—meaning too much jewelry and too many accessories. And it was
painfully obvious that the other students in their tailored skirts and silk
blouses thought we were hopeless and vulgar. The way they looked at us was
a taste of the cultural clash that awaited us in the real world, where prospective employers and men on the street would often misinterpret our tight skirts
and bright colors as a come-on.

It is custom, not chromosomes, that leads us to choose scarlet over pale   6
pink. Our mothers had grown up on a tropical island where the natural environment was a riot of primary colors, where showing your skin was one way
to keep cool as well as to look sexy. On the island, women felt freer to dress and
move provocatively since they were protected by the traditions and laws of a
Spanish/Catholic system of morality and machismo, the main rule of which
was: *You may look at my sister, but if you touch her I will kill you.* The extended
family and church structure provided them with a circle of safety on the island;
if a man "wronged" a girl, everyone would close in to save her family honor.

Off-island, signals often get mixed. When a Puerto Rican girl who is   7
dressed in her idea of what is attractive meets a man from the mainstream culture who has been trained to react to certain types of clothing as a sexual signal, a clash is likely to take place. She is seen as a Hot Tamale, a sexual
firebrand. I learned this lesson at my first formal dance when my date leaned
over and painfully planted a sloppy, overeager kiss on my mouth. When I
didn't respond with sufficient passion, he said in a resentful tone: "I thought
you Latin girls were supposed to mature early." It was only the first time
I would feel like a fruit or vegetable—I was supposed to *ripen*, not just grow
into womanhood like other girls.

These stereotypes, though rarer, still surface in my life. I recently stayed at   8
a classy metropolitan hotel. After having dinner with a friend, I was returning
to my room when a middle-aged man in a tuxedo stepped directly into my
path. With his champagne glass extended toward me, he exclaimed, "Evita!"[3]

Blocking my way, he bellowed the song "Don't Cry for Me, Argentina."   9
Playing to the gathering crowd, he began to sing loudly a ditty to the tune of
"La Bamba"[4]—except the lyrics were about a girl named Maria whose exploits
all rhymed with her name and gonorrhea.

I knew that this same man—probably a corporate executive, even worldly by   10
most standards—would never have regaled a white woman with a dirty song in
public. But to him, I was just a character in his universe of "others," all cartoons.

2. Star of a 1966–71 television comedy about a young woman living on her own in New York City.
3. Eva Perón, wife of Juan Perón, president of Argentina in the 1940s and 1950s. She is the subject of the musical *Evita.*
4. A song with Spanish lyrics popular in the late 1950s.

Still, I am one of the lucky ones. There are thousands of Latinas without the privilege of the education that my parents gave me. For them every day is a struggle against the misconceptions perpetuated by the myth of the Latina as whore, domestic worker or criminal. 11

Rather than fight these pervasive stereotypes, I try to replace them with a more interesting set of realities. I travel around the U.S. reading from my books of poetry and my novel. With the stories I tell, the dreams and fears I examine in my work, I try to get my audience past the particulars of my skin color, my accent or my clothes. 12

I once wrote a poem in which I called Latinas "God's brown daughters." It is really a prayer, of sorts, for communication and respect. In it, Latin women pray "in Spanish to an Anglo God/with a Jewish heritage," and they are "fervently hoping/that if not omnipotent,/at least He be bilingual." 13

Reacting to the Reading

1. Preview the essay. As you read it more carefully, highlight and annotate as needed to help you understand the writer's ideas.
2. Underline the essay's thesis statement. In the margins of the essay, number the examples Cofer uses to support this thesis.

Reacting to Words

*1. Define these words: *tamale* (title), *rendition* (paragraph 1), *microcosm* (2), *ornate* (4), *assailed* (5), *riot* (6), *machismo* (6), *firebrand* (7), *regaled* (10), *perpetuated* (11), *pervasive* (12), *omnipotent* (13). Can you suggest a synonym for each word that will work in the essay?
2. What does the phrase *hot tamale* suggest to you? What do you think Cofer intends it to suggest? Can you think of a word or phrase that might be more effective?

Reacting to Ideas

*1. Cofer states her thesis in paragraph 1: "You can leave the island of Puerto Rico, master the English language, and travel as far as you can, but if you're a Latina, . . . the island travels with you." Restate this thesis in your own words. Do you think this statement applies only to Latinas or to other ethnic groups as well? Explain.
2. How, according to Cofer, are the signals sent by dress and appearance interpreted differently in Puerto Rico and "off-island" (paragraph 7)? How does this difference create problems for Cofer? Do you think there is anything she can do to avoid these problems?

Reacting to the Pattern

1. What examples does Cofer use to support her thesis? Do you think she uses enough examples to convince readers that her thesis is reasonable?

2. Cofer begins her essay with an example. Do you think this is an effective opening strategy? Why or why not? How else might Cofer have begun her essay?

3. All of Cofer's examples are personal experiences. Are they as convincing as statistics or examples from current news articles would be? Are they *more* convincing? Explain.

Writing Practice

1. What kinds of examples can you think of to counteract the stereotype of the Latina as "whore, domestic worker or criminal" (paragraph 11)? Write a letter to a television network in which you propose the addition of several different Latina characters to actual programs in which they might appear.

2. What do you think Cofer can do to avoid being stereotyped? Write an essay that gives examples of specific things she might do to change the way others see her. In your thesis, state why she should (or should not) make changes.

3. Do you think others stereotype you because of your heritage—or because of your age, your gender, your dress, or where you live? Discuss some specific instances of such stereotyping.

THE SUSPECTED SHOPPER

Ellen Goodman

Journalist Ellen Goodman wrote "The Suspected Shopper" for her syndicated newspaper column. Note that although Goodman develops a single extended example of a "suspected shopper"—herself—throughout her essay, she supports her thesis with specific examples of incidents in which she was suspected. As you read, consider whether the essay (written in 1981) is still relevant to readers today—or whether it is perhaps even more relevant.

It is Saturday, Shopping Saturday, as it's called by the merchants who spread their wares like plush welcome mats across the pages of my newspaper.

But the real market I discover is a different, less eager place than the one I read about. On this Shopping Saturday I don't find welcomes, I find warnings and wariness.

At the first store, a bold sign of the times confronts me: SHOPLIFTERS WILL BE PROSECUTED TO THE FULL EXTENT OF THE LAW.

At the second store, instead of a greeter, I find a doorkeeper. It is his job, his duty, to bar my entrance. To pass, I must give up the shopping bag on my arm. I check it in and check it out.

At the third store, I venture as far as the dressing room. Here I meet another worker paid to protect the merchandise rather than to sell it. The guard of this dressing room counts the number of items I carry in and will count the number of items I carry out.

In the mirror, a long, white, plastic security tag juts out from the blouse tucked into the skirt. I try futilely to pat it down along my left hip, try futilely to zip the skirt.   6

Finally, during these strange gyrations, a thought seeps through years of dulled consciousness, layers of denial. Something has happened to the relationship between shops and shoppers. I no longer feel like a woman in search of a shirt. I feel like an enemy at Checkpoint Charlie.[1]   7

I finally, belatedly, realize that I am treated less like a customer these days and more like a criminal. And I hate it. This change happened gradually, and understandably. Security rose in tandem with theft. The defenses of the shopkeepers went up, step by step, with the offenses of the thieves.   8

But now as the weapons escalate, it's the average consumer, the innocent bystander, who is hit by friendly fire.   9

I don't remember the first time an errant security tag buzzed at the doorway, the first time I saw a camera eye in a dress department. I accepted it as part of the price of living in a tight honesty market.   10

In the supermarket, they began to insist on a mug shot before they would cash my check. I tried not to take it personally. At the drugstore, the cashier began to staple my bags closed. And I tried not to take it personally.   11

Now, these experiences have accumulated until I feel routinely treated like a suspect. At the jewelry store, the door is unlocked only for those who pass judgment. In the junior department, the suede pants are permanently attached to the hangers. In the gift shop, the cases are only opened with a key.   12

I am not surprised anymore, but I am finally aware of just how unpleasant it is to be dealt with as guilty until we prove our innocence. Anyplace we are not known, we are not trusted. The old slogan, "Let the Consumer Beware," has been replaced with a new slogan: "Beware of the Consumer."   13

It is no fun to be Belgium[2] in the war between sales and security. Thievery has changed the atmosphere of the marketplace. Merchant distrust has spread through the ventilation system of a whole business, a whole city, and it infects all of us.   14

At the cashier counter today, with my shirt in hand, I the Accused stand quietly while the saleswoman takes my credit card. I watch her round up the usual suspicions. In front of my face, without a hint of embarrassment, she checks my charge number against the list of stolen credit vehicles. While I stand there, she calls the clearinghouse of bad debtors.   15

Having passed both tests, I am instructed to add my name, address, serial number to the bottom of the charge. She checks one signature against another, the picture against the person. Only then does she release the shirt into my custody.   16

And so this Shopping Saturday I take home six ounces of silk and a load of resentment.   17

---

1. A military security checkpoint.
2. Country located between France and Germany, which were enemies in several wars.

Reacting to the Reading

1. Preview the essay. As you read it more carefully, highlight and annotate as needed to help you understand the writer's ideas.

2. Reread the essay, and review your highlighting and annotations. In the margins of the essay, supplement Goodman's examples with one or two examples from your personal experience (or from the experiences of your friends) that support her thesis.

Reacting to Words

*1. Define these words: *futilely* (paragraph 6), *gyrations* (7), *belatedly* (8), *tandem* (8), *errant* (10). Can you suggest a synonym for each word that will work in the essay?

2. What is Goodman's purpose in choosing words like *enemy* (paragraph 7) and *mug shot* (11)? How do they help to support her thesis? Can you find additional words or expressions that serve the same purpose?

Reacting to Ideas

*1. Goodman, a middle-class white woman, uses *we* in the sentence "Anyplace we are not known, we are not trusted" (paragraph 13). Who is this *we*? Do you think Goodman is really part of the group with which she identifies?

2. In paragraph 8, Goodman says the change in attitude she observes is understandable. Do you think she is right?

3. Do you think shoplifting is more or less of a problem today than it was in 1981 when Goodman wrote her essay? What makes you think so?

Reacting to the Pattern

1. In paragraph 8, Goodman states her thesis: "I finally, belatedly, realize that I am treated less like a customer these days and more like a criminal." However, she introduces a number of her examples even before she states this thesis. Why do you think she does this?

2. List the specific examples of times when Goodman was "treated less like a customer . . . and more like a criminal" (paragraph 8).

3. How does Goodman arrange the specific examples that support her thesis? Is each discussed in an individual paragraph, or are examples grouped together?

Writing Practice

1. Why do you think people shoplift? Write an exemplification essay in which you discuss a different reason in each body paragraph.

2. Have you ever been torn between giving in to peer pressure and maintaining your own sense of right and wrong? Develop an extended example that illustrates what it was like to be caught in the middle and explains how you resolved the problem.

3. What do you think merchants can do to reduce shoplifting without making shoppers feel like criminals? Using exemplification to organize your ideas, write a letter to a store where you are a regular customer.

For more on how to write a narrative essay, see 14B.

B   Narration

A **narrative** essay tells a story by presenting a series of events in chronological order. In the first of the two essays that follow, "The Sanctuary of School," Lynda Barry tells a story about home and family. In the second, "Thirty-Eight Who Saw Murder Didn't Call the Police," Martin Gansberg reports the story of a tragic murder.

THE SANCTUARY OF SCHOOL

Lynda Barry

In her cartoon strip "Ernie Pook's Comeek," which appears in a number of newspapers and magazines, Lynda Barry looks at the world through the eyes of children. Her characters remind adult readers of the complicated world of young people and of the clarity with which they see social situations. In "The Sanctuary of School," Barry tells a story from her own childhood. As you read this essay, note how Barry relates her personal experience to a broader issue.

I was 7 years old the first time I snuck out of the house in the dark. It was winter and my parents had been fighting all night. They were short on money and long on relatives who kept "temporarily" moving into our house because they had nowhere else to go. 1

My brother and I were used to giving up our bedroom. We slept on the couch, something we actually liked because it put us that much closer to the light of our lives, our television. 2

At night when everyone was asleep, we lay on our pillows watching it with the sound off. We watched Steve Allen's mouth moving. We watched Johnny Carson's mouth moving.[1] We watched movies filled with gangsters shooting machine guns into packed rooms, dying soldiers hurling a last grenade and beautiful women crying at windows. Then the sign-off finally came and we tried to sleep. 3

The morning I snuck out, I woke up filled with a panic about needing to get to school. The sun wasn't quite up yet but my anxiety was so fierce that I just got dressed, walked quietly across the kitchen and let myself out the back door. 4

---

1. Steve Allen and Johnny Carson were late-night television hosts.

It was quiet outside. Stars were still out. Nothing moved and no one was   5
in the street. It was as if someone had turned the sound off on the world.

I walked the alley, breaking thin ice over the puddles with my shoes. I didn't   6
know why I was walking to school in the dark. I didn't think about it. All I
knew was a feeling of panic, like the panic that strikes kids when they realize
they are lost.

That feeling eased the moment I turned the corner and saw the dark out-   7
line of my school at the top of the hill. My school was made up of about 15
nondescript portable classrooms set down on a fenced concrete lot in a run-
down Seattle neighborhood, but it had the most beautiful view of the Cascade
Mountains. You could see them from anywhere on the playfield and you could
see them from the windows of my classroom—Room 2.

I walked over to the monkey bars and hooked my arms around the cold   8
metal. I stood for a long time just looking across Rainier Valley. The sky was
beginning to whiten and I could hear a few birds.

In a perfect world my absence at home would not have gone unnoticed. I   9
would have had two parents in a panic to locate me, instead of two parents in
a panic to locate an answer to the hard question of survival during a deep
financial and emotional crisis.

But in an overcrowded and unhappy home, it's incredibly easy for any child   10
to slip away. The high levels of frustration, depression and anger in my house
made my brother and me invisible. We were children with the sound turned off.
And for us, as for the steadily increasing number of neglected children in this
country, the only place where we could count on being noticed was at school.

"Hey there, young lady. Did you forget to go home last night?" It was Mr.   11
Gunderson, our janitor, whom we all loved. He was nice and he was funny and
he was old with white hair, thick glasses and an unbelievable number of keys.
I could hear them jingling as he walked across the playfield. I felt incredibly
happy to see him.

He let me push his wheeled garbage can between the different portables as   12
he unlocked each room. He let me turn on the lights and raise the window
shades and I saw my school slowly come to life. I saw Mrs. Holman, our school
secretary, walk into the office without her orange lipstick on yet. She waved.

I saw the fifth-grade teacher Mr. Cunningham, walking under the breeze-   13
way eating a hard roll. He waved.

And I saw my teacher, Mrs. Claire LeSane, walking toward us in a red coat   14
and calling my name in a very happy and surprised way, and suddenly my
throat got tight and my eyes stung and I ran toward her crying. It was something that surprised us both.

It's only thinking about it now, 28 years later, that I realize I was crying   15
from relief. I was with my teacher, and in a while I was going to sit at my desk,
with my crayons and pencils and books and classmates all around me, and for
the next six hours I was going to enjoy a thoroughly secure, warm and stable
world. It was a world I absolutely relied on. Without it, I don't know where I
would have gone that morning.

Mrs. LeSane asked me what was wrong and when I said "Nothing," she   16
seemingly left it at that. But she asked me if I would carry her purse for her,

an honor above all honors, and she asked if I wanted to come into Room 2 early and paint.

She believed in the natural healing power of painting and drawing for troubled children. In the back of her room there was always a drawing table and an easel with plenty of supplies, and sometimes during the day she would come up to you for what seemed like no good reason and quietly ask if you wanted to go to the back table and "make some pictures for Mrs. LeSane." We all had a chance at it—to sit apart from the class for a while to paint, draw and silently work out impossible problems on 11 × 17 sheets of newsprint.   17

Drawing came to mean everything to me. At the back table in Room 2, I learned to build myself a life preserver that I could carry into my home.   18

We all know that a good education system saves lives, but the people of this country are still told that cutting the budget for public schools is necessary, that poor salaries for teachers are all we can manage and that art, music and all creative activities must be the first to go when times are lean.   19

Before- and after-school programs are cut and we are told that public schools are not made for baby-sitting children. If parents are neglectful temporarily or permanently, for whatever reason, it's certainly sad, but their unlucky children must fend for themselves. Or slip through the cracks. Or wander in a dark night alone.   20

We are told in a thousand ways that not only are public schools not important, but that the children who attend them, the children who need them most, are not important either. We leave them to learn from the blind eye of a television, or to the mercy of "a thousand points of light"[2] that can be as far away as stars.   21

I was lucky. I had Mrs. LeSane. I had Mr. Gunderson. I had an abundance of art supplies. And I had a particular brand of neglect in my home that allowed me to slip away and get to them. But what about the rest of the kids who weren't as lucky? What happened to them?   22

By the time the bell rang that morning I had finished my drawing and Mrs. LeSane pinned it up on the special bulletin board she reserved for drawings from the back table. It was the same picture I always drew—a sun in the corner of a blue sky over a nice house with flowers all around it.   23

Mrs. LeSane asked us to please stand, face the flag, place our right hands over our hearts and say the Pledge of Allegiance. Children across the country do it faithfully. I wonder now when the country will face its children and say a pledge right back.   24

Reacting to the Reading

1. Preview the essay. As you read it more carefully, highlight and annotate as needed to help you understand the writer's ideas.

2. Underline passages that describe Barry's home life in negative terms and her school life in positive terms. What specific features of the two places are contrasted?

---

2. Phrase used by former president George Bush to promote volunteerism rather than government programs.

Reacting to Words

*1. Define these words: *nondescript* (paragraph 7), *fend* (20). Can you suggest a synonym for each word that will work in the essay?

2. Look up the word *sanctuary* in a dictionary. Which of the listed definitions do you think comes closest to Barry's meaning?

Reacting to Ideas

1. In paragraph 10, Barry characterizes herself and her brother as "children with the sound turned off." What do you think she means?

2. List the ways in which Barry's home and school worlds are different.

*3. What is the main point of Barry's essay—the idea that she wants to persuade readers to accept? Is this idea actually stated in her essay? If so, where? If not, do you think it should be?

Reacting to the Pattern

1. Paragraphs 9–10 and 19–22 interrupt Barry's story. What purpose do these paragraphs serve? Do you think the essay would be more effective if paragraphs 9 and 10 came earlier? If paragraphs 19–22 came after paragraph 24? Explain.

2. What transitional words and phrases does Barry use to move readers from one event to the next? Do you think her essay needs more transitions? If so, where should they be added?

Writing Practice

1. Did you see elementary school as a sanctuary or as something quite different? Write a narrative essay that conveys to readers what school meant to you when you were a child.

2. In addition to school, television was a sanctuary for Barry and her brother. Did television watching (or some other activity) serve this function for you when you were younger? Is there some activity that fills this role now? In a narrative essay, tell about your own "sanctuary."

3. What role does college play in your life? Write an article for your school newspaper in which you use narration to illustrate what school means to you now that you are an adult.

THIRTY-EIGHT WHO SAW MURDER DIDN'T CALL THE POLICE

Martin Gansberg

This newspaper story uses objective language to tell about an incident that occurred in New York City in 1964. As Gansberg reconstructs a crime two weeks after it happened, he gives readers a detailed picture of the sequence of events that led up to a young woman's murder—in full view of thirty-eight of her "respectable, law-abiding" neighbors. As you read, consider how you might have acted if you had been a witness to this tragedy.

For more than half an hour 38 respectable, law-abiding citizens in Queens watched a killer stalk and stab a woman in three separate attacks in Kew Gardens. ₁

Twice their chatter and the sudden glow of their bedroom lights interrupted him and frightened him off. Each time he returned, sought her out, and stabbed her again. Not one person telephoned the police during the assault; one witness called after the woman was dead. ₂

That was two weeks ago today. ₃

Still shocked is Assistant Chief Inspector Frederick M. Lussen, in charge of the borough's detectives and a veteran of 25 years of homicide investigations. He can give a matter-of-fact recitation on many murders. But the Kew Gardens slaying baffles him—not because it is a murder, but because the "good people" failed to call the police. ₄

"As we have reconstructed the crime," he said, "the assailant had three chances to kill this woman during a 35-minute period. He returned twice to complete the job. If we had been called when he first attacked, the woman might not be dead now." ₅

This is what the police say happened beginning at 3:20 a.m. in the staid, middle-class, tree-lined Austin Street area: ₆

Twenty-eight-year-old Catherine Genovese, who was called Kitty by almost everyone in the neighborhood, was returning home from her job as manager of a bar in Hollis. She parked her red Fiat in a lot adjacent to the Kew Gardens Long Island Rail Road Station, facing Mowbray Place. Like many residents of the neighborhood, she had parked there day after day since her arrival from Connecticut a year ago, although the railroad frowns on the practice. ₇

She turned off the lights of her car, locked the door, and started to walk the 100 feet to the entrance of her apartment at 82-70 Austin Street, which is in a Tudor building, with stores on the first floor and apartments on the second. ₈

The entrance to the apartment is in the rear of the building because the front is rented to retail stores. At night the quiet neighborhood is shrouded in the slumbering darkness that marks most residential areas. ₉

Miss Genovese noticed a man at the far end of the lot, near a seven-story apartment house at 82-40 Austin Street. She halted. Then, nervously, she headed up Austin Street toward Lefferts Boulevard, where there is a call box to the 102nd Police Precinct in nearby Richmond Hill. ₁₀

She got as far as a street light in front of a bookstore before the man grabbed her. She screamed. Lights went on in the 10-story apartment house at 82-67 Austin Street, which faces the bookstore. Windows slid open and voices punctuated the early-morning stillness. ₁₁

Miss Genovese screamed: "Oh, my God, he stabbed me! Please help me! Please help me!" ₁₂

From one of the upper windows in the apartment house, a man called down: "Let that girl alone!" ₁₃

The assailant looked up at him, shrugged, and walked down Austin Street 14
toward a white sedan parked a short distance away. Miss Genovese struggled
to her feet.

Lights went out. The killer returned to Miss Genovese, now trying to make 15
her way around the side of the building by the parking lot to get to her apartment. The assailant stabbed her again.

"I'm dying!" she shrieked. "I'm dying!" 16

Windows were opened again, and lights went on in many apartments. The 17
assailant got into his car and drove away. Miss Genovese staggered to her feet.
A city bus, O-10, the Lefferts Boulevard line to Kennedy International Airport,
passed. It was 3:35 a.m.

The assailant returned. By then, Miss Genovese had crawled to the back 18
of the building, where the freshly painted brown doors to the apartment house
held out hope for safety. The killer tried the first door; she wasn't there. At the
second door, 82-62 Austin Street, he saw her slumped on the floor at the foot
of the stairs. He stabbed her a third time—fatally.

It was 3:50 by the time the police received their first call, from a man who 19
was a neighbor of Miss Genovese. In two minutes they were at the scene. The
neighbor, a 70-year-old woman, and another woman were the only persons on
the street. Nobody else came forward.

The man explained that he had called the police after much deliberation. 20
He had phoned a friend in Nassau County for advice and then he had crossed
the roof of the building to the apartment of the elderly woman to get her to
make the call.

"I didn't want to get involved," he sheepishly told police. 21

Six days later, the police arrested Winston Moseley, a 29-year-old business 22
machine operator, and charged him with homicide. Moseley had no
previous record. He is married, has two children and owns a home at 133-19
Sutter Avenue, South Ozone Park, Queens. On Wednesday, a court committed
him to Kings County Hospital for psychiatric observation.

When questioned by the police, Moseley also said that he had slain Mrs. 23
Annie May Johnson, 24, of 146-12 133d Avenue, Jamaica, on Feb. 29 and
Barbara Kralik, 15, of 174-17 140th Avenue, Springfield Gardens, last July. In
the Kralik case, the police are holding Alvin L. Mitchell, who is said to have
confessed to that slaying.

The police stressed how simple it would have been to have gotten in touch 24
with them. "A phone call," said one of the detectives, "would have done it."
The police may be reached by dialing "O" for operator or SPring 7-3100.

Today witnesses from the neighborhood, which is made up of one-family 25
homes in the $35,000 to $60,000 range with the exception of the two apartment
houses near the railroad station, find it difficult to explain why they didn't call
the police.

A housewife, knowingly if quite casually, said, "We thought it was a lovers' 26
quarrel." A husband and wife both said, "Frankly, we were afraid." They
seemed aware of the fact that events might have been different. A distraught
woman, wiping her hands in her apron, said, "I didn't want my husband to get
involved."

One couple, now willing to talk about that night, said they heard the first 27
screams. The husband looked thoughtfully at the bookstore where the killer
first grabbed Miss Genovese.

"We went to the window to see what was happening," he said, "but the 28
light from our bedroom made it difficult to see the street." The wife, still
apprehensive, added: "I put out the light and we were able to see better."

Asked why they hadn't called the police, she shrugged and replied: "I don't 29
know."

A man peeked out from a slight opening in the doorway to his apartment 30
and rattled off an account of the killer's second attack. Why hadn't he called
the police at the time? "I was tired," he said without emotion. "I went back
to bed."

It was 4:25 a.m. when the ambulance arrived to take the body of Miss Gen- 31
ovese. It drove off. "Then," a solemn police detective said, "the people came out."

Reacting to the Reading

1. Preview the essay. As you read it more carefully, highlight and annotate as
   needed to help you understand the writer's ideas.
2. Place a check mark beside each passage of dialogue Gansberg uses. Then,
   add brief marginal annotations next to three of these passages.

Reacting to Words

*1. Define these words: *staid* (paragraph 6), *shrouded* (9). Can you suggest a
   synonym for each word that will work in the essay?
2. What is Gansberg's purpose in using terms like *respectable* (paragraph 1),
   law-abiding (1), and *good people* (4)? What is your reaction to these
   words?

Reacting to Ideas

1. What reasons do the witnesses give for not coming to Kitty Genovese's
   aid? Why do *you* think no one helped her? Do you think the witnesses
   should be held accountable for their lack of action?
*2. Suppose Genovese's attack were to occur today. How do you think her
   neighbors would react? What might be different about the situation?

Reacting to the Pattern

1. What other patterns could Gansberg have used to develop his essay? For
   instance, could he have used comparison and contrast? Exemplification?
   Given the alternatives, do you think narration is the best choice? Why or
   why not?
*2. Gansberg uses many transitional words and phrases, including refer-
   ences to specific times, to move readers from one event to the next. List
   as many of these transitions as you can. Do you think more transitions
   should be added?

Writing Practice

1. Write a narrative essay about a time when you were a witness who chose not to become involved in events you were observing.
2. Find a brief newspaper article that tells a story about a similar incident in which bystanders witnessed a crime. Expand the article into a longer essay, inventing characters, dialogue, and additional details.
3. Retell Kitty Genovese's story—but this time, have a witness come to her rescue.

C   Description

A **descriptive** essay tells what something looks, sounds, smells, tastes, or feels like. It uses details to give readers a clear, vivid picture of a person, place, or object. In "Summer Picnic Fish Fry," Maya Angelou describes a community picnic. In "Guavas," Esmeralda Santiago describes a fruit.

For more on how to write a descriptive essay, see 14C.

SUMMER PICNIC FISH FRY

Maya Angelou

Maya Angelou is a poet, historian, actress, playwright, civil rights activist, producer, and director. At the request of President Clinton, she wrote and delivered a poem at his 1993 inauguration. "Summer Picnic Fish Fry," from her autobiographical *I Know Why the Caged Bird Sings* (1969), presents a vivid picture of a specific time (the 1930s) and place (the rural Arkansas town of Stamps). As you read, notice how Angelou, from her place on the grass, takes in the entire picnic, one scene at a time.

"Acka Backa, Sody Cracka
Acka Backa, Boo
Acka Backa, Sody Cracka
I'm in love with you."

The sounds of tag beat through the trees while the top branches waved in contrapuntal rhythms. I lay on a moment of green grass and telescoped the children's game to my vision. The girls ran about wild, now here, now there, never here, never was, they seemed to have no more direction than a splattered egg. But it was a shared if seldom voiced knowledge that all movements fitted, and worked according to a larger plan. I raised a platform for my mind's eye and marveled down on the outcome of "Acka Backa." The gay picnic dresses dashed, stopped and darted like beautiful

35 C

dragonflies over a dark pool. The boys, black whips in the sunlight, popped behind the trees where their girls had fled, half hidden and throbbing in the shadows.

The summer picnic fish fry in the clearing by the pond was the biggest out-door event of the year. Everyone was there. All churches were represented, as well as the social groups (Elks, Eastern Star, Masons, Knights of Columbus, Daughters of Pythias), professional people (Negro teachers from Lafayette county) and all the excited children.   2

Musicians brought cigar-box guitars, harmonicas, juice harps, combs wrapped in tissue paper and even bathtub basses.   3

The amount and variety of foods would have found approval on the menu of a Roman epicure. Pans of fried chicken, covered with dishtowels, sat under benches next to a mountain of potato salad crammed with hard-boiled eggs. Whole rust-red sticks of bologna were clothed in cheese-cloth. Homemade pickles and chow-chow, and baked country hams, aromatic with cloves and pineapples, vied for prominence. Our steady customers had ordered cold watermelons, so Bailey[1] and I chugged the striped-green fruit into the Coca-Cola box and filled all the tubs with ice as well as the big black wash pot that Momma used to boil her laundry. Now they too lay sweating in the happy afternoon air.   4

The summer picnic gave ladies a chance to show off their baking hands. On the barbecue pit, chickens and spareribs sputtered in their own fat and a sauce whose recipe was guarded in the family like a scandalous affair. However, in the ecumenical light of the summer picnic every true baking artist could reveal her prize to the delight and criticism of the town. Orange sponge cakes and dark brown mounds dripping Hershey's chocolate stood layer to layer with ice-white coconuts and light brown caramels. Pound cakes sagged with their buttery weight and small children could no more resist licking the icings than their mothers could avoid slapping the sticky fingers.   5

Proven fishermen and weekend amateurs sat on the trunks of trees at the pond. They pulled the struggling bass and the silver perch from the swift water. A rotating crew of young girls scaled and cleaned the catch and busy women in starched aprons salted and rolled the fish in corn meal, then dropped them in Dutch ovens trembling with boiling fat.   6

On one corner of the clearing a gospel group was rehearsing. Their har-mony, packed as tight as sardines, floated over the music of the county singers and melted into the songs of the small children's ring games.   7

"Boys, don'chew let that ball fall on none of my cakes, you do and it'll be me on you."   8

"Yes, ma'am," and nothing changed. The boys continued hitting the tennis ball with pailings snatched from a fence and running holes in the ground, col-liding with everyone.   9

---

1. The author's brother.

Reacting to the Reading

1. Preview the essay. As you read it more carefully, highlight and annotate as needed to help you understand the writer's ideas.

2. Circle all the words in the essay that designate colors. In the margin, write a brief note explaining what these words and phrases add to the essay.

Reacting to Words

*1. Define these words: *contrapuntal* (paragraph 1), *epicure* (4), *aromatic* (4), *vied* (4), *ecumenical* (5), *colliding* (9). Can you suggest a synonym for each word that will work in the essay?

2. Find several examples of vivid action verbs (for example, *sagged* in paragraph 5). What does each verb mean? What does it suggest?

*3. Angelou uses some unusual **metaphors** (for example, "boys, black whips in the sunlight" in paragraph 1) and **similes** (for example, "harmony, packed as tight as sardines" in paragraph 7). Find as many similes and metaphors as you can. Which ones are most effective? Why?

For more on metaphors and similes, see 20D.

Reacting to Ideas

1. What do you think Angelou means in paragraph 1 when she says that she "raised a platform for [her] mind's eye"?

2. What is it about the picnic that makes it so memorable to Angelou and the other townspeople?

Reacting to the Pattern

*1. In paragraph 2, Angelou says, "The summer picnic fish fry in the clearing by the pond was the biggest outdoor event of the year. Everyone was there." How do these statements establish her essay's dominant impression? What mood does Angelou want her details to convey?

2. Angelou, seated on the grass, begins her description with the sights and sounds of children playing tag and ends with her observation of another children's game. What does she see in between these two scenes? Trace her observations as she moves her gaze around the picnic.

3. Is this essay primarily subjective or objective description? Explain.

Writing Practice

1. Describe a large outdoor family or community event that you have attended. Be sure to include concrete, sensory details about the setting, food, guests, and activities, and make your description as visual and vivid as possible.

2. Describe a scene at which you, like Angelou, were an observer rather than a participant. Begin by describing the location from which you viewed the scene.

GUAVAS

Esmeralda Santiago

Writer Esmeralda Santiago grew up in Puerto Rico as the eldest of eleven children raised by a single mother. The family moved to New York when she was thirteen years old. She has written a childhood memoir, *When I Was Puerto Rican* (1993), and its sequel, *Almost a Woman* (1998), describing the family's move to Brooklyn. After graduating from the High School of the Performing Arts in Manhattan, Santiago spent eight years studying part-time at community colleges before being accepted on full scholarship to Harvard University. In recent years, Santiago has also founded a film and production company, helped found a shelter for battered women, and most recently worked as an editor. As you read this selection, take note of which of the five senses Santiago uses to describe the experience of eating a guava.

Barco que no anda, no llega a puerto.

A ship that doesn't sail, never reaches port.

1   There are guavas at the Shop & Save. I pick one the size of a tennis ball and finger the prickly stem end. It feels familiarly bumpy and firm. The guava is not quite ripe; the skin is still a dark green. I smell it and imagine a pale pink center, the seeds tightly embedded in the flesh.

2   A ripe guava is yellow, although some varieties have a pink tinge. The skin is thick, firm, and sweet. Its heart is bright pink and almost solid with seeds. The most delicious part of the guava surrounds the tiny seeds. If you don't know how to eat a guava, the seeds end up in the crevices between your teeth.

3   When you bite into a ripe guava, your teeth must grip the bumpy surface and sink into the thick edible skin without hitting the center. It takes experience to do this, as it's quite tricky to determine how far beyond the skin the seeds begin.

4   Some years, when the rains have been plentiful and the nights cool, you can bite into a guava and not find many seeds. The guava bushes grow close to the ground, their branches laden with green then yellow fruit that seem to ripen overnight. These guavas are large and juicy, almost seedless, their roundness enticing you to have one more, just one more, because next year the rains may not come.

5   As children, we didn't always wait for the fruit to ripen. We raided the bushes as soon as the guavas were large enough to bend the branch.

6   A green guava is sour and hard. You bite into it at its widest point, because it's easier to grasp with your teeth. You hear the skin, meat, and seeds crunching inside your head, while the inside of your mouth explodes in little spurts of sour.

7   You grimace, your eyes water, and your cheeks disappear as your lips purse into a tight O. But you have another and then another, enjoying the

crunchy sounds, the acid taste, the gritty texture of the unripe center. At night, your mother makes you drink castor oil, which she says tastes better than a green guava. That's when you know for sure that you're a child and she has stopped being one.

I had my last guava the day we left Puerto Rico. It was large and juicy, almost red in the center, and so fragrant that I didn't want to eat it because I would lose the smell. All the way to the airport I scratched at it with my teeth, making little dents in the skin, chewing small pieces with my front teeth, so that I could feel the texture against my tongue, the tiny pink pellets of sweet. 8

Today, I stand before a stack of dark green guavas, each perfectly round and hard, each $1.59. The one in my hand is tempting. It smells faintly of late summer afternoons and hopscotch under the mango tree. But this is autumn in New York, and I'm no longer a child. 9

The guava joins its sisters under the harsh fluorescent lights of the exotic fruit display. I push my cart away, toward the apples and pears of my adulthood, their nearly seedless ripeness predictable and bittersweet. 10

Reacting to the Reading

1. Preview the essay. As you read it more carefully, highlight and annotate as needed to help you understand the writer's ideas.
2. Circle all the words in the essay that convey information about guavas' physical appearance (how they look).

Reacting to Words

*1. Define these words: *guava* (title), *edible* (paragraph 3), *laden* (4), *enticing* (4), *spurts* (6), *grimace* (7), *pellets* (8). Can you suggest a synonym for each word that will work in the essay?
*2. Write an alternate one-word title for this selection.

Reacting to Ideas

1. How is the fruit in the Shop & Save different from the fruit of Santiago's childhood?
*2. Is this essay just about guavas, or is it really about something else? Explain.

Reacting to the Pattern

1. Santiago begins and ends her essay at the Shop & Save, but her imagination takes her somewhere else. Where? What sends her thoughts away from the supermarket?
2. Santiago describes several kinds of guavas. How are they different?
*3. In addition to describing how guavas look, Santiago also describes their smell, taste, and feel. Where does she use language that conveys how guavas taste? How they smell? How they feel?

4. If Santiago had written a purely objective description, what would she have left out? What might she have added?

Writing Practice

1. Write a subjective description of a food you loved when you were a child. Try to describe the smell, taste, and feel of the food as well as its appearance.

2. Write an essay about a friend or family member with whom you associate a particular food or meal. Include descriptions of that person engaged in eating or in preparing food.

3. How have your tastes in food changed since you were a child? Trace the development of your food preferences, beginning as far back as you can remember. Be sure to describe the foods that defined each stage of your life.

D   Process

For more on how to write a process essay, see 14D.

A **process** essay explains the steps in a procedure, telling how something is (or was) done. In "Slice of Life," Russell Baker gives a set of instructions for carving a turkey. In "Indelible Marks," Joyce Howe explains the routine of her family's laundry business.

SLICE OF LIFE

Russell Baker

Pulitzer Prize–winning columnist and author Russell Baker is known for his keen political insight and sharp social commentary. He is also known for being funny. The source of much of Baker's humor is his deadpan approach, in which he pretends to be completely serious. In the following essay, note how he uses this approach to turn what seems to be a straightforward set of instructions into a humorous discussion of a holiday ritual.

How to carve a turkey: 1

Assemble the following tools—carving knife, stone for sharpening carving   2
knife, hot water, soap, wash cloth, two bath towels, barbells, meat cleaver. If the house lacks a meat cleaver, an ax may be substituted. If it is, add bandages, sutures, and iodine to above list.

Begin by moving the turkey from the roasting pan to a suitable carving   3
area. This is done by inserting the carving knife into the posterior stuffed area of the turkey and the knife-sharpening stone into the stuffed area under the neck.

Thus skewered, the turkey may be lifted out of the hot grease with relative   4
safety. Should the turkey drop to the floor, however, remove the knife and

stone, roll the turkey gingerly into the two bath towels, wrap them several times around it and lift the encased fowl to the carving place.

You are now ready to begin carving. Sharpen the knife on the stone and insert it where the thigh joins the torso. If you do this correctly, which is improbable, the knife will almost immediately encounter a barrier of bone and gristle. This may very well be the joint. It could, however, be your thumb. If not, execute a vigorous sawing motion until satisfied that the knife has been defeated. Withdraw the knife and ask someone nearby, in as testy a manner as possible, why the knives at your house are not kept in better carving condition.

Exercise the biceps and forearms by lifting barbells until they are strong enough for you to tackle the leg joint with bare hands. Wrapping one hand firmly around the thigh, seize the turkey's torso in the other hand and scream. Run cold water over hands to relieve pain of burns.

Now, take a bath towel in each hand and repeat the above maneuver. The entire leg should snap away from the chassis with a distinct crack, and the rest of the turkey, obedient to Newton's law[1] about equal and opposite reactions, should roll in the opposite direction, which means that if you are carving at the table the turkey will probably come to rest in someone's lap.

Get the turkey out of the lap with as little fuss as possible, and concentrate on the leg. Use the meat cleaver to sever the sinewy leather which binds the thigh to the drumstick.

If using the alternate, ax method, this operation should be performed on a cement walk outside the house in order to preserve the table.

Repeat the above operation on the turkey's uncarved side. You now have two thighs and two drumsticks. Using the wash cloth, soap and hot water, bathe thoroughly and, if possible, go to a movie. Otherwise, look each person in the eye and say, "I don't suppose anyone wants white meat."

If compelled to carve the breast anyhow, sharpen the knife on the stone again with sufficient awkwardness to tip over the gravy bowl on the person who started the stampede for white meat.

While everyone is rushing about to mop the gravy off her slacks, hack at the turkey breast until it starts crumbling off the carcass in ugly chunks.

The alternative method for carving white meat is to visit around the neighborhood until you find someone who has a good carving knife and borrow it, if you find one, which is unlikely.

This method enables you to watch the football game on neighbors' television sets and also creates the possibility that somebody back at your table will grow tired of waiting and do the carving herself.

In this case, upon returning home, cast a pained stare upon the mound of chopped white meat that has been hacked out by the family carving knife and refuse to do any more carving that day. No one who cares about the artistry of carving can be expected to work upon the mutilations of amateurs, and it would be a betrayal of the carver's art to do so.

1. Sir Isaac Newton, seventeenth-century physicist and mathematician known for formulating the laws of gravity and light and for inventing calculus.

Reacting to the Reading

1. Preview the essay. As you read it more carefully, highlight and annotate as needed to help you understand the writer's ideas.
2. Underline or star the cautions and warnings Baker provides for readers.

Reacting to Words

*1. Define these words: *sutures* (paragraph 2), *gingerly* (4), *encased* (4), *torso* (5), *execute* (5), *testy* (5), *chassis* (7). Can you suggest a synonym for each word that will work in the essay?
2. In paragraph 14, Baker uses *herself* to refer to *somebody*. What is your reaction to this pronoun use? What other options did Baker have? Why do you think he chose to use *herself?*

Reacting to Ideas

1. This essay is not intended to be taken seriously or followed exactly. How can you tell?
*2. List the steps in Baker's essay. Then, cross out all nonessential or humorous material. Are the instructions that remain logically ordered? Clear? Accurate?

Reacting to the Pattern

1. What stylistic signals tell you that this essay is a set of instructions and not an explanation of a process?
*2. Do you think the phrase "How to carve a turkey" is an adequate introduction for this essay? What other kind of introduction might Baker have written?
3. Review the various cautions and warnings that you identified in Reacting to the Reading question 2. Are they all necessary? Explain.

Writing Practice

1. Write a new introductory paragraph for this essay. Then, turn Baker's instructions into a straightforward process explanation, deleting any material you consider irrelevant to your purpose. Be sure to include all necessary articles *(a, an, the)* and transitions.
2. List the steps in a recipe for preparing one of your favorite dishes. Then, expand your recipe into an essay, adding transitions and cautions and reminders. Finally, add opening and closing paragraphs that describe the finished product and tell readers why the dish is worth preparing.
3. Write an essay that explains to your fellow students how you juggle the demands of family, work, and school in a typical day. Organize your essay either as a process explanation or as a set of instructions.

INDELIBLE MARKS

Joyce Howe

Joyce Howe grew up in Queens, New York, in a neighborhood where everyone knew her father as "the man who ran the Chinese laundry." As his daughter, she had mixed feelings about his occupation and felt ashamed that she lived with her parents and sisters behind the store and helped in the laundry business. In this passage from a 1983 essay, she explains the process by which laundry was sorted, washed, dried, starched, ironed, folded, and wrapped. As you read, try to get a sense of what the process meant to Howe.

In Queens, on the block where we moved, my father was known as the man who ran the Chinese laundry, like Ernie who ran the deli, Benny the upholsterer, and the butcher a few doors down. To all of his customers he was Joe. And they—middle-aged housewives, young bachelors and students, mainly white—were known to him by a first name or by the unique indelible "mark" on their collars and hems. (This "mark," consisting of one or more characters, was written on each item for the duration of a customer's patronage; if he switched laundries, the new establishment usually did not bother changing it.) With all of them, as tickets, laundry bills, and change passed from hand to hand over the wide counter, my father exchanged comments: "Too much of this rain, huh?," "Yeah, the Mets looked lousy last night," or "How's the wife and the kids?"

Saturday was his busiest day. It was not only the day more customers came in and out, but it was also one of the three days on which the long and tedious job of laundry-sorting was done. The entire floor of the store became a dumping ground for soiled clothes. My father divided the laundry into piles: 10 to 15 sheets and pillowcases were bundled up into one sheet and the ticket stubs of the customers whose laundry made up the bundle were then stapled together and put aside for later identification. "Wet items," such as towels, underwear, and socks, were separated into two categories—light and dark; shirts were separated into four categories—colored, white, starch, and no starch. Each pile of "wet items" and shirts was then placed in a laundry bag with its respective tag.

The bags and bundles were picked up Sunday morning by the truck drivers, who had names like Rocky and Louie, from the wholesale laundry or "wet wash" contracted by my father. ("Hand laundry" has been a misnomer since the late 1930s and '40s, when a whole new industry of Chinese-operated wholesale laundries and pressing concerns sprang up and contracted to do the actual washing and pressing for laundrymen.) Every Sunday, we were awakened from our sleep by the sound of the drivers' keys turning in the front door's locks.

When the "wet wash" drivers returned Monday with the previous day's load, the sheets and pillowcases, or "flat pieces," were wrapped in a heavy brown paper which my mother later would use for tablecloths. The shirts returned in the same bags they went out in. My father pulled out the bag of shirts to be starched and hand-ironed, leaving the rest for the shirt-press truck to pick up that night. On Tuesday night, they returned—clean, pressed, folded—in large square cardboard boxes, each shirt ringed in its own pale blue paper band.

For a short time, we had our own automatic dryer to take care of the damp "wet items" when they returned. After it broke down, irreparably, the dryer retired, and was left to hold stacks of comic books and board games. My sisters and I took turns making pilgrimages to the local laundromat, our metal shopping cart bent from the weight of the load. We wheeled those three blocks three times a week. On my turn, I always hoped that no one I knew would see me as I struggled with two hands to keep laundry and cart intact when maneuvering the high curbs. Even then, the irony of going from the laundry to the laundromat was not lost. 5

Of course, there were days when the system was off, when the shirt press might return its load late, or when my father didn't feel well enough to wrap every package. On those days, we were all expected to help. We made sure that the promise my father had made to customers on Saturday that their shirts would be ready by Wednesday was kept. Behind the tan curtain drawn across our plate-glass window every evening at seven and the door's pulled venetian blind, we settled into a tableau. My family formed a late-night assembly line, each member taking his place amid the shelves, boxes, white cones of string, rolls of wrapping paper, and the familiar fragrance of newly laundered cloth. 6

Reacting to the Reading

1. Preview the essay. As you read it more carefully, highlight and annotate as needed to help you understand the writer's ideas.
2. In the margins of the essay, number the steps in the process that is presented in paragraphs 2 through 6.

Reacting to Words

*1. Define these words: *indelible* (paragraph 1), *duration* (1), *patronage* (1), *tedious* (2), *irreparably* (5), *pilgrimages* (5), *tableau* (6). Can you suggest a synonym for each word that will work in the essay?
2. Howe's father makes a "unique indelible 'mark'" (paragraph 1) on the collars of each customer's shirts. Where else does he make an indelible mark?

Reacting to Ideas

1. What does Howe achieve by describing this process?
2. Do you think Howe's memories of her childhood as the laundryman's daughter are largely positive or negative? Support your position with specific examples.

Reacting to the Pattern

1. Is this essay a set of instructions or an explanation of how a process is performed? How can you tell?

*2. Using the numbers you wrote in the margins for Reacting to the Reading question 2 as a guide, list the individual steps in the process Howe describes. Does the process vary at all, or is it always the same?

Writing Practice

1. Write a process essay explaining the daily routine you follow in a job you hold (or held). Include a thesis statement that tells readers how you feel about the job.

2. Write a process essay in which you tell how to perform a particular task at a job—for example, how to keep a potential customer on the phone during a sales call, how to clean a deep-fat fryer, or how to set up the housekeeping corner at a day-care center.

3. Write a process essay in which you take readers through the stages of a successful job search. In your conclusion, identify the job you found.

E   Cause and Effect

A **cause-and-effect** essay identifies causes or predicts effects; sometimes it does both. In "The 'Black Table' Is Still There," Lawrence Otis Graham focuses on a troubling situation from his junior high school days. In "Who Killed the Bog Men of Denmark? And Why?" Maurice Shadbolt unravels a two-thousand-year-old mystery.

For more on how to write a cause-and-effect essay, see 14E.

THE "BLACK TABLE" IS STILL THERE

Lawrence Otis Graham

A corporate lawyer and best-selling author, Graham is best known for "Invisible Man," an article he wrote about the racism he encountered while working as a busboy at an exclusive country club during a leave from his job as a lawyer. In the following 1991 essay, Graham reflects on the "black table," a situation that has continued in the school cafeteria since his junior high days. As you read, note how his conclusions about what motivates people to sit where they sit have changed over the years.

During a recent visit to my old junior high school in Westchester County,   1
I came upon something that I never expected to see again, something that was

a source of fear and dread for three hours each school morning of my early adolescence: the all-black lunch table in the cafeteria of my predominantly white suburban junior high school.

As I look back on 27 years of often being the first and only black person integrating such activities and institutions as the college newspaper, the high school tennis team, summer music camps, our all-white suburban neighborhood, my eating club at Princeton or my private social club at Harvard Law School, the one scenario that puzzled me the most then and now is the all-black lunch table.

Why was it there? Why did the black kids separate themselves? What did the table say about the integration that was supposedly going on in home rooms and gym classes? What did it say about the black kids? The white kids? What did it say about me when I refused to sit there, day after day, for three years?

Each afternoon, at 12:03 p.m., after the fourth period ended, I found myself among 600 12-, 13- and 14-year-olds who marched into the brightly lit cafeteria and dashed for a seat at one of the 27 blue formica lunch tables.

No matter who I walked in with—usually a white friend—no matter what mood I was in, there was one thing that was certain: I would not sit at the black table.

I would never consider sitting at the black table.

What was wrong with me? What was I afraid of?

I would like to think that my decision was a heroic one, made in order to express my solidarity with the theories of integration that my community was espousing. But I was just 12 at the time, and there was nothing heroic in my actions.

I avoided the black table for a very simple reason: I was afraid that by sitting at the black table I'd lose all my white friends. I thought that by sitting there I'd be making a racist, anti-white statement.

Is that what the all-black table means? Is it a rejection of white people? I no longer think so.

At the time, I was angry that there was a black lunch table. I believed that the black kids were the reason why other kids didn't mix more. I was ready to believe that their self-segregation was the cause of white bigotry.

Ironically, I even believed this after my best friend (who was white) told me I probably shouldn't come to his bar mitzvah because I'd be the only black and people would feel uncomfortable. I even believed this after my Saturday afternoon visit, at age 10, to a private country club pool prompted incensed white parents to pull their kids from the pool in terror.

In the face of this blatantly racist (anti-black) behavior, I still somehow managed to blame only the black kids for being the barrier to integration in my school and my little world. What was I thinking?

I realize now how wrong I was. During that same time, there were at least two tables of athletes, an Italian table, a Jewish girls' table, a Jewish boys' table (where I usually sat), a table of kids who were into heavy metal music and smoking pot, a table of middle class Irish kids. Weren't these tables just as segregationist as the black table? At the time, no one thought so. At the time, no one even acknowledged the segregated nature of these other tables.

Maybe it's the color difference that makes all-black tables or all-black   15
groups attract the scrutiny and wrath of so many people. It scares and angers
people; it exasperates. It did those things to me, and I'm black.

As an integrating black person, I know that my decision *not* to join the   16
black lunch table attracted its own kind of scrutiny and wrath from my classmates. At the same time that I heard angry words like "Oreo" and "white boy"
being hurled at me from the black table, I was also dodging impatient questions from white classmates: "Why do all those black kids sit together?" or
"Why don't you ever sit with the other blacks?"

The black lunch table, like those other segregated tables, is a comment on   17
the superficial inroads that integration has made in society. Perhaps I should
be happy that even this is a long way from where we started. Yet, I can't get
over the fact that the 27th table in my junior high school cafeteria is still
known as the "black table"—14 years after my adolescence.

Reacting to the Reading

1. Preview the essay. As you read it more carefully, highlight and annotate as
   needed to help you understand the writer's ideas.
2. Graham asks a number of questions in this essay—for example, in paragraph 3 and in paragraph 7. In marginal annotations, answer two or three
   of these questions.

Reacting to Words

*1. Define these words: *scenario* (paragraph 2), *espousing* (8), *bar mitzvah*
   (12), *incensed* (12), *blatantly* (13), *scrutiny* (15), *wrath* (15), *inroads* (17).
   Can you suggest a synonym for each word that will work in the essay?
2. What images does the phrase *black table* bring to mind? Does it have
   positive or negative connotations to you? Can you think of another term
   Graham might use to identify the black table?

Reacting to Ideas

*1. Why didn't Graham sit at the black table? Do you understand the forces
   that motivated him? Do you think he should have sat with the other
   African-American students?
2. When he was in junior high school, who did Graham think was at fault for
   the existence of the black table? Who does he now think was at fault? Do
   you agree with him?
3. In paragraph 14, Graham considers other lunch tables and asks, "Weren't
   these tables just as segregationist as the black table?" Answer his question.

Reacting to the Pattern

1. Is Graham's essay primarily about causes or about effects? Explain your
   answer.

*2. Graham focuses largely on his own experiences and actions. Where, if anywhere, does he consider other forces that could have created segregated lunch tables? Do you think he should have considered other causes? For example, should he have discussed the school administration's role? Housing patterns in his community? Explain your position.

Writing Practice

1. Graham's essay, written in 1991, describes his adolescence fourteen years earlier (1977). Try to recall the lunch tables in the cafeteria of your own junior high school or middle school. Were they segregated as they were in Graham's school? What factors do you believe led students to sit where they did? Write a cause-and-effect essay that discusses the possible causes of the seating patterns you remember.

2. What do you see as the *effects* of segregated lunch tables? Do you think they are necessarily a bad thing, or do they have advantages? Write a cause-and-effect essay that explores the possible results of such seating patterns.

3. What kinds of self-segregation (by race, gender, class, and so on) do you observe in your school, workplace, or community? In an essay, discuss both causes and effects.

WHO KILLED THE BOG MEN OF DENMARK? AND WHY?

Maurice Shadbolt

Maurice Shadbolt has published memoirs, short stories, plays, and historical novels, many of which center on family history and the local culture of his native New Zealand. His nearly fifty-year career as a writer began in 1959 with the publication of *The New Zealanders*, a collection of short stories, shortly after which he emigrated to Europe. His most recent books include *Selected Stories* (1998) and *From the Edge of the Sky* (1999), a memoir. In the following essay, note how Shadbolt works backward from the finding of the bog men to the cause of their deaths as discovered by the Højgaard brothers.

Every year in the Danish town of Silkeborg, thousands of visitors file past the face of a murder victim. No one will ever know his name. It is enough to know that 2000 years ago he was as human as ourselves. That face has moved men and women to poetry, and to tears.   1

Last summer I journeyed to the lake-girt Danish town and, peering at that face behind glass in a modest museum, I felt awe—for his every wrinkle and whisker tell a vivid and terrible tale from Denmark's distant past. The rope which choked off the man's breath is still around his neck. Yet it is a perplexingly peaceful face, inscrutable, one to haunt the imagination.   2

This strangest of ancient murder mysteries began . . . on May 8, 1950, when two brothers, Emil and Viggo Højgaard, were digging peat in Tollund   3

35 E

Shadbolt • Who Killed the Bog Men of Denmark? And Why?   **575**

Fen, near Silkeborg. Their spring sowing finished, the brothers were storing up the umber-brown peat for their kitchen range, and for warmth in the winter to come. It was a peaceful task on a sunny morning. Snipe called from the aspens and firs fringing the dank bowl of the fen, where only heather and coarse grass grew. Then, at a depth of nine feet, their spades suddenly struck something.

They were gazing, with fright and fascination, at a face underfoot. The corpse was naked but for a skin cap, resting on its side as if asleep, arms and legs bent. The face was gentle, with eyes closed and lips lightly pursed. There was stubble on the chin. The bewildered brothers called the Silkeborg police.   4

Quick to the scene, the police did not recognize the man as anyone listed missing. Shrewdly guessing the brothers might have blundered into a black hole in Europe's past, the police called in archeologists.   5

Enter Prof. Peter Glob, a distinguished scholar from nearby Aarhus University, who carefully dislodged a lump of peat from beside the dead man's head. A rope made of two twisted hide thongs encircled his neck. He had been strangled or hanged. But when, and by whom? Glob ordered a box to be built about the corpse and the peat in which it lay, so nothing might be disturbed.   6

Next day, the box, weighing nearly a ton, was manhandled out of the bog onto a horse-drawn cart, on its way for examination at Copenhagen's National Museum. One of Glob's helpers collapsed and died with the huge effort. It seemed a dark omen, as if some old god were claiming a modern man in place of a man from the past.   7

Bog bodies were nothing new—since records have been kept, Denmark's bogs have surrendered no fewer than 400—and the preservative qualities of the humic acid in peat have long been known. But not until the 19th century did scientists and historians begin to glimpse the finds and understand that the bodies belonged to remote, murky recesses of European prehistory. None survived long: the corpses were either buried again or crumbled quickly with exposure to light and air.   8

When peat-digging was revived during and after World War II, bodies were unearthed in abundance—first in 1942 at Store Arden, then in 1946, 1947 and 1948 at Borre Fen. Artifacts found beside them positively identified them as people of Denmark's Early Iron Age, from 400 B.C. to A.D. 400. None, then, was less than 1500 years old, and some were probably much older. The first of the Borre Fen finds—a full-grown male—was to prove especially significant: Borre Fen man, too, had died violently, with a noose about his neck, strangled or hanged. And his last meal had consisted of grain.   9

Peter Glob, alongside his artist father (a portraitist and distinguished amateur archeologist), had been digging into Denmark's dim past since he was a mere eight years old. For him, the Tollund man, who had by far the best-preserved head to survive from antiquity, was a supreme challenge. Since 1936, Glob had been living imaginatively with the pagan hunters and farmers of 2000 years ago, fossicking[1] among their corroded artifacts, foraging among   10

1. (Australian and New Zealand English) Searching for by picking through or rummaging.

the foundations of their simple villages; he knew their habits, the rhythms of their lives. Suddenly, here was a man of that very time. "Majesty and gentleness," he recalls, "seemed to stamp his features as they did when he was alive." What was this enigmatic face trying to tell him?

Glob was intrigued by the fact that so many of the people found in bogs 11 had died violently: strangled or hanged, throats slit, heads battered. Perhaps they had been travelers set upon by brigands, or executed criminals. But there might be a different explanation. These murder victims all belonged to the Danish Iron Age. If they were to be explained away as victims of robber bands, there should be a much greater spread in time—into other ages. Nor would executed criminals all have had so many common traits.

Glob considered the body with care. X rays of Tollund man's vertebrae, 12 taken to determine whether he had been strangled or hanged, produced inconclusive results. The condition of the wisdom teeth suggested a man well over 20 years old. An autopsy revealed that the heart, lungs and liver were well preserved; most important, the alimentary canal was undisturbed, containing the dead man's last meal—a 2000-year-old gruel of hand-milled grains and seeds: barley, linseed, flaxseed, knotgrass, among others. Knowledge of prehistoric agriculture made it possible to determine that the man had lived in the first 200 years A.D. The mixture of grains and seeds suggested a meal prepared in winter or early spring.

Since Iron Age men were not vegetarians, why were there no traces of 13 meat? Glob also marveled that the man's hands and feet were soft; he appeared to have done little or no heavy labor in his lifetime. Possibly, then, he was high-ranking in Iron Age society.

Then, on April 26, 1952, peat-digging villagers from Grauballe, 11 miles 14 east of Tollund, turned up a second spectacularly well-preserved body, and again Glob was fast to the scene. Unmistakably another murder victim, this discovery was, unlike Tollund man, far from serene. The man's throat had been slashed savagely from ear to ear. His face was twisted with terror, and his lips were parted with a centuries-silenced cry of pain.

Glob swiftly removed the body—still imbedded in a great block of 15 peat—for preservation and study. Carbon-dating of body tissue proved Grauballe man to be about 1650 years old, a contemporary of Constantine the Great. Grauballe man was in extraordinary condition: his fingerprints and footprints came up clearly. Tallish and dark-haired, Grauballe man, like Tollund man, had never done any heavy manual work. He had been slain in his late 30s. Another similarity came to light when Grauballe man's last meal was analyzed: it had been eaten immediately before death and like Tollund man's, like Borre Fen man's too, it was a gruel of grains and seeds, a meal of winter, or early spring. All three had perished in a similar season.

Who had killed these men of the bogs? Why in winter, or early spring? 16 Why should they—apparently—have led privileged lives? And why the same kind of meals before their sudden ends?

The bodies had told Glob all they could. Now he turned to one of his favorite 17 sources—the Roman historian Tacitus. Nearly 2000 years ago Tacitus recorded

35 E

Shadbolt • Who Killed the Bog Men of Denmark? And Why?   **577**

the oral traditions of Germanic tribes who inhabited northwest Europe. Tacitus' account of these wild, brave and generous blue-eyed people often shed light into dark corners of Denmark's past. Glob found these lines: "At a time laid down in the distant past, all peoples that are related by blood meet in a sacred wood. Here they celebrate their barbarous rites with a human sacrifice."

Elsewhere, Tacitus wrote: "These people are distinguished by a common worship of Nerthus, or Mother Earth. They believe that she interests herself in human affairs." Tacitus confirmed early spring as a time among the Germanic tribes for offerings and human sacrifice. They were asking the goddess to hasten the coming of spring, and the summer harvest. Men chosen for sacrifice might well have been given a symbolic meal, made up of plant seeds, before being consecrated through death to the goddess—thus explaining the absence of meat. The sacrificial men, with their delicate features, neat hands and feet, might have been persons of high rank chosen by lot for sacrifice, or priests, ritually married to Nerthus. 18

Tacitus supplied another essential clue: the symbol of Nerthus, he recorded, was a twisted metal "torque," or neck ring, worn by the living to honor the goddess. The leather nooses about the necks of Tollund man and the body from Borre Fen and some earlier bodies were replicas of those neck rings. Glob concluded that it was Nerthus—Mother Earth herself—who had preserved her victims perfectly in her peaty bosom long after those who had fed them into the bogs were dust. 19

Peter Glob was satisfied. He had found the killer and identified the victims. The centuries-old mystery of Denmark's bog bodies was no more. 20

Reacting to the Reading

1. Preview the essay. As you read it more carefully, highlight and annotate as needed to help you understand the writer's ideas.
2. Circle all the adjectives used to describe the bog man found by the Højgaard brothers.

Reacting to Words

*1. Define these words: *bog* (title), *perplexingly* (paragraph 2), *sowing* (3), *peat* (3), *fen* (3), *manhandled* (7), *murky* (8), *antiquity* (10), *pagan* (10), *brigands* (11). Can you suggest a synonym for each word that will work in the essay?
2. Review the adjectives used to describe the man discovered by the Højgaards. How do these words shape your reaction to him?

Reacting to Ideas

*1. Why do you think the face of the anonymous man found in the bog "has moved men and women to poetry, and to tears" (paragraph 1)?
2. Why does Shadbolt give readers so much information about Peter Glob and his role in the investigation? How would the essay be different without this information?

*3. Why do you suppose the "strangest of ancient murder mysteries" (paragraph 3) still might be of interest to modern readers?

Reacting to the Pattern

*1. Identify at least one *result* (or *effect*) of each of the following: the Højgaard brothers find a body; the box containing the body is moved; peat digging is revived after World War II.

*2. Identify at least one *cause* of each of the following: the man's hands and feet are soft; his last meal was grain; he died a violent death; he has a rope around his neck.

3. Is this essay's emphasis on causes, on effects, or on both causes and effects? Explain.

Writing Practice

1. Write a biography of the man the Højgaard brothers found, including an explanation of why he died. You may give the man a name and invent people and events.

2. Write an article for the Silkeborg daily newspaper in which you discuss the effect on the townspeople of the discovery of the bog man.

3. Write an essay that solves a "mystery" in your own life. For example, explain the causes of a friend's surprising actions or the reasons why your family settled where it did years (or generations) ago.

F Comparison and Contrast

For more on how to write a comparison-and-contrast essay, see 14F.

A **comparison-and-contrast** essay explains how two things are alike or how they are different; sometimes it discusses both similarities and differences. In "Words and People," linguist Richard Lederer compares the two items in his essay's title. In "Men Are from Mars, Women Are from Venus," John Gray compares men and women.

WORDS AND PEOPLE

Richard Lederer

After a twenty-seven-year teaching career, Richard Lederer earned a Ph.D. in English and Linguistics and began writing books and articles on the popular use and abuse of the English language. His books include *Anguished English* (1989), *Fractured English* (1996), and *The Miracle of Language* (1999); his weekly column, "Looking at Language," appears in newspapers and magazines across the country. He cohosts the National

Public Radio show *A Way with Words,* an on-air forum about issues of language ranging from pronunciation to puns. In the following essay, note all the different ways Lederer compares words with people.

Has it ever struck you how human words are?

Like people, words are born, grow up, get married, have children, and even die. They may be very old, like *man* and *wife* and *home.* They may be very young, like *veggies* and *househusband.* They may be newly born and struggling to live, as *netiquette, gangsta rap,* and *political correctness.* Or they may repose in the tomb of history, as *leechcraft,* the Anglo-Saxon word for the practice of medicine, and *murfles,* a long-defunct word for freckles or pimples.

Our lives are filled with people and words, and in both cases we are bound to be impressed with their vast numbers and infinite variety. Some words, like *OK,* are famous all over the world. Others, like *foozle* (a bungling golf stroke) and *groak* (to stare at other people's food, hoping that they will offer you some), are scarcely known, even at home.

There are some words that we will probably never meet, such as *schizocarps* (pinwheels that grow on maple trees) and *vomer* (the slender bone separating the nostrils), and others that are with us every day of our lives, such as *I, the, and, to,* and *of,* the five most frequently used English words.

As with people, words have all sorts of shapes, sizes, backgrounds, and personalities. They may be very large, like *pneumonoultramicroscopicsilicovolcaniosis,* a forty-one-letter *hippopotomonstrosesquipedalian* word for black lung disease. They may be very small, like *a* and *I.*

Some words are multinational in their heritage, as *remacadamize,* which is Latin, Celtic, Hebrew, and Greek in parentage. Some come of Old English stock, as *sun* and *moon* and *grass* and *goodness.* Some have a distinctly continental flavor—*kindergarten, lingerie, spaghetti.* Others are unmistakably American—*stunt* and *baseball.*

Words, like people, go up and down in the world. Some are born into low station and come up in life. With the passing of time, they may acquire *prestige* (which used to mean "trickery") and *glamour* (which began life as a synonym for "grammar"). Others slide downhill in reputation, such as *homely* (which originally meant "homelike, good around the home"), *awful* ("awe-inspiring"), and *idiot* ("one who did not hold public office").

Words like *remunerative, encomium,* and *perspicacious* are so dignified that they can intimidate us, whereas others, like *booze, burp,* and *blubber,* are markedly inelegant in character. Some words, such as *ecdysiast,* H. L. Mencken's Greek-derived name for a stripteaser, love to put on fancy airs; others, like *vidiot* and *palimony,* are winkingly playful. Certain words strike us as beautiful, like *luminous* and *gossamer,* others as rather ugly—*guzzle* and *scrod;* some as quiet—*dawn* and *dusk,* others as noisy—*thunder* and *crash.*

That words and people so resemble each other should come as no surprise. Words and people were created at the same time. Before language found a home in the mouths of humans, it was not fully language; before we possessed language, we were not fully human. Not only do we have language. We *are* language.

Reacting to the Reading

1. Preview the essay. As you read it more carefully, highlight and annotate as needed to help you understand the writer's ideas.
2. Number the similarities between words and people that Lederer identifies. (Note that in some paragraphs, he discusses more than one similarity.)

Reacting to Words

*1. Define these words: *repose* (paragraph 2), *defunct* (2), *multinational* (6), *stock* (6), *station* (7), *markedly* (8). Can you suggest a synonym for each word that will work in the essay?
2. Choose five unfamiliar words from those that Lederer uses as examples, and look them up in a dictionary. Then, use each word in a sentence.
*3. Give several additional examples for each kind of word Lederer discusses.

Reacting to Ideas

1. In your own words, list all the similarities Lederer identifies between words and people. Try to use complete sentences—for example, "Both words and people can be either famous or unknown."
2. Although Lederer is comparing words and people, all his examples are words. Why do you suppose he does not give examples of people to illustrate his parallels? Do you think he *should* have supplied examples of people? Explain.
*3. Supply an example of a person who corresponds to each kind of word Lederer discusses.

Reacting to the Pattern

1. Is Lederer's opening strategy of beginning his essay with a question effective? Why or why not? How might the opening paragraph be expanded?

For more on point-by-point and subject-by-subject comparison, see 14F.

2. Is this a subject-by-subject or a point-by-point comparison? Explain.
*3. Can you think of any similarities between words and people that Lederer does not list? Give examples of both words and people to make the similarities clear.

Writing Practice

1. Choose one paragraph of Lederer's essay, and expand it into an essay. Use his topic sentence as your thesis statement, and add examples to support it. (If Lederer does not include a clear topic sentence, write a new one.)
2. Find an unfamiliar word in the dictionary, and use its definition to help you write the word's biography, tracing the story of its different usages. Then, compare the word to a person you know—or to a famous person.

MEN ARE FROM MARS, WOMEN ARE FROM VENUS

John Gray

Marriage counselor, seminar leader, and author John Gray has written a number of books that examine relationships between men and women. His best-known book, *Men Are from Mars, Women Are from Venus* (1992), uses a two-planet model to show how, in his view, men and women are at times so different that they might as well come from different planets. In the following excerpt from this book, Gray contrasts the different communication styles that he believes are characteristic of men and women. As you read, consider whether Gray's comparison oversimplifies the gender differences he discusses.

1
The most frequently expressed complaint women have about men is that men don't listen. Either a man completely ignores [a woman] when she speaks to him, or he listens for a few beats, assesses what is bothering her, and then proudly puts on his Mr. Fix-It cap and offers her a solution to make her feel better. He is confused when she doesn't appreciate this gesture of love. No matter how many times she tells him that he's not listening, he doesn't get it and keeps doing the same thing. She wants empathy, but he thinks she wants solutions.

2
The most frequently expressed complaint men have about women is that women are always trying to change them. When a woman loves a man she feels responsible to assist him in growing and tries to help him improve the way he does things. She forms a home-improvement committee, and he becomes her primary focus. No matter how much he resists her help, she persists—waiting for any opportunity to help him or tell him what to do. She thinks she's nurturing him, while he feels he's being controlled. Instead, he wants her acceptance.

3
These two problems can finally be solved by first understanding why men offer solutions and why women seek to improve. Let's pretend to go back in time, where by observing life on Mars and Venus—before the planets discovered one another or came to Earth—we can gain some insights into men and women.

4
Martians value power, competency, efficiency, and achievement. They are always doing things to prove themselves and develop their power and skills. Their sense of self is defined through their ability to achieve results. They experience fulfillment primarily through success and accomplishment.

5
Everything on Mars is a reflection of these values. Even their dress is designed to reflect their skills and competence. Police officers, soldiers, businessmen, scientists, cab drivers, technicians, and chefs all wear uniforms or at least hats to reflect their competence and power.

6
They don't read magazines like *Psychology Today, Self,* or *People.* They are more concerned with outdoor activities, like hunting, fishing, and racing cars. They are interested in the news, weather, and sports and couldn't care less about romance novels and self-help books.

They are more interested in "objects" and "things" rather than people and feelings. Even today on Earth, while women fantasize about romance, men fantasize about powerful cars, faster computers, gadgets, gizmos, and new more powerful technology. Men are preoccupied with the "things" that can help them express power by creating results and achieving their goals.   7

Achieving goals is very important to a Martian because it is a way for him to prove his competence and thus feel good about himself. And for him to feel good about himself he must achieve these goals by himself. Someone else can't achieve them for him. Martians pride themselves in doing things all by themselves. Autonomy is a symbol of efficiency, power, and competence.   8

Understanding this Martian characteristic can help women understand why men resist so much being corrected or being told what to do. To offer a man unsolicited advice is to presume that he doesn't know what to do or that he can't do it on his own. Men are very touchy about this, because the issue of competence is so very important to them.   9

Because he is handling his problems on his own, a Martian rarely talks about his problems unless he needs expert advice. He reasons: "Why involve someone else when I can do it by myself?" He keeps his problems to himself unless he requires help from another to find a solution. Asking for help when you can do it yourself is perceived as a sign of weakness.   10

However, if he truly does need help, then it is a sign of wisdom to get it. In this case, he will find someone he respects and then talk about his problem. Talking about a problem on Mars is an invitation for advice. Another Martian feels honored by the opportunity. Automatically he puts on his Mr. Fix-It hat, listens for a while, and then offers some jewels of advice.   11

This Martian custom is one of the reasons men instinctively offer solutions when women talk about problems. When a woman innocently shares upset feelings or explores out loud the problems of her day, a man mistakenly assumes she is looking for some expert advice. He puts on his Mr. Fix-It hat and begins giving advice; this is his way of showing love and of trying to help.   12

He wants to help her feel better by solving her problems. He wants to be useful to her. He feels he can be valued and thus worthy of her love when his abilities are used to solve her problems.   13

Once he has offered a solution, however, and she continues to be upset it becomes increasingly difficult for him to listen because his solution is being rejected and he feels increasingly useless.   14

He has no idea that by just listening with empathy and interest he can be supportive. He does not know that on Venus talking about problems is not an invitation to offer a solution.   15

Venusians have different values. They value love, communication, beauty, and relationships. They spend a lot of time supporting, helping, and nurturing one another. Their sense of self is defined through their feelings and the quality of their relationships. They experience fulfillment through sharing and relating.   16

Everything on Venus reflects these values. Rather than building highways and tall buildings, the Venusians are more concerned with living together in har-   17 mony, community, and loving cooperation. Relationships are more important than work and technology. In most ways their world is the opposite of Mars.

They do not wear uniforms like the Martians (to reveal their competence). 18
On the contrary, they enjoy wearing a different outfit every day, according to how they are feeling. Personal expression, especially of their feelings, is very important. They may even change outfits several times a day as their mood changes.

Communication is of primary importance. To share their personal feelings 19
is much more important than achieving goals and success. Talking and relating to one another is a source of tremendous fulfillment.

This is hard for a man to comprehend. He can come close to understand- 20
ing a woman's experience of sharing and relating by comparing it to the satisfaction he feels when he wins a race, achieves a goal, or solves a problem.

Instead of being goal oriented, women are relationship oriented; they are 21
more concerned with expressing their goodness, love, and caring. Two Martians go to lunch to discuss a project or business goal; they have a problem to solve. In addition, Martians view going to a restaurant as an efficient way to approach food: no shopping, no cooking, and no washing dishes. For Venusians, going to lunch is an opportunity to nurture a relationship, for both giving support to and receiving support from a friend. Women's restaurant talk can be very open and intimate, almost like the dialogue that occurs between therapist and patient.

On Venus, everyone studies psychology and has at least a master's degree 22
in counseling. They are very involved in personal growth, spirituality, and everything that can nurture life, healing, and growth. Venus is covered with parks, organic gardens, shopping centers, and restaurants.

Venusians are very intuitive. They have developed this ability through cen- 23
turies of anticipating the needs of others. They pride themselves in being considerate of the needs and feelings of others. A sign of great love is to offer help and assistance to another Venusian without being asked.

Because proving one's competence is not as important to a Venusian, 24
offering help is not offensive, and needing help is not a sign of weakness. A man, however, may feel offended because when a woman offers advice he doesn't feel she trusts his ability to do it himself.

A woman has no conception of this male sensitivity because for her it is 25
another feather in her hat if someone offers to help her. It makes her feel loved and cherished. But offering help to a man can make him feel incompetent, weak, and even unloved.

On Venus it is a sign of caring to give advice and suggestions. Venusians 26
firmly believe that when something is working it can always work better. Their nature is to want to improve things. When they care about someone, they freely point out what can be improved and suggest how to do it. Offering advice and constructive criticism is an act of love.

Mars is very different. Martians are more solution oriented. If something is 27
working, their motto is don't change it. Their instinct is to leave it alone if it is working. "Don't fix it unless it is broken" is a common expression.

When a woman tries to improve a man, he feels she is trying to fix him.   28
He receives the message that he is broken. She doesn't realize her caring
attempts to help him may humiliate him. She mistakenly thinks she is just
helping him to grow.

Reacting to the Reading

1. Preview the essay. As you read it more carefully, highlight and annotate as needed to help you understand the writer's ideas.
2. In marginal annotations, number the specific characteristics of men and women that Gray identifies. Then, make an outline for a point-by-point comparison.

Reacting to Words

*1. Define these words: *empathy* (paragraph 1), *nurturing* (2), *autonomy* (8), *unsolicited* (9). Can you suggest a synonym for each word that will work in the essay?
2. Do you think referring to men as Martians and women as Venusians is an effective strategy? What other contrasting labels might work?

Reacting to Ideas

*1. Do you think Gray is serious? What makes you think so?
*2. Do you think Gray's specific observations about men and women are accurate? Is he stereotyping men and women? Explain.
*3. Do you agree with Gray's general point that men and women seem to be from two different planets? Why or why not?

Reacting to the Pattern

1. This essay is a subject-by-subject comparison. How does Gray signal the movement from the first subject to the second subject? Why do you suppose he chose to write a subject-by-subject rather than a point-by-point comparison?
*2. If you were going to add a more fully developed conclusion to sum up this selection's points, what closing strategy would you use? Do you think the selection needs such a conclusion?

Writing Practice

1. Are young (or adolescent) boys and girls also from two different planets? Take a position on this issue, and support it in a subject-by-subject comparison. In your thesis statement, try to account for the differences you identify between boys and girls.
2. Identify one general area in which you believe men's and women's attitudes, behavior, or expectations are very different—for example, dating, careers, eating habits, sports, housekeeping, or driving. Write a

comparison-and-contrast essay (serious or humorous) that explores the differences you identify.

3. Are men and women portrayed differently in television dramas (including soap operas) and comedies? Choose a program that has several well-developed male and female characters, and contrast the men and the women in terms of their actions and their conversations.

G   Classification

A **classification** essay divides a whole into parts and sorts various items into categories. Jo-Ellan Dimitrius and Mark Mazzarella's "Liars" considers four different kinds of liars. Scott Russell Sanders's "The Men We Carry in Our Minds" classifies the working men he has known.

For more on how to write a classification essay, see 14G.

LIARS

Jo-Ellan Dimitrius and Mark Mazzarella

Los Angeles lawyer Jo-Ellan Dimitrius is a jury-consultant who worked on some of the best-known criminal trials of the 1980s and 1990s, including the Rodney King, O. J. Simpson, and Reginald Denny cases. In the last fifteen years, Dimitrius has worked in civil and criminal trials to assist lawyers in selecting juries and evaluating witnesses by predicting human behavior. Mark Mazzarella is a practicing trial lawyer in San Diego, California, who writes about the formation and management of impressions in juries. He and Dimitrius have cowritten *Put Your Best Foot Forward* (2000) and *Reading People* (1998). As you read, think about how Dimitrius and Mazzarella's classification of liars could be useful beyond the courtroom.

If people were all honest with one another, reading them would be a lot easier. The problem is that people lie. I'm not talking about those who are wrong but sincerely believe they are correct, or about the delusional few who genuinely can't tell fact from fantasy. Rather, I'm referring to the one characteristic that is probably the most important in any relationship: truthfulness. And if we assume it's there when it's not—watch out! 1

Much of the information we gather about someone comes directly from the horse's mouth. If he is lying, the information is wrong, and we're likely to misjudge him. That's why it's so crucial to identify liars as soon as possible, and, if you have reason to doubt a person's honesty, to continue to test it until you're entirely at ease with your conclusion. 2

I have found that most liars fall into one of four basic categories: the occasional liar, the frequent liar, the habitual liar, and the professional liar. 3

The Occasional Liar

The occasional liar, like most of us, will lie now and then to avoid an unpleasant situation or because he doesn't want to admit doing something wrong or embarrassing. Also like most of us, he does not like to lie and feels very uncomfortable when he does. Because he's uncomfortable, he'll usually reveal his lie through his appearance, body language, and voice. The stress lying causes him will leak out through such things as poor eye contact, fidgeting, or a change in the tone, volume, or patterns of his speech.   4

The occasional liar often gives his lie some thought, so it may be logical and consistent with the rest of his story. Because it's well thought out, you probably won't be able to spot the lie by its content or context, or by information from third-party sources. In fact, the occasional liar will seldom lie about something that could be easily verified. Consequently, when dealing with an occasional liar, you need to focus on the various visual and oral clues he exhibits.   5

The Frequent Liar

The frequent liar recognizes what she's doing but doesn't mind it as much as the occasional liar does, so she lies more regularly. Practice makes perfect: the frequent liar is much less likely to reveal her lie through her appearance, body language, and voice. Also, since it doesn't bother her as much to lie, the typical stress-related symptoms won't be as obvious. Any clues in her appearance, voice, and body language might be rather subtle. Often a better way to detect a frequent liar is to focus on the internal consistency and logic of her statements. Since the frequent liar lies more often, and tends to think her lies through less carefully than the occasional liar, she can get sloppy.   6

The Habitual Liar

The habitual liar lies so frequently that he has lost sight of what he is doing much of the time. In most cases, if he actually thought about it, he would realize he was lying. But he doesn't much care whether what he's saying is true or false. He simply says whatever comes to mind. Because he doesn't care that he's lying, the habitual liar will give very few, if any, physical or vocal clues that he's being dishonest. But because he gives so little thought to his lies and they come so thick and fast, the habitual liar doesn't bother to keep track of them. As a result they are often inconsistent and obvious. So while it's hard to detect the physical and vocal clues in a habitual liar, it's easier to spot his inconsistencies. Listen carefully and ask yourself whether the liar is contradicting himself and whether what he's saying makes sense. Asking a third party about the liar's stories will also help you confirm your suspicions.   7

The habitual liar is fairly uncommon, so most of us are temporarily taken in when we encounter one. An acquaintance of mine told me she worked with   8 a woman for several months before her suspicions that the co-worker was a habitual liar were confirmed by an obvious and quite ridiculous lie. The liar, a brown-eyed brunette, came to work one day sporting blue contact lenses of an almost alien hue. When my friend commented on her lenses, the liar said, "These aren't contacts. They're my real eye color. It's just that I've always worn brown contact lenses before."

More than once, a client has told me that his adversary lies all the time   9 and will undoubtedly lie on the witness stand. I counsel my client not to worry: the habitual liar is the easiest target in a lawsuit. In real life, she can run from one person to another, from one situation to the next, lying as she goes, and no one compares notes. There are no court reporters or transcripts of testimony; no one reveals what every witness has said to every other witness, and nobody pores over everything the liar has written on the subject to see whether it's all consistent. But in litigation, that is exactly what happens — and suddenly the habitual liar is exposed. It's very rewarding to see.

The Professional Liar

The professional liar is the hardest to identify. He doesn't lie indiscriminately,   10 like the habitual liar. He lies for a purpose. For example, a mechanic who routinely cons motorists about their "faulty" transmissions will have his diagnosis carefully prepared. A real estate salesman who doesn't want to acknowledge a leaky roof will respond quickly to an inquiry about the stains on the ceiling with a rehearsed, very spontaneous sounding statement: "That was old damage from a water leak in the attic. All it needs is a little touch-up paint."

The professional liar has thought the lie through and knows exactly what   11 he's going to say, how it will fly, and whether the customer can easily verify it. Such a well-practiced lie will not be revealed by the liar's voice, body language, or appearance. The lie will be consistent, both internally and logically. The only sure way to detect it is to check the liar's statements against entirely independent sources. Have the roof inspected. Get a second opinion from another mechanic. Take nothing for granted.

Before you make a definitive call about someone who is truly important to   12 you, always ask yourself whether the information you have about him is reliable. Is he being truthful? If your goal is to accurately evaluate someone, you can't afford to skip this step.

Reacting to the Reading

1. Preview the essay. As you read it more carefully, highlight and annotate as needed to help you understand the writer's ideas.
2. In the margins of the essay, write a one-sentence definition of each of the four categories of liar the writers discuss. Be sure to use your own words for the definitions.

Reacting to Words

*1. Define these words: *delusional* (paragraph 1), *crucial* (2), *context* (5), *verified* (5), *adversary* (9), *pores* (9), *litigation* (9). Can you suggest a synonym for each word that will work in the essay?

2. When referring to the different types of liars, the writers alternate the pronouns *he* and *she*. Why do you think they do this? Do you find it confusing? What other alternatives do they have?

Reacting to Ideas

1. According to the authors, why is it so important to identify liars?

*2. Which kind of liar do you see as most dangerous? Why?

*3. Do you think a lie is ever acceptable? Explain.

Reacting to the Pattern

1. What determines the order in which the four kinds of liars are presented? Does this arrangement make sense to you?

2. The writers devote considerably more space to the "habitual liar" and the "professional liar" than to the other two kinds. What material do they include for these two categories and not for the other two? Why do you think they do this?

Writing Practice

1. Write an essay about the different kinds of lies told by "occasional liars." Be sure to include at least three different categories.

2. Using "Liars" as a model, write a classification essay that discusses three or four categories of cheaters. Give each category a name.

3. Write a classification essay about different kinds of heroes. In setting up your categories, consider what motivates people to perform heroic acts.

THE MEN WE CARRY IN OUR MINDS

Scott Russell Sanders

Scott Russell Sanders is a professor of English and an essayist. His essays are personal reflections that include social commentary and philosophical reflection and are often set in the Midwest, where he was born and raised. In "The Men We Carry in Our Minds," Sanders reflects on the working lives of the men he knew when he was a boy and classifies them according to their work. His essay discusses not only his boyhood impressions of the work these men did but also the direction his own professional life has taken. As you read, notice how Sanders moves from classifying men's work to comparing men's lives to women's lives.

The first men, besides my father, I remember seeing were black convicts and white guards, in the cottonfield across the road from our farm on the outskirts of Memphis. I must have been three or four. The prisoners wore dingy gray-and-black zebra suits, heavy as canvas, sodden with sweat. Hatless, stooped, they chopped weeds in the fierce heat, row after row, breathing the acrid dust of boll-weevil poison. The overseers wore dazzling white shirts and broad shadowy hats. The oiled barrels of their shotguns flashed in the sunlight. Their faces in memory are utterly blank. Of course those men, white and black, have become for me an emblem of racial hatred. But they have also come to stand for the twin poles of my early vision of manhood—the brute toiling animal and the boss.

When I was a boy, the men I knew labored with their bodies. They were marginal farmers, just scraping by, or welders, steelworkers, carpenters; they swept floors, dug ditches, mined coal, or drove trucks, their forearms ropy with muscle; they trained horses, stoked furnaces, built tires, stood on assembly lines wrestling parts onto cars and refrigerators. They got up before light, worked all day long whatever the weather, and when they came home at night they looked as though somebody had been whipping them. In the evenings and on weekends they worked on their own places, tilling gardens that were lumpy with clay, fixing broken-down cars, hammering on houses that were always too drafty, too leaky, too small.

The bodies of the men I knew were twisted and maimed in ways visible and invisible. The nails of their hands were black and split, the hands tattooed with scars. Some had lost fingers. Heavy lifting had given many of them finicky backs and guts weak from hernias. Racing against conveyor belts had given them ulcers. Their ankles and knees ached from years of standing on concrete. Anyone who had worked for long around machines was hard of hearing. They squinted, and the skin of their faces was creased like the leather of old work gloves. There were times, studying them, when I dreaded growing up. Most of them coughed, from dust or cigarettes, and most of them drank cheap wine or whiskey, so their eyes looked bloodshot and bruised. The fathers of my friends always seemed older than the mothers. Men wore out sooner. Only women lived into old age.

As a boy I also knew another sort of men, who did not sweat and break down like mules. They were soldiers, and so far as I could tell they scarcely worked at all. During my early school years we lived on a military base, an arsenal in Ohio, and every day I saw GIs in the guardshacks, on the stoops of barracks, at the wheels of olive drab Chevrolets. The chief fact of their lives was boredom. Long after I left the Arsenal I came to recognize the sour smell the soldiers gave off as that of souls in limbo. They were all waiting—for wars, for transfers, for leaves, for promotions, for the end of their hitch—like so many braves waiting for the hunt to begin. Unlike the warriors of older tribes, however, they would have no say about when the battle would start or how it would be waged. Their waiting was broken only when they practiced for war. They fired guns at targets, drove tanks across the churned-up fields of the military reservation, set off bombs in the wrecks of old fighter planes. I knew this was all play. But I also felt certain that when the hour for killing arrived, they would kill. When the real shooting started, many of them would die. This was what soldiers were *for,* just as a hammer was for driving nails.

Warriors and toilers: those seemed, in my boyhood vision, to be the chief destinies for men. They weren't the only destinies, as I learned from having a few male teachers, from reading books, and from watching television. But the men on television—the politicians, the astronauts, the generals, the savvy lawyers, the philosophical doctors, the bosses who gave orders to both soldiers and laborers—seemed as removed and unreal to me as the figures in tapestries. I could no more imagine growing up to become one of these cool, potent creatures than I could imagine becoming a prince.

A nearer and more hopeful example was that of my father, who had escaped from a red-dirt farm to a tire factory, and from the assembly line to the front office. Eventually he dressed in a white shirt and tie. He carried himself as if he had been born to work with his mind. But his body, remembering the earlier years of slogging work, began to give out on him in his fifties, and it quit on him entirely before he turned sixty-five. Even such a partial escape from man's fate as he had accomplished did not seem possible for most of the boys I knew. They joined the Army, stood in line for jobs in the smoky plants, helped build highways. They were bound to work as their fathers had worked, killing themselves or preparing to kill others.

A scholarship enabled me not only to attend college, a rare enough feat in my circle, but even to study in a university meant for the children of the rich. Here I met for the first time young men who had assumed from birth that they would lead lives of comfort and power. And for the first time I met women who told me that men were guilty of having kept all the joys and privileges of the earth for themselves. I was baffled. What privileges? What joys? I thought about the maimed, dismal lives of most of the men back home. What had they stolen from their wives and daughters? The right to go five days a week, twelve months a year, for thirty or forty years to a steel mill or a coal mine? The right to drop bombs and die in war? The right to feel every leak in the roof, every gap in the fence, every cough in the engine, as a wound they must mend? The right to feel, when the lay-off comes or the plant shuts down, not only afraid but ashamed?

I was slow to understand the deep grievances of women. This was because, as a boy, I had envied them. Before college, the only people I had ever known who were interested in art or music or literature, the only ones who read books, the only ones who ever seemed to enjoy a sense of ease and grace were the mothers and daughters. Like the menfolk, they fretted about money, they scrimped and made-do. But, when the pay stopped coming in, they were not the ones who had failed. Nor did they have to go to war, and that seemed to me a blessed fact. By comparison with the narrow, ironclad days of fathers, there was an expansiveness, I thought, in the days of mothers. They went to see neighbors, to shop in town, to run errands at school, at the library, at church. No doubt, had I looked harder at their lives, I would have envied them less. It was not my fate to become a woman, so it was easier for me to see the graces. Few of them held jobs outside the home, and those who did filled thankless roles as clerks and waitresses. I didn't see, then, what a prison a house could be, since houses seemed to me brighter, handsomer places than any factory. I did not realize because such things were never spoken of—how often women suffered from men's bullying. I did learn about the wretchedness of abandoned wives, single mothers, widows; but I also learned about the wretchedness of lone men. Even then I could see how exhausting it was for a mother to cater all day to the needs of young children. But if I had been asked, as a boy, to choose between tending a baby and tending a machine, I think I would have chosen the baby. (Having now tended both, I know I would choose the baby.)

So I was baffled when the women at college accused me and my sex of hav-   9
ing cornered the world's pleasures. I think something like my bafflement has been felt by other boys (and by girls as well) who grew up in dirt-poor farm country, in mining country, in black ghettos, in Hispanic barrios, in the shadows of factories, in Third World nations—any place where the fate of men is as grim and bleak as the fate of women. Toilers and warriors. I realize now how ancient these identities are, how deep the tug they exert on men, the undertow of a thousand generations. The miseries I saw, as a boy, in the lives of nearly all men I continue to see in the lives of many—the body-breaking toil, the tedium, the call to be tough, the humiliating powerlessness, the battle for a living and for territory.

When the women I met at college thought about the joys and privileges of   10
men, they did not carry in their minds the sort of men I had known in my childhood. They thought of their fathers, who were bankers, physicians, architects, stockbrokers, the big wheels of the big cities. These fathers rode the train to work or drove cars that cost more than any of my childhood houses. They were attended from morning to night by female helpers, wives and nurses and secretaries. They were never laid off, never short of cash at month's end, never lined up for welfare. These fathers made decisions that mattered. They ran the world.

The daughters of such men wanted to share in this power, this glory. So   11
did I. They yearned for a say over their future, for jobs worthy of their abilities, for the right to live at peace, unmolested, whole. Yes, I thought, yes yes. The difference between me and these daughters was that they saw me, because of my sex, as destined from birth to become like their fathers, and therefore as an enemy to their desires. But I knew better. I wasn't an enemy, in fact or in feeling. I was an ally. If I had known, then, how to tell them so, would they have believed me? Would they now?

Reacting to the Reading

  1. Preview the essay. As you read it more carefully, highlight and annotate as needed to help you understand the writer's ideas.
  2. In the margins of the essay, name and number the categories Sanders identifies. If he does not name a particular category, supply a suitable name.

Reacting to Words

*1. Define these words: *sodden* (paragraph 1), *acrid* (1), *overseers* (1), *tilling* (2), *finicky* (3), *toilers* (5), *savvy* (5), *expansiveness* (8), *undertow* (9), *yearned* (11). Can you suggest a synonym for each word that will work in the essay?

2. Suggest two or three alternative names for the categories *warriors* and *toilers* (paragraph 5). Do you think any of your suggestions are better than Sanders's choices?

Reacting to Ideas

1. When Sanders was young, what did he see as his destiny? How did he escape his fate? How else might he have escaped?
2. What were the grievances of the women Sanders met at college? Why did Sanders have trouble understanding these grievances?
*3. Who do you believe has an easier life—men or women? Explain.

Reacting to the Pattern

1. What two types of men did Sanders know when he was young? How are they different? What do they have in common?
2. What kinds of men discussed in the essay do not fit into the two categories Sanders identifies in paragraphs 2–4? Why don't they fit?
*3. Sanders does not categorize the women he discusses. Can you think of a few categories into which these women could fit?

Writing Practice

1. Write a classification essay in which you identify and discuss three or four categories of workers (females as well as males) you observed in your community when you were growing up. In your thesis statement, draw a conclusion about the relative status and rewards of these workers' jobs.
2. Consider your own work history as well as your future career. Write a classification essay in which you discuss your experience in several different categories of employment in the past, present, and future. Give each category a descriptive title, and include a thesis statement that sums up your progress.
3. Categorize the workers in your current place of employment or on your college campus.

H   Definition

For more on how to write a definition essay, see 14H.

A **definition** essay presents an extended definition, using other patterns of development to move beyond a simple dictionary definition. In "The Wife-Beater," Gayle Rosenwald Smith defines an item of clothing. In "Dyslexia," Eileen Simpson defines a reading disorder.

THE WIFE-BEATER

Gayle Rosenwald Smith

Philadelphia lawyer Gayle Rosenwald Smith, who specializes in family law, has coauthored *What Every Woman Should Know about Divorce and Custody* (1998). Her articles have been published in newspapers such as the *Chicago Tribune* and the *Philadelphia Inquirer.* She is currently working on a book about divorce and money, which will be published in 2004. As you read, think about the connotations of violence and masculinity in Smith's definition of a "wife-beater."

Everybody wears them. The Gap sells them. Fashion designers Dolce and Gabbana have lavished them with jewels. Their previous greatest resurgence occurred in the 1950s, when Marlon Brando's Stanley Kowalski wore one in Tennessee Williams' *A Streetcar Named Desire.* They are all the rage.   1

What are they called?   2

The name is the issue. For they are known as "wife-beaters."   3

A Web search shows that kids nationwide are wearing the skinny-ribbed white T-shirts that can be worn alone or under another shirt. Women have adopted them with the same gusto as men. A search of boutiques shows that these wearers include professionals who wear them, adorned with designer accessories, under their pricey suits. They are available in all colors, sizes and price ranges.   4

Wearers under 25 do not seem to be disturbed by the name. But I sure am.   5

It's an odd name for an undershirt. And even though the ugly stereotypes behind the name are both obvious and toxic, it appears to be cool to say the name without fear of (or without caring about) hurting anyone.   6

That the name is fueled by stereotype is now an academically established fact, although various sources disagree on exactly when shirt and name came together. The *Oxford Dictionary* defines the term *wife-beater* as:
"1. A man who physically abuses his wife and
2. Tank-style underwear shirts. Origin: based on the stereotype that physically abusive husbands wear that particular type of shirt."   7

The *World Book Dictionary* locates the origin of the term *wife-beater* in the 1970s, from the stereotype of the Midwestern male wearing an undershirt while beating his wife. The shirts are said to have been popular in the 1980s at all types of sporting events, especially ones at which one sits in the sun and develops "wife-beater marks." The undershirts also attained popularity at wet T-shirt contests, in which the wet, ribbed tees accentuated contestants' breasts.   8

In an article in the style section of the New York Times, Jesse Sheidlower, principal editor of the *Oxford English Dictionary*'s American office, says the association of the undershirt and the term *wife-beater* arose in 1997 from varied sources, including gay and gang subcultures and rap music.   9

In the article, some sources argued that the reference in the term was not to spousal abuse per se but to popular-culture figures such as Ralph Cramden and Tony Soprano. And what about Archie Bunker?   10

It's not just the name that worries me. Fashion headlines reveal that we ₁₁ want to overthrow '90s grunge and return to shoulder pads and hardware-studded suits. Am I reading too much into a fashion statement that the return is also to male dominance where physical abuse is acceptable as a means of control?

There has to be a better term. After all, it's a pretty rare piece of clothing ₁₂ that can make both men and women look sexier. You'd expect a term connoting flattery—not violence.

Wearers under 25 may not want to hear this, but here it is. More than ₁₃ 4 million women are victims of severe assaults by boyfriends and husbands each year. By conservative estimate, family violence occurs in 2 million families each year in the United States. Average age of the batterer: 31.

Possibly the last statistic is telling. Maybe youth today would rather ignore ₁₄ the overtones of the term *wife-beater*. It is also true, however, that the children of abusers often learn the behavior from their elders.

Therein lies perhaps the worst difficulty: that this name for this shirt ₁₅ teaches the wrong thing about men. Some articles quote women who felt the shirts looked great, especially on guys with great bodies. One woman stated that it even made guys look "manly."

So *manly* equals *violent?* Not by me, and I hope not by anyone on any side ₁₆ of age 25.

Reacting to the Reading

1. Preview the essay. As you read it more carefully, highlight and annotate as needed to help you understand the writer's ideas.
2. Smith's essay opens with the sentence, "Everybody wears them." Underline this sentence (if you have not already done so). Then, place a check mark beside each sentence in the essay that supports this opening statement.

Reacting to Words

*1. Define these words: *lavished* (paragraph 1), *resurgence* (1), *gusto* (4), *toxic* (6), *connoting* (12). Can you suggest a synonym for each word that will work in the essay?
2. Smith uses informal words and expressions—*kids* (4), *pricey* (4), and *Not by me* (16)—as well as contractions, in her essay. Do you think this informal style undercuts her serious message? Explain.

Reacting to Ideas

*1. Beyond simply defining the term *wife-beater*, what is Smith's purpose for writing this essay? How can you tell?
2. What does Smith actually propose or recommend to her readers? For example, does she think people should stop wearing "wife-beater" T-shirts?
*3. In paragraph 11, Smith asks, "Am I reading too much into a fashion statement . . . ?" Answer her question.

Reacting to the Pattern

*1. Where in her essay does Smith develop her definition with examples? Where does she use description? Can you identify any other patterns of development?

2. Where does Smith present a formal (dictionary) definition of *wife-beater?* Where does she give information about the term's origin? Why does she include these two sections?

Writing Practice

1. Define another article of clothing that, like the "wife-beater" T-shirt, has taken on some special significance. (For example, you could write about baggy jeans or baseball caps.) Focus on the garment and its wearers (not on its name), discussing the impression the article of clothing makes and the associations it has for its wearers and for others. You can use description, exemplification, or classification to develop your essay.

2. Think of an item or activity that has a name with a negative, even offensive, connotation—for example, the name *bobos* for generic-brand sneakers. Define the item, developing your definition with description and examples, and try in your definition to persuade people to stop using the negative term.

DYSLEXIA

Eileen Simpson

In *Reversals: A Personal Account of Victory over Dyslexia* (1979), psychotherapist and author Eileen Simpson tells the story of her own struggle with dyslexia. In her account, she describes how she was able to overcome dyslexia only when she understood what it was and how it made reading difficult. As you read the following excerpt from *Reversals,* watch for the various ways in which Simpson develops her definition, and note especially her use of exemplification.

Dyslexia (from the Greek, *dys,* faulty, + *lexis,* speech, cognate with the 1 Latin *legere,* to read), developmental or specific dyslexia as it's technically called, the disorder I suffered from, is the inability of otherwise normal children to read. Children whose intelligence is below average, whose vision or hearing is defective, who have not had proper schooling, or who are too emotionally disturbed or brain-damaged to profit from it belong in other diagnostic categories. They, too, may be unable to learn to read, but they cannot properly be called dyslexics.

For more than seventy years the essential nature of the affliction has been 2 hotly disputed by psychologists, neurologists, and educators. It is generally agreed, however, that it is the result of a neurophysiological flaw in the brain's ability to process language. It is probably inherited, although some experts are reluctant to say this because they fear people will equate "inherited" with "untreatable." Treatable it certainly is: not a disease to be cured, but a malfunction that requires retraining.

Reading is the most complex skill a child entering school is asked to develop. What makes it complex, in part, is that letters are less constant than objects. A car seen from a distance, close to, from above, or below, or in a mirror still looks like a car even though the optical image changes. The letters of the alphabet are more whimsical. Take the letter *b*. Turned upside down it becomes a *p*. Looked at in a mirror, it becomes a *d*. Capitalized, it becomes something quite different, a *B*. The *M* upside down is a *W*. The *E* flipped over becomes Ǝ. This reversed *E* is familiar to mothers of normal children who have just begun to go to school. The earliest examples of art work they bring home often have I LOVƎ YOU written on them.

Dyslexics differ from other children in that they read, spell, and write letters upside down and turned around far more frequently and for a much longer time. In what seems like a capricious manner, they also add letters, syllables, and words, or, just as capriciously, delete them. With palindromic words (was-saw, on-no), it is the order of the letters rather than the orientation they change. The new word makes sense, but not the sense intended. Then there are other words where the changed order—"sorty" for story—does not make sense at all.

The inability to recognize that g, *g*, and G are the same letter, the inability to maintain the orientation of the letters, to retain the order in which they appear, and to follow a line of text without jumping above or below it—all the results of the flaw—can make of an orderly page of words a dish of alphabet soup.

Also essential for reading is the ability to store words in memory and to retrieve them. This very particular kind of memory dyslexics lack. So, too, do they lack the ability to hear what the eye sees, and to see what they hear. If the eye sees "off," the ear must hear "off" and not "of," or "for." If the ear hears "saw," the eye must see that it looks like "saw" on the page and not "was." Lacking these skills, a sentence or paragraph becomes a coded message to which the dyslexic can't find the key.

It is only a slight exaggeration to say that those who learned to read without difficulty can best understand the labor reading is for a dyslexic by turning a page of text upside down and trying to decipher it.

While the literature is replete with illustrations of the way these children write and spell, there are surprisingly few examples of how they read. One, used for propaganda purposes to alert the public to the vulnerability of dyslexics in a literate society, is a sign warning that behind it are guard dogs trained to kill. The dyslexic reads:

Wurring

Guard God

Patoly

for

Warning

Guard Dog

Patrol

and, of course, remains ignorant of the danger.

Looking for a more commonplace example, and hoping to recapture the   9
way I must have read in fourth grade, I recently observed dyslexic children at
the Educational Therapy Clinic in Princeton, through the courtesy of Elizabeth Travers, the director. The first child I saw, eight-year-old Anna (whose red
hair and brown eyes reminded me of myself at that age), had just come to the
Clinic and was learning the alphabet. Given the story of "Little Red Riding
Hood," which is at the second grade level, she began confidently enough,
repeating the title from memory, then came to a dead stop. With much coax-
ing throughout, she read as follows:

> Grandma you a top. Grandma [looks over at picture of Red Riding
> Hood]. Red Riding Hood [long pause, presses index finger into the
> paper. Looks at me for help. I urge: Go ahead] the a [puts head close
> to the page, nose almost touching] on Grandma

for

> Once upon a time there was a little girl who had a red coat with a red
> hood. Etc.

"Grandma" was obviously a memory from having heard the story read   10
aloud. Had I needed a reminder of how maddening my silences must have
been to Miss Henderson, and how much patience is required to teach these
children, Anna, who took almost ten minutes to read these few lines, furnished
it. The main difference between Anna and me at that age is that Anna clearly
felt no need to invent. She was perplexed, but not anxious, and seemed to have
infinite tolerance for her long silences.

Toby, a nine-year-old boy with superior intelligence, had a year of tutoring   11
behind him and could have managed "Little Red Riding Hood" with ease. His
text was taken from the *Reader's Digest's Reading Skill Builder*, Grade IV. He
read:

> A kangaroo likes as if he had but truck together warm. His saw neck
> and head do not . . . [Here Toby sighed with fatigue] seem to feel happy
> back. They and tried and so every a tiger Moses and shoots from lone-
> some day and shouts and long shore animals. And each farm play with
> five friends . . .

He broke off with the complaint, "This is too hard. Do I have to read any   12
more?"

His text was: 13

A kangaroo looks as if he had been put together wrong. His small neck and head do not seem to fit with his heavy back legs and thick tail. Soft eyes, a twinkly little nose and short front legs seem strange on such a large strong animal. And each front paw has five fingers, like a man's hand.

An English expert gives the following bizarre example of an adult 14 dyslexic's performance:

An the bee-what in the tel mother of the biothodoodoo to the majoram or that emidrate eni eni Krastrei, mestriet to Ketra lotombreidi to ra from treido as that.

His text, taken from a college catalogue the examiner happened to have 15 close at hand, was:

It shall be in the power of the college to examine or not every licentiate, previous to his admission to the fellowship, as they shall think fit.

That evening when I read aloud to Auntie for the first time, I probably 16 began as Toby did, my memory of the classroom lesson keeping me close to the text. When memory ran out, and Auntie did not correct my errors, I began to invent. When she still didn't stop me, I may well have begun to improvise in the manner of this patient—anything to keep going and keep up the myth that I was reading—until Auntie brought the "gibberish" to a halt.

Reacting to the Reading

1. Preview the essay. As you read it more carefully, highlight and annotate as needed to help you understand the writer's ideas.
2. Underline the definition of *dyslexia* in the essay; in a marginal annotation, paraphrase the definition.

Reacting to Words

*1. Define these words: *process* (paragraph 2), *whimsical* (3), *capricious* (4), *orientation* (5), *replete* (8), *commonplace* (9), *perplexed* (10), *gibberish* (16). Can you suggest a synonym for each word that will work in the essay?
2. Can you think of a synonym or near-synonym for *dyslexia*? If not, try to coin a suitable word to describe the disorder.

Reacting to Ideas

1. What is dyslexia? How are children with dyslexia different from their peers?

2. What central point or idea do you think Simpson wishes to communicate to her readers? Does she ever actually state this idea? If so, where? If not, do you think she should?

*3. If you were dyslexic, how would your life be different?

Reacting to the Pattern

1. Simpson develops her definition of dyslexia with examples. Identify some of these examples. Do you find the material drawn from her own childhood struggle with dyslexia more or less effective than the examples of cases she observes as an adult? Explain.

*2. What other patterns does Simpson use to develop her definition?

Writing Practice

1. Choose a problem—physical, economic, or behavioral—that handicaps you as a student. Identify the problem, define it, and give examples to expand your definition.

2. Consider the tasks you do each day at home, at school, and at work. How would you manage these tasks differently if you were dyslexic? Write an essay in which you define *dyslexia* in terms of the things you, as a dyslexic adult, would not be able to do.

▌ Argument

An **argument** essay takes a stand on one side of a debatable issue, using facts, examples, and expert opinion to persuade readers to accept a position. The writers of the three essays that follow—Alan M. Dershowitz in "Why Fear National ID Cards?", Charles Krauthammer in "The New Prohibitionism," and Martin Luther King Jr. in "I Have a Dream"—attempt to persuade readers to accept their positions—or at least to acknowledge that they are reasonable.

For more on how to write an argument essay, see 14I.

WHY FEAR NATIONAL ID CARDS?

Alan M. Dershowitz

Alan M. Dershowitz is a Harvard Law School professor, columnist, and lawyer whose clients have included Klaus von Bulow, O. J. Simpson, Mia Farrow, and Mike Tyson. Dershowitz is the author of *The Best Defense* (1983), *The Abuse Excuse* (1995), *The Advocate's Devil* (1999), and *Supreme Injustice: How the High Court Hijacked Election 2000* (2001), among many others. His articles appear regularly in the *New York Times Magazine*, *The Nation*, the *Washington Post*, *Harper's*, the *Los Angeles Times*, and numerous law reviews. As you read, consider how Dershowitz acknowledges opposing viewpoints while still successfully arguing his case.

At many bridges and tunnels across the country, drivers avoid long delays   1
at the toll booths with an unobtrusive device that fits on a car's dashboard.
Instead of fumbling for change, they drive right through; the device sends a
radio signal that records their passage. They are billed later. It's a tradeoff
between privacy and convenience: the toll-takers know more about you—when
you entered and left Manhattan, for instance—but you save time and
money.

An optional national identity card could be used in a similar way, offering   2
a similar kind of tradeoff: a little less anonymity for a lot more security. Anyone who had the card could be allowed to pass through airports or building
security more expeditiously, and anyone who opted out could be examined
much more closely.

As a civil libertarian, I am instinctively skeptical of such tradeoffs. But I   3
support a national identity card with a chip that can match the holder's fin-
gerprint. It could be an effective tool for preventing terrorism, reducing the
need for other law-enforcement mechanisms—especially racial and ethnic
profiling—that pose even greater dangers to civil liberties.

I can hear the objections: What about the specter of Big Brother? What   4
about fears of identity cards leading to more intrusive measures? (The
National Rifle Association, for example, worries that a government that regis-
tered people might also decide to register guns.) What about fears that such
cards would lead to increased deportation of illegal immigrants?

First, we already require photo ID's for many activities, including flying,   5
driving, drinking, and check-cashing. And fingerprints differ from photographs only in that they are harder to fake. The vast majority of Americans
routinely carry photo ID's in their wallets and pocketbooks. These ID's are
issued by state motor vehicle bureaus and other public and private entities. A
national card would be uniform and difficult to forge or alter. It would reduce
the likelihood that someone could, intentionally or not, get lost in the cracks
of multiple bureaucracies.

The fear of an intrusive government can be addressed by setting criteria   6
for any official who demands to see the card. Even without a national card,
people are always being asked to show identification. The existence of a
national card need not change the rules about when ID can properly be
demanded. It is true that the card would facilitate the deportation of illegal
immigrants. But President Bush has proposed giving legal status to many of
the illegal immigrants now in this country. And legal immigrants would actually benefit from a national ID card that could demonstrate their status to government officials.

Finally, there is the question of the right to anonymity. I don't believe we   7
can afford to recognize such a right in this age of terrorism. No such right is
hinted at in the Constitution. And though the Supreme Court has identified a
right to privacy, privacy and anonymity are not the same. American taxpayers,
voters and drivers long ago gave up any right of anonymity without loss of our

right to engage in lawful conduct within zones of privacy. Rights are a function of experience, and our recent experiences teach that it is far too easy to be anonymous—even to create a false identity—in this large and decentralized country. A national ID card would not prevent all threats of terrorism, but it would make it more difficult for potential terrorists to hide in open view, as many of the Sept. 11 hijackers apparently managed to do.

A national ID card could actually enhance civil liberties by reducing the   8
need for racial and ethnic stereotyping. There would be no excuse for hassling someone merely because he belongs to a particular racial or ethnic group if he presented a card that matched his print and that permitted his name to be checked instantly against the kind of computerized criminal-history retrieval systems that are already in use. (If there is too much personal information in the system, or if the information is being used improperly, that is a separate issue. The only information the card need contain is name, address, photo and print.)

From a civil liberties perspective, I prefer a system that takes a little bit of   9
freedom from all to one that takes a great deal of freedom and dignity from the few—especially since those few are usually from a racially or ethnically disfavored group. A national ID card would be much more effective in preventing terrorism than profiling millions of men simply because of their appearance.

Reacting to the Reading

1. Preview the essay. As you read it more carefully, highlight and annotate as needed to help you understand the writer's ideas.
2. Underline Dershowitz's thesis statement. In the margin, rewrite it in your own words.

Reacting to Words

*1. Define these words: *unobtrusive* (paragraph 1), *anonymity* (2), *expeditiously* (2), *opted* (2), *skeptical* (3), *specter* (4), *intrusive* (4). Can you suggest a synonym for each word that will work in the essay?
2. In paragraph 3, Dershowitz identifies himself as a civil libertarian. What is a civil libertarian? Why do you think Dershowitz feels the need to identify himself in this manner?

Reacting to Ideas

*1. Do you agree with Dershowitz that trading "a little less anonymity for a lot more security" (paragraph 2) is a good idea? Why or why not?
2. Dershowitz believes that a system of national ID cards would reduce the threat of terrorism. Why does he think so?
3. Dershowitz believes that a system of national ID cards would "enhance civil liberties by reducing the need for racial and ethnic stereotyping" (paragraph 8). How does he explain this?

Reacting to the Pattern

*1. Dershowitz opens his essay with a discussion alluding to the EZ Pass system for collecting highway tolls. Why does he begin in this way? Is this an effective opening strategy?

 2. According to Dershowitz, what are the advantages of national identity cards?

*3. What opposing arguments does Dershowitz present? How does he refute (that is, argue against) them? Is his refutation of these arguments convincing?

Writing Practice

1. Reread paragraphs 4 through 7, and make a list of the objections Dershowitz identifies. Then, write a letter to your congressional representative in which you argue *against* instituting a system of national identity cards.

2. In recent years, many African Americans have been victims of unwarranted police stops for "driving while black"; in the wake of the September 11, 2001, terrorist attacks, some Arab Americans have faced a similar problem, which has been called "flying while brown." In both cases, the issue at hand is racial and ethnic stereotyping that inconveniences—and might even endanger—innocent people. Write an essay in support of national identity cards, focusing on their possible role in eliminating this kind of stereotyping. Use examples from your own experience if possible.

THE NEW PROHIBITIONISM

Charles Krauthammer

Charles Krauthammer is the author of a Pulitzer Prize–winning column for the *Washington Post* and a frequent contributor to various magazines. His work often discusses current political and social issues. In the following column, Krauthammer constructs an argument about the antismoking movement. Krauthammer's medical training (he was a practicing psychiatrist) and experience as a political and social commentator are evident in the way he develops his argument. As you read, note the ways in which he builds support for his thesis.

The oddest thing about the current national crusade against tobacco is not   1
its frenzy—our culture lives from one frenzy to the next—but its selectivity. Of course tobacco is a great national killer. It deserves all the pummeling it gets. But alcohol is a great national killer too, and it has enjoyed an amazingly free ride amid the fury of the New Prohibitionism.

Joe Camel[1] has been banished forever, but those beloved Budweiser frogs—succeeded by even cuter Budweiser lizards—keep marching along, right into the consciousness of every TV-watching kid in the country.   2

For 26 years[2] television has been free of cigarette ads. Why? Because TV persuades as nothing else, and we don't want young people—inveterate TV watchers—persuaded. Yet television is bursting with exhortations to drink. TV sports in particular, a staple of adolescents, is one long hymn to the glories of beer.   3

And the sports-worshipping years are precisely the time that kids learn to drink. The median age at which they start drinking is just over 13. A 1990 survey found that 56% of students in Grades 5 through 12 say alcohol advertising encourages them to drink. Surprise!   4

Am I for Prohibition? No. But I am for a little perspective. We tend to think of the turn-of-the-century temperance movement as little blue-haired ladies trying to prevent people from having a good time on Saturday night. In fact, the temperance movement was part of a much larger progressive movement seeking to improve the appalling conditions of the urban working class. These were greatly exacerbated by rampant alcoholism that contributed to extraordinary levels of spousal and child abuse, abandonment and destitution.   5

Alcohol is still a cause of staggering devastation. It kills 100,000 Americans a year—not only from disease but also from accidents. In 1996, 41% of all U.S. traffic fatalities were alcohol related. It causes huge economic losses and untold suffering. Why, then, do the Bud frogs get to play the Super Bowl while Joe Camel goes the way of the Marlboro Man[3]?   6

The most plausible answer is that tobacco is worse because it kills more people. Indeed it does. But 100,000 people a year is still a fair carnage. Moreover, the really compelling comparison is this: alcohol is far more deadly than tobacco *to innocent bystanders*. In a free society, should we not consider behavior that injures others more worthy of regulation than behavior that merely injures oneself? The primary motive for gun control, after all, is concern about homicide, not suicide.   7

The antitobacco folk, aware of this bedrock belief, try to play up the harm smokers cause others. Thus the attorneys general seeking billions of dollars in damages from the tobacco companies are claiming that taxpayers have been unfairly made to pay for the treatment of smoking-related illnesses.   8

A clever ploy. But the hardheaded truth is that premature death from smoking, which generally affects people in their late-middle and early retirement years, is an economic boon to society. The money saved on pensions and on the truly expensive health care that comes with old age—something these smokers never achieve—surely balances, if it does not exceed, the cost of treating tobacco-related diseases.   9

1. Retired cartoon image used to advertise Camel cigarettes; withdrawn by industry following complaints that it was aimed at underage smokers.
2. Cigarette commercials were banned from television in 1971; Krauthammer is writing in 1997.
3. Image of a rugged cowboy, used to advertise Marlboro cigarettes.

The alternative and more dramatic antitobacco tactic is to portray smok- 10
ing as an assault on nonsmokers via secondhand smoke. Now, secondhand
smoke is certainly a nuisance. But the claim that it is a killer is highly dubious. "The statistical evidence," reported the nonpartisan Congressional
Research Service in 1994, "does not appear to support a conclusion that there
are substantive health effects of passive smoking."

Unlike secondhand smoke, secondhand booze is a world-class killer. 11
Drunk driving alone kills 17,000 people a year. And alcohol's influence extends
far beyond driving: it contributes to everything from bar fights to domestic
violence. One study found that 44% of assailants in cases of marital abuse had
been drinking. Another study found that 60% of wife batterers had been under
the influence. Whatever claims you make against tobacco, you'd have quite a
time looking for cases of the nicotine-crazed turning on their wives with a
butcher knife.

Moreover, look at the *kinds* of people alcohol kills. Drunk drivers kill tod- 12
dlers. They kill teens. They kill whole families. Tobacco does not kill toddlers
and teens. Tobacco strikes late. It kills, but at a very long remove in time. Its
victims generally have already had their chance at life. Tobacco merely short-
ens life; alcohol can deprive people of it.

Still undecided which of the two poisons is more deserving of social dis- 13
approbation? Here's the ultimate test. Ask yourself this: If you knew your child
was going to become addicted to either alcohol or tobacco, which would you
choose?

Reacting to the Reading

1. Preview the essay. As you read it more carefully, highlight and annotate as
   needed to help you understand the writer's ideas.
2. Underline the transitional words and phrases that signal the movement
   from one part of the argument to another or that connect specific points
   to other points or to the thesis statement.

Reacting to Words

*1. Define these words: *prohibitionism* (title), *selectivity* (paragraph 1), *pummeling* (1), *inveterate* (3), *median* (4), *temperance* (5), *devastation* (6), *plausible* (7), *boon* (9), *dubious* (10), *disapprobation* (13). Can you suggest a
   synonym for each word that will work in the essay?
2. Krauthammer uses the word *kill* in many of the sentences of paragraph 12.
   Why does he do this? Would the paragraph be more effective if he used a
   different word in some sentences?

Reacting to Ideas

*1. Do you agree with Krauthammer when he says, "TV persuades as nothing
   else" (paragraph 3)? Do you believe that television advertising images like
   the Budweiser frogs can encourage children to drink?

2. How convincing is Krauthammer's argument that premature death from smoking "is an economic boon to society" (paragraph 9)? Can you think of another argument that might be more effective?

3. Krauthammer argues against the current "national crusade against tobacco" (paragraph 1) by maintaining that alcohol is far more deadly than tobacco. Does this line of reasoning make sense? Does the fact that alcohol may be more dangerous than tobacco eliminate the need for legislation against tobacco?

Reacting to the Pattern

*1. Throughout his essay, Krauthammer asks a series of questions. What function do these questions serve? Is this technique effective?

2. Krauthammer supports his position by contrasting alcohol and tobacco. What points does he make about each? What other points could he have made?

3. Krauthammer concludes by asking readers whether they would rather have their children addicted to tobacco or to alcohol. What is his purpose in doing so? Is this a reasonable question?

Writing Practice

1. Do you think government prohibition of smoking would work? Write an essay in which you argue for or against the banning of all tobacco products. Be sure to consider the problems that such a policy would create.

*2. Can you think of a product—firearms or over-the-counter medications, for example—whose sale should be controlled more strictly than it is now? Write an essay in which you present an argument for controlling this product's sale, discussing the problems that this product causes and suggesting ways that controls could improve the situation. Make sure your essay has a clearly stated thesis.

3. Instead of banning tobacco products, what can local and state governments do to discourage people from smoking? Write an essay in which you argue for a particular course of action—for example, charging smokers higher health-insurance premiums.

I HAVE A DREAM

Martin Luther King Jr.

On August 28, 1963, Martin Luther King Jr. delivered the following speech on the steps in front of the Lincoln Memorial in Washington, D.C. King used the occasion of this speech—the March on Washington, in which more than two hundred thousand people participated—to reinforce his ideas about racial equality and nonviolent protest. The speech itself is a deductive argument that makes a compelling case for racial justice in the United States. As you read, notice King's effective use of repetition.

Five score years ago, a great American, in whose symbolic shadow we stand, signed the Emancipation Proclamation. This momentous decree came as a great beacon light of hope to millions of Negro slaves who had been seared in the flames of withering injustice. It came as a joyous daybreak to end the long night of captivity.   1

But one hundred years later, we must face the tragic fact that the Negro is still not free. One hundred years later, the life of the Negro is still sadly crippled by the manacles of segregation and the chains of discrimination. One hundred years later, the Negro lives on a lonely island of poverty in the midst of a vast ocean of material prosperity. One hundred years later, the Negro is still languishing in the corners of American society and finds himself an exile in his own land. So we have come here today to dramatize an appalling condition.   2

In a sense we have come to our nation's capital to cash a check. When the architects of our republic wrote the magnificent words of the Constitution and the Declaration of Independence, they were signing a promissory note to which every American was to fall heir. This note was a promise that all men — yes, black men as well as white men — would be guaranteed the unalienable rights of life, liberty, and the pursuit of happiness.   3

It is obvious today that America has defaulted on this promissory note insofar as her citizens of color are concerned. Instead of honoring this sacred obligation, America has given the Negro people a bad check, a check which has come back marked "insufficient funds." But we refuse to believe that there are insufficient funds in the great vaults of opportunity of this nation. So we have come to cash this check — a check that will give us upon demand the riches of freedom and the security of justice. We have also come to this hallowed spot to remind America of the fierce urgency of *now*. This is no time to engage in the luxury of cooling off or to take the tranquilizing drugs of gradualism. *Now* is the time to make real the promises of Democracy. *Now* is the time to rise from the dark and desolate valley of segregation to the sunlit path of racial justice. *Now* is the time to open the doors of opportunity to all of God's children. *Now* is the time to lift our nation from the quicksands of racial injustice to the solid rock of brotherhood.   4

It would be fatal for the nation to overlook the urgency of the moment and to underestimate the determination of the Negro. This sweltering summer of the Negro's legitimate discontent will not pass until there is an invigorating autumn of freedom and equality; 1963 is not an end, but a beginning. Those who hope that the Negro needed to blow off steam and will now be content will have a rude awakening if the nation returns to business as usual. There will be neither rest nor tranquility in America until the Negro is granted his citizenship rights. The whirlwinds of revolt will continue to shake the foundations of our nation until the bright day of justice emerges.   5

But there is something that I must say to my people who stand on the warm threshold which leads into the palace of justice. In the process of gaining our rightful place we must not be guilty of wrongful deeds. Let us not seek to satisfy our thirst for freedom by drinking from the cup of bitterness and hatred. We must forever conduct our struggle on the high plane of dignity and   6 discipline. We must not allow our creative protest to degenerate into physical violence. Again and again we must rise to the majestic heights of meeting physical force with soul force. The marvelous new militancy which has engulfed the Negro community must not lead us to a distrust of all white people, for many of our white brothers, as evidenced by their presence here today, have come to realize that their destiny is tied up with our destiny and their freedom is inextricably bound to our freedom. We cannot walk alone.

And as we walk, we must make the pledge that we shall march ahead. We cannot turn back. There are those who are asking the devotees of civil rights, "When will you be satisfied?" We can never be satisfied as long as the Negro is the victim of the unspeakable horrors of police brutality. We can never be satisfied as long as our bodies, heavy with the fatigue of travel, cannot gain lodging in the motels of the highways and the hotels of the cities. We cannot be satisfied as long as the Negro's basic mobility is from a smaller ghetto to a larger one. We can never be satisfied as long as a Negro in Mississippi cannot vote and a Negro in New York believes he has nothing for which to vote. No, no, we are not satisfied, and we will not be satisfied until justice rolls down like waters and righteousness like a mighty stream.

I am not unmindful that some of you have come here out of great trials and tribulations. Some of you have come fresh from narrow jail cells. Some of you have come from areas where your quest for freedom left you battered by the storms of persecution and staggered by the winds of police brutality. You have been the veterans of creative suffering. Continue to work with the faith that unearned suffering is redemptive.

Go back to Mississippi, go back to Alabama, go back to South Carolina, go back to Georgia, go back to Louisiana, go back to the slums and ghettos of our northern cities, knowing that somehow this situation can and will be changed. Let us not wallow in the valley of despair.

I say to you today, my friends, that in spite of the difficulties and frustrations of the moment I still have a dream. It is a dream deeply rooted in the American dream.

I have a dream that one day this nation will rise up and live out the true meaning of its creed: "We hold these truths to be self-evident, that all men are created equal."

I have a dream that one day on the red hills of Georgia the sons of former slaves and the sons of former slaveowners will be able to sit down together at the table of brotherhood.

I have a dream that one day even the state of Mississippi, a desert state sweltering with the heat of injustice and oppression, will be transformed into an oasis of freedom and justice.

I have a dream that my four little children will one day live in a nation where they will not be judged by the color of their skin but by the content of their character.

I have a dream today.

I have a dream that one day the state of Alabama, whose governor's lips are presently dripping with the words of interposition and nullification, will be transformed into a situation where little black boys and black girls will be

able to join hands with little white boys and white girls and walk together as
sisters and brothers.

I have a dream today.   17

I have a dream that one day every valley shall be exalted, every hill and   18
mountain shall be made low, the rough places will be made plain, and the
crooked places will be made straight, and the glory of the Lord shall be
revealed, and all flesh shall see it together.

This is our hope. This is the faith with which I return to the South. With   19
this faith we will be able to hew out of the mountain of despair a stone of hope.
With this faith we will be able to transform the jangling discords of our nation
into a beautiful symphony of brotherhood. With this faith we will be able to
work together, to pray together, to struggle together, to go to jail together, to
stand up for freedom together, knowing that we will be free one day.

This will be the day when all of God's children will be able to sing with new   20
meaning

> My country, 'tis of thee,
> Sweet land of liberty,
>   Of thee I sing:
> Land where my fathers died,
> Land of the pilgrim's pride,
> From every mountainside,
>   Let freedom ring.

So let freedom ring from the prodigious hilltops of New Hampshire. Let   21
freedom ring from the mighty mountains of New York. Let freedom ring from
the heightening Alleghenies of Pennsylvania. Let freedom ring from the snow-
capped Rockies of Colorado. Let freedom ring from the curvaceous peaks of
California.

But not only that. Let freedom ring from Stone Mountain of Georgia. Let free-   22
dom ring from Lookout Mountain of Tennessee. Let freedom ring from every
hill and molehill of Mississippi. From every mountainside, let freedom ring.

When we let freedom ring, when we let it ring from every village and every   23
hamlet, from every state and every city, we will be able to speed up that day
when all of God's children, black men and white men, Jews and Gentiles,
Protestants and Catholics, will be able to join hands and sing in the words of
the old Negro spiritual, "Free at last! Free at last! Thank God almighty, we are
free at last!"

Reacting to the Reading

1. Preview the essay. As you read it more carefully, highlight and annotate as
   needed to help you understand the writer's ideas.
2. Highlight the passage in which King outlines his dream for the United
   States. In a marginal annotation, explain what he means when he says his
   dream is "deeply rooted in the American dream" (paragraph 10).

Reacting to Words

*1. Define these words: *score* (paragraph 1), *beacon* (1), *withering* (1), *languishing* (2), *appalling* (2), *promissory* (3), *unalienable* (3), *hallowed* (4), *gradualism* (4), *invigorating* (5), *inextricably* (6), *redemptive* (8), *wallow* (9), *prodigious* (21), *curvaceous* (21). Can you suggest a synonym for each word that will work in the essay?

2. King uses a number of words again and again in his speech. Identify some of these words. Why do you think he repeats them? Would the speech have been more (or less) effective without this repetition?

Reacting to Ideas

1. In paragraph 3, King says that he and the other marchers have come to Washington "to cash a check." How does this image convey what he and the other protesters want to achieve? Can you think of another image that might also work here?

2. In this speech, King addresses the marchers who have come to Washington. Whom else do you think he is addressing?

3. Do you think the current racial climate in the United States still warrants King's criticism? Are we any closer today than we were in 1963 to realizing his dream?

Reacting to the Pattern

*1. King uses a deductive argument to present his ideas about racial justice. Do you think an inductive argument would have been more effective?

2. King's argument reaches its conclusion in paragraph 4. What does he do in the rest of his speech?

For more on deductive arguments, see 14I.

3. Why do you think King chose to include only a few specific examples to illustrate his points? Should he have provided more evidence?

Writing Practice

1. In paragraph 4, King says, "America has defaulted on this promissory note. . . ." Can you think of some person or organization that has defaulted on its promissory note to you? Write an argument essay in which you make your case. If you wish, you may use King's image of a bad check.

2. Write an essay in which you argue that if King were alive today, he would (or would not) think his dream of racial justice had been realized.

3. Choose an issue you feel strongly about. Write a letter to the editor of your local paper in which you take a strong stand on this issue.

UNIT NINE

Writing with Sources

Writing a Research Paper **36**

PREVIEW

In this chapter, you will learn
- to choose a topic (36A)
- to look for sources (36B)
- to zero in on your topic (36C)
- to do research (36D)
- to take notes (36E)

- to watch out for plagiarism (36F)
- to draft a thesis statement (36G)
- to make an outline (36H)
- to write your paper (36I)
- to document your sources (36J)

When you write a research paper, you find material—from books, articles, television programs, the Internet, and other sources—to support your ideas.

A Choosing a Topic

The first step in writing a research paper is finding a topic to write about. Before you choose a topic, ask yourself the following questions.

- What is your page limit?
- When is your paper due?
- How many sources are you expected to use?
- What kind of sources are you expected to use?

The answers to these questions will help you tell if your topic is too broad or too narrow.

When Allison Rogers, a student in a composition course, was asked to write a three- to five-page research paper that was due in five weeks, she decided that she wanted to write about the violence she saw in society. She knew, however, that the general topic "violence" would be too broad for her paper. After considering a number of possible topics, Allison decided to write about the effect of violent movies on behavior. In her film class, she had just seen the movie *Natural Born Killers* and was shocked by its graphic violence. She remembered hearing that the movie had caused a great deal of controversy and that two teenagers who committed murder had actually used it as a defense in their trial. This is what led Allison to wonder about the link between film violence and behavior. She thought this topic would work well because she could discuss it in the required number of pages and because she would be able to finish her paper within the five-week time limit.

B Looking for Sources

To get an overview of your topic and to see whether you will be able to find enough material, quickly survey the resources of your library. (First, arrange a meeting with your college librarian, who can answer questions, give suggestions, and point you toward helpful resources.)

Begin by searching your library's catalog by subject to see what books it lists on your topic. For example, under the general subject of *violence*, Allison saw the related headings *movie violence* and *media violence*. Under each of these headings, she found a variety of books and government studies on the topic.

In addition to books, you can look for articles. To do this, consult an index such as *Readers' Guide to Periodical Literature*, which lists articles in newspapers and magazines, or *InfoTrac*, a computer database that contains the texts of many articles. (Your librarian can show you how to use these resources.) A quick look at *Readers' Guide* showed Allison that many articles had been written about violence in the media.

For information about using the Internet for research, see 37B.

The Internet can also help you get an overview of your topic. Begin by carrying out an Internet search with a **search engine**, a program that helps you find information available on the Internet. (The most popular search engines are Yahoo, Infoseek, and AltaVista.) When Allison entered the key words *movie violence* and *Natural Born Killers*, she found many articles that related to her topic. (Ask your librarian to demonstrate effective searching techniques.)

Note: For each source you find, record full publication information (for books: the title, author, and call number; for articles: the author, title, periodical name, date, and page number). If you do this, you can easily find the source again later.

C Zeroing In on Your Topic

As you skim the library's resources, the subject headings as well as the titles of books and articles should help you zero in on your topic. For example, Allison discovered that several of the books and a number of the articles she located focused on the effect of media violence on society. A few focused specifically on children, examining the effect of violent movies and television on their behavior. Because she was an early childhood education major, Allison decided to concentrate on the effect of media violence on children. Following her instructor's guidelines, she knew the purpose of her paper would be either to *present information* about media violence and children or *make a point* about it. She could present information by discussing some of the current research into the relationship between media violence and violent behavior in children, or she could make the point that media violence can have a negative effect on the behavior of children.

D   Doing Research

Once you have zeroed in on your topic, you need to gather information. Go back to the library, and check out any books you think will be useful. Photocopy relevant magazine articles, and make copies of material stored on microfilm or microfiche. If you use a computer database such as *InfoTrac,* print out the full text of any articles you plan to use. In addition, browse the World Wide Web for possible sources. Remember, the quality and reliability of material found on the Web can vary, so use only information from reliable sources — a Web site sponsored by a well-known national publication or organization, for example.

When Allison searched the Web using the key term *media violence,* she found the Web site produced by ERIC Counseling and Student Services Clearinghouse. This site contained "Children and Television Violence," an article posted by the American Psychological Association, a nationally recognized and reliable professional organization.

E   Taking Notes

Once you have gathered the material you will need, read it carefully, recording any information you think you can use in your paper. As you take notes, keep your topic in mind; this will help you decide what material is useful. Record your notes on three-by-five-inch cards, on separate sheets of paper, or in a computer file you have created for this purpose. When you use information from a source in your writing, you do not always *quote* the exact words of your source. More often, you *paraphrase* or *summarize* a source, putting its ideas into your own words. (You do not include your own ideas or opinions.)

Paraphrasing

When you **paraphrase**, you present the ideas of a source in your own words, following the order and emphasis of the original. You paraphrase when you want to make a discussion easier to understand while still conveying a clear sense of the original. Here is a passage from the article "Children and Television Violence," followed by Allison's paraphrase.

ORIGINAL

Children often behave differently after they've been watching violent programs on television. In one study done at Pennsylvania State University, about 100 preschool children were observed both before and after watching television; some watched cartoons that had many aggressive and violent acts; others watched shows that did not have any kind of violence. The researchers noticed real differences between the children who watched the violent shows and those who watched nonviolent ones.

PARAPHRASE

At Pennsylvania State University, researchers did a study. They divided 100 young children into two groups. One group watched television programs that contained a lot of violence. The other group watched programs that contained very little violence. Researchers found that the two groups of children behaved very differently.

Summarizing

When you write a **summary**, you also put the ideas of a source into your own words. Unlike a paraphrase, however, a summary condenses a passage, giving only the general idea of the original. Here is Allison's summary of the original passage above.

SUMMARY

According to a study conducted at Pennsylvania State University, young children who watched violent television shows behaved differently from those who watched nonviolent shows.

Quoting

When you **quote**, you use the exact words of a source, enclosing them in quotation marks. Because too many quotations can distract readers, quote only when an author's words are memorable or when you want to give readers the flavor of the original source.

According to the article "Children and Television Violence," "Children often behave differently after they've been watching violent programs on television."

Integrating Sources

To show readers why you are using a source and to integrate source material smoothly into your essay, introduce paraphrases, summaries, and quotations with a phrase that identifies the source or its author. You can position this identifying phrase at various places in a sentence. You should not use the same words over and over to introduce source material. Try using different words— for example, *points out, observes, comments, notes, remarks,* and *concludes.*

> According to the article "Children and Television Violence," "Children often behave differently after they've been watching violent programs on television."

> "Children often behave differently after they've been watching violent programs on television," observes one Pennsylvania State University study.

> "Children often behave differently," claim researchers in a study reported by the American Psychological Association, "after they've been watching violent programs on television."

F   Watching Out for Plagiarism

As a rule, you must **document** (acknowledge that you are borrowing) any words or ideas from an outside source that are not **common knowledge**, factual information widely available in reference works. When you present information from another source as if it is your own (whether you do it intentionally or unintentionally), you commit **plagiarism**—and plagiarism is theft. You can avoid plagiarism by understanding what you must document and what you do not have to document.

For information on documentation, see 36J.

FOCUS   Avoiding Plagiarism

You should document

- Word-for-word quotations from a source
- Ideas from a source that you put in your own words

(continued on the following page)

(continued from the previous page)
- Tables, charts, graphs, or statistics from a source

You do not need to document

- Your own ideas
- Common knowledge
- Familiar quotations

When you consult a source to get ideas for your writing, be careful to avoid the errors that commonly lead to plagiarism. The following paragraph from one of Allison's sources, Brian Siano's essay "Frankenstein Must Be Destroyed: Chasing the Monster of TV Violence," and the four rules that follow will help you understand and correct these common errors.

ORIGINAL

Of course, there are a few crazies out there who will be unfavorably influenced by what they see on TV. But even assuming that somehow the TV show (or movie or record) shares some of the blame, how does one predict what future crazies will take for inspiration? What guidelines would ensure that people write, act, or produce something that *will not upset a psychotic*? Not only is this a ridiculous demand, it's insulting to the public as well. We would all be treated as potential murderers in order to gain a hypothetical 5 percent reduction in violence.

Document Ideas from Your Sources

PLAGIARISM

Even if we were to control the programs that are shown on television, we would only decrease violence in society by perhaps 5 percent.

Even though Siano is not quoted directly, he must still be identified as the source of the paraphrased material.

CORRECT

According to Brian Siano, even if we were to control the programs that are shown on television, we would decrease violence in society by only perhaps 5 percent (24).

Place Borrowed Words in Quotation Marks

PLAGIARISM

According to Brian Siano, there will always be a few crazies out there who will be unfavorably influenced by what they see on television (24).

Although the writer cites Siano as the source, the passage incorrectly uses Siano's exact words without quoting them. The writer must either quote the borrowed words or rephrase the material.

CORRECT (BORROWED WORDS IN QUOTATION MARKS)

According to Brian Siano, there will always be "a few crazies out there who will be unfavorably influenced by what they see on TV" (24).

CORRECT (BORROWED WORDS REPHRASED)

According to Brian Siano, some unstable people will commit crimes because of the violence they see in the media (24).

Use Your Own Phrasing

PLAGIARISM

Naturally, there will always be people who are affected by what they view on television. But even if we agree that television programs can influence people, how can we really know what will make people commit crimes? How can we be absolutely sure that a show will not disturb someone who is insane? The answer is that we cannot. To pretend that we can is insulting to law-abiding citizens. We cannot treat everyone as if they were criminals just to reduce violence by a small number of people (Siano 24).

Even though the writer acknowledges Siano as her source, and even though she does not use Siano's exact words, her passage closely follows the order, emphasis, sentence structure, and phrasing of the original. In the following passage, the writer uses her own wording, quoting one distinctive phrase from her source. (Note that even though the paragraph ends with documentation, the quotation requires its own citation.)

CORRECT

> According to Brian Siano, we should not censor a televi-
> sion program just because "a few crazies" may be incited
> to violence (24). Not only would such censorship deprive
> the majority of people of the right to watch what they
> want, but it will not significantly lessen the violence
> in society (24).

Distinguish Your Ideas from the Source's Ideas

PLAGIARISM

> Any attempt to control television violence will quickly
> reach the point of diminishing returns. There is no way
> to make absolutely certain that a particular television
> program will not cause a disturbed person to commit a
> crime. It seems silly, then, to treat the majority of
> people as "potential murderers" just to control the
> behavior of a few (Siano 24).

In the preceding passage, it appears that only the quotation in the last sentence is borrowed from Siano's article. In fact, the ideas in the second sentence are also Siano's. The writer should use an identifying phrase (such as "According to Siano") to acknowledge the borrowed material in this sentence and to show where it begins. (Note that each quotation requires its own documentation.)

CORRECT

> Any attempt to control television violence will quickly
> reach the point of diminishing returns. According to
> Brian Siano, we cannot be absolutely certain that a
> particular television program will not cause a disturbed
> person to commit a crime (24). It seems silly, then, to
> treat the majority of people as "potential murderers"
> just to control the behavior of a few (24).

G   Drafting a Thesis Statement

For more on thesis statements, see 12D.

After you have taken notes, review the information you have gathered, and draft a thesis statement. Your **thesis statement** is a single sentence that states the main idea of your paper and tells readers what to expect. After reviewing her notes, Allison Rogers came up with the following thesis statement for her paper on media violence.

Thesis Statement

> For most adults, no amount of onscreen violence is an excuse for violent behavior; when it comes to young children, however, violent movies present a real danger.

H   Making an Outline

Once you have drafted a thesis statement, you are ready to make an outline. Your outline, which covers just the body paragraphs of your paper, can be either a **topic outline** (in which each idea is expressed in a word or a short phrase) or a **sentence outline** (in which each idea is expressed in a complete sentence). After reviewing her notes, Allison Rogers wrote the following sentence outline for her paper.

I. Teenagers claim the movie Natural Born Killers made them commit murder.
   A. According to John Grisham, the movie inspired the teenagers to commit their crimes.
   B. Grisham says that several murders have been committed by teenagers who say they were influenced by the movie.
II. The idea that movie violence causes violent behavior is not supported.
   A. Other factors could have influenced the teenagers.
   B. No clear link between media violence and aggressive behavior has been discovered.
III. Anecdotal evidence supporting the link between "copycat crimes" and media violence has two problems.
   A. Movies are seldom definitively linked to crimes.
   B. Anecdotal evidence is not representative.
IV. The right of the majority to watch movies and television shows of their choice should not be limited because some unbalanced people may commit crimes.

For more on outlining, see 12E.

```
      V. Still, young children should be protected from
         media violence.
         A. Parents should protect young children.
            1. Parents should monitor what children see on
               television and in the movies.
            2. Parents should discuss the content of movies
               and television shows with their children.
         B. The media should do more to protect young
            children.
            1. Movie theaters should enforce rating systems.
            2. Violent programs should not be shown on sta-
               tions whose audience is primarily children.
```

I Writing Your Paper

Once you have decided on a thesis and written an outline, you are ready to write a draft of your paper. Begin with an **introduction** that includes your thesis statement. Usually, your introduction will be a single paragraph, but sometimes it will be longer.

In the **body** of your research paper, you support your thesis statement, with each body paragraph developing a single point. These paragraphs should have clear topic sentences so that your readers will know exactly what points you are making. Use transitional words and phrases to help readers follow your ideas.

For more on introductions and conclusions, see 13A and 13B.

Finally, your **conclusion** should give readers a sense of completion. Like your introduction, your conclusion will usually be a single paragraph, but it could be longer. It should reinforce your thesis statement and should end with a memorable sentence.

Remember, you will probably write several drafts of your paper before you hand it in. You can use the Self-Assessment Checklists on page 147 to help you revise and edit your paper.

Allison Rogers's completed paper on media violence begins on page 630.

J Documenting Your Sources

When you **document** your sources, you tell readers where you found the ideas that you used in your paper. The Modern Language Association (MLA) recommends the following documentation style for research papers. This format consists of *parenthetical references* within the paper that refer to a *Works Cited* list at the end of the paper.

Parenthetical References in the Text

A parenthetical reference should include just enough information to lead readers to a specific entry in your Works Cited list. A typical parenthetical reference consists of the author's last name and the page number (Grisham 2). If you use more than one work by the same author, include a shortened form of the title in the parenthetical reference (Grisham, "Killers" 4). Notice that there is no *p* or *p.* before the page number.

Whenever possible, introduce information from a source with a phrase that includes the author's name. (If you do this, include only the page number in parentheses.)

    As John Grisham observes in "Unnatural Killers," Oliver
    Stone celebrates gratuitous violence (4).

Place documentation so that it does not interrupt the flow of your ideas, preferably at the end of a sentence.

In three special situations, the format for parenthetical references departs from these guidelines.

1. When You Are Citing a Work by Two Authors

    Film violence has been increasing during the past ten
    years (Williams and Yorst 34).

2. When You Are Citing a Work without a Listed Author

    Ever since cable television came on the scene, shows
    with graphically violent content have been common
    ("Cable Wars" 76).

3. When You Are Citing an Indirect Source

If you use a statement by one author that is quoted in the work of another author, show this by including the abbreviation *qtd. in* ("quoted in").

    When speaking of television drama, Leonard Eron, of the
    University of Illinois, says "perpetrators of violence
    should not be rewarded for violent acts" (qtd. in Siano
    23).

FOCUS   Formatting Quotations

- **Short quotations** Quotations of no more than four typed lines are run in with the text of your paper. End punctuation comes after the parenthetical reference (which follows the quotation marks).

  According to Grisham, there are "only two ways to curb the excessive violence of films like Natural Born Killers" (576).

- **Long quotations** Quotations of more than four lines are set off from the text of your paper. Begin a long quotation ten spaces (or one inch) from the left-hand margin, and do not enclose it in quotation marks. Do not indent the first line of a single paragraph or part of a paragraph. If a quoted passage has more than one paragraph, indent the first line of each paragraph (including the first) three additional spaces (or one-quarter inch). Introduce a long quotation with a complete sentence followed by a colon, and place the parenthetical reference one space *after* the end punctuation.

  Grisham believes that eventually the courts will act to force studio executives to accept responsibility for the effects of their products:

  > But the laughing will soon stop. It will take only one large verdict against the likes of Oliver Stone, and his production company, and perhaps the screenwriter, and the studio itself, and then the party will be over. The verdict will come from the heartland, far away from Southern California, in some small courtroom with no cameras. (577)

FOCUS   Preparing the Works Cited List

- Begin the Works Cited list on a new page after the last page of your paper.
- Number the Works Cited page as the next page of your paper.

(continued on the following page)

(continued from the previous page)

- Center the heading *Works Cited* one inch from the top of the page; do not underline or italicize the heading or place it in quotation marks.
- Double-space the list.
- List entries alphabetically according to the author's last name.
- Alphabetize unsigned works according to the first major word of the title.
- Begin typing each entry at the left-hand margin.
- Indent second and subsequent lines five spaces (or one-half inch).
- Separate each division of the entry—author, title, and publication information—by a period and one space.

The Works Cited List

The Works Cited list includes all the works you cite (refer to) in your paper. Use the guidelines in the box above to prepare your list.

The following sample Works Cited entries cover the situations you will encounter most often. Follow the formats exactly as they appear here.

Note: For more examples of MLA documentation style, see the *MLA Handbook for Writers of Research Papers,* 5th ed. (New York: MLA, 1999) or the MLA Web site <http://www.mla.org>.

Books

Book by One Author

List the author, last name first. Underline the title. Include the city of publication and a shortened form of the publisher's name—for example, *Prentice* for *Prentice Hall* or *Bedford* for *Bedford/St. Martin's*. Use the abbreviation *UP* for *University Press*, as in *Princeton UP* and *U of Chicago P.* End with the date of publication.

```
Brown, Charles T. The Rock and Roll Story. Englewood
     Cliffs: Prentice, 1983.
```

Book by Two or Three Authors

List second and subsequent authors, first name first, in the order in which they are listed on the book's title page.

```
Coe, Sophie D., and Michael D. Coe. The True History of
     Chocolate. New York: Thames, 1996.
```

Book by More Than Three Authors

List only the first author, followed by the abbreviation *et al.* ("and others").

Sklar, Robert E., et al. <u>Movie-Made America: A Cultural
    History of American Movies</u>. New York: Random, 1999.

Two or More Books by the Same Author

List two or more books by the same author in alphabetical order according to title (not counting *A, An,* or *The* at the beginning of the title). In each entry after the first, use three unspaced hyphens (followed by a period) instead of the author's name.

Angelou, Maya. <u>Even the Stars Look Lonesome</u>. New York:
    Bantam, 1997.

---. <u>I Know Why the Caged Bird Sings</u>. New York: Bantam,
    1985.

Edited Book

Dickinson, Emily. <u>The Complete Poems of Emily Dickinson</u>.
    Ed. Thomas H. Johnson. New York: Little, 1990.

Translation

García Márquez, Gabriel. <u>Love in the Time of Cholera</u>.
    Trans. Edith Grossman. New York: Knopf, 1988.

Revised Edition

Gans, Herbert J. <u>The Urban Villagers</u>. 2nd ed. New York:
    Free, 1982.

Anthology

Kirszner, Laurie G., and Stephen R. Mandell, eds.
    <u>Patterns for College Writing</u>. 8th ed. New York:
    Bedford, 2001.

Essay in an Anthology

Grisham, John. "Unnatural Killers." <u>Patterns for College
    Writing</u>. Ed. Laurie G. Kirszner and Stephen R.
    Mandell. 8th ed. New York: Bedford, 2001. 566-75.

Note: Record full publication information (including page numbers) for all information you photocopy or download; you will need this information when you document your sources.

More Than One Essay in the Same Anthology

List each essay separately with a cross-reference to the entire anthology.

Grisham, John. "Unnatural Killers." Kirszner and Mandell
    566-75.

Kirszner, Laurie G., and Stephen R. Mandell, eds.
     <u>Patterns for College Writing</u>. 8th ed. New York:
     Bedford, 2001.

Stone, Oliver. "Memo to John Grisham: What's Next--
     'A Movie Made Me Do It'?" Kirszner and Mandell
     576-79.

Section or Chapter of a Book

Gordimer, Nadine. "Once upon a Time." <u>"Jump" and Other
     Stories</u>. New York: Farrar, 1991. 23-30.

Periodicals

Article in a Journal with Continuous Pagination throughout an Annual Volume

Some scholarly journals have continuous pagination; that is, one issue might
end on page 234, and the next would then begin with page 235. In this case,
the volume number is followed by the year of publication in parentheses.

Allen, Dennis W. "Horror and Perverse Delight:
     Faulkner's 'A Rose for Emily.'" <u>Modern Fiction
     Studies</u> 30 (1984): 685-96.

Note: When one title enclosed in quotation marks falls within another, use single quotation marks for the inside title.

Article in a Journal with Separate Pagination in Each Issue

For a journal in which each issue begins with page 1, the volume number is
followed by a period and the issue number and then by the year. Leave no
space after the period.

Lindemann, Erika. "Teaching as a Rhetorical Art." <u>CEA
     Forum</u> 15.2 (1985): 9-12.

Article in a Monthly or Bimonthly Magazine

If an article does not appear on consecutive pages—for example, if it begins
on page 43, skips to page 47, and continues on page 49—include only the first
page, followed by a plus sign.

O'Brien, Conor Cruise. "Thomas Jefferson: Radical and
     Racist." <u>Atlantic Monthly</u> Oct. 1996: 43+.

Article in a Weekly or Biweekly Magazine (Signed or Unsigned)

Miller, Arthur. "Why I Wrote <u>The Crucible</u>." <u>New Yorker</u>
     21 Oct. 1996: 158-63.

```
"Real Reform Post-Enron." The Nation 4 Mar. 2002: 3.
```

Note: An entry with no listed author begins with the title flush with the left margin. The remaining elements follow the normal order.

Article in a Newspaper

```
Gelles, Jeff. "New Tool to Aid Identity-theft Victims."
    Philadelphia Inquirer 6 Feb. 2002, late ed.: D1.
```

Editorial or Letter to the Editor

```
"Support for the Saudi Struggle." Editorial. New York
    Times 28 Feb. 2002, late ed.: A26.
```

Internet Sources

When citing Internet sources appearing on the World Wide Web, include both the date of electronic publication (if available) and the date you accessed the source. (Some of the following examples include only the date of access; this indicates that the date of publication was not available.) In addition, include the electronic address (URL) enclosed in angle brackets.

Professional Site

```
Words of the Year. American Dialect Society. 18 Jan.
    2002 <http://www.americandialect.org/woty.html>.
```

Personal Site

```
Lynch, Jack. Home page. 21 Dec. 2001 <http://
    andromeda.rutgers.edu/~jlynch>.
```

Article in an Online Reference Book or Encyclopedia

```
"Croatia." The World Factbook 2001. 30 Mar. 2002.
    Central Intelligence Agency. 30 Dec. 2002
    <http://www.odci.gov/cia/publications/factbook>.
```

```
"Empire State Building." Britannica Online. Vers.
    98.1.1. Nov. 1997. Encyclopaedia Britannica. 8 Mar.
    1999 <http://www.eb.com>.
```

Article in a Newspaper

```
Lohr, Steve. "Microsoft Goes to Court." New York
    Times on the Web 19 Oct. 1998. 9 Apr. 1999
    <http://archives.nytimes.com/archives/search/
    fastweb?search>.
```

Editorial

```
"Be Serious." Editorial. Washington Post 25 Mar. 1999.
    9 Apr. 1999 <http://newslibrary.Krmediastream.com/
    cgi-bin/search/wp>.
```

Article in a Magazine

```
Nobel, Philip. "Head for the Hills." Metropolis
    Magazine Feb. 2002. 20 Feb. 2002 <http://
    www.metropolismag.com/html/content_0202/far/
    index.html>.
```

Posting to a Listserv or Newsgroup

Be sure to include the phrase "Online posting."

```
Thune, W. Scott. "Emotion and Rationality in Argument."
    Online posting. 23 Mar. 1997. CCCC/97 Online. 11
    Nov. 1997 <http://www.missouri.edu/HyperNews/get/
    cccc98/proplink/12.html>.
```

Other Nonprint Sources

Television or Radio Program

```
"Prime Suspect 3." Writ. Lynda La Plante. Perf. Helen
    Mirren. Mystery! WNET, New York. 28 Apr. 1994.
```

Videotape, Movie, Record, or Slide Program

```
Updike, John. Interview. "Comments on 'A&P.'" Dir. Bruce
    Schwartz. Videocassette. Harcourt, 1997.
```

Personal Interview

```
Garcetti, Gilbert. Personal interview. 7 May 2000.
```

Material Accessed through a Computer Service

When citing information from a commercial computer service such as
CompuServe, America Online, or Prodigy, include the name of the computer
service (America Online, for example), the date you accessed the material, and
the keyword you entered to find the material.

```
Glicken, Natalie. "Brady Defends Gun Law in Court."
    Congressional Quarterly. America Online. 10 Oct.
    1996. Keyword: CQ.
```

If instead of entering a keyword, you followed a series of topic labels, indicate
the path you used.

```
Yiddish King Lear, The. America Online. 2 July 2002.
    Path: Research and Learning; Arts; Films and
    Movies; Internet Movie Database; King Lear.
```

Material Accessed on a CD-ROM or a DVD

In addition to the publication information, include the medium (CD-ROM),
the vendor (UMI-Proquest, for example), and the date you accessed the
information.

Braunmiller, A. R., ed. <u>Macbeth</u>. By William Shakespeare.
CD-ROM. New York: Voyager, 1994.

If the material you are citing has appeared in print, include the print publication information before the electronic information. Use the abbreviation *n. pag.* ("no pagination") if no pages are given.

Sample Research Paper in MLA Style

Following is Allison Rogers's completed essay on the topic of media violence. The essay follows the conventions of MLA documentation style. Note that it has been reproduced in a narrower format than a standard (8½″ × 11″) sheet of paper.

Rogers 1

Allison Rogers
English 122-83
Prof. Pressman
8 April 2001

                    Violence in the Media
        Mickey and Mallory, two characters in
Oliver Stone's film <u>Natural Born Killers</u>, travel
across the Southwest, killing a total of fifty-
two people. After watching this movie, two
teenagers went on a crime spree of their own
and killed one person and wounded another, para-
lyzing her for the rest of her life. At their
trial, their defense was that watching <u>Natural
Born Killers</u> had made them commit their crimes
and that Hollywood, along with the director of
the movie, Oliver Stone, was to blame. As creative as this defense is, it is hard to accept.
For most adults, no amount of onscreen violence
is an excuse for violent behavior; when it
comes to young children, however, violent movies
present a real danger.
        According to John Grisham, Oliver Stone's
<u>Natural Born Killers</u> "inspired" two teenagers
"to commit murder" (5). Grisham goes on to say
that since the movie was released, several

> Introduction

> Thesis statement

> Paragraph combines quotation and paraphrase from Grisham article with Allison's own observations

Rogers 2

murders have been committed by troubled young
people who claimed they were "under the influence" of Mickey and Mallory (5). This type of
defense keeps reappearing as the violence in our
everyday lives increases: "I am not to blame,"
says the perpetrator. "That movie (or television
show) made me do it."

The idea that violence in the media causes
violent behavior is not supported by the facts.
When we look at Ben and Sarah, the two
teenagers who supposedly imitated Mickey and
Mallory, it is clear that factors other than
Natural Born Killers could have influenced their
decision to commit murder. Both young adults had
long histories of drug and alcohol abuse as
well as psychiatric treatment (Stone 39). In
addition, no clear experimental link between
violent movies and television shows and aggressive behavior has been established. Many studies
have shown that after watching violent television shows, children tend to act aggressively,
but after about a week they return to their
normal pattern of behavior (Siano 22).

What, then, are we supposed to make of
crimes that seem to be inspired by the media? As
Siano points out, a body of anecdotal evidence
supports the link between these "copycat crimes"
and media violence (24). Two problems exist with
this type of "evidence," however. The first problem is that in most cases, the movie or television show is never definitely linked to the
crime. For example, after the movie The Money
Train was released, a clerk in a New York City
subway token booth was set on fire in much the
same way a subway token clerk was in the movie.
Naturally, it appeared as if the movie had
inspired the crime. But at the time of the crime,
several newspapers reported that the violent act

> Paragraph combines
> clearly documented para-
> phrases of Stone and
> Siano articles with
> Allison's own conclusions

> Phrase "As Siano points
> out" introduces Allison's
> summary of source's
> ideas

> No documentation
> necessary for common
> knowledge

36 J

Rogers 3

shown in the movie had occurred at least twice in the year before the movie's release. So the question remains: Did the movie cause the violence, or did it simply reflect a kind of violent behavior that was already present in society? The truth is that we cannot answer this question.

The second problem with anecdotal evidence is that it is not representative. Crimes that are inspired by the media--killers imitating the characters in slasher movies, for example--are unusual. As Siano says, most people who watch violent movies do not go out and commit crimes (24). Only a few people will have such extreme reactions, and because they are mentally unbalanced, we cannot predict what will set them off. It could be a movie like Natural Born Killers, but it could also be a Bugs Bunny cartoon or a Three Stooges movie. Siano's point is that society should not limit the right of the majority to watch the movies and television shows they want to see just because a few unbalanced individuals might go out and commit crimes (24-25).

Even if the link between media violence and violent behavior is not clear, most people agree that young children are easily influenced by what they see. One study has shown that young children who watch violent movies and television shows behave differently from those who do not (American Psychological Association). For this reason, young children should be protected. First, parents need to understand their responsibility for monitoring what their children see on television and in the movies. Second, as the American Psychological Association suggests, parents should take the time to discuss the content of movies and television shows with their children. Parents should be sure to teach

This and the following paragraph combine paraphrases from an article with Allison's own observations

Rogers 4

their children what is real and what is not
real and what is right and what is not right.

The media have already taken steps to protect children. For example, rating systems now
in place can help. These give parents the ability to judge the content of movies before children go to see them and to evaluate television
shows before they are turned on. Clearly, however, more needs to be done to protect young
children. For one thing, these rating systems
must be enforced. If an R movie is being shown
at a theater, for example, the management must
require proof of age. In addition, movies or
television shows containing violence should not
be shown on stations whose audience is primarily
children, such as the Disney Channel, even at
night. The time of day should not matter. When
we think of Disney, Mickey Mouse should come to
mind, not Dirty Harry (American Psychological
Association).

There is no doubt that violence is learned
and that violent media images encourage violent
behavior in young children. It is not clear,
however, that violent movies and television
shows will actually cause an adult to commit a
crime. Placing the blame on the media is just
an easy way to sidestep the hard questions,
such as what is causing so much violence in our
society and what can we do about it. If we
prohibit violent programs, we will only
deprive many people of their right to view the
programs of their choice, and we will prevent
artists from expressing themselves freely.
In the process, these restrictions will also
deprive society of a good deal of worthwhile
entertainment.

> Conclusion

> This paragraph needs
> no documentation
> because it represents
> Allison's own ideas

Rogers 5

Works Cited

American Psychological Association. "Children
    and Television Violence." <u>School Violence
    Virtual Library</u> 6 June 1997. 19 Oct. 2001
    <http://www.uncg.edu/edu/ericcass/
    violence/index.htm>.

Grisham, John. "Unnatural Killers." <u>The Oxford
    American</u> Spring 1996: 2-5.

Siano, Brian. "Frankenstein Must Be Destroyed:
    Chasing the Monster of TV Violence." <u>The
    Humanist</u> Jan.-Feb. 1994: 20-25.

Stone, Oliver. "Memo to John Grisham: What's
    Next--'A Movie Made Me Do It'?" <u>LA Weekly</u>
    29 Mar.-4 Apr. 1996: 39.

Sources for Writing

PREVIEW

In this chapter, you will learn
- to identify and locate books, periodical articles, and other data in your college library (37A)
- to search for and access sources on the Internet (37B)

Both libraries and the Internet offer vast amounts of information. A library provides users with material written by authorities and then evaluated, purchased, and arranged by experienced librarians, who are there to help you. The Internet, however, presents a particular challenge. It not only provides material that may be suitable for research, but it also provides material that may be inaccurate or biased. As a result, users sometimes have difficulty determining what material is appropriate for their research and what is not. Still, as this chapter explains, the Internet can be a valuable tool that you can learn to use to supplement the information that you find in your college library.

A   Library Sources

Your college library is most likely computerized. Whether you use a computer in the library building itself or connect to the library's computer system from your dorm room or at home, you can easily find information both about how your library works and about subjects that interest you or have been assigned to you.

The Library's Home Page

From your college library's home page, you may select a tutorial explaining how to access information in the library. Or you may choose to move directly to searching the library's electronic resources for the information you need. By following instructions that take you to other screens, you can explore electronic materials such as reference books; fiction and nonfiction books; and databases or indexes to magazines, journals, and newspapers. If you want to locate and examine materials available only in print—not yet in digital form — you will need to access the library's online catalog from the library's home page. These resources are discussed on the following pages.

Electronic Reference Books

You may want to begin your research into a particular subject by looking at one or more electronic reference books. On the library's home page, look for a choice such as "Reference Books," which will take you to a listing of electronic encyclopedias, atlases, almanacs, and many other kinds of data. Then, you can use the computer to carry out a search of one or more of these resources for the information you need. (You can ask the reference librarian to help you decide which reference sources to consult.) *Note:* Some libraries' home pages place reference materials under the label "Electonic Databases," where they also place periodicals (see pages 637–639).

FOCUS   **Efficient Electronic Searches**

- Whenever you are asked to type in what you are looking for, you can usually find quick onscreen guidelines about how to word your request—for example, when you should use a word such as *and* or *or.* If you need more help, ask a librarian, or attend an orientation provided by the library staff to help students with searches and other questions about the library's computers.
- In general, you have to strike a balance between typing in a subject that is too broad and one that is too narrow. If your topic is too broad (*cars*, for example), the computer will give you a list with so many items that you will not know where to begin. If your topic is too narrow (*Chevy Impala Convertibles*, for example), the computer may not find much to list. With practice, you will begin to figure out the wording (for example, *car repair*) that will lead you to the information you are looking for.
- In general, use only nouns, adjectives, and connectors such as *and* and *or.* Usually, extra words such as *how, very, the,* and *in* are not useful and, in fact, may slow down the search process.

Electronic Fiction and Nonfiction Books

In addition to or instead of reference materials, you may want to find fiction or nonfiction books about the subject you are researching. In that case, go to the library's home page, and click on a choice such as *Full-Text E-books* or *netLibrary.* Either of these sites give you access to a collection of thousands of online full-text books purchased by your college for your use at a computer. Following directions on the E-books or netLibrary screen, type in what you are looking for. For example, a student researching violence in the media decided to begin by looking for a general introduction to mass media. After typing *mass media* on the search screen of netLibrary, the student saw a list of electronic books dealing with that subject, including *Essentials of Mass Communication Theory,* written by Arthur Asa Berger and published by Sage Publications in 1995.

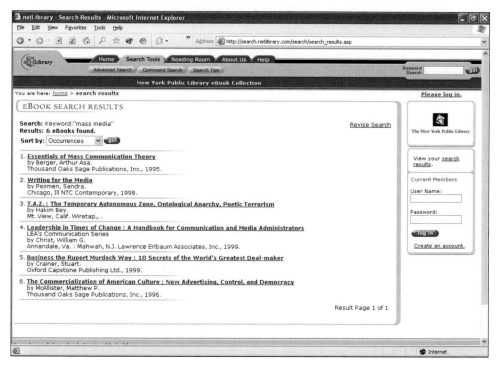

netLibrary E-book Search Results

The student first browsed briefly through the book and then borrowed it electronically for a while. In Chapter 3 he quickly discovered a section called "The Problem of Violence," which provided a helpful overview of exactly the subject the student wanted to explore.

Electronic Databases and Indexes to Periodical Articles

In addition to expecting you to read about your subject in reference books or in fiction and nonfiction books, your instructors expect you to read articles in periodicals that the library subscribes to. **Periodicals** include general newspapers and consumer magazines such as *Newsweek,* which are published for the general public. **Trade magazines**—such as *Golf Digest,* aimed at people with a particular hobby, or *Entrée: Tennessee's Restaurant, Bar, and Foodservice Trade Magazine,* aimed at people in a particular business—are another kind of periodical. Finally, scholarly periodicals called **journals** are published for doctors, lawyers, and people in related professions. These periodicals range from the *American Journal of Bioethics* to the *Yale Journal of Criticism.*

To search for periodical articles about your subject, begin on the library's home page, where you will find one or more of the following choices: (1) a general category such as "Magazine/Newspaper Articles" or "Electronic Databases and Indexes"; (2) a list of disciplines—for example, "accounting" or "health"; (3) the name of one or more specific databases or indexes to periodicals—such as *InfoTrac, ProQuest,* and *EBSCOhost.* (The library computer will tell you what kinds of periodicals each database or index will lead you to; for example, *EBSCOhost* is "for general reference, business, consumer health, general science, humanities, and multi-cultural periodicals.")

Next, the screen will ask what you are looking for. The following example shows the results that came up when a student asked the *EBSCOhost* database to list articles about the subject "movie violence." The database found articles in six periodicals: *The Chronicle of Higher Education, School Library Journal, Newsweek, American Spectator, Maclean's,* and *The Nation.*

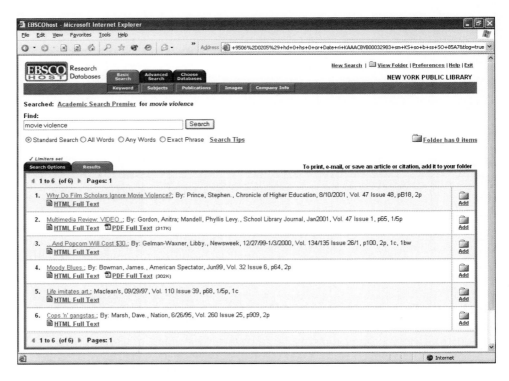

EBSCO Database Periodical Search Results

Often, with just one more click, you can make the full text of an article appear on the screen. You may then read it on screen and take notes (see Chapter 36); or you may print the article, e-mail it to yourself, or save it to your own disk for reading and note taking at another time.

If you find an article listed by the software but not available as full text in electronic form, print out or copy the information about where it appears. With that information, you will be able to find out if your library carries hard copies of the periodical you want; if so, you can locate for yourself (or ask the library staff to find for you) the printed and bound periodicals or **microforms** that contain the articles you need. (A microform is a card or film reel that contains the miniaturized contents of periodicals. With a special reader, you can project the miniature images back to full-size pages so that you can read the contents.)

Print Indexes to Periodical Articles

If you are looking for an old issue of a periodical, you will need to use old print indexes. Such print indexes include the popular index to general periodicals — *Readers' Guide to Periodical Literature* — as well as print indexes to more specialized periodicals — for example, *Social Science Index, General Science Index, Applied Science and Technology Index,* and *Business Periodicals Index.* (For recent or current articles, all these indexes are available online.)

The Library's Catalog to Printed Books and Recordings

Beyond its wealth of online materials, your college library has many printed books and recorded audio and video offerings. Until recently, libraries had card catalogs in which users would look up a subject, title, or author's name to see which materials were available. Some libraries still have card catalogs for their oldest books. Currently, though, most libraries have computer catalogs.

To find out which printed books and recorded materials your library has on your subject, go to the library's home page, select "Library Catalog," and type in the subject you are researching. For example, the student interested in "media violence" typed that phrase on the library catalog's search screen; the computer responded by listing several items. Here is the detailed entry that the catalog provided about a book that the student decided to examine. (This entry would also have come up if the student had known and typed in the author's name, last name first, or the title.)

CALL #:	P 96 .V5 B65 1998
AUTHOR:	Bok, Sissela
TITLE:	Mayhem: violence as public entertainment

(continued on the following page)

(continued from the previous page)

PUBLISHER: Reading, Mass.: Perseus, © 1998.

SUBJECTS: violence in mass media

NOTES: includes bibliographic references (pp. 159–181) and index.

ISBN: 0201489791

LOCATION: circulation stacks

CHECKED IN: yes

To examine the book itself, note if it is available (that is, "checked in"), and then print out the catalog entry, or copy by hand the call number and other essential information about the book. Then, search the library shelves for the book with that call number printed or typed on its spine.

FOCUS   **Call Numbers and Library Classification Systems**

Books in a library are arranged according to fields: all the books on accounting are together in one section of the shelves, and all the books on zoology are together in another section. When you know the call number of a book, you can go to the correct section of shelves (or stacks) to get the book.

Most college libraries use the Library of Congress Classification System, which divides books into twenty-one fields and assigns each field a call number beginning with a letter of the alphabet. For example, a book carrying the letter H will be about social sciences. If the book's call number has a second letter, that indicates a subcategory of the field. For example, a call number beginning with the code HF indicates a book about commerce, a subcategory of all the H books.

Most public libraries use the Dewey Decimal Classification System, which divides and codes books differently but also uses call numbers.

Other Library Terms

Here are a few additional terms that you may come across as you do library research.

closed stacks   Some libraries do not store books where users can get them for themselves. Instead, the books stay in areas called closed stacks, where only authorized library workers can retrieve them. To read such books, you have to submit their call numbers and author and title information and wait while library personnel get the books for you.

interlibrary loan   A library that does not own a particular item but that is part of a larger library system—say, part of a university system that has campuses throughout an entire state—can arrange to borrow that item for you by means of an interlibrary loan.

reserve materials   When all the students in a class need to read a particular printed article at approximately the same time, the instructor may ask the library to photocopy the article and keep the photocopies on reserve in a special place in the library. Students can read the article in the library, or they can borrow it for a short time (perhaps just overnight). Sometimes instructors also put a book or photocopies of part of a book on reserve. Professors put materials on reserve so students will not have to purchase a book to read only one chapter.

specialized libraries   If you were looking for a good deal of material on one particular subject, you might not be able to find it in your college library. In this case, you might go to a specialized library, such as the National Library of Medicine in Bethesda, Maryland, or the Helen Fowler Library at the Denver Botanic Gardens.

◆ PRACTICE 37-1

Be prepared to discuss your answers to each of the following questions in class.

1. Of the following reference titles, which ones do you think might have information about the writer Tom Clancy? *Book Review Digest, Contemporary Authors, Current Biography, Encarta* (the Microsoft encyclopedia), *Encyclopaedia Britannica, Encyclopedia of Computer Science and Technology, Statistical Abstract of the United States, Times Atlas of the World,* or *The World Almanac and Book of Facts.*

2. Using your library's catalog, identify two books about jazz.

3. A student wants to find books about movie directors who have won Oscars. He is trying to decide if he should search netLibrary and the library catalog for *movies* or *Oscar movies* or *directors* or *how to direct and win*. Which term would you advise him to type on a search screen? Why?

◆ PRACTICE 37-2

1. Using an electronic database or a printed index, find the title of an article about rebuilding on the site of the World Trade Center towers in New York City. Note the author, if identified; the name of the periodical; and as much publication information (date, volume, issue, and page numbers) as possible. Be prepared to explain how you found your source.

2. On each blank in the left column, write the letter of the item in the right column that correctly identifies or defines it.

1. works to be borrowed for a limited time and to be read in the library _____

2. area from which only library workers can retrieve books _____

3. specialized library _____

4. system that makes books from one branch or institution available to another _____

a. Folger Shakespeare Library in Washington, D.C.

b. reserve materials

c. interlibrary loan

d. closed stacks

B   Internet Sources

The **Internet** is a network of millions of computers at colleges and universities, government agencies, research institutions, businesses, and libraries all over the world. The Internet can give you access to a world of information—information that can help you in school and in your everyday life. Here are some of the things you can do on the Internet.

■ Send and receive messages via e-mail
■ Send and receive text files (for example, assignments), graphics, sound, animation, film clips, and live video
■ Read articles and other documents about practically any subject, from asteroids to engineering to Zen Buddhism
■ Send messages to electronic "bulletin boards" set up for your classes or for other groups, and read messages sent by others

When people refer to the Internet, they often mean the **World Wide Web**. The Web, which forms an important part of the Internet, is a collection of millions of documents on every imaginable topic. The Web relies on **hypertext links**—specially highlighted words and phrases. By clicking your computer's mouse on these links, you can move easily from one part of a document to another, or from one **Web site** (collection of documents) to another.

For example, a Web article discussing immigration might have the word *Cuban* highlighted in a different color from the rest of the text. Clicking on this word might take you to a discussion of Cuban immigration. This discussion, in turn, might include links to articles, bulletin board postings, or other material about Cuban history, Cuban politics, Fidel Castro, Cuban cultural life in the United States, and so on.

Finding Information on the Internet

To use the Internet, you need an Internet **browser**, a tool that enables you to display Web pages. The most popular browsers are Netscape Navigator and Microsoft Internet Explorer. Most new computers come with one of these browsers already installed.

Before you can access the Internet, you have to be **online**—that is, connected to an **Internet service provider (ISP)**. Many colleges and universities provide Internet access free of charge to students. In addition, companies such as America Online provide access for a monthly fee. Once you are online, you need to connect to a **search engine**, a program that helps you find information by sorting through the millions of documents that are available on the Internet. Among the most popular search engines are AltaVista <www.altavista.com>, Google <www.google.com>, and Yahoo <www.yahoo.com>.

There are three ways to use a search engine to find information.

1. *You can enter a Web site's URL.* All search engines have a box in which you can enter a Web site's electronic address, or **URL**. When you click on the URL or hit your computer's Enter or Return key, the search engine connects you to the Web site. For example, to find information about family members who entered the United States through Ellis Island, you would enter this URL: *www.ellisislandrecords.com.*

2. *You can do a keyword search.* All search engines let you do a **keyword search**: you type a term into a box, and the search engine looks for documents that contain the term, listing all the **hits** (documents containing one or both of these words) that it found. If you type in a broad term like *civil war,* you might get hundreds of thousands of hits—more than you could possibly consider. If this occurs, do not give up. Narrow your search by using a more specific term—*Battle of Gettysburg,* for example. You can focus your search even further by putting quotation marks around the term *("Battle of Gettysburg").* When you do this, the search engine will search only for documents that contain this phrase.

Computer Tip

It is a good idea to **bookmark** useful sites by selecting the Bookmark or Favorites option at the top of your browser screen. Once you bookmark a site, you can easily return to it whenever you want.

---

3. *You can do a subject search.* Some search engines, such as Yahoo, let you do a **subject search**. First, you choose a broad subject from a list of subjects: The Humanities, The Arts, Entertainment, Business, and so on. Each of these general subjects leads you to more specific subjects, until eventually you get to the subtopic that you want. For example, you could start your search on Yahoo with the general topic *Entertainment*. Clicking on this topic would lead you to *Movies* and then to *Movie Reviews*. Finally, you would get to a list of movie reviews that might link to a review of the specific movie you are interested in.

FOCUS   **Accessing Web Sites: Troubleshooting**

Sometimes your computer will tell you that a site you want to visit is unavailable or does not exist. When this occurs, consider the following possibilities before moving on to another site.

- *Check to make sure the URL is correct.* To reach a site, you have to type its URL accurately. Do not add spaces between items in the address or put a period at the end. Any error will send you to the wrong site—or to no site at all.
- *Check to make sure you are connected to the Internet.* To reach a site, you have to be connected to the Internet. If you are not properly connected, your computer will indicate this.
- *Check to make sure your computer is connected to your phone line.* A loose connection or an unplugged phone jack will make it impossible for you to access the Internet. If your computer is not connected to a phone line, it will indicate that it is not receiving a dial tone.
- *Check to make sure the site still exists.* Web sites, especially those maintained by individuals, frequently disappear because people either cannot afford to maintain a site or lose interest in doing so. If you entered a URL correctly, your computer is functioning properly, and you still cannot access a site, chances are that the site no longer exists.
- *Try revisiting the site later.* Sometimes Web sites experience technical problems that prevent them from being accessed. Your computer will tell you if a site is temporarily unreachable.

Evaluating Web Sites

Not every Web site is a valuable source of information. In fact, anyone can put information on the Internet. For this reason, it is a good idea to approach Web sites with skepticism. In a sense, Web sites are like strangers knocking at your door: before you let them in, you need to be sure they are honest and trustworthy. To determine whether information you find on the Internet is believable and useful, you must evaluate the Web site where you found the information.

FOCUS **Evaluating Web Sites**

To decide whether to use information from a particular Web site, try to answer the following questions:

- *Is the site reliable?* Never rely on information by an unidentified author; always try to determine the author of material on a Web site. Also, try to determine the author's qualifications. For example, say you are looking at a site that discusses Labrador retrievers. Is the author a breeder? A veterinarian? Someone who has had a Lab as a pet? The first two authors would probably be authorities on the subject; the third author might not be.
- *Does the site have a hidden purpose?* When you evaluate a Web site, be sure to consider its purpose. For example, a site discussing the health benefits of herbal medicine would have one purpose if it were sponsored by a university and another if it were sponsored by a company selling herbal remedies. Researchers who post information on a university site are trying to inform others about their findings. Retailers, however, put information online to sell a product; therefore, they sometimes make exaggerated claims about its usefulness.

Computer Tip

A Web site's URL can give you information about the site's purpose. For example, the suffix *.edu* indicates that the site is sponsored by an educational institution; *.gov* indicates a government agency; *.org* indicates a nonprofit organization; and *.com* indicates a business.

- *Is the site up-to-date?* If a site has not been recently updated, you should question the information it contains. A discussion of foot-and-mouth disease in England, for example, would be out of date if it were written before the widespread outbreak in 2001. You would have to continue your search until you found a more current discussion.

(continued on the following page)

(continued from the previous page)

◾ *Is the information on the site trustworthy?* A site should include evidence to support what it says. If it does not, consider the information to be unsupported personal opinion. Points should be supported with facts, examples, statistics, and expert opinions—not rumors or thirdhand opinions.

◾ *Does the site contain needlessly elaborate graphics?* With Web sites, substance counts more than style. When you come across a site that has slick visuals—animation, bright colors, and lots of pictures—don't be misled. Make sure that these graphic elements do not mask weak logic or uninformed opinion.

Using the Internet to Locate Information for Assignments

You can use the Internet to find information about the subjects you are studying. For example, if in your communication class you were discussing early television sitcoms, you could go to the Internet and find Web sites devoted to this subject. You could also find specific sites for shows such as *I Love Lucy*, *The Honeymooners*, and *The Brady Bunch*. The following sites can help you access information that will be useful for many of your courses.

Academic Subjects on the Web

The Humanities

Art history
Art History Resources on the Web
<http://witcombe.sbc.edu/
ARTHLinks.html>

Film
The Internet Movie Database
<http://www.imdb.com>

History
HyperHistory Online
<http://www.hyperhistory.com/
online_n2/History_n2/a.html>

Literature
The On-Line Books Page
<http://digital.library.upenn.edu/
books/>

Philosophy
Stanford Encyclopedia of
Philosophy
<http://plato.stanford.edu>

The Natural Sciences

Biology
Biodiversity and Biological
Collections Web Server
<http://biodiversity.uno.edu>

Chemistry
WWW Chemistry Resources
<http://www.chem.ucla.edu/
chempointers.html>

Engineering
The Engineer's Reference
<http://www.eng-sol.com>

(continued on the following page)

(continued from the previous page)

Mathematics
Math.com
<http://www.math.com>

Physics
Web Links: Physics around the World
<http://www.physicsweb.org/resources/>

The Social Sciences

Education
Education World®
<http://www.education-world.com/>

Political science
Political Resources on the Net
<http://www.politicalresources.net>

Psychology
PsychCrawler
<http://www.psychcrawler.com>

Sociology and social work
Social Work and Social Services Web Sites
<http://gwbweb.wustl.edu/websites.html>

FOCUS   **Avoiding Plagiarism**

When you transfer information from Web sites into your notes, you may be tempted to "cut and paste" text without noting where the text comes from. If you then copy this text into a draft of your paper, you are committing plagiarism—the theft of ideas. Every college has rules that students must follow when using words, ideas, and visuals from books, articles, and Internet sources. Consult your school's Web site or student handbook for information on the appropriate use of such information.

Using the Internet to Improve Your Writing

The Internet has many Web sites that can help you with your writing. Sites like the following ones include links to other useful sites.

Writing Help on the Web

The *Writing in Context* site
<http://www.bedfordstmartins.com/writingincontext>

Help with the writing process
Principles of Composition
<http://webster.commnet.edu/
(continued on the following page)

(continued from the previous page)
grammar/composition/
composition.htm>
The UVic Writer's Guide
<http://web.uvic.ca/wguide>

Help finding something to say
*Paradigm Online Writing
Assistant: Choosing a Subject*
<http://www.powa.org/
whtfrms.htm>

Help writing paragraphs
Purposes of Paragraphs
<http://www.fas.harvard.edu/
~wricntr/para.html>
Writing Paragraphs
<http://www.uottawa.ca/
academic/arts/writcent/
hypergrammar/paragrph.html>

Advice on revision
*Paradigm: Global and Local
Perspectives*
<http://www.powa.org/
revifrms.htm>

Tips on grammar
The Online English Grammar
<http://www.edunet.com/
english/grammar>
Guide to Grammar and Writing
<http://webster.commnet.edu/
grammar/index.htm>

Tips on proofreading
Tips for Effective Proofreading
<http://www.ualr.edu/~owl/
tipsforproofreading.htm>
Proofreading
<http://www.bgsu.edu/
departments/writing-lab/
goproofreading.html>

Online writing centers
LEO: Literacy Education Online
<http://leo.stcloudstate.edu>
Online Writing Lab
<http://owl.english.purdue.edu>

Using the Internet to Locate Everyday Information

The Internet can make your daily life easier. For example, you can use the
Internet to access news and weather reports, download voter registration
forms, get travel information, find directions, obtain consumer information,
locate people, find movie reviews—or even find a job. The following sites are
just a sample of the many resources available on the Internet.

Everyday Information on the Web

The Bible
The Unbound Bible
<http://www.unboundbible.org>

Book reviews
The New York Times *on the
Web: Books*
<http://www.nytimes.com/books>
(continued on the following page)

(continued from the previous page)

Calendars

Calendar Zone

<http://www.calendarzone.com>

Census data

U.S. Census Bureau Newsletter: Census and You

<http://www.census.gov/prod/www/abs/cen-you.html>

City and county data

U.S. Census Bureau: County and City Data Book

<http://www.census.gov/statab/www/ccdb.html>

Computers

Free On-Line Dictionary of Computing

<http://foldoc.doc.ic.ac.uk/foldoc/index.html>

Dictionaries

yourDictionary.com™

<http://www.yourdictionary.com>

Employment

America's Job Bank

<http://www.ajb.dni.us>

Encyclopedias

Britannica.com®

<http://www.britannica.com>

Genealogy

Lineages

<http://www.lineages.com>

Insurance company ratings

A. M. Best Insurance Information

<http://ambest.com/insurance>

Law and legal information

American Law Sources On-line

<http://lawsource.com/also>

Maps and directions

MapBlast!

<http://www.mapblast.com/myblast/index.mb>

Movie reviews

The Internet Movie Database

<http://www.imdb.com>

Newspapers

Newspapers.Com

<http://www.newspapers.com>

Telephone directories

AnyWho

<http://www.tollfree.att.net>

Switchboard.com

<http://www.switchboard.com>

Weather forecasts and information

National Weather Service Home Page

<http://www.nws.noaa.gov>

◆ **PRACTICE 37-3**

At home or in your school's computer lab, practice entering five of the URLs listed on pages 646–649. Make sure you enter the URLs exactly as they appear on the page. If a URL you enter does not take you to the appropriate Web site, check to make sure that you entered the URL correctly. (If the site is no longer active, choose another URL from the list.)

◆ PRACTICE 37-4

Working in a group of four students, select one of the Web sites listed on pages 646–649. At home or in your school's computer lab, access the site, and make a list of three things you like and three things you dislike about it. Then, exchange lists with another student in your group. In what ways do you agree? In what ways do you disagree?

◆ PRACTICE 37-5

Access the following Web site, which focuses on evaluating Web resources: <http://www2.widener.edu/Wolfgram-Memorial-Library/webevaluation/ webeval.htm>. Do you think this site is useful? Why or why not? Write a few sentences explaining your answer.

◆ PRACTICE 37-6

Working in a group of three or four students, access two or three of the Web sites listed on pages 646–649. Choose one site, and evaluate it according to the guidelines listed on pages 645–646. Present your group's findings to the class.

◆ PRACTICE 37-7

Use one of the search engines listed on page 643 to locate a Web site that focuses on a topic you know a lot about—for example, your hometown, a famous person, or a sport. Evaluate the site according to the guidelines listed on pages 645–646.

Strategies for College Success

Learning the time-tested strategies discussed in this appendix can help to make your life as a college student more productive and less stressful.

1 Learning Orientation Strategies

Some strategies come in handy even before school begins, as you orient yourself to life as a college student. In fact, you may already have discovered some of them.

- Make sure you have a college catalog, a photo ID, a student handbook, a parking permit, and any other items that entering students at your school are expected to have.
- Read your school's orientation materials (distributed as handouts or posted on the school Web site) very carefully. These materials will help you to familiarize yourself with campus buildings and offices, course offerings, faculty members, extracurricular activities, and so on.
- Be sure you know your academic adviser's name (and how to spell it), e-mail address, office location, and office hours. Copy this information into your personal address book.
- Get a copy of the library's orientation materials. These will tell you about the library's hours and services and explain procedures such as how to use the online catalog.
- Be sure you know where things are—not just how to find the library and the parking lot, but also where you can do photocopying or buy a newspaper. You might as well learn to find your way around before things get too hectic.

2 Learning First-Week Strategies

College can seem like a confusing place at first, but from your first day as a college student, there are steps you can take to help you get your bearings.

1. *Make yourself at home.* Find places on campus where you can get something to eat or drink, and find a good place to study or relax before or between classes. As you explore the campus, try to locate all the things you need to feel comfortable—for example, pay phones, ATMs, and rest rooms.

2. *Know where you are going and when you need to be there.* Check the building and room number for each of your classes and the days and hours the class meets. Copy this information onto the front cover of the appropriate notebook. Pay particular attention to classes with irregular schedules (for example, a class that meets from 9 a.m. to 10 a.m. on Tuesdays but from 11 a.m. to 12 noon on Thursdays).

3. *Get to know your fellow students.* Get the name, phone number, and e-mail address of two students in each of your classes. If you miss class, you will need to get in touch with someone to find out what material you missed.

4. *Familiarize yourself with each course's syllabus.* At the first meeting of every course, your instructor will hand out a **syllabus**, an outline or summary of course requirements, policies, and procedures. (The syllabus may also be posted on the course's Web page.) A syllabus gives you three kinds of useful information.

   - Practical information, such as the instructor's office number and e-mail address and what books and supplies to buy
   - Information that can help you plan a study schedule—for example, when assignments are due and when exams are scheduled
   - Information about the instructor's policies on absences, grading, class participation, and so on

   Read each syllabus carefully, ask questions about anything you do not understand, refer to all your course syllabi regularly—and do not lose them.

5. *Buy books and supplies.* When you buy your books and supplies, be sure to keep the receipts, and do not write your name in your books until you are certain that you are not going to drop a course. (If you write in a book, you will not be able to return it.) If your roster of courses is not definite, wait a few days to buy your texts. You should, however, buy some items right away: a separate notebook and folder for each course you are taking, a college dictionary, and a pocket organizer (see A8). In addition to the books and other items required for a particular course (for example, a lab notebook, a programmable calculator, art supplies), you should buy pens and pencils in different colors, blank computer disks, paper clips or a stapler, Post-it notes, highlighter pens, and so on. (Remember to buy a backpack or bookbag in which to keep all these items!)

6. *Set up your notebooks.* Establish a separate notebook (or a separate section of a divided notebook) for each of your classes. Copy your instructor's name, e-mail address, phone number, and office hours and location

into the inside front cover of the notebook; write your own name, address, and phone number on the outside.

FOCUS **Using a Dictionary**

Even though your computer has a spell checker, you still need to buy a dictionary. A college dictionary tells you not only how to spell words but also what words mean and how to use them.

---

3 **Learning Day-to-Day Strategies**

As you get busier and busier, you may find that it is hard to keep everything under control. Here are some strategies to help you as you move through the semester.

1. *Find a place to study.* As a college student, you will need your own private place to work and study. Even if it is just a desk in one corner of your dorm room (or, if you are living at home, in one corner of your bedroom or at the back of your basement or garage), you will need a place that is yours alone, a place that will be undisturbed when you leave it. (The kitchen table, which you share with roommates or family members, will not work.) This space should include everything you will need to make your work easier—quiet, good lighting, a comfortable chair, a clean work surface, storage for supplies, and so on.

2. *Set up a bookshelf.* Keep your textbooks, dictionary, calculator, supplies, and everything else you use regularly for your coursework in one place— ideally, in your own work space. That way, when you need something, you will know exactly where it is.

3. *Set up a study schedule.* Identify thirty- to forty-five-minute blocks of free time before, between, and after classes. Set this time aside for review. Remember, studying should be part of your regular routine, not something you do only the night before an exam.

4. *Establish priorities.* It is very important to understand what your priorities are. Before you can establish priorities, however, you have to know which assignments are due first, which ones can be done in steps, and which tasks or steps will be most time consuming. Then, you must decide which tasks are most pressing. For example, studying for a test to be given the next day is more pressing than reviewing notes for a test scheduled for the following week. Finally, you have to decide which tasks are more important than others. For example, studying for a midterm is more important than studying for a quiz, and the midterm for a course you are

in danger of failing is more important than the midterm for a course in which you are doing well. Remember, you cannot do everything at once; you need to know what must be done immediately and what can wait.

FOCUS **Skills Check**

Do not wait until you have a paper to write to discover that your computer skills need improvement. Be sure your basic word-processing skills are at the level you need for your work. If you need help, get it right away.

5. ***Check your mail.*** Check your campus mailbox or e-mail account regularly—if possible, several times a day. If you miss a message, you may miss important information about changes in assignments, canceled classes, or rescheduled quizzes.

6. ***Schedule conferences.*** Try to meet with each of your instructors during the semester even if you are not required to do so. You might schedule one conference during the second or third week of school and another a week or two before a major exam or paper is due. Your instructors will appreciate and respect your initiative.

7. ***Become familiar with the student services available on your campus.*** College is hard work, and you cannot do everything on your own. There is nothing shameful about getting help from your school's writing lab or tutoring center or from the center for disabled students (which serves students with learning disabilities as well as physical challenges), the office of international students, or the counseling center, as well as from your adviser or course instructors. Think of yourself as a consumer. You are paying for your education, and you are entitled to—and should take advantage of—all the available services you need.

FOCUS **Asking for Help**

Despite all your careful planning, you may still run into trouble. For example, you may miss an exam and have to make it up; you may miss several days of classes in a row and fall behind in your work; you may have trouble understanding the material in one of your courses; or a family member may get sick. Do not wait until you are overwhelmed to ask for help. If you have an ongoing personal problem or a family emergency, let your instructors know immediately.

4   Learning Note-Taking Strategies

Learning to take notes in a college class takes practice, but taking good notes is essential for success in college. Here are some basic guidelines that will help you develop and improve your note-taking skills.

During Class

1. *Come to class.* If you miss class, you miss notes—so come to class, and come on time. In class, sit where you can see the board or screen and hear the instructor. Do not feel you have to keep sitting in the same place in each class every day; change your seat until you find a spot that is comfortable for you.

2. *Date your notes.* Begin each class by writing the date at the top of the page. Instructors frequently identify material that will be on a test by dates. If you do not date your notes, you may not know what to study.

3. *Know what to write down.* You cannot possibly write down everything an instructor says. If you try, you will miss a lot of important information. Listen carefully *before* you write, and listen for cues to what is important. For example, sometimes the instructor will tell you that something is important, or that a particular piece of information will be on a test. If the instructor emphasizes an idea or underlines it on the board, you should do the same in your notes. Of course, if you have done the assigned reading before class, you will recognize important topics and know to take especially careful notes when these topics are introduced in class.

4. *Include examples.* Try to write down an example for each general concept introduced in class—something that will help you remember what the instructor was talking about. (If you do not have time to include examples as you take notes during class, add them when you review your notes.) For instance, if your world history instructor is explaining *nationalism*, you should write down not only a definition but also an example, such as "Germany in 1848."

5. *Write legibly, and use helpful signals.* Use dark (blue or black) ink for your note-taking, but keep a red or green pen handy to highlight important information, jot down announcements (such as a change in a test date), note gaps in your notes, or question confusing points. Do not take notes in pencil, which is hard to read and not as permanent as ink.

6. *Ask questions.* If you do not hear (or do not understand) something your instructor said, or if you need an example to help you understand something, *ask!* But do not immediately turn to another student for clarification. Instead, wait to see if the instructor explains further, or if he or she pauses to ask if anyone has a question. If you are not comfortable asking a question during class, make a note of the question and ask the instructor—or send an e-mail—after class.

After Class

1. *Review your notes.* After every class, try to spend ten or fifteen minutes rereading your notes, filling in gaps and examples while the material is still fresh in your mind.
2. *Recopy information.* When you have a break between classes, or when you get home, recopy important pieces of information from your notes.

For information on calendars and organizers, see A8.

   ■ Copy announcements (such as quiz dates) onto your calendar.
   ■ Copy reminders (for example, a note to schedule a conference before your next paper is due) into your organizer.
   ■ Copy questions you have to ask the instructor onto the top of the next blank page in your class notebook.

Before the Next Class

1. *Reread your notes.* Leave time to skim the previous class's notes once more just before each class. This strategy will get you oriented for the class to come and will remind you of anything that needs clarification or further explanation.
2. *Ask for help.* Call a classmate if you need to fill in missing information; if you still need help, see the instructor during his or her office hours, or come to class early so that you can ask your question before class begins.

5   Learning Homework Strategies

Doing homework is an important part of your education. Homework gives you a chance to practice your skills and measure your progress. If you are having trouble with the homework, chances are you are having trouble with the course. Ask the instructor or teaching assistant for help *now;* do not wait until the day before the exam. Here are some tips for getting the most out of your homework.

1. *Write down the assignment.* Do not expect to remember an assignment; copy it down. If you are not sure exactly what you are supposed to do, check with your instructor or another student.
2. *Do your homework, and do it on time.* Teachers assign homework to reinforce classwork, and they expect homework to be done on a regular basis. It is easy to fall behind in college, but trying to do three—or five—days' worth of homework in one day is not a good idea. If you do several assignments at once, you not only overload yourself, but you also miss important day-to-day connections with classwork.

3. *Be an active reader.* Get into the habit of highlighting your textbooks and other material as you read.

4. *Join study groups.* A study group of three or four students can be a valuable support system for homework as well as for exams. If your schedule permits, do some homework assignments—or at least review your homework—with other students on a regular basis. In addition to learning information, you will learn different strategies for doing assignments.

For information on specific reading strategies, see the Introduction.

6   Learning Exam-Taking Strategies

Preparation for an exam should begin well before the exam is announced. In a sense, you begin this preparation on the first day of class.

Before the Exam

1. *Attend every class.* Regular attendance in class—where you can listen, ask questions, and take notes—is the best possible preparation for exams. If you do have to miss a class, arrange to copy (and read) another student's notes *before the next class* so you will be able to follow the discussion.

2. *Keep up with the reading.* Read every assignment, and read it before the class in which it will be discussed. If you do not, you may have trouble understanding what is going on in class.

3. *Take careful notes.* Take careful, thorough notes, but be selective. If you can, compare your notes on a regular basis with those of other students in the class; working together, you can fill in gaps or correct errors. Establishing a buddy system will also force you to review your notes regularly instead of just on the night before the exam.

4. *Study on your own.* When an exam is announced, adjust your study schedule—and your priorities—so that you have time to review everything. (This is especially important if you have more than one exam in a short period of time.) Over a period of several days, review all your material (class notes, readings, and so on), and then review it again. Make a note of anything you do not understand, and keep track of topics you need to review. Try to predict the most likely questions, and—if you have time—practice answering them.

5. *Study with a group.* If you can set up a study group, you should certainly do so. Studying with others can help you understand the material better. However, do not come to group sessions unprepared and expect to get everything from the other students. You must first study on your own.

6. *Make an appointment with your instructor.* Set up an appointment with the instructor or with the course's teaching assistant a few days before the exam. Bring to this conference any specific questions you have about

course content and about the format of the upcoming exam. (Be sure to review all your study material before the conference.)

7. ***Review the material one last time.*** The night before the exam is not the time to begin your studying; it is the time to review. When you have finished your review, get a good night's sleep.

During the Exam

By the time you walk into the exam room, you will already have done all you could to get ready for the test. Your goal now is to keep the momentum going and not do anything to undermine all your hard work.

FOCUS   **Writing Essay Exams**

If you are asked to write an essay on an exam, remember that what you are really being asked to do is write a **thesis-and-support essay**. Chapter 12 of this text tells you how to do this.

---

1. ***Read through the entire exam.*** Be sure you understand how much time you have, how many points each question is worth, and exactly what each question is asking you to do. Many exam questions call for just a short answer—*yes* or *no, true* or *false*. Others ask you to fill in a blank with a few words, and still others require you to select the best answer from among several choices. If you are not absolutely certain what kind of answer a particular question calls for, ask the instructor or the proctor *before* you begin to write. (Remember, on some tests there is no penalty for guessing, but on other tests it is best to answer only those questions you have time to read and consider carefully.)

2. ***Budget your time.*** Once you understand how much each section of the exam and each question are worth, plan your time and set your priorities, devoting the most time to the most important questions. If you know you tend to rush through exams, or if you find you often run out of time before you get to the end of a test, you might try putting a mark on your paper when about one-third of the allotted time has passed (for a one-hour exam, put a mark on your paper after twenty minutes) to make sure you are pacing yourself appropriately.

3. ***Reread each question.*** Carefully reread each question *before* you start to answer it. Underline the **key words**—the words that give specific information about how to approach the question and how to phrase your answer.

  Remember, even if everything you write is correct, your response is not acceptable if you do not answer the question. If a question asks you to *compare* two novels, writing a *summary* of one of them will not be acceptable.

FOCUS	Key Words

Here are some helpful key words to look for on exams.

analyze	explain	suggest results,
argue	give examples	effects, outcomes
compare	identify	summarize
contrast	illustrate	support
define	recount	take a stand
demonstrate	suggest causes,	trace
describe	origins,	
evaluate	contributing factors	

4. ***Brainstorm to help yourself recall the material.*** If you are writing a paragraph or an essay, look frequently at the question as you brainstorm. (You can write your brainstorming notes on the inside cover of the exam book.) Quickly write down all the relevant points you can think of—what the textbook had to say, your instructor's comments, and so on. The more you can think of now, the more you will have to choose from when you write your answer.

5. ***Write down the main idea.*** Looking closely at the way the question is worded and at your brainstorming notes, write a sentence that states the main idea of your answer. If you are writing a paragraph, this sentence will be your topic sentence; if you are writing an essay, it will be your thesis statement.

6. ***List your main points.*** You do not want to waste your limited (and valuable) time writing a detailed outline, but an informal outline that lists just your key points is worth the little time it takes. An informal outline will help you plan a clear direction for your paragraph or essay.

7. ***Draft your answer.*** You will spend most of your time actually writing the answers to the questions on the exam. Follow your outline, keep track of time, and consult your brainstorming notes when you need to—but stay focused on your writing.

8. ***Reread, revise, and edit.*** When you have finished drafting your answer, reread it carefully to make sure it says everything you want it to say—and that it answers the question.

For more on brainstorming, see 1C and 12C.

For more on topic sentences, see 2A and 2C.

7	**Learning Public-Speaking Strategies**

In college classes, you may be called on to speak not only informally in one-on-one situations or in small groups but also more formally in front of an audience. Even though for many people the thought of speaking in public is terrifying, there are a number of things you can do to make the process easier and less stressful. The following strategies can help you plan and deliver your presentation.

Before an Individual Oral Presentation

1. *Know your purpose.* When an instructor gives you a speaking assignment, be sure you know your purpose: Do you have to recount an experience, take a stand on a controversial issue, or do something else?

2. *Know your audience.* As with written communication, you have to figure out what listeners already know (and how they feel) about the topic of your speech. If some listeners are more knowledgeable and sophisticated than others, you have to figure out how to appeal to both groups without insulting one or confusing the other.

3. *Identify your main idea.* Using invention strategies such as those discussed in Chapter 1 should lead you to a clear statement of your speech's main idea. Keep this statement simpler and clearer than the thesis statement you might put in a piece of writing that you prepare for readers. Remember, readers can reread a passage they cannot understand; however, in an oral presentation, you have only one chance to communicate your ideas to your audience.

4. *Gather support for your main idea.* Do not expect listeners to accept your main idea without facts, examples, or other details to support it. Even with such support, be prepared for listeners who will challenge you or ask you to explain your ideas in more depth.

5. *Think of your presentation in three parts.* A time-tested piece of advice for speakers is "Tell them what you're going to tell them; tell them; tell them what you told them." The point behind this advice is that listening is hard work, so a speaker needs not only to state the main idea—a simple idea—in simple terms but also to repeat the idea throughout the course of a speech. The speech's main idea should be evident at the beginning of the speech, in the body of the speech, and in the conclusion. An effective speaker figures out how to accomplish this goal and how to help the audience understand the main idea without making the speech monotonous.

6. *Develop notes and an outline for each part.* Usually, instructors in public-speaking classes want you to give **extemporaneous** presentations: speeches that you have planned and practiced but that you do not read word for word from a fully written-out essay. These teachers will direct you to prepare notes—usually on index cards—to keep in front of you as you speak to your audience. The simplest way to arrange these notes is in the form of an outline.

7. *Use clear signals to guide your listeners.* Be sure to give readers cues about where you are in the speech—for example, when you are about to present the main idea, when you will present support for the main idea,

and when you are about to finish. Because it is more difficult to follow a speech than a piece of writing, you will need to include more transitions than you would in your writing.

Transitions to Use in Speeches

I believe that . . . ; I can cite three examples to support my point that . . . ; First . . . , Second . . . , In addition to the preceding two examples, here is the third and most significant example . . . Now that you have heard my three examples . . . ; I want to end with the following anecdote . . . ; I hope you agree that . . .

8. ***Prepare visual aids.*** You will not always need visual aids, but sometimes—for example, when you are explaining a process or tracing causes— you may communicate your main idea and supporting points more clearly if you give the audience something to look at. If you are explaining how an abacus works, for example, you may want to show one to your listeners. If you are talking about a dance, you may want to have someone perform its steps during your presentation. Or you may show photos, drawings, maps, posters, or even a videotape.

Alternatively, you may use presentation software such as Microsoft PowerPoint to produce graphs, charts, or lists that you can project from your computer. Or you can print these visuals on acetate sheets and, with an overhead projector, enlarge and display them on a wall or screen.

FOCUS   Designing and Displaying Visual Aids

- Do not clutter your slides with pictures or, in the case of PowerPoint, special effects. Use a clear typeface such as Chicago or New York.
- Do not use visuals that your audience cannot see clearly. Use images that are large enough for your audience to see and that will reproduce clearly.
- Do not make lettering too small. Use 40- to 50-point type for titles, 25- to 30-point type for major points, and 20- to 25-point type for other points.
- Do not include full sentences or paragraphs. Use bulleted lists.
- Do not put too many points on one visual. Four is a good upper limit.
- Do not use too many colors and too many styles of type. Make sure that there is a clear contrast between the background and the lettering. (See the sample PowerPoint slide on the next page.)

(continued on the following page)

(continued from the previous page)

■ Do not let the audience see the visual before you introduce it or after you finish talking about it.

■ Do not talk to the visual. Look at and talk to your audience. Even if you have to point to the visual on the screen, make sure you are looking at your audience when you speak.

A college student used PowerPoint to prepare this slide for a presentation on how he landed a job. He selected two easy-to-read typefaces—one for the main head and another for the two levels of subheads. He used 44-point, 28-point, and 20-point type sizes. Notice that the three bulleted subheads are parallel: they are all nouns. If the student were to add a verb to the first— "Studied company literature," for example—he would have to add a verb to the other two also—maybe "Checked library" and "Practiced networking."

9. ***Integrating a visual aid.*** Do not just show or read the visual to your audience. Tell your audience more than they can see or read for themselves. For example, on a map, you might point out the route of the trip you are reporting on; for a bar graph, you might convert the raw numbers to a proportion and state how much more ice cream sells in July than in January.

10. ***Practice. Practice. Practice.*** Be sure to rehearse enough times to guarantee that you know the order of points in your presentation (including

when to show visual aids) and how to move from one point to the next. You must rehearse enough so that even though you have only notes in front of you, you are confident that you can convert the words and phrases to full sentences. Leave time for a trial run with a friend, and ask for feedback on content and delivery; then take time to apply the friend's feedback and improve your presentation. Finally, leave time to rehearse more—cutting and adding as necessary—until you know you can stay within the required time limit.

During an Individual Oral Presentation

1. *Accept nervousness as part of the process.* The trick is to convert this fear into the positive energy that will catch and hold your audience's attention.

FOCUS **Dealing with Anxiety**

Your goal should not be to eliminate anxiety totally. The complete absence of anxiety in a speaker leads to overconfidence, which can irritate and even bore an audience. Instead, learn to cope with anxiety by doing enough preparation so that you feel you *own* your speech. In other words, work on the speech to the point where you are comfortable with—but not smug about—your main idea and supporting points. You want to be so familiar with the material that you can relax enough to sound natural, not stiff.

---

2. *Do not begin speaking while you are still looking at your notes.* Look first at your audience. Most coaches advise speakers to pick a few people in different parts of the room and to alternate eye contact among them during the speech.
3. *Speak slowly.* No matter how slowly you think you are speaking, chances are you can slow down further. Take your time.
4. *Make every movement count.* Do not pace as you speak or move your hands erratically. Stand in one spot, and gesture to emphasize a point or to display a visual aid. (Arrange in advance to have someone in the audience perform certain tasks—for example, distributing handouts.) Depending on the topic and level of formality of your speech (and your instructor's guidelines), you may stand directly in front of your audience or behind a lectern.
5. *Do not get flustered if someone asks you to speak louder.* In addition, do not get upset if some people in your audience look bored; you might

change your pace or volume to get more attention, but remember that a bored person may be overtired, preoccupied, or just a poor listener.

6. ***Do not sit down too quickly.*** Leave time for questions. Your audience may want to ask questions or challenge what you have said. If someone asks a question that you have already answered in your speech, repeat the information as briefly as possible. And do not be upset if someone begins to argue with you; an appropriate response might be "I never thought of that angle," "I respectfully disagree because . . .," or "I need to think about that point more."

FOCUS   **Group Presentations**

Sometimes a public speaking assignment will involve group work. A group presentation requires you to cooperate with other students to bring a discussion or a performance to an audience. Whether you are participating in a panel discussion about college services or performing a dramatic reading of a one-act play, a group presentation involves intensive behind-the-scenes work. You must understand your own role as well as those of everyone else: Who is in charge? Who sets the pace? Who prepares and displays the visuals? Furthermore, everyone in a group situation must bear responsibility for sticking to a schedule for research and rehearsal. After rehearsals and after the actual presentation, everyone should contribute to evaluations of the group effort and figure out how to improve the next time around.

---

8   Learning Time-Management Strategies

Learning to manage your time is very important for success in college. Here are some strategies you can adopt to make this task easier.

1. ***Use an organizer.*** Whether you prefer a print organizer or an electronic one, you should certainly use one—and use it *consistently*. If you are most comfortable with paper and pencil, purchase a "week-on-two-pages" academic year organizer (one that begins in September, not January); the "week-on-two-pages" format (see pages 665–666) gives you more writing room for Monday through Friday than for the weekend, and it also lets you view an entire week at once.

    Carry your organizer with you at all times. At the beginning of the semester, copy down key pieces of information from your course syllabi—for example, the date of every quiz and exam and the due date of every paper. As the semester progresses, continue to write in assignments and deadlines. Also, enter information such as days when a class will be canceled or will meet in the computer lab or in the library, reminders to bring a particular book or piece of equipment to class, and appointments with instructors or other college personnel. You can also jot down reminders and schedule appointments that are not related to school—for example, changes in your work hours, a dentist appointment, or lunch with a friend. (In addition to writing notes on the pages for each date, some students like to keep a separate month-by-month "to do" list. Crossing out completed items can give you a feeling of accomplishment—and make the road ahead look shorter.)

The first sample organizer below shows how you can use an organizer to keep track of deadlines, appointments, and reminders. The second sample organizer (page 666) includes not only this information but also a study schedule, with notes about particular tasks to be done each day.

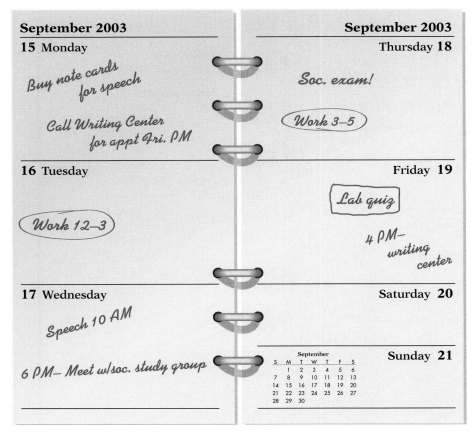

Sample Organizer Page: Deadlines, Appointments, and Reminders Only

2. *Use a calendar.* Buy a large calendar, and post it where you will see it every morning—on your desk, in your car, or on the refrigerator. At the beginning of the semester, fill in important dates such as school holidays, work commitments, exam dates, and due dates for papers and projects. When you return from school each day, update the calendar with any new information you have entered into your organizer.

3. *Plan ahead.* If you think you will need help from a writing lab tutor to revise a paper that is due in two weeks, do not wait until day thirteen to make an appointment; all the time slots may be filled by then. To be safe, make an appointment for help about a week in advance.

4. *Learn to enjoy downtime.* One final—and very important—point to remember is that you are entitled to "waste" a little time. When you have a free minute, take time for yourself—and do not feel guilty about it.

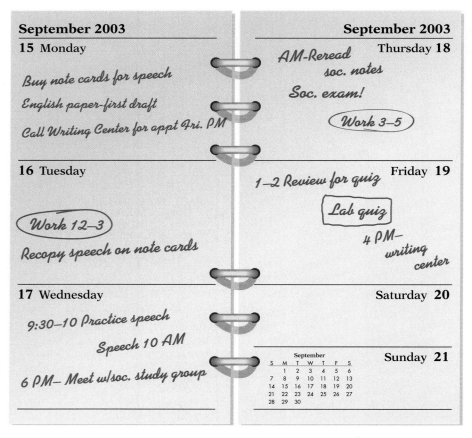

Sample Organizer Page: Deadlines, Appointments, Reminders, and Study Schedule

9   Learning Job Application Strategies

Seeking a job—whether to earn money and gain experience while you are in school or to pursue a career after you have finished school—requires that you understand your goals, look for job leads in the right places, learn about companies and organizations that might employ you, and—most important—learn how to market yourself.

Defining Your Goals

1. *Determine how much time you have.* How many hours do you think you need to work? How many hours a week *can* you work while still in school? Are those hours distributed throughout the week, or are they all on one or two days—for example, Saturday and Sunday? Can you work during conventional business hours, or will you need to work evenings? In addition to conventional full-time jobs demanding a minimum of 35 hours per week, part-time jobs and special short-term assignments are increasingly available as employers replace expensive staff with more affordable freelance workers.

2. *Consider unpaid work.* If you can afford to fill a low-paying or unpaid internship, you can gain the experience you need to land a paying position later on. In addition to exploring established internships, you can create your own internship by offering to work at an organization without pay so that you can learn how the organization operates. In either case, you should take your internship seriously—showing up regularly (and on time), volunteering for unglamorous tasks, and seeking out contacts with whom you can network.

FOCUS   **Advice for Finding Part-time and Short-term Jobs**

- Think carefully about balancing school and part-time work. Do not let work get in the way of school assignments or pull down your grades.
- Be honest from the outset with a potential employer. For a part-time job, be clear about the maximum number of hours you can work each week. For a summer or other short-term job, explain when you will leave to return to school.
- Consider industries that often look for people who want to work 8 to 20 hours a week or on special projects but who do not need the employment benefits. These industries include publishing, public relations, and event planning for sports, performing arts, and trade organizations. Many small offices look for college students who can help with paperwork and administrative duties one or two days a week.

A 9

Learning about Job Openings

1. *Check your college placement office.* Placement offices generally list both part-time and full-time jobs as well as short-term and temporary positions. Sometimes these lists are available only in the office; sometimes they are accessible online. In addition to placement offices, individual academic departments may use real or virtual bulletin boards to list job openings for students.

2. *Scan newspaper and Web listings.* Many people find jobs through classified advertisements in newspapers or on Web sites, so you may want to check them out. Commercial Web sites also post listings and invite job seekers to post their résumés for employers to scan. (See "Marketing Yourself," page 669.)

3. *Network.* Networking is a powerful tool for learning about job openings and for learning the values and priorities of employers. Basically, networking involves telling instructors, friends, and relatives about your goals and qualifications and finding out who may have helpful information for you.

4. *Keep your eyes open.* Many jobs are never advertised. Some small businesses, for example, rely on word of mouth, signs put in store windows, or flyers posted on campus or community bulletin boards. If you are looking for work, you need to be on the alert for job possibilities at all times.

Researching Companies and Organizations

1. *Explore Web sites of companies, organizations, and their competitors.* Even though Web sites exist to enhance companies' images, they can be useful to you. First, they tell you how a company or organization sees itself. Second, they usually identify key personnel. Third, they often contain news releases that can keep you up to date about new projects or possible plans for expansion.

2. *Use library resources.* In your campus library, in the library section of your college placement service, or in a local public library, you can find books and electronic resources that can help you with your job search. Ask a librarian which books he or she recommends. Also, ask about electronic services such as *Career Search*. These resources will help you to identify places where you might want to work; they will also help you to answer the questions about the organization that an interviewer or a network acquaintance might ask you. The library is also the place where, by using one or more electronic databases, you can locate and read magazine, journal, and newspaper articles about the organizations of interest to you. (See Chapter 37, "Sources for Writing.")

3. *Expand your network.* Once you have identified companies and organizations that appeal to you and that may be hiring, use the resources in your college placement office or the alumni office to find out if graduates of your school already work there. Sometimes these graduates will be will-

ing to take the time to share information that can help you learn if a company is right for you—or if it will be hiring in the near future.

Marketing Yourself

1. *Prepare your résumé.* Here is one of the harshest facts about job searching: the résumé that you spend hours perfecting usually gets no more than a few seconds' review. To increase your résumé's chance of generating interest, you need to include everything an employer expects to see. Beyond the essential contact information, a résumé should include most of the following items (the asterisks identify the sections you *must* include):

   - OBJECTIVE or GOAL to help a screener who may have several positions to fill
   - SUMMARY to emphasize your greatest strengths or the most relevant facts about you and to serve as a bridge to the rest of the résumé
   - EDUCATION* and EXPERIENCE* to demonstrate qualifications (under *Experience*, be sure to include internships and volunteer work, summer and campus jobs, temporary work, entrepreneurial undertakings, and extracurricular positions)
   - SPECIAL SKILLS to illustrate how you are different from others who are applying for the job (under *Special Skills*, be sure to include proficiency in languages other than English as well as specific computer experience)
   - ACTIVITIES, ACHIEVEMENTS, HONORS, LEADERSHIP, and INTERESTS to highlight exceptional accomplishments
   - REFERENCES who will support what you have written about yourself

   Your school placement officer can tell you which of the above items to include. The placement office will also have the latest information on résumé formats and on variations required for submitting a résumé electronically. Be prepared to update your résumé on a regular basis as your experiences and preferences change.

2. *Prepare a cover letter.* Do not simply repeat in the cover letter what your résumé already says. Instead, use the cover letter to make yourself stand out from the crowd by showing what you know about the organization's needs, identifying how you can benefit the organization, and respectfully requesting an interview. If possible, address your letter to a specific individual rather than to a general audience such as "Dear Sir or Madam." The company's Web site, the job ad or posting, or your networking contacts can help you identify the person to whom you should write. (Keep in mind that when you post a résumé online, there usually is no cover letter.)

3. *Prepare for an interview.* During the job interview, you will listen to an interviewer, answer his or her questions, and ask questions of your own. Interviews take place in person or by phone; they may occur on campus or in an employer's office. The interviewer wants to see if you are suited for the job and if you can think on your feet. Go into an interview prepared

to answer standard questions (see page 674). Dress neatly and conservatively, make eye contact, smile comfortably, demonstrate common-sense behavior (arrive on time, do not smoke, and so on), and be honest about your qualifications. (But do not undersell yourself.)

4. *Write the follow-up letter.* A strong follow-up letter—one that is both respectful and enthusiastic—will make a favorable impression on a potential employer. If you want to expand on or adjust an answer that you gave in the interview, this is your chance.

FOCUS   **Coping with Application Forms**

Large organizations often require job applicants to fill out an application form even though they are carrying carefully prepared résumés. Usually, these forms ask for information not provided on the résumé— for example, a Social Security number, the telephone number of someone to call in case of an emergency, or the reasons for leaving former jobs. Arrive prepared to fill in those blanks. Sometimes the human resources office will allow an applicant to attach his or her résumé to the form after he or she has filled it out.

The following résumé, cover letter, and follow-up letter were written by a student for a full-time, permanent position in the field of hotel management.

Rolando J. Matta

UNTIL JUNE 1, 2003	AFTER JUNE 1, 2003
321 Topland Avenue	c/o Fried
Johnson City, NY 13790	6543 Lincoln Street, 6D
607 737-1111	Chicago, IL 60666
rjmatta@fhcc.edu	312 787-5555
	rjmatta@hotmail.com

OBJECTIVE   Associate innkeeper position in the Chicago area

Summarize key strengths discussed below →

SUMMARY   Employment in moderate-priced and upscale hotels; skill in spoken and written communication

EDUCATION   Fox Hollow Community College, Johnson City, NY 13790

(continued on the following page)

(continued from the previous page)

```
        Major: Hospitality Management
        Expected Date of Graduation: June 2003
        GPA of 3.4 on a 4.0 scale
        Major courses (partial list)
        Hotel and Restaurant Accounting
        Hotel-Restaurant Organization and Management
        Food Purchasing
        Principles of Food Preparation
        Executive Housekeeping
        Hotel Front-Office Operations
        Hospitality Law
```

Omit if under 3.0; explain grades if asked

EXPERIENCE

**Hospitality Internship,
  May 2002 to August 2002
Grande Hotel, New York, NY**

- Rotated through Front Desk, Housekeeping, and Room Service departments in hands-on and supervisory positions
- Participated in weekly question-and-answer sessions with key managers
- Reported on satisfaction of American Bar Association conventioneers
- Researched cost savings on alternative gifts for returning guests

**Assistant to Meetings Supervisor,
  August 2001 to May 2002
VIP Executive Suites, Binghamton, NY**

- Coordinated and reviewed setup and breakdown of furniture and refreshments for all meeting rooms
- Liaised with audiovisual department
- Reviewed all billing against contracts
- Scheduled appointments for prospective clients with supervisor

Use boldface and bullets to highlight data

OTHER SKILLS

Proficiency with MS Office, the Internet; good communication with computer technicians; bilingual (English, Spanish)

ACTIVITIES

Travel in Latin America; registration in summer cooking classes, New York

REFERENCES

Available on request

Or give names, titles, and phone numbers here

Sample Résumé

321 Topland Avenue
Johnson City, NY 13790
607 737-1111
rjmatta@fhcc.edu

April 1, 2003

Ms. Jennifer T. White
Manager
Rotunda Hotel and Sports Club
88990 Airport Highway
Chicago, IL 60677

Dear Ms. White:

Try writing to referrals rather than sending a blind mailing

Mr. Luigi Cuenca of the Grande Hotel in New York, where I worked last summer, tells me that you will shortly be interviewing candidates for management assistants. I believe my experience in Mr. Cuenca's facility and elsewhere have prepared me for the challenge of working at the Rotunda.

Tell what you know about the organization and what you can bring to it

Since your hotel is at O'Hare Airport, I know that many of your guests stay at the Rotunda because of last-minute flight cancellations due to weather. For this reason, my experience in responding to frustrated travelers will be of use to you. In addition, I have been reading about services that boutique hotels in Europe and Australia offer to business travelers. I would like to have the opportunity of implementing such services for business travelers in the States.

Politely indicate what comes next

I have enclosed my résumé, and I look forward to talking with you at your convenience. I will be available for an interview anytime after my final exams on May 30th.

Sincerely,

Rolando J. Matta

Remember to sign above your typed name

Rolando J. Matta

Sample Cover Letter

321 Topland Avenue
Johnson City, NY 13790
607 737-1111
rjmatta@fhcc.edu

June 10, 2003

Ms. Jennifer T. White
Manager
Rotunda Hotel and Sports Club
88990 Airport Highway
Chicago, IL 60677

Dear Ms. White:

Thank you for meeting with me earlier today. I appreciated the opportunity to speak with you. I especially enjoyed hearing how your facility is similar to and different from the Grande Hotel in New York City.

Thank the interviewer

The Web site for the boutique hotel in Sydney that we discussed is www.medusa.com.au. On this Web site you will find photos of the wall units that each room contains. These units not only make an attractive appearance, but they also save space in the closet and in the mini-kitchen.

Provide information offered or requested

I am extremely interested in joining your staff and feel certain that I could contribute much to your organization.

State enthusiasm directly and briefly

Sincerely,

Rolando J. Matta

Rolando J. Matta

Sample Letter after an Interview

FOCUS **Interviews: Frequently Asked Questions**

Prepare short but focused answers to the following common interview questions. Go over your answers with someone you can trust to provide honest feedback.

1. Tell me about yourself.
2. Where do you see yourself in five years?
3. How do you respond to criticism?
4. What accomplishment have you been most proud of? How did you solve problems along the way to the accomplishment?
5. Are you a team player? More a leader or a follower?
6. What have you learned about handling conflict?
7. What is your greatest strength? What is your greatest weakness?
8. Why did you go to [name of college]? What did you like about it? What did you not like?
9. Why isn't your GPA higher?
10. What do you know about this organization?
11. Are you willing to relocate or travel?

Answers to Odd-Numbered Exercise Items

Chapter 15

◆ **PRACTICE 15-1, page 230**

Answers: **(1)** Complete subject: Derek Walcott **(3)** Complete subject: Walcott's early years; simple subject: years **(5)** Complete subject: His early poems; simple subject: poems **(7)** Complete subject: Walcott **(9)** Complete subject: the renowned poet; simple subject: poet **(11)** Complete subject: the sixty-two-year-old Caribbean poet; simple subject: poet

◆ **PRACTICE 15-2, page 231**

Possible answers: **(1)** pets **(3)** Pets **(5)** Social workers/Nurses/Doctors **(7)** patients **(9)** dogs

◆ **PRACTICE 15-3, page 231**

Answers: **(1)** Sixteen nations; plural **(3)** Living quarters; plural **(5)** They; plural **(7)** Russia and the United States; plural **(9)** An international crew; singular

◆ **PRACTICE 15-4, page 233**

Answers: **(1)** Prepositional phrases: With more than 27 percent, of the vote, in history; subject: Theodore Roosevelt **(3)** Prepositional phrases: Until Roosevelt, of votes; subject: candidate **(5)** Prepositional phrases: For example, of the Progressive Party, about 16 percent, of the vote, in the 1924 race; subject: Robert M. LaFollette **(7)** Prepositional phrases: In 1980, of the vote; subject: John B. Anderson **(9)** Prepositional phrases: In 2000, with the support, of many environmentalists, for the presidency; subject: Ralph Nader

◆ **PRACTICE 15-5, page 236**

Answers: **(1)** see **(3)** offers **(5)** enters; wins **(7)** realizes **(9)** enjoy

◆ **PRACTICE 15-6, page 236**

Answers: **(1)** are **(3)** is **(5)** is **(7)** becomes **(9)** are

◆ **PRACTICE 15-7, page 237**

Answers: **(1)** wrote **(3)** is; seems **(5)** lives **(7)** dies **(9)** works

◆ **PRACTICE 15-8, page 238**

Answers: **(1)** Complete verb: had become; helping verb: had **(3)** Complete verb: had become; helping verb: had **(5)** Complete verb: would get; helping verb: would **(7)** Complete verb: did cause; helping verb: did **(9)** Complete verb: would remain; helping verb: would

Chapter 16

◆ **PRACTICE 16-1, page 244**

Answers: **(1)** , and **(3)** , and **(5)** , and **(7)** , so/ and **(9)** , for

◆ **PRACTICE 16-2, page 245**

Answers: **(1)** , for **(3)** , or **(5)** , but **(7)** , for **(9)** , and

◆ **PRACTICE 16-3, page 245**

Possible edits: Diet, exercise, and family history may account for centenarians' long lives, but this is not the whole story. Recently, a study conducted in Georgia showed surprising common traits among centenarians. They did not necessarily avoid tobacco and alcohol, nor did they eat low-fat diets. In fact, they ate relatively large amounts of fat, cholesterol, and sugar, so diet could not explain their long lives. They did, however, share four key survival characteristics. First, all of the centenarians were optimistic about life, and all of them were positive thinkers. They were also involved in religious life and had deep religious faith. In addition, all the centenarians had continued to lead physically active lives, and they remained mobile even as elderly people. Finally, all were able to adapt to loss. They had all experienced the deaths of friends, spouses, or children, but they were able to get on with their lives.

◆ PRACTICE 16-4, page 246
Answers will vary.

◆ PRACTICE 16-5, page 248
Answers: **(1)** Sometimes runners-up are better remembered than winners; the triumphant are forgotten. **(3)** Robert Falcon Scott was a British naval officer; Roald Amundsen was a Norwegian explorer. **(5)** Amundsen's men buried food along the trail; Scott's men left food in only a few locations. **(7)** Amundsen's men made it to the Pole in December 1911; Scott's party arrived in January 1912. **(9)** Scott's exhausted party could not get to their scarce provisions; none of the men survived the trek to the Pole.

◆ PRACTICE 16-6, page 249
Answers will vary.

◆ PRACTICE 16-7, page 252
Answers: **(1)** Andrew F. Smith, a food historian, wrote a book about the tomato; subsequently, he wrote a book about ketchup. **(3)** The word *ketchup* may have come from a Chinese word; however, Smith is not certain of the word's origins. **(5)** Ketchup has changed a lot over the years; for example, special dyes were developed in the nineteenth century to make it red. **(7)** Ketchup is now used by people in many cultures; still, salsa is more popular than ketchup in the United States. **(9)** Some of today's ketchups are chunky; in addition, some ketchups are spicy.

◆ PRACTICE 16-8, page 252
Possible edits: **(1)** *Time* selects the Man of the Year to honor the person who has most influenced the previous year's events; consequently, the choice is often a prominent politician. **(3)** During the war years, Hitler, Stalin, Churchill, and Roosevelt were all chosen; in fact, Stalin was featured twice. **(5)** In 1956, The Hungarian Freedom Fighter was Man of the Year; then, in 1966, *Time* editors chose The Young Generation. **(7)** In 1975, American Women were honored as a group; nevertheless, the Man of the Year has nearly always been male. **(9)** The Man of the Year has almost always been one or more human beings; however, the Computer was selected in 1982 and Endangered Earth in 1988.

◆ PRACTICE 16-9, page 253
Possible answers: **(1)** Living at home gives students access to free home-cooked meals; in contrast, dorm residents eat dining hall food. **(3)** Being at home means the commuters get to take part in family life; however, they may also miss out on social activities on campus. **(5)** At most colleges, commuters have access to social activities such as dances, clubs, and games; in fact, many campuses have their own commuter social groups. **(7)** Commuter students might have to help take care of younger or older family members; for example, the student might baby-sit for a younger brother or sister. **(9)** Commuters are always under the watchful eye of their parents; moreover, their parents are likely to be stricter than the dorm counselor.

◆ PRACTICE 16-10, page 255
Answers will vary.

Chapter 17

◆ PRACTICE 17-1, page 260
Answers: **(1)** Independent clause **(3)** Dependent clause **(5)** Independent clause **(7)** Independent clause **(9)** Dependent clause

◆ PRACTICE 17-2, page 261
Answers: **(1)** Independent clause **(3)** Independent clause **(5)** Dependent clause **(7)** Dependent clause **(9)** Independent clause

◆ **PRACTICE 17-3, page 263**

Possible answers: **(1)** When/As **(3)** Although **(5)** Because **(7)** Even though **(9)** wherever

◆ **PRACTICE 17-4, page 264**

Possible edits: **(1)** Although professional midwives are used widely in Europe, in the United States, they usually practice independently only in areas with few doctors. **(3)** Stephen Crane powerfully describes battles in *The Red Badge of Courage* even though he never experienced a war. **(5)** After Jonas Salk developed the first polio vaccine in the 1950s, the incidence of polio began to decline rapidly in the United States. **(7)** Before the Du Ponts arrived from France in 1800, American gunpowder was inferior to French gunpowder. **(9)** Because Thaddeus Stevens thought plantation land should be distributed to freed slaves, he disagreed with Lincoln's peace terms for the South.

◆ **PRACTICE 17-5, page 266**

Answers: **(1)** Most Japanese learn English in high school by reading passages from textbooks that are designed to get them into universities. **(3)** Some Japanese who could not understand spoken English have been killed or injured in the United States. **(5)** This case has led many Japanese to learn "usable English" that will help them when they travel to the United States.

◆ **PRACTICE 17-6, page 267**

Possible answers: **(1)** MTV's very first music video, which was performed by a group called the Buggles, made the claim "Video Killed the Radio Star." **(3)** Recording executives, who had been suspicious of MTV at first, soon realized the power of music videos in selling records. **(5)** Today, MTV, which devotes less and less time to music videos, produces many hours of original programming aimed at young people.

◆ **PRACTICE 17-7, page 268**

Answers will vary.

Chapter 18

◆ **PRACTICE 18-1, page 274**

Answers will vary.

◆ **PRACTICE 18-2, page 277**

Answers: **(1)** Adverb: sometimes; edited sentence: Sometimes, job applicants feel tongue-tied or even ill when asked questions. **(3)** Adverb: first; edited sentence: First, applicants should realize that interviewers expect nervousness. **(5)** Adverb: ultimately; edited sentence: Ultimately, job applicants must trust their own abilities during interviews.

◆ **PRACTICE 18-3, page 277**

Answers will vary.

◆ **PRACTICE 18-4, page 278**

Answers: **(1)** Prepositional phrase: during World War II; edited sentence: During World War II, many male factory workers became soldiers. **(3)** Prepositional phrase: in the war's early years; edited sentence: In the war's early years, the U.S. government encouraged women to take factory jobs. **(5)** Prepositional phrase: in unprecedented numbers; edited sentence: In unprecedented numbers, they entered the industrial workplace.

◆ **PRACTICE 18-5, page 278**

Answers will vary.

◆ **PRACTICE 18-6, page 279**

Answers: **(5)** After graduation, these professors can also write letters of recommendation for them. **(7)** In addition, the study recommends that students study in groups and that they take courses that require writing, preferably several short papers rather than one long one. **(9)** Throughout their college careers, students should give themselves a chance to become involved in outside activities.

◆ **PRACTICE 18-7, page 280**

Possible edits: **(7)** Of course, the fans also share the blame for the violence of football.

◆ **PRACTICE 18-8, page 282**

Answers: **(1)** Growing up in the slums of London, Charlie Chaplin began his acting career in vaudeville shows. **(3)** Adding writing and directing to acting, Chaplin made his first famous film, *The Tramp*, in 1915. **(5)** Continuing to play the little tramp in other silent films, Chaplin starred in *The Kid* (1921) and *The Gold Rush* (1925). **(7)** Charming audiences in *City Lights*, the little tramp was last seen in *Modern Times* (1936). **(9)** Departing from Hollywood in the 1950s, Chaplin settled in England.

◆ PRACTICE 18-9, page 283

Answers will vary.

◆ PRACTICE 18-10, page 284

Answers: **(1)** Captured as a young girl by a rival tribe, Sacajawea was later sold into slavery. **(3)** Hired by the explorers Lewis and Clark in 1806, Charbonneau brought his pregnant wife along on their westward expedition. **(5)** Guided by Sacajawea's knowledge of the rugged terrain, the expedition also benefited from her familiarity with native food plants. **(7)** Protected by the presence of a Shoshone woman and her infant, Lewis and Clark encountered little hostility from the tribes they met. **(9)** Celebrated for many years as an American hero, Sacajawea recently received an additional honor.

◆ PRACTICE 18-11, page 286

Answers will vary.

◆ PRACTICE 18-12, page 287

Answers: **(1)** American tourists and foreign visitors flock to Orlando's theme parks. **(3)** At the Magic Kingdom, the roller coaster Space Mountain and the Pirates of the Caribbean ride draw large crowds. **(5)** Children and adults enjoy having their pictures taken with Mickey Mouse.

◆ PRACTICE 18-13, page 288

Answers: **(1)** Despite his lack of formal education, Edison had a quick mind and showed a talent for problem solving. **(3)** Edison patented the earliest phonograph in 1878 and created the first practical light bulb the following year. **(5)** Edison held many patents and made a fortune from his inventions.

◆ PRACTICE 18-14, page 288

Answers: **(1)** These college presidents and their supporters want to improve the academic performance of college athletes. **(3)** A second proposal requires athletes to earn a certain number of credits every year and mandates a minimum grade point average for them. **(5)** Many Big East coaches believe standardized test scores are biased and want

their use in screening student athletes banned. **(7)** According to supporters, however, many athletes under the current system fail to advance academically and often finish their eligibility fifty or more hours short of graduation. **(9)** In the supporters' view, poor supervision by athletic directors and lack of support for academic excellence are to be blamed for the poor performance of student athletes.

◆ PRACTICE 18-15, page 290

Answers: **(1)** A playwright who wrote the prize-winning *A Raisin in the Sun*, Lorraine Hansberry was born in Chicago in 1930. **(3)** Hostile neighbors there were responsible for throwing a brick through a window of their house, an act Hansberry never forgot. **(5)** Lena Younger, the mother of the family, is about to receive a ten-thousand-dollar insurance payment following her husband's death. **(7)** Her dream for the family, a house with a yard her grandson can play in, leads her to purchase a home in a white neighborhood. **(9)** One of their new white neighbors has offered to pay the Younger family a bribe not to move into the neighborhood, an offer Walter now decides to accept.

◆ PRACTICE 18-16, page 292

Possible edits: Kente cloth is made in western Africa and produced primarily by the Ashanti people. It has been worn for hundreds of years by African royalty, who consider it a sign of power and status. Many African Americans wear kente cloth because they see it as a link to their heritage. Each pattern on the cloth has a name, and each color has a special significance. For example, red and yellow suggest a long and healthy life, while green and white suggest a good harvest. Although African women may wear kente cloth as a dress or head wrap, African-American women, like men, usually wear strips of cloth around their shoulders. Men and women of African descent wear kente cloth as a sign of black pride; in fact, it often decorates college students' gowns at graduation.

Chapter 19

◆ PRACTICE 19-1, page 297

Answers: **(1)** Parallel **(3)** They also admit that cigarettes are expensive, smelly, and dangerous.

(5) Being happy in life is more important to me than making a lot of money. **(7)** Judges must care about justice, uphold the laws, and treat defendants fairly. **(9)** Love is blind, but hate is blinder.

◆ **PRACTICE 19-2, page 300**
Answers will vary.

◆ **PRACTICE 19-3, page 300**
Answers: **(1)** Pasadena, Claremont, and Pomona are major cities in the valley. **(3)** Watching the big Tournament of Roses parade is more exciting than viewing the Macy's Thanksgiving Parade. **(5)** Judges rate the rose-covered floats on their originality, artistic merit, and overall impact. **(7)** The Rose Bowl game is not only America's oldest collegiate championship but also the country's most popular bowl game. **(9)** Visitors come to play challenging skill games and enjoy various ethnic foods.

Chapter 20

◆ **PRACTICE 20-1, page 306**
Answers: **(1)** three fifty-watt bulbs; coal oil; baking bread **(3)** wooden table; unfinished game of checkers; apple-tree stump

◆ **PRACTICE 20-2, page 307**
Answers will vary.

◆ **PRACTICE 20-3, page 307**
Answers will vary.

◆ **PRACTICE 20-4, page 309**
Possible edits: **(1)** Adult children can become frustrated because their parents seem to treat them as if they were not capable of making their own decisions. **(3)** When this happens, the children may begin to whine childishly or even throw a temper tantrum although such behavior only reinforces their parents' attitude. **(5)** To get parents to stop being critical, an adult child might turn the tables and encourage his or her parents to talk about their own childhoods. **(7)** Adult children might also explain that while they value their parents' opinion, they are still going to make their

own decisions. **(9)** Although parents may have been telling these stories the same way for years, the child may have a very different perspective on the event.

◆ **PRACTICE 20-5, page 311**
Possible edits: **(1)** Clichés: working like a dog, living high on the hog; edited sentence: Many people think that a million-dollar lottery jackpot allows the winner to stop working long hours and start living a comfortable life. **(3)** Cliché: hit the jackpot; edited sentence: For one thing, lottery winners who win big prizes do not receive their winnings all at once; instead, payments—for example, $50,000—are usually spread out over twenty years. **(5)** Clichés: with their hands out, between a rock and a hard place; edited sentence: Next come relatives and friends who ask for money, leaving winners with difficult choices to make. **(7)** Cliché: Adding insult to injury; edited sentence: Even worse, many lottery winners have lost their jobs because employers thought that once they were "millionaires," they no longer needed to draw a salary. **(9)** Cliché: In their hour of need; edited sentence: Faced with financial difficulties, many would like to sell their future payments to companies that offer lump-sum payments of forty to forty-five cents on the dollar.

◆ **PRACTICE 20-6, page 312**
Answers will vary.

◆ **PRACTICE 20-7, page 313**
Answers will vary.

◆ **PRACTICE 20-8, page 315**
Answers: **(1)** Many people today would like to see more police officers patrolling the streets. **(3)** The attorneys representing the plaintiff are Geraldo Diaz and Barbara Wilkerson. **(5)** Travel to other planets will be a significant step for humanity.

Chapter 21

◆ **PRACTICE 21-1, page 322**
Answers: **(1)** Run-on **(3)** Run-on **(5)** Run-on **(7)** Comma splice **(9)** Correct

◆ **PRACTICE 21-2, page 325**

Possible edits: **(1)** Nursing offers job security and high pay; therefore, many people are choosing nursing as a career.   **(3)** The Democratic Republic of the Congo was previously known as Zaire; before that, it was the Belgian Congo.   **(5)** Millions of Jews were killed during the Holocaust; in addition, Catholics, Gypsies, homosexuals, and other "undesirables" were killed.   **(7)** Japanese athletes play various positions on American baseball teams; however, until recently all Japanese players were pitchers.   **(9)** Père Noel is the French name for Santa Claus; he is also known as Father Christmas and St. Nicholas.

◆ **PRACTICE 21-3, page 326**

Possible edits: **(1)** Harlem, which was populated mostly by European immigrants at the turn of the last century, saw an influx of African Americans beginning in 1910.   **(3)** Many African-American artists and writers created a settlement in Harlem during the 1920s, which led to a flowering of African-American art.   **(5)** When scholars of the era recognize the great works of the Harlem Renaissance, they point to the writers Langston Hughes and Countee Cullen and the artists Henry Tanner and Sargent Johnson.   **(7)** Because Harlem was an exciting place in the 1920s, people from all over the city went there to listen to jazz and to dance.   **(9)** While contemporary African-American artists know about the Harlem Renaissance, it is still not familiar to many others.

◆ **PRACTICE 21-4, page 327**

Possible edits: In the late nineteenth century, Coney Island was famous; in fact, it was legendary. Every summer, it was crowded, and people mailed hundreds of thousands of postcards from the resort on some days. Coney Island, which was considered exotic and exciting, even had a hotel shaped like an elephant. Although some people saw Coney Island as seedy, others thought it was a wonderful, magical place. It had beaches, hotels, racetracks, and a stadium; however, by the turn of the century, it was best known for three amusement parks. These parks were Luna Park, Steeplechase, and Dreamland. Even though gaslight was still the norm in New York, a million electric lights lit Luna Park. While Steeplechase offered many rides, its main attraction was a two-mile ride on mechanical horses. At Dreamland, people could see a submarine; in addition, they could travel through an Eskimo village or visit Lilliputia, with its three hundred midgets. Today, the old Coney Island no longer exists. Fire destroyed Dreamland in 1911, and Luna Park burned down in 1946. In 1964, Steeplechase closed. The once-grand Coney Island is gone. Still, its beach and its boardwalk endure. Its famous roller coaster, the Cyclone, still exists, and its giant Ferris wheel, the Wonder Wheel, keeps on turning. Now, a ballpark has been built for a new minor league baseball team. The new team is called the Brooklyn Cyclones.

Chapter 22

◆ **PRACTICE 22-1, page 332**

Answers: **(1)** Add a verb.   **(3)** Add a subject and a verb.   **(5)** Add a subject and a verb.   **(7)** Add a verb.   **(9)** Add a subject.

◆ **PRACTICE 22-2, page 333**

Answers: Items 2, 4, 6, and 7 are fragments. Rewrite: Sara Paretsky writes detective novels, such as *Burn Marks* and *Guardian Angel*. These novels are about V. I. Warshawski, a private detective. V. I. lives and works in Chicago, the Windy City. Every day as a detective, V. I. takes risks. V. I. is tough. She is also a woman.

◆ **PRACTICE 22-3, page 335**

Answers: **(1)** Most scholars agree that the United States flag was designed by Francis Hopkinson, a New Jersey delegate to the Continental Congress.   **(3)** The United States has adopted a number of other patriotic symbols, such as the Pledge of Allegiance.   **(5)** Congress officially recognized the pledge in 1942, the first year the United States participated in World War II.

◆ **PRACTICE 22-4, page 336**

Answers: **(1)** First-borns and only children often display distinct leadership qualities as children and later as adults.   **(3)** In large families, middle-born children often form close personal relationships among themselves or with friends outside of the family.   **(5)** Youngest children can be charming and funny but sometimes manipulative in their relationships with other family members.

◆ **PRACTICE 22-5, page 337**

Answers will vary.

◆ **PRACTICE 22-6, page 339**

Answers will vary.

◆ **PRACTICE 22-7, page 339**

Answers will vary.

◆ **PRACTICE 22-8, page 340**

Answers: **(1)** Prior to the 1990s, most animated films were hand-drawn, requiring painstaking skill. **(3)** Computer animation has gained a wide audience, impressed by its range of visual possibilities. **(5)** For decades after that, the Disney studios provided the very best in animated storytelling, focusing on fairy tales and classics of children's literature.

◆ **PRACTICE 22-9, page 341**

Answers: **(1)** Emergency medical technicians receive intensive training. This training is meant to prepare them for saving lives. **(3)** Retailers often locate frequently purchased items at the back of their stores. They do this to increase customer traffic. **(5)** Japan's Tokyo Zoo is closed for two months each year. This is done to give the animals a vacation from visitors. **(7)** More and more, people rely on e-mail to keep in touch with family and friends. **(9)** Early telephone users said "Ahoy" instead of "Hello" to greet incoming calls.

◆ **PRACTICE 22-10, page 344**

Possible edits: **(1)** Many homeless people are mentally ill. **(3)** People disagree about the effects of violent video games. **(5)** Competition for athletic scholarships increased.

◆ **PRACTICE 22-11, page 345**

Answers will vary.

Chapter 23

◆ **PRACTICE 23-1, page 351**

Answers: **(1)** know **(3)** include **(5)** sell; top **(7)** surprises; gives **(9)** hosts; draws

◆ **PRACTICE 23-2, page 352**

Answers: **(1)** write **(3)** supervise **(5)** give **(6)** contain **(7)** put; read **(9)** hates

◆ **PRACTICE 23-3, page 352**

Answers: **(1)** fill **(3)** survey **(5)** plays **(7)** smell **(9)** greets

◆ **PRACTICE 23-4, page 354**

Answers: **(1)** have **(3)** has **(5)** do **(7)** is **(9)** has

◆ **PRACTICE 23-5, page 356**

Answers: **(1)** Prepositional phrase: in the painting; subject: cupids; verb: symbolize **(3)** Prepositional phrase: in the kitchen; subject: appliances; verb: make **(5)** Prepositional phrase: of skis and poles; subject: set; verb: costs **(7)** Prepositional phrase: in the city; subject: Workers; verb: pay **(9)** Prepositional phrase: including people like my father; subject: Volunteers; verb: help

◆ **PRACTICE 23-6, page 358**

Answers: **(1)** has **(3)** wants **(5)** takes **(7)** seems **(9)** is

◆ **PRACTICE 23-7, page 359**

Answers: **(1)** Subject: Bering Straits; verb: are **(3)** Subject: twins; verb: are **(5)** Subject: this; verb: has **(7)** Subject: people; verb: are **(9)** Subject: reasons; verb: are

◆ **PRACTICE 23-8, page 361**

Answers: (1) Subject: story; verb: has (3) Subject: narrator; verb: has (5) Subject: Madeline; verb: lives (7) Subject: vault; verb: is (9) Subject: Roderick; verb: is

Chapter 24

◆ **PRACTICE 24-1, page 366**

Answers: **(1)** When Beverly Harvard became the chief of the Atlanta police force, she was the first African-American woman ever to hold that title in a major U.S. city. **(3)** Now, more than half the department is African American, and women make up about a quarter of the force. **(5)** Her husband even agreed to pay her $100 if she made it onto the force.   **(7)** In fact, when she entered the police academy, she did not really plan to be a police officer; she just wanted to prove her husband wrong and to win the $100 bet.   **(9)** When her promotion was announced, some veteran officers criticized her appointment as police chief, but most younger officers praised the choice.

◆ **PRACTICE 24-2, page 368**

Answers: **(1)** Young people who want a career in the fashion industry do not always realize how hard they will have to work.   **(3)** In reality, no matter how talented he or she is, a recent college graduate entering the industry is paid only about $22,000 a year.   **(5)** A young designer may receive a big raise if he or she is very talented, but this is unusual.   **(7)** Employees may be excited to land a job as an assistant designer but then find that they color in designs that have already been drawn.   **(9)** If a person is serious about working in the fashion industry, he or she has to be realistic.

◆ **PRACTICE 24-3, page 370**

Possible edits: **(1)** According to recent studies, a juror may have his or her mind made up before the trial even begins.   **(3)** This unfounded conclusion often depends on which attorney makes his or her initial description of the case the most dramatic.   **(5)** Jurors with poor decision-making skills are also not likely to listen to challenges to their opinions during the deliberation phase of the trial.   **(7)** Correct   **(9)** For example, one juror argued that a man being tried for murder was acting in his own defense because the victim was probably carrying a knife, but no knife was mentioned during the trial.

◆ **PRACTICE 24-4, page 372**

Answers: **(1)** A local university funded the study, and Dr. Alicia Flynn led the research team.   **(3)** Two-thirds of the subjects relied on instinct alone, and only one-third used logical analysis.   **(5)** Many experts read the report, and most of them found the results surprising.

Chapter 25

◆ **PRACTICE 25-1, page 377**

Answers: **(1)** Present participle modifier: Tracing their origins to the late 1700s; modifies: organiza-

tions   **(3)** Present participle modifier: Focusing on academics; modifies: fraternities   **(5)** Present participle modifier: Evolving out of these; modifies: fraternities and sororities   **(7)** Present participle modifier: Reflecting members' interests; modifies: fraternities and sororities   **(9)** Present participle modifier: Taking various forms; modifies: hazing

◆ **PRACTICE 25-2, page 379**

Answers: **(1)** Past participle modifier: The best-preserved fossil ever found; modifies: it   **(3)** Past participle modifier: excited by the find; modifies: hunters   **(5)** Past participle modifier: Supported by previous rulings; modifies: judge   **(7)** Past participle modifier: Questioned by the press; modifies: hunters   **(9)** Past participle modifier: Shocked by the ruling; modifies: dealer

◆ **PRACTICE 25-3, page 381**

Answers will vary.

◆ **PRACTICE 25-4, page 381**

Answers will vary.

◆ **PRACTICE 25-5, page 384**

Answers: **(1)** Frightened by a noise, the cat broke the vase.   **(3)** Lori looked at the man with red hair sitting in the chair.   **(5)** People are sometimes killed by snakes with their deadly venom.   **(7)** I ran outside in my bathrobe and saw eight tiny reindeer.   **(9)** Wearing a mask, the exterminator sprayed the insect.

Chapter 26

◆ **PRACTICE 26-1, page 393**

Answers: **(1)** owned   **(3)** browsed   **(5)** turned; wanted   **(7)** insisted   **(9)** kicked

◆ **PRACTICE 26-2, page 395**

Answers: **(1)** broke   **(3)** beat   **(5)** let; felt   **(7)** kept; took   **(9)** won

◆ **PRACTICE 26-3, page 396**

Answers: **(1)** was   **(3)** Correct   **(5)** was   **(7)** was; were   **(9)** Correct

◆ **PRACTICE 26-4, page 398**

Answers: **(1)** could   **(3)** will   **(5)** could   **(7)** would   **(9)** could

Chapter 27

◆ **PRACTICE 27-1, page 403**
Answers: **(1)** started **(3)** appeared **(5)** expanded **(7)** consumed **(9)** changed

◆ **PRACTICE 27-2, page 407**
Answers: **(1)** found **(3)** drawn **(5)** seen **(7)** gotten; grown **(9)** begun

◆ **PRACTICE 27-3, page 407**
Answers: **(1)** become **(3)** come; found **(5)** Correct; made **(7)** spoken; Correct **(9)** Correct

◆ **PRACTICE 27-4, page 409**
Answers: **(1)** have been **(3)** named **(5)** had **(7)** adopted **(9)** have given

◆ **PRACTICE 27-5, page 410**
Answers: **(1)** have presented **(3)** developed **(5)** has become **(7)** have begun

◆ **PRACTICE 27-6, page 411**
Answers: **(1)** had left **(3)** had arrived **(5)** had lied **(7)** had decided **(9)** had been

◆ **PRACTICE 27-7, page 413**
Answers: **(1)** surprised; preapproved **(3)** inscribed **(5)** stuffed **(7)** concerned **(9)** cherished

Chapter 28

◆ **PRACTICE 28-1, page 419**
Answers: **(1)** lives (irregular) **(3)** chains (regular) **(5)** honeys (regular) **(7)** loaves (irregular) **(9)** beaches (regular)

◆ **PRACTICE 28-2, page 419**
Answers: **(1)** friends **(3)** husbands-to-be; catches; senses **(5)** Correct; personalities; lives **(7)** sexes; species.

◆ **PRACTICE 28-3, page 420**
Answers: **(1)** I **(3)** they; I **(5)** she; I **(7)** it

◆ **PRACTICE 28-4, page 422**
Answers: **(1)** Antecedent: campuses; pronoun: they **(3)** Antecedent: students; pronoun: their **(5)** Antecedent: Joyce; pronoun: she **(7)** Antecedent: friends; pronoun: them

◆ **PRACTICE 28-5, page 422**
Answers: **(1)** they **(3)** it **(5)** He **(7)** It

◆ **PRACTICE 28-6, page 424**
Answers: **(1)** Compound antecedent: Larry and Curly; connecting word: and; pronoun: their **(3)** Compound antecedent: Laurel and Hardy; connecting word: and; pronoun: their **(5)** Compound antecedent: *MASH* or *The Fugitive*; connecting word: or; pronoun: its **(7)** Compound antecedent: film or videotapes; connecting word: or; pronoun: their **(9)** Compound antecedent: popcorn and soft drinks; connecting word: and; pronoun: their

◆ **PRACTICE 28-7, page 426**
Answers: **(1)** Indefinite pronoun antecedent: Either; pronoun: its **(3)** Indefinite pronoun antecedent: Everything; pronoun: its **(5)** Indefinite pronoun antecedent: Neither; pronoun: her **(7)** Indefinite pronoun antecedent: Several; pronoun: their **(9)** Indefinite pronoun antecedent: Anyone; pronoun: his or her

◆ **PRACTICE 28-8, page 427**
Possible edits: **(1)** Everyone has the right to his or her own opinion. **(3)** Somebody forgot his or her backpack. **(5)** Someone in the store has left his or her car's lights on. **(7)** Each of the applicants must have his or her driver's license. **(9)** Either of the coffeemakers comes with its own filter.

◆ **PRACTICE 28-9, page 428**
Answers: **(1)** Collective noun antecedent: company; pronoun: its **(3)** Collective noun antecedent: government; pronoun: its **(5)** Collective noun antecedent: army; pronoun: its

◆ **PRACTICE 28-10, page 428**
Answers: **(3)** Correct **(5)** its; their **(7)** his or her **(9)** its; correct

◆ **PRACTICE 28-11, page 431**

Answers: **(1)** Subjective; Possessive **(3)** Objective; Possessive; Possessive **(5)** Subjective; Subjective; Possessive; Objective **(7)** Objective; Subjective; Possessive **(9)** Possessive

◆ **PRACTICE 28-12, page 434**

Answers: **(1)** me **(3)** him **(5)** I **(7)** Correct; me **(9)** They

◆ **PRACTICE 28-13, page 435**

Answers: **(1)** she [is] **(3)** she [does] **(5)** we [have] **(7)** they [serve] **(9)** [it fits] me

◆ **PRACTICE 28-14, page 435**

Answers: **(1)** who **(3)** who **(5)** who **(7)** whoever **(9)** who

◆ **PRACTICE 28-15, page 437**

Answers: **(1)** themselves **(3)** himself **(5)** yourself **(7)** itself **(9)** themselves

Chapter 29

◆ **PRACTICE 29-1, page 443**

Answers: **(1)** poorly **(3)** truly **(5)** really **(7)** specifically **(9)** important; immediately

◆ **PRACTICE 29-2, page 444**

Answers: **(1)** good **(3)** good **(5)** good **(7)** well **(9)** good

◆ **PRACTICE 29-3, page 447**

Answers: **(1)** more slowly **(3)** healthier **(5)** more loudly **(7)** more respectful **(9)** wilder

◆ **PRACTICE 29-4, page 448**

Answers: **(1)** largest **(3)** most successful **(5)** most powerful **(7)** most serious **(9)** most popular

◆ **PRACTICE 29-5, page 449**

Answers: **(1)** better **(3)** better; worse **(5)** better **(7)** best **(9)** better

Chapter 30

◆ **PRACTICE 30-1, page 454**

Possible edits: **(1)** When the first season of the reality show *Survivor* aired, it was an immediate hit. **(3)** For a while, *Survivor* became a cultural phenomenon—probably because it was seldom in bad taste. **(5)** It was surprising to see the controversial shows that suddenly appeared on the air. **(7)** A recent poll asked viewers: "Do you enjoy reality TV, or has it gone too far?" **(9)** It turns out that reality TV is nothing new.

◆ **PRACTICE 30-2, page 456**

Possible answers: **(1)** By the 1700s, there were thirteen British colonies in North America. **(3)** The Revolutionary War went on for eight years. **(5)** For the first congress, the colonies sent representatives to Philadelphia in 1787. **(7)** One of their goals was to protect the rights of individuals. **(9)** The Constitution works because it was written to allow additions or amendments.

◆ **PRACTICE 30-3, page 457**

Answers: **(1)** species; sharks **(3)** Sharks **(5)** No plural nouns **(7)** sharks; meat-eaters; species; people **(9)** 1950s; sharks

◆ **PRACTICE 30-4, page 459**

Answers: **(1)** Count: approaches **(3)** Noncount **(5)** Count: shortages **(7)** Count: individuals **(9)** Count: systems

◆ **PRACTICE 30-5, page 461**

Answers: **(1)** every **(3)** A few violent **(5)** their **(7)** Many **(9)** some

◆ **PRACTICE 30-6, page 465**

Answers: **(1)** the; a **(3)** No article needed **(5)** the; the; the; No article needed **(7)** No article needed **(9)** a **(11)** a; No article needed; No article needed; the

◆ **PRACTICE 30-7, page 467**

Answers: **(1)** Is converting metric measurements to English measurements difficult? **(3)** Was that family very influential in the early 1900s? **(5)** Has the winner of the presidential election always been the candidate who got the most votes? **(7)** The prosecutor cannot verify the accuracy of the witness's story. **(9)** Customs officers at the border have not been requiring motorists to show proof of citizenship.

◆ **PRACTICE 30-8, page 470**

Answers: **(1)** is being [is] **(3)** are knowing [know]; is [Correct] **(5)** are having [have] **(7)** are changing [Correct]; are becoming [Correct] **(9)** was showing [showed]; are [Correct]

◆ **PRACTICE 30-9, page 471**

Answers: **(1)** a brand-new high-rise apartment building **(3)** numerous successful short-story collections **(5)** the publisher's three best-selling works **(7)** a strong-willed young woman **(9)** an exquisite white wedding gown

◆ **PRACTICE 30-10, page 475**

Answers: **(1)** in; in **(3)** in; at; to **(5)** in; in; in **(7)** to; in; with; from; to; with; with **(9)** with; at; of

◆ **PRACTICE 30-11, page 478**

Answers: **(1)** Some people who have dreams of going to college have to set them aside for a variety of reasons. **(3)** Correct **(5)** "Distance learning" takes place when a teacher and student are separated by physical distance, and technology hooks them up. **(7)** Correct **(9)** Teachers can distribute assignments, and students can hand them in by fax or e-mail.

Chapter 31

◆ **PRACTICE 31-1, page 486**

Answers: **(1)** A talented musician, he plays guitar, bass, and drums. **(3)** Correct **(5)** The remarkable diary kept by young Anne Frank while her family hid from the Nazis is insightful, touching, and sometimes humorous. **(7)** Most coffins manufactured in the United States are lined with bronze, copper, or lead. **(9)** California's capital is Sacramento, its largest city is Los Angeles, and its oldest settlement is San Diego.

◆ **PRACTICE 31-2, page 488**

Answers: **(1)** In recent years, many Olympic athletes have been disqualified because they tested pos-

itive for banned drugs. **(3)** Correct **(5)** Banned by the rules of the Olympics, these drugs still appeal to athletes because they supposedly enhance performance. **(7)** Often called dietary supplements, these alternative chemicals are supposed to enhance athletic performance in the same way steroids supposedly do. **(9)** Instead of enhancing performance, they often cause considerable damage to the body.

◆ **PRACTICE 31-3, page 489**

Answers: **(1)** For example, the African-American celebration of Kwanzaa is less than forty years old. **(3)** By the way, the word *Kwanzaa* means "first fruits" in Swahili. **(5)** This can, in fact, be demonstrated in some of the seven principles of Kwanzaa. **(7)** The focus, first of all, is on unity *(umoja).* **(9)** In addition, Kwanzaa celebrations emphasize three kinds of community responsibility *(ujima, ujamaa,* and *nia).*

◆ **PRACTICE 31-4, page 491**

Answers: **(1)** Traditional Chinese medicine is based on meridians, channels of energy believed to run in regular patterns through the body. **(3)** Herbal medicine, the basis of many Chinese healing techniques, requires twelve years of study. **(5)** Correct **(7)** Nigeria, the most populous country in Africa, is also one of the fastest-growing nations in the world. **(9)** The Yoruban people, the Nigerian settlers of Lagos, are unusual in Africa because they tend to form large urban communities.

◆ **PRACTICE 31-5, page 493**

Answers: **(1)** Correct **(3)** Correct **(5)** The Japanese had just landed in the Aleutian Islands, which lay west of the tip of the Alaska Peninsula. **(7)** As a result, they made them work under conditions that made construction difficult. **(9)** In one case, white engineers who surveyed a river said it would take two weeks to bridge.

◆ **PRACTICE 31-6, page 495**

Answers: **(1)** The American Declaration of Independence was approved on July 4, 1776. **(3)** At 175 Carlton Avenue, Brooklyn, New York, is the house where Richard Wright began writing *Native Son.* **(5)** Correct **(7)** The Pueblo Grande Museum is located at 1469 East Washington Street, Phoenix, Arizona. **(9)** St. Louis, Missouri, was the birthplace of writer Maya Angelou, but she spent most of her childhood in Stamps, Arkansas.

◆ PRACTICE 31-7, page 497

Answers: **(1)** The capital of the Dominican Republic is Santo Domingo. **(3)** Chief among these are sugarcane, coffee, cocoa, and rice. **(5)** Correct **(7)** Tourists who visit the Dominican Republic remark on its tropical beauty. **(9)** Correct

Chapter 32

◆ PRACTICE 32-1, page 502

Answers: **(1)** We're all trying hard to watch our diets, but it's not easy. **(3)** Maybe we shouldn't be so tempted, but it's hard to resist the lure of the fast-food chains and their commercials. **(5)** When we're away from home and hungry, it's the picture of that burger that pops into our minds. **(7)** It shouldn't be so hard to find a fast, healthy meal. **(9)** It's still not the perfect meal for a dieter, but it isn't too bad.

◆ PRACTICE 32-2, page 504

Answers: **(1)** the singer's video **(3)** the writer's first novel **(5)** the players' union **(7)** the children's bedroom **(9)** everyone's dreams

◆ PRACTICE 32-3, page 506

Answers: **(1)** Parents; theirs **(3)** its; weeks **(5)** Ryans; years **(7)** classes; Correct; your **(9)** tests; Correct

Chapter 33

◆ PRACTICE 33-1, page 513

Answers: **(1)** Midwest; Lake Michigan; Chicago; O'Hare International Airport; nation's **(3)** north; Soldier Field; Chicago Bears; Wrigley Field; Chicago Cubs; National League; baseball team **(5)** John Kinzie **(7)** United States; Mrs.; cow **(9)** mother; Aunt Jean; Uncle Amos

◆ PRACTICE 33-2, page 515

Answers: **(1)** "We who are about to die salute you," said the gladiators to the emperor. **(3)** "The

bigger they are," said boxer John L. Sullivan, "the harder they fall." **(5)** Lisa Marie replied, "I do." **(7)** When asked for the jury's verdict, the foreman replied, "We find the defendant not guilty." **(9)** "Yabba dabba doo!" Fred exclaimed. "This brontoburger looks great."

◆ PRACTICE 33-3, page 516

Answers: **(1)** Essayist Simone de Beauvoir wrote, "One is not born a woman; one becomes one." **(3)** "When I'm good, I'm very good," said actress Mae West in the classic film *I'm no Angel*. "When I'm bad, I'm better." **(5)** "If a man hasn't discovered something he will die for, then he isn't fit to live," said Martin Luther King Jr.

◆ PRACTICE 33-4, page 518

Answers: **(1)** *Plan Nine from Outer Space* **(3)** *Born to Sing;* "You Don't Have to Worry"; "Time Goes On"; "Just Can't Stay Away" **(5)** *The Weakest Link; Friends; Law and Order*

◆ PRACTICE 33-5, page 519

Answers: **(1)** Sui Sin Far's short story "The Wisdom of the New," from her book Mrs. Spring Fragrance, is about the clash between Chinese and American cultures in the early twentieth century. **(3)** Interesting information about fighting skin cancer can be found in the article "Putting Sunscreens to the Test," which appeared in the magazine Consumer Reports. **(5)** Ang Lee has directed several well-received films, including Crouching Tiger, Hidden Dragon. **(7)** The title of Lorraine Hansberry's play A Raisin in the Sun comes from Langston Hughes's poem "Harlem."

◆ PRACTICE 33-6, page 521

Answers: **(1)** New Orleans has two nicknames: the "Crescent City" and the "City that Care Forgot." **(3)** The French Quarter is famous for several attractions: its unique buildings, its fine food, its street musicians, and its wild nightlife. **(5)** The Square—a gathering place for artists and other merchants—centers on a monument to Andrew Jackson. **(7)** Its popular beignets (pronounced ben-*yeas*) are deep-fried pastries covered with sugar. **(9)** New Orleans visitors—people from all over the world—particularly enjoy the laid-back atmosphere of the city.

Chapter 34

◆ PRACTICE 34-1, page 528

Answers: **(1)** weigh; Correct **(3)** Correct; deceive; believing **(5)** Correct; veins; Correct **(7)** Their; Correct; grief **(9)** variety; foreign

◆ PRACTICE 34-2, page 530

Answers: **(1)** unhappy **(3)** preexisting **(5)** unnecessary **(7)** impatient **(9)** overreact

◆ PRACTICE 34-3, page 531

Answers: **(1)** lonely **(3)** revising **(5)** desirable **(7)** microscopic **(9)** ninth

◆ PRACTICE 34-4, page 532

Answers: **(1)** happiness **(3)** denying **(5)** readiness **(7)** destroyer **(9)** fortyish

◆ PRACTICE 34-5, page 533

Answers: **(1)** hoped **(3)** revealing **(5)** cramming **(7)** referring **(9)** fatter

◆ PRACTICE 34-6, page 534

Answers: **(1)** effects; already **(3)** buy; Correct **(5)** Correct; Correct

◆ PRACTICE 34-7, page 536

Answers: **(1)** here; every day **(3)** Correct; conscience **(5)** conscious; its

◆ PRACTICE 34-8, page 537

Answers: **(1)** past; knew **(3)** peace; Correct **(5)** Correct; laid

◆ PRACTICE 34-9, page 539

Answers: **(1)** plane; quite **(3)** supposed; quiet **(5)** principal; Correct

◆ PRACTICE 34-10, page 540

Answers: **(1)** There; Correct **(3)** threw; Correct **(5)** to; they're

◆ PRACTICE 34-11, page 541

Answers: **(1)** whose; Correct **(3)** where; Correct **(5)** Correct; whether; Correct

Acknowledgments

Picture acknowledgments

   Introduction: Bob Daemmrich/Stock, Boston; *Chapter 1:* David Butow/Corbis/Saba; *Chapter 2:* Bachman/Photo Researchers; *Chapter 3:* Andy Levin/Photo Researchers; *Chapter 4:* Illustration for *The Three Little Pigs* by Leonard Leslie Brooks/Penguin Putnam, Inc.; *Chapter 5:* Cathy Ursillo/eStock; *Chapter 6:* TWISTER® and © 2002 Hasbro, Inc. Used with permission; *Chapter 7:* IT International, Ltd./eStock; *Chapter 8:* Photofest; *Chapter 9:* Tom Hauck/ALLSPORT/Getty Images; *Chapter 10:* Tony Freeman/PhotoEdit; *Chapter 11:* David Young-Wolff/PhotoEdit; *Chapter 12:* Photofest; *Chapter 13:* Photofest; *Chapter 14:* Bob Daemmrich; *Practice 14-3:* Bill Aron/PhotoEdit; *Practice 14-6:* Culver Pictures; *Practice 14-9:* Frank Siteman; *Practice 14-12:* Photofest; *Practice 14-15:* Buddy Norris/Newport News Daily Press/AP/Wide World Photos; *Practice 14-18:* (upper) Dennis MacDonald/Index Stock Imagery, (lower) Richard Pasley/Stock, Boston; *Practice 14-21:* David Young-Wolff/PhotoEdit; *Practice 14-24:* (top left) Ken Kavanaugh/Photo Researchers, (top right) Sybil Shackman, (bottom left) Bob Daemmrich/Stock, Boston, (bottom right) James Wilson/Woodfin Camp & Associates; *Practice 14-27:* Bob Daemmrich/Stock, Boston; *Chapter 15:* Jonathan Daniel/ALLSPORT/Getty Images; *Chapter 16:* Joel Gordon; *Chapter 17:* Dan Loh/AP/Wide World Photos; *Chapter 18:* AP/Wide World Photos; *Chapter 19:* James Leynse/Corbis/Saba; *Chapter 20:* Ellen Senisi/The Image Works; *Chapter 21:* Jeff Greenberg/Photo Researchers; *Chapter 22:* Courtesy, Ford Motor Co., Thunderbird Division; *Chapter 23:* Edgar Degas, *A Woman Seated Beside a Vase of Flowers*, 1865, oil on canvas. The Metropolitan Museum of Art, H. O. Havemeyer Collection, Bequest of Mrs. H. O. Havemeyer, 1929. Photo, c. 1998, MMA; *Chapter 24:* David Young-Wolff/PhotoEdit; *Chapter 25:* Lawrence Migdale/Stock, Boston; *Chapter 26:* Courtesy, De Roo Family Archives; *Chapter 27:* Bob Stern/The Image Works; *Chapter 28:* ™ and © 20th Century Fox Film Corp./Photofest; *Chapter 29:* James Marshall/The Image Works; *Chapter 30: Fourth of July, 1916* by Frederick C. Hassam (detail)/Christie's Images, NY; *Chapter 31:* Monika Graff/The Image Works; *Chapter 32:* Tony Freeman/PhotoEdit; *Chapter 33:* Photofest; *Chapter 34:* Eric Fowke/PhotoEdit.

Text acknowledgments

   Maya Angelou, "Summer Picnic Fish Fry." From *I Know Why the Caged Bird Sings* by Maya Angelou. Copyright © 1969 and renewed 1997 by Maya Angelou. Used by permission of Random House, Inc.
   Russell Baker, "Slice of Life." From *The New York Times*, November 24, 1974. Copyright © 1974 by the New York Times Company. Reprinted by permission.
   Lynda Barry, "The Sanctuary of School." From *The New York Times*, January 5, 1992. Copyright © 1992 by the New York Times Company. Reprinted by permission.
   Judith Ortiz Cofer, "Don't Call Me a Hot Tamale." Originally titled "The Myth of the Latin Woman: I Just Met a Girl Named Maria" from *Latin Deli: Prose and Poetry* by Judith Ortiz Cofer. Copyright © 1993 by Judith Ortiz Cofer. Reprinted by permission of University of Georgia Press.

Index

690

Correction Symbols

This chart lists symbols that many instructors use to point out writing problems in student papers. Next to each problem is the chapter or section of *Writing in Context* where you can find help with that problem. If your instructor uses different symbols from those shown here, write them in the space provided.

YOUR INSTRUCTOR'S SYMBOL	STANDARD SYMBOL	PROBLEM
_____	adj	problem with use of adjective 29
_____	adv	problem with use of adverb 29
_____	agr	agreement problem (subject-verb) 23
_____		agreement problem (pronoun-antecedent) 28D, 28E
_____	apos	apostrophe missing or used incorrectly 32
_____	awk	awkward sentence structure 24, 25
_____	cap	capital letter needed 33A
_____	case	problem with pronoun case 28F
_____	cliché	cliché 20C
_____	coh	lack of paragraph coherence 2C
_____	combine	combine sentences 18C
_____	cs	comma splice 21
_____	d	diction (poor word choice) 20A
_____	dev	lack of paragraph development 2B
_____	frag	sentence fragment 22
_____	fs	fused sentence 21
_____	ital	italics or underlining needed 33C
_____	lc	lower case; capital letter not needed 33A
_____	para or ¶	indent new paragraph 2
_____	pass	overuse of passive voice
_____	prep	nonstandard use of preposition 30K, 30L, 30M
_____	ref	pronoun reference not specific 28E
_____	ro	run-on sentence 21
_____	shift	illogical shift 24
_____	sp	incorrect spelling 34
_____	tense	problem with verb tense 26, 27
_____	thesis	thesis unclear or not stated 12D–G
_____	trans	transition needed 2C
_____	unity	paragraph not unified 2A
_____	w	wordy, not concise 20B
_____	//	problem with parallelism 19
_____	(;)	problem with comma use 31
_____	(;)	problem with semicolon use 16B, 16C
_____	" "	problem with quotation marks 33B–C
_____	⌒	close up space
_____	^	insert
_____	ℓ	delete
_____	∼	reversed letters or words
_____	X	obvious error
_____	✓	good point, well put